Syllabus

BUSINESS STATISTICS

(B.Com, Course, Bangalore University)

PAPER VI : BUSINESS STATISTICS

1. **Conceptual Framework**
   - *(a)* Definition of Stastics as Statistical Data and Science of Statistics – Main Divisions of Statistics – Objects of Statistics.
   - *(b)* Functions, Importance and Limitations of Statistics. Distrust of Statistics (brief reference).
2. **Statistical Investigation**
   - *(a)* Meaning and Stages of Statistical Investigation.
   - *(b)* Collection of Data – Methods of Collection of Primary and Secondary Data – Census and Sample Method. Statistical Errors – Law of Statistical Regularity and Law of Inertia of large numbers.
   - *(c)* Classification, Seriation and Tabulation – Meaning and Objects of Tabulation, Construction of Statistical Tables. Meaning, Objects and Types of Classification – Meaning and Types of Statistical Series.
3. **Diagrammatic and Graphic Representation of Statistical Data**
   Utility and Limitations of Statistical Diagrams and Graphs, Types of Statistical Diagrams, Simple, Subdivided, Multiple and Percentage Bars – Rectangular Bars, Piechart, Histogram, Frequency Polygon and Ogive.
4. **Measures of Central Tendency (Statistical Averages)**
   - *(a)* Meaning and Objects of Statistical Averages – Requisites of an Ideal Average – Limitations of Averages.
   - *(b)* Types of Statistical Averages (i) Arithmetic Mean – Simple and Weighted – Combined and Corrected Mean, Miscellaneous Problems on Weighted and Unweighted Arithmetic Mean; (ii) Geometric and Harmonic Mean (individual observations only) – Calculation and Applicability; (iii) Median and Quartiles; (iv) The Mode.
5. **Measures of Variation**
   - *(a)* Meaning, Absolute and Relative Measures of Variation.
   - *(b)* Types : (i) Range, (ii) Quartile Deviation, (iii) Mean Deviation, (iv) Standard Deviation, Co-efficient of Variation (exclusive of combined and corrected standard deviation).

6. Skewness

(a) Meaning and Tests of Skewness; Absolute and Relative Measures of Skewness.

(b) Types : Karl Pearson's Coefficient of Skewness and Bowley's Coefficient of Skewness.

7. Correlation Analysis

Meaning and Methods of Studying Correlation – Degree of Correlation – Karl Pearson's Coefficient of Corrleation (ungrouped data only), Probable Error, Spearman's Rank Correlation.

8. Regression Analysis

Meaning, Difference between Correlation and Regression – Regression Coefficients, Regression Equations.

9. Analysis of Time Series

Significance and Components of Time Series. Computation of Trend Values by the Method of Moving Averages and Least Squares and Graphic Representation of Trend Values (in the case of least squares method problems having $\Sigma x = 0$ only).

10. Index Numbers

(a) Meaning, Purpose and Limitations of Index Numbers. Steps in the Construction of General Index Number.

(b) Unweighted and Weighted Index Numbers : Weighted Aggregative Method, Weighted Average of Price Relatives Method and Fisher's Ideal Index Number (Including time reversal test and factor reversal test).

(c) Cost of Living Index Number : Meaning and Uses of Cost of Living Index Numbers, Calculation of Cost of Living Index Numbers by Aggregative Expenditure Method and Family Budget Method.

11. Interpolation and Extrapolation

Meaning and Assumptions of Interpolation – Difference between Interpolation and Extrapolation. Methods of Interpolation – Binomial Expansion Method and Newton's Method of Advancing Differences.

Preface

This textbook is meant for the Bangalore and other Indian Universities. Each topic is treated in a systematic and logical manner. Statistical concepts are introduced in a sequential way with full explanations and illustrations. On the whole, the book fulfills the needs of students and teachers for whom it is intended.

The book contains the solved question papers of the past sixteen years. It widely recognises the necessity for equipping the II year B.Com. students with an elementary knowledge of the Statistical techniques.

All care has been taken to make the book free of conceptual errors. However, inspite of best efforts, some typographical, numerical and other human errors might have escaped our attention; these should cause no problem to the discerning reader. Constructive criticism, comments and suggestion are most welcome.

We wish to express our gratitude to Mrs. Meena Pandey of Himalaya Publishing House for taking keen interest in the publication of the book.

Our special appreciation goes to Sri. Guruprasad, Sri H.S. Vishweshwar and Miss B.S. Sandhya for their excellent computer-type setting work and we also like to express thanks to Sri Amit Kumar C.C. for his help and interest in compiling the materials of the subject.

We are also grateful to the teachers and students who have encouraged us to write this book.

Prof. C.M. Chikkodi, M.Com, L.L.B
Prof. B.G. Satyaprasad, M.Com, Ph. D.

BUSINESS STATISTICS

Prof. C.M. Chikodi
M.Com., LL.B.
Department of Commerce,
K.L.E.'s S. Nijalingappa College,
Rajajinagar, Bangalore - 10.

Prof. B.G. Satyaprasad
M.Com., Ph.D.
Department of Commerce,
Abbas Khan College for Women,
O.T.C. Road, Bangalore - 02.

Himalaya Publishing House

ISO 9001:2015 CERTIFIED

First Edition : 1998
Second Revised Edition : 1999
Reprint : 2002, 2003, 2006, 2013, 2014, 2015, 2016
Reprint : 2018, 2021
Reprint : 2023

Published by : Mrs. Meena Pandey
for **HIMALAYA PUBLISHING HOUSE PVT. LTD.,**
"Ramdoot", Dr. Bhalerao Marg, Girgaon, Mumbai - 400 004.
Phone: 022-23860170, 23863863; **Fax:** 022-23877178
E-mail: himpub@bharatmail.co.in; **Website:** www.himpub.com

Branch Offices :

New Delhi : "Pooja Apartments", 4-B, Murari Lal Street, Ansari Road, Darya Ganj, New Delhi - 110 002.
Phone: 011-23270392, 23278631; Fax: 011-23256286

Nagpur : Kundanlal Chandak Industrial Estate, Ghat Road, Nagpur - 440 018. Phone: 0712-2738731, 2721216

Bengaluru : Plot No. 91-33, 2nd Main Road Seshadripuram, Behind Nataraja Theatre, Bengaluru - 560 020.
Phone: 080-41138821; Mobile: 09379847017, 09379847005

Hyderabad : No. 3-4-184, Lingampally, Besides Raghavendra Swamy Matham, Kachiguda, Hyderabad - 500 027.
Phone: 040-27560041, 27550139

Chennai : No. 34/44, Motilal Street, T. Nagar, Chennai - 600 017.
Mobile: 09380460419

Pune : First Floor, "Laksha" Apartment, No. 527, Mehunpura, Shaniwar Peth (Near Prabhat Theatre), Pune - 411 030.
Phone: 020-24496323, 24496333; Mobile: 09370579333

Cuttack : Plot No 5F-755/4, Sector-9, CDA Market Nagar, Cuttack - 753 014, Odisha. Mobile: 09338746007

Kolkata : 3, S.M. Bose Road, Near Gate No. 5, Agarpara Railway Station, North 24 Parganas, West Bengal - 700 109. Mobile: 09674536325

Printed at : M/s. Charita Impressions, Hyderabad on behalf of HPH.

Contents

1

Conceptual Framework

The subject of statistics is not a new discipline. In the olden days, it was regarded as the **"Science of Statecraft"** and was the by-product of the administrative activity of the state.

The word statistics seems to have been derived from the Latin word *'Status'* or the Italian word *'Statista'* or the German word *'Statistik'* or the French word *'Statistique'*, each of which means a political state.

In days of yore, statistics was once known as the **"Science of Kings"**. The kings or ruling chiefs used to take censuses of population and property within their domain to determine their man-power and material wealth . They used to plan their fiscal and military policies. So collection of data regarding all the national resources became the main function of the state. The data or information so collected was useful in the distribution of land, introduction of tax system and formation of social and economic policies. Thus, the science of statistics is the by-product of state.

In the 18th century, mathematics was introduced in the collection, classification and presentation of data. The data so presented was further analysed to make the conclusions. The modern science of statistics is no longer synonymous with *"political arithmetic"*. It has extended its scope to a number of departments of human knowledge. It is concerned not merely with matters of state but also with every branch of human knowledge. Nowadays, its methods are applied to all those fields of enquiry where a study of large numbers is involved. Thus, the science of statistics is relating to mathematics that is applied to observational data.

I. Definition of Statistics

The term 'Statistics' is used in a plural as well as singular meaning. Used in a plural sense, it refers to the description of numerical facts that are presented systematically. Used in a singular sense, it refers to the statistical methods and principles used for the classification and analysis of a quantitative data so as to arrive valid conclusions. Statistics has been defined by many writers from time to time. It is practically impossible to enumerate all the definitions given to statistics. However, we give below some selected definitions:

A. Statistics as Numerical Data (Plural)

The term *'Statistics'*, as a plural noun, means a collection of numerical facts - the figures themselves. It also includes the percentages, averages and coefficients derived from the numerical facts. The numerical facts or statistics relate to the quantitative aspects of things, concern with the numerical description of facts, involve counting of the items and include the various mathematical measurements.

(i) *"Statistics are the classified facts representing the conditions of the people in a state... specially those facts which can be stated in number or in tables of numbers or in any tabular or classified arrangement."* – **Webster.**

This definition considers only numerical facts and restricts the domain of statistics to the affairs of a state i.e. to social sciences. It is a very old and narrow definition, and is inadequate for modern times.

(ii) *"Statistics are numerical statement of facts in any department of enquiry placed in relation to each other."* – **Bowely.**

This definition is more general than the one given by Webster. It is related to numerical data in any department of enquiry. It also provides for comparative study of the figures.

(iii) *"By Statistics we mean quantitative data affected to a marked extent by multiplicity of causes."*– **Yule and Kendall.**

This definition is not exhaustive and it fails to provide for comparative study of the figures and their arrangement.

(iv) *"Statistics may be defined as the aggregate of facts affected to a marked extent by multiplicity of causes, numerically expressed, enumerated or estimated according to a reasonable standard of accuracy, collected in a systematic manner, for a predetermined purpose and placed in relation to each other."* – **Prof. Horace Secrist.**

This definition seems to be the most exhaustive of all the definitions. By examining this definition, we can draw the following essentials of *"Statistics"*:

(a) Aggregate of Facts : Statistics are a part of aggregate of facts relating to any particular field of enquiry. No single or isolated items can be termed as statistics.

(b) Affected by Multiplicity of Causes: The facts are hardly ever traceable to a single cause. They are affected by multiplicity of causes or factors. The joint effect of all the causes on a single item is studied with the help of the statistical techniques. We are more concerned with the facts rather than their causes

(c) Numerically Expressed: Statistics are quantitatively expressed. The facts having qualitative characters cannot be termed as 'statistics'. However, the qualitative aspects, which can be expressed numerically by assigning scores or ranks or standards, can be treated as 'Statistics'.

(d) Enumerated or Estimated According to Reasonable Standard of Accuracy: Statistics are made available by maintaining reasonable standard of accuracy. For precise results, statistics must be accurately compiled. When a complete enumeration or estimation is not possible, the sampling method is adopted and a reasonable standard of accuracy is maintained in collecting, classifying and analysing the data. It all depends upon the nature and purpose of the enquiry for which statistics are to serve.

(e) Collected in a Systematic Manner: The facts about the particular phenomenon are collected systematically. A proper plan is prepared, and it is executed effectively by the trained investigators.

(f) Collected for a Pre-determined Purpose: The objectives or purpose of the enquiry must be defined in clear and concrete terms well in advance. This avoids the collection of irrelevant data.

(g) Comparable: From practical point of view, the statistics are capable of being compared with other concerned figured. They are being placed in relation to each other. They are all comparable, homogeneous and related to the same phenomenon or subject.

Thus, from the definition of Prof. Horace Secrist and its discussion above, we may conclude that:

"All statistics are numerical statements of facts but all numerical statements of facts are not statistics." The numerical statements of facts, to be designed as statistics, must possess some of the characteristics given in the definition of Prof. Horace Secrist.

B. Statistics as a Science (Singular)

The term *'Statistics'*, as a singular noun, means a body of theories and techniques or methods employed in analysing the numerical information. It is a branch of scientific method and deals with the mathematical process to yield finished product. It is concerned with the collection, classification, tabulation, presentation and analysis of data relating to a particular field of study.

(i) (a) *"Statistics may be called the science of counting."*
– Dr. Bowley A.L.

(b) *"Statistics may rightly be called the science of averages."*
– Dr. Bowley A.L.

(c) *"Statistics is the science of the measurement of social organism, regarded as a whole in all its manifestation."*
– Dr. Bowley A.L.

The above three definitions are inadequate to give the exact meaning of the word 'Statistics'.

(ii) *"Statistics is the science of estimates and probabilities."*
– Prof. Boddington.

This definition is also inadequate as it fails to describe the meaning and functions of statistics. It is confined only to probabilities and estimates. It does not describe the other statistical tools.

(iii) *"The science of statistics is the method of judging collective, natural or social phenomenon from the results obtained from the analysis or enumeration or collection of estimates."*
– King W.I.

This definition is also inadequate as it confines statistics to only social sciences and it does not consider natural sciences.

(iv) *"Statistics is the science which deals with classification and tabulation of numerical facts as the basis for explanation, description and comparison of phenomenon."* **– Prof. Lovitt.**

This definition is fairly satisfactory. However, it fails to describe all the functions completely.

(v) *"Statistics is the science which deals with the methods of collecting, classifying, presenting, comparing and interpreting numerical data collected to throw some light on any sphere of enquiry."* **– Seligman.**

This definition is very short, simple and quite comprehensive.

(vi) *"Statistics may be defined as the science of collection, presentation, analysis and interpretation of numerical data."* **– F.E. Croxton and D.J. Cowden.**

This definition is the best of all the above definitions. It is satisfactory and complete in giving the correct meaning of the term 'statistics'.

(vii) *"Statistics may be regarded as a body of methods for making wise decisions in the face of uncertainty."* **– Wallis and Roberts.**

This definition is quite modern since the statistical methods enable us to arrive at valid decisions.

(viii) *"Statistics is a method of decision making in the face of uncertainty on the basis of numerical data and calculated risks."* **– Prof. Ya-Lun-Chou.**

This definition is a modified form of the definition of Wallis and Roberts.

(ix) *"Statistics is the science and art of handling aggregate of facts – observing, enumerating, recording, classifying and otherwise systematically treating them."* **– Harlow.**

This definition describes statistics as both a science and an art. It provides tools and laws for analysis of data, so it is a science. It involves requisite skill, experience and patience while applying statistical tools, so it is an art.

Thus, a study and analysis of various definitions of statistics helps us to draw the following essentials of "Statistics":

(a) It is a science and an art as well.

(b) It deals with the quantitative mass data.

(c) It includes collection, classification, tabulation and presentation of data.

(d) It is a system of analysis and synthesis of numerical data.

(e) It is a device of summarization, comparison, treatment and interpretation of numerical data.

(f) It is a process of observing, recording, describing and enumerating the quantitative data.

(g) Its purpose is to obtain and explore knowledge.

(h) It involves a technique of drawing conclusions and making wise decisions on the face of uncertainty.

(i) It is a body of methods for obtaining information (i.e. a branch of scientific method).

Thus, the science of statistics is widely employed as a tool of analysing the problems in the field of natural and social sciences. It provides tools and techniques for research students. It is not studied for its own sake but for the sake of developing new sciences. It is a method of research in which statistical method (experiment method in natural sciences) is adopted in studying the problems concerned with the social sciences.

II. Main Divisions of Statistics

The domain of statistics or the subject-matter of statistics can be generally classified into two main divisions - Statistical Methods and Applied Statistics.

1) Statistical Methods: Statistical methods are concerned with the formulation of the general rules and principles applicable in handling different branches of data - Collection, Classification, Organisation, Tabulation, Presenting, Analysing and Interpreting data relating to any field of enquiry. They are tools in the hands of statistical investigators in achieving predetermined objectives. They help in extracting truths which are hidden in a mass of data. They are again divided into two groups:

(a) ***Descriptive Statistics:*** It is confined to the treatment of data for the purpose of describing their characteristics. It involves techniques for summarizing data and presenting them in a usable form.

(b) ***Inferential Statistics:*** It is an inductive statistics which involves making forecasts, estimations or judgments, about some larger group of data, from sample data. Inferences about population drawn from sample measures may involve some error or discrepancy.

2) Applied Statistics: Applied statistics deals with the application of statistical rules and principles to concrete factors like wages, prices, income, trade, population and other variables, as they exist. Quality control, sample surveys, quantitative analysis for business decisions and other applications are included in this division.

III. Objects of Statistics

The main object of statistics is to study the population and the variables therein for the pu. pose of reducing the population to the possible extent which helps to make decisions and solve problems. Following are the various objects of statistics:

1. To *make sense* from the population or mass.
2. To *take action* on the basis of available data.
3. To *bear light* on the complexity of the problem.
4. To *forecast the future* trend from the data.
5. To *prove unknown* from the known data.
6. To *examine* the changes in particular activities.
7. To *draw* conclusions from the information.
8. To *provide basis* for the formation of knowledge relating to a particular field of study.

Thus, the quantitative data are processed for the purpose of doing something and making use of them. They are utilised to examine the problems concerning a field of enquiry in their true perspective, to find out the causes of changes and to estimate their probable effects. The statistical methods are employed as a tool for comparison between past and present events to throw light on the reasons of changes.

IV. Functions of Statistics

The main function of statistics is to enlarge our knowledge of complex phenomenon and to lend precision to our ideas that would otherwise remain vague and indeterminate. Statistics increases the field of mental vision as an opera glass or telescope that increases the filed of physical vision. It widens our knowledge because of its following functions:

1. It *simplifies* unwieldy (awkward) and complex mass of data in an intelligible manner.
2. It *enlarges* individual experience that helps in making decisions.
3. It *indicates* tendencies or trends or positions or directions of changes in data.

4. It *collects* the data systematically in a definite form, as information, useful for various purposes.
5. It *presents* data in a most suitable manner that can be understood at a glance.
6. It *compares* one set of data with the other and discloses the comparative position.
7. It *studies* or establishes relationship between the two related aspects of particular phenomenon.
8. It *guides* the management in formulating the plans and policies.
9. It *acts* as a guide in measuring the effects of government policies and business.
10. It *assists* in testing the hypothesis in theory and discovering new theories.
11. It *helps* in estimating the present and forecasting the future activities.

Thus, the important functions of statistics are *simplifying, enlarging, indicating, collecting, presenting, comparing, studying, guiding and helping in the process of statistical investigation and interpretation.* It discloses the hidden facts and enlarges the field of all the branches of human knowledges.

V. Importance of Statistics

Statistics has been termed as the *"Science of Kings"*. Indeed in ancient times, it kept the Kings informed about the man power and riches of domain. Nowadays, it is treated as the *"Arithmetic of Human Welfare"*. It is indispensable for a clear appreciation of any problem affecting the welfare of mankind.

In modern times, *planning without statistics cannot be imagined.* Statistics is the light bearer that enlightens the way to life's adventure. It unravels the crowded complexities of life and thought. Without its support man has to Wander aimlessly through this perplexing universe. It discloses casual connection between related facts. Such a study of statistics is at the bottom of all sound human endeavour.

Statistics are *the eyes of administration*. All the businessmen and statesmen can tender sound advice on a problem to their administrative machinery with the help of adequate data before them to base their judgments.

Statistics *are aids to supervision.* The present days of impersonal relationship between the employer and employees, statistics are becoming tools for the supervision of work in obtaining efficiency of the employees. The supervisors or officers are provided with accurate and concise information to supervise the work of their subordinates.

Statistics are *invaluable in business.* To be successful, a businessman estimates demand for his products in the market. His business runs on estimates and probabilities. Statistics help him in planning and policy making.

Statistical methods are *indispensable in a quantitative study.* They are useful in marketing, accounting, producing and operating activities. They bring truth to light and correct the faulty observations. They are extensively applicable to all the branches of human knowledge – governing, managing, accounting, business, research, social studies, planning and other fields. They are closely associated with the progress of civilization.

VI. Scope of Statistics

The importance of statistics makes it clear that the science of statistics includes in its fold all quantitative analysis concerned with any department of enquiry. Its scope, therefore, is stretched over all those branches of human knowledge in which a grasp of the significance of large numbers is looked for. Its methods provide an important manner of measuring numerical changes in complex groups and judging collective phenomenon. Its scope is, thus, wide, the limiting factor being its applicability to studies of quantitative aspects alone.

"Sciences without statistics bear no fruits,
Statistics without sciences have no roots."

There is hardly any field of human knowledge where statistical methods are not applicable. Thus the significance of statistics has increased from the "Science of Kings" to the "Science of Universe".

VII. Limitations of Statistics

It is necessary to note carefully the limitations of statistics. Otherwise one might make too much of this delicate science. There is no doubt that science of statistics has universal applicability but still it suffers from limitations. Statistical Tools can be misused by a few prejudiced persons. For proper use of statistics, it is essential to keep in mind the following limitations:

1. Statistics Ignores Qualitative Aspects : Statistical methods cannot study those qualitative phenomena which cannot be expressed quantitatively. However, the qualitative phenomenon, to which quantitative standards or scores can be assigned, is included in the study

2. Statistics does not Study Individual Items: A single or isolated figure cannot be regarded as 'statistics'. Statistical methods do not study or recognize an isolated fact. Statistics is confined only to those problems where group characteristics are to be studied.

3. Statistical Laws are not Exact: Statistical laws are true only on the average or in the long run. They are not like the exact laws of physical sciences which are said to hold true in every individual case. Statistical laws only show approximate tendencies.

4. Statistics does not Reveal Entire Story: Statistics provides solution to a problem. It does not study the problem itself. Its results are depending upon many other evidences. It cannot give the entire story of the problem. Too much dependence on statistics may lead to wrong conclusions. *"Statistics is only a means to an end but not an end itself."*

5. Statistics is Liable to be Misused: Statistical tools are dangerous in the hands of those who do not know their use and deficiencies. They can be misused to serve one's own purpose. Statistics is the useful servant but only of great value to those who realize them properly.

Thus the use of statistics by the experts, who are well experienced and skilled in the analysis and interpretation of statistical data for drawing correct and valid inferences, very much reduces the chances of disgrace to the mass popularity of this important science.

VIII. Distrust of Statistics

There exists today a great prejudice or personal feeling against statistics. Some people have simply blind faith in it and ready to swear to tell anything by it. Others have no faith at all and they think adversely of statistics. The science of statistics is often commented by some as under,

"An ounce of truth will produce tons of statistics."

"Statistics can prove anything."

"Figures do not lie. Liars figure."

"Statistics is an unreliable science."

"What statistics reveal is ordinary but what they hide is important."

"History asserts without evidence, while statistics asserts contrary to the evidence."

"Statistics are like clay of which one can make god or devil as he pleases."

Following are the two interesting statements made by the great men:

"There are three kinds of lies – lies, damned lies and statistics."

– Mark Twain.

"Statistics can be compared to miniskirts because they are short enough to make a thing interesting and long enough to cover the subject-matter." **– Paris Banker**

All the above statements bring discredit to the science of statistics. Statistics by nature are innocent and easily believed. They may be incomplete, inaccurate and manipulated deliberately by prejudiced persons. The difficulty lies not with the science of statistics but with the users who misuse it. It is merely a tool in the hands of a statistician just as operating tools in the hands of a surgeon. The derogatory statements about the science of statistics are due to ignorance, resulting from unhappy experience being misled by figures in the past. One may knowingly mishandle the statistical tools to serve his own purpose, but statistics is not to prove or disprove anything. It is to describe a particular phenomenon quantitatively which prepares the ground for a logical inference. It is only a tool liable to be misused. That is why great skill and accumulated experience are required to safeguard the proper diagnosis of figures. One should not blame the tools; the operator of the tools should be blamed. The fault lies with the manner in which the statistical tools are used and persons using them but not with the science of statistics. Statistical methods are not entirely automatic in their operation; the progress in knowledge depends to a considerable degree on the personal qualities of an investigator.

Utmost care and precautions should be taken in the interpretation of statistical data in all its manifestations. Whatever be the distrust of statistics, it does not imply that statistics have no value. No doubt, statistics do not supply conclusions but they do furnish, in part, the basis on which conclusions may be drawn. With he study of statistics as a science, with the recognition of its limitations and with improvements in its techniques, the cause for its distrust is gradually waning.

STATISTICS

Statistical Investigation

Collection of Raw Data

Processing of Data

Elimination of irrelevant and defective data	Scrutinizing and editing of the data	Correcting, Adjusting and refining of the data

Presentation

Classification and Tabulation

Identification, Assessment and Grouping of the Characteristics of Data	Simplification and Arrangement of data in Columns and Rows

Analysis and Interpretation

Averages, Dispersion, Skewness Correlation, Regression, Time Series Indices, Interpolation, Extrapolation Diagrams and Graphs.	Unearthing the trends and relations. Drawing conclusions, Interpreting meaning and Making Decisions.

Questions

1. Explain the term "Statistics". (BU - A83, N87, A91, A96)
2. Is it correct to say that figures do not lie but liars figures? (BU-A83, N91, A95, A97)
3. Mention any four functions of statistics. (BU-N83, A85, N89, N90, N96, N97)
4. "Statistics is the Science of Counting" – Comment. (BU-N83, A88, A92)
5. What is Statistics? (BU - A84, N84, N97)
6. State any two limitations of statistics. (BU - N84, N86, N89, A91, A96)
7. Give Prof. Bowley's definition of Statistical Methods. (BU - N85, N96)
8. Explain the scope of statistics. (BU - A86)
9. "Statistics can prove anything". Comment. (BU - A86, A89, N95)

10. "Statistics is the Science of Estimates and Probabilities". Comment. (BU - N89, A93)
11. Comment on Distrust of Statistics. (BU - A88, A94)
12. Define "statistics" in singular sense.
13. Define "statistics" in plural sense. (BU - A89)
14. State any two objects of statistics. (BU - N91)
15. "Statistics are like clay of which one can make a God or Devil as he pleases". Comment. (BU - N92)
16. Comment on Prof. Horace Secrist's definition of Statistics. (BU - N93, A97)
17. "Statistics should be handled by experts". Comment. (BU - A94)
18. How has Boddington defined statistics? (BU - N86)
19. What is the scope of statistics? (BU- A98)

2

Statistical Investigation

"Statistical Investigation" means an `enquiry' or `inquiry' or `survey' or `search for knowledge' that can be expressed in quantitative terms. It implies a search of knowledge or information through statistical devices. It is a technical job which requires specilized knowledge and skill. It is a comprehensive process involving the following stages:

A. Planning the Enquiry

(i) Purpose of Enquiry.
(ii) Scope of Enquiry.
(iii) Units of Data Collection.
(iv) Sources of Data (primary and secondary).
(v) Techniques of Data Collection(census and sample).
(vi) Types of Enquiry.
(vii) Choice of Frame.
(viii) Degree of Accuracy.
(ix) Miscellaneous considerations.

B. Execution of the Enquiry

(i) Organizational Set Up.
(ii) Designing the Forms.
(iii) Staffing.
(iv) Controlling.
(v) Follow Up Work.
(vi) Presentation.
(vii) Analysis.
(viii) Reporting.

A statistical investigation may be either a *general* purpose enquiry or a *special* purpose enquiry. In a general purpose enquiry we obtain data which are useful for several purposes. The best example of this type of enquiry is the census taken every ten years in India. A special purpose enquiry is that in which data obtained may be useful in analysing a particular problem.

A. Planning the Enquiry

Though the collection of data constitutes the first step in all the statistical enquiries, planning the enquiry occupies as the preliminary to the collection of data. Following are the points to be considered in the planning of enquiry:

(i) Purposes of Enquiry: The objectives of the enquiry must be clearly and concretely defined. This determines the nature of data to be collected and the techniques for the analysis of data to be employed. This avoids wastage and confusion in collecting the data. This would also help in eliminating the collection of irrelevant information. So the purpose of enquiry should be decided specifically.

(ii) Scope of Enquiry: The scope of enquiry should be determined well in advance. It relates to the coverage with respect to the type of information, subject matter and geographical area. It fixes the area within which the enquiry is to be conducted. It helps in deciding the exact quantum of data to be collected for the purpose. The larger the scope of enquiry, the more the resources are required.

(iii) Units of Data Collection: A statistical unit is the basis in terms of which data are collected, analysed and interpreted. It is a thing or object or quantity which is well defined and identified, and with which counts or measurements are associated.

It is an amount or quantity used as a standard measurement. It should be unambiguous, specific, stable, appropriate and uniform.

The statistical units may be broadly classified as follows:

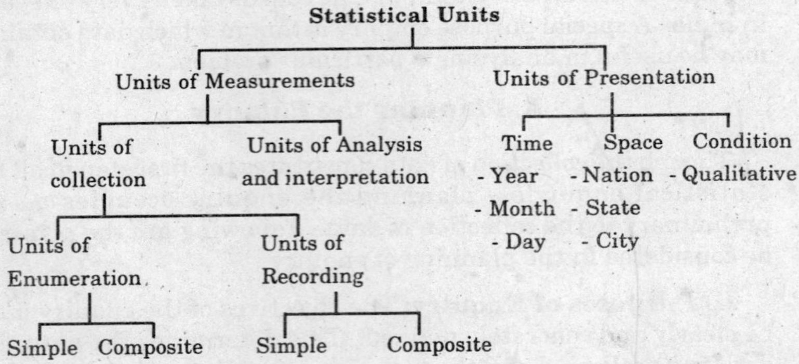

(a) Units of Measurements: These units are used for counting or measuring the data in the process of collection, analysis and interpretation.

(i) Units of Collection are used while collecting the data. They are further divided into two classes- Units of Enumeration and the Units of Recording.

A unit of enumeration is the basic unit on which the observations are to be made. Examples of simple units are a person, a shop, a company, a family and an animal. Examples of composite(complex) units are a rich person, a medical shop, a limited company, a muslim family and a farm animal.

A *unit of recording* is the secondary unit by which the data are to be recorded. Examples of simple units are a ton, a kilowatt, an hour, a month and a kilometer. Examples of composite(complex) units are a ton kilometer, a kilowatt hour, an hour kilowatt, a monthly wage, a passenger kilometer.

(ii) Units of Analysis and Interpretation are those units in the form of which the data are ultimately analysed and interpreted.

They facilitate comparisons between the two sets of data with respect to time, space or conditions. They include Rates, Ratios, Percentages and Coefficients. A "Rate' is a standard of reckoning which is obtained by bringing two numbers or amounts into relationship. They are usually expressed per thousand. For instance, birth rates and death rates per thousand are used in the analysis of population data. Ratios and percentages are used where quantities compared are of the same kind. For instance the ratio of literates to illiterates is 1:4 or 'Literates are 20% of the population'. Rate per unit is called a 'Coefficient'. For example, if it is stated that the death(mortality) rate in India 1.6% or 16 per thousand, the coefficient of deaths is 1.6/100 or 0.016.

(b) Units of Presentation: These units are used for presenting the data. They are of three types : Time, Space and Condition. The data may be measured by years, by location or by efficiency. The turnover may be shown monthwise, statewise or naturewise.

We can also classify the statistical units as Physical and Arbitrary. The physical units like a Rupee, a kilo and a meter do not need any explanation. The Arbitrary units like Wages, Literacy, poverty and Educated need explanation. For example, the wages may be real wages, money wages, time wages and monthly wages.

(iv) Sources of Data: The various sources from which data are collected should be carefully determined. The data to be collected may be either primary or secondary.

The data which are collected originally by the investigator for the given enquiry are termed as "Primary Data". The data which had been collected earlier by some one else and the investigator makes use of them are called "Secondary Data".

The data which are collected from the internal records of the organization are called "internal data". The data which are collected from the sources outside the organization are called "external data".

(v) Techniques of Data Collection: The problem in collecting the data does not arise if the secondary data are to be used. But if the primary data are to be collected, a decision has to be taken whether the census method or the sample method is to be used for data collection.

The "census method" is a complete enumeration and recording of every unit of universe or population or mass. The "sample method" is a selection of representative and adequate fraction(finite subset) of the universe or population or mass. The choice of the method or technique depends on a number of factors- source of the data, nature of the data, purpose of the enquiry, availability of funds and time and other conditions.

(vi) Types of Enquiry: There are various types of enquiries among which the investigator has to deal with one.

If an enquiry is conducted by or on behalf of the government, it is termed as an "*Official Enquiry*". If it is conducted by institutions patronized by the government, it is termed as a "*Semi-official Enquiry*". If an enquiry is conducted by the private organizations, it is termed as an "*Unofficial Enquiry*".

If an enquiry is conducted for the first time it is called an "*Initial or Original Enquiry*". If an enquiry is carried on in continuation or repetition of some previously conducted enquiry, it is called a "*Repetitive Enquiry*".

If an enquiry to be conducted is to be kept confidential, it is known as a "*Confidential Enquiry*". An enquiry whose results are to be published and made known to the general public is known as a "*Non-confidential Enquiry*".

If the enquiry to be conducted involves the study of phenomenon capable of being quantitatively measured such as age, weight, income and prices, is termed as a "*Direct Enquiry*". If the enquiry to be conducted involves the study of phenomenon not capable of being quantitatively measured such as honesty, beauty and intelligence(and expressed quantitatively by assigning appropriate standards or ranks), it is termed as an "*Indirect Enquiry*".

If the enquiry is conducted periodically at equal intervals of time(monthly, quarterly or yearly) it is said be a "*Regular Enquiry*". If an enquiry is conducted as and when necessary without any regularity or periodicity, it is said to be an "*Ad-hoc Enquiry*".

If the enquiry involves adoption of census method in collecting the data, it is called a "*Census Enquiry*". If the enquiry involves adoption of sample method in collecting the data, it is called a "*Sample Enquiry*".

If the enquiry relates to the collection of primary data, it is called a "*Primary Enquiry*". If the enquiry relates to the collection of secondary data, it is called a "*Secondary Enquiry*".

If the enquiry to be dealt with the many aspects of the problem under study, it is called an "*Extensive Enquiry*". If the enquiry to be dealt with only one or two aspects of the problem under study, it is called a "*Limited Enquiry*".

If the enquiry is conducted not in detail or is conducted summarily, it is termed as a "*Pilot (brief) Enquiry*". If the enquiry is conducted in detail, it is termed as a "*Comprehensive Enquiry*".

(vii) Choice of Frame : A "frame is a structure, or border or outline which refers to the list, map or specification. Within such particular frame the data available is referred. The frame may be a "Directory", "Voters' List", "City plan" or "Ration cardholders List". The frame determines the whole structure of enquiry. While selecting the frame, a proper examination of it has to be made regarding its reliability.

(viii) Degree of Accuracy: A decision regarding the degree of accuracy or precision desired by the investigator in his estimates or results is essential before starting any statistical enquiry. An investigator has to decide at what degree the accuracy be maintained. In any statistical enquiry, perfect accuracy in final results is practically impossible to achieve. So the necessary degree of accuracy in counting or measuring is desired and maintained. It all depends upon the practical value of accuracy in relation to its cost. A strict watch should also be made on all the possible inaccuracies and a reasonable standard of accuracy should be aimed at.

(ix) Miscellaneous Considerations: The various considerations-time-fixation, arrangement of funds, appointment of staff, government polices, economic conditions and other contingencies are to be taken into account while planning the enquiry. It all depends upon the nature and type of enquiry that is to be conducted.

Thus a proper planning, with due consideration of various aspects of enquiry, is very essential before we take the task of collecting the data.

B . Execution of the Enquiry

Once the plan is prepared for collecting the data, an investigator should proceed with the execution of the plan. A plan should be put into action. Following are the various stages in the execution of the plan:

(i) Organizational Set Up: A suitable organization to carry out the planned performance is set up for the statistical investigation. The nature and scope of enquiry will determine the size of the organization. Generally the existing organizations are used for this purpose on temporary basis.

(ii) Designing the Forms: A number of forms are required to collect the data and record the same in a systematic manner. Different types of forms are designed and got them printed which can be used in the process of enquiry,. especially the forms of questionnaire.

(iii) Staffing: The appointment of required staff is very important task in the statistical investigation. The proper selection and training of staff, and assigning the jobs to them should be carefully made. There must be an adequate number of field investigators, supervisors and other staff for the execution of the enquiry.

(iv) Controlling: A planned performance of the enquiry is regularly compared with the actual performance of the enquiry for the purpose of controlling the various activities. A strict watch on all the activities should be kept. The variations between the planned and actual performances are examined and corrective measures are taken.

(v) Follow Up Work: In spite of taking corrective steps and controlling measures, it is possible, sometimes, that there would not be any response. Under such circumstances, a proper arrangements should be made to deal with the cases of non-response. So, every effort should be made to collect the information as per schedule having the follow-up.

(vi) Presentation: The data collected is to be classified, simplified, edited and finally tabulated, presented or represented in the form graphs and diagrams. It is the most important task of the statistician to present the data in a suitable form.

(vii) Analysis: The presented data has to be properly analysed which needs a special skill. The statistical analysis involves the application of the mathematical techniques to reduce the presented data and represent them in a single value. A heap of data is reduced to some kind of mathematical measures for the purpose of decision making.

(viii) Reporting: The analysed data should be properly understood and carefully interpreted to make accurate conclusions. Then it becomes necessary to embody the results in the form of a report. A preparation of report constitutes the last stage in the execution of enquiry. A report so prepared should contain all the details of the enquiry and it should be submitted to the concerned higher authorities for action.

Thus the statistical investigation is a long process of planning the activities and executing the plan effectively.

Questions

1. What is a statistical Survey? (BU-A83, A86, N90, A97)
2. Give any four requisites of a good statistical unit. (BU-A83, N92, N95)
3. Enumerate any four aspects that need careful consideration while planning the survey. (BU-N83, A90, N96, A97, A98)
4. Mention the types of statistical units. (BU-N83, N84, N91, A95)
5. Explain the term "Units of Measurement". (BU-N84)
6. What is a 'frame' in a statistical survey? (BU-A85)
7. Mention any four phases of executing a statistical survey. (BU-N85)
8. Define a statistical unit? Give examples. (BU-A88, A89, A92)
9. State the four stages in the planning a statistical survey. (BU-A90, A95)
10. What do you mean by "Units of Collection" and "Units Analysis"? (BU-A93)
11. Distinguish between the general purpose survey and the special purpose survey. (BU-A96)

3

Collection of Data

The raw material of statistics originates from the operation of counting or enumeration or measurement. For any statistical enquiry, the basic problem is to collect facts and figures relating to a particular phenomenon under study. A statistician conducts the statistical enquiry and he begins his work with the counting or measuring the data i.e. collection of data.

The process of counting or enumerating or measuring together with the recording of results is called the **"Collection of Data."** It is the preliminary step of the statistical enquiry or investigation.

I. Sources of Data

Having determined the purpose and scope of statistical enquiry, a statistician or investigator has to determine the best method of collecting the data. The sources of data collection are classified, on the basis of the nature of data, into two groups - Primary and Secondary.

"Primary Data" are those data which are originally collected for the first time, for a specific purpose by an investigator. They are collected directly from the people to whom the enquiry is related. They are original in character. They are primary to the institution which collects them; they are secondary to all other institutions which refer such data.

"Secondary Data" are those data which are already collected, processed and used by someone else for their own purpose. They are either published or unpublished. They are finished products. They are secondary to all those institutions except the one which has collected them.

It may be observed that the distinction between primary and secondary data is a matter of degree or relativity only. The same set of data may be primary in the hands of one and secondary in the hands of others. The sources of collecting the data, thus, are also classified as - Primary Sources and Secondary Sources.

A. Primary Sources: The data which are originally collected for the first time are called "primary data." The methods of collecting the primary data are as under:

(i) Direct Personal Observation.

(ii) Indirect Oral Interviews.

(iii) Information Through Local Agencies.

(iv) Mailed Questionnaire Method.

(v) Schedules Through Enumerators.

(i) Direct Personal Observation: This method consists in the collection of data personally by the investigator or organising agency who has to go to the field personally for making observations or enquiries and soliciting information from the informants or respondents. Such a method is suited only if the enquiry is intensive rather than extensive. It is used only if the investigation is local or regional. It requires the personal attention of the investigator. Generally, the information gathered is original in nature. It involves personal face to face contact with the informants or respondents.

The information is first hand one, more reliable and accurate. Because of personal approach, there will be a good response from the informants. The investigator can get additional information, if any, from the informants and he can adjust his plan of observation according the nature and behaviour of the informants.

This method is restrictive in nature and is suited only for intensive studies and not for extensive enquiry. It is handicapped due to lack of time, money and manpower since the informants are to be approached at their residence or office at their convenience. It requires skilled and experienced investigator for enquiry.

(ii) Indirect Oral Interviews: This method consists in collection of the data through enumerators appointed for the purpose. A small list of questions pertaining to the subject matter of the enquiry is prepared. These listed questions are then put to the informants or witnesses who are closely connected or concerned with the subject matter. The enumerators collect all the answers from the informants and record them systematically. This method is adopted by the commissions appointed by the government.

The information collected by the enumerators is correct and relevant. It is less expensive and requires less time for conducting the enquiry. If necessary, the expert views and suggestions can be obtained in order to formulate and conduct the enquiry more efficiently and effectively.

This method suffers from lack of personal touch and supervision by the investigator as the information is collected through the enumerators from the informants. The accuracy of data collected much depends upon the nature and skill of the informants who may give a wrong information. The informants may be prejudiced persons. It is very difficult to find the informants who are more concerned with the subject matter of the enquiry. Some of them even may not really possess the knowledge in answering the questions.

(iii) Information Through Local Agencies: This method consists in the appointment of local agents or correspondents by the investigators in different parts of field of enquiry. These agencies or correspondents in different regions collect the information according to their own ways, fashions, likings and decisions, and then submit their reports periodically to the central or head office where the data are finally collected. This method is usually employed by the newspaper or periodical agencies and the various departments of the government.

This method works out to be very cheap and economical for extensive investigations particularly when the data are obtained by part-time correspondents or agents. Moreover, the information can be obtained expeditiously since only rough estimates are required.

This method suffers from personal prejudices and whims of the correspondents in different fields of the enquiry and consequently the data so obtained will not be very reliable. This method is not suitable for collecting the accurate and exact information.

(iv) Mailed Questionnaire Method: This method consists in preparing a **'Questionnaire'** (a list of questions) relating to the field of enquiry and providing space for the answers to be filled in by the respondents or informants or addressees to whom the questionnaire is mailed with a request for quick response within the specified time. A very polite covering note or letter explaining the aims and objects of enquiry is attached. Respondents are also requested to extend their full co-operation by furnishing information and returning the questionnaire duly filled in. Respondents are are taken into confidence by ensuring them that the information so supplied by them will be kept strictly confidential and secrete. In order to ensure quick and better response, the return postal expenses are usually borne by the investigating organization by sending the self-addressed stamped envelope. This method is usually used by the research workers, private individuals, non-official agencies and government departments.

In this method, the questionnaire plays an important role. Due skill, efficiency, care and experience are required in framing the questionnaire. The questions asked must be clear, short, brief, corroborative, non-offending, courteous, unambiguous and suitable for answering in the form of **"Yes"** or **"No"**. They should not be too confidential and hurt the feelings of the respondents. They must be arranged in a logical order. They must suit the general educational level of the respondents.

This method is by far the most economical method in terms of time, money and manpower. It is used for extensive enquiries covering a very wide area. The information obtained is original and much more authentic.

The most serious drawback of this method is that it is used only if the audience is educated. It is not at all useful when the informants are illiterate. Even if they are literate, they may not take interest in answering and returning the questionnaire. Quite often, the correct information may be suppressed. It is very difficult to verify the authenticity of the answers given by them in the questionnaire. Sometimes the informants may hesitate to disclose their income, property and habits in writing. There is also no scope for obtaining supplementary information by putting additional questions for cross checking the answers. Moreover, the informants are not given any opportunity for clearing the doubts that are in their minds.

(v) Schedules Through Enumerators: A **schedule** is the device of obtaining answers to the questions in the form which is filled in by the enumerators in a face to face situation with the respondents. Schedules are sent through the enumerators. A questionnaire is a list of questions which is sent directly to and filled in by the informants. A schedule is a list of questions which is filled in by the enumerators.

The enumerators visit the respondents personally with the list of questions (schedules), ask them the questions therein and record the answers from the informants. This method is generally used by the big business houses, large public undertakings and research institutions.

The enumerators can explain in detail the objective and scope of the enquiry to the informants and impress upon them the need and utility of furnishing the correct information.. This method is useful in extensive enquiries and it yields reliable and dependable results. There will be a good and quick response from the informants whether they are literates or illiterates. The enumerators can effectively check the accuracy of the information by cross-questioning and putting additional questions.

This method is fairly expensive as the team of enumerators is to be highly paid for the work. It is also more time consuming as compared to the "mailed questionnaire" method. The success of the method largely depends upon the efficient, skilled and trained enumerators. Inefficient and biased enumerators may suppress or even twist the information supplied by the informants or respondents. There will be variation in the information recorded by different enumerators with different personal views. If the schedule is not correctly and carefully framed, the enumerators may get incomplete and wrong information from the respondents.

From all the above sources the primary data can be collected. However, there are other methods - Local Reports, Enquiries , Telephone Calls and Fax - which are used in most of the advanced countries for collecting the data.

B. Secondary Sources: The data which have already been collected by someone else are called "secondary data" which have gone through the statistical process at least once. They may be either finished or semi-finished and published or unpublished.

Published sources are those publications which belong to the government, national and international organisations, trade associations and chambers of commerce. The various government departments also publish Journals, Bulletins and Periodicals which contain valuable and ready information. Even research centres and educational institutions are publishing various types of information.

Unpublished sources are those publications which are not openly circulated in the public. The data are just maintained, as records, by the private firms or business concerns. They are not at all published as they are meant for private purposes. Even the various units or departments of the government can circulate the information within the departments. Such secondary data may be made available to others. The secondary data should be used with extra caution. The investigator must satisfy himself as regards the reliability, accuracy, adequacy and suitability of the data.

II. Techniques of Collecting Data

Statistical data are collected for the purpose of analysis and interpretation. The data are collected by techniques - Census and Sample. The problem of application of techniques will arise only in case of collecting the primary data.

A. Census Method: In a census technique of collecting the data every element of the population is included in the investigation. It involves a complete count in which information is collected about every unit of the universe relating to the subject mater of the enquiry. It is the oldest method of collecting the data. It is a straight forward technique in which an investigator observes each and every item within the scope of enquiry. Not a single item is left unnoticed by him. All the items of the population are observed and recorded. The results from such method are more accurate and reliable. This method helps in making available the intensive knowledge. It is useful (suitable) where units of diverse nature constitute universe or population or mass. However, this technique is more expensive and required more labour and time. It is the most difficult and giant task to count all the items in the population as they are always subject to changes.

B. Sample Method: In a sample technique of collecting the data a selection of the part of the universe is made for the purpose of study. Only the representative items from the mass are collected. The number of items selected generally represent the entire population. It is very essential to select the adequate number of items so that each one shall have the characteristics of the mass to the possible extent. A finite subset of the population is called **"sample"**. The number of units in the sample is called the **"sample size"**. Sampling enables us to draw conclusions. This method is economical, time-saving, convenient and practicable. However, the samples selected may not represent the mass and they may be false and influenced by the personal bias of the selector.

As the census method is too cumbersome and costly, in most of the cases the sampling method is used in statistical enquiries. There are two methods of taking the samples - Random sampling and Non-random sampling.

(a) Random Sampling: It refers to the chance selection but it does not mean that the selection should be made in a haphazard manner. A few mechanical devices are used in a sample selection so that every item selected on random basis has equal probability of entering the sample. It is a blind chance alone that determines whether one or the other item may or may not be selected. The term **"random"**, is not used in the sense of *'hit or miss'* method. There shall be no room for discrimination to be exercised by the investigator. In fact, sampling is a scientific way of getting items selected from the mass. The selection of the items should be free from personal bias or judgment. The various methods of sampling - Drawing chips from the bowl, rotating the drum and use of a table of random digits - are used in collecting the data. The most important method adopted nowadays is the **"lottery"** draws that are based on purely random sampling.

(b) Non-random Sampling: It involves a deliberate selection of the samples and refers to the personal bias and discretion of the investigator while selecting the specific items. It is also called a purposeful sampling in which an investigator exercises human judgment. There is scope for bias or personal interest and no element of chance in selection of the items.

There are many more **other methods** of taking the samples. They are as under:

In a *"Systematic or Quasi-random"* sampling, a list of universe is prepared either on the basis of alphabetical, geographical or numerical order. The first item is selected at random from each set, then eleventh item, then twenty first and so on.

In a *"Stratified Sampling"*, different strata or segments are made in the population on the basis of homogeneous characteristics. Each stratum is called sub-population from which selection of the items are made.

In a *"Cluster Sampling"*, various clusters having heterogeneous characteristics are made. It involves selection of some of the clusters on random basis.

In a "*Double Sampling*", samples are taken in two stages. If the first set of sample is inconclusive, the second set is added to the first one to strengthen the results.

In a "*Multiple Sampling*", a sample procedure is carried out in several stages - the first stage, the second stage and so on. For example, in the first stage a few districts from the state are selected. In the second stage, a few talukas are selected from the sample districts. In the third stage, a few villages are selected from the sample talukas. In the next stage, a few families are selected from the sample villages. In this process, the size of the sample goes on reducing at each stage.

In a "*Quota Sampling*", the investigator is directed to collect information from an assigned quota or number of individuals in each of several groups characterised in the universe.

In a "*Convenience Sampling*", a sample is obtained from the readily available lists such as telephone directory, ration card-holders' list and voters' list.

In a "*Sequential Sampling*", a number of samples are drawn from the universe one after another depending on the results of previous samples. If the first sample is not acceptable, the lot from which the first samples are made is rejected. Then the second lot is taken from which again samples are selected. After each lot of items, we have to decide whether to accept or reject or to reserve the judgement or continue the process until a final decision is taken.

Thus, the choice of sampling technique depends upon the nature of the universe, the sampling unit, the size of sample and the other factors.

III. Principles of Sampling

In all the statistical enquiries, generally the random sampling is employed as it assumes equal chances of inclusion and exclusion of different characteristics of the data of the population. This makes the selection balanced and it is purely based on the various mathematical theories. Following are the theories or principles or laws of the statistical methods:

(i) Theory of Probability: The method of random sampling is based on the mathematical "theory of probability". The theory implies that if from a very large number of items (population), a moderately large number of items is chosen at random, such items are almost sure, on the whole, to possess the characteristics of the population.

If a rupee coin is tossed twelve times, the probability is that it will fall six times with its head upwards and six times its tail upwards. Similarly, if a die has been cast, consisting of six sides, it is certain that one side will land uppermost. If we throw it twenty four times, each side will land upward probably four times. (i.e. each of the outcome is 1/6). On this theory only the gamblers run risk continuously and the insurance companies undertake to indemnify the loss. Thus, the theory says that in the samples chosen from the population, every item has an equal chance of selection.

(ii) Law of Statistical Regularity: The law indicates that a moderately large number of items chosen at random from a large group are almost sure to possess, on an average, the characteristics of the large group or population. The **"Theory of Probability"** gave rise to the **"Law of Statistical Regularity"**. The former tells us of mathematical expectation of happening and not happening of events having equal chances in a sample selection. The latter tells us that random selection from the universe is likely to give a representative character of the population.

The "Law of Statistical Regularity" provides the basis of sampling investigation. It guarantees at least reasonable accuracy in results because there is a marked regularity in probability of having same results in each and every set of samples. It directs our attention to the desirability of choosing the sample at random because of regularity in natural phenomena of having the probability of representative character. So it impresses upon the large sample size and random selection.

(iii) Law of Inertia of Large Numbers: It is a corollary to the "Law of Statistical Regularity". It states that, other things being equal, larger the size of the sample, it is likely that the results will be more accurate. It lays down that large aggregates are more stable than small ones. The large numbers have an `inertia' or great stability, steadiness and consistency than that possessed by small ones. For example, the quantity of wheat produced in a year varies immensely from month to month in any one country, but the wheat production of the world as a whole relatively remains stable for decades. The movements in individual components of a population have a tendency to cancel out the positive and negative variances one another. When very large numbers are involved, changes are likely to be more gradual and regular than when relatively small numbers are considered. It is based on the fact that the behaviour of a phenomenon on a large scale is generally stable.

IV. Editing the Data

The mass data collected is in the form of raw material. They should be edited, or scrutinized to detect errors, omissions and inconsistencies. The defective data may be either altered or rejected completely. It is very essential that the data should be examined whether they are appropriate or not. It requires a high degree of skill in editing the data as the accuracy of the results of an enquiry depends upon it.

In the process of editing, inconsistent data are corrected or rejected, uniformity is maintained in statistical units, reliability of the information is confirmed and accuracy is maintained reasonably.

Perfect accuracy in the data is rarely attainable. In statistical enquiries, accuracy is neither possible nor desirable. Reasons for it are obvious; the observer and the observing instruments are both sources of error. Statistical methods do not, therefore, aim at arithmetical precision. A statistician has to be satisfied with Reasonable Accuracy of the figures because statistics deals with estimates and probabilities.

Accuracy is a relative term; absolute accuracy is not possible and not desired, but for all practical purposes a reasonable degree of accuracy is maintained.

Approximation of the figures is extensively used in the statistical methods. Numerous digits confuse the mind. They may be expressed in round numbers, even though exact figures may be available. For example, the figure 2,64,785 may be expressed as 2,64,790 or 2,64,800 or 2,65,000, but not as 2,64,700 or 2,64,000. In this process a rough calculation, estimation or guess is made.

Generally, **'approximation to the nearest whole number'** method is regarded as the best method, because it is scientific and reasonable. The previous digital value is unchanged, when the next digital value is less than half (0.5). All fractions more than half should be counted as whole numbers and all numbers less than half should be discarded. For example

Original Number	Approximation
15.039	15.0
15.049	15.1
15.449	15.5
15.349	15.4
15.444	15.4
15.4445	15.5

Approximation of the figures is made only when the importance of the figures do not change. Figures should be approximated to the least point. The fact of approximation should be indicated. The most important point to be borne in mind is that the **approximation should be done at the last stage of analysis or computation.**

Thus, a method of approximation is commonly adopted to ignore fractions less than half and count fractions more than half as full. Fractions equal to exactly half may be counted as full or dropped at the discretion of the investigator.

V. Statistical Errors

An "error", in general, refers to a mistake. An **"error"**, in statistics, denotes the difference between the true value (a result of census) and the estimated value (a result of sampling). So, in statistics, an error does not mean mistake but a difference.

After the collection and editing of the data, there still remains the difference between the true value and the estimated value. Such errors are called statistical errors which arise due to inadequacy of data, unintentional acts of the investigators, random sampling and editing of the data. Statistical errors are of two types - sampling errors and non-sampling errors.

(a) Sampling Errors: These errors arise due to drawing inference about the population or universe on the basis of samples or observations, because samples are seldom perfect miniature of the population. These sampling errors may be classified, further, as biased and unbiased (purposeful and unpurposeful).

"Biased Errors" exist due to biased views of the informants and investigators, defective measurements, defective sampling and prejudiced treatment of data collected. These errors are constant, cumulative, persistent and systematic. They are not compensating and they move in the same direction. They can be checked by examining their sources carefully and taking proper precautions at each stage in the process of investigation.

"Unbiased Errors" exist naturally and suddenly without any bias or prejudice. They arise due to the principles of statistics - "Theory of Probability", "Law of Statistical Regularity" and "Law of Inertia of Large Numbers". The excess errors in one direction is almost balanced by the excess errors in the other direction. Such errors, therefore, are compensating. They are non-cumulative and compensating. They lie in both the directions - positive and negative.

Thus in the sampling enquiry we find both the sampling and non-sampling errors.

(b) Non-sampling Errors: These errors occur in the sampling enquiry and the census enquiry as well. But in the census enquiry we find only non-sampling errors. Non-sampling errors included both statistical errors and mistakes. They creep in during the process of collecting the information. They arise due to the negligence of the investigators in asking the questions or in recording the answers. They also arise due to the lack of knowledge in the investigation. Even they are also the result of the approximation, faulty definitions and defective system of collecting the data. They increase as the number of units included in the census enquiry. They are greater in a census enquiry than in a sample.

All the statistical errors can be measured absolutely or relatively. So the statistical errors may be either Absolute or Relative.

(i) Absolute Error: It is the difference between the true value and the estimated value. It is the difference between the origin figure and the approximated figure. To put it in a formula form:

$$\text{Absolute Error} = \text{Actual Value} - \text{Estimated Value}$$

$$AE = AV - EV$$

(The result may be positive or negative)

(ii) Relative Error: It is the ratio of the absolute error to the estimated value. It can also be expressed in a percentage.

$$\text{Relative Error} = \frac{\text{Actual Value - Estimated Value}}{\text{Estimated Value}}$$

$$= \frac{\text{AV - EV}}{\text{EV}} = \frac{\text{Absolute Error}}{\text{Estimated Values}}$$

For example, if there are three workers having daily wages Rs 44, Rs 84 and Rs 164. Their estimated daily wages will be Rs 40, Rs 80 and Rs 160 respectively. Then the errors are;

Absolute Errors	**Relative Errors**
44 - 40 = 4	4/40 = 0.1 = 10%
84 - 80 = 4	4/80 = 0.05 5%
164 - 160 = 4	4/160 = 0.025 = 2.5%

Thus, to make the secondary data fit for analysis and interpretation, we should edit them to suit the purpose of enquiry. The errors and irregularities in them are to be removed. The suitability, adequacy and reliability of the secondary are examined carefully. When they are satisfactory and reliable, they may be used for analysis and interpretation.

Questions

1. What do you mean by a "Statistical Error"? (BU-A83, N86, N87, N89, N90)
2. What is "Primary Data"? Give example. (BU-A83, N84, N87, N96)
3. Give any two merits and demerits of direct personal investigation. (BU - A83, N93)
4. State the principle of "Statistical Regularity". (BU - A83, A87, N87, A97)
5. What is "Secondary Data"? Give example. (BU - N83, A87, A96)
6. Mention any four qualities of a good questionnaire. (BU-N83, N86, A89)
7. State the principle of "Inertia of Large Numbers". (BU-N83, N89, A96).
8. Explain the term "Sample Design". (BU-A84)
9. State any four factors that influence the choice between "Primary and Secondary Data". (BU-A85, A93)
10. What do you mean by "Secondary Data"? What are the precautions to be taken in their use? (BU - N85, N92)
11. What do you mean by a "Census" and "Sampling"? (BU-A86)

12. Give two methods of collecting primary data. (BU-A86, N89, A91)
13. Distinguish between primary and secondary data. (BU-A88, A92, N94, A97)
14. Distinguish between a "Census" and "Sampling". (BU-N89, A98)
15. What is a questionnaire? (BU-N89, A91, A95, A98)
16. Mention two principles of sampling . (BU-N84)
17. Name the sources of secondary data. (BU-N91, N97)
18. What are the merits and demerits of collecting data through the schedule method? (BU-A92)
19. What are the merits and demerits of collecting data through the questionnaire method? (BU - N92)
20. Distinguish between "Questionnaire" and "Schedule". (BU-A93)
21. Mention various methods of sampling? (BU-N93)
22. Distinguish between random sampling and non-random sampling. (BU-N96)

4

Classification of Data

The data collected in any statistical enquiry are voluminous, huge and in a raw form. They are unwieldy and uncomprehensible. An overwhelming mass of raw data should go through some statistical process. Because the data collected is unorganized and not capable of being rapidly or easily assimilated or interpreted. Some process of condensation is necessary to make the data organized so that they could be easily understood. A crude data should be made fit for any analysis and interpretation. Such data require proper arrangements and modification. They should be grouped or classified under appropriate classes or heads systematically. Thus, the complex mass data should be organized systematically. There are three steps in organizing the raw data – Classification, Tabulation and Analysis.

"Classification" is a process of arranging things (either actually or notionally) in groups or classes according to their resemblances and affinities. It gives expression to the unity of attributes that may subsist amongst a diversity of individuals. All the items with similarities are brought together. Following are the definitions.

"Classification is the process of arranging data into sequences and groups according to their common characteristics, or separating them into different but related parts". – **Secrist**

"Classification is a scheme for breaking a category into a set of parts, called classes, according to some precisely defined differing characteristics possessed by all the elements of the category".

– Tuttle.A.M.

Thus, the process of classification involves the arrangements of the data into different classes which are to be determined depending upon the nature, objectives and scope of the enquiry. It involves grouping of related facts into classes. It refers to the sorting out of a heterogeneous mass of data into a number of homogeneous groups and sub-groups. The grouping is done with respect to some characteristics or attributes. It eliminates unnecessary details and brings in the unity of attributes within the diversity. It makes distinction between the points of similarity and dissimilarity. It allows comparison for inference easily.

I. Objects of Classification

The objects of classification are as under:

(i) To present the facts in a simple form: Classification makes the unorganized mass of data simple, brief, logical and understandable. It helps in understanding the structure and nature of data.

(ii) To bring out points of similarity and dissimilarity: Classification brings out clearly the points of similarity and dissimilarity existing among the data. Different attributes of data are placed in different classes.

(iii) To facilitate comparison: Classification helps in making comparisons between the two series which enables one to draw inferences. Without classification it is very difficult to have a comparative study and take decisions.

(iv) To bring out relationship: Classification helps to establish relationship between the two series. With the help of such a relationship, one can conclude about the cause and effect relationship.

(v) To present a mental picture: Classification makes one to have a mental picture of the mass data. It gives a clear picture of the complex data in a condensed form.

(vi) To prepare the basis for tabulation: Classification makes the process of tabulation easy. Without classification it is very difficult to tabulate the data.

(vii) To eliminate unnecessary data: Classification eliminates the unnecessary and irrelevant data for further study. It gives prominence to the important information only and drops out the unwanted elements.

(viii) To bring in uniformity among attributes out of the diversities persistent in the collected raw data. This helps to understand the data easily.

II. Functions of Classification

The functions of classification may be briefly summarized as follows:

(i) It condenses the data: Classification presents the huge unwieldy data in a condensed form which is readily comprehensible to the mind and attempts to highlight the significant features contained in the data.

(ii) It facilitates comparisons: Classification enables us to make meaningful comparisons depending on the basis or criterion of classification. For instance, the classification of the students in a university according to sex enables us to make comparative study of the prevalence of university education among males and females.

(iii) It helps to study the relationships: The classification of the given data with respect to two or more criteria – sex, faculty and area will enable us to study the relationship between the two criteria.

(iv) It facilitates the statistical treatment of the data: The arrangement of the voluminous heterogeneous data, into relatively homogeneous groups or classes according to their points of similarities, introduces uniformity amidst diversity. Such an arrangement makes the data intelligible, useful and readily amenable for further processes like tabulation, analysis and interpretation.

Thus, in statistics, the importance of classification cannot be overemphasized. It requires skill and patience to classify the raw data. Experience alone will convince one of the requisite care that should be taken to avoid blunders and save time. However, there are no precise rules to be followed in classifying the data. It may be noted that an ideal classification should possess the merits of being unambiguous, stable and flexible. It should not leave room for any doubt; it should be stable enough to render comparisons easy and it should be flexible to incorporate new ideas as they would be materialized in future. It should be exhaustive and the classes made in it should not overlap. The items included in one class should be homogeneous. The total of the items, included in different classes should tally with the total or the items collected.

III. Bases of Classification

The basis or the criteria with respect to which the data are classified primarily depend on the objectives and the purpose of the enquiry. Generally, the data are classified as under:

Bases of Classification

- Attributes (Qualitative or Descriptive)
  - Simple (two-fold)
  - Composite (manifold)
  - Arbitrary (notional)
- Variables (Quantitative or Numerical)
  - Discrete (integers)
  - Continuous (fractional)

(i) Qualitative Classification: Under this method, data are classified according to attributes or qualities or characteristics or some properties. Generally, the qualitative phenomena are not capable of quantitative measurements such as honesty, beauty, employment, intelligence, occupation, sex, literacy and other attributes. However, they can be studied either in the form of presence or in the form of absence of a particular quality for example, the classification can be made like married and unmarried, educated and uneducated, tall and short, fat and lean and so on. So descriptive characteristics of the data can be classified by means of some natural or physical lines of demarcation.

"Simple Classification" involves presence or absence of a single attribute. There are only two classes with reference to a single attribute only. Examples of such classification are male and female, honest and dishonest trained and untrained or black and white. Only one pair is considered under the simple classification. It is a two fold classification.

"Composite Classification" involves presence or absence of more than one attribute. It starts with a simple (two-fold) classification and extends further with other attributes of the same data. Examples of such classification are Male and Female, among these both attributes again we have Male-Married and Unmarried, and Female-Married and Unmarried. Likewise we can have again sub classification in Married class as Graduates and Non-graduates, and in Unmarried class as Graduates and Non-graduates. A number of divisions and sub divisions are made in the attributes under the composite classification. It is a manifold classification.

Following is the scheme of classification made in the population:

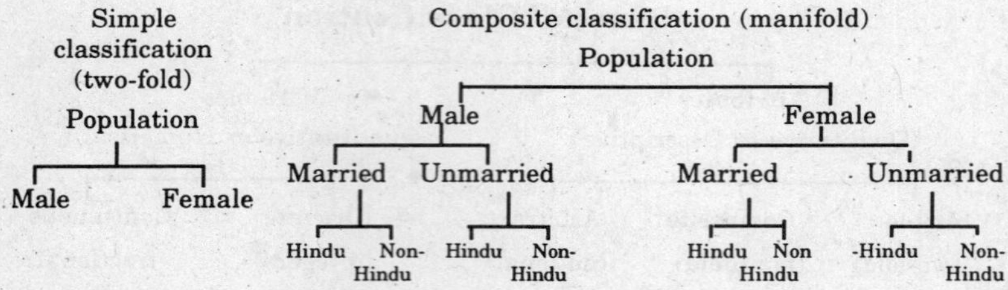

"Arbitrary classification" refers to those attributes which are not clearly defined and in which no demarcation can be made. Opinions regarding the meaning of such attributes differ from person to person. So it is necessary to define these attributes precisely and clearly without having doubts and ambiguity. For example, tall persons and short persons literates and illiterates, young and old and so on. Such attributes require specific definitions. They are called "notional attributes".

(ii) Quantitative Classification: Under this method data are classified according to quantitative measurements like age, height, marks, weight, prices, production, income, wages, expenditure, sales and profits. The quantitative phenomenon under study is known as 'variable', hence this classification is also sometimes called "classification by variables"

A *'variable'* is a quantitative phenomenon which can assume any numerical value within a particular range. It is a thing or quantity or factor which varies in value from one individual to another. It is an item which can be described and expressed in numerical terms. Such a measurable quantity can be taken as the basis for classification. It varies in amount and magnitude and assumes numerical values or a range of values. It is also called a "variate" on the basis of which the classification can be made.

The observations which are recorded as differences in magnitude or number are called "Values of Variable". Following are the examples:

Table 4.1

Variable A Marks	Variable B Wages(Rs)	Variable C Weight(Kg)	Variable D Age
25	50	52.650	29.00
36	60	55.650	29.50
47	70	58.247	31.25
52	80	62.279	32.00
63	90	63.008	33.50

There are four variables - A, B, C and D. In each variable there are six values. The units are marks in `A' variable, rupees in `B' variable, kilograms in `C' variable and years in `D' variable. Variables are of two kinds – Discrete and Continuous.

(a) Discrete Variable: The variable which cannot take all the possible values within a given specified range is called a discrete variable. It takes only integers (values) characterised by jumps and gaps between the one value and the next. The values, generally, change with particular gap constantly. In the Variable 'B' (as above), we can find such values. So variable 'B' (wages) is a discrete variable. There are no values like 53, 72.5, 84, 87 and 96.98. From value 50 to 60 there is no continuity. So it is also called a discontinuous variable. It takes a definite integer (value). There is a constant gap between the two values. Thus a variable, which shows definite breaks between one value and the other succeeding it, is called a "Discrete Variable."

(b) Continuous Variable: The variable which takes all the possible values, integer as well as fractional, is called a continuous variable. It is capable of passing from any given value (integer and fractional) to the next value by infinitely small gradations. The values are progressing from one to the next without any break continuously. In the variable 'C' and 'D' (as above), we can find such values. So variable 'C' and 'D' are continuous variables. They take any partial values within a given range.

Thus, a discrete variable cannot manifest every conceivable fractional value and a continuous variable can manifest every conceivable fractional value. The values in a discrete variable are obtained just by counting and the values in a continuous variable are obtained through the specified measurements. Following are the two examples of series based on discrete and continuous variables.

Table - 4.2

Discrete (variable) Series		Continuous (Variable) Series	
No. of Children	No. of Families	Weights (lbs)	No. of Students
1	15	80 - 90	50
2	60	90 - 100	45
3	43	100 - 110	160
4	25	110 - 120	90
5	8	120 - 130	40
6	4	130 - 140	15
	Total = 155		Total = 400

In a discrete series, we find isolated real numbers, most frequently positive integers or zero, such as 1, 2, 3 and so on, or 0, 10, 20, 30 and so on, or 5, 10, 15 and so on. There are only whole numbers. In a continuous series, we cannot find isolated real numbers. The values are required to be measured theoretically to any desired degree of fitness, such as weights (lbs) 82, 83.6, 84, 84.9, 86, 87 and 88 which can be accommodated in a class "80-90" for convenience. Although, the theoretical distinction between the two variables is clear and precise, in practical statistical analysis, it is only a question of approximation.

IV Seriation

Seriation is concerned with the logical listing or arrangement of the data into a particular sequence. The data are listed orderly in different categories. The things or attributes are measured, counted or weighted and then they are placed one after another in the process of seriation. Thus, 'seriation' means a logical or systematic arrangement of data with reference to time or area or condition.

Statistical series may be defined as things, events or attributes arranged in a particular or logical or systematic order. There are three types of series based on time, area or condition - Time Series, Geographical Series and Condition Series. Statistical series are prepared to present the classified data in a properly arranged way. Classification is concerned with the division of data into different groups and sub-groups, whereas seriation is related with the arrangement of data in a systematic manner. Both the processes aim at presenting the data for further analysis.

Types of Statistical Series
(Bases)

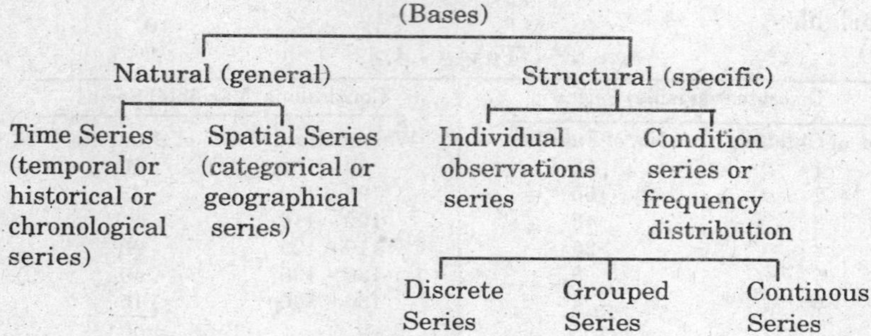

"Time Series" (historical or chronological or temporal) is one in which data are arranged on the basis of differences in time or period. The values of variable are placed in this series with reference to days, weeks, months, years, decades or centuries. Such series are found quite frequently in economics and business studies. Time is the most important factor according to which data are arranged.

"Spatial Series" (geographical or categorical) is one in which data are arranged on the basis of locational differences or geographical area. The values of variable are placed with reference to villages, cities, districts, regions, zones, states or nations and presented in an alphabetical order or ascending order of values.

"Individual Series" is one in which data are shown as they are observed. The values of variable are small in size or limited in number. The observations are just recorded and presented as they are collected. generally, they are in raw form and unorganized. However, by arranging them in an **"array"** (ascending or descending order of values) form, they can be organised. As the values of variables are small in size, there is no need to condense the collected data. So individual observations or series are ungrouped.

"Condition Series" is one in which data are arranged with reference to the physical condition such as age, height and weight with respect to their occurrence (frequency) at a given time. In this series, data are shown with their variations in size and amount of things. The values of variable are large in size or unlimited in number. They are required to be condensed before presenting them for analysis. A frequency distribution is to be formed to reduce the size of the data collected. The condition series are of three types:

(i) Discrete (Discontinuous or Ungrouped) Series: When the values of variable in the data are individually distinct and integers, we can have the discrete form of frequency distribution. The values of variable are smaller in size as compared to the number of observations. Because, each value is occurring in the series repeatedly. There is a definite gap between the variables which makes the series discontinuous in values. There are no fractional values at all. Each value takes a definite frequency against it according to the repetitions of the same in the series.

(ii) Grouped Series: When the values of variable in the data are individually distinct and integers, we can have the discrete form of frequency distribution. It is possible only when the size of the values of the variable is smaller as compared to the number of observations. If the values of variable and the number of observations are both large in size, we can have the grouping of the values for the purpose of condensing the data.

All the definite integers (values) are classified into different classes (class-intervals) by dividing the entire range of the values of the variable. There are two limits for each class-interval - **lower limit and upper limit**. Both the limits are included while counting the observations in the particular class interval. The class intervals are **arrayed** in one column and their frequencies in another. By this process, the collected data are condensed considerably and presented. The class intervals, under this series, are called **"inclusive class intervals"**. There is a gap of **1** value between the upper limit of the preceding class interval and the lower limit of the succeeding class interval.

(iii) Continuous Series: When the values of variable in the data are not integers, we cannot have the grouped series (inclusive method of class intervals). Instead of integers, we find the values of the variable in fractions. Inclusive method of forming the class intervals is not suitable for the fractional values of variable. Under such circumstances we form continuous class intervals which are called **"exclusive method of class intervals"**. The lower limit of the each class interval is only included while counting the observations in the particular class interval. The upper limit is excluded in the process of counting.

All the values of variable (integers as well as fractional) are continuous and take intermediate values within a given range. The class intervals (exclusive method) are linked with each other from the beginning to the end without any break and they are arrayed in one column. The respective frequencies are taken in another column. By this process, the collected data are condensed considerably and presented. There is no gap between the upper limit of the preceding class interval and the lower limit of the succeeding class interval, as they are one and the same.

V. Formation of Statistical Series

In the process of organising the data, pertaining to a quantitative phenomenon, the following four series are considered:

(i) Individual series **(ii)** Discrete series **(iii)** Grouped series **(iv)** Continuous series.

We shall explain the various stages of presenting the data by means of a numerical illustration. Let us consider the following marks of 100 students in an examination, arranged in order of roll numbers.

Table 4.3

Marks of 100 students (out of 20) (raw, unorganised or ungrouped data)

5	14	10	16	8	15	1	14	9	6
11	3	8	12	6	4	11	17	7	10
18	10	15	9	8	14	8	5	15	4
10	13	4	18	2	6	10	7	13	8
16	7	14	11	9	4	11	9	3	7
1	8	10	5	13	7	15	8	19	16
6	17	11	15	6	3	18	12	9	4
14	11	9	4	14	11	8	7	19	10
15	8	19	11	7	16	10	3	6	14
10	19	3	20	8	11	20	14	9	19

The data recorded as above are called the **"raw or unorganised"** data. The marks are so unwieldy and scattered. Even after a careful reading, the various details contained in them are not clear. The marks are recorded as they are collected. They are not organised. However, they can be organised and presented in a better way in an "array form". The raw data can be arranged in an ascending or descending order of the values. This arrangement is called "arraying". The format of arraying the data is called an **"array"**. The marks of 100 students in the examination are now presented in an organised form as under:

Table 4.4

Marks of 100 students (out of 20) (organised and arrayed) (Ref. Table 4.3)

S.No	Marks	S.No.	Marks	S.No.	Marks	S.No.	Marks	S.No	Marks
1	1	21	6	41	9	61	11	81	15
2	1	22	6	42	9	62	11	82	15
3	2	23	6	43	9	63	11	83	15
4	3	24	7	44	9	64	11	84	15
5	3	25	7	45	9	65	11	85	16
6	3	26	7	46	9	66	12	86	16
7	3	27	7	47	9	67	12	87	16
8	3	28	7	48	10	68	13	88	16
9	4	29	7	49	10	69	13	89	17
10	4	30	7	50	10	70	13	90	17
11	4	31	8	51	10	71	14	91	18
12	4	32	8	52	10	72	14	92	18
13	4	33	8	53	10	73	14	93	18
14	4	34	8	54	10	74	14	94	19
15	5	35	8	55	10	75	14	95	19
16	5	36	8	56	10	76	14	96	19
17	5	37	8	57	11	77	14	97	19
18	6	38	8	58	11	78	14	98	19
19	6	39	8	59	11	79	15	99	20
20	6	40	8	60	11	80	15	100	20

In arraying the raw data, we have to use the serial numbers instead of roll numbers to maintain the order of the values of variable. By arraying, the data is not condensed. The size of the observations remain the same. However, the presentation of data looks better than that of the raw data. Such a type of presentation of data is essential for the purpose of statistical analysis.

Though the presentation of data in an array form gives a better view than that of the raw data, it is difficult to grasp the true significance of the data at a glance. So we can make the data further presented, still more attractive and condensed, with the help of a "Frequency Distribution".

"Frequency" is a number of times each value of variable occurs in the series. It refers to the number of repetitions of a particular value of variable. It is shown, with the help of counting, against the particular value or class. So it is the rate of occurrence of a particular event or thing or value.

"Frequency Distribution" is a summary presentation of values of variable (or attributes) arranged according to their magnitudes either individually or in groups or classes. It depicts the different values of variable in one column and their respective frequencies in another. It is a mode of classification of data made on the basis of phenomenon which is capable of quantitative measurement. It is also called a "Frequency Table" or "Frequency Chart" or "Frequency Series".

On the basis of statistical series, we can construct the three types of frequency distributions as under:

(i) Discrete (discontinuous) Frequency Distribution.

(ii) Grouped Frequency Distribution.

(iii) Continuous Frequency Distribution.

(i) Discrete Frequency Distribution: The variables which can take only definite or particular integers are called 'discrete variable. They do not take all the possible fractional values in between the two integers. While constructing the discrete frequency distribution, we count the number of times each value of variable occurs in the series. This is facilitated through the technique of "Tally bars" or "Tally marks".

"Tally bars" or **"Tally marks"** are small vertical bars scored parallel to each other. They are put opposite to the particular value or class to facilitate the counting of the frequencies. Usually a bloc of five bars is used in the counting process, as " 𝍸 " (four bars vertical and one bar crossed over the all). This procedure makes the counting process more easy in the form of a unit of five frequencies.

Table 4.5

Marks of 100 students (out of 20) (Discrete Frequency Distribution) (Ref. Table 4.4)

Marks	Tally bars	Frequencies	Marks	Tally bars	Frequencies
1	||	2	11	𝍸 ||||	9
2	|	1	12	||	2
3	𝍸	5	13	|||	3
4	𝍸 |	6	14	𝍸 |||	8
5	|||	3	15	𝍸 |	6
6	𝍸 |	6	16	||||	4
7	𝍸 ||	7	17	||	2
8	𝍸 𝍸	10	18	|||	3
9	𝍸 ||	7	19	𝍸	5
10	𝍸 ||||	9	20	||	2
				Total =	100

The values of variable are twenty in number (out of 20 marks score). Whereas the number of observations (students) is one hundred. In this discrete form of distribution (Table 4.5), the entire data is considerably condensed and shown in which we count the number of times each value of variable occurs. The phenomenon of marks is called a variable. The marks themselves are called values of variable. The number of students scoring marks is called a frequency. This type of distribution is suitable when the values of variable are less and the number of observations are more.

(ii) Grouped Frequency Distribution: When the number of observations and the number of values of variable both are large in size, the discrete frequency distribution is not suitable. The entire range of the values of variable is to be condensed by dividing it into a suitable groups or classes. Each class is having two limits - **lower limit and upper limit**. As the values of variable are integers or whole numbers (not fractional), 'inclusive method' of classes are prepared. Both the limits are included while counting the number of observations against the particular class. However, there is a gap of **1** between the upper limit of the preceding class interval and the lower limit of the succeeding class interval.

Let us consider the marks of 100 students presented already in Table 4.3. Though the values of variable are 20 in number, assuming that they are large in size, we can divide them into different classes suitably as 1-3, 4-6, 7-9 ... so on. The next step is to count the number of observations with the use of **"Tally bars"** to form the frequency distribution. The tally bars are scored against the respective classes to which the values are referred.

Table 4.6

Marks of 100 students (Out of 20) (Ref. Table 4.4) Inclusive Method of class

Class interval	Tally marks	Frequency (f)
1- 3	𝍸 III	8
4- 6	𝍸 𝍸 𝍸	15
7- 9	𝍸 𝍸 𝍸 𝍸 IIII	24
10-12	𝍸 𝍸 𝍸 𝍸	20
13-15	𝍸 𝍸 𝍸 II	17
16-18	𝍸 IIII	9
19-21	𝍸 II	7
		Total = 100

In a grouped frequency distribution, the identity of the units (students in the above example) about whom a particular information is collected (marks in the above example) is not relevant but the condensation of data is important. The data is classified in to different classes (class intervals) by dividing the entire range of the value of the variables into a suitable number of groups or classes. All the observations are recorded in the respective groups or classes. In the above example, we have divided the entire range (1 to 21) of the values of variable into seven groups of size 3 each. The length of the group or class interval is 3 which is also called the **"width"** or **"magnitude"** of the classes. The two values specifying the class are called the **"class limits"** - the lower limit and the upper limit. The classes of this type - 4-6, 7-9, 10-12 and so on - are called **"inclusive classes"**. The lower and upper limits are included while counting the frequencies and classifying them. For instance, the class interval 16-18 includes all the three values 16, 17 and 18. Here the value 16 (lower limit) and the value 18 (upper limit) are included in marking the tally bars for counting frequencies. The next value 19 is included in the next class 19-21. Generally, the fractional values between 18 and 19 (i.e. 18.20, 18.65, 18.78 so on) are not at all considered and counted under this type of classification. Only those variables which take integers are taken in this type of classification such as a number of cars, a number of families, a number of accidents and so on.

The inclusive method is not in general usage. That is why the inclusive method is converted into the exclusive method for all the purposes. There is a gap of **1** between the upper limit of the preceding class and the lower limit of the succeeding class. This gap is adjusted by a correction factor, computed as under

$$\text{Correction Factor} = \frac{\text{Lower Limit of the succeding class} - \text{Upper limit of the preceding class}}{2}$$

The correcting factor is generally 0.5 which is adjusted as under.

Inclusive method of classes (Marks)	Converted into exclusive method of classes (Marks)
1 - 3	0.5 - 3.5
4 - 6	3.5 - 6.5
7 - 9	6.5 - 9.5
10 - 12	9.5 - 12.5
13 - 15	12.5 - 15.5
16 - 18	15.5 - 18.5
19 - 21	18.5 - 21.5

Note:

Correcting factor 0.5 is deducted from all the lower limits and added to all the upper limits.

The magnitude of the class interval is 2, before the adjustment, but it is 3 after the adjustment. However, the mid-value in both the cases remains the same.

(iii) Continuous Frequency Distribution: When the number of observation and the number of values of variable both are large in size, and the values of variable are both integers and fractionals, the grouped frequency distribution is not suitable. The entire range of values of variable is to be condensed by dividing it into suitable groups or classes. Each class is having two limits - lower limit and upper limit. As the values of variable are integers and fractionals, "exclusive method" of classes are prepared. The upper limit of the class is excluded while counting the number of observations against the particular class. There will not be a gap of 1 between the upper limit of the preceding class and the lower limit of the succeeding class. Because both the limits are same.

Let us consider the weekly wages of 100 workers of factory A.

Table 4.7

Weekly Wages (in Rs) of Workers - Factory A

96	62	41	90	52	37	78	48	85	30
52	36	53	26	112	61	133	55	108	43
44	54	80	51	43	104	75	98	60	34
45	97	38	69	56	122	31	46	125	52
28	109	42	89	68	26	79	105	59	38
35	125	57	70	120	34	137	47	130	50
95	48	101	27	136	132	48	140	87	40
32	134	63	43	58	138	148	34	114	65
39	117	142	48	148	29	149	49	148	116
64	143	33	147	150	44	150	86	150	32

In the above table, the lowest weekly wage is Rs 26 and the highest weekly wage is Rs 150. Let us take a class interval with the magnitude 10. Thus we have about 14 number of classes starting with 20-30 and ending with 140-160. We are dealing with a continuous variable. Though the values are integers, the range in which they exist extends from 26 to 150. There are no definite values like 25, 30, 35, 45 and so on. We find the values continuous in between the definite values. So we should assume that they are just like fractional values which exist in between the two definite values. The number of values of variable are large in size. It requires grouping as under:

Table 4.8

Weekly wages of 100 workers (Factory A) (Continuous Frequency Distribution) (Ref. Table 4.7) Exclusive Method of Class.

Class interval Wages (Rs)	Tally Marks	No. of Workers (f)
20- 30	~~IIII~~	5
30- 40	~~IIII~~ ~~IIII~~ IIII	14
40- 50	~~IIII~~ ~~IIII~~ ~~IIII~~ I	16
50- 60	~~IIII~~ ~~IIII~~ II	12
60- 70	~~IIII~~ III	8
70- 80	IIII	4
80- 90	~~IIII~~	5
90-100	~~IIII~~	5
100-110	~~IIII~~	5
110-120	IIII	4
120-130	IIII	4
130-140	~~IIII~~ II	7
140-150	~~IIII~~ IIII	8
150-160	III	3
		Total = 100

The measurement of values of variable, their magnitude and volume which are capable of sub-division (like fractionals) constitute the continuous series. The class intervals are formed without any gaps in between them. They are of exclusive type in which the upper limits are excluded while counting the observations to mark the tally bars. It means the lower limits are only included in the process of counting. For example, in the above distribution, there are three workers getting Rs 150 weekly wages. They are grouped in the class interval 150-160, but not in the class interval 140-150. Because 150, as the upper limit of the class interval 140-150, is excluded and 150, as the lower limit of the class interval 150-160, is included.

The variable can take any intermediate value between the two limits of the class intervals which continue from the beginning to the end of the whole range of values without any break.

Construction of Continuous Series

Formation of continuous frequency distribution is most popular in practice nowadays. There are no hard and fast rules laid down for constructing the continuous series. A statistician has to use his discretion for classifying the data in a continuous frequency distribution. Experience, wisdom, skill and aptness are required for an appropriate classification of the data. However, the following terms and guidelines are to be borne in mind while constructing the continuous frequency distribution:

(A) Important Terms: The following technical terms are to be studied while forming the continuous frequency distribution.

(i) Class interval: It is a size of each group of the data beginning with the lower limit and ending with the upper limit. So it is a group constituted by the two limits. Examples of inclusive method of class intervals are 10-19, 20-29, 30-39 and so on. Examples of exclusive method of class intervals are 10-20, 20-30, 30-40 and so on.

(ii) Ideal number of class interval: There are no hard and fast rules regarding the determination of number of class intervals in any given observations. However, **Prof H.A. Sturges** has given a formula by which we can compute the ideal number of class intervals to be formed in any series. His formula is,

$$n = 1 + 3.222 \log N$$

n = number of class intervals

N = number of observations

Accordingly, on the basis of the above **Sturges Rule**, we can determine the magnitude of the class interval as under:

$$i = \frac{L - S}{1 + 3.222 \log N} = \frac{\text{Range}}{\text{No. of Classes}}$$

L = Largest Value, i = Magnitude of the class interval

S = Smallest Value.

When we apply the **Sturges Formula**, the number of classes are determined within the range of 4 and 20 in general. It is a fairly reasonable range within which we get the number of class intervals. However, the number of classes should be a whole number (integer) preferably 5 or multiples of 5 such as 10, 15, 20 and so on. Such integers are readily perceptible to the mind and quite convenient for numerical computations in the analysis of data. Similarly, the magnitude of the class intervals should also be taken preferably in 5 or least common multiples of 5 such as 0-5 or 15-25 or 20-40 and so on.

(iii) Types of Class Interval: The data is classified into class intervals which are of two types - inclusive classes and exclusive classes.

(a) Inclusive Class Intervals: Under this method each class is specified by the two extreme values called the class limits. The smaller limit is called "lower limit" and the larger limit the "upper limit". Both the limits are included while counting the observations for such class interval. For instance, the class interval 40-49 includes all the values from 40 to 49, both inclusive. The next value 50 is included in the next class interval 50-59 and so on. However the fractional values between 49 and 50 cannot be accounted for in such a classification. This method of class interval (inclusive) is used for those variables whose values are integers (whole numbers). Generally, this method can be adopted in the grouped series in which there are no fractional values of variable.

However, the inclusive method of class interval, with some corrections, can also be used in continuous series. The class limits are adjusted and converted into the exclusive class intervals as under,

Inclusive Method of Class Intervals	Converted into Exclusive Method of Class Intervals
10-19	9.5 - 19.5
20-29	19.5 - 29.5
30-39	29.5 - 39.5
40-49	39.5 - 49.5
50-59	49.5 - 59.5

Note:

Correcting factor 0.5 is deducted from all the lower limits and added to all the upper limits.

$$\text{Correction Factor} = \frac{\text{Lower Limit of the succeding class} - \text{Upper limit of the preceding class}}{2}$$

$$= \frac{20 - 19}{2} = \frac{1}{2} = 0.5$$

In the above example, the new class limits are computed. Generally, these limits are called **"Class Boundaries"**.

(b) Exclusive Class Intervals: Under this method each class is specified by the two extreme values called the class limits. The smaller limit is called "lower limit" and the larger limit the "upper limit". The lower limit is included and the upper limit is excluded while counting the observations for such class interval. For instance, the class interval 40-50 includes all the values from 40 to 49, excluding the value 50 which is included in the next class interval 50-60.

In this method, the upper limit of the preceding class will become the lower limit of the succeeding class. The class intervals are formed continuously without any gap or break. It is presumed that the values of variable are both integers and fractionals. This method ensures continuity of data and it is widely followed in practice.

The following example illustrates the exclusive method of class interval:

Weekly wages (Rs) C.I.	No. of workers (f)	Weekly wages (Rs) C.I.	No. of workers (f)
40-50	8	80- 90	12
50-60	13	90-100	9
60-70	15	100-110	2
70-80	10	110-120	1
		Total	= 70

A difficulty may arise while counting and classifying the wages like Rs 50, Rs 60 and Rs 70 which are appearing in two classes as an upper limit and a lower limit as well. To avoid such type of confusion regarding overlapping limits, the distribution can be presented in a better way as under:

Weekly Wages (Rs)	No. Of Workers (f)
Rs 40 but under Rs 50	8
Rs 50 but under Rs 60	13
Rs 60 but under Rs 70	15
Rs 70 but under Rs 80	10
Rs 80 but under Rs 90	12
Rs 90 but under Rs 100	9
Rs 100 but under Rs 110	2
Rs 110 but under Rs 120	1
Total =	70

The above presentation does not lead to any confusion. It is free from any ambiguity about the allocation of size of items into various classes.

(iv) Empty Class Interval: It is the class interval which is having no frequency. It means there are no observations against this class interval.

(v) Class Limits: Each class interval is having two limits - lower limit and upper limit. The lowest value is the lower limit and the highest value the upper limit. They are the two ends by which the class interval is constituted.

(vi) Class Boundaries: In a grouped series we are forming inclusive method of class intervals. There are gaps between the upper limits of the preceding class and the lower limits of the succeeding classes. Such gaps are corrected by a correcting factor (0.5) which is deducted from the lower limit and added to the upper limit. Thus the inclusive method is converted into the exclusive method. The new corrected class limits are called “class boundaries”.

$$\text{Correcting Factor} = \frac{\text{Lower Limit of the succeding class} - \text{Upper Limit of the preceding class}}{2}$$

$$= \frac{20 - 19}{2} = \frac{1}{2} = 0.5$$

$$= 0.5 \text{ or } \frac{1}{2} \text{ of the difference.}$$

Upper Class Boundary = Upper Class Limit + 1/2 d.

Lower Class Boundary = Lower Class Limit - 1/2 d.

d= the difference between the lower class limit of the succeding class and the upper class limit of the preceding class. 1/d = the correcting factor.

The technique of correcting the class limits and converting them into the class boundaries will help us extensively in computing the statistical measures.

(vii) Magnitude and Width of the Class: The "magnitude" is the difference between the lower limit and the upper limit of the class interval, whereas the "width" is the difference between the lower boundary and the upper boundary of the class interval.

Let us take the example of inclusive method of class interval and its conversion into the exclusive method as under:

Inclusive method of class	Conversion with the class boundaries	Magnitude of class	Width or size or length of class
10-19	9.5 - 19.5	9	10
20-29	19.5 - 29.5	9	10
30-39	29.5 - 39.5	9	10
40-49	39.5 - 49.5	9	10

In case of exclusive method, we can have the magnitude as the difference between the two limits the class interval. For example,

Exclusive Method of class	Magnitude of class
10-20	10
20-30	10
30-40	10
40-50	10

Note:
We are not coming accross the terms "boundaries" and "width" in this method.

(viii) Open-end Series: Under this series, the lower limit of the first class interval and the upper limit of the last class interval are not specified. The first class interval begins with the words "less than (upper limit) value" and the last class interval ends with the words "more than (lower limit) value". For example,

Class Interval	Frequencies
Less than 20	15
20-30	20
30-40	13
40-50	8
50-60	9
More than 60	10

Note:
"below 20" and "above 60" words can also be used

(ix) Closed-end Series: Under this series, all the class limits of all the class intervals are specified. There are no open-end class intervals either in the beginning or in the end of the series.

(x) Broken-end Series: Under this series, both the types of series - discrete and continuous - are found. It is the combination of discrete and continuous frequency distribution. For example,

Values (x)	Frequencies (f)
10	8
20	3
20-30	15
30-40	11
40	7
50	4
50-60	2

Note:
Such series is used when there are most fluctuations in the values of variable.

The broken end series are rarely formed as the distribution is not suitable for statistical analysis.

(xi) Mid-value (Mid-point or Class Mark): It is the central point of the class interval which is exactly at the middle of the two extreme limits of the class interval. It is determined as under:

$$\text{Mid - value} = \frac{\text{Lower Limit - Upper Limit}}{2}$$

For example,

Class interval	Class boundaries	Magnitude of C.I.	Width of C.I.	Mid-value of C.I
10-19	9.5-19.5	9	10	14.5
20-29	19.5-29.5	9	10	24.5
30-39	29.5-39.5	9	10	34.5
40-49	39.5-49.5	9	10	44.5

Class Interval	Magnitude of C.I.	Mid-value of C.I
10-20	10	15
20-30	10	25
30-40	10	35
40-50	10	45

Note:
The difference between the two types class intervals

Mid-values differ with the differences in the types of class-interval. They lie half-way between the two extreme limits or boundaries as the case may be.

(xii) Class Frequency: It is the number of the observations corresponding to the specific class. It is the rate of occurrence of a particular event or value relating to a particular class interval.

(xiii) Derived Frequencies: From the class frequency we can derive a number of other frequencies for different purposes in the process of statistical analysis. Following are the derived frequencies:

(a) Frequency Density: It is the ratio of the class frequency to the width of that class interval. It is derived as under:

$$\text{Frequency Density} = \frac{\text{Class Frequency}}{\text{Width of the class}}$$

Class interval	Frequency	Frequency Density
0 - 9	5	5÷10 = 0.5
10-19	7	7÷10 = 0.7
20-29	14	14÷10 = 1.4
30-39	18	18÷10 = 1.8
40-49	6	6÷10 = 0.6
	Total = 50	

Frequency density is the frequency per unit width of the class. Such frequency densities are used for comparing the concentration of frequencies in the classes. It is essential that all the classes should be of equal width. While preparing the histogram, if the classes are of unequal width, frequency densities are of much use.

(b) Percentage Frequency: It is the ratio of the class frequency expressed as a percentage of the total frequency. It is derived as under:

$$\text{Percentage frequency} = \text{Relative Frequency} \times 100$$

$$= \frac{\text{Class frequency}}{\text{Total frequency}} \times 100$$

Considering the frequencies given in the (xiii) (a) above illustration, the percentage frequencies are,

$$(5 \div 50) \times 100 = 10\%$$
$$(7 \div 50) \times 100 = 14\%$$
$$(14 \div 50) \times 100 = 28\%$$
$$(18 \div 50) \times 100 = 36\%$$
$$(6 \div 50) \times 100 = 12\%$$
$$\text{Total} = \underline{100\%}$$

(c) Cumulative Frequency: It is a modified form of the class frequency given in the distribution. It is derived by adding the frequencies successively when the frequencies are recorded in the ascending order of the values or classes. There are two types of cumulative frequencies - "less than" and "more than".

"Less than" cummulative frequencies are derived by adding the class frequencies which are arranged in an ascending order of values or classes. The frequencies of all the values or classes are successively added including the frequency of the value of variable or class against which the cummulative totals are written. So it is the sum of all the frequencies for each value or class written against the value or class as "less than" value or upper limit of the class.

"More than" cummulative frequencies are derived by adding the class frequencies, from the last (bottom) frequency in opposite direction, which are arranged in an ascending order. It means we should start with the total frequency and go on deducting the frequencies at each stage. So it is the sum of all the frequencies for each value or class written against the value or class as "more than" value or lower limit of the class

Class interval	Frequency (f)	Less than values	Cumulative frequencies c.f.	More than values	Cumulative frequencies c.f.
5-15	8	less than 15	8	more than 5	140
15-25	19	less than 25	27	more than 15	132
25-35	22	less than 35	49	more than 25	113
35-45	27	less than 45	76	more than 35	91
45-55	32	less than 55	108	more than 45	64
55-65	24	less than 65	132	more than 55	32
65-75	7	less than 75	139	more than 65	8
75-85	1	less than 85	140	more than 75	1
Total	= 140				

Thus a cummulative frequency is the progressive total of each frequency at each stage - up to and including the frequency of that class interval or value of variable. It presents for each value or class, the total number of observations in that value or class below and above it.

(xiv) Bivariate Frequency Distribution: When the data is classified with reference to two bases or criterias simultaneously we can call such distribution as "bivariate frequency distribution". For example, weights and heights of a group, marks in accountancy and statistics of 10 students, ages of husbands and wives for a group of couples and so on are bivariate frequency distributions. Such type of distribution can be summarised in the form of a "two-way frequency table". It is commonly known as a "correlation table."

In a bivariate frequency distribution, the values of each variable are grouped into various classes keeping in view the same considerations as applied to a univariate distribution. There will be class intervals for one set of values of variable as columns and for other set of values of variable as rows. For example,

Marks in									
Accountancy:	24	22	21	25	23	26	21	22	23
Statistics:	12	18	17	14	11	15	13	16	12
Accountancy:	24	25	22	26	24	21	22	21	23
Statistics:	13	16	18	12	14	17	18	11	12

Statistics (y) / (x) Accountancy	11	12	13	14	15	16	17	18	Total
21	I		I				II		4
22						I		III	4
23	I	III							3
24		I	I	I					3
25				I		I			2
26		I			I				2
Total	2	4	2	2	1	2	2	3	18

The boxes are formed at the intersection of columns and rows which represent joint-values or joint-classes. The frequency of the joint-values is the number of items that has the value of the first variable in the column and the value of the second variable in the row (i.e. 2 and 4).

(B) Guidelines: The following general guidelines may be considered for ensuring an ideal frequency distribution:

(i) The number of classes should be minimum five and maximum fifteen.

(ii) It is better to have the magnitude (or width) of the class intervals in the least common factors of 5, 10, 15, 20, 50 or 100. For example, 5-10 or 10-20 or 0-50, 100-200 and so on.

(iii) It is better to adopt exclusive method of class interval instead of inclusive method to ensure continuity in classification. The inclusive method may be converted into the exclusive by adjusting the correcting factor.

(iv) The class limits chosen should be in such a way that the observations in any class interval are evenly distributed.

(v) The open-end class intervals are avoided as far as possible, because the computation of mid-value for such group could not be easily determined.

(vi) The class interval should have a uniform or equal magnitude throughout the series.

(vii) In case of open-end class intervals, the magnitude will be considered as equivalent to the magnitude of the succeeding or preceding class interval for the purpose of statistical analysis.

The above guidelines or basic principles will help us in constructing the frequency distribution.

Thus, the voluminous and huge raw data collected is edited and organised in the process of classifying the data. The data is presented in a readily comprehensible and condensed form, which highlights the important characteristics of data; this is possible only by the process of classification. A classification is a process in which the raw data is organized according to some precisely defined differing characteristics and is grouped in a systematic manner useful for further statistical analysis.

Questions

1. Define "Classification". (BU-N83)
2. State any four objects of classification. (BU-N84, N85)
3. State any four types of classification. (BU-A85)
4. What are open-end class intervals? (BU-N86)
5. What is a frequency distribution? (BU-N89)
6. What are the methods of classification? (BU-N91)
7. What is classification? What are the usual bases used? (BU-A92)

8. What do you mean by a class interval? What is the rule suggested by Prof. Sturges? (BU-N92)
9. Define classification and mention the bases of classification. (BU-A93)
10. Explain the terms "Mid-value" and "Open-end Classes" with suitable examples. (BU-N93)
11. What are the objects of classification. (BU-A95, A97)
12. Define a frequency. (BU-A84)
13. Define a statistical series. (BU-A90)

5
Tabulation

The collected and classified data can also be presented in a tabular form. The term "tabulation" stands for the systematic and scientific presentation of quantitative data in such a form as to elucidate the problem under consideration. It is a function of arranging the data in an orderly manner through the table. Tables are intended to summarize the information obtained in course of an investigation.

Thus, "tabulation" is an orderly arrangement of data in columns and rows systematically in a tabular form. It is the logical listing of related quantitative data in vertical columns and horizontal rows with explanatory and qualifying words, phrases and statements along with titles, headings and notes. It is one of the old methods of presenting the data in a condensed and readily comprehensible form. It attempts to furnish the maximum information in the minimum possible space, without sacrificing the quality and usefulness of the data. It is an intermediate process between the collection of the data and the statistical analysis.

In fact, tabulation is the final stage in the collection and compilation of the data and forms the gateway for further statistical analysis and interpretation. It makes the data comprehensible and facilitates comparisons. It overcomes the drawbacks of presenting the data in a narrative form, and presents the data neatly in true perspective highlighting the significant features of data. Tabulated data attracts a common reader and leaves a lasting impression on his mind as compared to the data in a textual form. So the tabulation enables us to draw attention of a common observer to specific items by means of comparisons, emphasis and arrangement of the layout. It also facilitates the detection of the errors and the omissions that are not detected easily.

I. Objects of Tabulation

A statistical table is a systematic format having columns and rows. It is a means of recording the data attractively.

Tabulation is a process of recording the data in the form of a table that could be understood easily. Its purpose is to summarize the complex and mass data in a simple form. It aims at communicating the data effectively and economically. Following are the objects of tabulation:

(i) *To summarize the data systematically.*

(ii) *To clarify the data in a simple form.*

(iii) *To facilitate the data for a comparative study.*

(iv) *To present the data in a minimum space.*

Thus the statistical table not only presents the data in a simple form but also serves as a useful tool for statistical analysis. It provides answers to all problems under study at a glance.

II. Classification and Tabulation

The process of classification and tabulation are interrelated. However, the classification is the first step and the tabulation is the next. The data are classified before they are put in a tabular form. Hence classification forms the basis for tabulation. Still, there are some differences between the two processes as under,

(i) The process of classification begins when the process of collection ends, whereas the process of tabulation begins when the process of classification ends.

(ii) In the process of classification data are arranged according to attributes and variables, whereas in the process of tabulation data are arranged in columns and rows.

(iii) The classification process refers to the arrangement of data into classes or groups, whereas the tabulation process refers to the placement of data in a tabular form. One refers to the identification of data and the other presentation of the data.

Thus the main object of tabulation is to summarise the narrative form of data into a tabular form which can be easily understood and interpreted.

III. Advantages of Tabulation

Tabulation plays an important role after the collection and classification of data. It makes the data suitable for their interpretation. Following are the advantages of tabulation.

(i) It simplifies the data: Tabulation simplifies the complex data by presenting them systematically in columns and rows in a condensed form. It avoids all the unnecessary data that is found in a narrative form.

(ii) It uses less space: Tabulation achieves economy in using the space for presenting the data. The textual matter is presented neatly in a short form without sacrificing utility of the data.

(iii) It facilitates comparison: The data presented in a tabular form is helpful for a comparative study. The relationship among the various items can be easily understood.

(iv) It reveals the data at a glance: Tabulation depicts the data and their significance at first sight in the form of figures, which cannot be understood when the same data are in a narrative form.

Thus the tabulated data are very useful sources for future references. They are fit for further statistical analysis and interpretation.

IV. The Parts of a Table

A table is an orderly arrangement of data in columns and rows. Following are the different parts of table:

(i) Table number: When a number of tables are used in a report, each table should be numbered for the purpose of identification and reference. Generally, the number is placed at the top of the table conveniently.

(ii) Title: A table should have a suitable title which is placed at the top in bold letters. The title describes the contents of the table briefly. As far as possible, the title should be complete and unambiguous as regards the subject matter of the data. It should be clear, properly worded and self-explanatory.

(iii) Captions: They refer to the heading of the information shown at the top of the vertical columns. Under the captions, there may be sub-headings. They are written in small letters along with the units if any.

(iv) Stubs: They refer to the headings of the information shown at the extreme left of the horizontal rows. They perform the similar functions as are performed by the captions. Captions and stubs are interchangeable.

(v) Body: It refers to the numerical information that are presented in the captions and stubs. It is the most important part of the table which describes the entire data attractively and precisely. It covers the major portion of the table.

(vi) Headnote: It is a brief note preferably placed in brackets just below the title. It is a preparatory or supplementary note to the title. It is used to explain some of the important facts relating to the statistical units or measurements such as "in 000's", "in millions", "in crores", "in quintals" and so on.

(vii) Footnote: It is a brief note given at the foot of the table. Footnotes are meant to clarify certain terms in detail. They may be attached to any part of the table by using the asterisk(*) to show that explanation is given below.

(viii) Source Note: When the secondary data are used, a source note is given at the bottom of the table, below the footnote. It contains the name of the publication and the journal or periodical from which the data are collected.

There are no hard and fast rules for preparing a statistical table. Construction of a table requires common sense, experience and skill. The data must be so presented in a condensed and concise form that they are capable of easy and quick reception to eyes. Preparation of a table is an art and a specilised process. However, the following guide-lines are borne in mind while preparing a good table:

(i) The table should be precise and simple so that the data presented should be easily understood. It should be free from irrelevant information, overlappings and ambiguities.

(ii) The table should contain all the important materials of the data. It should highlight the desired and relevant information.

(iii) The table should suit the size of the paper used. The width of the columns should be reasonable. Different types of letterings may be used to distinguish points of special emphasis.

(iv) Suitable title, captions and stubs are given to make the data more descriptive and self-explanatory.

(v) The averages, percentages, totals and grand totals are given both horizontally and vertically making approximations with no digital values.

(vi) All the items can be arranged either in an alphabetical, chronological or geographical order. Sometimes we may arrange them according to size, importance, emphasis or relationship.

(vii) Explanatory notes can be given wherever possible in the table. All the entries should be checked after they are made in the table. Over-writing should be avoided. Abbreviations should not be used.

Thus the use of common sense is essential while planning a table which is used and studied by a common reader. The table should be easy to read and understand. It should be of a reasonable size and complete in all the respects. It should be attractive and appealing to the eyes and minds of the readers.

V. Types of Tables

The statistical tables are prepared in different ways the choice of which depends upon objectives, scope, nature and extent of the enquiry. Following are the types of tables:

(i) *General Purpose Tables:* They are reference tables which are also called "information tables". They are designed for use by research workers, statisticians and government agencies. They serve as a repository of information and are arranged for easy reference. They tell facts in general with no particular purpose.

(ii) *Special Purpose Tables:* They are summary tables which are also called "interpretative tables". They are analytical in nature and prepared with an idea of making comparative studies. They are derived from the general purpose tables to serve specific purpose. So they are also called "derived or derivative" tables.

(iii) *Primary Tables:* The primary tables are those tables in which facts are expressed in the original form. They contain actual and absolute figures. They are also called "original tables".

(iv) *Secondary Tables:* They are nothing but derived tables. They contain figures and results derived from the primary tables. They express the information in terms of ratios, percentages, aggregates, averages and other statistical measures.

(v) *Simple Tables:* The simple tables are those tables which furnish information about only a single characteristic of the data. They are popularly known as "one-way tables".

(vi) *Two-way Tables:* They are called "double tables" which furnish information about two characteristics of the data. The two attributes of the data are interrelated for e.g., the number of students - male and female, male - married and unmarried, and female - married and unmarried.

(vii) *Three-way Tables:* The three-way tables are those tables in which the data are classified with reference to three characteristics. They furnish information regarding three interrelated attributes of the same data. For example, the number of students - male and female, married and unmarried, and graduates and undergraduates.

(viii) *Manifold Tables:* They are also called complex tables which furnish a number of characteristics of the same data. They are high order tables having more than three characteristics of the same data which are interrelated.

Thus, as the order of the table goes on increasing with attributes of the data, the table becomes more and more complex. In practice, three-way tables are used generally.

Following are the forms of tables:

1. Simple Table:

Table Showing the Number of Employees in Canara Bank According to Age Group.

Age (in years)	No. of Employees
Below 30	15
30-40	18
40-50	9
50 & above	3
	Total = 45

2. Two-way Table:

Table Showing the Number of Employees in Canara Bank According to Age and Sex.

Age (in years) \ Sex	No. of Employees		Total
	Male	Female	
Below 30	9	6	15
30-40	10	8	18
40-50	2	7	9
50 & above	–	3	3
Total	21	24	45

3. Three-way Table:

Table Showing the Number of Employees in Canara Bank According to Age, Sex and Marital Status.

Sex \ Marital status	No. of Employees						Grand Total
	Male			Female			
Age Group	Mrd	Un. Mrd	Total	Mrd.	Un.Mrd	Total	
Below 30	3	6	9	2	4	6	15
30 - 40	2	8	10	4	4	8	18
40 - 50	1	1	2	7	–	7	9
50 & above	–	–	–	3	–	3	3
Total	6	15	21	16	8	24	45

Example 5.1. *Draw a neat blank table to present data relating to the college students according to faculty (Arts, Commerce and Science), Class (P.U.C and Degree), Sex (Male and Female) and Years (1982-1983).* *(BU-N84)*

Solution:

The number of students studying in the A.B. college, Bangalore During the year 1982 and 1983.

(Head note: ....)

Faculty/Class \ Year/Sex		1982			1983			Grand Total
		Male	Female	Total	Male	Female	Total	
Arts	P.U.C.							
	Degree.							
Commerce	P.U.C.							
	Degree.							
Science	P.U.C.							
	Degree.							
Total								

Footnote: Source Note:

Example 5.2. *In a sample study about coffee habit in two towns the following information was received:*

Town A: *Females were 40%; Total coffee drinkers were 45% and Males non-coffee drinkers were 20%.*

Town B: *Males were 55%; Males non-coffee drinkers were 30% and Female coffee drinkers were 15%.*

Present the above data in a tabular form. *(BU-A89)*

Solution:

Coffee Drinkers in Town A and B. (Figures are in %).

Sex / Drinking Habit	Town A			Town B			Grand Total		
	Male	Female	Total	Male	Female	Total	Male	Female	Total
Coffee Drinkers	40	5	45*	25	15*	40	65	20	85
Coffee Non-drinkers	20*	35	55	30*	30	60	50	65	115
Total	60	40*	100*	55*	45	100*	115	85	200

Hints: Asterisk (*) figures are given. Other figures are arrived by common sense by additions and subtractions. Towns A and B totals are assumed as 100 each.

Example 5.3. *In the house of Loksabha there were 600 members present. During the discussion on a motion put to vote, 400 voted in favour of the resolution.*

The government members in the house were 380, 65 members belonging to the opposition voted for the resolution. All the members are belonging to either of the two groups and there were no absentees.

Tabulate the above information. (BU-A91)

Solution:

Table showing the details of voting taken place in the Loksabha during the discussion on a motion put to vote.

Members / Voting	Ruling Party	Opposition Party	Total
In Favour	335	65	400
Against	45	155	200
Total	380	220	600

Example 5.4. *The number of workers in a large factory in 1986 was 540 of which 30% were female and the rest males. In 1988, the strength of the workers increased by 100 females and 200 males. In 1990, the total number of workers increased by 25% over its value in 1988. The female workers were 340. Tabulate the data.*

(BU-N91)

Solution:

Table showing the number of workers in a factory for 1986, 1988 and 1990.

Members / Voting	1986	1988	1990
Male	378	578	710
Female	162	262	340
Total	540	840	1050

Example 5.5. *Convert the given ratios into corresponding numbers and prepare a complete table for the following information:*

In the year 1994, the total strength of three colleges A, B and C in a city was in the ratio of 3:1:4. The strength of the A college was 3000. The proportion of girls and boys in all the colleges was in the ratio of 1:3. The facultywise distribution of girls and boys in the faculties of Arts, Science and Commerce was in the ratio of 2:1:2 respectively in all the colleges. (BU-A95)

Solution:

Table showing the number of girls and boys studying in A, B & C collegs in different faculties during 1994.

College / Sex / Faculty	A			B			C		
	Girls	Boys	Total	Girls	Boys	Total	Girls	Boys	Total
Arts	300	900	1200	100	300	400	400	1200	1600
Science	150	450	600	50	150	200	200	600	800
Commerce	300	900	1200	100	300	400	400	1200	1600
Total	750	2250	3000	250	750	1000	1000	3000	4000

Example 5.6. *Out of total number of 1807 women, who were interviewed for employment in a textile factory Bombay, 512 were from the textile areas and the rest were from the non-textile areas.*

Amongst the married women, who belonged to textile areas, 247 were experienced and 73 were inexperienced, while for non-textile areas the corresponding figures were 49 and 520 respectively.

The total number of inexperienced women was 1341 of whom 111 resided in the textile areas. Of the total number of women, 918 were unmarried, and of these, the number of experienced women in the textile and non-textile areas were 154 and 16 respectively. Tabulate the data.

Solution:

Marital status of women residing in textile areas and their interview in a textile factory, Bombay.

Area& Marital Status / Experience	Textile Area			Non-Textile Area			Grand Total		
	Mrd.	Unm.	T	Mrd.	Unm	T	Mrd.	Unm.	T
Experienced	247 *	154 *	401	49 *	16 *	65	296	170	466
Inexperienced	73 *	38	111 *	520 *	710	1230	593	748	1341*
Total	320	192	512 *	569	726	1295 *	889	918*	1807*

Mrd. = Married. Unm. = Unmarried T = Total

(Hints: * asterisk figures are given)

Example 5.7. *The number of accidents in Southern Railway in 1970 was 3,500, and it was decreased by 300 in 1971 and by 700 in 1972. The total number of accidents in meter gauge section showed 245 in 1970, 346 in 1971 and 428 in 1972.*

In the meter gauge, "non-compensated" cases were 49 in 1970, 77 in 1971 and 108 in 1972. "Compensated cases" in broad gauge were 2867 in 1970, 2587 in 1971 and 2152 in 1972.

Tabulate the above information. (BU-A90)

Solution:

Number of accidents in Southern railway during the period 1970-72 (Classified according to broad guage and meter guage).

Year Guage / Compensation	1970			1971			1972		
	BG	MG	Total	BG	MG	Total	BG	MG	Total
Compensated	2867 *	196	3063	2587 *	269	2856	2152 *	320	2472
Noncompen sated	388	49 *	437	267	77 *	344	220	108*	328
Total	3255	245 *	3500*	2854	346 *	3200 *	2372	428*	2800*

BG = Broad Gauge MG = Meter Gauge

(Hints: Asterisk * figures are given)

Example 5.8. *A super market is divided into five main sections - grocery, vegetables, medicine, textile and novelty. All the sections recorded the following sales in 1981, 1982 and 1983.*

In 1981, sales in grocery were Rs. 6,25,000, in vegetable Rs. 4,05,000 less than grocery, in medicine Rs. 4,88,000 which is double the sales of novelty. Textiles accounted for 30% of the total sales during the year.

In 1982, the total sales showed 10% increase over the previous year while grocery and vegetables registered 8% and 10% increase over their corresponding figures of 1981, medicine dropped by Rs. 13,000 and textile stood at Rs. 5,36,000.

In 1983, though the total sales remained the same as in 1982, grocery fell by Rs. 22,000, vegetable by Rs. 32,000, medicine by Rs 10,000. Sales of textiles are more by Rs. 4,81,000 as compared to that of novelties. *(BU-A85)*

Solution:

Table showing sales of super market in different sections during 1981, 1982 and 1983 (sales in Rs.).

Year / Sections	1981 Rs.	1982 Rs.	1983 Rs.
Grocery	6,25,000	6,75,000	6,53,000
Vegetable	2,20,000	2,42,000	2,10,000
Medicine	4,88,000	4,75,000	4,65,000
Textile	6,75,857	5,36,000	8,15,572
Novelty	2,44,000	5,50,143	3,34,571
Total	22,52,857	24,78,143	24,78,143

(Hints for calculation)

Sections	1981		1982		1983	
Grocery		625000	6,25,000 +50,000	675000	675000 -22,000	653000
Vegetable	625000 -405000	220000	220000 +22000	242000	242000 -32000	210000
Medicine		488000	488000 -13000	475000	475000 -10000	465000
Textile	30%*	675857		536000	Diff	815572
Novelty	488000/2	244000	Diff	5,50,000		334571
Total	(100%)	2252857	2252857 + 225286	2478143		2478143
* (1577000x30)/70=675857 (G+V+M+N = 15,77,000) or (15,7700x100)/70=2252857			10% increse in total	4,81,000 3,34,572 3,34571	Diff*	1150143 -481000 669143

Example 5.9. *A survey was conducted among 1,00,000 music listeners who were asked to indicate their preference for classical, light music, folk songs, film songs and pop varieties of music. The male listeners interviewed were as many as female listeners.*

The survey indicated that while the percentage of listeners who preferred classical, light music and folk songs were 8, 13 and 4 respectively. The actual number of females for each of the first two kinds were 6,000.

Of the listeners who liked folk songs, the number of male listeners was same as that of female listeners. While film songs were liked by number one and half times that of all other varieties put together; the number of pop varieties was only fourth of the number of film songs listeners. Sixty percentage of the listeners of pop music were females.

Prepare a table showing the distribution of music listeners according to sex and type of music. (BU-N85)

Solution:

Table showing the number of music listeners (males and females) in different types of music.

Sex / Music	%	Male	Female	Total
Classical	8*	2,000	6,000*	8,000*
Light	13	7,000	6,000*	13,000*
Folk songs	4*	2,000*	2,000*	4,000*
Film songs	60	33,000	27,000	60,000
Pop varities	15	6,000	9,000	15,000
Total	100*	50,000*	50,000*	1,00,000*

Hints: $C + L + F0 + Fi + P = 100$ $\quad$ $P = 1/4\ Fi$ (given)

$$8 + 13 + 4 + Fi + P = 100$$
$$25 + Fi + P = 100$$
$$Fi + P = 75$$
$$Fi + 1/4\ Fi = 75$$
$$4Fi + Fi = 300$$
$$5\ Fi = 300$$
$$Fi = 60$$

$\therefore P = 15$

* asterisk figures are given

Example 5.10. *Present the following information in the form of a table with suitable captions as clearly and as conveniently as you can. In1965 out of a total 1750 workers of a factory, 1200 workers were members of a trade union. The number of women employed was 200 of which 175 did not belong to a trade union.*

In 1970, the number of union workers increased to 1510 of which 1290 were men. On the other hand, the number of non-union workers fell down to 208 of which 180 were men.

In 1975, there were on the pay rolls of the factory 1800 employees who belonged to a trade union and 50 who did not. Of all employees in 1975, 300 were women of whom only 8 did not belong to trade union. (BU-A86, N89)

Solution:

Comparative study of the members of trade union in a factory in 1965, 1970 and 1975.

Membership / Sex / Year	Members of Trade Union			Non- members of Trade Union			Grand Total
	Male	Female	Total	Male	Female	Total	
1965	1,175	25*	1,200*	375	175*	550	1,750*
1970	1,290*	220	1,510*	180*	28	208*	1,718
1975	1,508	292*	1,800*	42	8*	50*	1,850
Total	3,973	537	4510	597	211	808	5,318

Hints: Asterisk figures are given and remaining figures are derived.

Example 5.11. *In April, 1986, examinations of Bangalore University, 4000 appeared for the B.Com examinations of which 60% were from Bangalore city colleges and the rest were from rural colleges.*

Of the total students appearing for the examination, 75% were boys and the rest were girls. The results of the examination revealed a total pass of 40%. The ratio of boys and girls passing in the examination was 2:3. (BU-A87)

Solution:

Number of students appeared for the Bangalore University B.com. examination April, 1986.

Bangalore / Sex / Results	City Colleges			Rural Colleges			Total		
	Boys	Girls	Total	Boys	Girls	Total	Boys	Girls	Total
Pass	384	576	960	256	384	640	640	960	1600
Fail	1416	24	1440	944	16	960	2360	40	2400
Total	1800	600	2400	1200	400	1600	3000	1000	4000

Example 5.12. *In a trip organized by a college there were 80 persons, each of whom paid Rs 15.50 on an average. There were 60 students each whom paid Rs 16. Members of the teaching staff were charged at a higher rate. The number of servants was 6 (all males) and they were not charged anything. The number of ladies was 20% of the total participants in the trip of which one was a lady staff member.*

Tabulate the above information. (BU-N87)

Solution:

Table showing the members of the trip and their contribution.

Members	Sex		Total	Contribution per member	Total
	Male	Female			
Students	45	15	60	16.00	960
Staff	13	1	14	20.00	280
Servants	6	-	6	-	-
Total	64	16	80	15.50	1,240

Hints:

The total contribution = Average contribution x 15.50

= Rs 1240

Staff contribution is the remaining amount after the students have contributed = 1240 - 960 = 280.

Example 5.13. *In a newspaper account describing the incidence of influenza among tuberculosis persons living in the same family the following paragraph appears:*

"Exactly a fifth of the 1,00,000 inhabitants showed the signs of tuberculosis and no fewer than 5,000 among them had an attack of influenza; but among them only 1,000 lived in infected houses.

In contrast with this, 1/15 of the tubercular persons who did not have influenza were still exposed to infection.

Altogether 21000 were attacked by influenza and 41,000 were exposed to risk of infection, but the number, who having influenza but not tubercular lived in houses where no other cases of influenza occurred, was only 2000."

Prepare the table showing the above information, with an appropriate title. (BU-N86)

Solution:

Table showing incidence of influenza among tubercular persons living in the same family.

Infection / Attack	Attacked by Influenza			Not-attacked by Influenza			Grand Total
	Living in IH	Living in UIH	Total	Living in IH	Living in UIH	Total	
Attacked by TB	1,000	4,000	5,000	1,000	14,000	15,000	20,000
Not attachked	14,000	2,000	16,000	25,000	39,000	64,000	80,000
Total	15,000	6,000	21,000	26,000	53,000	79,000	1,00,000

TB = tuberculosis, IH = infected houses, UIH = uninfected houses.

The statistical table is a layout of figures in rectangular form with appropriate headings to describe various columns and rows. It is the most interesting task to prepare a tabular form of data. There are no rigid rules to be followed in the tabulation. However, general guide-lines are borne in mind along with common sense, experience and skill. Nevertheless, the following considerations should be kept in view while tabulating the data:

1. Identify the attributes of data and prepare the rough draft of a table.
2. Read the information carefully and proceed with making the entries with figures in the body of the table.
3. After having filled in the figures in rectangles, a few rectangles will remain vacant.
4. Try to arrive the figures by additions and subtractions with the help of available data and fill in the remaining rectangles which are vacant.
5. Always, provide for the table the total columns, total rows and grand total column with all the attributes, which will help in deriving the unknown figures.

Thus, in the tabulation of data, common sense is the chief requisite and experience the chief teacher. Practice makes one perfect; keep the habit of practicing the tabulation.

Questions

1. What is a statistical table? (BU-A83)
2. Mention any four main parts of a statistical table. (BU-N83. A85. N97)

3. What are the elements of tables? (BU-A84, A91)
4. Explain the term "Primary Table". (BU-N84)
5. "In the tabulation of the data common sense is the chief requisite and experience the chief teacher". Comment. (BU-A92)
6. Distinguish between classification and tabulation. (BU-N92, A96)
7. What is a statistical table? What are its parts? (BU-A93, N96)
8. What are the requisites of a good table? (BU-N95)
9. In 1995, the total number of visitors is 250. Among them male visitors who belong to foreign countries are 65 and who belong to India are 86. In all there are 35 foreign female visitors. In 1996, the total number of visitors is increased by 20% and that of Indian visitors is increased by 10%. Among them there are 80 male foreign visitors and 60 female Indian visitors. Tabulate the above information.
10. In 1995, out of total customers visiting the hotel 75 are non-vegetarians and 125 are vegitarians. In total there are 55 male non vegitarian customers and 30 female vegitarian customers. In 1996, the total number of customers increased by 25%, of non-vegitarian customers increased by 20%. In all there are 170 male customers among them 65 are non-vegitarions. Present the given information in the form of table.
11. Prepare a blank table to show the exports of three companies A, B & C to five countries, The U.K, The U.S.A, The U.S.S.R, France and West Germany in each of the years 1970 to 1974. [I.C.W.A (intermediate) Dec 75)
12. Examine the format of this table and give your suggestions.
    Table showing the details of number of employees of A factory according to their designation, age and sex.

Clerks	Age group	Male	Female	Total
Supervisors Managers	Below 30 30 - 40 40 & above			
Total				

6

Diagrammatic Representation of Data

The statistical data can be presented in a readily intelligible manner through the diagrams. Diagrammatic presentation of data enables one to grasp the entire information at a glance. For a common man numbers are not so interesting; he is more attracted by charts, pictures or diagrams than the figures. Diagrams are comparable and appealing both to the eye and the intellect. Computation of various statistical measures constitutes further step in the direction of condensing the classified and tabulated data. But still the condensed material is presented in a numerical form. For many people, figures are dull and confusing; a long list of figures would make the reader monotonous. The readers could not make the differences between the two series easily. Therefore it is necessary to adopt a device which may present a huge mass of quantitative data in a condensed form which can be comparable and appealing at once.

"Diagrams" are visual aids which comprise of presenting statistical materials in pictures, geometric figures and curves. They present complex and unwiedly data in a simple and attractive manner. They carry with them the merits of attraction and effective impression. A common reader would not like to take his eyes away from a picture relating to the particular information. Even he might invite others to have a look at the picture. It is all based on human psychology which is best exploited by a successful advertiser or propagandist to influence the minds of the people.

I. Utilities of Diagrams

Diagrams carry with them the merits of **"attraction"** and **"effective impression"**. They have also the merit of rendering the whole idea **"readily intelligible"**. Another merit of diagrams is the **"ease"** with which they make comparison possible. Yet another feature of diagrams is that they **"save much valuable time"**, which would otherwise be lost in studying the numerical data. Lastly, a chief merit of diagrams is that the entire data are **"visible at a glance"**. For all these merits, the diagrams are useful in economic and social studies. Following are the utilities of diagrams:

(i) They give a more attractive presentation of data than is given by figures.

(ii) They create more stable effects on the minds of the readers.

(iii) They simplify the complex data and present the information attractively.

(iv) They save time which is otherwise needed in drawing inferences from the figures.

Thus, diagrams are of great help in all types of studies. An economist finds in them the basis for logical reasoning and easily explaining the economic laws. He may make his ideas impressive through the diagrams. A social reformer appears on the platform with diagrams which make his speech interesting, lively and impressive. A businessman has hardly any time to devote to the study of a huge mass of figures however well arranged. But, if he is presented with diagrams showing the tendencies of figures, he will grasp the subject matter within a few minutes.

II. Limitations of Diagrams

Diagrams can be as much misused as they are useful. They never replace the classification and tabulation. Because they serve just as a complementary to classification and tabulation. They give only a rough idea of the subject matter. Their presentation is risky in the hands of those who draw inferences from diagrams without making a careful study. Diagrams are delicate tools liable to be easily misused. A true statistician has to guard himself against misrepresentation. Hence general guide-lines and directions for drawing diagrams can help in making them more and more useful. Care has to be taken while using diagrams and interpreting them. However, diagrams have certain limitations as under:

(i) They are useful only to a common man; their utility to an expert is limited.

(ii) They show only a limited size of information; they fail to furnish detailed information.

(iii) They disclose only approximate values; they do not give accurate facts and figures.

(iv) They present the data only in a particular range of values of variable; they cannot present the data having extreme values of variable with the large gap i.e. from 50 to 50,00,000.

(v) They take into account only two or three sets of data; they cannot take into account more than four sets of data.

(vi) They are not subject to further mathematical analysis; they are not useful for any other statistical processes.

(vii) They are sometimes based on false-base lines; they are illusory when a proper scale is not maintained in drawing them.

(viii) They are not reliable sources; they are only a means to draw conclusions.

Thus it is necessary to take into account carefully a number of precautions while drawing the diagrams; otherwise they may create wrong impression and lead to false conclusions. They should be drawn neatly and attractively. The geometrical figures used in diagrams should be proportional and accurate. The diagram should be neither too small nor too big in size. Every diagram must have a suitable but short heading. All the figures, drawn according to scale, should be clearly explained. Different colours, dots, cross-lines, horizontal lines, vertical lines and other marks are used to show different attributes of the data. As far as possible the original data shall be depicted in the diagrams along with the diagrammatic figures. The diagram should be drawn artistically and scientifically. The selection of the most suitable type of diagram is also an important factor to make the diagram attractive. It all depends upon the speed with which the data can be accurately studied with the help of the type of diagram selected.

III. Types of Diagrams

There are various forms of presenting the data diagrammatically. Any one among the following forms or types or methods can be suitably selected according to the nature of the data available. The following are the common methods of diagrams:

1. On the Bases of Dimension:

(A) One-dimensional diagrams (lines and bars)

(B) Two-dimensional diagrams (squares and rectangles)

(C) Three-dimensional diagrams (cubes, cylinders and blocks)

2. On the Bases of View:

(A) Pictograms (B) Cartograms (Mapograms)

1. A. One-dimensional Diagrams (Bar diagrams)

In one-dimensional diagrams, only one dimension of the figure is taken into account. Bars are drawn with different widths and lengths. A bar is merely a thick line in one way. A line is merely a thin bar in another way. In bar diagrams only the length or height is taken into consideration. The bar diagrams are further classified as under:

(i) Line Diagrams.

(ii) Simple Bar Diagrams.

(iii) Multiple Bar Diagrams (compound bars).

(iv) Sub-divided Bar Diagrams (component bars).

(v) Sub-divided Percentage Bar Diagrams.

(vi) Deviation Bars.

(vii) Duo-directional Bars.

(viii) Paired Bars.

(ix) Broken Bars.

(i) Line Diagrams: These diagrams are used when there is a large number of values of variable with variations in their values within a small range. They are in the form of vertical lines relating to respective values of variable. A proper space should be left uniformly in between the two lines. The line diagrams are most suitable for the comparative study of related items.

Example 6.1. *Represent the following data in a suitable diagram:*

Profits (Rs. in laks) :	5	10	15	20	25	30	35	40	45	50
No. of Firms :	35	80	20	30	50	68	90	40	25	10

Solution: Line diagram is suitable for the above data.

Diagram Showing Profits of the Firms

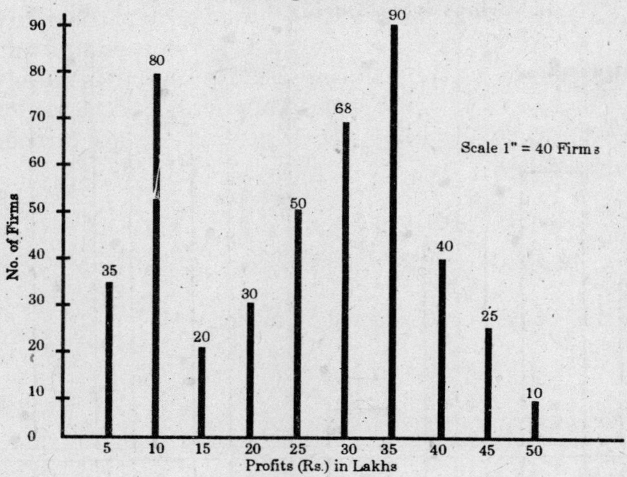

(ii) Simple Bar Diagrams: These diagrams can be drawn either vertically or horizontally. The bars must have the similar width and uniform space should be kept between the two bars. The values of variable are taken either in ascending order or in descending order. Individual observations, time series and other series are generally represented in the simple bar diagram. We can use different colours or shades or dots for each bar if necessary to identify the data and to make the diagram attractive.

Example 6.2. *Draw a vertical simple bar diagram from the following data relating to the number of small scale industrial units in various states during the year 1997.*

States:	Karnataka	T.Nadu	Kerala	Andra	Maha-rastra	M.P.	U.P
No. of Small scale units('000)	55	68	60	40	80	75	85

Solution:

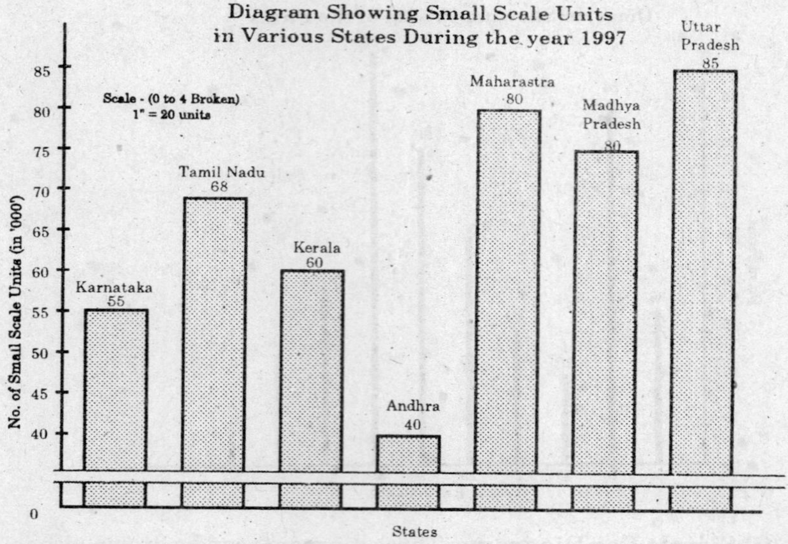

Note: There are wide variations only in the second part of the values i.e. from 40,000 to 85,000. The space between 0 to 40,000 is reduced by "Broken Bars".

Example 6.3. *The incomes of persons sitting in the Raj-darbar are given below:*

Persons sitting in Raj-darbar:	Peon	Dancer	Minister I	Minister II	King
Incomes(Rs):	450	500	2,000	3,000	5,000

Represent the data by a suitable diagram. (BU-N83)

Solution:

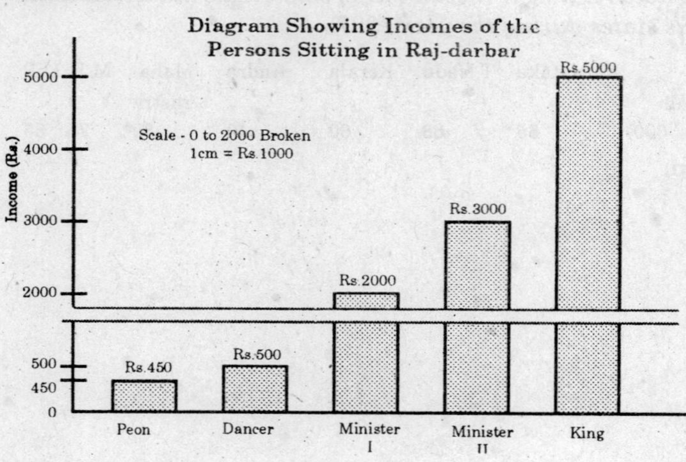

Example 6.4 *Draw a bar diagram from the following data about the raw materials imported by a country "A":*

Raw Materials	Import in Crores Rs
Aluminium	135
Copper	120
Iron	170
Silver	80

(BU-N91)

Solution:

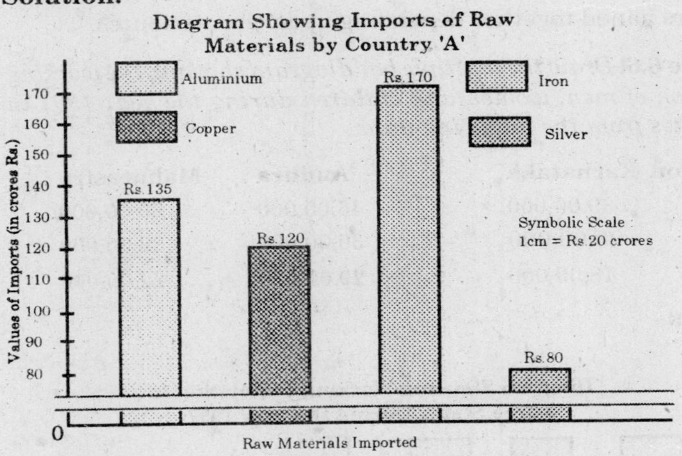

Example 6.5. *The following table gives the proportion of married women of India under various ages. Represent the data by bar diagrams.*

Age	: 18	20	22	24	26
Married Women (in %)	: 17	36.2	50.7	62	65.7

(BU-A95)

Solution:

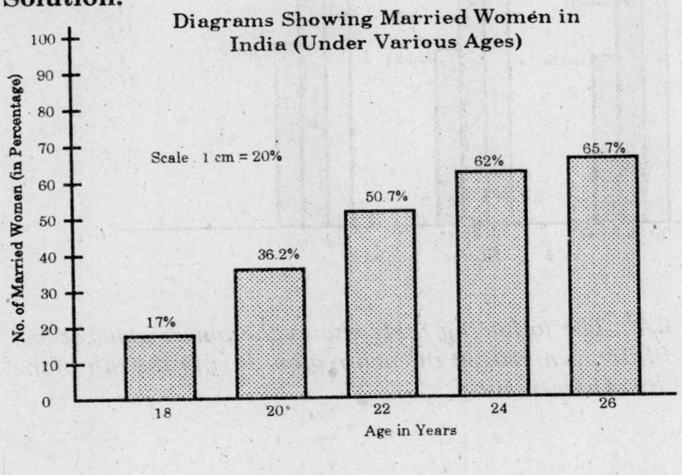

(iii) Multiple Bar Diagrams: These diagrams are also known as "compound bar diagrams". They are adopted when two or more phenomena over a number of years are compared with each other. Similar attributes in each period are presented for the purpose of comparison. Different colours or shades or dots are used for each attribute in each set of period. For the identification of different attribute , an index is prepared. In each set, we may have two or more bars joined together depending upon the attributes.

Example 6.6. *Draw the multiple bar diagram showing the working population of men, women and children during the year 1997 in three states from the following data:*

Population	Karnataka	Andhra	Maharastra
Men	39,00,000	45,00,000	50,00,000
Women	25,00,000	30,00,000	38,00,000
Children	18,00,000	20,00,000	22,00,000

Solution:

Diagram Showing Working Population in Three States During the year 1997

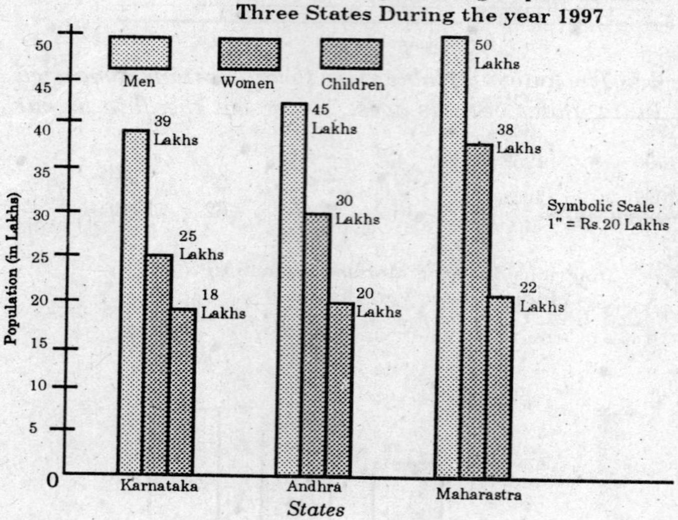

Example 6.7. *The following table shows the power generation capacity additions envisaged in each region during the 6th plan period and its achievements:*

Region :	Northern	Western	Southern	Eastern	North-Eastern
Target (in MWs) :	5172	5937	4565	3323	669
Achievement (in MWs):	3082	4450	2555	1443	346

Present the above data in multiple bars. *(BU - A90)*

Diagram Showing MWs Power Generation in Different Regions

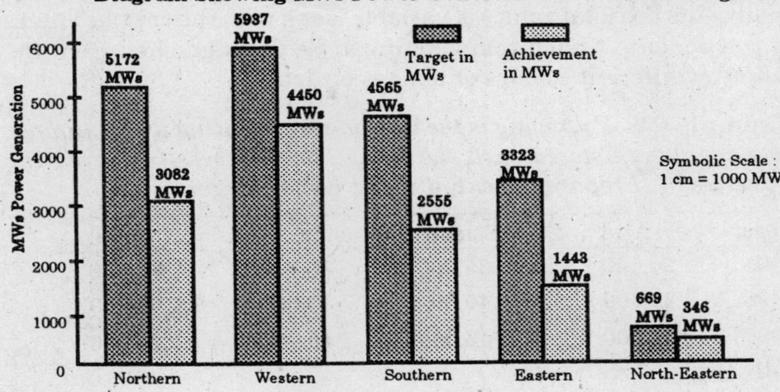

Example 6.8. *Present the following data of results of II B.Com statistics examination of Bangalore University held in November 1995, 1996 and 1997.*

Year	I Class	II Class	III Class	Failed
November 1995	100	300	500	300
November 1996	120	400	600	280
November 1997	100	500	700	300

Solution: (BU-N84, A88) (Refer Example 6.10)

Bangalore University II B.Com., Statistics Results During 1995-1997

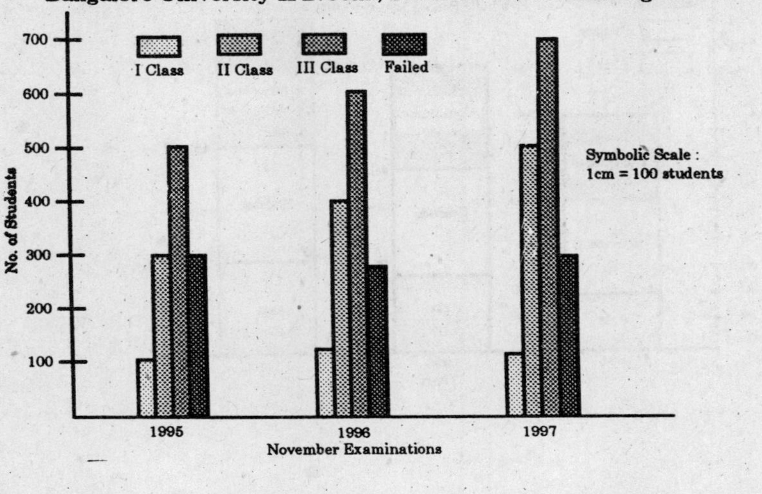

(iv) Sub-divided Bar Diagrams: These diagrams are also known as "component bar diagrams". Each bar is sub-divided according to the components consisting in it. A given magnitude of the phenomenon can be broken into parts of which it is composed. From each bar, the different portions are made from the bottom of the bar to distinguish different components. The complete bar represents the total values of variable along with the various values of components. Each component can be distinguished from the other by different colours or shades or dots.

Example 6.9. *Following is the information relating to the number of students registered with the Bangalore University during the three years. Prepare the sub-divided bar diagram:*

Year	Arts	Science	Commerce	Total
1995	20,000	35,000	30,000	85,000
1996	28,000	40,000	37,000	1,05,000
1997	32,000	45,000	45,000	1,22,000

Solution:

The above data is to be converted into cumulative figures for showing the different components and their break up.

Year	A	A + S	A + S + C
1995	20,000	55,000	85,000
1996	28,000	68,000	1,05,000
1997	32,000	77,000	1,22,000

Diagrams showing the number of students Registered wth the Bangalore University During the three years

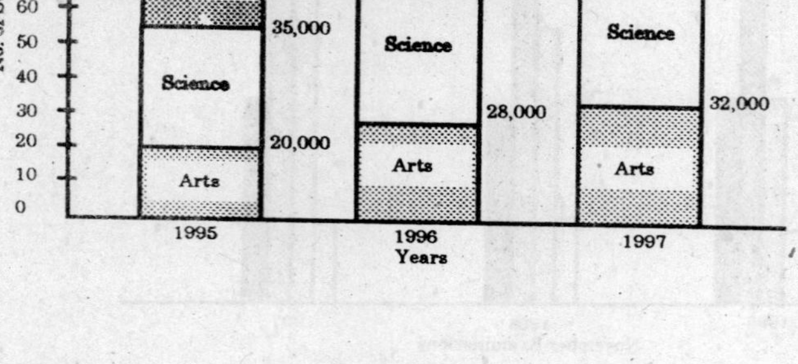

Example 6.10. *The following table shows the results of M.B.A. students of a university for the last three years. Represent the data in a suitable diagram. (The data can also be shown by multiple bar diagram - refer example 6.8).* (BU-N84, A88)

Year	I. Class	II. Class	III. Class	Failed	Total
1995	60	160	260	163	643
1996	70	210	310	150	740
1997	60	260	360	160	840

(No. of students in '000 s).

Solution:

The above data is to be converted into cumulative figures for showing the different components and their break up.

Year	I. Class	I & II Class	I,II & III Class	All + Failed
1995	60	220	480	643
1996	70	280	590	740
1997	60	320	680	840

Bangalore University M.B.A Results of a University for Three Years

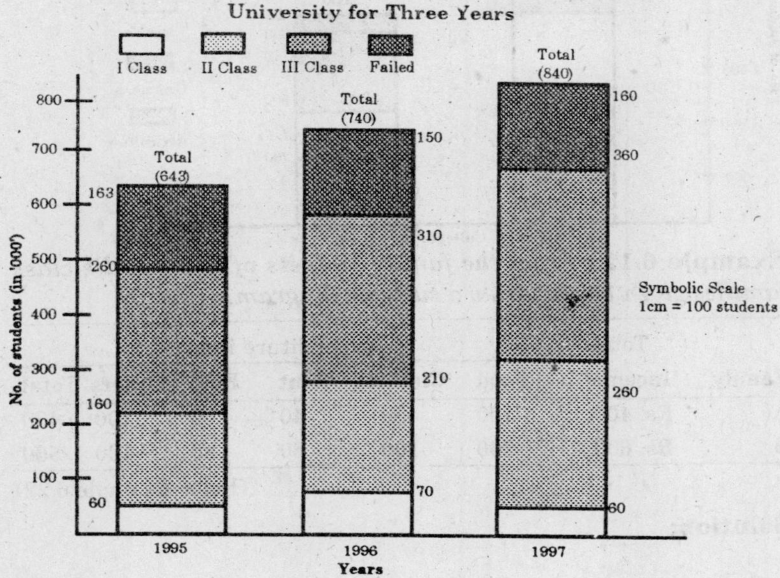

Example 6.11. *Construct a suitable bar diagram for the following data of number of students in two colleges in different faculties:*

College	Arts	Science	Commerce	Agriculture	Total
A	1,200	800	600	400	3,000
B	700	500	600	200	2,000

(BU-A93)

Solution:

The above data is to be converted into cumulative figures for showing the different components and their break up.

College	A	A + S	A + S + C	A + S + C + A
A	1200	2000	2600	3000
B	700	1200	1800	2000

Diagrams Showing Number of Students in A and B Colleges in Different Faculties

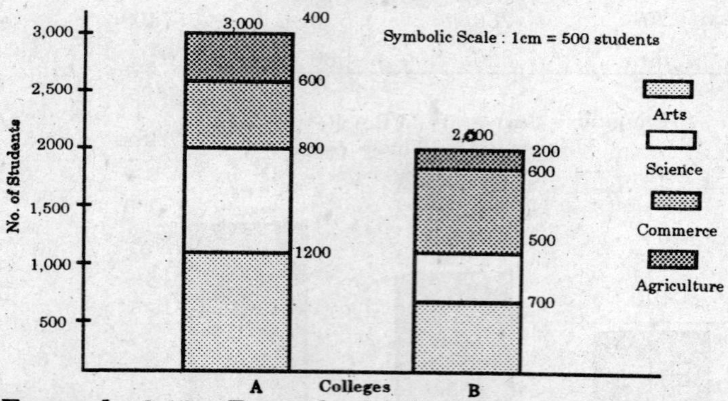

Example 6.12. *From the family budgets of two middle class families given below, draw a suitable diagram.*

Family	Total Income	Food	Clothing	Rent	Fuel	Others	Total
		Expenditure items					
A	Rs. 400	150	80	40	60	100	430
B	Rs. 600	200	100	60	80	120	560

(Refer Example 6.22)

Solution:

Diagram Showing Incomes and Expenditure of Family A and B

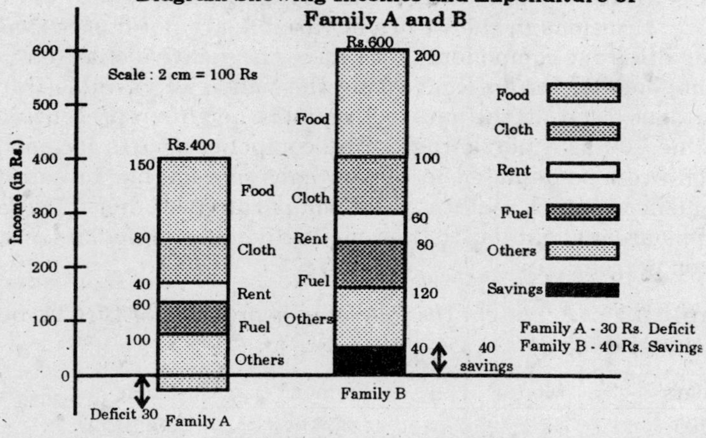

Note: The above data can also be represented by two-dimensional diagram. Ref. Example 6.19.

Example 6.13. *Represent the following information in a suitable diagram.*

(Figures in '000)

District	Males	Females	Total
Bangalore	2400	1650	4000
Tumkur	800	700	1500
Kolar	500	600	1100
Mandya	800	1000	1800

(BU-N84)

Solution:

Diagram Showing Population in Four Districts

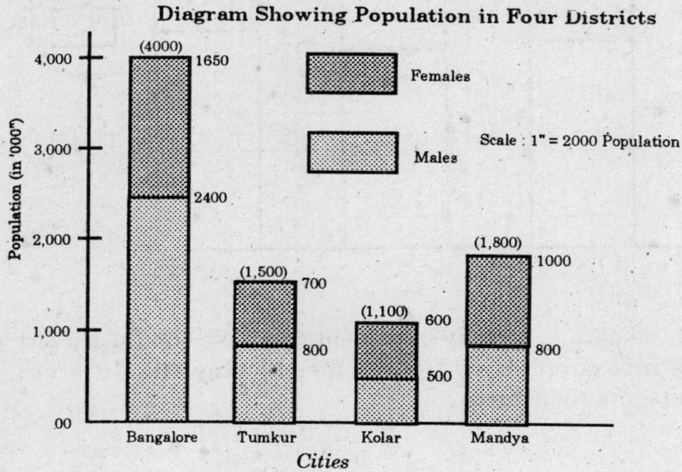

(v) Sub-divided Percentage Bar Diagrams: In these bars, absolute variations in the values of variable are not depicted as regards different components. To have the relative changes in the components, we are converting the values of variable into percentages. Now all the bars look equal in heights representing the value 100 as a percentage. The component parts for each division are also depicted in percentages in each bar or set of phenomenon, "which facilitates for comparative studies. These diagrams are just similar to that of sub-divided simple bars, but based on percentages.

Example 6.14. *Represent the following population of City 'A' by a percentage diagram:*

Years	Men	Women	Children
1995	45%	35%	20%
1996	44%	34%	22%
1997	48%	36%	16%

(BU-A91)

Solution:

Diagram Showing the Composition of Population in City A During the Three Years

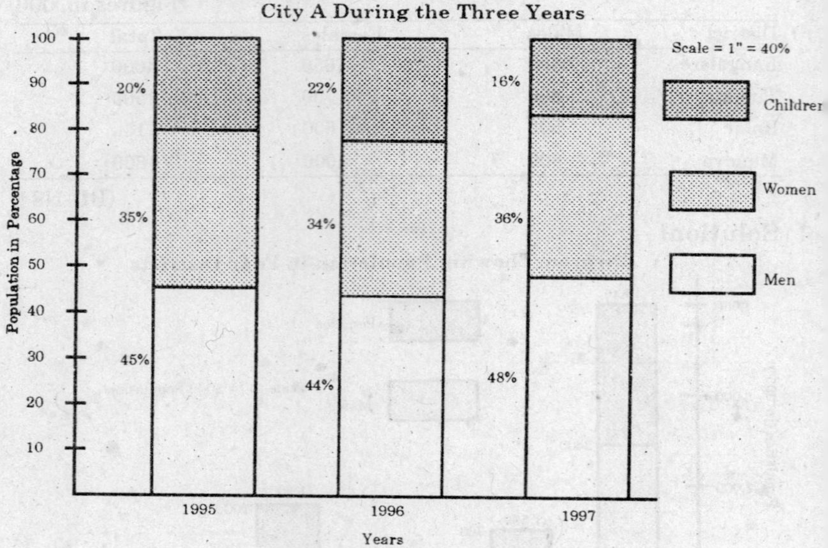

The above data is already in percentages. We should convert the same into cumulative figures for showing the different components and their break up.

Years	M	M+W	M+W+C
1995	45%	80%	100%
1996	44%	78%	100%
1997	48%	84%	100%

Example 6.15. *Proportion of males and females in India are given below according to occupation. Draw a suitable diagram.*

S.No.	Occupation	Males	Females
1.	Industrial Labour	45%	55%
2.	Agricultural Labour	55%	45%
3.	Household Industries Labour	61%	39%
4.	Miscellaneous Labour	88%	12%

(BU-A89)

Solution:

Diagram Showing Male & Female Labour in Different Sectors

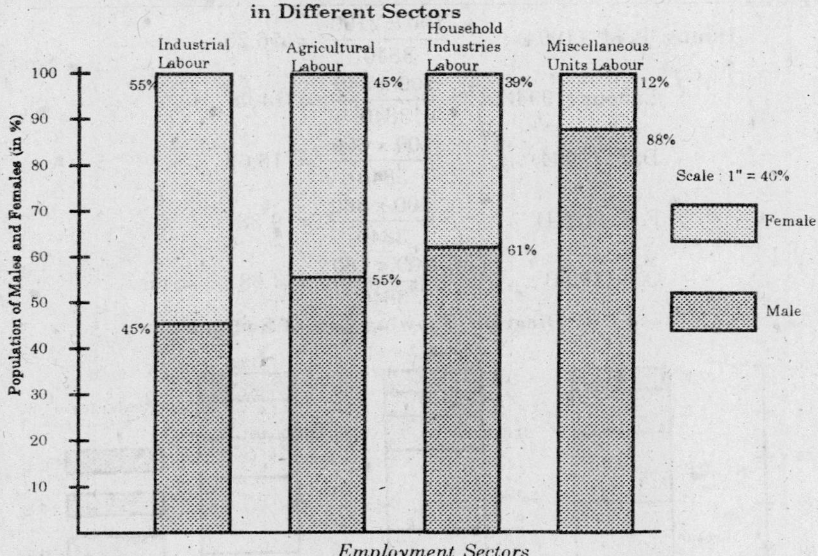

Example 6.16. *Represent the following data by means of Percentage Sub-divided bar diagrams:*

Cost Per Equipment	1994 Rs.	1995 Rs.	1996 Rs
Raw Materials	2,160	2,600	2,700
Labour	540	700	810
Direct Expenses	600	300	350
Factory Expenses	360	200	360
Office Expenses	180	200	270
Total	3,840	4,000	4,490

(BU-A98)

Solution:

The figures are first converted into the percentages and then cummulative percentages are prepared to draw the sub-divided bar diagrams.

Cumulative Percentages of Cost of Equipment

Elements	1994		1995		1996	
of Cost	%	c.f.%	%	c.f.%	%	c.f.%
Raw Materials	56.25	56.25	65.00	65.00	60.13	60.13
Labour	14.06	70.31	17.50	82.50	18.04	78.17
Direct Expenses	15.63	85.94	7.50	90.00	7.80	85.97
Factory Expenses	9.38	95.32	5.00	95.00	8.02	93.99
Office Expenses	4.68	100.00	5.00	100.00	6.01	100.00
	100.00		100.00		100.00	

Hints: R. M. (1994) .... $\frac{100 \times 2160}{3840} = 56.25$

Labour (1994) .... $\frac{100 \times 540}{3840} = 14.06$

D. E. (1994) .... $\frac{100 \times 600}{3840} = 15.63$

F. E. (1994) .... $\frac{100 \times 360}{3840} = 9.38$

O. E (1994) .... $\frac{100 \times 180}{3840} = 4.68$ ... so on

Diagram Showing Cost of Equipment

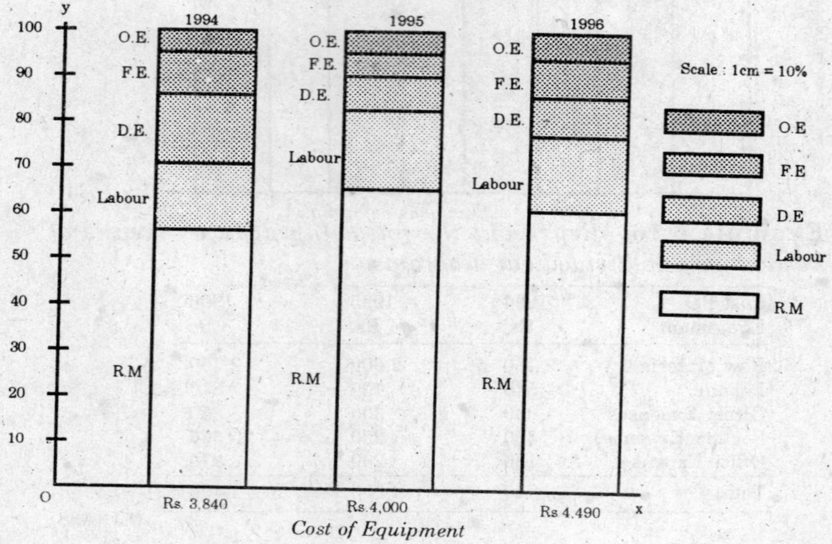

(vi) Deviation Bars: These bars depict the net deviations in different values. The positive deviations are taken above the 'OX' axis and the negative deviations taken below it. The two opposite phenomena - Profits or Losses, Favourable Balance of Trade or Unfavourable Balance of Trade and Surplus or Deficit - are depicted by deviation bar diagrams. These diagrams are also known as "Bilateral Bar Diagrams".

Example 6.17. *Following are the figures relating to exports and imports for six years. Represent the information by deviation bars.*

Year	Exports (in lakhs) Rs.	Imports (in lakhs) Rs	Balance of payment (in lakhs)Rs
1991	25	5	+ 20
1992	110	70	+ 40
1993	80	110	- 30
1994	130	90	+ 40
1995	90	140	- 50
1996	150	130	+ 20

Solution:

Diagram Showing Balance of Payment (in lakhs of Rs.) For Six Years

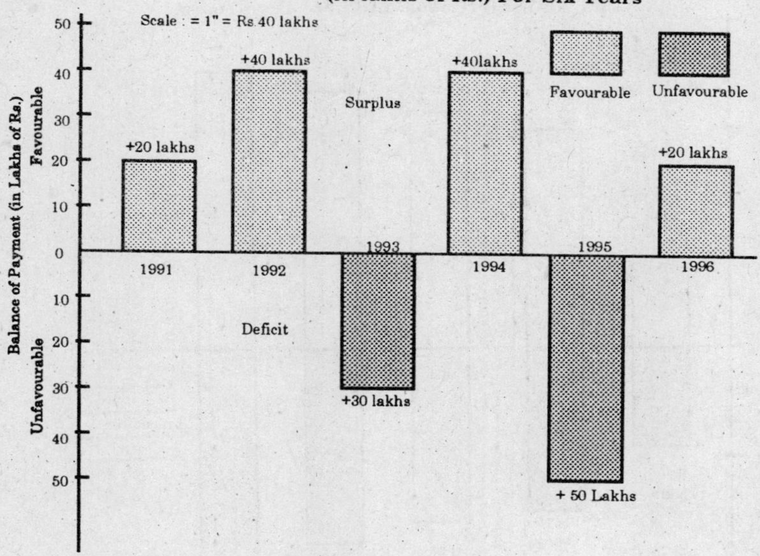

(vii) Duo-directional Bars: These diagrams are drawn to show an aggregate result of different and opposite components of the same phenomenon. The total gross value of the variable is separated into two parts so that one part lies above the 'OX' axis and the other below it. Both the parts added together give us the gross result of the value of variable.

Example 6.18. *Following is the data relating to the Gross Profits and Expenses (in lakhs of Rs) of M / s Amit Electricals Ltd. for five years. Represent the data by a duo-directional diagram.*

Years	Gross profit (in lakhs of Rs)	Expenditure (in lakhs of Rs)	Net Profit (in lakhs of Rs)
1991	200	90	110
1992	350	150	200
1993	380	160	220
1994	420	180	240
1995	460	200	260

Solution:

Diagram Showing Gross Profits and Net Profits of M/s. Amit Electricals Ltd., For Five Years

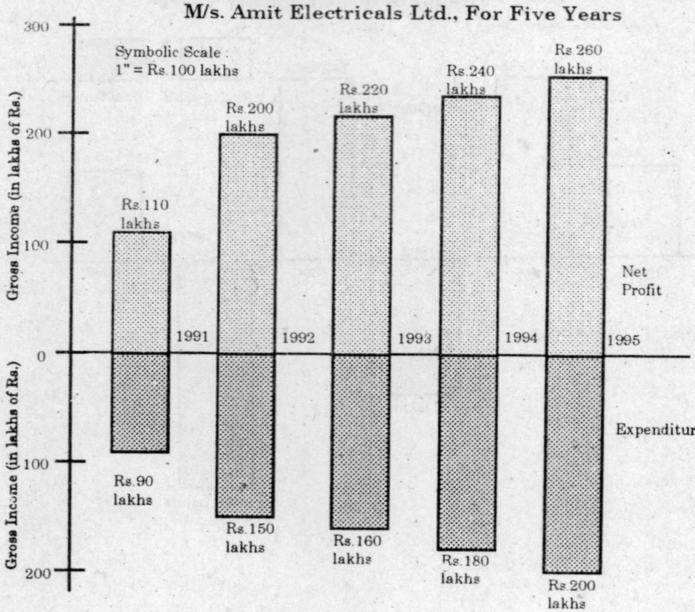

(viii) Paired Bars: These diagrams are drawn to show related data of the same phenomenon. The paired bars relate to each other and they are jointly studied. They also look like duo-directional bars. The duo-directional bars are separated by OX axis vertically whereas the paired bars are separated horizontally by the items to which the data are related. Naturally it gives the impression of stretched arms.

Example 6.19. *Represent the following data by paired bars showing area and production of rice during 1997.*

Country :	Italy	Spain	Portugal	Greece	France
Area (000 hectares):	200	150	100	60	30
Production (000 metric tons):	700	600	400	300	100

Solution:

Diagram Showing Production of Rice and Cultivated Area in Five Countries in 1997

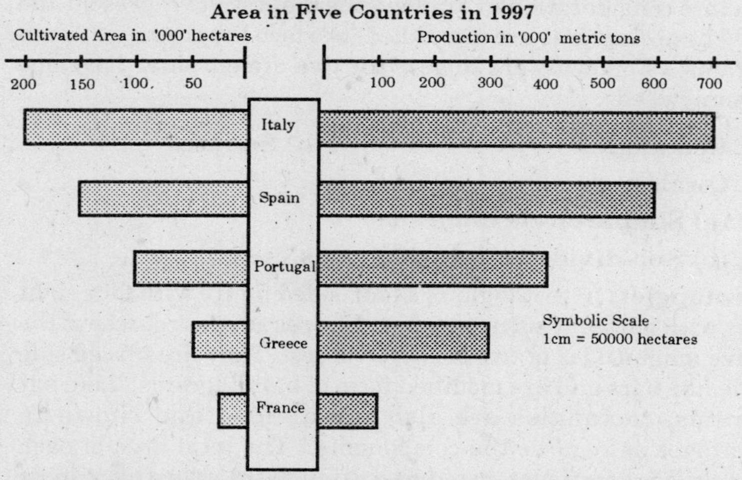

(ix) Broken Bars: These bars do not refer to any method of diagram in particular. It is a device of adjusting the scale while drawing the bars when there is a large gap between the '0' and the value from which the values start varying (refer examples 6.2, 6.3 and 6.4). The bars are broken at a particular point and the space is reduced. We may also show a few bars only reduced in scale by breaking them. Such broken bars must be read carefully. They are shown as illustrated below:

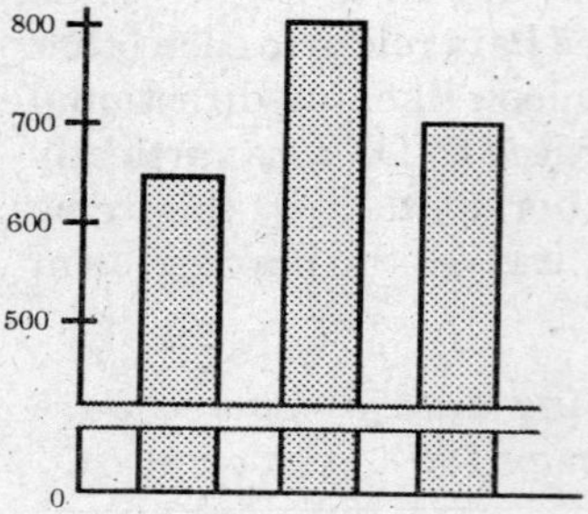

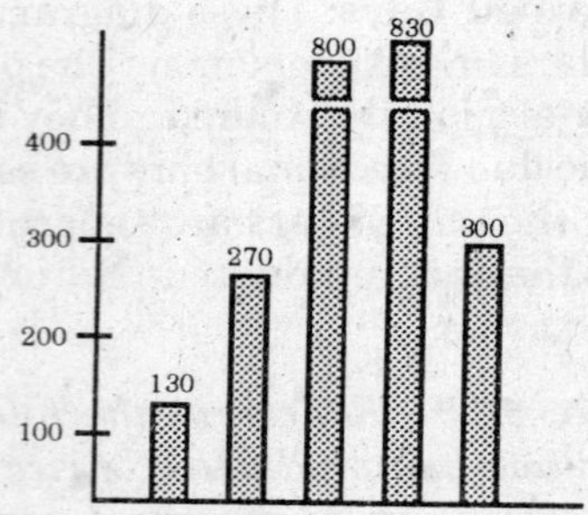

1.B Two-dimensional Diagrams

In two-dimensional diagrams, both the length and breadth are taken into consideration in drawing the diagram to represent the data. These diagrams are also called "Surface Diagrams" or "Area Diagrams". Following are some of the two-dimensional diagrams commonly used:

(i) Rectangles **(ii) Squares**

(iii) Circles:

(a) Simple circle diagrams

(b) Sub-divided circle diagrams.

(i) Rectangles: A `rectangle' is a four-sided figure with four right angles with adjacent sides unequal. The rectangles represent the relative magnitudes of two or more values. They are placed side by side like bars and are modified form of bar diagrams. Like bar diagrams, rectangles are also sub-divided and shown in percentages as regards the components. The total area of each rectangle is proportionately reduced through the adjustment in its breadth and height as per its value. There are two types of rectangle diagrams.

(a) Simple sub-divided rectangles

(b) Percentage sub-divided rectangles.

(a) Simple sub-divided rectangles: Under this method, the breadth and height of the bars vary according to the values proportionately. The figures are represented as they are given. Such diagrams are generally used to show three related phenomena – Per unit cost, Quantity of sales and Value of sales.

Example 6.20: *Present the following data by a suitable diagram*

Commodities:	A	B
Quantity Sold	200 units	240 units
Price per Unit	Rs. 500	Rs. 600
Cost of Raw Materials Per unit	Rs. 200	Rs. 300
Wages Per unit	Rs. 150	Rs. 120
Other Costs Per Unit	Rs. 100	Rs. 90
Profit Per Unit	Rs. 50	Rs. 90

Solution: (BU-A95)

Cost Elements	Commodity A		Commodity B	
	Per Unit Rs.	200 Units Rs.	Per units Rs.	240 Units Rs.
Raw Material	200	40,000	300	72,000
Labour	150	30,000	120	28,800
Overheads	100	20,000	90	21,600
Profit	50	10,000	90	21,600
	500	1,00,000	600	1,44,000

Cumulative Totals	A (Rs.)	B (Rs.)
Raw material	40,000	72,000
Labour	70,000	1,00,800
Overheads	90,000	1,22,400
Profit	1,00,000	1,44,000

Diagram Showing Details of Cost and Profit of A and B Commodities

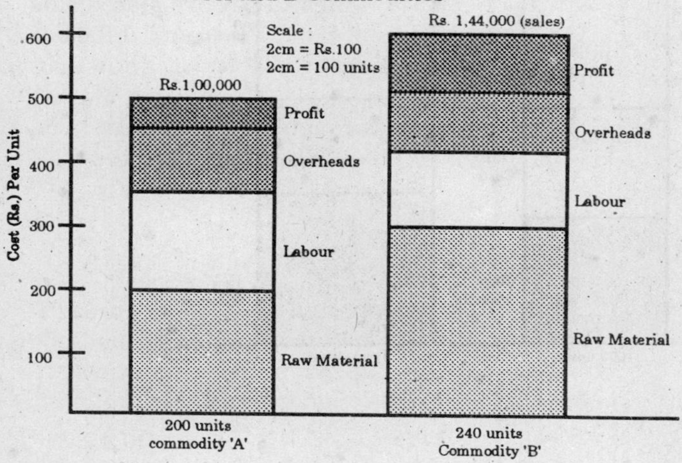

Example 6.21. *Draw a rectangular diagram to represent the following information:*

Particulars	Factory A	Factory B
Price Per Unit	Rs. 15.00	Rs. 12.00
Units Sold	1000	1,200
Cost of Raw materials ...	Rs. 5.00 Per Unit	Rs. 5.00 Per Unit
Other Costs	Rs. 4.00 Per Unit	Rs. 3.00 Per Unit

(BU - N89)

Solution:

	Factory A			Factory B		
Cost Elements:	Per Unit Rs.	1000 Units Rs.	C.f	Per Unit Rs.	1200 Units Rs.	C.f
Raw materials	5.00	5,000	5	5.00	6,000	6
Other Costs	4.00	4,000	9	3.00	3,600	9.6
		9,000			9,600	
Profits	6.00	6,000	15	4.00	4,800	14.4
Sales	15.00	15.000		12.0	14,400	

Diagram Showing Details of Cost and Profits of Factories A & B. Products

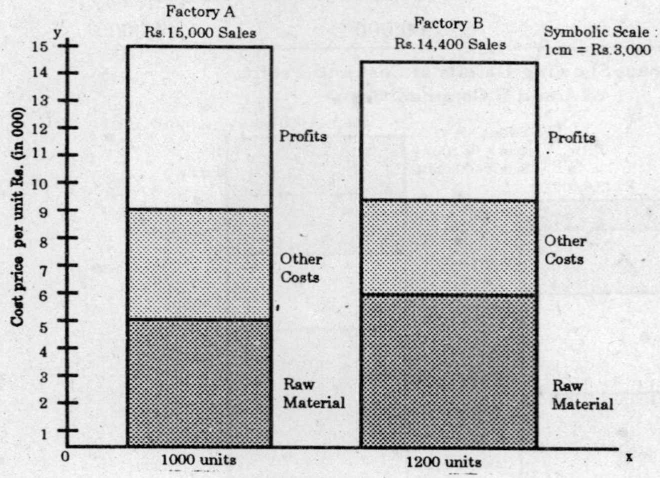

Example 6.22. *From the family budgets of two middle class families are given below, draw a suitable diagram.*

Family	Total Income	Expenditure Items					
		Food	Clothing	Rent	Fuel	Others	Total
A	Rs. 400	150	80	40	60	100	430
B	Rs. 600	200	100	60	80	120	560

Solution:

Diagram Showing Incomes and Expenditure of Family A and B

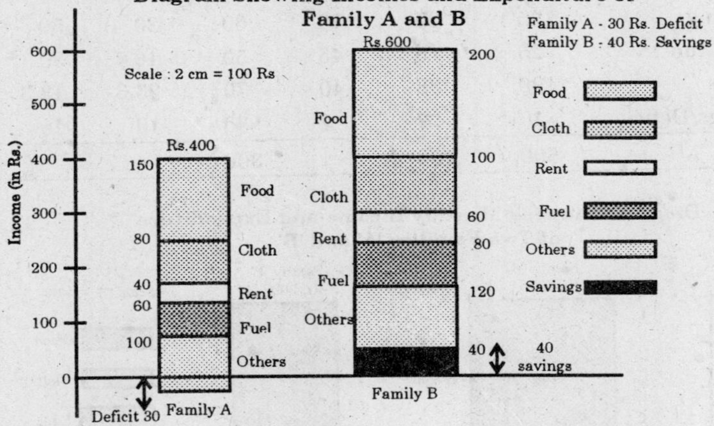

(**Note:** The above data can also be represented by sub-divided bar diagrams. Ref. Example 6.12).

(b) Percentage Sub-divided Rectangles: Under this method, the widths of the rectangles are kept proportionately according to the total values in the ratio. As regards the length of the rectangles, all the values are converted into percentages. The data can also be shown by simple sub-divided rectangles.

Example 6.23. *Represent the following data by a percentage sub-divided bar diagram.*

Items of Expenditure:	Food	Clothing	Education	Others	Savings/ Deficit	Total
Family 'A' Income Rs. 500	150	125	25	190	+10	500
Family 'B' Income Rs. 300	150	60	50	70	-30	300

(BU-N87)

Solution: The widths of the rectangles are taken in the ratio of the total incomes viz., 500:300 i.e., 5:3

Values are converted into percentages as under:

Item of Expenditure	Family 'A'			Family 'B'		
	Expenditure (Rs.)	%	Cumulative	Expenditure (Rs.)	%	Cumulative
Food	150	30	100	150	50	100
Clothing	125	25	70	60	20	50
Education	25	5	45	50	16.7	30
Others	190	38	40	70	23.3	13.3
Savings/Deficit	+10	2	2	-30	-10	-10
Total	500	100		300		

Diagram Showing Monthly Income and Expenditure of Two Families 'A' and 'B'

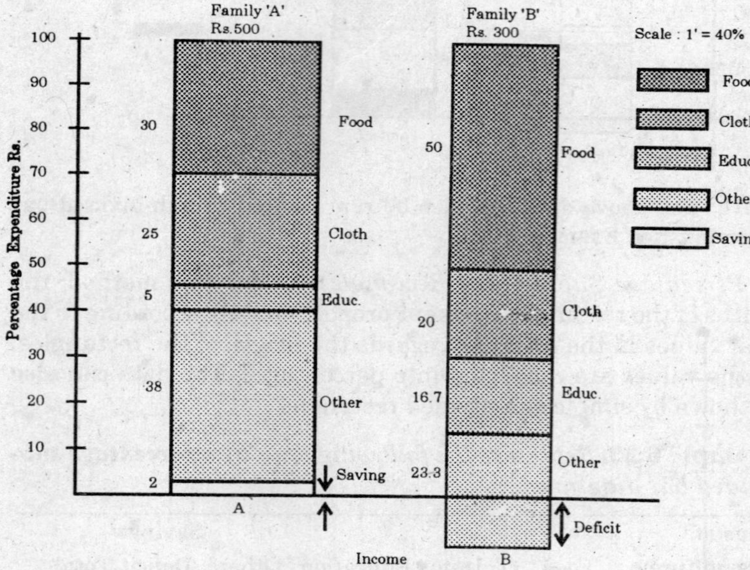

Example 6.24. *Present the following data by a percentage sub-divided rectangle diagram.*

Items	Family 'A' Income Rs. 4500 p.m	Family 'B' Income Rs. 3500 p.m
Food	1300	1200
Clothing	800	700
Rent	700	500
Education	300	350
Fuel	400	100
Others	600	250

(BU- N91)

Solution: The widths of the rectangles are taken in the ratio of 4.5 : 3.5

Values are converted into percentages as under:

Items	Family A Expenditure	%	Cumulative	Family B Expenditure	%	Cumulative
Food	1300	28.90	100.00	1200	34.30	100.00
Clothing	800	17.80	71.10	700	20.00	65.70
Rent	700	15.50	53.30	500	14.30	45.70
Education	300	6.70	37.80	350	10.00	31.40
Fuel	400	8.90	31.10	100	2.90	21.40
Others	600	13.30	22.20	250	7.10	18.50
Savings/Deficit	+400	8.90	8.90	+400	11.40	11.40
	Rs. 4,500	100.00		Rs. 3,500	100.00	

Diagram Showing Monthly Income and Expenditure of Two Families 'A' and 'B'

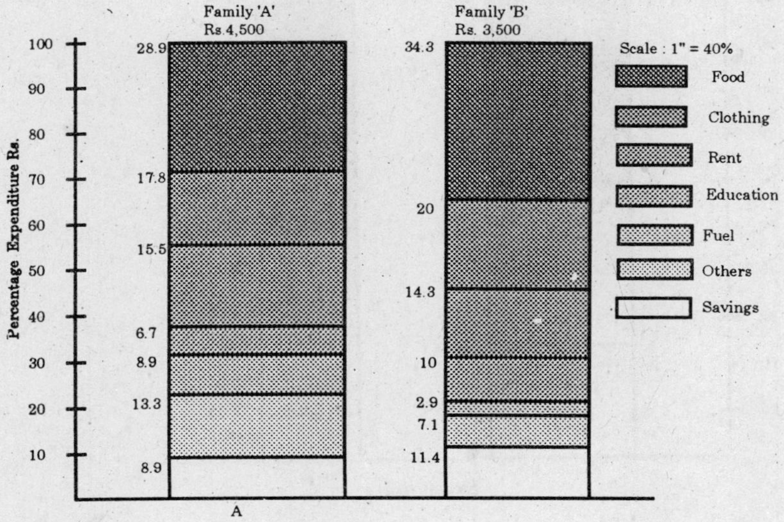

Example 6.25. *The following data relate to monthly expenditure of two families A and B.*

Items of Expenditure	Expenditure (in Rs.) Family A	Family B
Food	160	100
Clothing	80	30
Rent	60	40
Fuel	20	10
Others	80	20
Total	Rs. 400	Rs. 200

Represent the data by a suitable percentage diagram. (BU - N92)

Solution: The widths of the rectangles are taken in the ratio of 2:1

Values are converted into percentages as under:

Items	Family 'A' Expenditure(Rs)	%	Cumulative	Family 'B' Expenditure(Rs)	%	Cumulative
Food	160	40	100	100	50	100
Clothing	80	20	60	30	15	50
Rent	60	15	40	40	20	35
Fuel	20	5	25	10	5	15
Others	80	20	20	20	10	10
Total	400	100		200	100	

Diagram Showing Monthly Expenditure of Two Families 'A' and 'B'

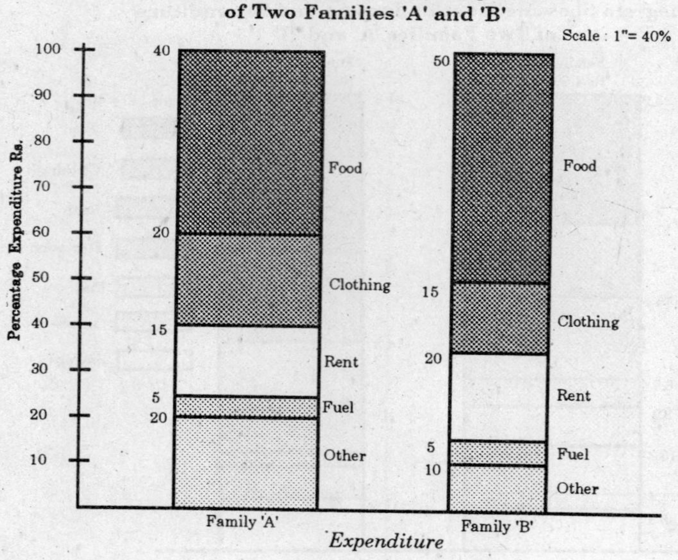

Example 6.26. *Present the following data by a suitable percentage diagram:*

Particulars	1992	1993	1994
Material Cost	Rs. 320	Rs. 320	Rs. 450
Labour Cost	" 240	" 280	" 400
Polishing	" 160	" 200	" 250
Total Cost	" 720	" 800	" 1,100
Sale Proceeds	" 800	" 800	" 1,000
Profit or Loss	" +80	" Nil	" (-100)

(BU - N95)

Solution: the widths of the rectangles are taken in the ratio of 4:4:5 for 1992, 1993 and 1994 respectively.

Values are converted into percentages as under:

Particulars of Cost	1992 Rs.	%	Cumu lative	1993 Rs.	%	Cumu lative	1994 Rs.	%	Cumu lative
Material	320	40	100	320	40	100	450	45	100
Labour	240	30	60	280	35	60	400	40	55
Polishing	160	20	30	200	25	25	250	25	15
Profit/Loss	80	10	10	-	-	-	(-100)	(-10)	(-10)
Total Rs.	800	100		800	100		1,000		

Diagram Showing Cost, Sales Proceeds and Profit or Loss Per Unit During 1992, 1993 and 1994

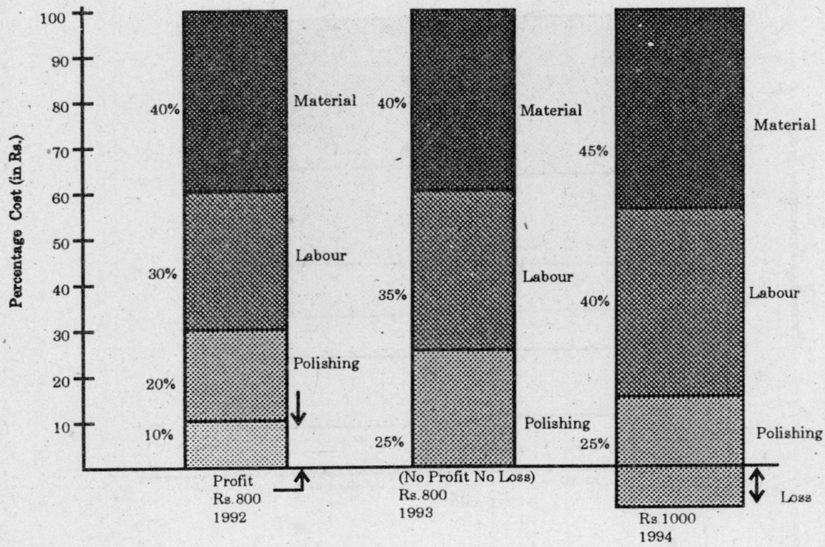

Example 6.27. *Represent the following monthly expenditure of two families A and B by means of Rectangular diagrams:*

Items of Expenditure:	Food	Clothing	Rent	Fuel	Education	Others
Expenses of						
Family A:	105	60	30	24	45	36
Family B:	128	88	48	32	64	40

(BU - A 97)

Solution: The widths of the rectangles are taken in the ratio of 3 : 4. Values are converted into percentages as under:

Items of Expenditure	Family 'A'			Family 'B'		
	Rs.	%	Cumulative	Rs.	%	Cumulative
Food	105	35	100	128	32	100
Clothing	60	20	65	88	22	68
Rent	30	10	45	48	12	46
Fuel	24	8	35	32	8	34
Education	45	15	27	64	16	26
Others	36	12	12	40	10	10
Total	300	100		400	100	

Diagram Showing Expenditure of Two Families - 'A' and 'B'

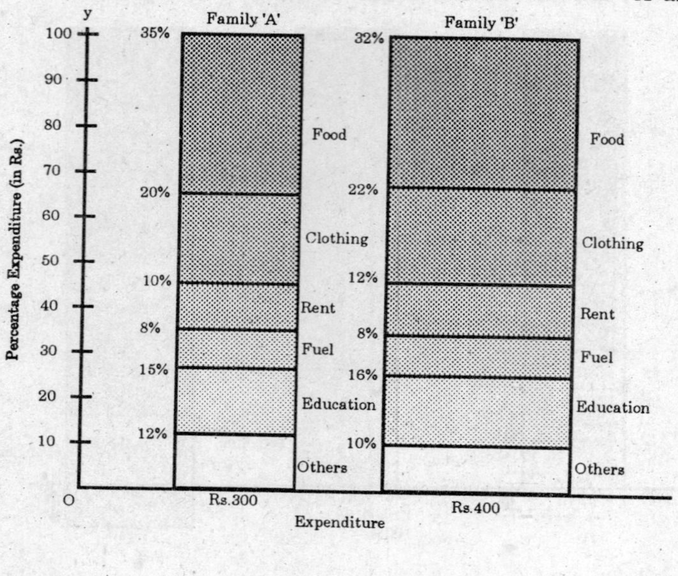

Example 6.28. *Family Budget of two middle - class families is given below:*

Total Income (Rs. per. month):	Family 'A' Rs. 800	Family 'B' Rs. 1200
Expenditure (Rs. per. Month)		
Food	440	600
Clothing	144	144
Fuel	40	60
Rent	96	120
Education	64	120
Others	56	96
Total	Rs. 840	Rs. 1,140

Represent the above data by a Rectangular Diagram drawn on percentage basis. (BU - N97)

Solution: The widths of the rectangles are taken in the ratio of 2 : 3. Values are converted into percentages as under:

Items of Expenditure	Family 'A' Rs.	%	Cumulative	Family 'B' Rs.	%	Cumulative
Food	440	55	100	600	50	100
Clothing	144	18	45	144	12	50
Fuel	40	5	27	60	5	38
Rent	96	12	22	120	10	33
Education	64	8	10	120	10	23
Others	56	7	2	96	8	13
Deficit/Savings	(-40)	(-5)	-5	+60	5	5
Total	Rs. 800	100		Rs. 1,200	100	

Diagram Showing Expenditure of Two Families 'A' and 'B'

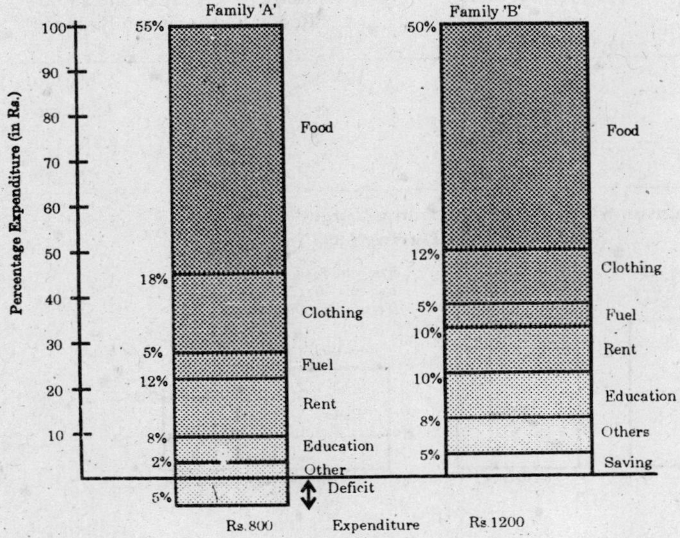

(ii) Squares: "Squares" are figures with four equal sides and four right angles. When the values of variables bear the long range of ratios like 1 : 100 or 4 : 400 or 10 : 1000, the rectangles fail to answer the purpose of drawing the diagrams. In such cases bars and rectangles are replaced by squares. In a square, its size varies as the square root of its area changes. Therefore, two comparable values of variable can be represented by square root of the area as one side of the square. For example, if the values are 400, 81 and 16, we can represent them by drawing three squares having their each side 20, 9 and 4 respectively i.e., $\sqrt{400}$, $\sqrt{81}$ and $\sqrt{16}$. We may convert them into ratio as 10, 4.5 and 2. As far as possible we can reduce the values of ratio to the minimum. Since the area of the square is given by the square of its side, the side of the square diagram will be in proportion to the square root of the given observations.

Example 6.29. *Following is the information relating to the production of sugar-cane in four countries during the year 1997. Represent the data by a suitable diagram.*

Countries:	India	Jawa	Hawai	Columbia
Production of Sugar-Cane (in'000' Quintals):	3600	2500	1600	900

Solution: The following calculations are made to obtain the side of square measurement:

Country	Sugar-Cane Production/ (in '000' Quintals)	Square Roots	Side of the square (Ratio Reduced)
India	3,600	60	3.0. cm.
Jawa	2,500	50	2.5 cm.
Hawai.	1,600	40	.2.0 cm.
Columbia	900	30	1,5 cm.

Diagram Showing Production of Sugar-Cane in Four Countries During 1997

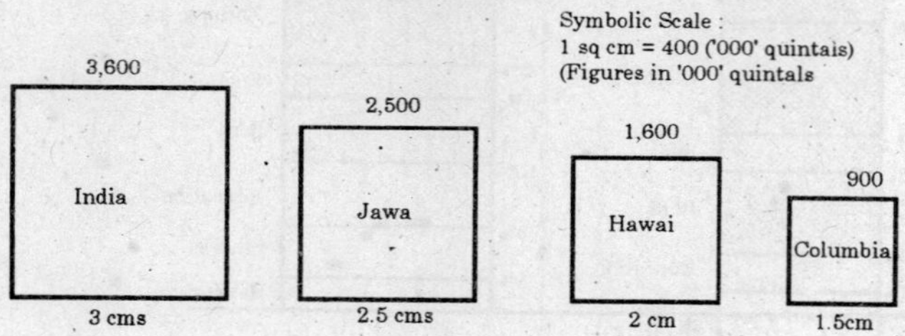

(iii) Circles: A 'circle' refers to the space enclosed by a curved line which keeps the same distance from the centre. The area of a circle is given as under.

Area of a circle = πr^2 (Where π =22/7 and r= radius)

The area of a circle is proportional to the square of its radius. `π' is the common factor that can be avoided. The circle diagrams are also called "Circular Diagrams". They are of two types:

(A) Simple Circle Diagrams.

(B) Sub-divided Circle Diagrams (Pie Charts, Sector Charts or Angular charts).

(A) Simple Circle Diagrams: The area of a circle varies as the square of its radius. If the area of circle 'A' is four times of the area of circle 'B' the radius of the Circle 'A' is twice the radius of circle 'B'. It follows that it the radii of several circles are in the same proportion as the sides of the squares, the areas of the circles would also be in the same proportion as the areas of the squares. Therefore, the same procedure may be used either as the radii of several circles or the sides of several squares. Let us take the figures given in the Example 6.29 for drawing the circle diagrams as under.

Countries:	India	Jawa	Hawai	Columbia
Production of Sugar-Cane (in '000' Quintals) :	3,600	2,500	1,600	900
Radii of circles :	3 cm.	2.5 cm.	2.0 cm	1.5 cm.

Solution:

Sugar-Cane Production

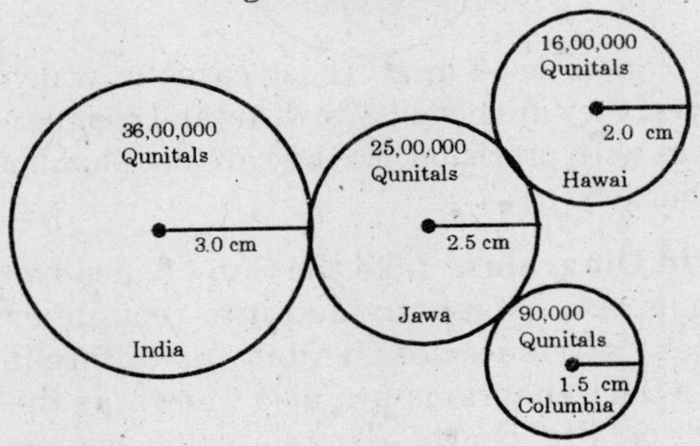

Example 6.30. *Per capita incomes of three countries are given below:*

Country	Per Capital Income (in Rs.)
Australia	7,744
United Kingdom	5,929
Newzeland	4,356

Represent the data by means of circular diagrams. (BU - A87)

Solution. Let us find the square roots of the per capita of income figures to know the radii of three circles as under.

Country	P.C.Income (Rs)	Square Roots	Radii
Australia	7,744	88	4
United Kingdom	5,929	77	3.5
Newzeland	4,356	66	3

Circular Diagrams Showing Per Capita Income of Three Countries

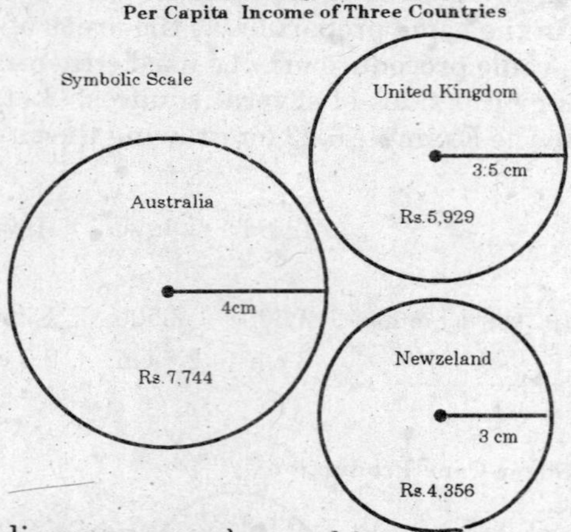

The circle diagrams can be used in all those cases in which squares are used. However, they are not easy to draw and compare to the relative magnitudes with precision. So they are not popular in statistical presentation.

(B) Sub-divided Circle Diagrams: Like the Sub-divided bar diagrams, the circles can also be sub-divided into rectangles according to the different attributes of the data as different segments of the circles. Such diagrams are also known as the **"Circular"** or **"Angular"** or **"Pie"** charts. There are 360 degrees at the centre of a circle. Taking the entire data equal to 360 degrees, the proportionate sectors are cut representing the different attributes of the same data. Such diagrams are used to the break-up of a total value into component parts. Following are the steps to be followed in constructing the pie diagrams:

(i) Express entire data into the percentages according to different attributes. For example, cost of production into raw material, labour and overheads - 50%, 30% and 20% respectively.

(ii) The percentages so obtained are converted into degrees by multiplying 360/100 or 3.6. so we get 180^0, 108^0 and 72^0.

(iii) The circle is drawn with appropriate radius and it is divided into 3 angular parts from the centre forming 180^0, 108^0 and 72^0 with the help of a protractor.

Cost of Production

Elements	Amount	%	Degrees
R.M. -	Rs 100	50	180
Labour	60	30	108
Overheads	40	20	72
Total	Rs. 200		

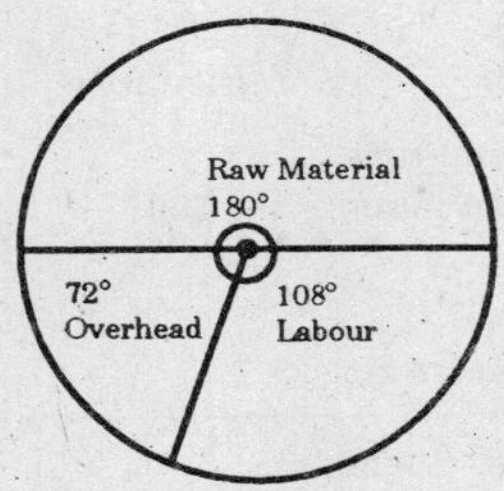

It is a common practice to present the largest sector at the top, the next largest in sequence running clockwise. The pie chart should contain explanatory note to each sector for identification.

Example 6.31. *Draw a Pie diagram to represent the following data of investment pattern in the Third Five year plan.*

Agriculture and Community Development	Irrigation and Power	Industries and Minerals	Transport and Communication	Social Services and Miscellaneous
15%	20%	30%	10%	25%

(BU-A83)

Solution:

S.No	Items	% Investment	Degree
1.	Agriculture and Community Development.	15%	15x360/100 = 54^0
2.	Irrigation and Power	20%	20x360/100 = 72^0
3.	Industries and Minerals	30%	30x360/100 = 108^0
4.	Transport and Communication	10%	10x360/100 = 36^0
5.	Social Servicesand Miscellaneous	25%	25x360/100 = 90^0
	Total	100%	360^0

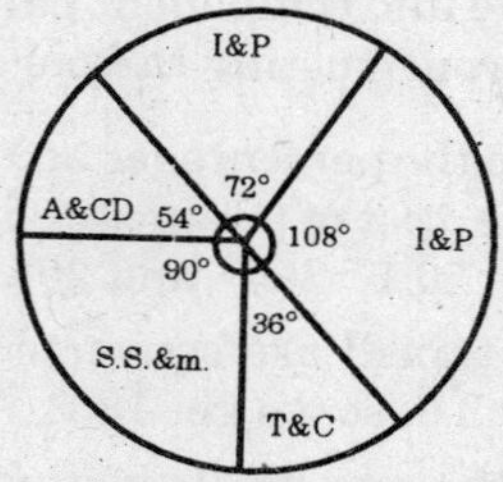

Example 6.32. *Draw a Pie chart to represent the following data of the proposed expenditure by the Karnataka Governor for 1985-86.*

Items:	Agriculture	Industry	Irrigation	Education	Miscellaneous
Expenditure (Rs. in lakhs):	600	400	450	300	250

(BU-A85)

Solution:

S.No.	Items	% Investment	Degrees
1.	Agriculture	(600x100)/2000 = 30%	(30x360)/100 = 108°
2.	Industry	(400x100)/2000 = 20%	(20x360)/100 = 72°
3.	Irrigation	(450x100)/2000 = 22.5	(22.5x360)/100 = 81°
4.	Education	(300x100)/2000 = 15%	(15x360)/100 = 54°
5.	Miscellaneous	(250x100)/2000=12.5%	(12.5x360)/100 = 45°
		Total 100%	Total 360°

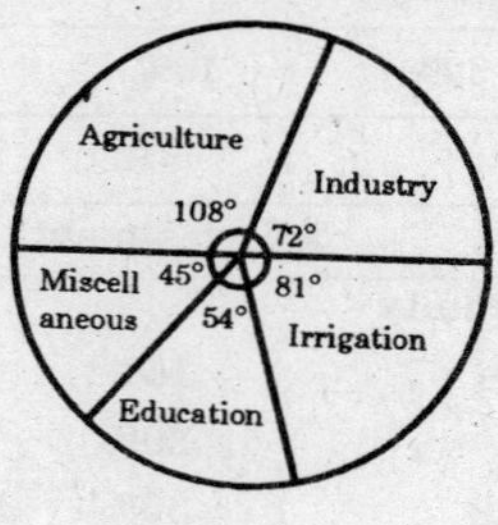

Example 6.33. *Represent the following data of Family 'A' by a pie diagram:*

Items of Expenditure:	Food	Rent	Clothing	Education	Lighting	Misce.	saving
Expenditure :	540	180	180	90	40	40	10

(BU-A92)

Solution: The expenditures are converted into degrees directly as under.

Items	Expenditure	Conversion into Degrees
Food	Rs. 540	$540 \times 360/1080 = 180^0$
Rent	Rs. 180	$180 \times 360/1080 = 60^0$
Clothing	Rs. 180	$180 \times 360/1080 = 60^0$
Education	Rs. 90	$90 \times 360/1080 = 30^0$
Lighting	Rs. 40	$40 \times 360/1080 = 13.33^0$
Miscellaneous	Rs. 40	$40 \times 360/1080 = 13.33^0$
Savings	Rs. 10	$10 \times 360/1080 = 3.34^0$
Total	1080	Total 360.00^0

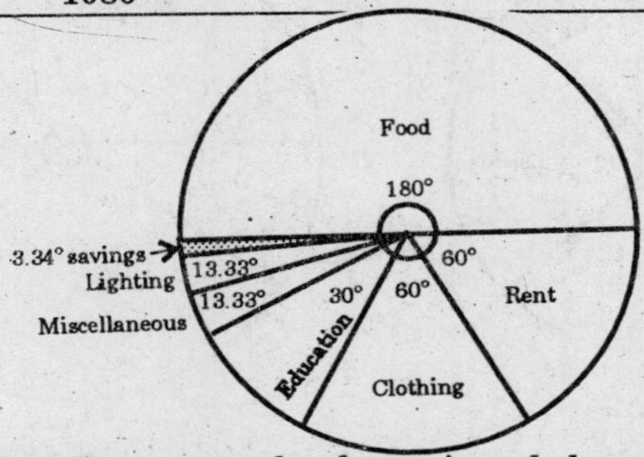

Example 6.34. *Represent the data given below with a suitable diagram:*

Items	1988 Rs. per Unit	1998 Rs. Per Unit
Raw Material	150	350
Labour	100	200
Overheads	120	250
Profits	30	100
Total Sales	400	900

Solution: Let us have the two circles for 1988 and 1988 having the radii 2 cm and 3 cm respectively (i.e $\sqrt{4}$ and $\sqrt{9}$) in proportion of the sales per unit.

For sub-division into various elements of cost, we should convert the figures into degrees as under:

Items	1988		1998	
	Rs. Per Unit	Degrees	Rs. per Unit	Degrees
Raw Material	150	150x0.9=135^0	350	350x0.4 = 140^0
Labour	100	100x0.9 = 90^0	200	200x0.4 = 80^0
Overheads	120	120x0.9 =108^0	250	250x0.4=100^0
Profits	30	30x0.9 = 27^0	100	100x0.4 = 40^0
Total Sales	400	360^0	900	360^0

Common Factor = 360/400 = 0.9 Common Factor = 360/900=0.4

Pie Diagrams Showing Sales Per Unit for the Year 1988 and 1998

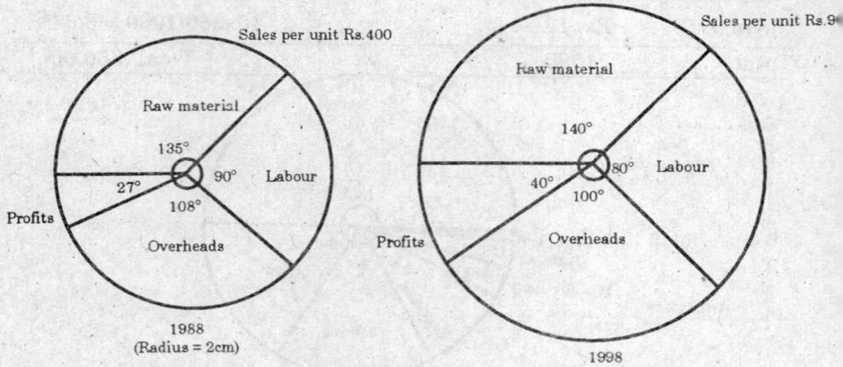

1.C. Three - dimensional Diagrams

When it is desired to compare the quantities which bear the ratio 8 : 27 : 64 and 125 or 8 and 512, we find a large gap among the values of variable. In such cases, the two-dimensional diagrams fail to depict the data conveniently. So it is preferable to have the three - dimensional diagrams such as Cones, Blocks, Spheres, Cubes and other things.

The Cubes are the most popular devices used in drawing the three-dimensional diagrams. A 'Cube' means a solid body having six equal square sides. The sides of cubes are equal to the cub root of the data to be presented. The sides of two cubes representing 1 and 216 will be $\sqrt[3]{1}$ and $\sqrt[3]{216}$ or 1 and 6. Cubes are used only when there is a biggest gap between the two or more values of variable.

Example 6.35: *Following data is relating the tea production (in Kg) during the week in three states:*

States:	Bengal	Kerala	Madras
Tea Production(in Kg.):	1,25,000	64,000	3,375

Solution: The figures are converted into Cube roots as under:

States	Tea Production (in Kg.)	Cube Root	Sides of Each Square
Bengal	1,25,000	50	5 cm.
Kerala	64,000	40	4 cm.
Madras	3,375	15	1.5 cm.

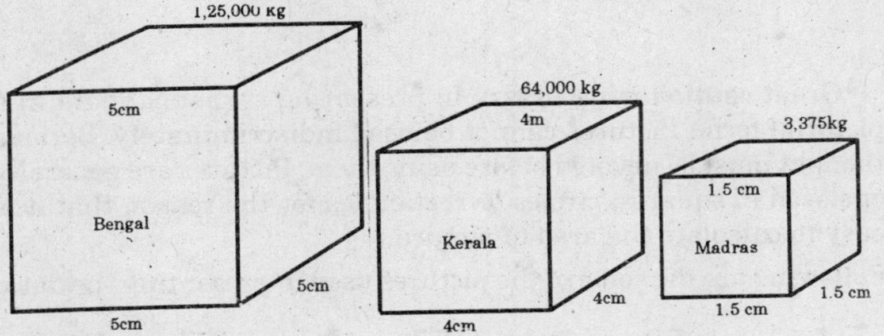

2.A. Pictograms

"Pictogram" is a device of picture by which the data can be presented. This technique was developed by Dr. Otto Neurath, a resident of Vienna. That, is why the device is called "Vienna Method" or "Isotype Method". Pictures are profusely used for comparing statistical data. To convert the dull data into an interesting and attractive view through objects of daily observation. The image of the entire data is fixed in the picture. Relationship between figures and their comparison can be studied with the help of pictograms easily.

Example 6.36. *Following are the figures relating to bank deposits as on June 30, 1998, in Kolar and Bangalore Districts.*

Districts	Deposits as on June 31, 1998
Kolar :	Rs. 81,00,000
Bangalore :	Rs. 256,00,000

Solution: The deposit figures are Rs. 81 lakhs and Rs. 256 lakhs respectively. We can show the 'Money Bags' pictures enclosed in squares whose areas are in the proportion of 81 and 256 or whose sides are in the proportion of $\sqrt{81}$ and $\sqrt{216}$ i.e., 9 and 16. We can further reduce the ratio to 2.25 and 4 respectively.

Picture of Deposites in Two districts as on June 30, 1998

2.25 cm Kolar

4 cm Bangalore

Great caution is necessary in presenting statistical data in a pictorial form. Pictures cannot be used indiscriminately. Serious thought must be devoted before using them. Pictures are generally enclosed in squares, circles or rectangles for the reason that it is easy to calculate the area of picture.

Following are the some of the pictures used in presenting the data:

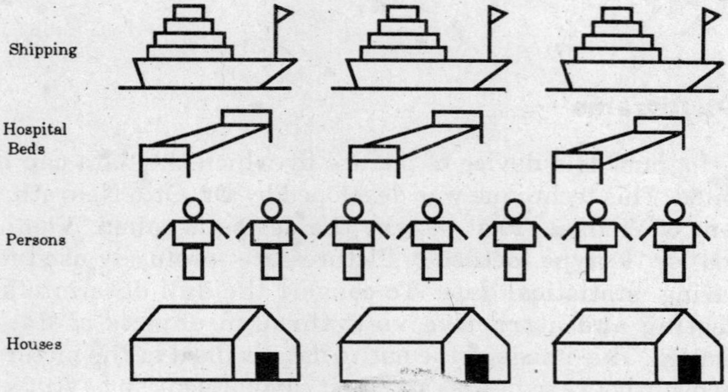

The number of pictures drawn or the size of the pictures should be proportional to the values of the different magnitudes to be presented. A symbol must represent a general concept which can be understood clearly and easily. A symbol should be neither too small nor too large.

2.B Cartograms or Mapographs

Instead of using pictures, different types of maps are used to present the data. Maps represent the regional data like languages spoken, religion belonging, education achieved and other characteristics. On a map, the data are shown with different colours, shades or points or dots having different attributes. We can study the **Atlas Book** and realize how the maps are depicting the data relating to the various parts of the world.

Thus, several devices are used in representing the data diagrammatically - One-dimensional, Two-dimensional, Three-dimensional, Pictograms and Cartograms. Forethought with regard to the suitability of a particular form in a given case and practice in drawing diagrams are essential factors. Bars and Circles are the easiest to draw and suitable for general use. A particular case, however, may make necessary to draw a square, a rectangle or a cube. Attention, in drawing diagrams, should always be fixed upon their neatness and on the precision with which they represent facts. Diagrams are preferably used in representing the time series. Thus, the selection of a method of drawing a diagram depends on the nature of data.

Questions

1. Give any four general rules of construction of diagrams. (BU-N83, A93, A95)
2. What is a scatter diagram? (BU-A84,N94)
3. What is a bar diagram? (BU-N86,N89,N93,N94)
4. What are the utilities of diagrams? (BU.A88,N91)
5. What are the advantages of diagrammatical presentation of data? (BU-A91,N92,N95)
6. What are the special merits of Bar Diagram? (BU-N93)
7. What is a Pie-Chart? When do you use it? (BU-A90, N97)
8. Under what circumstances do you use Sub-divided and multiple bar diagram? (BU - N90)
9. What are the limitations of Bar Diagrams? (BU-A98)

10. Represent the following data by means of a suitable diagram:

Year	Number Employed			
	Men	Women	Children	Total
1990	2,00,000	1,50,000	1,00,000	4,50,000
1991	4,00,000	2,00,000	1,50,000	7,50,000
1992	5,00,000	3,00,000	2,00,000	10,00,000

11. Prepare a rectangular diagram from the following data relating to the cost of production of a commodity in 1995.

	Particulars	Amount Rs
i)	Raw materials	5000
ii)	Labour	2500
iii)	Factory overheads	1500
iv)	Office overheads	1000
v)	No. of units produced	1000

12. Represent the following in a suitable diagram.

Items of expenditure	Expenditure in rupees
Food	500
Clothing	150
Housing	200
Fuel	50
Miscelleneous	100
	1,000

13. Represent the following by a sub-divided bars drawn on percentage basis.

Particulars	1990	1991
Cost Per Chair:		
i) Wages	24	18
ii) Indirect Cost	12	12
iii) Polishing	4	6
Total Cost :	40	36
Proceeds Per Chair	44	30
Profit (+)/Loss(-)	+ 4	− 6

7

Graphic representation of Data

Graphs and charts set an extremely visual aid for explaining, interpreting and analysing statistical data by means of points, lines, areas and other geometric configurations. For clear and effective exposition and appreciation of quantitative data, graphical presentations play an important role by facilitating comparison of values, trends and relationships.

A **'Graph'** is a vivid or intense or bright form of presentation of data. It is a simplest and commonest aid to the numerical reading which gives a picture of numbers in such a way that the relations between the two series can be easily compared.

I. Utilities of Graphs

A graph depicts the data more attractively than a table. It does not require the knowledge of mathematics to understand the data. The data presented by graph will be more simple than any other way of presentation of data. Two or more series can be depicted in a graph for comparisons. Well designed graphs are more effective in creating interest in the minds of the readers. The mass data can be visualised at a glance from the graphs. Graphical presentation of data very often brings out hidden facts and relationships existing in the data.

II. Limitations of Graphs

Graphic techniques, however, are not under all circumstances and for all purposes complete substitutes for tabular and other forms of presentation. In some of the cases, the graphs fail to give satisfactory information. The graph-maker may give undue emphasis on certain facts which may not be justified. Graphs fail to give detailed values of variables. The presented facts and figures may be, sometimes, misleading. Graphs may be based on defective scales. Accuracy cannot be maintained perfectly in graphs.

In spite of the limitations, graphic representation of data is considered as the most important technique of presenting the data.

Its use is of immense value.

Distinction Between Diagrams and Graphs

The diagrams and graphs are statistical techniques of representing the data. However, we can make the following distinctions between the two :

(i) Diagrams can be drawn on plane papers and graph papers as well, where as graphs can only be drawn on graph papers.

(ii) In diagrams, lines, bars, rectangles, circles, cubes, pictures and maps are used. On the other hand, in graphs, dots, dashes, dot-dashes and curves are used.

(iii) Diagrams furnish only approximate information as compared to the graphs. Graphs furnish more accurate information than the diagrams.

(iv) Diagrams depict categorical and geographical data, whereas graphs depict time series and frequency distribution.

(v) Diagrams are drawn not so easily and it requires some drawing skill to draw them. Graphs can be drawn easily.

Thus graphs are extremely useful visual aids for explaining, interpreting and analysing the statistical data.

III. Construction of Graph

A **'Graph Sheet'** is a paper in which lines are drawn dividing every inch or centimeter into 10 equal parts. A set of intersecting lines are also drawn at right angles. The horizontal lines are used as **'X'**-axis (abscissa) and vertical lines are as **'Y'**-axis (ordinates). These two axes divide the region of the plane into four parts which are called **'quadrants'**.

Following chart indicates the basic structural characteristics of a rectangular co-ordinate system:

Rectangular Co-ordinate System Graph drawn when Y = +4.5 and X = +4

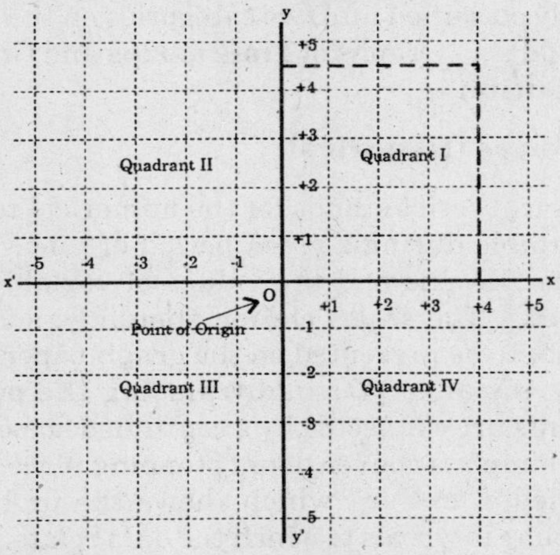

In quadrant I, the values on both X and Y axes are positive. In quadrant II, the values on Y axis are positive and the values on 'X'-axis, are negative. In quadrant III, the values on both X and Y axis are negative. In quadrant IV, the values on Y axis are negative and the values on X-axis are positive.

Most of the statistical data are represented in the quadrant I and IV. Generally independent values of variable are taken on **OX**-axis and dependent are taken on **OY**-axis.

A suitable scale is selected so as to accommodate the available data. The graph drawn should have the suitable data so as to cover the explanation. If the data available covers unnecessarily the large space, a portion of the scale unwanted may be omitted and it is indicated by a **'false base line'**. An index should also be given to show the scales and meaning of different curves. A note, if necessary, may also be given regarding the sources from which the data are collected.

Thus, graphic method of representation of data is becoming more effective and powerful than the diagrammatic representation. Graphs bring to light the facts that are hidden. They are becoming more and more powerful in all the fields of study.

IV. Types of Graphs

Graphs are generally classified into two categories on the basis of the characteristics of data - Graphs of **Time series** and Graphs of **Frequency Distribution**.

A. Graphs of Time Series (Historical)

Time series or historical series stands for the numerical record of the changes in a variable during a given period of time. Time units are placed on the OX-axis and the values of variable are measured on the OY-axis. The scales chosen should be such as would allow the full data to be presented on the graph paper. The data is plotted on the OX and OY axis by placing the points accordingly. All the points are connected by a continued smoothed lines, each point being simply a conventional stopping place such a smoothed line is called a **'curve'**. which shows the probable changes at all possible time intervals to which the data relate. This curve is also known as a **'Historigram'** which is distinguished from a histogram. Drawing a smooth curve requires practice and skill which everyone does not possess usually. Therefore, all the points are connected by straight lines as an alternative method to a curve.

The time series graphs depict the historical data and they are easy to draw and understand. They do not require much skill and experience in drawing. They are of three types as under,

(a) One Variable Graph.

(b) Two Variable Graph.

(c) Three Variable Graph.

(a) One Variable Graph: In one variable graph, only one factor is shown on the OY-axis and the time is measured on OX-axis. Following is the production of rice (in '000' tonnes) in Kerala in different years,

Year :	1991-1992	1992-1993	1993-1994	1994-1995	1995-1996	1996-1997	1997-1998
Rice Production (in '000' tonnes):	220	270	220	290	250	280	240

Graph Showing Rice Production in Kerala During Seven Years

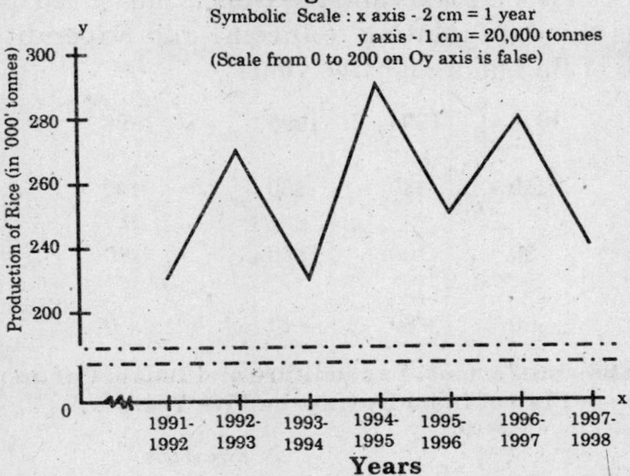

(b) Two Variable Graph: In two variable graph, there are factors on the OY-axis and the time is measured on OX-axis. Following is the data relating to foreign trade of India during the seven years:

Year :	1991-1992	1992-1993	1993-1994	1994-1995	1995-1996	1996-1997	1997-1998
Exports (in Crores of Rs.) :	3300	4000	5700	6300	6700	6000	6500
Imports (in Crores of Rs.) :	2000	2500	2800	3000	3500	3800	4000

Graph showing Imports and Exports of India (in crores of Rs.) During the seven years

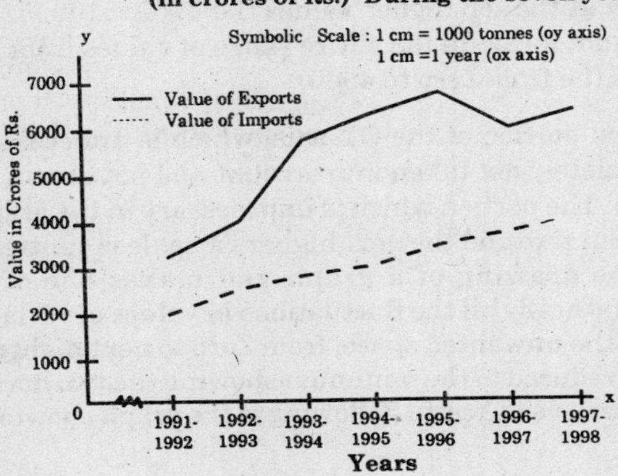

(c) Three Variable Graph: In three variable graph, there are three factors on the OY-axis and the time is measured on OX-axis. Following is the data relating to Income and Expenditure of the Sports Club of Bangalore for five years,

Year :	1993	1994	1995	1996	1997
Income (in '000' Rs.) :	150	180	160	190	170
Expenditure (in '000' Rs.) :	90	100	120	190	200
Profit/Loss (in '000' Rs.) :	+60	+80	+40	0	-30

Graph Showing Income, Expenditure and Balance of Sports Club of India During the Five Years

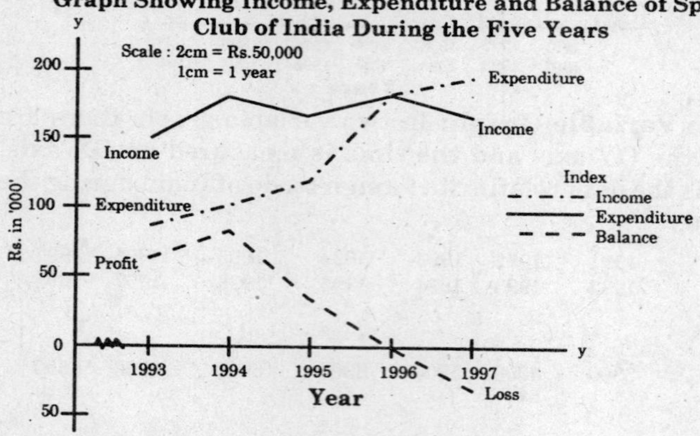

False Base Line : Generally we measure the values on OY-axis starting from Zero. When the values of variable vary or fluctuate only at the top higher values (i.e 4900, 5100, 5250 and 5280), we cannot measure the entire range of values from Zero to higher values (i.e from Zero to 4900).

The vertical portion of the OY-axis, which is unnecessary for curve, is completely not taken into account and not drawn as it is not attractive. The portion which is unnecessary in the graph and is lying between zero and the next higher variable is omitted. This simplifies the drawing of a graph and makes use of space economical. Naturally all the fluctuations in values of variable are amplified. So the unwanted space, from Zero to next higher value of variable, is reduced to the minimum showing the two horizontal lines in the form of saw teeth. Following is the graph showing false base line:

Graph Showing Population in Bangalore District During the Four Years

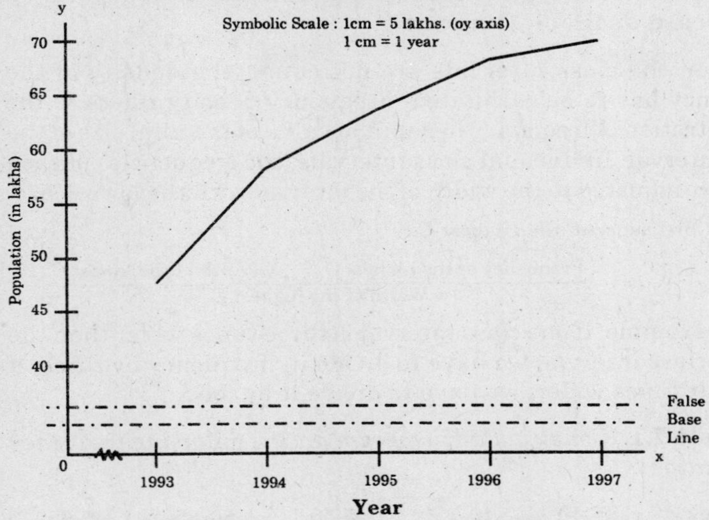

The use of false base line saves enough space on the graph sheet. It gives more emphasis on the data in which there are major fluctuations.

B. Graphs of Frequency Distribution

When the data is expressed in terms of occurrence of frequencies, it is essential to draw a frequency graph. Frequency distribution, whether discrete or continuous, can be graphically represented. The values of variable or mid-values of the class interval are measured on OX-axis and the frequencies on OY-axis. There are four types of frequency graphs:

(a) Histogram (c) Frequency Curve

(b) Frequency Polygon (d) Ogive Curves

(a) Histogram : The histogram is a device of graphic representation of a frequency distribution. It is constructed by erecting a set of rectangles on each class-interval on the horizontal respective class frequencies. Frequencies are shown on **OY**-axis. The height of rectangle represents the frequency of the respective class interval. The height should be measured on **OY**-axis from the point of the 'upper class limit' of the concerned class interval. The area of all the rectangles joined together represents the total frequencies. This type of graphic representation is also called **"Staircase or Block Diagram"**.

When the class intervals are not equal, the density of the frequency has to be calculated. Frequency density refers to the concentration of frequency in a unit of value of the total size of the class interval. In unequal class intervals, the frequencies of each class are adjusted to the width of the interval with the lowest size.

Adjusted Frequency of the Highest C.I

$$= \frac{\text{Frequency of the highest C. I. X Wdith of the lowest C. I.}}{\text{Width of the highest C. I.}}$$

For example, if one class interval is three times wider than the lowest class interval, we have to divide its frequency by three, if it is four times wider, we have to divide it by four.

Example 7.1. *Construct a Histogram for the following frequency distribution:*

Variable :	35-40	40-45	45-50	50-55	55-65
Frequency:	12	30	22	30	28

(BU-A89)

Solution: The first four class intervals are equal, whereas the last class interval is not. The lowest class interval is 5. We have to reduce the last class interval as under,

Adjusted Frequency of the Highest C.I

$$= \frac{\text{Frequency of the highest C. I. X Wdith of the lowest C. I.}}{\text{Width of the highest C. I.}}$$

$$= \frac{28 \times 5}{10} = 14$$

Histogram Showing the Frequency Distribution

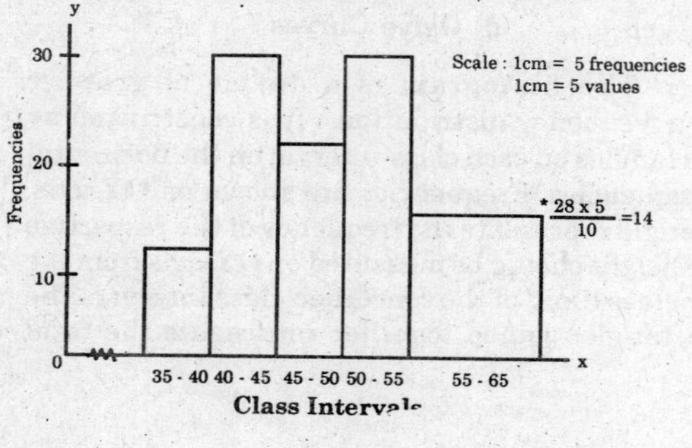

Example: 7.2.: *Prepare a frequency distribution of the following data taking a class interval of 10(exclusive method).*

12	30	29	22	35	39	40	42	40	16
30	18	12	5	15	3	4	9	45	50
0	5	6	8	15	25	22	3	4	9
12	5	9	3	4	30	32	29	1	8

Draw a Histogram.

(BU-A94)

Solution:

Let us have the continuous series having class intervals with tally bars to count the frequencies as under.

Class Interval	Tally Bars	Frequencies
0-10	~~IIII~~ ~~IIII~~ ~~IIII~~ II	17
10-20	~~IIII~~ II	7
20-30	~~IIII~~	5
30-40	~~IIII~~ I	6
40-50	IIII	4
50-60	I	1
	Total	40

Histogram Showing Frequency Distribution

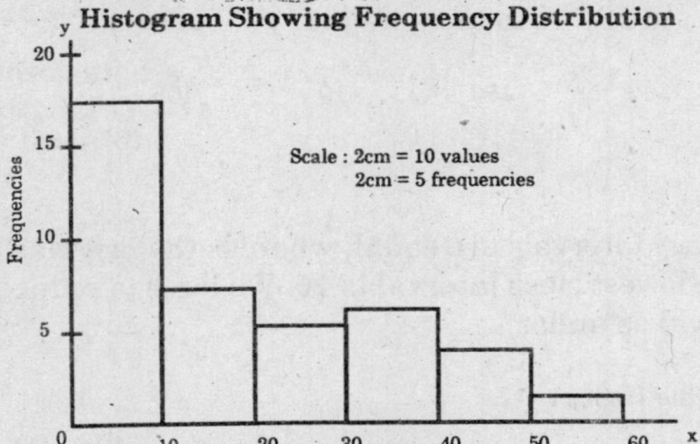

Class Interval

Example 7.3. *Represent the following data by means of a Histogram:*

Weekly Wages(in Rs.):	20-25	25-30	30-35	35-40	40-45	45-50
No. of Workers :	6	18	25	14	10	8

(BU-A84)

Solution:

Histogram Showing Weekly Wages

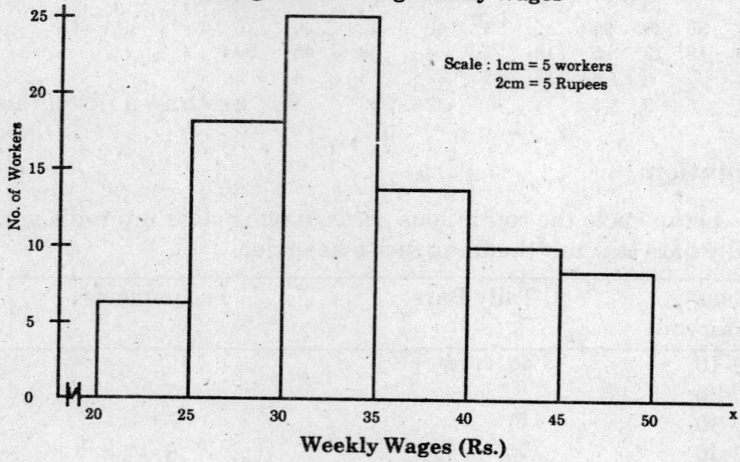

Example 7.4. *Draw a Histogram for the following frequency distribution:*

Age Group:	0-10	10-20	20-30	30-40	40-60
No. of persons:	60	40	150	110	100

(BU-A96)

Solution:

The first four class intervals are equal, whereas the last class interval is not. The lowest class interval is 10. We have to reduce the last class interval as under,

Adjusted Frequency of the Highest C.I.

$$= \frac{\text{Frequency of the highest C. I. X Wdith of the lowest C. I}}{\text{Width of the highest C. I.}}$$

$$= \frac{100 \times 10}{20} = 50$$

Histogram Showing the Frequency Distribution of Age

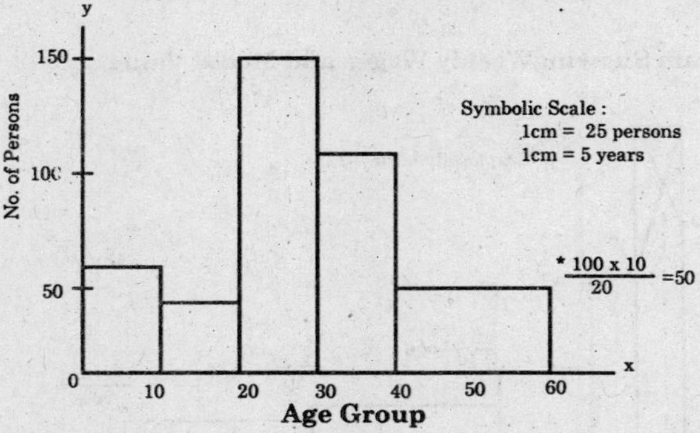

Example 7.5. *Determine the mode graphically from the following series and verify the results.*

Weekly Wages(in Rs.):	10-15	15-20	20-25	25-30	30-40	40-60	60-80
No. of Workers :	7	19	27	15	12	12	8

(BU-A91)

Solution:

The first four class intervals are equal whereas the last three class intervals are not. The lowest class interval is 5. We have to reduce the last three class intervals as under,

C.I.	Adjusted Frequency
30-40	$\frac{12 \times 5}{10} = 6$
40-60	$\frac{12 \times 5}{20} = 3$
60-80	$\frac{8 \times 5}{20} = 2$

$f_o = 19$

$f_1 = 27$ (Highest Frequency)

$f_2 = 15$

$$Z = l + \frac{f_1 - f_o}{2f_1 - f_0 - f_2} \times C = 20 + \frac{27 - 19}{54 - 19 - 15} \times 5$$

$$= 20 + \frac{8}{20} \times 5 = 20 + \frac{40}{20} = 20 + 2 = \mathbf{22}$$

Histogram ShowingWeekly Wages and Modal Value

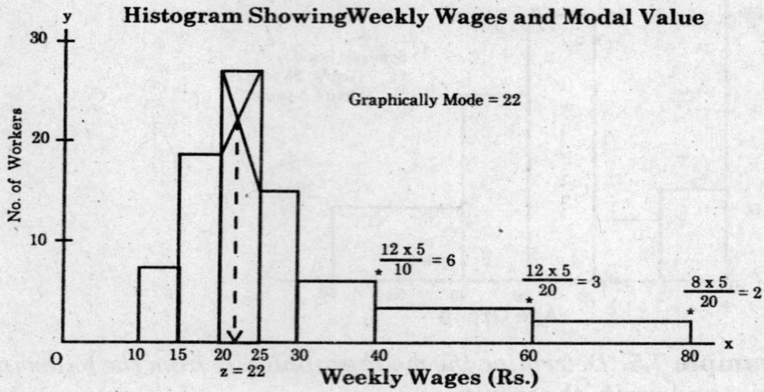

Example 7.6. *Construct a Histogram from the following and the locate the Mode.*

Marks:	0-10	10-20	20-40	40-50	50-70
Number of Students:	10	30	80	64	56

(BU-A83)

Solution:

The third class interval and the last class interval are different. Their frequencies are to be adjusted as under:

C.I.	Adjusted Frequency
20-40	$\frac{18 \times 10}{20} = 40$
50-70	$\frac{56 \times 10}{20} = 28$

$f_o = 40$

$f_1 = 64$ (Highest Frequency)

$f_2 = 28$ (Modal Class is 40-50)

$$Z = l + \frac{f_1 - f_o}{2f_1 - f_0 - f_2} \times C = 40 + \frac{64 - 40}{128 - 40 - 28} \times 10$$

$$= 40 + \frac{24}{60} \times 10$$

$$= 40 + \frac{240}{60} = 40 + 4 = \mathbf{44}$$

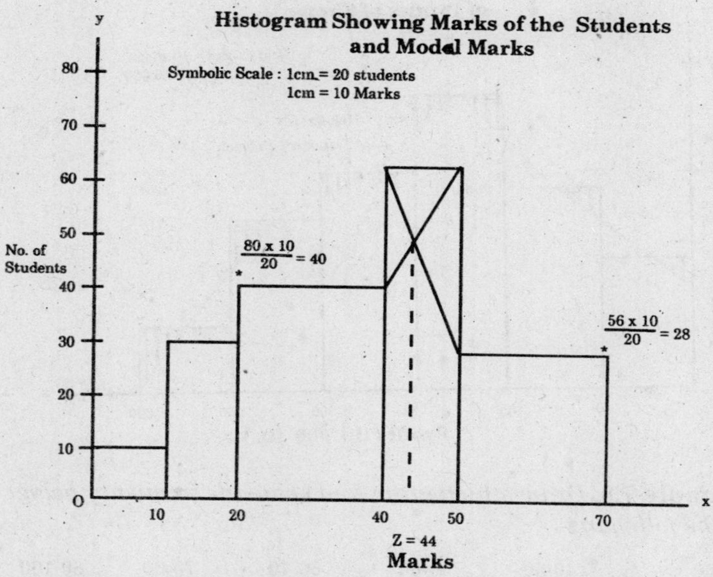

(b) Frequency Polygon: It is a device of graphic representation of a frequency distribution. It is a simple method of drawing the graph with the help of histogram. First, construct the histogram. Then plot the mid-points of the top of each rectangle. To make a frequency polygon we have to connect the mid-points of the top of all the rectangles by straight lines. This is done under the assumption that the frequencies in each class interval are evenly distributed.

The area of the frequency polygon is equal to the area of the histogram, as the area left outside is geometrically equal to the area included in it.

Example 7.7. *Monthly profits of 100 shops are distributed as follows:*

Profits per shop: (in '000' Rs.)	0-50	50-100	100-150	150-200	200-250	250-300
No. of Shops:	12	18	27	20	17	6

Draw a histogram and a frequency polygon for it. (BU-N86)

Solution:

Graph Showing Histogram and Frequency Polygon of Profits of Shops

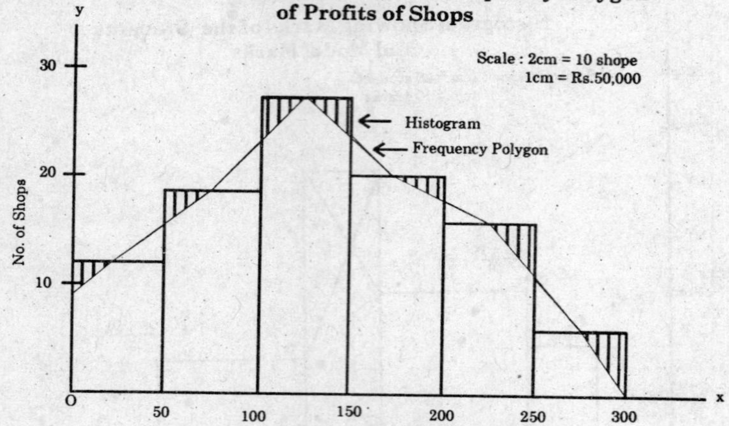

Example 7.8. *Draw a histogram and show the frequency polygcn for the following:*

Marks:	40-50	50-60	60-70	70-80	80-100
No. of Students:	5	12	20	13	8

(BU-N94)

Solution:

The last class interval is not equal as compared to the others. So the frequency of the last class interval is adjusted as under:

Adjusted Frequency of the Highest C.I.

$$= \frac{\text{Frequency of the highest C. I. X Wdith of the lowest C. I.}}{\text{Width of the highest C. I.}}$$

$$= \frac{8 \times 20}{20} = 4$$

Graph Showing Histogram and Frequency Polygon of Marks Scored by the Students

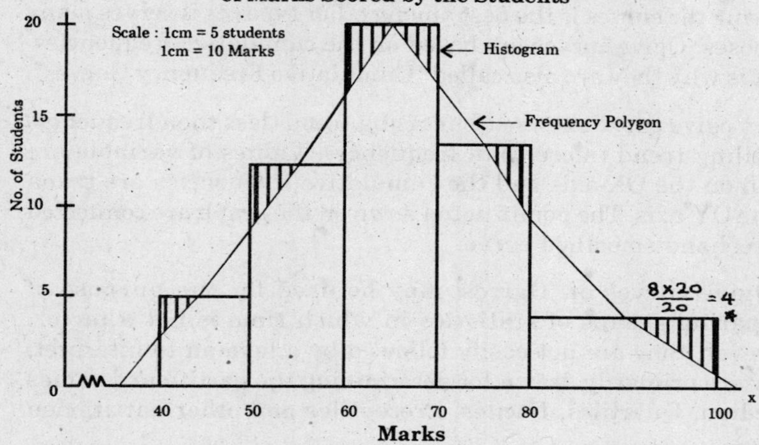

(c) Frequency Curve: With the help of the histogram and Frequency polygon, we can also draw a smoothed curve to iron out or eliminate the accidental irregularities in the data. A smoothed frequency curve represents a generalized characterisation of the data collected from the population or mass. In smoothing a curve, it is important to note that the total area under the curve be equal to the area under the histogram or polygon. When the curve is accurately drawn, we can use it for interpolation of the figure also.

Generally, we should take into account only the mid-points of all the top sides of the rectangles of the histograms for the frequency curve. Let us take the Example No 7.8 as under.

Smoothed Frequency Curve (Refer Example No.7.8)

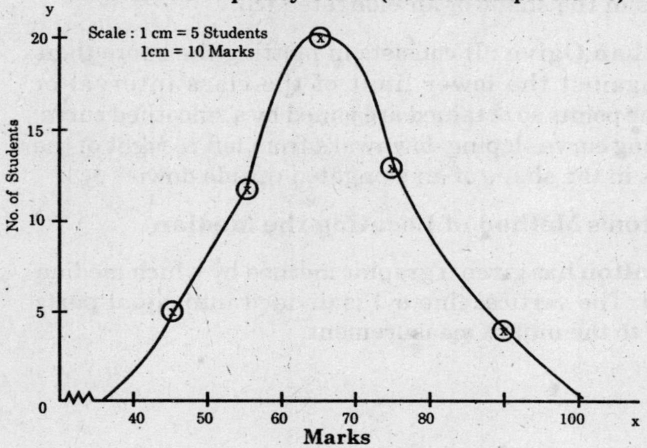

(d) Ogive Curves: These curves refer to a continuous form of the cumulative frequency curves-less than cumulative frequency curve and more than cumulative frequency curve. This method of drawing the curves is the best among other types as it serves many purposes. Ogive curves are based on the cumulative frequencies. That is why they are also called "Cumulative Frequency Curves".

An ogive curve shows either rising trend (less then frequency) or falling trend (more than frequency). Values of variable are taken on the OX-axis and the cumulative frequencies are taken on the OY-axis. The points noted down on the graph are connected by freehand smoothed curve.

Ogive curves or 'Ogives' may be used for the purpose of comparing groups of statistics in which time is not a factor. However, they are not easily followed by a layman to interpret. They are primarily drawn for determining the partitioned values - Median, Quartiles, Deciles, Precentiles and other partitioned values.

Ogive (pronounced as Ojive) is a graphic presentation of cumulative frequency distribution of a continuous series. Since there are two types of cumulative frequencies, we have accordingly two types ogives – Less Than Frequency Curve(Ogive) and More Than Frequency Curve (Ogive).

(i) Less than Ogive : It consists in plotting the 'less than' frequencies against the upper limit of the class interval or boundaries. The points so obtained are joined by a smoothed curve. It is an increasing curve sloping upward from left to right of the graph and it is in the shape of an elongated-(S).

(ii) More than Ogive : It consists in plotting the 'more than' frequencies against the lower limit of the class interval or boundaries. The points so obtained are joined by a smoothed curve. It is a decreasing curve sloping downward from left to right of the graph and it is in the shape of an elongated upside down - (S).

Galton's Method of Locating the Median

Francis Galton has given a graphic method by which median can be located. The vertical line(oy) is divided into equal parts corresponding to the unit of measurement.

From the half of the OY-axis, a horizontal line is drawn from the left to the right. This line cuts the "less than" frequency curve in a particular point. From this point draw a perpendicular line on OX-axis. The intersecting point on OX-axis will be the median value. In a similar way we can also find all the other partitioned values such as Quartiles, Deciles, Percentiles and others.

Characteristics of Ogives:

Following are the characteristics of "Less Than" and "More Than" ogives:

(i) When both the ogives are plotted on the same graph, they intersect at a particular point. From this intersecting point, if we draw a perpendicular line on OX-axis, it gives the value of median.

(ii) Less than Ogive is useful in computation of Quartiles, Median and other partitioned values.

(iii) Ogives give a clear picture about the data by which we can have the comparative study.

(iv) Ogive partitioned values are always in consistency with the positional averages.

Thus, the two ogives are playing on important role in presenting the data relating to cumulative frequencies.

Example 7.9. *Draw an "Ogive" and from it read the median and quartiles.*

Marks:	0-20	20-30	30-40	40-50	50-60	60-70	70-80
No. of Students:	21	19	60	42	24	18	17

(BU-A84)

Solution:

To find the partitioned values we have to convert the data into a less than frequency distribution.

Marks Less than:	20	30	40	50	60	70	80
No. of Students:	21	40	100	142	166	184	201

Graph Showing Median and Quartile Marks of the Students

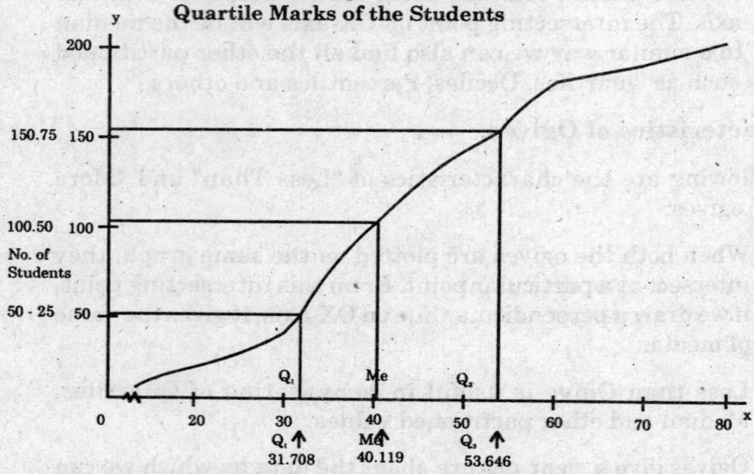

Example 7.10. *Draw the two ogives from the following data, and locate the median value.*

Marks:	20-40	40-60	60-80	80-100	100-120	120-140	140-160
No. of Students:	4	6	10	16	12	7	3

(BU-N85)

Solution:

For the ogive curves we have to convert the data into two cumulative frequencies.

Marks C.I.	No. of Students	Marks	LT. Cf.	Marks	MT. Cf.
20- 40	4	Less than 40	4	More than 20	58
40- 60	6	,, ,, 60	10	,, ,, 40	54
60- 80	10	,, ,, 80	20	,, ,, 60	48
80-100	16	,, ,, 100	36	,, ,, 80	38
100-120	12	,, ,, 120	48	,, ,, 100	22
120-140	7	,, ,, 140	55	,, ,, 120	10
140-160	3	,, ,, 160	58	,, ,, 140	3

Graph Showing O gives of Marks obtained by Students

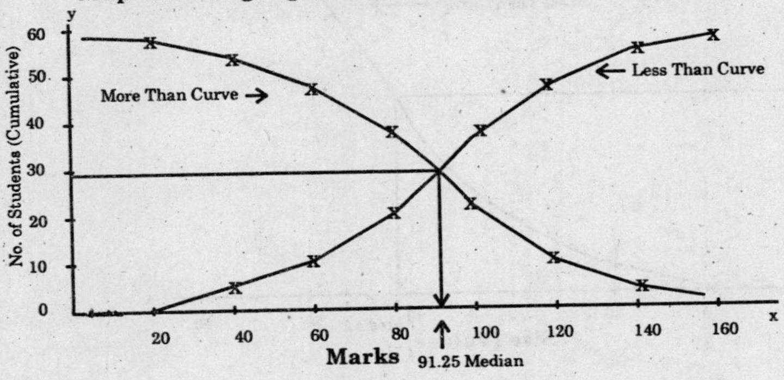

Example 7.11. *Draw a 'Less Than Ogive" from the from the following and locate the median:*

Size :	10-20	20-30	30-40	40-50	50-60
Frequency :	20	60	100	150	75

(BU-A88)

Solution:

Let us convert the data into a less than value distribution.

Size C.I.	f	Size	LT.Cf.
10-20	20	Less than 20	20
20-30	60	,, ,, 30	80
30-40	100	,, ,, 40	180
40-50	150	,, ,, 50	330
50-60	75	,, ,, 60	405

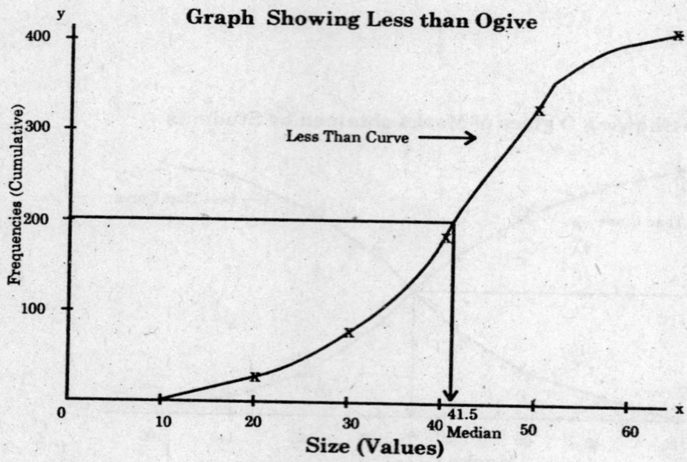

Example 7.12. *Draw the two ogives from the following data and locate median:*

Class :	100-200	200-300	300-400	400-500	500-600	600-700
Frequency :	20	40	60	80	100	120

(BU-N89)

Solution:

Let us convert the data into 'Less Than' and "More Than" frequency distribution.

C.I.	f	Size	LT.Cf.	Size	MT.Cf.
100-200	20	Less Than 200	20	More Than 100	420
200-300	40	,, ,, 300	60	,, ,, 200	400
300-400	60	,, ,, 400	120	,, ,, 300	360
400-500	80	,, ,, 500	200	,, ,, 400	300
500-600	100	,, ,, 600	300	,, ,, 500	220
600-700	120	,, ,, 700	420	,, ,, 600	120

Graph Showing O gives and Median value

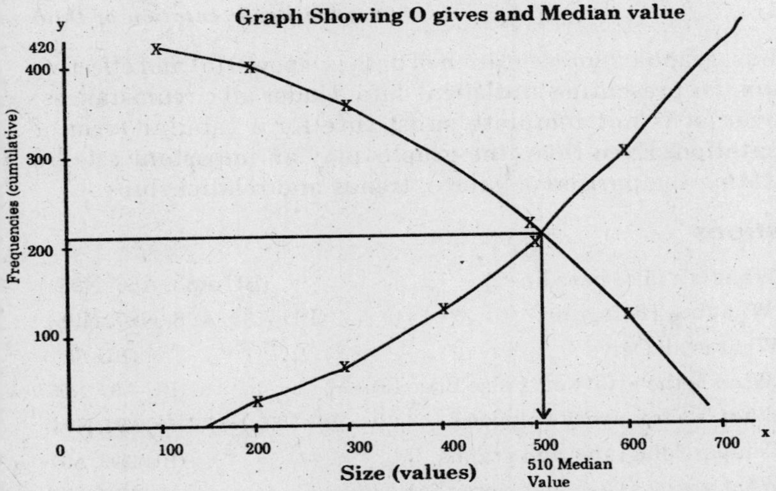

Example 7.13. *Draw a less than ogive and find the value of quartiles for the following;* (BU-N97)

Wages(R) Less Than :	20	40	60	80	100	120	140
No. of Workers :	3	8	20	38	52	58	60

Solution: The frequencies are already in the form of "Less than" Values.

Graph Showing Less Than O give and Quartiles

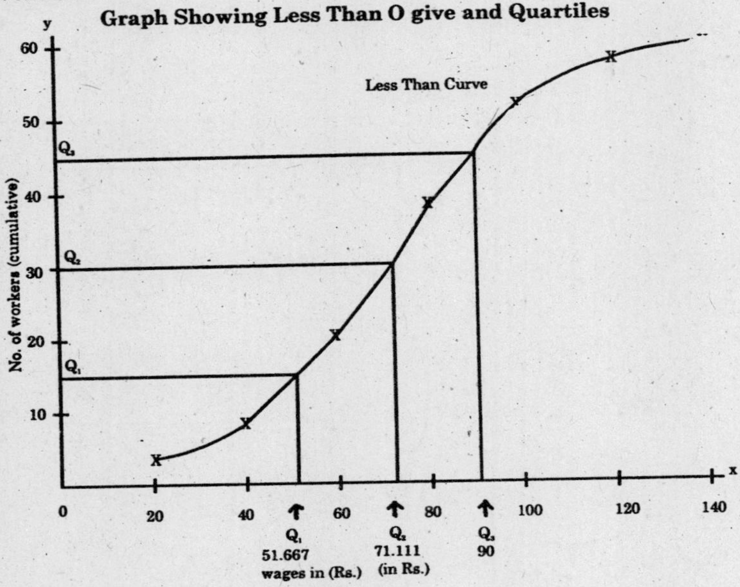

Thus, graphic representation of data is a powerful and effective medium for presenting statistical data. Under all circumstances, however, it is not complete substitute for a tabular form of presentation. Even then, the graphs play an important role by facilitating comparison of values, trends and relationships.

Questions

1. What is a false base line ? (BU-A83, A86, N91)
2. What is a Histogram ? (BU-A84, A86, N87, N96)
3. What is an Ogive ? (BU-A85)
4. What is the utility of "False Base Line" ? (BU-A87, N95)
5. What is a frequency Polygon ? (BU-N85, N87, N89, A91, N94)
6. Compare diagrams and graphs. (BU-A92, A97)
7. What are less than and more than ogives ? (BU-A96)
8. When ogive curve is given how do you locate median? (BU-N94)

8

Measures of Central Tendency (I)

Mass data are collected, classified, tabulated and presented systematically. The data so presented is analysed further to bring its size to a single representative figure. It is the **"Descriptive Statistics"** which describes the presented data in a single number. It is concerned with the analysis of a frequency distribution or other form of presentation mathematically by which a few constants or representative numbers are arrived. These constants are the integral parts of the statistical language. The entire process of analysing the presented data ranges from the simple observation to the intricate and highly mathematical techniques.

Descriptive statistics deals with the two types of data - **Univariate and Bivariate**. In the univariate data there is only one variate for measurement. In the bivariate data there are two variates for measurements.

Measures of central Tendency or Location (Averages of First Order) and Measures of Dispersion (Averages of Second Order) deal with the univariate data. Correlation, Regression and other measures deal with the bivariate data.

I Meaning of Statistical Averages :

An **'average'** is a figure which represents the large number of observations in a concise or single numerical data. It is a typical size which describes the central tendency. It is a representative value around which all the values of variable cluster or concentrate.

"Measures of central Tendency" or "Measures of Central Location" or "Averages of First Order" describe the concentration of large numbers adequately around the central tendency. An average is a set of summary figures. It is a single value which represents all the items. It is a single simple expression in which the net result of a complex group or large numbers is concentrated.

Thus an average brushes off the *irregularaies* of a series, levels all differences of the individual items and presents complex data in a few significant figures. It follows that an average may be computed for its own sake (averages of first order), or as a means to another end (averages of second order).

II. Objectives of Statistical Averages:

An average' is of great significance in all the fields of human knowledge, because it depicts the characteristics of the whole group of data under study. Following are the objects of computing the statistical averages:

(i) To give or present the complex data in a simple manner and concise form.

(ii) To facilitate the data for comparative study of two different series.

(iii) To study the mass data (population) from the sample.

(iv) To establish relationship between the two series.

(v) To provide basis for decision - making.

(vi) To calculate the representative single value from the given data.

The main objects are to describe the distribution in a single figure, to study the different distributions comparatively and to compute the various other (second order) measures.

III. Requisites of a Good and Ideal Average:

Any statistical average to be a good and ideal average must possess some of the characteristics as it is a single value representing a group of values. Following are the requisite properties of a good and ideal average:

(i) It should be easily understood.

(ii) It should be simple in calculation.

(iii) It should be based on all the observations.

(iv) It should not be unduly affected by the extreme values.

(v) It should be rigidly defined.

(vi) It should be capable of further algebraic treatment.

(vii) It should have sampling stability. (Three or four sampling sets must give the same or similar results).

Thus a statistical average should have all the above requisites to be an ideal and good average.

IV. Limitations of Statistical Averages:

Although an average is useful in studying the complex data and is very widely used in almost all the spheres of human activity, it is not without limitations that restrict its scope and applicability. Following are the limitations of statistical averages:

(i) The extreme values, if any, will affect the averageable figure disproportionately.

(ii) The composition of the data cannot be viewed with the help of the average.

(iii) The average does not represent always the characteristics of individual items.

(iv) The average gives only a representative figure of the mass but fails to depict the entire picture of the data.

In spite of the limitations, the statistical averages still are useful measures which play an important role in analysing the mass data as there is no alternative left for statistical analysis.

V. Types of Statistical Averages:

Broadly speaking, there are five types of statistical averages which are commonly used in practice. They are,

(i) Arithmetic Mean (ii) Geometric Mean
(iii) Harmonic Mean (iv) Median
(v) Mode.

The following chart shows the detailed classification of averages:

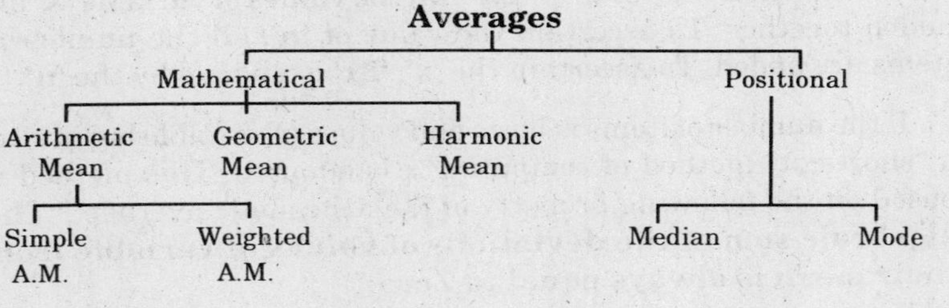

A. Arithmetic Mean:

Arithmetic Mean is the most widely used measurement which represents the entire data. Generally it is termed as an 'Average' to a layman. It is the quantity obtained by dividing the sum of the values of the items in a variable by their number. It is denoted by a symbol $\overline{X}$. Arithmetic mean may be either:

(i) Simple A.M. or **(ii) Weighted A.M.**

Simple Arithmetic Mean is the quotient of the sum of the values divided by their number. Weighted Arithmetic Mean is an average in which the items are multiplied by the weights assigned to them according to their importence. It means, in simple Arithmetic Mean, all the items are treated alike, each item being considered only once. In weighted Arithmetic Mean, each item is differently by assigning weights.

A Greek symbol `**Σ**' (sigma) is used as summation notation. **'X'** is the value of variable and **'n'** the number of items or observations. **'f'** stands for frequency.

(i) Simple Arithmetic Mean

As has been explained above, the simple arithmetic mean is the quotient obtained by dividing the sum of the values by the number of items. Algebraically we can have the formula as under:

a) For individual observations

$$\overline{X} = \frac{x_1 + x_2 + x_3 + \ldots + x_n}{n} = \frac{\Sigma X}{n}$$

b) For Discrete and Continuous Series

$$\overline{X} = \frac{fx_1 + fx_2 + fx_3 + \ldots + fx_n}{n} = \frac{\Sigma fX}{n}$$

(*Note:* In Continuous Series x is the mid-value of the class interval)

To ascertain the value of '**ΣX**', all the values of variable **'X'** are added together. To ascertain the value of **'n'**, all the number of items are added. To ascertain the **'x'**, **'Σx'** is divided by the **'n'.**

If the number of items is large and values of variable big in size, a "short-cut" method of computing x is adopted. This method is based on the following property of the arithmetic average, **"The algebraic sum of the deviations of values of variable from their mean is always equal to Zero."**

Let us assume the difference figure **'A'** (generally the integer or whole number), as assumed mean. Take deviations of values of variable from the assumed mean denoted as **'d'**. Obtain the sum of these deviations denoted as **'Σd'**. Substitute the values of these symbols in the short-cut formula as under,

$$\overline{X} = A + \frac{\Sigma d}{n} \quad \ldots \text{ for individual observations}$$

$$\overline{X} = A + \frac{\Sigma fd}{n} \quad \ldots \text{ for discrete \& continuous series}$$

(*Note*: 'fd' is the product of frequency and deviation.)

The **'step deviation'** method is the only additional adjustment to the 'short cut' method. Under this method, the deviations are divided by a single common factor to reduce the figures to the minimum size. It is, in a way , a deliberate error and it is compensated by multiplying the quotient. The adjusted or reduced value of **'d'** is now termed as **'d''** so the formula stands as under.

$$\overline{X} = A + \frac{\Sigma d'}{n} \times c \quad \ldots \text{ for individual observation.}$$

$$\overline{X} = A + \frac{\Sigma fd'}{n} \times c \quad \ldots \text{ for discrete \& continous series.}$$

(*Note:* 'c' the common factor or width of the class interval is used for dividing and multiplying).

Let us have the marks of 7 students in a class as 131, 150, 96, 114, 125, 142, 103.

Marks (x)	Direct Method	Marks (x)	d (x-A)
131	$\overline{x} = \frac{\Sigma x}{n}$	96	- 24
150		103	-17
96	$= \frac{861}{7}$	114	-6
114		125	+ 5
125	= 123	131	+ 11
142		142	+ 22
103		150	+ 30
Σx = 861			+ 68
			- 47
n = 7			Σd = 21

Short-cut Method

A = Assumed Mean = 120

$$\overline{x} = A + \frac{\Sigma d}{n}$$

$$= 120 + \frac{21}{7}$$

$$= 120 + 3 = \mathbf{123}$$

n = 7

Example 8.1. *In a class of 50 students, 10 have failed and their average marks is 2.5. The total marks secured by the entire class was 281. Find the average marks of those who have passed.*

(BU-A86)

Solution:

(a) Total Marks of 50 students

$\Sigma x_{50} = 281$ (given)

(b) Total Marks 10 students failed

$$\bar{x} = \frac{\Sigma x}{n}$$

$$2.5 = \frac{\Sigma x}{10}$$

$$\Sigma x_{10} = 25$$

(c) Total Marks of 40 students passed

$$\Sigma x_{50} - \Sigma x_{10} = \Sigma x_{40}$$

$$281 - 25 = 256$$

Therefore, the average marks of students passed is ...

$$\bar{x}_{100} = \frac{\Sigma x_{40}}{n} = \frac{256}{40} = \mathbf{6.4}$$

Example 8.2. *The arithmetic mean age of the first group of 80 boys is 10 years and that of the second group of 20 girls is 15 years. Find the arithmetic mean of the boys and girls together* (BU-A85)

Solution:

(a) Total age of 80 boys

$$\bar{x} = \frac{\Sigma x}{n}$$

$$10 = \frac{\Sigma x}{80}$$

$$\Sigma x_{80} = 800$$

(b) Total age of 20 girls

$$\bar{x} = \frac{\Sigma x}{n}$$

$$15 = \frac{\Sigma x}{20}$$

$$\Sigma x_{20} = 300$$

(c) Total age of boys and girls together

$$\Sigma x_{80} + \Sigma x_{20} = \Sigma x_{100}$$

$$800 + 300 = 1100$$

Therefore, the average age of boys and girls together is ...

$$\bar{x}_{100} = \frac{\Sigma x_{100}}{n} = \frac{1100}{100} = \mathbf{11\ years}$$

Example 8.3. *The mean age of 100 persons is 30 years. If the mean age of the group of men is 32 years and that for the group of women is 27 years, find the number of men and women.*

(BU-A95)

Solution:

We have to assume the number of men as 'M' and women as 'W'. Then we can have the following two equations:

(a) M + W = 100 ... it is given.

(b) (i) Total age of men

$$\bar{x} = \frac{\Sigma x}{n}$$

$$32 = \frac{\Sigma x}{M}$$

$$\Sigma x = 32\ M$$

(ii) Total age of women

$$\bar{x} = \frac{\Sigma x}{n}$$

$$27 = \frac{\Sigma x}{W}$$

$$\Sigma x = 27\ W$$

(iii) Total age of men and women

$$\bar{x} = \frac{\Sigma x}{n}$$

$$30 = \frac{\Sigma x}{100}$$

$$\Sigma x = 3000$$

Therefore

$$32M + 27W = 3000$$

Using the simultaneous equations,

(a) $M + W = 100$ Multiply (a) by 32

(b) $32M + 27W = 3{,}000$

(a) x 32.... $32M + 32W = 3200$

$\underline{-32\ M \pm 27W = -3000}$

$5W = 200$

$W = \mathbf{40}$

Substituting the value of W in(a)

$M + W = 100$

$M + 40 = 100$

$M = 100 - 40$

$M = \mathbf{60}$

So, the number of men is 60 and the number of women is 40.

Example 8.4. *The average weight of the 10 different balls was 25.686 gms. The average of the first four was 25.680 gms. and that of the last three was 25.686 gms. If the average of the fifth and the sixth balls was 0.042 gms greater than the weight of the seventh ball, what was the weight of the seventh ball?* (BU-N93)

Solution:

(a) Total weight of the ten balls

$$\bar{x}_{10} = \frac{\Sigma x}{n}$$

$$25.686 = \frac{\Sigma x}{10}$$

$$\Sigma x_{10} = 256.860\text{gms}$$

(b) Total weight of the first four balls

$$\bar{x}_4 = \frac{\Sigma x}{n}$$

$$25.680 = \frac{\Sigma x}{4}$$

$$\Sigma x_4 = 102.720\text{gms}$$

(c) Total weight of last three balls

$$\bar{x}_3 = \frac{\Sigma x}{n}$$

$$25.686 = \frac{\Sigma x}{3}$$

$$\Sigma x_3 = 77.058\text{gms}$$

(d) Total weight of the seventh ball was assumed to be as A.

(e) **Total weight of the fifth and sixth balls:**

The average of these two balls was 0.042 greater than the weight of the seventh ball. So,

$$\bar{x}_2 = A + 0.042 \text{ gms}$$

$$A + 0.042 = \frac{\Sigma x}{2} \text{ ... (fifth and sixth balls)}$$

$$\Sigma x_2 = 2A + 0.084 \text{ gms (total weight of two balls)}$$

Now we can have the final equation as under

$$\Sigma x_{10} = \Sigma x_4 + \Sigma x_2 + A + \Sigma x_3$$

$$256.860 = 102.720 + 2A + 0.084 + A + 77.058$$

$$3A = 256.860 - 102.720 - 0.084 - 77.058$$

$$3A = 76.998 \text{ gms} \quad \therefore \quad A = \mathbf{25.666 \text{ gms}}$$

So the weight of the seventh ball is 25.666 gms.

Example 8.5. *The mean weight of 100 workers in a factory is 50 Kgs. If the mean weight of men in the factory is 55 Kgs., and that of the women is 45 Kgs., find the number of men and women in the factory.* (BU-A90, N97)

Solution:

We have to assume the number of men as 'M' and women as 'W". Then we can have the following two equation:

(a) M + W = 100 .... it is given

(b) (i) total weight of men and women

$$\bar{x} = \frac{\Sigma x}{n}$$

$$50 = \frac{\Sigma x}{100}$$

$$\Sigma x_{100} = 5000$$

(ii) Total weight of men

$$\bar{x} = \frac{\Sigma x}{n}$$

$$55 = \frac{\Sigma x}{M}$$

$$\Sigma x = 55 M$$

(iii) Total weight of women

$$\bar{x} = \frac{\Sigma x}{n}$$

$$45 = \frac{\Sigma x}{W}$$

$$\Sigma x = 45W$$

Therefore

$$55M + 45W = 5000$$

Using the Simultaneous equations.

(a) $M + W = 100$ Multiply (a) by 55

(b) $55M + 45W = 5{,}000$

(a) x 55... $55M + 55W = 5500$

$\pm 55M \pm 45W = -5000$

$10W = 500$

$W = \mathbf{50}$

Substituting the value of W in(a)

$M + W = 100$

$M + 50 = 100$

$M = 100 - 50$

$M = \mathbf{50}$

So, the number of men worker is 50 and the number of women worker is 50.

Example 8.6. *If* $\bar{x}_1$ *= Rs 275,* N_1 *= 100,* $\bar{x}_2$ *= Rs 225 and* N_2 *= 80, what is the value of* $\bar{x}_{1.2}$ *?* (BU-N96)

Solution:

(i) Total Value of 100 items

$$\bar{x}_1 = \frac{\Sigma x}{n}$$

$$275 = \frac{\Sigma x}{100}$$

$$\Sigma x_1 = 27{,}500$$

(ii) Total value of 80 items

$$\bar{x}_2 = \frac{\Sigma x}{n}$$

$$225 = \frac{\Sigma x}{80}$$

$$\Sigma x_2 = 18{,}000$$

(iii) Average of 180 items

$$\bar{x}_{1.2} = \frac{\Sigma x_1 + \Sigma x_2}{180}$$

$$= \frac{27{,}500 + 18{,}000}{180} = \frac{45{,}500}{180} = 252.777$$

So, the value of $\bar{x}_{1.2}$ = **Rs 252.7777.**

Example 8.7. *The mean wages paid to 1000 workers in a factory was found to be Rs. 180.40. Later on it is discovered that the wages of the two employees were taken wrongly as 297 and 165 instead 197 and 185. Find the correct mean wages.*

Solution:

We can use the following equation,

Correct Σx = Incorrect Σx - Wrong Items + Correct Items.

$$=(180.40 \times 1000) - (297 + 165) + (197 + 185)$$

$$=1,80,400 - 462 + 382 = 1,80,320$$

So, the correct total wages are Rs 1,80,320 and the correct mean wage is,

$$\bar{x} = \frac{\Sigma x}{n} = \frac{1,80,320}{1,000} = \textbf{Rs 180.32.}$$

Example 8.8. *Mean height of 50 students is 5' – 8". The heights of 10 students are given below,*

5'-6", 5'-2", 5'-4", 5'-0", 4'-10", 4'-8", 6'-2", 5'-8", 5'-9", 5'-3"

Find the mean height of remaining students.

Solution:

All the heights are converted into inches as the inches are not in the metric system.

(a) The total height of 50 students is,

$$5' - 8'' = 68'' = \frac{\Sigma x}{50}$$

$$\Sigma x_{50} = 3400''$$

(b) The total height of 10 students is given,

x		Conversion into inches
5'-6"	...	66"
5'-2"	...	62"
5'-4"	...	64"
5'-0"	...	60"
4'-10"	...	58"
4'-8"	...	56"
6'-2"	...	74"
5'-8"	...	68"
5'-9"	...	69"
5'-3"	...	63"
	Σx_{10} =	640"

(c) To find the total height of remaining 40 students we have to compute as under:

$$\Sigma x_{50} = 3400''$$

$$\Sigma x_{10} = 640''$$

$$\Sigma x_{40} = 2760''$$

$$\bar{x}_{40} = \frac{\Sigma x}{n} = \frac{2760}{40} = 69''$$

"69" = **6' - 9"** is the mean height of 40 students.

Example 8.9. Answer *the following qeustions.*

(a) The average marks of statistics in a class of 30 students was 52. The top six students hold an average of 31. What was the average marks of other students?

(b) The mean weight of 150 workers in a factory is 56 Kgs. If the mean weight of Men in the factory is 64 Kgs and that of the Women is 48 Kgs. Find the number of men and women in the factory.
(BU-A98)

Solution:

(a) Let us calculate the total marks of 30 students and the total marks of the top 6 students to obtain the total marks of the remaining students.

(i) Total Marks of the 30 students (Σx_{30})

$$\bar{x}_{30} = \frac{\Sigma x_{30}}{30} \qquad 52 = \frac{\Sigma x_{30}}{30}$$

$$\therefore \quad \Sigma x_{30} = 52 \times 30 = \mathbf{1560}$$

(ii) Total Marks of the top 6 students (Σx_6)

$$\bar{x}_6 = \frac{\Sigma x_6}{6} \qquad 31 = \frac{\Sigma x_6}{6}$$

$$\therefore \quad \Sigma x_6 = 31 \times 6 = \mathbf{186}$$

(iii) Total average of remaining students

Remaining students = 30 - 6 = 25.

The total marks of 24 students will be,

$$\Sigma x_{30} - \Sigma x_6 = \Sigma x_{24}$$

$$1560 - 186 = 1374$$

$$\therefore \quad \bar{x}_{24} = \frac{\Sigma x_{24}}{24} = \frac{1374}{24} = \mathbf{57.25}$$

Thus the average marks of 24 students is **57.25**.

(b) Let us assume that the number of men in a factory is `M' and the number of women in a factory is `W', to obtain the following equations,

(i) M + W = 150 .... (given)

(ii) Total weight of 150 workers

$$\bar{x}_M = 64 \qquad \text{and} \qquad \bar{x}_W = 48$$

$$\bar{x}_M = \frac{\Sigma x_M}{M} \qquad \bar{x}_W = \frac{\Sigma x_W}{W}$$

$$64 = \frac{\Sigma x_M}{M} \qquad 48 = \frac{\Sigma x_W}{W}$$

$$\Sigma x_M = 64M \qquad \Sigma x_W = 48W.$$

Total weight of 150 students will be, 56 x 150 = 8,400.

$$\therefore \quad \Sigma x_M + \Sigma x_W = 8,400$$

$$64M + 48W = 8,400$$

Using the simultaneous equations,

(ii) ... $64M + 48W = 8,400$

(i) ... $M + W = 150$

Multiplying (i) by 48,

$$\begin{aligned} 64M + 48W &= 8,400 \\ \_48M \pm 48W &= \_7,200 \\ \hline 16M &= 1,200 \\ M &= 75 \end{aligned}$$

Substituting the value of M in (i).

$$75 + W = 150 \;...\; W = 150\text{-}75 = 75.$$

Thus, the number of Men and Women in a factory are 75 and 75.

Example 8.10. *Mr. Satish has appeared for 3 Tests of the values - 20, 50 and 30 marks. In the first he scored 75%, in the second 60% and in all the tests together, he scored aggregate of 60% marks. Find the % of marks in the third test.*

Solution:

(a) Total marks scored in all the tests: 60% out of 100 i.e 60 marks.

(b) Total marks scored in the first test: 75% out of 20 i.e 15 marks.

(c) Total marks scored in the second test: 60% out of 50 i.e 30 marks.

(d) Total marks scored in the third test:

(i)	Total marks Scored in all the tests	60
(ii)	Less total Marks scored in the first and the second tests 15 + 30	- 45
	Total marks scored in the third test	15

So, if satish scored 15 marks in the third test out of 30 total the % of marks is $\frac{100 \times 15}{30}$ = **50%**.

Example 8.11. *In the city, 30 members were surveyed as to how many domestic appliances they have purchased, the replies were is as follows:*

1, 2, 5, 1, 5, 2, 1, 4, 2, 3, 4, 2, 4, 3, 2,
6, 3, 2, 4, 3, 6, 2, 2, 3, 3, 7, 2, 3, 0, 2

prepare the Discrete series and find the mean. (BU-A91)

Solution:

Values (x)	Tally Bars	Frequencies (f)	fx
0	—	1	0
1	III	3	3
2	~~IIII~~ ~~IIII~~	10	20
3	~~IIII~~ II	7	21
4	IIII	4	16
5	II	2	10
6	II	2	12
7	I	1	7
		n = 30	Σfx = 89

$$\bar{x} = \frac{\Sigma fx}{n}$$

$$\bar{x} = \frac{89}{30}$$

$$\bar{x} = \mathbf{2.9667}$$

Example 8.12. *100 students appeared for an examination. The results of those who failed were given below:*

Marks :	5	10	15	20	25	30
No. of Students:	4	6	8	7	3	2

If the average marks of all the 100 students is 68.6, find out the average marks of those who have passed. *(BU-A91)*

Solution:

Marks (x)	No. of students (f)	fx
5	4	20
10	6	60
15	8	120
20	7	140
25	3	75
30	2	60
	n = 30	Σfx = 475

(i) Total marks of 100 students

$$\bar{x} = \frac{\Sigma fx}{n}$$

$$68.6 = \frac{\Sigma fx}{100}$$

$$\Sigma fx_{100} = 6860$$

(ii) Total marks of 30 students

$$\Sigma fx_{30} = 475$$

Therefore,

The total marks of 70 students 6860

Passed in the Examination is - 475

$$\Sigma fx_{70} = 6385$$

So mean marks of 70 students passed is $\bar{x}_{70} = \frac{\Sigma fx}{n} = \frac{6385}{70}$

$= \mathbf{91.2143}$

Example 8.13. *From the following data calculate the missing value when the mean is 115.86.*

Wages(in Rs.) :	110	112	113	117	(?)	125	128	130
No. of workers :	25	17	13	15	14	8	6	2

(BU-A83, N87)

Solution:

Let us assume the missing value as 'A'

Wages (in Rs.) (x)	No. of Workers (f)	fx
110	25	2,750
112	17	1,904
113	13	1,469
117	15	1,755
A	14	(14A)
125	8	1,000
128	6	768
130	2	260
	n = 100	Σfx = 9906 + 14A

$$\bar{x} = \frac{\Sigma fx}{n}$$

$$115.86 = \frac{9{,}906 + 14A}{100}$$

$$9{,}906 + 14A = 11{,}586$$

$$14A = 11{,}586 - 9{,}906$$

$$14A = 1{,}680$$

$$A = \frac{1680}{14} = \mathbf{120}$$

So the missing value is 120.

Example 8.14. *Rainfall for a month as observed and recorded is as follows:*

"Sundays 87 mm; Mondays 63 mm; Tuesdays 74mm; Wednesdays 56 mms; Thursdays 62mm; Fridays 85 mm and Saturdays 73 mm.

There are 5 mondays, Tuesdays and Wednesdays, and 4 Sundays, Thursdays, Fridays and Saturdays during the month. What is the daily average rainfall during the month? (BU-N96)

Solution:

Days		No. of Days (f)	Rain fall (x)mm	fx
Sundays	...	4	87	348
Mondays	...	5	63	315
Tuesdays	...	5	74	370
Wednesdays	...	5	56	280
Thursdays	...	4	62	248
Fridays	...	4	85	340
Saturdays	...	4	73	292
		n = 31		Σfx = 2,193

Average rainfall .... $\bar{x} = \frac{\Sigma fx}{n}$

$= \frac{2193}{31}$

$=$ **70.7419mm**

Example 8.15. *Find the missing frequency from the following distribution if its mean is 15.25.*

x :	10	12	14	16	18	20
f :	3	7	(?)	20	8	5

Solution:

Let us assume the missing frequency as 'A'

x	f	fx
10	3	30
12	7	84
14	(A)	(14A)
16	20	320
18	8	144
20	5	100
	n = 43+A	Σfx = 678+14A

$$\bar{x} = \frac{\Sigma fx}{n}$$

$$15.25 = \frac{678 + 14A}{43 + A}$$

$$(43 + A)\,15.25 = 678 + 14A$$

$$655.75 + 15.25A = 678 + 14A$$

$$1.25A = 678 - 655.75$$

$$1.25A = 22.25$$

$$A = \frac{22.25}{1.25} = \mathbf{17.8}$$

Therefore the missing frequency equal to 17.8 or 18 approximately.

Example 8.16. *If the average wages paid to 25 workers is Rs. 79.60, find the missing frequencies.*

Wages (Rs.):	50	60	70	80	90	100	110
No. of Workers :	1	3	–	–	6	2	1

Solution:

Assume that the missing frequencies are 'A' and 'B'. Total frequencies are 25. So, 1+3+A+B+6+2+1 = 25. A + B = 25 - 13 = 12.
∴ A + B = 12 B = 12 - A.

Wages(Rs.) x	No. of workers(f)	fx
50	1	50
60	3	180
70	(A)	(70A)
80	(12-A)	(960-80A)
90	6	540
100	2	200
110	1	110
	n = 25	Σfx = 2040 - 10A

$$\bar{x} = \frac{\Sigma fx}{n}$$

$$79.60 = \frac{2040 - 10A}{25}$$

$$1990 = 2040 - 10A$$

$$10A = 2040 - 1990$$

$$10A = 50$$

$$A = 5$$

Substituting the value of 'A' in ... A + B = 12

A + B = 12

5 + B = 12

B = 12-5

B = 7. So missing frequencies are A = **5**, B = **7**.

Example 8.17. *Calculate the average marks from the following distribution.*

Marks :	0-5	5-10	10-15	15-20	20-25	25-30	30-35
No. of Students :	2	4	5	3	2	4	5

(BU-A84)

Solution:

Marks C.I.	No. of Students(f)	Mid-value (x)	(x-A)/5 d'	fd'
0- 5	2	2.5	-3	-6
5-10	4	7.5	-2	-8
10-15	5	12.5	-1	-5
15-20	3	17.5	0	0
20-25	2	22.5	+1	+2
25-30	4	27.5	+2	+8
30-35	5	32.5	+3	+15
	n = 25			+ 25
				- 19
				Σfd' + 6

$$\bar{x} = A + \frac{\Sigma fd'}{n} \times c$$

$$= 17.5 + \frac{6}{25} \times 5 \qquad = 17.5 + 1.2 = 18.7$$

$$= 17.5 + \frac{30}{25}$$

∴ **Rs 18.70** is the mean wage.

Note: 1. The step devia- tion formula is used.

2. Assumed mean is 17.5.

3. Common factor is 5.

Example 8.18. *You are given the following incomplete information and its mean 25. Find out the missing frequencies.*

Class Interval :	0-10	10-20	20-30	30-40	40-50	Total
No. of Frequencies :	5	-	15	-	5	=45

(BU-A93)

Solution:

Assume that the missing frequencies are 'A' and 'B'. Total frequencies are 45. so,

5 + A + 15 + B + 5 = 45. A + B = 45 - 25 = 20

∴ A + B = 20 B = 20 - A

C.I	f	MV x	fx
0-10	5	5	25
10-20	(A)	15	(15A)
20-30	15	25	375
30-40	(20-A)	35	(700-35A)
40-50	5	45	225
	n = 45		Σfx = 1325 - 20A

$$\bar{x} = \frac{1325 - 20A}{45}$$

$$25 = \frac{1325 - 20A}{45}$$

$$1125 = 1325 - 20A$$

$$20A = 1325 - 1125$$

$$20A = 200$$

$$A = 10$$

Substitute the value of A in ... $A + B = 20$

$$10 + B = 20$$

$$B = 20\text{-}10$$

$$B = 10$$

∴ Missing frequencies are A = **10** & B = **10**.

Example 8.19. *Arrange the following information into a frequency distribution and obtain the arithmetic mean assuming the range of wages Rs. 0 to 500.*

For a group of wage earners, 20%, 40%, 70%, 80% of the wage earners receive wages less than Rs. 50, 120, 300 and 350 respectively and 5% are receiving Rs. 400 and over. (BU-N85)

Solution:

Let us prepare the table showing 'less than' frequencies, frequencies and the remaining frequency.

Wages Rs.		No. of Workers	Conversion Into C.I	f	MV x	fx
Less than	50	20%	0 - 50	20	25	500
,, ,,	120	40%	50-120	20	85	1,700
,, ,,	300	70%	120-300	30	210	6,300
,, ,,	350	80%	300-350	10	325	3,250
,, ,,	400	*95%	350-400	15	375	5,625
,, ,,	500	100%	400-500	5	450	2,250
				n = 100		Σfx = 19,625

1. Information given is as under.

(a) Range is 0-500.

(b) Less than 350 is 80% and more than 400 is 5%.

(c) Total No. of workers is assumed to be 100.

2. * Information Derived is
(a) Less than 400 is 95% and
(b) Less than 500 is 100%

$$\bar{x} = \frac{\Sigma fx}{n} = \frac{19,625}{100}$$

= **196.25 mean wage**

Example 8.20. *A limited company wants to pay bonus to the members of the staff. The bonus is to be paid as under,*

Monthly Salary (Rs.) :	100	120	140	160	180	200	220 &
Not exceeding :	120	140	160	180	200	220	over.
Bonus (Rs.) :	50	60	70	80	90	100	110

Actual salary of the members of the staff is given as under:
200, 180, 195, 218, 187, 160, 250, 168, 190, 168, 170, 178, 175, 140, 120, 148, 165, 155, 145, 125, 110, 162, 130, 150, 185.

What is the total bonus paid? What is the average bonus paid to the members of the staff?

(BU-N87 and Rajastan-1960)

Solution:

Let us prepare the continuous series and frequencies in respect of bonus payable.

Class Interval	Bonus x	Members Eligible	f	fx
100-120	50		1	50
120-140	60		3	180
140-160	70		5	350
160-180	80		8	640
180-200	90		5	450
200-220	100		2	200
220 & Over	110		1	110
			n = 25	Σfx = 1980

Average Bonus

$$\bar{x} = \frac{\Sigma fx}{n} = \frac{1980}{25}$$

= Rs 79.2

Total bonus **Rs 1980**.

Example 8.21. *A college management wanted to give monthly scholarship to B.Com. Students securing 50% and above marks in the following manner:*

Percentage of Marks:	50-55	55-60	60-65	65-70	70-75
Scholarship (in Rs.)	25	30	35	40	45

The percentage of marks of 20 students who were eligible for scholarship are given below:

52, 62, 51, 71, 54, 61, 53, 51, 50, 57, 64, 56, 54, 69, 63, 65, 59, 58, 68, 57.

Calculate the monthly scholarship payable to the students as well as the average scholarship. (BU-N90)

Solution:

Let us prepare the continuous series and frequencies in respect of scholarship payable.

Class Interval	Scholarship x	Students Eligible	f	fx
50-55	25	𝍸 ||	7	175
55-60	30	𝍸	5	150
60-65	35	||||	4	140
65-70	40	|||	3	120
70-75	45	|	1	45
			n = 20	Σfx = 630

Average Scholarship

$$\bar{x} = \frac{\Sigma fx}{n}$$

$$= \frac{630}{20} = \textbf{Rs 31.5}$$

Total Scholarship **Rs 630.**

Example 8.22. *Find the class intervals if the arithmetic mean of the following distribution is 30.1, and assumed mean 31.5.*

Step Deviation:	-3	-2	-1	0	+1	+2
Frequency:	5	10	25	30	20	10

Solution:

Assumed Mean = 31.5 and actual Mean = 30.1.

Step Deviation d'	f	fd'
-3	5	-15
-2	10	-20
-1	25	-25
0	30	0
+1	20	+20
+2	10	+20
	n = 100	- 60
		+ 40
		Σfd' = -20

$$\bar{x} = A + \frac{\Sigma fd'}{n} \times c$$

$$30.1 = 31.5 + \frac{-20}{100} \times c$$

$$-1.4 = \frac{-20}{100} \times c$$

$$1.4 = 0.2\,C$$

$$C = \frac{1.4}{0.2} = \textbf{7 magnitude}$$

As the common factor is 7, the differences of the mid-points of the classes will also be 7 and the mid-points would be

← Deduct 7 ← Assumed mean → Add 7 →
↓
10.5, 17.5, 24.5 ← 31.5 → 38.5 45.5

To find out the classes half of the interval is added (i.e 7/2 or 3.5) to the mid-points and deducted from the mid-points. So we can obtain the upper limits and lower limits of the class intervals as under:

Lower Limit			← Mid-Points →					C.I
7	=	3.5 -	10.5	+	3.5	=	14	7-14
14	=	3.5 -	17.5	+	3.5	=	21	14-21
21	=	3.5 -	24.5	+	3.5	=	28	21-28
28	=	3.5 -	31.5	+	3.5	=	35	28-35
35	=	3.5 -	38.5	+	3.5	=	42	35-42
42	=	3.5 -	45.5	+	3.5	=	49	42-49

Example 8.23. *Find mean for the following data.* (KU-A77)

ClassInterval :	50-59	40-49	30-39	20-29	10-29	0-9
Frequency :	1	3	8	10	15	3

Solution :

It is not necessary to convert the data into exclusive class-interval series. Even we need not arrange them in ascending order. Let us have the assumed mean 34.5.

Class Interval	f	MV x	x - A/10 d'	fd'
50-59	1	54.5	+2	+2
40-49	3	44.5	+1	+3
30-39	8	34.5	0	0
20-29	10	24.5	-1	-10
10-19	15	14.5	-2	-30
0-09	3	4.5	-3	-9
	n = 40			- 49
				+ 5
				Σfd' - 44

$$\bar{x} = A + \frac{\Sigma fd'}{n} \times c$$

$$= 34.5 + \frac{-44}{40} \times 10$$

$$= 34.5 - 11$$

$$= \mathbf{23.5}$$

Example 8.24. *Find out the missing frequencies from the following data, if the Mean of it 67.45.* *(BU-A94)*

Height (inches) :	60-62	63-65	66-68	69-71	72-74	Total
No. Of Students :	5	18	-	-	8	= 100

Solution:

Less assume the frequencies as A and B

C.I	f	MV x	fx
60-62	5	61	305
63-65	18	64	1152
66-68	A	67	(67A)
69-71	B	70	(70B)
72-74	8	73	584
	n = 100		Σfx = 2041 + 67A + 70B

$$\bar{x} = \frac{\Sigma fx}{n}$$

$$67.45 = \frac{2041 + 67A + 70B}{100}$$

$$6745 = 2041 + 67A + 70B$$

$$67A + 70B = 6745 - 2041$$

$$67A + 70B = 4704$$

We have two equations. Using simultaneous equations,

(a) $A + B = 69$ .. Multiply by 70

(b) $67A + 70B = 4704$

$$\begin{aligned} 70A + 70B &= 4830 \\ -67A \pm 70B &= 4704 \\ \hline 3A &= 126 \\ A &= \mathbf{42} \end{aligned}$$

Substituting the value of A in (a)

$A + B = 69$ ... $42 + B = 69$ ... $B = 69 - 42 = \mathbf{27}$

Example 8.25. *Calculate the mean wages of the following three factories:*

Factory A		Factory B		Factory C	
Weekly Wages(Rs.)	No. of Workers.	Weekly Wages(Rs.)	No. of Workers	Weekly Wages(Rs.)	No. of Workers
Below 20	3	Below 20	2	Below 40	4
20-40	7	20-50	5	40-60	8
40-60	10	50-90	11	60-100	12
60-80	6	90-140	9	100-130	5
Above 30	4	Above 140	3	Above 130	1

Solution:

The series are open end class interval series. They are adjusted with reference to the succeeding and preceding magnitudes. In some cases the increasing trend of magnitudes is also considered.

Factory A

Note: The magnitudes of C.I increase gradually at even rate. So the same pattern is adopted.

C.I	x	f	fx
0-20	10	3	30
20-40	30	7	210
40-60	50	10	500
60-80	70	6	420
80-100	90	4	360
		n = 30	Σfx=1520

$$\bar{x} = \frac{\Sigma fx}{n} = \frac{1520}{30} = \textbf{Rs. 50.667}$$

Factory B

Note : The magnitudes of class interval increase by 10 successively. So the same pattern is adopted.

C.I	x	f	fx
0-20	10	2	20
20-50	35	5	175
50-90	70	11	770
90-140	115	9	1035
140-200	170	3	510
		n = 30	Σfx=2510

$$\bar{x} = \frac{\Sigma fx}{n} = \frac{2510}{30} = \textbf{Rs. 83.667}$$

Factory C

Note: The magnitudes of class interval are varying and there is no consistency. So the First C.I should be formed on the basis of second, and the last C.I on the basis of previous.

C.I	x	f	fx
20-40	30	4	120
40-60	50	8	400
60-100	80	12	960
100-130	115	5	575
130-160	145	1	145
		n = 30	Σfx=2200

$$\bar{x} = \frac{\Sigma fx}{n} = \frac{2200}{30} = \textbf{Rs. 73.333}$$

Example 8.26. *From the following information relating to a certain industry consisting of 32 firms, calculate the average salary paid in the whole industry:*

Income Group :	50-75	75-100	100-150	150-200	200-300
No. of Firms :	30	26	24	20	28
Average No. of Workers :	5	8	5.5	6.5	1

(BU-A90)

Solution:

We should obtain the total number of workers by multiplying 'Firms' by 'Average' number of workers.

Income Group C.I		No. of Workers (f)	MV (x)	fx
50- 75 ..	(32 x 5) ..	160	62.5	10,000
75-100 ..	(26 x 8) ..	208	87.5	18,200
100-150 ..	(24 x 5.5) ..	132	125.0	16,500
150-200 ..	(20 x 6.5) ..	130	175.0	22,750
200-300 ..	(28 x 1) ..	28	250.0	7,000
		n = 658		Σfx = 74,450

$$\bar{x} = \frac{\Sigma fx}{n} = \frac{74,450}{658} = \mathbf{113.14589.}$$

So, the average salary paid in the whole industry is, Rs. 113.15

(ii) Weighted Arithmetic Mean

In computing simple arithmetic mean, it is assumed that all the items are of equal importance. This may not always be the case. Where items vary in importance they must be assigned some weights in proportion to their importance. The value of each item is then multiplied by its weight. The products are summated and divided by the number of weights, and not by the number of items. The quotient is the weighted arithmetic mean or average. Symbolically,

$$\bar{x}_w = \frac{\Sigma WX}{\Sigma W} \quad . . . \quad WX = X \times W.$$

$$W = \text{Weight}$$

'Weights' are numbers or percentages which stand for the relative importance of items. Such a relative importance may be real or estimated, or actual or approximated. These weights are assigned to each item under the following circumstances:

(i) When the results of the series are studied comparatively,

(ii) When the computation involves ratios or percentages i.e, Death Rates and Birth Rates.

(iii) When we compute the Index Numbers involving prices of essential commodities having different importance to each one.

Thus weight of a variate is numerical multiplier assigned to it in order to indicate its relative importance.

Example 8.27. *Calculate simple and weighted average price of coal purchased by an industry for the half-year and account for the difference between the two.*

Month :	Jan.	Feb.	March	April	May	June
Price per Ton (Rs.) :	42.50	51.25	50.00	52.00	44.25	54.00
Tons Purchased :	25	30	40	50	10	45

(BU-A97)

Solution:

(A) The simple arithmetic average price of coal purchased will be computed (Without Weights) as under.

$$\bar{x} = \frac{\Sigma x}{n} = \frac{42.50 + 51.25 + 50.00 + 52.00 + 44.25 + 54}{6}$$

$$= \frac{294}{6} = \text{Rs 49 per ton}$$

(B) The weighted arithmetic average price of coal purchased will be computed by considering the tons purchased as weights as under,

Prices Per Ton Rs. (X)	Tons Purchased (W)	Wx
42.50	25	1,062.50
51.25	30	1,537.50
50.00	40	2,000.00
52.00	50	2,600.00
44.25	10	442.50
54.00	45	2,430.00
	ΣW=200	ΣWx=10,072.50

$$\bar{x}_w = \frac{\Sigma WX}{\Sigma W} = \frac{10,072.50}{200} = \textbf{Rs 50.3625}$$

Difference between Simple Arithmetic Mean and Weighted Arithmetic Mean is 50.3625–49 = 1.3625.

Example 8.28. *A contractor employs three types of workers male, female and children. To a male worker he pays Rs. 30 per day, to a female worker Rs. 20 per day and to a child worker Rs. 10 per day. What is the average wage paid by the contractor?* (BU-N93)

Solution: In the example, the numbers of male, female and children workers are not given. So we can take arbitrary weights or numbers as 20,15 and 5 respectively,

(A) The simple Arithmetic Mean is

$$\bar{x} = \frac{\Sigma x}{n} = \frac{30 + 20 + 10}{3} = \text{Rs } 20 \text{ per day}$$

(B) The weighted Arithmetic Mean is

Wage Per Day (Rs) X	No. of Workers W	WX
30	20	600
20	15	300
10	5	50
	ΣW = 40	ΣWX = 950

$$\bar{x}_w = \frac{\Sigma WX}{\Sigma W} = \frac{950}{40} = \textbf{Rs 23.75} \text{ per day.}$$

Example 8.29. *The following table gives the marks of two candidates :*

Subjects	Weights	Marks by Candidates x	y
A -	1	70	80
B -	2	65	64
C -	3	58	56
D -	4	63	60

Find the weighted average marks of each candidate. By which figure would the second candidate have had to increase his marks in subject 'B', all other marks remaining same, in order that both the candidates have the same place? (BU-A96)

Solution:

Subjects	Weights(W)	Marks by X	Y	WX	WY
A	1	70	80	70	80
B	2	65	64	130	128
C	3	58	56	174	168
D	4	63	60	252	240
	ΣW=10			ΣWX=626	ΣWY=616

X average marks is $\bar{x}_w = \frac{\Sigma WX}{\Sigma W} = \frac{626}{10} = 62.6.$

Y average marks is $\bar{x}_w = \frac{\Sigma WY}{\Sigma W} = \frac{616}{10} = 61.6.$

As Y has scored 10 less (i.e 626 - 616) marks in total, he would have increased these marks in subject B where the weight is 2. So 10/2 will be the marks he has to score in the subject B, in order to be equal with the total marks of x. (i.e. 5 marks *)

Thus, Y's marks are now,

Y's marks = (80 x 1) + (64 + *5)2 + (56 x 3) + (60 x 4)

= 80 + 138 + 168 + 240 = **626.**

Example 8.30. *A train runs 25 Kilometers at a speed of 30 Km.p.h., another 50 Km. at a speed of 40 Km.p.h., then due to repairs of the track it travels for 6 minutes at a speed of 10 Km.p.h. and finally covers the remaining distance of 24 Kilometers at a speed of 24 km. p.h. What is the average speed in Kilometers per hour?* (BU-N83)

Solution :

Time taken in covering the distance at each stage will be treated as weights.

Speed Km.p.h.(X)	Time taken in minutes(W)	WX
30	50	1,500
40	75	3,000
10	06	60
24	60	1,440
	ΣW=191	ΣWX=6,000

$\bar{x}_w = \frac{\Sigma WX}{\Sigma W} = \frac{6000}{191}$ = **31.41** Km. p.h.

Example 8.31. *Comment on the performance of the students of the two universities given below using simple and weighted averages:*

Universities	Bombay		Madras	
Courses:	% Pass	No. of Students	% Pass	No. of Students
M.A.	75	300	68	280
M.Com.	80	400	83	370
M.Sc.	72	500	76	490

Solution:

Note: % are converted as fractional figures i.e 75/100 = 0.75 (in WXx).

Courses	Bombay University			Madras University		
	%Pass(X)	No. of Stu(W)	WX	%Pass(X)	No. of Stu(W)	WX
M.A	75	300	225	68	280	190.4
M.Com	80	400	320	83	370	307.1
M.Sc.	72	500	360	76	490	372.4
	227	ΣW=1200	ΣWX=905	227	ΣW=1140	ΣWX=869.9

Simple and weighted Arithmetic Means are

Bombay University

$$\bar{x} = \frac{\Sigma X}{n} = \frac{227}{3} = \mathbf{75.667\%}. \qquad \bar{x}_w = \frac{\Sigma WX}{\Sigma W} = \frac{905}{1200} = \mathbf{0.75417} \text{ (i.e. 75.417\%)}$$

Madras University

$$\bar{x} = \frac{\Sigma X}{n} = \frac{227}{3} = \mathbf{75.667\%}. \qquad \bar{x}_w = \frac{\Sigma WX}{\Sigma W} = \frac{869.9}{1140} = \mathbf{0.7631} \text{ (i.e. 76.31\%)}$$

The arithmetic mean is the same for both the Universities, i.e 75.667 % and hence it may be concluded that the performance of the students is alike.

On comparing the weighted arithmetic mean, we find that for Madras University, the mean value is slightly more and hence we can say that the performance of the Madras University Students is better.

Algebraic Properties of Arithmetic Mean.

The arithmetic mean is having the number of properties as under:

(1) The sum of the deviations of the items from the arithmetic mean is always Zero. i.e. $\Sigma(x - \bar{x})$ or $\Sigma d = 0$

(2) The sum of the squared deviations of the items from the arithmetic mean is minimum or least.

i.e. $\Sigma(x - \bar{x})^2$ or Σd^2 = Minimum

(3) If arithmetic and the number of items of two or more than two related groups are known, then their combined mean can be computed.

Combined mean.... $\bar{x} = \dfrac{N_1\bar{X}_1 + N_2\bar{X}_2 + N_3\bar{X}_3 + N_4\bar{X}_4}{N_1 + N_2 + N_3 + N_4}$

Merits of Arithmetic Mean: Arithmetic mean is commonly used by one and all as it has the following advantages:

(1) It is simple to understand and easy to compute.

(2) It is computed correctly and the figure is exact and suitable for further mathematical treatment.

(3) It takes into consideration every item in the series in computation.

(4) It is not necessary to arrange the values in an array form.

(5) It is the centre of gravity which balances the values on either side.

Demerits (Limitations) of Arithmetic Mean: Arithmetic Mean suffers from the following limitations:

(1) Extreme items affect the average figure disproportionately.

(2) It may not be the one item among the given values of variable. It may represent fractional figures(persons or animals or machines)

(3) It may give wrong impression, if proper weights are not given.

(4) In case of open end class intervals, mid-points are arrived by making assumptions, which may be wrong.

In spite of the limitations, the arithmetic mean is still treated as a fairly stable average and it is useful in analysing the data on economic and business statistics, in averaging data on production, consumption, sales and prices over a period of time.

B. Geometric Mean

Geometric Mean or Average is the **'n'th** root of the product of the **'n'** quantities of a series. It is obtained by multiplying the values of the items together and extracting the root of the product corresponding to the number of items. Thus, the square root of the product of two items and the cube root of the product of three items are the geometric means.

In the field of business and management, various problems often arise relating to **"Average Percentage"** rate of change over a period of time. In such cases, the arithmetic mean is not an appropriate average to employ. So, we can suitably apply the geometric mean in such cases. Symbolically,

$$G.M = \sqrt[n]{x_1 \times x_2 \times x_3 \times \ldots \times x_n}$$

where **'G.M'** stands for the geometric mean; 'n' for the number of items and $\mathbf{x_1, x_2, x_3 \ldots x_n}$ for the values of variable. The actual product of the values of the series (i.e. 2 x 4 x 8 = 64) will remain unchanged when the value of Geometric Mean is substituted (i.e 4 x 4 x 4 = 64) for each individual value, similarly the geometric mean of 4 and 9 is 6. i.e. $\sqrt[2]{4 \times 9} = \sqrt[2]{6 \times 6}$

When the number of items in a series is larger than three, the process of computing the geometric mean is difficult to follow. To obviate this difficulty, logarithm of each size is obtained from the Mathematical (logarithm) Table. The logarithms of all the values are added up and divided by the number of items. The anti-logarithm of the quotient so obtained is the required geometric mean. The formula is

$$G.M. = \text{Anti-log}\left[\frac{\log x_1 + \log x_2 + \ldots + \log x_n}{n}\right]$$

$$= \text{Anti-log of } \frac{\Sigma \log x}{n}$$

Example: G.M. of 2, 4, 8

$$G.M. = \text{Anti-log of } \frac{\log 2 + \log 4 + \log 8}{n}$$

$$= \text{Anti-log of } \frac{0.3010 + 0.6012 + 0.9031}{3}$$

$$= \text{Anti-log of } \frac{1.8062}{3}$$

$$= \text{Anti-log of } 0.6012 = 3.999 = 4.$$

Example 8.32. *Yield in sugar mill (in quintals) of 10 farms in Mandya District is given below, find the Geometric Mean.*

Farm Number:	1	2	3	4	5	6	7	8	9	10
Yield (in quintals):	7.5	13	18.5	20.5	5.2	23	24	25	26	28

(BU-A84)

Solution:

x		log.x
7.5	...	0.8751
13.5	...	1.1139
18.5	...	1.2672
20.5	...	1.3118
5.2	...	0.7160
23.0	...	1.3617
24.0	...	1.3802
25.0	...	1.3979
26.0	...	1.4150
28.0	...	1.4472
	Σ log x =	12.2860

$$\text{G.M.} = \text{Anti-log of } \frac{\Sigma \log x}{n}$$
$$= \text{Anti-log of } \frac{12.2860}{10}$$
$$= \text{Anti-log of } 1.2286$$
$$= \mathbf{16.92.}$$

Example 8.33. *Calculate the Geometric Mean of the following data.*

3884, 382, 63, 8, 0.4, 0.03, 0.009, 0.0005

(BU-N86)

Solution:

x		log.x
3884	...	3.5893
382	...	2.5821
63	...	1.7993
8	...	0.9031
0.4	...	$\bar{1}.6021$
0.03	...	$\bar{2}.4771$
0.009	...	$\bar{3}.9542$
0.0005	...	$\bar{4}.6990$
	Σ log x =	1.6062

$$\text{G.M.} = \text{Anti-log of } \frac{\Sigma \log x}{n}$$
$$= \text{Anti-log of } \frac{1.6062}{8}$$
$$= \text{Anti-log of } 0.200775$$
$$= \mathbf{1.588.}$$

Example 8.34. *Calculate Geometric Mean for the following,*

35, 250, 18.7, 234.6, 1.06, 98.72, 0.987

(BU-N91, N95)

x		log x
35	...	1.5441
250	...	2.3979
18.7	...	1.2718
234.6	...	2.3703
1.06	...	0.0253
98.72	...	1.9944
0.987	...	$\bar{1}.9943$
		$\Sigma \log x = 9.5981$

$$\text{G.M.} = \text{Anti-log of } \frac{\Sigma \log x}{n}$$

$$= \text{Anti-log of } \frac{9.5981}{7}$$

$$= \text{Anti-log of } 1.37115$$

$$= \mathbf{23.51}.$$

Example 8.35. *Find the Geometric Mean from the following.*

S.No.	1	2	3	4
Values :	1000	20	8	0.6

(BU-A93)

Solution :

x		log x
1000	...	3.0000
20	...	1.3010
8	...	0.9031
0.6	...	$\bar{1}.7782$
		$\Sigma \log x = 4.9823$

$$\text{G.M.} = \text{Anti-log of } \frac{\Sigma \log x}{n}$$

$$= \text{Anti-log of } \frac{4.9823}{4}$$

$$= \text{Anti-log of } 1.24557 = \mathbf{17.60}$$

Example 8.36. *Calculate the G.M of the following*

375, 0.05, 0.5672 and 0.0854 (BU-A96, A98)

Solution:

x		log x
375	...	2.5740
0.05	...	$\bar{2}.6990$
0.5672	...	$\bar{1}.7538$
0.0854	...	$\bar{2}.9315$
		$\Sigma \log x = \bar{1}.9583$

$$\text{G.M.} = \text{Anti-log of } \frac{\Sigma \log x}{n}$$

$$= \text{Anti-log of } \frac{-4}{4} + \frac{3.9583}{4}$$

$$= \text{Anti-log of } \bar{1}.98957$$

$$= \mathbf{0.9763}$$

(*Note:* $\bar{1}$ is converted into -4 and +3)

Example 8.37. *Compute the geometric mean of the following,*

475, 0.8974, 12.5 and 0.0081 (BU-N96)

Solution:

x		log x
475	...	2.6767
0.8974	...	$\bar{1}.9530$
12.5	...	1.0969
0.0081	...	$\bar{3}.9085$
		Σ log x = 1.6351

$$\text{G.M.} = \text{Anti-log of } \frac{\Sigma \log x}{n}$$

$$= \text{Anti-log of } \frac{1.6351}{4}$$

$$= \text{Anti-log of } 0.40877 = \mathbf{2.564}$$

Example 8.38. *Calculate G.M of the following*

2574, 75, 0.8, 0.075 (BU-A97)

Solution :

x		log x
2574	...	3.4106
75	...	1.8751
0.8	...	$\bar{1}.9031$
0.075	...	$\bar{2}.8751$
		Σ log x = 4.0639

$$\text{G.M.} = \text{Anti-log of } \frac{\Sigma \log x}{n}$$

$$= \text{Anti-log of } \frac{4.0639}{4}$$

$$= \text{Anti-log of } 1.01597 = \mathbf{10.37}$$

Example 8.39. *Calculate the Geometric Mean of the following.*

224, 13.65, 0.0456, & 0.5431 (BU-N97)

Solution:

x		log x
224	...	2.3502
13.65	...	1.1351
0.0456	...	$\bar{2}.6590$
0.5431	...	$\bar{1}.7349$
		Σ log x = 1.8792

$$\text{G.M.} = \text{Anti-log of } \frac{\Sigma \log x}{n}$$

$$= \text{Anti-log of } \frac{1.8792}{4}$$

$$= \text{Anti-log of } 0.4698 = \mathbf{2.949}$$

Example 8.40. *Compared to the previous year the overhead expenses went up by 32% in 1961; then increased by 40% in the next year and 50% in the following year. Calculate the average rate of increase in overhead expenses over the three years. Explain clearly the reason for the choice of the average.* (BU-A83)

Solution: As geometric mean is more appropriate for ratios and percentages, we can select the same as under for computing average,

Year	Rate of Change	Conversion x	log x
1960 ...	Base Year	100	–
1961 ...	32%	132	2.1206
1962 ...	40%	140	2.1461
1963 ...	50%	150	2.1761
		$\Sigma \log x$ =	6.4428

$$G.M. = \text{Anti - log of } \frac{\Sigma \log x}{n}$$

$$= \text{Anti - log of } \frac{6.4428}{3}$$

$$= \text{Anti - log of } 2.1476$$

$$= 140.5$$

∴ The average % increase in overheads is (140.5-100) = **40.5%**

Example 8.41. *Find the average, rate of increase in population which in the first decade has increased by 20%, in the next by 30% and in the third by 45%.* (BU-N86)

Solution:

Decade	Rate of Increase	Conversion x	log x
Base ...	Year	100	–
First ...	20%	120	2.0792
Second ...	30%	130	2.1139
Third ...	45%	145	2.1614
		$\Sigma \log x$ =	6.3545

$$G.M. = \text{Anti - log of } \frac{\Sigma \log x}{n}$$

$$= \text{Anti - log of } \frac{6.3545}{3}$$

$$= \text{Anti - log of } 2.11816$$

$$= 131.3$$

∴ The average % increase in population is (131.30-100) = **31.30%**

Example 8.42. *The price of a commodity increased by 8% from 1978 to 79, 12.5% from 1979 to 80 and 77% from 1980 to 1981. What is the average increase?* (BU-A92)

Solution:

Year	Rate of Increase	Conversion x	log.x
1977-78	Base Year	100	–
1978-79	8%	108	2.0334
1979-80	12.5%	112.5	2.0511
1980-81	77%	177	2.2480
		$\Sigma \log x$ =	6.3325

$$G.M. = \text{Anti - log of } \frac{\Sigma \log x}{n}$$

$$= \text{Anti - log of } \frac{6.3325}{3}$$

$$= \text{Anti - log of } 2.1108$$

$$= 129.0$$

∴ The average increase in price of a commodity is (129.00-100) = **29%.**

Example 8.43. *The annual growth rates of a factory in 3 years are 5.0, 7.5 and 2.5.* (BU-N92)

Solution:

The growth rate are 5%, 7.5% and 2.5%

Years	Rate of Increase	Conversion x	log x
1	Base Year	100	–
2	5%	105	2.0212
3	7.5%	107.5	2.0315
4	2.5%	102.5	2.0107
		Σ log x =	6.0634

$$\text{G.M.} = \text{Anti - log of } \frac{\Sigma \log x}{n}$$
$$= \text{Anti - log of } \frac{6.0634}{3}$$
$$= \text{Anti - log of } 2.02113$$
$$= 105.00$$

∴ The average grow rate is (105.00 - 100) = **5%**.

Example 8.44. *Consider the following time series for annual sales of Star and Company Ltd., for four years and find the average rate of change per year in sales,*

Rs. 10,000, Rs. 8,000, Rs. 12,000 and Rs. 15,000

Solution:

Year	Sales(Rs.)	Increase/ Decrease	Conversion x	log x
First	10,000	Base Year	–	–
Second	8,000	–20%	80	1.9031
Third	12,000	+50%	150	2.1761
Fourth	15,000	+25%	124	2.0969
			Σ log x =	6.1761

$$\text{G.M.} = \text{Anti - log of } \frac{\Sigma \log x}{n}$$
$$= \text{Anti - log of } \frac{6.1761}{3}$$
$$= \text{Anti - log of } 2.0587 = 114.50$$

∴ The average increase of sales is (114.50 - 100) = **14.50%**

Example 8.45. *Compute the geometric mean for the following:*

0.067, 0.008, 0.0809, 0.005, 0.125

Solution:

x	log x
0.067	$\bar{2}.8261$
0.008	$\bar{3}.9031$
0.0809	$\bar{2}.9036$
0.005	$\bar{3}.6990$
0.125	$\bar{1}.0969$
	$\Sigma \log x = \bar{8}.4287$

$$\text{G.M.} = \text{Anti-log of } \frac{\Sigma \log x}{n}$$

$$= \text{Anti-log of } \frac{\bar{8}.4287}{5}$$

$$= \text{Anti-log of } \frac{\bar{10}}{5} + \frac{2.487}{5}$$

$$= \text{Anti-log of } \bar{2}.4974 = \mathbf{0.03144}$$

Algebraic Properties of Geometric Mean.

The geometric mean has the properties as under:

(1) If G.M is placed in place of each value, there will be no difference in the product of given values and the product of G.M Values.

(2) The sum of deviations of logs of the values from the log of the G.M is equal to Zero.

x	log.x	log.G.M = (.91417) (d)
3	0.4771	-0.43707
7	0.8451	-0.06907
12	1.0792	+0.16503
18	1.2553	+0.34113
	$\Sigma \log x = 3.6567$	$\Sigma d = 0$

$$\text{G.M.} = \text{Anti-log of } \frac{3.6567}{4} = \text{Anti-log of } 0.91417 = \mathbf{8.208}$$

Merits of Geometric mean. Geometric mean is used in special cases as it has the following advantages:

(1) It is determinate, provided the values of the variable are greater than zero.

(2) It is based on all the data in the group.

(3) It gives less weight to large items and more to small ones.

(4) It is particularly useful when we are dealing with the ratios.

(5) It is amenable to arithmetic and algebraic manipulations.

Demerits(limitations) of Geometric Mean. Geometric mean suffers from the following limitations:

(1) It cannot be used when any one of the items is '0' or negative; because when the item '0' is multiplied, all the items' product will be '0'

(2) It may be found to lie at a point where very few (or even none) of the actual measurements lie.

(3) It entails much work of calculation and is difficult to compute.

(4) It is less easily understood than the arithmetic mean.

It spite of the limitations, the geometric mean is suitable for studying various social and economic phenomena where it is desired to give large weight to small items. The geometric mean is particularly useful in dealing with relative as against absolute differences while computing index numbers.

C. Harmonic Mean

Harmonic Mean or Average is the total number of items of a variable divided by the sum of the reciprocals of the values of the variable. It is a specialised average which solves problems involving variable expressed in 'time rates' that vary according to time-Km. Per Hour, Hour per Km., Units per Day, Price per Unit and so on. Harmonic Mean is suitable only when,

"Time factor is variable and the act being performed remains constant."

Thus, the Harmonic Mean provides the same result as that of the Weighted Arithmetic Mean, when the act being performed remains the same otherwise not. Symbolically,

$$\text{H.M.} = \frac{n}{\frac{1}{x_1} + \frac{1}{x_2} + \frac{1}{x_3} + \ldots + \frac{1}{x_n}}$$

$$= \text{Reciprocal of} \ldots \frac{\frac{1}{x_1} + \frac{1}{x_2} + \frac{1}{x_3} + \ldots + \frac{1}{x_n}}{n}$$

$$= \frac{n}{\Sigma Rx} \text{ or R. of } \frac{\Sigma Rx}{n}$$

Example 8.46. *Calculate the Harmonic Mean for the following:*

35, 250, 18.7, 234.6, 1.06, 98.72, 0.987 (BU-M91, N95)

Solution:

x		Rx
35	...	0.02857
250	...	0.00400
18.7	...	0.05348
234.6	...	0.00426
1.06	...	0.94340
98.72	...	0.01013
0.987	...	1.01317
	Σ Rx =	2.05701

$$\text{H.M.} = \frac{n}{\Sigma Rx} = \frac{7}{2.05701} = 3.402998$$

Example 8.47. *Calculate the Harmonic Mean for the following,*

375, 0.05, 0.5672 and 0.0854 (BU-A96)

Solution:

x		Rx
375	...	0.002667
0.05	...	20.000000
0.05672	...	1.763045
0.0854	...	11.709601
	ΣRx =	33.475313

$$\text{H.M.} = \frac{n}{\Sigma Rx} = \frac{4}{33.475313} = \mathbf{0.119491}$$

Example 8.48. *Compute the Harmonic Mean for the following.*

475, 0.8974, 12.5, and 0.0081 (BU-N96)

Solution:

x		Rx
475	...	0.0021052
0.8974	...	1.1143302
12.5	...	0.0800000
0.0081	...	123.4567900
	Σ Rx =	124.6532254

$$\text{H.M.} = \frac{n}{\Sigma Rx} = \frac{4}{124.6532254} = \mathbf{0.032089}$$

Example 8.49. *Calculate the Harmonic Mean for the following,*

2574, 75, 0.8, 0.075 (BU-A97)

Solution:

x		Rx
2574	...	0.0003885
75	...	0.0133333
0.8	...	1.2500000
0.075	...	13.3333333
	Σ Rx =	14.5970551

$$H.M. = \frac{n}{\Sigma Rx} = \frac{4}{14.5970551} = \mathbf{0.2740278}$$

Example 8.50. *A man traveled by a car for 3 days. He covered 480 Kms. Each day. On the first day he drove for 10 hours at 48 Kms. per hour, on the second day he drove for 12 hours at 40 Kms. per hour and on the last day he drove for 15 hours at 32 Kms per hour. What was his average speed?* (BU-A77, A86)

Solution:

In this problem, the distance travelled is the same. We can solve the problem by both the methods, i.e., Weighted A.M and Harmonic Mean.

(i) Weighted A.M

Speed Kms per Hour X	Hours Traveled W	WX
48	10	480
40	12	480
32	15	480
	$\Sigma W = 37$	$\Sigma WX = 1440$

$$\bar{x}_w = \frac{\Sigma WX}{\Sigma W} = \frac{1440}{37} = \mathbf{38.92} \text{ Km. per. Hour}$$

(ii) Harmonic Mean

x		Rx
48	...	0.02083
40	...	0.02500
32	...	0.03125
	$\Sigma Rx =$	0.07708

$$H.M. = \frac{n}{\Sigma Rx} = \frac{3}{0.07708} = \mathbf{38.92} \text{ Km. per. Hour}$$

Example 8.51. *An aeroplane flies around a square whose side is 100 Kms. long, covering the first side at 100 Kms. per hour, the second side at 200 Kms. per hour, the third side at 300 Kms per hour and the fourth at 400 Kms per hour. What is the average speed of the aeroplane?* (BU-A92)

Solution:

In this problem, the distance travelled is the same. We can solve the problem by both the methods, i.e., Weighted A.M and Harmonic Mean.

(i) Weighted A.M

Speed KmsP/H X	Minutes Travelled W	WX
100	60	6,000
200	30	6,000
300	20	6,000
400	15	6,000
	ΣW = 125	ΣWx = 24,000

$$\bar{x}_w = \frac{\Sigma WX}{\Sigma W} = \frac{24000}{125} = \textbf{192} \text{ Km. per. Hour}$$

(ii) Harmonic Mean

x	Rx
100 ...	0.01000
200 ...	0.00500
300 ...	0.00333
400 ...	0.00250
	Σ Rx = 0.02083

$$\text{H.M.} = \frac{n}{\Sigma Rx} = \frac{4}{0.02083} = \textbf{192} \text{ Km. per. Hour}$$

Example 8.52. *An investor buys Rs. 1,200 worth of shares in a company each month. During the first four months he bought shares at a price of Rs. 10, Rs. 12, Rs. 15 and Rs. 20. Calculate the average price paid.* (BU-N92)

Solution:

In this problem, the amount invested is the same. We can solve the problem by both the methods i.e., Weighted A.M and Harmonic Mean.

(i) Weighted A.M

Price (Rs.) per Share X	No. of Shares Purchased W	WX
10	120	1200
12	100	1200
15	80	1200
20	60	1200
	ΣW = 360	ΣWX = 4800

$$\bar{x}_w = \frac{\Sigma WX}{\Sigma W} = \frac{4800}{360} = \textbf{Rs 13.33} \text{ per share}$$

(ii) Harmonic Mean

x	Rx
10	0.100000
12	0.083333
15	0.066666
20	0.050000
	ΣRx= 0.299999

$$\text{H. M.} = \frac{n}{\Sigma Rx} = \frac{4}{0.299999} = \text{Rs } 13.33 \text{ per share}$$

Example 8.53. *In a factory, a unit of work is completed by A in 4 minutes, by B in 5 minutes, by C in 6 minutes and by D in 10 minutes. What is their average time taken per unit?* (BU-A93, A98)

Solution:

Minutes per unit x	Rx
4 ...	0.25000
5 ...	0.20000
6 ...	0.16666
10 ...	0.10000
ΣRx =	0.71666

$$\text{H. M.} = \frac{n}{\Sigma Rx} = \frac{4}{0.71666}$$

= **5.58145** minutes per unit.

Example 8.54. *Typist A can type a letter in five minutes, B in ten minutes, and C in fifteen minutes. What is the average number of letter typed per hour per unit?* (BU-A94)

Solution:

Minutes per Letter x	Rx
5 ...	0.20000
10 ...	0.10000
15 ...	0.06666
	0.36666

$$\text{H. M.} = \frac{n}{\Sigma Rx} = \frac{3}{0.36666}$$

= **8.18197** minutes per unit.

Average no. of letters per hour is $= \frac{60 \times 1}{8.18197}$

= 7.3332 letters per hour.

Characteristics of Harmonic Mean

The harmonic mean is having the following characteristics,

(1) The harmonic mean is determinate and considers the largest weight to the smallest values and the smallest weight to the largest values.

(2) The harmonic mean is the reciprocal of the arithmetic mean of the reciprocals of the given items.

Merits of Harmonic Mean. Harmonic mean is used in special cases where one factor is constant and another being variable. Following are the advantages,

(1) It is rigidly defined and based on all the observations.

(2) It is suitable for further mathematical manipulations.

(3) It gives best results where time and rates are under study.

Demerits (Limitations) of Harmonic Mean. Harmonic suffers from the following limitations:

(1) It is not easy to compute.

(2) It cannot be used when any one of the items is '0' or negative; because when the item '0' is used as a divider, the item will be zero.

(3) It is not representing the distribution unless weightages are given disproportionately.

In spite of the limitations, the harmonic mean is suitable in averaging of rates and time. Though not used in general, it is of much importance in very special cases.

Relationship Among the Averages.

When all the values of variables are equal, the A.M., G.M. and H.M are equal for example,

x	log x	Rx
3	0.4771	0.3333
3	0.4771	0.3333
3	0.4771	0.3333
ΣX=9	Σlog x=1.4313	ΣRx=0.9999

$$\bar{x} = \frac{\Sigma x}{n} = \frac{9}{3} = \mathbf{3}$$

$$G.M = \text{Anti-log of } \frac{\Sigma \log x}{n}$$

$$= \text{Anti-log of } \frac{1.4313}{3}$$

$$= \text{Anti-log of } 0.4771 = \mathbf{3}$$

$$H.M. = \frac{n}{\Sigma Rx} = \frac{3}{0.9999} = \mathbf{3}$$

When all the values of variable are not equal, then we can establish the following relationship,

A.M. > G.M. > H.M,

For example, if 'a' and 'b' are two positive values which are not equal in size, the averages are computed as under,

AM	**GM**	**HM**
$\bar{x} = \dfrac{a+b}{2}$	$\sqrt[2]{a \times b}$	$\dfrac{2}{\frac{1}{a}+\frac{1}{b}}$ or $\dfrac{2ab}{a+b}$

Case 1: *The A.M of two observations is 25 and their G.M is 15, find their H.M.* (BU-A92, A98)

$$\text{A.M.} = \frac{a+b}{2}$$
$$25 = \frac{a+b}{2}$$
$$a + b = 50$$

$$\text{G.M.} = \sqrt[2]{a \times b}$$
$$15 = \sqrt[2]{a \times b}$$
$$ab = 15^2 = 225$$

$$\text{H.M.} = \frac{2ab}{a+b}$$
$$= \frac{2(225)}{50} = \frac{450}{50}$$
$$= \mathbf{9}$$

Case 2. *If the G.M is 60, H.M is 28.24 of the two observations, what is their A.M?* (BU-N92)

$$\text{G.M.} = \sqrt[2]{a \times b}$$
$$60 = \sqrt[2]{a \times b}$$
$$ab = 60^2 = 3600$$

$$\text{H.M.} = \frac{2ab}{a+b}$$
$$28.24 = \frac{2(3600)}{a+b}$$
$$a + b = \frac{7200}{28.24}$$
$$a + b = 254.9575$$

$$\text{A.M.} = \frac{a+b}{2}$$
$$= \frac{254.9575}{2}$$
$$= \mathbf{127.47875}$$

Case 3. *If A.M of two observations is 25 and their H.M is 9, find their G.M* (BM-A93, N93, A95)

$$\text{A.M.} = \frac{a+b}{2}$$
$$25 = \frac{a+b}{2}$$
$$a + b = 50$$

$$\text{H.M.} = \frac{2ab}{a+b}$$
$$9 = \frac{2ab}{50}$$
$$2ab = 450$$
$$ab = 225$$

$$\text{G.M.} = \sqrt[2]{a \times b}$$
$$= \sqrt[2]{225}$$
$$= \mathbf{15}$$

Case 4. *A.M of two observations is 12.5 and their G.M is 12. Find the H.M.*

$$\text{A.M.} = \frac{a+b}{2}$$
$$12.5 = \frac{a+b}{2}$$
$$a + b = 25$$

$$\text{G.M.} = \sqrt[2]{a \times b}$$
$$12 = \sqrt[2]{ab}$$
$$ab = 12^2 = 144$$

$$\text{H.M.} = \frac{2ab}{a+b}$$
$$= \frac{2(144)}{25} = \frac{288}{25}$$
$$= \mathbf{11.52}$$

Thus, in any distribution when the values of variable differ in size, A.M is greater G.M and G.M is greater than H.M.

We can have also the following formula in which the relationship among the three averages can be presented,

$$G.M. = \sqrt{\bar{x} \times H.M.} \qquad \text{or} \qquad G.M^2 = \bar{x} \times H.M.$$

Case 1: The A.M. of the two observations is 25 and their G.M. is 15, find their H.M. (BU-A92, A98)

$$(G.M)^2 = A.M. \times H.M.$$

$$H.M. = \frac{(G.M.)^2}{A.M.} = \frac{15^2}{25} = \frac{225}{25} = \mathbf{9}$$

Case 2: If the G.M. and the H.M. of the two observations are respectively 60 and 28.24, find the A.M. (BU-92)

$$(G.M)^2 = A.M. \times H.M.$$

$$60^2 = 28.24\ A.M.$$

$$A.M. = \frac{60^2}{28.24.} = \frac{3600}{28.24} = \mathbf{127.47875}$$

Case 3: If A.M. and H.M. of the two observations are respectively 25 and 9, find the G.M. (BU-A93, N93, A95)

$$G.M. = \sqrt{A.M. \times H.M} = \sqrt{25 \times 9}$$

$$= \sqrt{225} = \mathbf{15}$$

Case 4: If A.M. and G.M. of the two observations are respectively 12.5 and 12, find the H.M.

$$G.M^2 = A.M. \times H.M.$$

$$12^2 = 12.5\ H.M.$$

$$H.M. = \frac{12^2}{12.5} = \frac{144}{12.5} = \mathbf{11.52}$$

Questions

1. Give any four requisites of a good average. (BU-A83,A88, N90, N92)
2. State the relationship between Mean, G.M and H.M (BU-N83)
3. Define Geometric Mean. (BU-N84, A91, A95, A98))
4. State any two limitations of harmonic Mean. (BU-N84)
5. What are the algebraic properties of arithmetic average? (BU-N89)
6. What are the merits of arithmetic mean? (BU-A92)

7. What are the uses of averages? (BU-A95)
8. What are the characteristics of a good measure of central tendency? (BU-N95, N97)
9. Give four uses of mean. (BU-A86)
10. Given below is the distribution of 140 candidates obtaining marks 'X' or higher in a certain examination. Calculate the mean marks.

X:	10	20	30	40	50	60	70	80	90	100
C.f:	140	133	118	100	75	45	25	9	2	0

(Hint: It is a cumulative frequency. $\overline{X}$= 51.22)

11. Calculate the geometric mean of the following figures: 27.74, 475, 75, 5, 0.8 0.08, 0.005, 0.009 (G.M = 1.394)
12. A man travels from Lucknow to Delhi at an average speed of 30 miles per hour and returns along the same route at an average speed of 60 miles per hour. Find the average speed for the entire trip. (H.M = 40 m.p.h)
13. Let the values of variable be 1, 2, 3, 4, 5, 6, 7 and the weights assigned are 7, 6, 5, 4, 3, 2, 1 respectively. Find the simple mean and weighted mean ($\overline{X}$ = 4, $\overline{X}$W = 3)
14. The mean of the distribution is 4.9. Find the missing frequency of the following:

x:	0	1	2	3	4	5	6	7
f:	2	36	250	972	2269	?	2471	823

($\overline{x}$ = 3177)

15. The mean monthly salary paid to all the workers in a concern is Rs. 92. The means of monthly salary paid to skilled and unskilled workers are Rs. 100 and Rs. 80 respectively. Find out the percentage of skilled and unskilled workers employed in the concern. (60% Sk and 40% Unsk).
16. The mean of 100 items is found to be 30. If at the time of calculation, two items are wrongly taken as 32 and 12 instead of 23 and 11, find the correct mean. ($\overline{x}$= 29.90%)
17. The price of a commodity increased by 5% from 1995 to 1996, by 9% from 1996 to 1997 and by 73% from 1997 to 1998. Find the average increase in the price (G.M = 25.6%)
18. Compute the hormonic mean of the following values 4257, 700, 77.3 9.25, 0.787, 0.04238, 0.004728, 0.0004527 (H.M = 0.03272)

9

Measures of Central Tendency (II)

I. Median

"Median" is the value of that item in a series which divides the array into two equal parts, one consisting of all the values less than it and the other consisting of all the values more than it. It means, when the values of variable are arranged in an array form (in an ascending or descending order of their magnitude), the value of middle item of the array is the median.

Median is a positional average. The number of items below it is equal to the number of items above it. It occupies the central position. So it is the middle most value in the arrayed distribution. It may be the original value (one of the items in the series) or it may be interpolated between the two values. It is denoted by a symbol **'Me'**.

If the students of a class, 23 (odd) in number, are asked to stand in order of their heights, the 12th student from either side shall be the one whose height will be the median height of the class. This method of picking of the median value can be symbolically expressed as follows:

"Me is the size of $\left(\frac{n+1}{2}\right)^{th}$ item" where 'Me' represents the median (middle item), and 'n' the number of items.

A. Individual Observations

If the students of a class, 24(even) in number, are asked to stand in order of their heights, the size of $\left(\frac{n+1}{2}\right)^{th}$ item will be falling in between 12th and 13th student i.e, 12.5th item. Then, we have to take the average of the heights of the 12th student and the 13th student as the Median height of the class.

Case I :- Find the median value of the following data:

43, 62, 15, 80, 56, 72, 34, 8, 25

Solution: Arrange the data in an array form with serial number.

S.No. :	1	2	3	4	5	6	7	8	9
X :	8	15	25	34	43	56	62	72	80

Median is the size of $\frac{n+1}{2}$ th item

$\therefore \frac{9+1}{2}$ th item = 5th item

Me = **43**

Case II :- Find the median value of the following:

36, 5, 19, 26, 6, 28, 56, 18, 63, 4

Solution: Arrange the data in an array form with serial numbers.

S.No. :	1	2	3	4	5	6	7	8	9	10
X :	4	5	6	18	19	26	28	36	56	63

Median is the size of $\frac{n+1}{2}$ th item.

$\therefore \frac{10+1}{2}$ th item = 5.5 th item,

The item lies in between 5th & 6th item.

So there are two values i.e 19 & 26.

Then the median value will be mean of these two values i.e.,

$$\frac{19+26}{2} = \frac{45}{2} = 22.5$$

Me = **22.5**

B. Discrete Series

In discrete series, the values are already in the form of array and the frequencies are recorded against each value. However, for determining the size of $\left(\frac{n+1}{2}\right)$ th item, a separate column is to be prepared for cumulative frequencies. The median size is first located with reference to the cumulative frequency which covers the size first. Then, against that cumulative frequency, the value will be located as the median value. For example,

Following is the frequency distribution.

Marks x		No. of Students f	C.f.
10	...	10	10
20	...	16	26
30	...	18	44
→40	...	13	57←
50	...	6	63
60	...	3	66
70	...	8	74
80	...	4	78
90	...	6	84
100	...	6	90
		n = 90	

Median is the size of $\frac{n+1}{2}$ th item

$\therefore \frac{90+1}{2}$ th = 45.5th item

It lies in 57 c.f..

Against 57 c.f. the value is 40

$\therefore$ Median Marks is **40**

Note: Median value is identified by locating the respective c.f. in which $\frac{n+1}{2}$ th item falls.

Example 9.1. *In a class of 15 students, 5 students failed in a test. The marks of 10 students who have passed were 9, 6, 7, 8, 9, 6, 5, 4, 7 and 8. What was the median marks of the 15 students.* (BU-N91)

Solution : Let us have the marks arranged in order and the frequencies recorded respectively.

x		f	c.f.
0, 1, 2, 3		5 failed	5
4	...	1	6
5	...	1	7
6	...	2	9
7	...	2	11
8	...	2	13
9	...	2	15
		n = 15	

(* 5 failed + 10 passed)

Median is the size of $\frac{n+1}{2}$ th item.

$\therefore \frac{15+1}{2}$ th item = 8th item

It lies in 9 c.f..

Against 9 c.f. the value is 6

$\therefore$ Median is **6** marks.

The above exercise can also be solved assuming that the data is in Individual Observation Form.

S.No. :	1	2	3	4	5	6	7	8 (Me)	9	10	11	12	13	14	15
X :	5 Students Failed					4	5	6	6	7	7	8	8	9	9

Median is the $\frac{n+1}{2}$ th item. So it is $\frac{15+1}{2}$ th item i.e., 8th item. 8th item is having **6** marks.

(C) Continuous Series

A different procedure is adopted to find out the Median value under continuous series. The class intervals are already in the form of array and the frequencies are recorded against each class interval. For determining the size, we should take $\frac{n}{2}$ th item and median class is located accordingly with reference to the cumulative frequency, which covers the size first. When the Median class is located, the median value is to be interpolated with the help of the following formula:

$$Me = l + \frac{\frac{n}{2} - m}{f} \times c \quad \text{or} \quad Me = l + \frac{c}{f}\left(\frac{n}{2} - m\right)$$

l = lower limit of the median class.

m = cumulative frequency of the class preceding the median class.

n = total number of the frequencies.

c = magnitude of the median class.

f = frequency of the median class.

Following are the examples,

Case I :- *Find the Median value of the following data:*

C.I.	:	10-15	15-20	20-25	25-30	30-35	35-40
f	:	6	18	9	10	4	3

Solution:

	C.I.	f	c.f.
	10-15	6	6
	15-20	18	24(m)
(l)	20-25	9 (f)	33 ←
	25-30	10	43
	30-35	4	47
	35-40	3	50
		n = 50	

Median is the size of $\frac{n}{2}$ th item.

$\therefore \frac{50}{2}$ th = 25th item.

It lies in 33 c.f..

Against 33 c.f. the median class is (20-25).

l = 20 n = 50 f = 9

m = 24 c = 5

$$Me = l + \frac{\frac{n}{2} - m}{f} \times c$$

$$= 20 + \frac{\frac{50}{2} - 24}{9} \times c = 20 + \frac{25 - 24}{9} \times 5 = 20 + \frac{1}{9} \times 5$$

$$= 20 + \frac{5}{9} = 20 + 0.5555 = \mathbf{20.5555}$$

Case II :- *Find the Median value of the following data:*

C.I.	:	4-7	8-11	12-15	16-19	20-23	24-27
f	:	12	23	40	65	17	3

Solution: Since there is an inclusive class interval distribution, we shall convert it into exclusive class interval series.

	C.I.	f	c.f.
	3.5 - 7.5	12	12
	7.5 - 11.5	23	35
	11.5 - 15.5	40	75(m)
(l)	15.5 - 19.5	65 (f)	140←
	19.5 - 23.5	17	157
	23.5 - 27.5	3	160
		n = 160	

Median is the size of $\frac{n}{2}$ th item.

$\therefore \frac{160}{2}$ th = 80 th item.

It lies in 140 c.f..

Against 140 c.f. the median class is (15.5-19.5).

$l = 15.5$ $n = 160$ $f = 65$ $m = 75$ $c = 4$

$$Me = l + \frac{\frac{n}{2} - m}{f} \times c$$

$$= 15.5 + \frac{\frac{160}{2} - 75}{65} \times 4 = 15.5 + \frac{80 - 75}{65} \times 4 = 15.5 + \frac{5}{65} \times 4$$

$$= 15.5 + \frac{20}{65} = 15.5 + 0.30769$$

$$= \mathbf{15.80769}$$

Example 9.2. *Calculate the Median of the following data:*

Less than	: 10	20	30	40	50	60	70	80
Frequency	: 4	16	40	76	96	112	120	125

Solution: Let us convert the data from less than frequency distribution into normal distribution.

C.I.	f	c.f
less than.10	4	4
10-20	12	16
20-30	24	40 (m)
(l) 30-40	36 (f)	76←
40-50	20	96
50-60	16	112
60-70	8	120
70-80	5	125
	n = 125	

Median is the size of $\frac{n}{2}$ th item

$\therefore \frac{125}{2}$ th = 62.5 th item

It lies in 76 c.f..

Against 76 c.f. the median class is (30-40).

$$Me = l + \frac{\frac{n}{2} - m}{f} \times c$$

$$= 30 + \frac{\frac{125}{2} - 40}{36} \times 10 = 30 + \frac{62.5 - 40}{36} \times 10$$

$$= 30 + \frac{22.5}{36} \times 10 = 30 + \frac{225}{36} = 30 + 6.25$$

$$= \mathbf{36.25}$$

Example 9.3. *Calculate the median of the following data.*

More Than :	10	20	30	40	50	60	70	80
Frequencies:	115	103	88	68	43	23	13	3

Solution: Let us convert the data from more than frequency distribution into normal distribution.

C.I.	f	c.f.
10-20	12	12
20-30	15	27
30-40	20	47 (m)
(l) 40-50	25 (f)	72←
50-60	20	92
60-70	10	102
70-80	10	112
80 & above	3	115
	n = 115	

Median is the size of $\frac{n}{2}$ th item.

$\therefore \frac{115}{2}$ th = 57.5th item

It lies in 72 c.f..

Against 72 c.f. the Median class is (40-50)

$$Me = l + \frac{\frac{n}{2} - m}{f} \times c$$

$$= 40 + \frac{\frac{115}{2} - 47}{25} \times 10 = 40 + \frac{57.5 - 47}{25} \times 10 = 40 + \frac{10.5}{25} \times 10$$

$$= 40 + \frac{105}{25} = 40 + 4.2 = \mathbf{44.2}$$

Example 9.4. *From the following data find out the missing frequency if the median is 50.*

Class intervals :	10-20	20-30	30-40	40-50	50-60	60-70
Frequencies :	2	8	6	--	15	10

(BU - N 83)

Solution : Let us assume the missing frequency as `A'

	C.I	f	c.f.
	10-20	2	2
	20-30	8	10
	30-40	6	16
	40-50	(A)	16 + A (m)
(l)	50-60	15 (f)	31 + A ←
	60-70	10	41 + A
		n = 41 + A	

Median is given as 50.

∴ Median class is (50-60)

$$Me = l + \frac{\frac{n}{2} - m}{f} \times c$$

$$50 = 50 + \frac{\frac{41 + A}{2} - (16 + A)}{15} \times 10$$

$$0 = \frac{\frac{41 + A}{2} - 16 - A}{15} \times 10$$

$$0 = \frac{205 + 5A - 160 - 10A}{15}$$

$$0 = 205 + 5A - 160 - 10A$$

$$5A = 205 - 160$$

$$5A = 45$$

$$A = 9$$

∴ Missing Frequency is **9**

Example 9.5. *In a group of 1000 wage earners, the monthly wages of 4% are below Rs. 60 and those of 15 % are under Rs. 62.50. 15% earned Rs. 95 and over, and 5% got Rs. 100 and over. Find the median wage.* (BU - A85, A97)

Solution : Let us prepare the table showing different types of % frequencies and then convert it into the original frequencies.

Monthly wages (Rs.)	Frequencies f	C.I	F (%)	(1000) f	c.f
Less than 60	4%	0 - 60	4%	40	40
Less than 62.50	15%	60 - 62.5	11%	110	150 (m)
62.50 – 95	(Diff)	62.5 - 95	70%	700 (f)	850 ⟵
More than 95	15%	95 - 100	10%	100	950
100 & over	5%	100 & over	5%	50	1000
		Total	100%	n=1000	

Median is the size of $\frac{n}{2}$ th item. $\therefore$ $\frac{1000}{2}$ th = 500 th item.

It lies in 850 c.f..

Against 850 c.f. the Median class is (62.5-95)

$$Me = l + \frac{\frac{n}{2} - m}{f} \times c$$

$$= 62.5 + \frac{\frac{1000}{2} - 150}{700} \times 32.5 = 62.5 + \frac{500 - 150}{700} \times 32.5$$

$$= 62.5 + \frac{350}{700} \times 32.5 = 62.5 + (0.5)32.5$$

$$= 62.5 + 16.25 = \mathbf{78.75}$$

Example 9.6. *10 percent of the workers in a firm, employing a total of 1000 workers, earn between Rs. 5 and 9.99, 30 per cent between Rs.10 and Rs.14.99, 250 workers between Rs.15 and Rs.19.99 and the rest Rs.20 and above. What is the median wage?*

Solution: Let us prepare the frequency table adjusting the class intervals and frequencies.

Wages Rs. (C.I)	No. of workers	(1000) workers (f)	c.f.
4.995 – 9.995	10%	100	100
9.995 – 14.995	30%	300	400 (m)
14.995 – 19.995	(250)	250 (f)	650 ⟵
19.995 & above	(Diff)	350	1000
		n = 1000	

Median is the size of $\frac{n}{2}$ th item. $\therefore$ $\frac{1000}{2}$ th = 500 th item.

It lies in 650 c.f..

Against 650 c.f. the median class is (14.995 -- 19.995)

$$Me = l + \frac{\frac{n}{2} - m}{f} \times c$$

$$= 14.995 + \frac{\frac{100}{2} - 400}{250} \times 5 = 14.995 + \frac{500 - 400}{250} \times 5$$

$$= 14.995 + \frac{100}{250} \times 5 = 14.995 + \frac{500}{250} = 14.995 + 2$$

$$= \mathbf{16.995} \quad \text{(Rs.17 Approximately)}$$

Example 9.7. *An incomplete distribution is as follows:*

Variable	: 10-20	20-30	30-40	40-50	50-60	60-70	70-80	Total
Frequency	: 12	30	--	65	--	25	18	= 229

Complete the distribution, if its median is 46. (BU – N92)

Solution: Assume the two frequencies as A & B. So A + B = 79

	C.I.	f		c.f
	10 – 20	12	...	12
	20 – 30	30	...	42
	30 – 40	(A)	...	42 + A (m)
(l)	40 – 50	65 (f)	...	107 + A ⟵
	50 – 60	(B)	...	107 + A + B
	60 – 70	25	...	132 + A + B
	70 – 80	18	...	150 + A + B
	n =	229		

Median Value is given, i.e. 46

Median class is (40 – 50)

$$Me = l + \frac{\frac{n}{2} - m}{f} \times c$$

$$46 = 40 + \frac{\frac{229}{2} - (42 + A)}{65} \times 10$$

$$6 = \frac{114.5 - 42 - A}{65} \times 10$$

$$390 = 1145 - 420 - 10A$$

$$10A = 1145 - 420 - 390$$

$$10A = 335$$

$$A = \mathbf{33.5}$$

Substitute the value of

A in ... A + B = 79

33.5 + B = 79

B = 79 - 33.5

B = 45.5

So the frequencies are 33.5 and 45.5

As the frequencies are in integers,

A = **3[illegible]** and B = **45** ... approximately.

Example 9.8. *20% of the workers in a firm, employing a total of 4,000 workers, earn less than Rs.4 per hour, 880 earn from Rs.4 to Rs.4.24 per hour, 24% earn from Rs.4.25 to Rs.4.49 per hour, 740 earn from Rs.450 to Rs.4.74 per hour, 12% earn from Rs.4.75 to Rs.4.99 per hour and rest earn Rs.5 or more per hour. Set up a frequency table and calculate median.* (BU - N94)

Solution: We have to adjust the class intervals into inclusive method as under.

	Wages per hour(Rs.)	No. of Workers	f	c.f
	0 - 3.995	20%	800	800
	3.995 - 4.245	880	880	1,680(m)
(l)	4.245 - 4.495	24%	960	2,640
	4.495 - 4.745	740	740	3,380
	4.745 - 4.995	12%	480	3,860
	4.995 & above	Diff→	140	4,000
			n = 4,000	

Median is the size of the $\frac{n}{2}$ th item. $\therefore$ $\frac{4000}{2}$ th = 2000 th item.

It lies in 2640 c.f..

Against 2640 c.f. the Median class is (4.245-4.495)

$$Me = l + \frac{\frac{n}{2} - m}{f} \times c = 4.245 + \frac{\frac{4000}{2} - 1680}{960} \times 0.25$$

$$= 4.245 + \frac{2000 - 1680}{960} \times 0.25 = 4.25 + \frac{320}{960} \times 0.25$$

$$= 4.245 + \frac{80}{960} = 4.245 + 0.833 = \mathbf{4.32833}$$

= Rs. **4.33** ps. approximately

Example 9.9. *An incomplete distribution is given below:*

Height (in inches)	: 5.1-6.0	6.1-7.0	7.1-8.0	8.1-9.0	9.1-10	10.1-11	11.1-12
No.of Plants	: 3	8	27	--	17	11	9

It is known that the median height of a plant is 8.53 inches. Calculate the missing frequency. (BU - A96)

Solution: Let us assume that the missing frequency is 'A'. We have to adjust the class intervals into inclusive method as under,

	Height (in inches) C.I.	f	c.f.
	5.05 - 6.05	3	3
	6.05 - 7.05	8	11
	7.05 - 8.05	27	38 (m)
(l)	8.05 - 9.05	(A) (f)	38 + A ⟵
	9.05 - 10.05	17	55 + A
	10.05 - 11.05	11	66 + A
	11.05 - 12.05	9	75 + A
		n = 75 + A	

Median value is given i.e. 8.53

∴ Median Class is (8.05 – 9.05)

$$M = l + \frac{\frac{n}{2} - m}{f} \times c$$

$$8.53 = + \frac{\frac{75 + A}{2} - 38}{A} \times 1 \qquad 0.48 = \frac{\frac{75 + A}{2} - 18}{A} \times 1$$

$$0.48A = \frac{75 + A}{2} - 38 \qquad 0.48A - \frac{75 + A}{2} = -38 \quad ......(\times 2)$$

$$0.96A - 75 - A = -76 \qquad -0.04A = -76 + 75 = -0.04A = -1$$

$$A = \frac{1}{0.04} = \mathbf{25}$$

Missing frequency is **25**.

Example 9.10. *Using a suitable formula calculate the median from the following:*

Mid-values :	115	125	135	145	155	165	175	185	195
Frequencies :	6	25	48	72	116	60	38	22	3

(BU - N96)

Solution : The interval of mid-values of the class intervals and the magnitudes of the class intervals are same i.e. 10. So half of 10 is deducted from and added to the mid -values will give us the lower and upper limits. Thus classes are ... 115 - 5 = 110 L.L. & 115 + 5 = 120 ... so on.

Class Intervals	f	c.f.
110 – 120	6	6
120 – 130	25	31
130 – 140	48	79
140 – 150	72	151 (m)
(l) 150 – 160	116 (f)	267 ←
160 – 170	60	327
170 – 180	38	365
180 – 190	22	387
190 – 200	3	390
	n = 390	

Median is the size of the $\frac{n}{2}$ th item.

$\therefore \frac{390}{2}$ th = 195th items

It lies in 267 c.f.. Against 267 the median class is (150 – 160)

$$Me = l + \frac{\frac{n}{2} - m}{f} \times c = 150 + \frac{\frac{390}{2} - 151}{116} 10$$

$$= 150 + \frac{195 - 151}{116} \times 10 = 150 + \frac{44}{116} \times 10 = 150 + \frac{440}{116}$$

$$= 150 + 3.793 = \mathbf{153.8}$$

Example 9.11. *Find Mean and Median from the following.*

X :		f	X		f
Less than 5	...	7	20-25	...	20
Less than 10	...	20	25 and above	...	5
5 – 15	...	38	30 and above	...	1
15 and above		55			

(BU - N97)

Solution : Let us convert the table into the normal distribution.

X	f	C.I	f	x	fx	c.f
Less than 5 ...	7	0- 5	7	2.5	17.50	7
Less than 10 ...	20	5-10	13	7.5	97.50	20
(5 - 15) ...	38	10-15	25	12.5	312.50	45(m)
15 and above ...	55 (l)	15-20	30 (f)	17.5	525.00	75 ←
20-25 ...	20	20-25	20	22.5	450.00	95
25 and above ...	5	25-30	4	27.5	110.00	99
30 and above ...	1	30-35	1	32.5	32.50	100
			n = 100		Σfx = 1545.00	

$\bar{x} = \frac{\Sigma fx}{n} = \frac{1545}{100} = \mathbf{15.45}$ Median is the size of $\frac{n}{2}$ th item

$\therefore \frac{100}{2}$ th = 50 th item

It lies in 75 c.f..

Against 75 c.f. the Median class is (15 - 20)

$$Me = l + \frac{\frac{n}{2} - m}{f} \times c = 15 + \frac{\frac{100}{2} - 45}{30} \times 5 = 15 + \frac{50 - 45}{30} \times 5$$

$$= 15 + \frac{5}{30} \times 5 = 15 + \frac{25}{30} = 15 + 0.8333 = \mathbf{15.8333}$$

Properties of Median.

The median has the following characteristics:

(i) The sum of the deviations of the items from the median (ignoring the negative signs) will be the least or smaller than the one obtained from any other value.

(ii) It is only a positional average calculated with the help of mathematical formula based on interpolation.

Merits of the Median :- Median is useful when we require to measure the position of the item.

Following are the advantages of the median:

(i) It is easy to calculate and simple to understand.

(ii) It eliminates the effect of extreme values to variable by which it is not affected.

(iii) It is capable of further algebraic treatment for analysing other measures.

(iv) It can be determined just by inspection of the arrayed data.

(v) It can be determined graphically with the help of Ogives (less than and more than frequency curves).

(vi) It is the best-suited average where direct quantitative measurement is not possible.

(vii) It indicates the value of the middle item in the distribution.

Demerits (Limitations) of the Median :- Median suffers from the following limitations:

(i) It may not be always the representative of the items as it ignores the extreme values.

(ii) It cannot be determined precisely when its size falls between the two values.

(iii) It is not capable of being located by any simple mathematical process.

(iv) It is not useful in those cases where large weights are given to extreme values, for it treats all frequencies alike.

(v) It requires the data to be arrayed, before it can be determined, which involves a considerable amount of work.

(vi) It is erratic (unusual) if the number of items is very small.

In spite of the limitations, the median is useful and it is an accurate measure in cases like distributions having open end class intervals. It is frequently used where the values of variable are highly fluctuating as compared to the number of items and where such values distort the mean.

II. Other Partitioned Values

The same procedure, according to which median is determined, can also be extended to divide a series into any number of parts. The partitioned values are useful to know the exact composition of series in the educational and psychological studies. The following are the different partitioned values which divide the given data into different parts :

Measures	Values	Parts	Symbols	Remark
Quartiles	Three	Four	Q_1, Q_2, Q_3	Q_2 = Me.
Median	One	Two	Me -	
Quintiles	Four	Five	Qt_1, Qt_2, Qt_3 Qt_4, Qt_5	
Deciles	Nine	Ten	$D_1, \ldots D_9$	D_5 = Me
Percentiles	Ninety Nine	Hundred	$P_1 \ldots. P_{99}$	P50 = Me

Similarly there are seven `octiles' dividing the series into eight parts. So we can have as many partitioned values as required for the purpose.

A. Quartiles

The quartiles are also positional averages like the median. As the median value divides the entire distribution into two equal parts, the quartiles (Q_1, Q_2 and Q_3) divide the entire distribution into four equal parts.

First Quartile (Lower Quartile) is the value below which there are one fourth of the items and above which there are three fourth of the items.

Second Quartile (Median) divides the total distribution into two halves.

Third Quartile (Upper Quartile) is the value below which there are three fourth of the items and above which there are one fourth of the items.

The quartile values are located on the same principle as is followed in case of locating the median value. Following is the procedure to be followed in determining the sizes:

Measure	Individual and Discrete Series	Continuous Series
Q_1	$\frac{n+1}{4}$ th item	$\frac{n}{4}$ th item
Q_2	$\frac{2(n+1)}{4}$ th or $\frac{n+1}{2}$ th item	$\frac{2n}{4}$ th or $\frac{n}{2}$ th item
Q_3	$\frac{3(n+1)}{4}$ th item	$\frac{3n}{4}$ th item

Example 9.12. *Find the quartiles from the following values,*

19, 27, 24, 39, 57, 44, 56, 50, 59, 67
62, 42, 47, 60, 26, 34, 57, 51, 59, 45

Solution : Let us arrange the data in an array form.

	S.No.		x		S.No.		x
	1	...	19		11	...	50
	2	...	24		12	...	51
	3	...	26		13	...	56
	4	...	27		14	...	57
(Q_1) →	5	...	34	(Q_3) →	15	...	57
	6	...	39		16	...	59
	7	...	42		17	...	59
	8	...	44		18	...	60
	9	...	45		19	...	62
Me →	10	...	47		20	...	67
	Here n =		20				

Q_1 is the size of $\frac{n+1}{4}$ th item.

$\therefore \quad \frac{20+1}{2}$ th = 5.25th item.

5.25th item lies between 5th and 6th ... i.e. 34 and 39

Q_1 = 5th item + 0.25 of the difference between the two values.

$= 34 + 0.25(39 - 34) = 34 + 0.25(5)$
$= 34 + 1.25 = \mathbf{35.25}$

Q_2 or Median is the size of $\frac{n+1}{2}$ th item.

$\therefore \frac{20+1}{2}$ th = 10.5th item.

10.5th item lies between 10 and 11 ... i.e. 47 and 50

Me = 10th item + 0.5 of the Difference between the two values.

= 47 + 0.5 (50 - 47) = 47 + 0.5 (3) = 47 + 1.5 = **48.5**

Q_3 is the size of $\frac{3(n+1)}{4}$ th item

$\frac{3(20+1)}{4}$ th = 15.75th item

15.75th item lies between 15 and 16 ... i.e. 57 and 59

Q_3 = 15th item + 0.75 of the Difference between the two values.

= 57 + 0.75(59 - 57) = 57 + 0.75(2) = 57 + 1.50 = **58.50**

Example 9.13. *From the following marks find Q_1, Median and Q_3 marks,*

23, 48, 34, 68, 15, 36, 24, 54, 65, 75
92, 10, 70, 61, 20, 47, 83, 19, 77

Solution : Let us arrange the data in an array form.

	S.No.		x	
	1	...	10	
	2	...	15	
	3	...	19	
	4	...	20	
Q_1 →	5	...	23	← Q_1
	6	...	24	
	7	...	34	
	8	...	36	
	9	...	47	
Me →	10	...	48	← Me
	11	...	54	
	12	...	61	
	13	...	65	
	14	...	68	
Q_3 →	15	...	70	← Q_3
	16	...	75	
	17	...	77	
	18	...	83	
	19	...	92	
Here			n = 19	

Q_1 is the size of $\frac{n+1}{4}$ th item.

$\therefore \frac{19+1}{4}$ th = 5th item

5th item is 23 Q_1 = **23**

Me is the size of $\frac{n+1}{2}$ th item

$\frac{19+1}{2}$ th = 10th item

10th item is 48 Me = **48**

Q_3 is the size of $\frac{3(n+1)}{4}$ th item

$\frac{3(19+1)}{4}$ th = 15 th item.

15th item is **70** Q_1 = **70**

Example 9.14. *Locate Median and Quartiles from the following data.* (BU - N84)

Sizes of shoes :	4.0	4.5	5.0	5.5	6.0	6.5	7.0	7.5	8.0
Frequencies :	20	36	44	50	80	30	30	16	14

Solution : Let us prepare the table showing cumulative frequencies for locating he partitioned values.

	X	f	c.f	
	4.0	20	20	
	4.5	36	56	
Q_1 →	5.0	44	100	← Q_1
	5.5	50	150	
Me →	6.0	80	230	← Me
Q_3 →	6.5	30	260	← Q_3
	7.0	30	290	
	7.5	16	306	
	8.0	14	320	
		n = 320		

Q_1 is the the size of $\frac{n+1}{4}$ th item

$\therefore \frac{320+1}{4}$ th 80.25th

80.25th item lies in 100 c.f..

Against 100 c.f. the value is 5.0

Q_1 = **5.0**

Me is the size of $\frac{n+1}{2}$ th item.

$\therefore \frac{320+1}{2}$ th = 160.50 th item

160.50 th item lies in 230 c.f.. Against 230 c.f. the value is 6. Q_2 or Me = **6.0**

Q_3 is the size of $\frac{3(n+1)}{4}$ th item.

$\therefore \quad \frac{3(320+1)}{4}$ th = 240.75th

240.75 th item lies in 260 c.f.. Against 260 c.f. the value is 6.5. Q_3 = **6.5**

Example 9.15. *Compute the quartiles from the following data:*

C.I	0-10	10-20	20-30	30-40	40-50	50-60	60-70	70-80
f	5	8	7	12	28	20	10	10

Solution:

	C.I.	f	c.f
	0-10	5	5
	10-20	8	13
	20-30	7	20 $(m)_1$
$(l)_1$	30-40	12 $(f)_1$	32 $(m)_2$
$(l)_2$	40-50	28 $(f)_2$	60 $(m)_3$
$(l)_3$	50-60	20 $(f)_3$	80
	60-70	10	90
	70-80	10	100
		n = 100	

Q_1 is the size of $\frac{n}{4}$ th item. $\quad \therefore \quad \frac{100}{4}$ th = 25 th item.

25th item lies in 32 c.f..

Against 32 c.f. the class interval is (30-40).

$$Q_1 = l + \frac{\frac{n}{4} - m}{f} \times c = 30 + \frac{\frac{100}{4} - 20}{12} \times 10$$

$$= 30 + \frac{25 - 20}{12} \times 10 = 30 + \frac{5}{12} \times 10$$

$$= 30 + \frac{50}{12} = 30 + 4.1667 = \mathbf{34.1667}$$

Q_2 or Me is the size of $\frac{n}{2}$ th item. $\therefore$ $\frac{100}{2}$ th = 50 th item.

50th item lies in 60 c.f..

Against 60 c.f. the class interval is (40-50).

$$Me = l + \frac{\frac{n}{2} - m}{f} \times c = 40 + \frac{\frac{100}{2} - 32}{28} \times 10$$

$$= 40 + \frac{50 - 32}{28} \times 10 = 40 + \frac{18}{28} \times 10$$

$$= 40 + \frac{180}{28} = 40 + 6.4286 = \mathbf{46.4286}$$

Q_3 or Me is the size of $\frac{3n}{4}$ th item. $\therefore$ $\frac{3(100)}{4}$ th = 75 th item.

75th item lies in 80 c.f..

Against 80 c.f. the class interval is (50-60).

$$Q_3 = l + \frac{\frac{3n}{4} - m}{f} \times c = 50 + \frac{\frac{3(100)}{4} - 60}{20} \times 10$$

$$= 50 + \frac{75 - 60}{20} \times 10 = 50 + \frac{15}{20} \times 10$$

$$= 50 + \frac{150}{20} = 50 + 7.5 = \mathbf{57.5}$$

B. Deciles

The deciles divide the arrayed set of variates into ten portions of equal frequency, and they are some times used to characterise the data for some specific purpose. In this process, we get nine decile values. The fifth decile is nothing but a median value. We can calculate other deciles by following the procedure which is used in computing the quartiles.

In case of individual observations and discrete series, the size can be determined by using the $\frac{n+1}{10}$ th item for D_1, $\frac{2(n+1)}{10}$ th item for D_2 and so on. In case of continuous series we have to use the different procedure. For example,

$$D_4 = l + \frac{\frac{4n}{10} - m}{f} \times c \text{.........} D_7 = l + \frac{\frac{7n}{100} - m}{f} \times c$$

C. Percentiles

The percentiles divide the arrayed set of variates into hundred portions of equal frequency, and they are some times used to decide the educational and psychological problems. In this process, we get ninety-nine percentile values. The 25th, 50th and 75th percentiles are nothing but quartile first, median and quartile third values respectively. We can calculate other percentiles by following the procedure which is used to compute the quartiles.

In case of individual observations and discrete series, the size can be determined by using the $\frac{n+1}{100}$th item for P_1, $\frac{34(n+1)}{100}$th item for P_{34} and so on. In case of continuous series we have to use different procedure.

For example,

$$P_{58} = l + \frac{\frac{58n}{100} - m}{f} \times c \text{ .... } P_{63} = l + \frac{\frac{63n}{100} - m}{f} \times c$$

III. Mode

It is the value which occurs with the maximum frequency. It is the most typical or common value that receives the highest frequency. It represents fashion and often it is used in business. Thus, it corresponds to the value of the variable which occurs most frequently. The modal class of a frequency distribution is the class with the highest frequency. It is denoted by a symbol 'Z'.

Mode is the value of variable which is repeated the greatest number of times in the series. It is the usual, and not casual, size of item in a series. It lies at the position of greatest density. If we say that modal marks obtained by students in a class are 40, we mean that the largest number of students have secured 40 marks. It means around 40 the number of students tend to be heavily concentrated. When we talk of 'most common wage', 'most common height' or 'most common marks', we have in our mind `Modal Value'. When a doctor makes a statement that the usual duration of cold-fever getting cured is one week, he means that it is the modal duration.

If each observation occurs the same number of times, we can say that there is *'no mode'*. If two observations occur the same number of times, we can say that it is a *'Bi-modal'* case. If three or more observations occur the same number of times, we can say that it is a *'Multi-modal'* case. When there is a single observation which occurs the most number of times, we can say that it is the case of a *'Uni-modal'*.

A. Determination of Mode

When a distribution is **'unimodal'**, it is very easy to locate the mode. Sometimes it is probable that there may be number of irregularities in the distribution and it would become difficult to determine the mode. In such cases frequencies are adjusted by the process of *'grouping'* i.e. by widening the groups into which the frequencies fall until a modal size of item or a modal group presents itself.

(i) Individual Observations :- The modal value is determined just by inspection. Generally an array helps to identify and count the values quickly. For example,

Case I :- Following are the values of variable,

54, 66, 42, 64, 44, 86, 104, 94, 100, 80
72, 64, 64, 44, 64, 72, 54, 48, 52, 50

The mode is '**64**' as it occurs the highest number of times (i.e. 4 times) in the series. So the mode is clearly defined and it is a `Uni-modal' case.

Case II :- Following are the values of variable.

122, 234, 638, 410, 512, 270, 900, 175
365, 195, 283, 234, 175, 115, 310, 208
175, 410, 638, 195, 512, 234, 600, 415

There are two modes i.e. **175** and **234** each occurring three times. So the mode is not clearly defined. It is a *'Bi-modal'* case.

When the number of items increase, we may convert the data into a discrete form. Then, the value having the maximum frequency will be treated as the mode.

(ii) Discrete Series :- The modal value can be determined just by 'inspection' of the the frequency column. It is that value which occurs with the maximum frequency. If there is regularity and homogencity in the series, the mode can be located easily by inspection.

If there is no regularity and no homogencity in the frequency distribution, the location of mode will be a difficult task. Then, a grouping process can be resorted to identify the modal value, or class.

Grouping :- Under this process, the frequencies are adjusted by widening the groups into which they fall until a modal size of item or a group presents itself.

Treat the frequency column as the first column and mark the highest frequency (or frequencies of same number). In the second column, referring the first column, add the 1st and 2nd frequencies, 3rd and 4th frequencies and so on, and record the frequencies. In the third column, referring the first column once again, add the 2nd and 3rd frequencies, 4th and 5th frequencies and so on, and record the frequencies. In the fourth column, referring the first column again, add 1st, 2nd and 3rd frequencies, 4th, 5th and 6th frequencies and so on, and record the frequencies, This process is followed, till the 6th column is obtained. Finally, we can set up an **'analysis table'** to know the frequencies that affect the highest total in each column. This analysis table helps us to identify the modal value affected by the highest concentration of frequencies.

Case I :- *Following are the distributions.*

A. Series			B. Series			C. Series		
x	f		x	f		x	f	
1	... 2	Highest Frequency is 18 ∴ z = 4	10 ...	50	Highest Frequency is 180 ∴ z = 20	8 ...	2	Concentrat - ion of frequency is around 19 ∴ z = 32
2	... 8		15 ...	95		16 ...	4	
3	... 11		z → 20 ...	180 ←		24 ...	20	
z → 4	... 18 ←		25 ...	63		z → 32 ...	19 ←	
5	... 9		30 ...	24		40 ...	10	
6	... 7		35 ...	5		48 ...	5	

Case II :- *Following are the distributions.*

A. Series.

x	f
2	6
4	8
6	16_1
z → 8	16_2 ←
10	12
12	6

Concentration is around the frequency 16_2 but not 16_1 considering the neighbouring frequencies of each one, the totals are arrived as under,

8 + (16) + 16 = 40 ... 16 + (16) + 12 = 44.

Around 16_2, we find the concentration more and the mode is 8 (but not 6).

B. Series.

x	f
4	18
8	22
12	19
16	4
20	7
24	20
28	22
32	17
36	8

In this series there are two highest frequencies having the concentration also in the same degree (i.e. 18 + (22) + 19 = 59 and 20 + (22) + 17 = 59). There is no apparent mode clearly revealed by the frequency distribution. So it is necessary to adopt the grouping procedure.

Grouping Table

x		f_1	f_2	f_3	f_4	f_5	f_6
4	...	18					
			(40)				
8	...	(22)			(59)		
				41			
12	...	19				45	
			23				
16	...	4					30
				11			
20	...	7			31		
			27				
24	...	20				(49)	
				(42)			
28	...	(22)					(59)
			39				
32	...	17			47		
				25			
36	...	8					

Analysis Table

Column Number	Values of Variable.								
	4	8	12	16	20	24 →	28 ←	32	36.
f_1		1					1		
f_2	1	1							
f_3						1	1		
f_4	1	1	1						
f_5					1	1	1		
f_6						1	1	1	
Total	2	3	1		1	3 →	4 ←	1	

From the above tables, it is clear that the mode is **28** as it participating four times in the highest frequency in he grouping procedure. Here, we can say that the mode is clearly defined only after grouping the frequencies.

(iii) Continuous Series :- Under the continuous series, the modal class is located with the help of highest frequencies or grouping or inspection (maximum concentration of frequencies). The same procedure is adopted as it is followed in case of discrete series. After locating the modal class, we have to interpolate the value of the mode within the modal class by using the following formulas:

1. ***General Formula*** is used, when the distribution is normal. (i.e. Mode against the highest frequency)

(a) $z = l + \dfrac{f_1 - f_0}{2f_1 - f_0 - f_2} \times c$ or $z = l + \dfrac{(f_1 - f_0)}{(f_1 - f_0) - (f_2 - f_1)} \times c$

l = lower limit of the modal class interval.

f_0 = frequency of the class interval preceding the modal class interval.

f_1 = frequency of the modal class interval.

f_2 = frequency of the class interval succeeding the modal class interval.

c = magnitude of the modal class interval.

Sometimes, due to the concentration of frequencies, we may find f_1 is less than f_0 or f_2. Then the above general formula gives us negative results. So we can put the above formula for all the purposes as under,

(b) $z = l + \frac{\Delta_1}{\Delta_1 + \Delta_2} \times c$ Δ_1 = Difference between f_1 and f_0

Δ_2 = Difference between f_1 and f_2

Case I :-

$f_0 = 260$

$f_1 = 240$ (Note : Negative sign is neglected)

$f_2 = 252$

$$z = l + \frac{\Delta_1}{\Delta_1 + \Delta_2} \times c = l + \frac{20}{20 + 12} \times c$$

[The formula is applicable even when $2f_1 = f_0 + f_2$]

This formula is preferably used safely to avoid the negativ answers. It is giving the same result as is given by the 1(c above.

2. If the difference between the neighbouring frequencies (and f_0) and the modal frequency is not relatively very larg the following formula is preferably used,

Case II:- $f_0 = 740$ (750-740 = 10) and (750 - 745 = 5)

$f_1 = 750$ relatively the small difference

$f_2 = 745$

$$z = l + \frac{f_2}{f_2 + f_0} \times c = l + \frac{745}{745 + 740} \times c$$

3. When $f_0 = f_2$, we should simply take the mid-point of t modal class interval as the Mode (i.e. Mean of the Low and Upper Limits).

Case III :- $f_0 = 155$

$f_1 = 198$ $z = \frac{\text{Upper limit + Lower limit}}{2}$

$f_2 = 155$

Thus, the above formulas help us in determining the mc under different circumstances. However, **1(b)** formula, preferably used in most of the cases.

Example 9.16. *Calculate the Arithmetic Mean and Mode fr the following data:*

Central value	:	1	2	3	4	5	6	7
Frequency	:	7	11	31	17	16	5	2

Solution: (BU - N94)

	x	f	fx
	1	7	7
	2	11	22
z	3	31 ←	93
	4	17	68
	5	16	80
	6	5	30
	7	2	14
		n = 89	Σfx = 314

$$\bar{x} = \frac{\Sigma fx}{n} = \frac{314}{89} = \mathbf{3.5281}$$

Highest frequency is 31.

So the mode is 3 z = **3**

Example 9.17. Twenty per cent of the workers in a firm employing a total of 2000 workers earn less than Rs.2.00 per hour, 440 earn from Rs.2.00 to Rs.2.24 per hour, 24% earn from Rs.2.25 to Rs.2.49 per hour, 370 earn from Rs.2.50 to Rs.2.74 per hour, 12% earn from Rs.2.75 to Rs.2.99 per hour and rest Rs.3.00 or more per hour. Set up a frequency table and calculate modal wage. (BU - N89)

Solution : Let us prepare the table adjusting the class intervals and frequencies.

Wages per hour (Rs.)	No. of workers	C.I	F	
Less than 2.00	20%	Less than 1.995	400	
2.00 – 2.24	440	1.995 – 2.245	440	
2.25 – 2.49	24%	2.245 – 2.495	480	f_0
2.50 – 2.74	370	2.495 – 2.745	370	f_1
2.75 – 2.99	12%	2.745 – 2.995	240	f_2
3.00 and above	Rest	2.995 and above	30	
	n = 2,000		n = 2000	

$$z = l + \frac{\Delta_1}{\Delta_1 + \Delta_2} \times c = 2.245 + \frac{(480 - 440)}{(480 - 440) + (480 - 370)} \times 0.25$$

$$= 2.245 + \frac{40}{40 + 110} \times 0.25 = 2.245 + \frac{10}{150} = 2.245 + 0.0667 = \mathbf{2.3117}$$

Example 9.18 From the following data compute the mean and mode marks of all the students of 50 schools in a city:

Marks obtained	35 and above	30–35	25 – 30	20 – 25	15 – 20	Less than 15
No. of schools	7	10	15	9	5	4
Average No. of students in a school	200	250	300	200	150	100

(BU · A89)

Solution: Let us rearrange the data in order and obtain the frequencies.

Marks C.I	No. of schools	Avg. students	No. of students (f)		C.I.	x	fx
Less than 15	4	100	400		10-15	12.5	5,000
15-20	5	150	750		15-20	17.5	13,125
20-25	9	200	1800	f_0	20-25	22.5	40,500
25-30	15	300	4500	f_1	25-30	27.5	1,23,750
30-35	10	250	2500	f_2	30-35	32.5	81,250
35 and above	7	200	1400		35-40	37.5	52,500
			n=11,350				Σfx = 3,16,125

$$\bar{x} = \frac{\Sigma fx}{n} = \frac{3,16,125}{11,350} = 27.8524 = \mathbf{27.85} \text{ marks}$$

$$z = l + \frac{(f_1 - f_0)}{(f_1 - f_0) + (f_1 - f_2)} \times c$$

$$= 25 + \frac{(4500 - 1800)}{(4500 - 1800) + (4500 - 2500)} \times c$$

$$= 25 + \frac{2700}{2770 + 2000} \times 5 = 25 + \frac{13,500}{4700} = 25 + 2.87234$$

$= \mathbf{27.87}$ marks

Example 9.19. *Calculate mode from the following data:*

Value	: 0-4	5-9	10-19	20-29	30-39	40-49	50-59	60-69
Frequency	: 328	350	720	664	598	524	378	244

Solution: The class intervals in the distribution are unequal. The class intervals for the three frequencies f_0, f_1 and f_2 - must be same. (* two classes are joined)

C.I.	f
0- 9 *	678 f_2
10-19	720 f_1
20-29	664 f_3
30-39	598
40-49	524
50-59	378
60-69	244

The real boundaries of classes are 0-9.5, 9.5 - 19.5, 19:5- 29.5 and so on.

$$z = 9.5 + \frac{(720-678)}{(720-678)+(720-664)} \times 10$$

$$= 9.5 + \frac{42}{42+56} \times 10 = 9.5 + \frac{420}{98}$$

$$= 9.5 + 4.2857 = \mathbf{13.7857}$$

Example 9.20 : Find the Mode and Median from the following :

No. of days Absent	No. of Students	No. of days Absent	No. of Students
Less than 5	29	Less than 30	644
Less than 10	224	Less than 35	650
Less than 15	465	Less than 40	653
Less than 20	582	Less than 45	655
Less than 25	634		

Solution : The cumulative frequencies are to be converted into frequencies by obtaining class intervals.

(BU-A98)

C.I.	No. of Students (f)	c.f.
0 – 5	29	29
5 – 10	195	224 (m)
(l) 10 – 15	241 (f)	465
15 – 20	117	582
20 – 25	52	634
25 – 30	10	644
30 – 35	6	650
35 – 40	3	653
40 – 45	2	655
	n=655	

$$\begin{bmatrix} f_0 = 195 \\ f_1 = 241 \\ f_2 = 117 \end{bmatrix}$$

(a) Median Value :

Median is the size of the $\frac{n}{2}$ th item.

It lies in 465 c.f..

Against 465 c.f. the Median Class is (10 – 15)

$$Me = l + \frac{\frac{n}{2} - m}{f} \times c = 10 + \frac{327.50 - 224}{241} \times 5 = 10 + \frac{103.50}{241} \times 5$$

$$= 10 + \frac{517.50}{241} = 10 + 2.14731 = \mathbf{12.14731}$$

(b) Modal Value :

Mode is clearly defined. Highest frequency is 241 and the Modal Class is (10 – 15).

$$Z = l + \frac{(f_1 - f_0)}{(f_1 - f_0) + (f_1 - f_2)} \times c = 10 + \frac{(241 - 195)}{(241 - 195) + (241 - 117)} \times 5$$

$$= 10 + \frac{46}{(46) + (124)} \times 5 = 10 + \frac{230}{170} = 10 + 1.35294 = \mathbf{11.3529}$$

B. Ill - defined Mode

When there are two items having the same maximum frequency, we call it a **'bi-modal distribution'**. When there are more than two items having, the same maximum frequency, we call it a **'multi-modal distribution'**. In all these distributions the mode is ill defined. The following distribution does not have a mode clearly defined:

Size of item	Frequencies f_1	Grouping f_2	f_3	f_4	f_5	f_6
40- 49	7					
		16				
50- 59	9			26		
			19			
60- 69	10				25	
		16				
70- 79	6					29
			19			
80- 89	(13)			(29)		
		(23)				
90- 99	10				(36)	
			(23)			
100-109	(13)					(33)
		(23)				
110-119	10					

Analysis Table

Column No.	60-69	70-79	80-89	90-99	100-109	110-119
1			1		1	
2			1	1	1	1
3			1	1	1	
4		1	1	1		
5			1	1	1	
6				1	1	1
Total		1	5	5	5	5

From the above Grouping and Analysis process, we can conclude that the distribution is having mode ill-defined. Hence, mode is determined with the help of Mean and Median.

In fact, there is no relationship at all among the three averages $\bar{x}$, **Me** and **Z**. However, in an ideally and positively skewed distribution, a particular degree of empirical relationship can be established among the averages.

Empirical Relationship Among the Averages:

When mode is ill-defined, it is difficult to find the value of mode. In an ideally and positively skewed distribution, a sort of empirical relationship among the averages can be established. Let us study the three different types of distributions graphically as under :

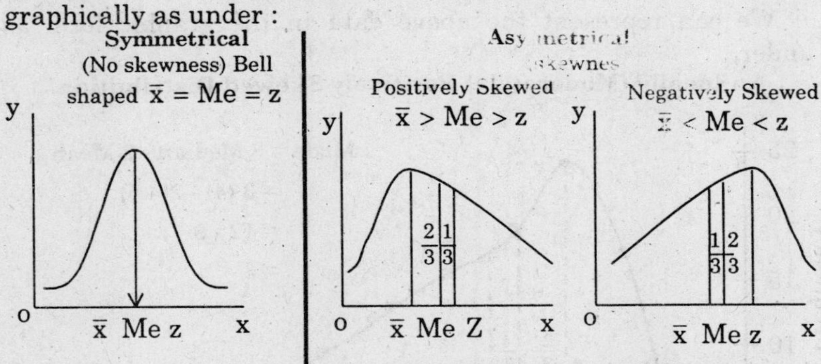

(Such variable is rarely found)

(Such variable is generally found)

The above graphical study reveals that in an ideally or moderately and positively skewed distribution, the Median lies between the Mode and the Mean. The Mode departs (to the left) two - third distance from the Median, and the Mean departs (to the right) one third distance from the Median. This tendency gives rise to an `**empirical formula**' as under,

z = 3Me – 2$\overline{\mathbf{x}}$ (Based on Positive Skewness)

The above empirical relationship can be explained with the help of the following example :

x	:	1	2	3	4	5	6	7	8	9
f	:	2	15	23	16	14	10	9	7	4 = 100

Solution: we can prove that $\overline{x}$ > Me > z

	x	f	fx	c.f
	1	2	2	2
	2	15	30	17
z	3 ←	23 ←	69	40
Me	4 ←	16 ←	64 ←	56 ←
	5	14	70	70
	6	10	60	80
	7	9	63	89
	8	7	56	96
	9	4	36	100
	n =	100	=450 Σfx	

(1) $\overline{x} = \frac{\Sigma fx}{n} = \frac{450}{100} = \mathbf{4.5}$

(2) Median is the size of $\frac{n+1}{2}$ th item.

$\therefore \quad \frac{100+1}{2}$ th = 50.5th item.

It lies in 56 c.f..

Against 56 c.f. Median = **4**

(3) The highest frequency is 23.

Against 23 frequency, the Mode is 3

So $\quad \overline{x}$ = **4.5**, Me = **4**, and Z = **3**

We can represent the above data in the graphic form as under,

An Ideally (Moderately) Positively Skewed Distribution.

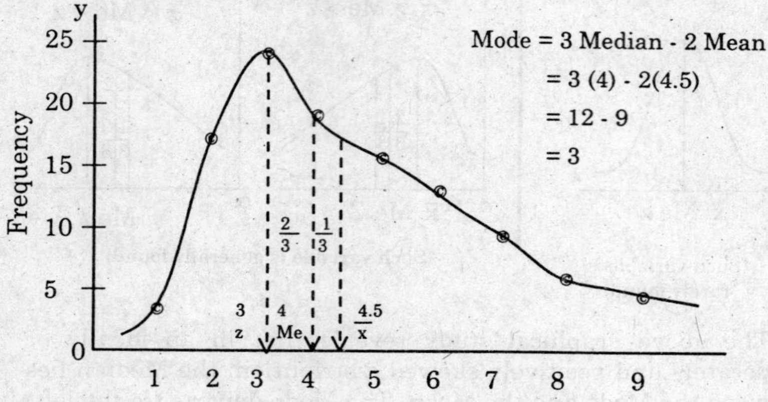

Thus, in an ideally (moderately) positively skewed distribution, $\bar{x}$ lies on one end and **z** on the other. In between the $\bar{x}$ and **z**, the **Me** lies. $\bar{x}$ lies one-third distance right of the **Me** and **z** lies two-third distance left of the **Me**. On the basis of this relationship among the averages, we can have the "Empireical Relationship Formula" ... **Mode = 3 Median -2 Mean**. This empirical relationship is founded by **Prof. Karl Pearson**. It is useful to find any one of the three averages, when two among them are given. From this formula, we can have the other equations as under:

Basic formula ..... $z = 3Me - 2\bar{x}$

We can prove the following equations by simplifying the basic formula

(1) $\bar{x} = \frac{1}{2}(3Me - z)$

$$z = 3Me - 2\bar{x}$$
$$2\bar{x} = 3Me - z$$
$$\bar{x} = \frac{1}{2}(3Me - z)$$

(2) $Me = \frac{2}{3}(\bar{x} - z) + z$

$$z = 3Me - 2\bar{x}$$
$$3Me = 2\bar{x} + z$$
$$Me = \frac{1}{3}(2\bar{x} + z)$$
$$Me = \frac{2}{3}\bar{x} + \frac{1}{3}z$$
$$Me = \frac{2}{3}\bar{x} - \frac{2}{3}z + z$$
$$Me = \frac{2}{3}(\bar{x} - z) + z$$

(3) $\bar{x} - z = 3(\bar{x} - Me)$

$$z = 3Me - 2\bar{x}$$
$$z = 3Me - 3\bar{x} + \bar{x}$$
$$-z = -3Me + 3\bar{x} - \bar{x}$$
$$\bar{x} - z = 3(\bar{x} - Me)$$

(4) $\bar{x} - Me = \frac{1}{3}(\bar{x} - z)$

$$z = 3Me - 2\bar{x}$$
$$3Me - 2\bar{x} = z$$
$$3Me - 3\bar{x} + \bar{x} = z$$
$$\bar{x} - z = 3\bar{x} - 3Me$$
$$\bar{x} - z = 3(\bar{x} - Me)$$
$$3(\bar{x} - Me) = \bar{x} - z$$

(5) $\bar{x} - Me = \frac{1}{2}(Me - z)$

$$z = 3Me - 2\bar{x}$$
$$2\bar{x} = 3Me - z$$
$$\bar{x} = \frac{1}{2}(3Me - z)$$
$$\bar{x} = \frac{3}{2}Me - \frac{1}{2}z$$
$$\bar{x} = \frac{1}{2}Me + Me - \frac{1}{2}z$$
$$\bar{x} = \frac{1}{2}Me - \frac{1}{2}z + Me$$
$$\bar{x} - Me = \frac{1}{2}Me - \frac{1}{2}z$$
$$\bar{x} - Me = \frac{1}{2}(Me - z)$$

Example 9.21. *From the following two averages given, find the third average :*

(a) z = 50 and Me = 45, $\bar{x}$ = ? ... (BU-N85)

(b) $\bar{x}$ = 20.2 and Me = 22.1, z = ? ... (BU-A96)

(c) Me = 42 and z = 40, x = ? ... (BU-N96)

(d) z = 500 and $\bar{x}$ = 450, Me = ? ... (BU-N97)

(e) $\bar{x}$ = 20 and Me = 22, z = ? ... (BU-A98)

Solution :

(a) $\mathbf{z = 3Me - 2\bar{x}}$

$50 = 3(45) - 2\bar{x}$

$50 = 135 - 2\bar{x}$

$2\bar{x} = 135 - 50$

$2\bar{x} = 85$

$\bar{x} = \mathbf{42.5}$

(b) $\mathbf{z = 3M - 2\bar{x}}$

$z = 3(22.1) - 2(20.2)$

$z = 66.3 - 40.4$

$z = \mathbf{25.9}$

(c) $\mathbf{z = 3Me - 2\bar{x}}$

$40 = 3(42) - 2\bar{x}$

$40 = 126 - 2\bar{x}$

$2\bar{x} = 126 - 40$

$2\bar{x} = 86$

$\bar{x} = \mathbf{43}$

(d) $\mathbf{z = 3Me - 2\bar{x}}$

$500 = 3Me - 2(450)$

$3M = 500 + 900$

$3M = 1400$

$M = \frac{1400}{3} = \mathbf{466.67}$

(e) $\mathbf{z = 3M - 2\bar{x}}$

$z = 3(22) - 2(20)$

$z = 66 - 40$

$z = \mathbf{26}$

Example 9.22. *From the following monthly incomes of 8 families, find* $\bar{x}$ *, Me and Z.*

Families	: A	B	C	D	E	F	G	H
Incomes(Rs.)	: 70	10	500	75	08	250	08	42

(BU - A88)

Solution: Let us arrange the values in order.

Sl. No	x
1	08
2	08
3	10
4	42
5	70
6	75
7	250
8	500
	$\Sigma fx = 963$

Median is the size of $\frac{n+1}{2}$ th item.

$\therefore \frac{8+1}{2}$ th = 4.5th.

It lies in between 42 and 70.

$$Me = \frac{42+70}{2} = \frac{112}{2} = \mathbf{56}$$

z is having the highest frequency.

$\therefore$ Value 8 only occurs two times. $\therefore$ Z = 8

$$\bar{x} = \frac{\Sigma x}{n} = \frac{963}{8} = \mathbf{120.375}$$

$$\bar{x} = 120.375 > Me = 56 > z = 8$$

C. Locating Mode by Curve Fitting

The various formulas for computing mode are applicable when there are class intervals of equal magnitude. However, the process of grouping, in case of ill-defined mode, is not quite justified always. To have the ideal method of calculating the mode is to have the curve fitting. The curve fitting process arises only in case of continuous series. The values of variable are represented in a graph. The peak of the curve signifies the modal value on the **`ox'**- axis.

Example 9.23. *Fit the curve and locate the mode from the following data:*

C.I.	:	0-10	10-20	20-30	20-40	40-50	50-60	60-70
Frequencies	:	5	30	90	180	250	260	130

Solution : Let us use the formula first to compute the mode. The concentration of frequencies is found to be in the class interval 40-50 but not in 50-60 (though the highest frequency is 260)

$$z = l + \frac{(f_1 - f_0)}{(f_1 - f_0) + (f_1 - f_2)} \times c \qquad \text{(Diff. only)}$$

$f_0 = 180$

$f_1 = 250$

$f = 260$

$$= 40 + \frac{70}{70+10} \times 10 = 40 + \frac{700}{80}$$

Let us have the data in a curve fitting process as under

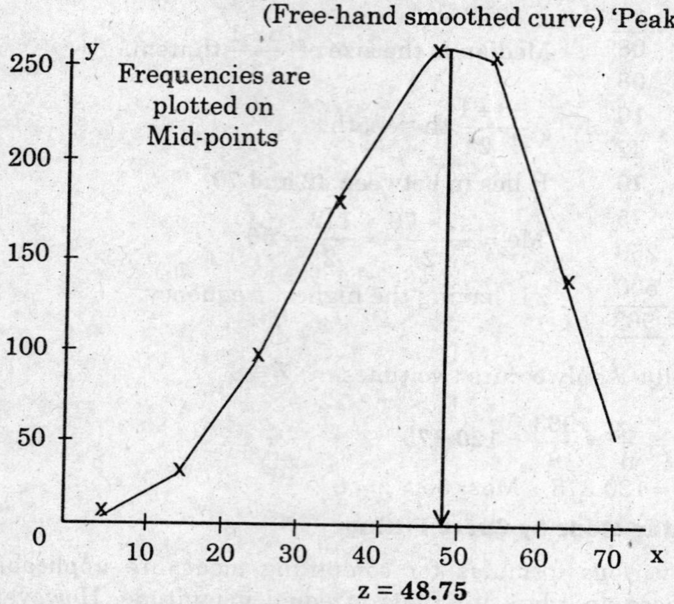

D. Locating Mode By Histogram.

One more graphic method of locating mode from the continuous series is the **"Histogram"**. Prepare the histogram by erecting the rectangles on 'OX'- axis. Join the top of the corner of the rectangle of the modal class with the top of the right corner of the rectangle of the pre-modal class. Then the same procedure is adopted in an opposite direction drawing the cross line. From the point, at two cross lines, draw a perpendicular line on the 'OX'- axis. The meeting point of the line on the 'OX'- axis gives us the Mode.

Example 9.24 *Draw a histogram from the following and locate the mode:*

C.I:	0-10	10-20	20-30	30-40	40-50	50-60
f :	14	23	35	20	8	5

Solution : Let us prepare the Histogram as under.

Histogram Showing Mode

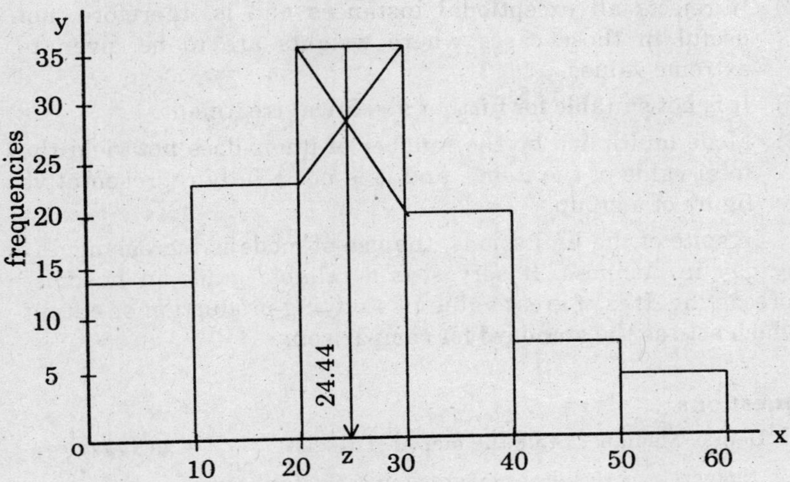

Applying the formula for mode we get the modal value same as under :

$$z = l + \frac{(f_1 - f_0)}{(f_1 - f_0) + (f_1 - f_2)} \times c = 20 + \frac{(35 - 23)}{(35 - 23) + (35 - 20)} \times 10$$

$$= 20 + \frac{12}{12 + 15} \times 10 = 20 + \frac{120}{27} = \mathbf{24.444}$$

Merits of Mode : The concept of mode is readily intelligible, and is applied in many cases in daily routine. Following are the advantages of mode:

1) It is easily understood and has a general and precise usage.
2) It eliminates extreme values of variables and it is not affected by stray items.
3) It is concerned with only the highest frequency and not other items.
4) It can be located by mere inspection in most of the cases.

Demerits of Mode: The mode suffers from the following limitations:

1) It is frequently ill-defined and indefinite.
2) It is often indeterminate and, therefore, difficult to locate.

3) It is incapable of being located by any simple arithmetic process.
4) It rejects all exceptional instances and is, therefore, not useful in those cases where weights are to be given to extreme values.
5) It is not suitable for further algebrical treatment.
6) Mode multiplied by the number of items does not yield the total value of the items, and it is not a fully representative figure of a group.

In spite of the limitations, the use of mode is increasing day by day in business. It serves as a reliable guide in business forecasting. It is of great value in studying production or output which acts as the standard for comparison.

Questions

1. Define `Median' ? State the merits of Median. (BU – A84, A98)
2. Suggest a more suitable average in each of the following cases:
   (a) Average intelligence of students in a class, and
   (b) Average change in the cost of living of workers. (BU - A85)
   (c) Average rate of increase in sales, and
   (d) Average size of slippers sold in a chappal shop. (BU - N85)
3. State the empirical relationship among the Mean, Median and Mode. (BU - A87, A88, N90, N92)
3. State the nature of a symmetry in the following cases:
   (i) when median is greater than mean, and
   (ii) when mean is greater than median. (BU- A89)
4. Suggest with reasons a suitable average to study the following :
   (i) Rate of growth of population.
   (ii) Production efficiency of workers. (BU-A89)
5. Suggest a more suitable average in each of the following cases:
   (i) Average size of ready-made garments, and
   (ii) Average speed of the train. (BU-N91)
7. Mention the demerits of Median. (BU-N93)
8. Make any four demerits of Mode. (BU-A94)
9. The following table gives the monthly incomes of twelve families in a town:

S.No.	: 1	2	3	4	5	6	7	8	9	10	11	12
Monthly Income (Rs.)	: 280	180	96	98	104	75	80	94	100	75	600	200

Calculate the arithmetic mean, the median and the mode of the above incomes. ($\bar{x}$ = 165.2, Me = 99, z = 75)

10. The marks obtained by 15 students in a class test are given below:

6, 9, 10, 12, 18, 19, 23, 23, 24, 28, 37, 48, 49, 53 and 60

Find $\bar{x}$, Me, z, Q_1 and Q_3.

($\bar{x}$, = 27.93, Me = 23, z =23, Q_1 = 12 and Q_3 = 48)

11. In a moderately skewed distribution $\bar{x}$ = 24.6 and z= 26.1, Find the Median. (Me = 25.1)

12. Compute the mode of the following distribution:

Size	: 0-5	5-10	10-15	15-20	20-25	25-30	30-35
Frequency	: 24	32	28	16	37	10	8

(z = 13.3)

13. The number of telephone calls received in 245 successive one minute intervals at an exchange are shown below:

No. of calls :	0	1	2	3	4	5	6	7	
Frequency :	14	21	25	43	51	40	39	12	= 245

Calculate $\bar{x}$, Me and Z. ($\bar{x}$ = 3.76, Me = 4 and Z = 4)

14. Find out the missing figures:

Mean = ? (3 Median - Mode) (1/2)

Mean - Mode = ? (Mean - Mode) (3)

Median = Mode + ? (Mean-Mode) (2/3)

Mode = Mean - ? (Mean- Median) (3)

15. From the following values of variable, find Me, Q_1, Q_3, D_4, D_7, P_{23} and P_{82}.

3, 7, 12, 15, 25, 37, 48, 52, 69, 70, 73, 80, 82, 88, 92

(Me = 52, Q_1 = 15, Q_3 = 80, D_4 = 41.4, D_7 = 74.4 P_{23}= 14.04 and P_{82} = 82.72)

16. Calculate the Median, the Mode, the two Quartiles and the Mean from the following data:

Age	: 20-25	25-30	30-35	35-40	40-45	45-50	50-55	55-60
No. of Persons	: 100	140	200	360	300	240	140	120

(Me = 40, z = 38.64, Q1 = 34, Q_3 = 47.8 and $\bar{x}$ = 40.31)

17. Find the missing frequency from the following distribution of sales of shops, given that the median sales of shops is Rs.2400.

Sales (in`100' Rs.)	:	0-10	10-20	20-30	30-40	40-50
No. of Shops	:	5	24	-	18	7

(Missing Frequency is 20)

10

Measures of Dispersion

Measures of Dispersion (Variation) are the **'averages of second order'**. They are based on the average of deviations of the values obtained from the central tendencies $\overline{x}$, **Me** or **z**. The variability is the basic feature of the values of variables. Such type of variation or dispersion refers to the 'lack of uniformity'.

Following are the distinctions between the Central Tendencies and Dispersions.

Central tendencies	Dispersions
1. Averages of first order.	1. Averages of second order.
2. Do not throw light on the formation of series.	2. Throw light on the formation of series or distribution.
3. Do not give detailed features of observations .	3. Give detailed characteristics of observations
4. Do not establish relationship with the items.	4. Establish relationship with the individual items.
5. Do not reveal entire picture of distribution.	5. Reveal the entire picture of the distribution.
6. Give only the idea of concentration of items.	6. Give the idea of deviation from central tendencies.

An average of second order is an average of the difference of all the items of the series from an average of those items. In averaging these differences or deviations, their irregularities are brushed off and a representative figure of depression results in.

All the distributions are not similar. They differ in numerical size of their averages and in their respective formations. Let us observe the following series carefully:

Series i :	15	15	15	15	15	15	15	15	15
Series ii :	11	12	13	14	15	16	17	18	19
Series iii :	3	6	9	12	15	18	21	24	27

Arithmetic Mean and Median in all the series are same i.e 15, but items in series differ widely. So the central tendencies fail to describe the scatterdness of the values. For measuring the nature of formation, we require the averages of second order, in support of the first order. The **objectives** of computing the average of second order are,

i. To ascertain the suitability of the first order averages.

ii. To decide the consistency of performance ,and

iii. To reveal the degree of uniformity in the series.

In the three series, as given above, are constituted differently though their mean median are same. The first series is uniformly distributed and there is no dispersion at all. The second series is having some sort of dispersion from the central tendency and the uniformity is disturbed. The third series shows a high degree of dispersion and there is no uniformity among the items. Thus, we can conclude that the larger the dispersion is, the lower will be the uniformity in the distribution.

The term *'Dispersion' or' Variation' or' deviation'* is studied with reference to two measures -**Absolute** and **Relative**. The absolute measures are expressed in terms of original units and they are not suitable for comparative studies. The relative measures are expressed in ratios or percentage and they are suitable for comparative studies. Following are the various types of measures of dispersions:

Measures of Dispersion

- Positional (Based on Limits)
  - Range
  - Quartile Deviation
- Arithmetic (Based on Difference)
  - Mean Deviation
  - Standard Deviation
- Graphic Based on Graph
  - Lorenz Curve

I. Range

"Range" represents the difference between the values of the extremes -- the largest value and the smallest value. The values in between the two extremes are not at all taken into consideration.

The 'Range' gives an extremely simple indicator of the variability of a set of observations. It is denoted symbolically by **'R'**.

(i) Range = largest value - smallest value

R = L – S .... Absolute Measure

(ii) Coefficient of Range $= \dfrac{\text{Largest value} - \text{Smallest value}}{\text{Largest value} + \text{Smallest value}}$

C. of R $= \dfrac{L-S}{L+S}$ ... Relative measure

Example 10.1. *Compute the range and the Coefficient of Range of the series, and state which one is more dispersed and which one is more uniform.*

Series	*Values of variables*					
i.	*13,*	*14,*	*15,*	*16,*	*17 ... ($\bar{x}$ = 15)*	"Central tendency is same but formation differs"
ii.	*9,*	*12,*	*15,*	*18,*	*21 ... ($\bar{x}$ = 15)*	
iii.	*1,*	*8,*	*15,*	*22,*	*29 ... ($\bar{x}$ = 15)*	

Solution :

	(I)	(II)	(III)
Range ...	R = L – S	R = L – S	R = L – S
	=7 – 13	= 21 – 9	= 29 – 1
	= 4	**= 12**	**= 28**
Coefficient of Range ...	C of R $= \dfrac{L-S}{L+S}$	C of R $= \dfrac{L-S}{L+S}$	C of R $= \dfrac{L-S}{L+S}$
	$= \dfrac{17-13}{17+13}$	$= \dfrac{21-9}{21+9}$	$= \dfrac{21-1}{29+1}$
	$= \dfrac{4}{30}$	$= \dfrac{12}{30}$	$= \dfrac{28}{30}$
	= 0.1333	**= 0.4**	**= 0.9333**

Series (I) is **less** dispersed and **more** uniform.

Series (III) is **less** uniform and **more** dispersed.

Example 10.2. *Compute the range and the Coefficient of Range of the series, and state which one is more dispersed and which one is more uniform.*

Solution :

Series	*Values of variables*					
A :	*10,*	*11,*	*12,*	*13,*	*14 ... ($\bar{x}$ = 12)*	"Central tendency differs but formation is same"
B :	*40,*	*41,*	*42,*	*43,*	*44 ... ($\bar{x}$ = 42)*	
C :	*100,*	*101,*	*102,*	*103,*	*104 ... ($\bar{x}$ = 102)*	

Solution :

	A	**B**	**C**
Range ...	R = L – S = 14–10 = **4**	R = L – S = 44–44 = **4**	R = L – S = =104–100 = **4**
Coefficient of Range ...	$C \text{ of } R = \frac{L-S}{L+S}$ $= \frac{14-10}{14+10}$ $= \frac{4}{24}$ = **0.1667**	$C \text{ of } R = \frac{L-S}{L+S}$ $= \frac{44-40}{44+40}$ $= \frac{4}{84}$ = **0.0476**	$C \text{ of } R = \frac{L-S}{L+S}$ $= \frac{104-100}{104+100}$ $= \frac{4}{204}$ = **0.0196**

Series (C) is **less** dispersed and **more** uniform.

Series (A) is **less** uniform and **more** dispersed.

Example 10.3. *From the following distriubtion find the Range and the Coefficient of Range.*

X :	*6*	*12*	*18*	*24*	*30*	*36*	*42*
F :	*20*	*130*	*80*	*60*	*210*	*1500*	*600*

Solution : In finding the range, the frequencies are never taken into account.

Range = L – S = 42 – 6 = **36**

$$\text{Coefficient of Range} = \frac{L-S}{L+S} = \frac{42-6}{42+6} = \frac{36}{48} = \mathbf{0.75}$$

Example 10.4. *Compute the Range and the Coefficient of Range from the following distribution :*

C. I :	120 - 130	130 – 140	140 – 150	150 – 160	160 – 170
F :	2	9	16	12	5

Solution : In finding the range, the frequencies are never taken into account. The upper limit of the highest class and the lower limit of the smallest class are only taken into account.

Range = L – S = 170 – 120 = **50**

$$\text{Coefficient of Range} = \frac{L-S}{L+S} = \frac{170-120}{170+120} = \frac{50}{290} = \mathbf{0.1724}$$

Merits of Range : Following are the merits of Range :

a) It is the simplest measure of dispersion.
b) It is regidly defined and the easiest measure of dispersion to compute.
c) It is readily comprehensible and it requires very little calculations.
d) It is useful in statistical methods of quality control techniques.
e) It is useful in studying the variations in the prices of share and stocks.
f) It is useful in studying weather conditions (weatheriology or meteorology) where minimum and maximum temperature is identified.

Demerits of range : In spite of the uses of range the range suffers from the following limitations :

a) Unfortunately, it is not a stable measure of dispersion, because it is affected by the extreme values only.
b) It is not a suitable measure of dispersion where the class intervals are open in the distribution.
c) It is completely depending upon the two extreme values but not on the other values.
d) It is not suitable for mathematical treatment.
e) It is very sensitive to the fluctuations in the sampling size. As the size of the sample increases, it tends to increase not in proportion.

II. Quartile Deviation

It is nothing but a *"Semi-interquartile Range"*. With some modifications , it is similar to the range. In the distribution, we consider $\mathbf{Q_3}$ as the largest value and $\mathbf{Q_1}$ as the smallest. It means, the items below the lower quartile and the items above the upper quartile are not at all included in the computation. Thus we are considering only the middle half portion of the distribution. The range so obtained is divided by two as we are considering only half of the data. Thus the Quartile deviation measures the difference between the values of Q_1 and Q_3 . It is denoted symbolically by 'Q.D'.

a) Quartile Deviation $= \text{Q.D.} = \dfrac{Q_3 - Q_1}{2}$ ... Absolute Measure.

b) Coefficient of C of Q. D. $= \dfrac{Q_3 - Q_1}{Q_3 + Q_1}$ ... Relative Measure.

For example, if $Q_1 = 15$ and $Q_3 = 40$

$$\text{Q.D.} = \frac{Q_3 - Q_1}{2} = \frac{40-15}{2} = \frac{25}{2} = \mathbf{12.5}$$

(BU – N 85)

$$\text{C of Q.D.} = \frac{40-15}{40+15} = \frac{25}{55} = \mathbf{45.45}$$

The Quartile Deviation gives the average amount by which the two quartiles differ from median in an asymmetrical distribution. Rigorously speaking quartile deviation is only a positional average. It does not exhibit any scatter around an average. It is a measure of partition rather than a measure of dispersion. The smallest the value of Q.D., the minimum is the dispersion of middle half of the distribution around the median. However, it provides no indication of the, degree of dispersion lying beyond the limits of the two quartiles.

Example 10.5. *From the following marks of the 12 students, compute the Quartile Deviation and its Coefficient.*

S.No :	*1*	*2*	*3*	*4*	*5*	*6*	*7*	*8*	*9*	*10*	*11*	*12*
Marks :	*25*	*30*	*37*	*43*	*48*	*54*	*61*	*67*	*72*	*80*	*84*	*89*

Solution: **Computation of Quartile Deviation**

S.No.	Marks
1	25
2	30
3	37
4	43
5	48
6	54
7	61
8	67
9	72
10	80
11	84
12	89

Q_1 is the size of $\frac{n+1}{4}$ th item.

$\therefore \frac{12+1}{4}$ th = 3.25th item.

Q_1 = 3rd item + 0.25 (43 − 37)

= 37 + 0.25(43 − 37) = 37 + 0.25(6) = 37 + 1.5

= **38.5**

Q_3 is the size of $\frac{3(n+1)}{4}$ th item.

$\therefore \frac{3(12+1)}{4}$ th = 9.75th item.

Q_3 = 9th item + 0.75(80 − 72)

= 72 + 0.75(80 − 72) = 72 + 0.75(8) = 72 + 6 = **78**

$$\text{Q.D.} = \frac{Q_3 - Q_1}{2} = \frac{78 - 38.5}{2} = \frac{39.5}{2} = \mathbf{19.75}$$

$$\text{Coefficient of Q.D.} = \frac{Q_3 - Q_1}{Q_3 + Q_1} = \frac{78 - 38.5}{78 + 38.5} = \frac{39.5}{116.5} = \mathbf{0.339}$$

Example 10.6. *Calculate the Quartile Deviation and its Coefficient from the following data:*

X :	*58*	*59*	*60*	*61*	*62*	*63*	*64*	*65*	*66*
F :	*15*	*20*	*32*	*35*	*33*	*22*	*20*	*10*	*8*

Solution : **Computation of Quartile Deviation**

X	f	C.f
58	15	15
59	20	35
(Q_1) 60	32	67←
61	35	102
62	33	135
(Q_3) 63	22	157←
64	20	177
65	10	187
66	8	195
	n = 195	

Q_1 is the size of $\frac{n+1}{4}$ th item.

$\therefore \frac{195+1}{4}$ th = 48.78 th .

It lies in 67 c.f.. Against 67 C.f.. Q_1 = **60**

Q_3 is the size of $\frac{3(n+1)}{4}$ th item

$\therefore \frac{3(195+1)}{4}$ th = 146.33 th

It lies in 157 c.f. Against 157 c.f.. Q_3 = **63**

$$\text{Q.D.} = \frac{Q_3 - Q_1}{2} = \frac{63 - 60}{2} = \frac{3}{2} = \mathbf{1.5}$$

$$\text{Coefficient of Q.D.} = \frac{Q_3 - Q_1}{Q_3 + Q_1} = \frac{63-60}{63+60} = \frac{3}{123} = \mathbf{0.02439}$$

Example 10.7. *From the following compute Quartile Deviation and the Coefficient of Quartile Deviation.* *(BU-A86)*

Weekly Wages (Rs.) :	*4–8*	*8–12*	*12–16*	*16–20*	*20–24*	*24–28*	*28–32*	*32–36*	*36-40*
No.of Workers :	*6*	*10*	*18*	*30*	*15*	*12*	*10*	*6*	*2*

Solution :

Computation of Quartile Deviation

Weekly Wages (Rs.)	No. of Workers (f)	C. f.
4 – 8	6	6
8 – 12	10	16 (m)
(*l*) 12 – 16	18 (f)	34 ← Q_1
16 – 20	30	64
20 – 24	15	79 (m)
(*l*) 24 – 28	12 (f)	91 ← Q_3
28 – 32	10	101
32 – 36	6	107
36 – 40	2	109
	n = 109	

Q_1 is the size of $\frac{n}{4}$ th item. $\therefore \frac{109}{4}$ th = 27.25 th item .

It lies in 34 c.f. Against 34 c.f. the Q_1 class is (12 – 16)

Q_3 is the size of $\frac{3n}{4}$ th item. $\therefore \frac{3(109)}{4}$ th = 81.75 th items

It lies in 91 c.f. Against 91 c.f. the Q_3 class is (24 – 28).

$$Q_1 = l + \frac{\frac{n}{4} - m}{f} \times c = 12 + \frac{\frac{109}{4} - 16}{18} \times 4 = 12 + \frac{27.25 - 16}{18} \times 4$$

$$= 12 + \frac{11.25}{18} \times 4 = 12 + \frac{45}{18} = 12 + 2.5 = \mathbf{14.5}$$

$$Q_3 = l + \frac{\frac{3n}{4} - m}{f} \times c = 24 + \frac{\frac{3(109)}{4} - 79}{12} \times 4 = 24 + \frac{81.75 - 79}{12} \times 4$$

$$= 24 + \frac{2.75}{12} \times 4 = 24 + \frac{11}{12} = 24 + 0.9167 = \mathbf{24.9167}$$

$$Q.D. = \frac{Q_3 - Q_1}{2} = \frac{24.9167 - 14.5}{2} = \frac{10.4167}{2} = \mathbf{5.208}$$

Coefficient of Q.D. =

$$\frac{Q_3 - Q_1}{Q_3 + Q_1} = \frac{24.9167 - 14.5}{24.9167 + 14.5} = \frac{10.4167}{39.4167} = \mathbf{0.26427}$$

Example 10.8. *Compute Quartile Deviation and its Coefficient from the following data:* *(BU – A95)*

Size	*5 – 7*	*8 – 10*	*11 – 13*	*14 - 16*	*17 - 19*
Frequency	*14*	*24*	*38*	*20*	*4*

Solution: For partitioned values the class intervals are converted from inclusive to exclusive method.

Computation of Quartile Deviation

C.I	F	C.f	
4.5 – 7.5	14	14 (m)	
(l) 7.5 – 10.5	24 (f)	38 (m)	Q_1 ←
(l) 10.5 – 13.5	38 (f)	76	Q_3 ←
13.5 - 16.5	20	96	
16.5 – 19.5	4	100	
	n = 100		

Q_1 is the size of $\frac{n}{4}$ th item. $\therefore \frac{100}{4}$ th = 25 th item.

It lies in 38 c.f. Against 38 c.f. the Q_1 class is (7.5 – 10.5).

Q_3 is the size of $\frac{3n}{4}$ th item. $\therefore \frac{3(100)}{4}$ th = 75 th items.

It lies in 76 c.f. Against 76 c.f. the Q_3 class is (10.5 – 13.5).

$$Q_1 = l + \frac{\frac{n}{4} - m}{f} \times c = 7.5 + \frac{\frac{100}{4} - 14}{24} \times 3 = 7.5 + \frac{25 - 14}{24} \times 3$$

$$= 7.5 + \frac{11}{24} \times 3 = 7.5 + \frac{33}{24} = 7.5 + 1.375 = \mathbf{8.875}$$

$$Q_3 = l + \frac{\frac{3n}{4} - m}{f} \times c = 10.5 + \frac{\frac{3(100)}{4} - 38}{38} \times 3 = 10.5 + \frac{75 - 38}{38} \times 3$$

$$= 10.5 + \frac{37}{38} \times 3 = 10.5 + \frac{111}{38} = 10.5 + 2.921 = \mathbf{13.421}$$

$$\text{Q.D.} = \frac{Q_3 - Q_1}{2} = \frac{13.421 - 8.875}{2} = \frac{4.546}{2} = \mathbf{2.273}$$

Coefficient of Q.D. =

$$\frac{Q_3 - Q_1}{Q_3 + Q_1} = \frac{13.421 - 8.875}{13.421 + 8.875} = \frac{4.546}{22.296} = \mathbf{0.2039}$$

Merits of Quartile Deviation : Following are the merits of Quartile Deviation:

a) It is very easy to calculate and simple to understand.
b) It is not affected by extreme values of variable as it is concerned with the central half portion of the distribution.
c) It is not at all affected by open end class intervals.

Demerits of Quartile Deviation: In spite of the importance, the quartile deviation suffers from the following limitations:

a) It ignores completely the portions below the lower quartile and above the upper quartile.
b) It is not capable of further mathematical treatment.
c) It is greatly affected by the fluctuations in the sampling
d) It is only a positional average but not mathematical average.

III. Mean Deviation (δ)

Mean deviation is the average difference among the items in a series from the mean itself or median or mode of that series. It is concerned with the extent to which the values are dispersed about the mean or the median or the mode. It is found by the averaging all the deviations from the central tendency. These deviations are taken into computations with regard to negative sign (i.e., all the deviations assumed as positive).

Theoretically, the deviations of items are taken preferably from median instead than from the mean or the mode. Median is supposed to be the suitable central tendency for calculating deviations because the sum of the deviations from the median is less than the sum of the deviations from the mean. It is not a common practice to calculate the deviation from the mode as its value is sometimes not clearly defined.

In aggregating the deviations, the algebraic negative signs are not taken into account. It means all the deviations are treated **as positive ignoring the negative signs.** It is the deviation not the mathematical difference. Suppose city 'A' is away from city 'B' by 250 kms. 'A' is deviated geographically by 250 kms from 'B' and 'B' is deviated geographically by 250 kms from 'A'. There is no point in saying that one is positive deviation and the other the negative. Since the purpose is to study the variation of items from a central tendency, it does not matter in the least weather it is **'plus'** 'or **'minus'**.

Mean deviation or *average deviation* or *first moment of dispersion* is denoted symbolically by the Greek small alphabet 'δ' (delta).

A : Individual Observations: $\delta = \frac{\Sigma d}{n}$ ... Absolute Measure

Coefficient of $\delta = \frac{\delta}{Me}$ or $\frac{\delta}{\bar{x}}$ or $\frac{\delta}{z}$ ... Relative Measure

B : Discrete and Continuous Series:

$\delta = \frac{\Sigma fd}{n}$ ..... Absolute Measure

Coefficient of $\delta = \frac{\delta}{Me}$ or $\frac{\delta}{\bar{x}}$ or $\frac{\delta}{z}$ ... Relative Measure

(**Note :** **Σd** is the sum of the deviations and **Σfd** is the sum of the products 'f' and 'd'.)

When the averages are in fractions, the calculation of mean deviation becomes a tedious job. So, to make the things more simplified, a short-cut method or formula is used as under :

A : Individual Observations : $\delta = \frac{\Sigma xA - \Sigma xB - (\Sigma A - \Sigma B)Me^*}{n}$

B : Discrete and Continuous series :

$$\delta = \frac{\Sigma fxA - \Sigma fxB - (\Sigma fA - \Sigma fB)Me^*}{n}$$

(**Note:** In place of Me* we can take $\bar{x}$ or z as the deviations are concerned.)

Steps to be followed in the short cut method :

(i) Make two sections in the entire distribution, as **A and B**, so that all the items greater than average (including average) should fall in *'A section'* and all the items smaller than average should fall in the *'B section'*.

(ii) Terms used in the formula:

ΣxA : the sum of the values grater than average.
ΣxB : the sum of the values smaller than average.
ΣA : the total number of items greater than average.
ΣB : the total number of items smaller than average.
n : the total number of items.
ΣfxA : the sum of the 'fx' greater than average.
ΣfxB : the sum of the 'fx' smaller than the average.
ΣfA : the sum of the frequencies greater than average.
ΣfB : the sum of frequencies smaller than average.

Though the formula looks lengthy, it is useful in all the respects and makes the calculations easiest.

Example 10.9. *From the following variables find the Mean Deviation and Coefficient of Mean Deviation from the mean.*

X : 68 49 32 21 54 38 59 66 41

Solution: *Arrange the data in an ascending order to have the short cut method applicable.*

Computation of Mean Deviation

X	$(x - \bar{x})$ d
21	26.56
32	15.56
38	9.56
41	6.56
49	1.44
54	6.44
59	11.44
66	18.44
68	20.44
428	116.44
Σx	Σd

$$\bar{x} = \frac{\Sigma x}{n} = \frac{428}{9} = \mathbf{47.56}$$

$$\delta = \frac{\Sigma d}{n} = \frac{116.44}{9} = \mathbf{12.9378}$$

Coefficient of

$$\delta = \frac{\delta}{\bar{x}} = \frac{12.9378}{47.56} = \mathbf{0.272}$$

Short – cut method

X		
21		
32	ΣB = 4	ΣxB = 1.32
38	B	
41		
49	ΣA = 5	ΣxA = 296
54	A	
59		
66		
68		

$\bar{x}$ = 47 56 It is merged in 49, from which we can have the division

$$\delta = \frac{\Sigma xA - \Sigma xB - (\Sigma A - \Sigma B)\bar{x}}{n} = \frac{296 - 132 - (5-4)47.56}{9}$$

$$= \frac{164 - (1)47.56}{9} = \frac{164 - 47.56}{9} = \frac{116.44}{9} = \mathbf{12.9378}$$

Example 10.10. *Following are the wages of the workers. Find the Mean Deviation from the median and its Coefficient.*

Wages(Rs) : 59 32 67 43 22 17 64 55 47 80 25

Solution *:* Arrange the data in an ascending order for computing the median.

Computation of Mean Deviation

Median is the size of $\frac{n+1}{2}$ th item

$\therefore \frac{11+1}{2}$ th = 6th ∴ 6th item is 47. Me = **47**

S.No.	Wages (Rs.) X	(x – Me) d
1	17	30
2	22	25
3	25	22
4	32	15
5	43	4
→ 6	→ 47	0
7	55	8
8	59	12
9	64	17
10	67	20
11	80	33
		Σd = 186

$$\delta = \frac{\Sigma d}{n} = \frac{186}{11} = \mathbf{16.91}$$

Coefficient of

$$\delta = \frac{\delta}{\bar{x}} = \frac{16.91}{47} = \mathbf{0.36}$$

Short – cut method

X		
17		
22		ΣB = 5.
25		
32	B	ΣxB = 139
43 →		
47		
55		
59	A	
64		ΣA = 6.
67		ΣxA = 372
80		

$$\delta = \frac{\Sigma xA - \Sigma xB - (\Sigma A - \Sigma B)Me}{n} = \frac{372 - 139 - (6-5)47}{n}$$

$$= \frac{233 - (1)47}{11} = \frac{233 - 47}{11} = \frac{186}{11} = \mathbf{16.91}$$

Example 10.11. *Following are the runs scored by the batsmen in different innings of cricket tests.*

Runs :	*20*	*40*	*60*	*80*	*100*	*120*	*140*	*160*	*180*
No of batsmen :	*6*	*19*	*40*	*23*	*65*	*83*	*55*	*20*	*9*

Compute the Mean Deviation from mode and its Coefficient.

Solution : Computation of Mean Deviation

X	f	$(x-z)=d$	fd
20	6	100	600
40	19	80	1,520
60	40	60	2,400
80	23	40	920
100	65	20	1,300
120	83	0	0
140	55	20	1,100
160	20	40	800
180	9	60	540
	n = 320		Σfd = 9,180

The highest frequency is 83.

$\therefore$ z = **120**

$$\delta = \frac{\Sigma fd}{n} = \frac{9180}{320} = \mathbf{28.69}$$

Coeffecient of δ

$$= \frac{\delta}{z} = \frac{28.69}{120} = \mathbf{0.239}$$

Short-cut Method

X	f	fx	
20	6	120	B
40	19	760	B
60	40	2,400	B
80	23	1,840	B
100	65	6,500	B
120	83	9,960	A
140	55	7,700	A
160	20	3,200	A
180	9	1,620	A
		Σfx = 34,100	

ΣfB = **153** ΣfxB = **11620**

ΣfA = **167** ΣfxA = **22480**

$$\delta = \frac{\Sigma fxA - \Sigma fxB - (\Sigma fA - \Sigma fB)z}{n}$$

$$= \frac{22480 - 11620 - (167-153)\,120}{320}$$

$$= \frac{10860 - (14)120}{320} = \frac{10860 - 1680}{320}$$

$$= \frac{9180}{320} = \mathbf{28.69}$$

Example 10.12. *Find out the Mean Deviation from the information given below :* *(BU-A92)*

Salaries (Rs.) :	*40*	*50*	*50-100*	*100-200*	*200-400*
No. of employes :	*22*	*18*	*10*	*8*	*2*

Solution: As the distribution involves both the discrete and continuous values of variable, mean deviation is computed preferably from median.

Computation of Mean Deviation

Salaries Rs.	X (m.v.)	f	Cf	(x – Me) d	fd
40	40	22	22	10	220
50	50	18	40	0	0
50 –100	75	10	50	25	150
100 – 200	150	8	58	100	800
200 – 400	300	2	60	250	500
		n = 60			Σfd = 1,770

Median is the size of $\frac{n+1}{2}$ th item.

$\therefore \frac{60+1}{2}$ th item = 30.5

It lies in 40 c.f..

Against 40 c.f. the discrete value is 50.

$\therefore$ Me = **50**

$\delta = \frac{\Sigma fd}{n} = \frac{1770}{60} = \mathbf{29.5}$

Coefficient of δ

$= \frac{\delta}{Me} = \frac{29.5}{50} = \mathbf{0.59}$

Assumed Mean Method

When the average is in fraction and values of variable or mid-points are increasing at regular intervals and computation involves big multiplications, we can use the following formula coveniently:

$$\delta = \frac{\Sigma fd'(c) + (^{*}\bar{x} - A)(\Sigma fB - \Sigma fA)}{n} \text{ .... * Any average}$$

A = Assumed Average. ('c' is in case of step-deviation)

Example 10.13. *From the following marks of 100 students compute the Mean Deviation from median and its Coefficient.*

Marks	*20-25*	*25-30*	*30-35*	*35-40*	*40-45*	*45-50*	*50-55*	*55-60*	*60-65*
No of students	*6*	*12*	*17*	*30*	*10*	*10*	*8*	*5*	*2*

Solution: **Computation of Mean Deviation**

C.I	f	c.f.	x	$(x-A)/5$ d'	fd'	
20 – 25	6	6	22.5	3	18	
25 – 30	12	18	27.5	2	24	ΣfB = 63
30 – 35	17	35 (m)	32.5	1	17	
(*l*)35 – 40	28(f)	63←	37.5	0	0	
40 – 45	12	75	42.5	1	12	
45 – 50	10	85	47.5	2	20	ΣfA = 37
50 – 55	8	93	52.5	3	24	
55 – 60	5	98	57.5	4	20	
60 – 65	2	100	62.5	5	10	
	n=100				Σfd' = 145	

Me is the size of $\frac{n}{2}$ th item. $\therefore \frac{100}{2}$ th = 50th item.

It lies in 63 c.f.. Against 63 c.f. median class is (35 – 40).

$$\text{Me} = l + \frac{\frac{100}{n} - m}{f} \times c = 35 + \frac{50-35}{28} \times 5 = 35 + \frac{15}{28} \times 5$$

$$= 35 + \frac{75}{28} = 35 + 2.6786 = \mathbf{37.6786}$$

Assumed Median = 37.5 (one among the mid-points)

$$\delta = \frac{\Sigma fd'(c) + (\text{Me} - A)(\Sigma fB - \Sigma fA)}{n} = \frac{145(5) + (37.6786 - 37.5)(63.}{100}$$

$$= \frac{725 + 0.1786(26)}{100} = \frac{725 + 4.6436}{100} = \frac{729.6436}{100} = \mathbf{7.296}$$

$$\text{Coefficient of } \delta = \frac{\delta}{\text{Me}} = \frac{7.296}{37.6786} = \mathbf{0.19365}$$

Merits of Mean Deviation : Following are the merits of Mean Deviation:

i) It is rigidly defined and easy to compute and understand.

ii) It takes all the items into consideration and gives weight to deviation according to their size.

iii) It is less affected by extreme values of variables.

iv) It removes all the irregularities by obtaining deviations and provides a correct measures.

Demerits of Mean Deviation : In spite of the importance, the Mean Deviation suffers from the following limitations:

i) It does not lend itself readily to algebraic treatment.

ii) It ignores the negative deviation and treats them as positive which is not justified mathematically.

iii) It is not a satisfactory measure when the deviations are taken from the mode.

iv) It is rarely used in social sciences.

v) It is not suitable when the class intervals are open end.

IV. Standard Deviation (σ)

'Standard deviation' is the root of the sum of the squares of the deviations divided by their number. It is also called *"Mean Error Deviation"*, *'Mean Square Error Deviation'* or *"Root Mean*

Square Deviation". It is a second moment of a dispersion. Since the sum of the squares of the deviations from the mean is minimum, *the deviations are taken only from mean* (but not from median or mode).

Standard Deviation is the root-mean-square average of all the deviations from the mean. It is proposed by **Prof. Karl Pearson** in 1893, and it is denoted by ' σ ' (sigma)

A : Individual Observations :

$$\sigma = \sqrt{\frac{\Sigma d^2}{n}} \text{ or } \sqrt{\frac{\Sigma(x-\bar{x})^2}{n}} \quad \text{... Absolute Measure}$$

$$\text{Coefficient of Variation } \frac{\sigma}{\bar{x}} \times 100 \quad \text{... Relative Measure}$$

B : Discrete and Continuous series :

$$\sigma = \sqrt{\frac{\Sigma fd^2}{n}} \text{ or } \sqrt{\frac{\Sigma f(x-\bar{x})^2}{n}} \quad \text{... Absolute Measure}$$

$$\text{Coefficient of Variation } = \frac{\sigma}{\bar{x}} \times 100 \text{ ... Relative Measure}$$

Steps to be followed :

(i) Calculate the $\bar{x}$.

(ii) Note down the deviations $[\text{ i.e., } (x-\bar{x}) \text{ or } d]$.

(iii) Square the deviations $\left[\text{i.e., } (x-\bar{x})^2 \text{ or } d^2\right]$.

(iv) Multiply d^2 by f $\left(\text{ i.e, } fd^2\right)$

(v) Total the fd^2 column $\left(\text{i.e, } \Sigma fd^2\right)$

(vi) Divide Σfd^2 by n (i.e., $\Sigma fd^2/n$)

(vii) Obtain the roots of $\Sigma fd^2/n$ $\left(\text{i.e., } \sqrt{\Sigma fd^2/n}\right)$

Short-cut Method :

Sometimes the mean will be a fractional figure. Then we should take the deviations from the assumed mean and the direct method formula will be having some adjustment. As the deviations are not taken from the actual mean, we get the 'Σ**d**' as some value instead zero. The short cut formula works as under,

A : Individual Observations $: \sigma = \sqrt{\frac{\Sigma d^2}{n} - \sqrt{\left(\frac{\Sigma d}{n}\right)^2}}$

B : Discrete and Continuous series $: \sigma = \sqrt{\frac{\Sigma fd^2}{n} - \left(\frac{\Sigma fd}{n}\right)^2}$

Step -deviation Method

The deviations are further divided by the common factor in case of assumed mean. This deliberate error is compensated by multiplying the entire formula by the same factor . The formula works as under,

A : Individual Observations : C = Common Factor

$$\sigma = \sqrt{\frac{\Sigma d'^2}{n} - \left(\frac{\Sigma d'}{n}\right)^2} \times c$$

B : Discrete and Continues series :

$$\sigma = \sqrt{\frac{\Sigma fd'^2}{n} - \left(\frac{\Sigma fd'}{n}\right)^2} \times c$$

Example10.14. *Ten students of B.A. class have obtained the following marks in Kannada major out of 100. Calculate the Standard Deviation of marks obtained.* *(BU – A84)*

S.No. :	*1*	*2*	*3*	*4*	*5*	*6*	*7*	*8*	*9*	*10*
Marks :	*5*	*10*	*20*	*25*	*40*	*42*	*45*	*48*	*70*	*80*

Solution : Computation of Standard Deviation

x	$(x - \bar{x}) = d$	d^2	$(x - A) = d$	d^2
5	-33.5	1122.25	-35	1225
10	-28.5	812.25	-30	900
20	-18.5	342.25	-20	400
25	-13.5	182.25	-15	225
40	+1.5	2.25	0	0
42	+3.5	12.25	+2	4
45	+6.5	42.25	+5	25
48	+9.5	90.25	+8	64
70	+31.5	992.25	+30	900
80	+41.5	1722.25	+40	1600
$\Sigma x = 385$	$\Sigma d = 0$	$\Sigma d^2 = 5,320.50$	$\Sigma d = -15$	$\Sigma d^2 = 5343$

$$\bar{x} = \frac{\Sigma x}{n} = \frac{385}{10} = \mathbf{38.5}$$

$$\sigma = \sqrt{\frac{\Sigma d^2}{n} - \left(\frac{\Sigma d}{n}\right)^2} = \sqrt{\frac{5343}{10} - \left(\frac{-15}{10}\right)^2} = \sqrt{534.3 - (-1.5)^2}$$

$$= \sqrt{534.3 - 2.26} = \sqrt{532.05} = \mathbf{23.066} \quad \text{... Short - cut Method}$$

$$\sigma = \sqrt{\frac{\Sigma d^2}{n}} = \sqrt{\frac{5320.50}{10}} = \sqrt{532.05} = \mathbf{23.066} \quad \text{... Direct Method}$$

$$c.v = \frac{\sigma}{\bar{x}} \times 100 = \frac{23.066}{38.5} \times 100 = 0.5991 \times 100 = \mathbf{59.91\%}$$

Example 10.15. *Following are the runs scored by the two batsmen named NEKO and DECO in ten innings. Find who is better scorer and who is more consistent.* *(BU-N84)*

NEKO:	101	22	0	36	82	45	7	13	65	14
DECO:	97	12	40	96	13	8	85	8	56	16

Solution: **Computation of Standard Deviation**

NECO x	$(x-\bar{x})$ d	d^2	DECO x	$(x-\bar{x})$ d	d^2
0	-38.5	1482.25	8	- 35.1	1232.01
7	-31.5	992.25	8	- 35.1	1232.01
13	-25.5	650.25	12	- 31.1	967.21
14	-24.5	600.25	13	- 30.1	906.01
22	-16.5	272.25	16	- 27.1	734.41
36	-2.5	6.25	40	-3.1	9.61
45	+6.5	42.25	56	+12.9	166.41
65	+26.5	702.25	85	+41.9	1755.61
82	+43.5	1892.25	96	+52.9	2798.41
101	+62.5	13906.25	97	+53.9	2905.21
385 $\Sigma x =$	$\Sigma d = 0$	10546.50 $\Sigma d^2 =$	$\Sigma x = 431$	$\Sigma d = 0$	12706.90 $\Sigma d^2 =$

$$\bar{x} = \frac{\Sigma x}{n} = \frac{385}{10} = \mathbf{38.5} \qquad \sigma = \sqrt{\frac{\Sigma d^2}{n}} = \sqrt{\frac{10546.50}{10}} = \sqrt{1054.65} = \mathbf{32.475}$$

$$c.v = \frac{\sigma}{\bar{x}} \times 100 = \frac{32.475}{38.5} \times 100 = \mathbf{84.35\%}$$

$\overline{x} = \frac{\Sigma x}{n} = \frac{431}{10} = \mathbf{43.1}$ $\sigma = \sqrt{\frac{\Sigma d^2}{n}} = \sqrt{\frac{12706.90}{10}} = \sqrt{12706.90} = \mathbf{35.647}$

$c.v = \frac{\sigma}{\overline{x}} \times 100 = \frac{34.647}{43.1} \times 100 = \mathbf{82.71\%}$

DECO is a better run scorer and more consistent player than NEKO .(because his average is more and variation is less)

Example 10.16. *Following are the marks obtained by two students 'A' and 'B' in 10 tests of 100 marks each.*

Tests :	1	2	3	4	5	6	7	8	9	10
A :	44	80	76	48	52	72	72	51	60	54
B :	48	75	54	60	63	69	72	51	57	66

Find who is better in studies and if consistency is the criterion for awarding a prize, who should get the prize.

(BU-N85)

Solution: **Computation of Standard Deviation**

A x	$(x - \overline{x})$ d	d^2	B x	$(x - \overline{x})$ d	d^2
44	-16.9	285.61	48	-13.5	182.25
48	-12.9	166.41	51	-10.5	110.25
51	-9.9	98.01	54	-7.5	56.25
52	-8.9	79.21	57	-4.5	20.25
54	-6.9	47.61	60	-1.5	2.25
60	-0.9	0.81	63	+1.5	2.25
72	+11.1	123.21	66	+4.5	20.25
72	+11.1	123.21	69	+7.5	56.25
76	+15.1	228.01	72	+10.5	110.25
80	+19.1	364.81	75	+13.5	182.25
609 Σx =	$\Sigma d = 0$	1516.90 Σd^2 =	615 Σx =	$\Sigma d = 0$	742.50 Σd^2 =

$\overline{x} = \frac{\Sigma x}{n} = \frac{609}{10} = \mathbf{60.9}$

$\sigma = \sqrt{\frac{\Sigma d^2}{n}} = \sqrt{\frac{1516.90}{10}} = \sqrt{151.69} = \mathbf{12.316}$

$c.v = \frac{\sigma}{\overline{x}} \times 100 = \frac{12.316}{60.9} \times 100 = \mathbf{20.22\%}$

$\overline{x} = \frac{\Sigma x}{n} = \frac{615}{10} = \mathbf{61.5}$

$\sigma = \sqrt{\frac{\Sigma d^2}{n}} = \sqrt{\frac{742.50}{10}} = \sqrt{74.25} = \mathbf{8.617}$

$c.v = \frac{\sigma}{\overline{x}} \times 100 = \frac{8.617}{61.5} \times 10 = \mathbf{14.01\%}$

B is better in studies and he should get a prize aslo as his average is more and variance is less.

Example 10.17. *Prices of particular commodity in five years in two cities are given below:*

City A :	*20*	*22*	*19*	*23*	*16*
City B :	*10*	*20*	*18*	*12*	*15*

Find from the table which city had more stable prices. (BU-N87)

Solution : Computation of Standard Deviation

A X	$(x-\bar{x})$ d	d^2	B X	$(x-\bar{x})$ d	d^2
16	-4	16	10	-5	25
19	-1	1	12	-3	9
20	0	0	15	0	0
22	+2	4	18	+3	9
23	+3	9	20	+5	25
$\Sigma x = 100$	$\Sigma d = 0$	$\Sigma d^2 = 30$	$\Sigma x = 75$	$\Sigma d = 0$	$\Sigma d^2 = 68$
$\bar{x} = \frac{\Sigma x}{n}$	$\sigma = \sqrt{\frac{\Sigma d^2}{n}}$	$c.v = \frac{\sigma}{\bar{x}} \times 100$	$\bar{x} = \frac{\Sigma x}{n}$	$\sigma = \sqrt{\frac{\Sigma d^2}{n}}$	$c.v = \frac{\sigma}{\bar{x}} \times 100$
$= \frac{100}{5}$	$= \sqrt{\frac{30}{5}}$	$= \frac{2.45}{20} \times 100$	$= \frac{75}{5}$	$= \sqrt{\frac{68}{5}}$	$= \frac{3.688}{15} \times 100$
= 20	$= \sqrt{6}$	**= 12.25%**	**= 15**	$= \sqrt{13.6}$	**= 24.585%**
	= 2.45			**= 3.688**	

Coefficient of variation is less in prices of city A: the prices of city A are more stable than city B.

Example 10.18. *Following are the runs scored by two batsmen A and B:* *(BU-N94)*

A :	*70*	*90*	*80*	*50*	*40*
B :	*70*	*90*	*60*	*50*	*30*

Find who is a better run getter and more consistent player.

Solution : Corporation of Standard Deviation

10.22

A X	$(x-\bar{x})$ d	d^2	B X	$(x-\bar{x})$ d	d^2
70	+4	16	70	+10	100
90	+24	576	90	+30	900
80	+14	196	60	0	0
50	-16	256	50	-10	100
40	-26	676	30	-30	900
$\Sigma x = 330$	$\Sigma d = 0$	$\Sigma d^2 = 1720$	$\Sigma x = 300$	$\Sigma d = 0$	$\Sigma d^2 = 2000$

$$\bar{x} = \frac{\Sigma x}{n} = \frac{330}{5} = \mathbf{66} \qquad \sigma = \sqrt{\frac{\Sigma d^2}{n}} = \sqrt{\frac{1720}{5}} = \sqrt{344} = \mathbf{18.547} \qquad c.v = \frac{\sigma}{\bar{x}} \times 100 = \frac{18.547}{66} \times 100 = \mathbf{28.10\%}$$

$$\bar{x} = \frac{\Sigma x}{n} = \frac{300}{5} = \mathbf{60} \qquad \sigma = \sqrt{\frac{\Sigma d^2}{n}} = \sqrt{\frac{2000}{5}} = \sqrt{400} = \mathbf{20} \qquad c.v = \frac{\sigma}{\bar{x}} \times 100 = \frac{20}{60} \times 100 = \mathbf{33.33\%}$$

Batsman A is better run getter and more consistent as his average is more and variation is less.

Example 10.19. *From the prices of shares of x and y given below, state which share prices are more stable.* *(BU – N95, A98)*

X (Rs) :	*55*	*54*	*53*	*53*	*56*	*68*	*52*	*50*	*51*	*49*
Y (Rs) :	*108*	*107*	*105*	*105*	*106*	*107*	*104*	*103*	*104*	*101*

Solution: Values are arranged in ascending order

Computation of Standard Deviation

'X' price x	$(x-\bar{x})$ d	d^2	'Y' price x	$(x-\bar{x})$ d	d^2
49	-5.1	26.01	101	-4	16
50	-4.1	16.81	103	-2	4
51	-3.1	9.61	104	-1	1
52	-2.1	4.41	104	-1	1
53	-1.1	1.21	105	0	0
53	-1.1	1.21	105	0	0
54	-0.1	0.01	106	+1	1
55	+0.9	0.81	107	+2	4
56	+1.9	3.61	107	+2	4
68	+13.9	193.21	108	+3	9
$\Sigma x = 541$	$\Sigma d = 0$	$\Sigma d^2 = 256.90$	$\Sigma x = 1050$	$\Sigma d = 0$	$\Sigma d^2 = 40$

$$\bar{x} = \frac{\Sigma x}{n} = \frac{541}{10} = \mathbf{54.1} \qquad \sigma = \sqrt{\frac{\Sigma d^2}{n}} = \sqrt{\frac{256.90}{10}} = \sqrt{25.69} = \mathbf{5.069} \qquad c.v = \frac{\sigma}{\bar{x}} \times 100 = \frac{5.069}{54.1} \times 100 = \mathbf{9.369\%}$$

$$\bar{x} = \frac{\Sigma x}{n} = \frac{1050}{10} = \mathbf{105} \qquad \sigma = \sqrt{\frac{\Sigma d^2}{n}} = \sqrt{\frac{40}{10}} = \sqrt{4} = \mathbf{2} \qquad c.v = \frac{\sigma}{\bar{x}} \times 10 = \frac{2}{105} \times 10 = \mathbf{1.905\%}$$

'Y' share prices are more stable than 'X' as the variation is less.

Example 10.20. *The number of employees, wage per employee and the variance of the wages per employee for two factories are given below:*

		Factory A	*Factory B*
No. of employees	...	*50*	*100*
Average wages per employee per month	...	*Rs.120*	*Rs. 85*
Variance of wages per employee permonth	...	*Rs. 9*	*Rs. 16*

In which factory is there greater variation in the distribution of wages per employee. Which factory pays more wages?

(BU-A83,N86)

Solution :

Factory A

$\sigma = \sqrt{\text{variance}}$ c.v. $= \dfrac{\sigma}{\bar{x}} \times 100$

$= \sqrt{9}$ $= \dfrac{3}{120} \times 100$

$= \mathbf{3}$ $= \mathbf{2.5\%}$

$\Sigma x = 120 \times 50 =$ Rs.**6000**

= Total wages

In factory **B** there is greater variation.

Factory B

$\sigma = \sqrt{\text{variance}}$ c.v. $= \dfrac{\sigma}{\bar{x}} \times 100$

$= \sqrt{16}$ $= \dfrac{4}{85} \times 100$

$= \mathbf{4}$ $= \mathbf{4.71\%}$

$\Sigma x = 100 \times 85 =$ **Rs.8500**

= Total wages

Factory **B** pays more wages

Example 10.21 : *An analysis of the monthly wages paid to the worker in two firms A and B belonging to the same industry gives the following results:* *(BU – N90)*

		Firm A	*Firm B*
No. of workers	...	*500*	*600*
Average monthly wages	...	*Rs. 186*	*Rs. 175*
Variance of distribution of wages	...	*Rs. 81*	*Rs. 100*

(i) Which of the firms A or B has a larger wage bill? and

(ii) In which of the firms A or B, is there greater variability in individual wages?

Solution:

Firm A

$\sigma = \sqrt{\text{variance}}$ c.v. $= \frac{\sigma}{\bar{x}} \times 100$

$= \sqrt{81}$ $= \frac{9}{186} \times 100$

= 9 **= 4.84%**

$\Sigma x = 186 \times 500 =$ **Rs.93,000**

= Total wages

Firm B

$\sigma = \sqrt{\text{variance}}$ c.v. $= \frac{\sigma}{\bar{x}} \times 100$

$= \sqrt{100}$ $= \frac{10}{175} \times 100$

= 10 **= 5.71%**

$\Sigma x = 175 \times 600 =$ **Rs.1,05,000**

= Total wages

Firm **B** has larger wage bill, and it also has greater variability in individual wages.

Example 10.22. *An analysis of the monthly wages paid to workers in two firms A and B belonging to the same industries gives the following results:*

		Firm A	*Firm B*
No. of wage earners	...	*586.00*	*648.00*
Average monthly wage	...	*Rs. 52.50*	*Rs. 47.50*
Variance of the distribution	...	*Rs.100.00*	*Rs.121.00*

i) Which firm pays out the larger amount as monthly wages? and
ii) In which firm is there greater variability in individual wage?

(BU-A85)

Solution:

Firm A

$\sigma = \sqrt{\text{variance}}$ c.v. $= \frac{\sigma}{\bar{x}} \times 100$

$= \sqrt{100}$ $= \frac{10}{52.50} \times 100$

= 10 **= 19.05%**

$\Sigma x = 586 \times 52.50 =$ **Rs.30,765**

= Total wages

Firm B

$\sigma = \sqrt{\text{variance}}$ c.v. $= \frac{\sigma}{\bar{x}} \times 100$

$= \sqrt{121}$ $= \frac{11}{47.50} \times 100$

= 11 **= 23.16%**

$\Sigma x = 648 \times 47.50 =$ **Rs.30,780**

= Total wages

Factory **B** pays out more wages than factory A, and at the same it has greater variability also.

Example 10.23. *Following are the marks scored by 2 students in a class test.* *(BU – N91)*

X :	*25*	*29*	*35*	*39*	*39*
Y :	*28*	*23*	*32*	*40*	*49*

Find who is more consistent student.

Solution : Computation of Standard Deviation

x Student			y Student		
X x	$(x-\bar{x})$ d	d^2	Y x	$(x-\bar{x})$ d	d^2
25	-10.4	108.16	23	-11.4	129.96
29	-6.4	40.96	28	-6.4	40.96
35	-0.4	0.16	32	-2.4	5.76
39	+3.6	12.96	40	+5.6	31.36
49	+13.6	184.96	49	+14.6	213.16
$\Sigma x = 177$	$\Sigma d = 0$	$\Sigma d^2 = 347.20$	$\Sigma x = 172$	$\Sigma d = 0$	$\Sigma d^2 = 421.20$

$\bar{x} = \frac{\Sigma x}{n}$	$\sigma = \sqrt{\frac{\Sigma d^2}{n}}$	$c.v = \frac{\sigma}{\bar{x}} \times 100$	$\bar{x} = \frac{\Sigma x}{n}$	$\sigma = \sqrt{\frac{\Sigma d^2}{n}}$	$c.v = \frac{\sigma}{\bar{x}} \times 100$
$= \frac{177}{5}$	$= \sqrt{\frac{347.20}{5}}$	$= \frac{8.333}{35.4} \times 100$	$= \frac{172}{5}$	$= \sqrt{\frac{421.20}{5}}$	$= \frac{9.178}{34.4} \times 100$
$= \mathbf{35.4}$	$= \sqrt{69.44}$	$= \mathbf{2.54\%}$	$= \mathbf{34.4}$	$= \sqrt{84.24}$	$= \mathbf{26.681\%}$
	$= \mathbf{8.333}$			$= \mathbf{9.178}$	

'X' student is more consistent than **'Y'** as his variation is less.

Example 10.24. *A study of large number of workers revealed an average pulse rate of 81 beats per minute and standard deviation 12.2 beats. Measurement of heights gave averages 66.9 inches and standard deviation 2.7 inches. Are the industrial workers more variable in respect of pulse rate?* *(BU-94)*

Solution :

Pulse Rate	Height in inches
$\bar{x} = 81$	$\bar{x} = 66.9$
$\sigma = 12.2$	$\sigma = 2.7$
$\therefore$ c.v. $= \frac{\sigma}{\bar{x}} \times 100$	$\therefore$ c.v. $= \frac{\sigma}{\bar{x}} \times 100$
$= \frac{12.2}{81} \times 100 = \mathbf{15.06\%}$	$= \frac{2.7}{66.9} \times 100 = \mathbf{4.036\%}$

Yes the industrial workers are more variable in pulse rate.

Example 10.25. *The goals scored by two teams A and B in the football matches were as follows:*

Goals	:	*0*	*1*	*2*	*3*	*4*
Matches A	:	*27*	*9*	*8*	*4*	*5*
B	:	*17*	*9*	*6*	*5*	*3*

Find the team which is more consistent. *(BU-A86)*

Solution: **Computation of Standard Deviation**

(A)

No. of Goals (x)	f	fx	d	fd	fd^2
0	27	0	-2	-54	108
1	9	9	-1	-9	9
2	8	16	0	0	0
3	4	12	+1	+4	4
4	5	20	+2	+10	20
	n = 53	$\Sigma fx = 57$		$\Sigma fd = -49$	$\Sigma fd^2 = 141$

$$\bar{x} = \frac{\Sigma fx}{n} = \frac{57}{53} = \mathbf{1.0755}$$

$$\sigma = \sqrt{\frac{\Sigma fd^2}{n} - \left(\frac{\Sigma fd}{n}\right)^2} = \sqrt{\frac{141}{53} - \left(\frac{-49}{53}\right)^2} = \sqrt{2.66 - (-0.925)^2}$$

$$= \sqrt{1.8052} = \mathbf{1.3436}$$

$$\text{c.v.} = \frac{\sigma}{\bar{x}} \times 100 = \frac{1.3436}{1.0755} \times 100 = \mathbf{124.93\%}$$

Computation of Standard Deviation

(B)

No. of Goal (x)	f	fx	d	fd	fd^2
0	17	0	-2	-34	68
1	9	9	-1	-9	9
2	6	12	0	0	0
3	5	15	+1	+5	5
4	3	12	+2	+6	12
	n = 40	$\Sigma fx = 48$		$\Sigma fd = -32$	$\Sigma fd^2 = 94$

$$\bar{x} = \frac{\Sigma fx}{n} = \frac{48}{40} = \mathbf{1.2}$$

$$\sigma = \sqrt{\frac{\Sigma fd^2}{n} - \left(\frac{\Sigma fd}{n}\right)^2} = \sqrt{\frac{94}{40} - \left(\frac{-32}{40}\right)^2} = \sqrt{2.35 - (-0.8)^2}$$

$$= \sqrt{2.35 - 0.64} = \sqrt{1.71} = \mathbf{1.308}$$

$$\text{c.v.} = \frac{\sigma}{\bar{x}} \times 100 = \frac{1.308}{1.2} \times 100 = \mathbf{109\%}$$

Team **B** is more consistent as it has less variation.

Example 10.26. *The following table gives the age distribution of boys and girls in a high school. Find which of the two groups is more variable in age.* *(BU – A90)*

Age in years	:	*13*	*14*	*15*	*16*	*17*
No. of students						
(boys)	:	*12*	*15*	*15*	*5*	*3*
(girls)	:	*13*	*10*	*12*	*2*	*1*

Solution : Computation of Standard Deviation

Age (x) in years	f	fx	(Boys) d	fd	fd^2
13	12	156	-2	-24	48
14	15	210	-1	-15	15
15	15	225	0	0	0
16	5	80	+1	+5	5
17	3	51	+2	+6	12
	n = 50	Σfx = 722		Σfd = –28	Σfd^2 = 80

$$\bar{x} = \frac{\Sigma fx}{n} = \frac{722}{50} = \mathbf{14.44}$$

$$\sigma = \sqrt{\frac{\Sigma fd^2}{n} - \left(\frac{\Sigma fd}{n}\right)^2} = \sqrt{\frac{80}{50} - \left(\frac{-28}{50}\right)^2} = \sqrt{1.6 - (-0.56)^2}$$

$$= \sqrt{1.6 - 0.3136} = \sqrt{1.28641} = \mathbf{1.1342}$$

$$\text{c.v.} = \frac{\sigma}{\bar{x}} \times 100 = \frac{1.342}{14.44} \times 100 = \mathbf{7.855\%}$$

Computation of Standard Deviation

Age (x) in years	f	fx	d (Girls)	fd	fd^2
13	13	169	-2	-26	52
14	10	140	-1	-10	10
15	12	180	0	0	0
16	2	32	+1	+2	2
17	1	17	+2	+2	4
	n = 38	$\Sigma fx = 538$		$\Sigma fd = -32$	$\Sigma fd^2 = 68$

$$\bar{x} = \frac{\Sigma fx}{n} = \frac{538}{38} = \mathbf{14.16}$$

$$\sigma = \sqrt{\frac{\Sigma fd^2}{n} - \left(\frac{\Sigma fd}{n}\right)^2} = \sqrt{\frac{68}{38} - \left(\frac{-32}{38}\right)^2} = \sqrt{1.7895 - (-0.842)^2}$$

$$= \sqrt{1.7895 - 0.7091} = \sqrt{1.0804} = \mathbf{1.039}$$

$$\text{c.v.} = \frac{\sigma}{\bar{x}} \times 100 = \frac{1.039}{14.16} \times 100 = \mathbf{7.341\%}$$

Age of boys is more variable as its variation is more.

Example 10.27. *Calculate the Standard Deviation from the following data:* *(BU – N84)*

Midpoint	*1*	*2*	*3*	*4*	*5*	*6*	*7*	*8*	*9*
Frequency	*4*	*120*	*202*	*304*	*410*	*310*	*158*	*80*	*2*

Solution : Computation of Standard Deviation

M.P	f	d	fd	fd^2
1	4	-4	-16	64
2	120	-3	-360	1080
3	202	-2	-404	808
4	304	-1	-304	304
5	410	0	0	0
6	310	+1	+310	310
7	158	+2	+316	632
8	80	+3	+240	720
9	2	+4	8	32
	n = 1590	$\Sigma d = 0$	$\Sigma fd = -210$	$\Sigma fd^2 = 3950$

$$\bar{x} = A + \frac{\Sigma fd}{n} = 5 + \frac{-210}{1590} = 5 - 0.1321 = \mathbf{4.868}$$

$$\sigma = \sqrt{\frac{\Sigma fd^2}{n} - \left(\frac{\Sigma fd}{n}\right)^2} = \sqrt{\frac{3950}{1590} - \left(\frac{}{1590}\right)^2} = \sqrt{2.484 - (-0.1321)^2}$$

$$= \sqrt{2.484 - 0.1745} = \sqrt{2.4665} = \mathbf{1.571}$$

$$\text{c.v.} = \frac{\sigma}{\bar{x}} \times 100 = \frac{1.571}{4.868} \times 100 = \mathbf{32.26\%}$$

Example 10.28. *Compute the Coefficient of Variation from the following data :* *(BU-N87)*

Profit/Loss (in '000' Rs.)	No. of Shops	Profit/Loss (in '000' Rs.)	No. of Shops
-4 -- -3	4	+1 -- +2	56
-3 -- -2	10	+2 -- +3	40
-2 -- -1	22	+3 -- +4	24
-1-- 0	28	+4 -- +5	18
0 -- +1	38	+5 -- +6	10

Solution: **Computation of Standard Deviation**

Profit / Loss C.I.	f	m.v	2(mv) x	fx	fx²
-4 -- - 3	4	-3.5	-7	-28	196
-3 -- - 2	10	-2.5	-5	-50	250
-2 -- - 1	22	-1.5	-3	-66	198
-1 -- 0	28	-0.5	-1	-28	28
0 -- +1	38	+0.5	+1	+38	38
+1 -- +2	56	+1.5	+3	+168	504
+2 -- +3	40	+2.5	+5	+200	1000
+3 -- +4	24	+3.5	+7	+168	1176
+4 -- +5	18	+4.5	+9	+162	1458
+5 - +6	10	+5.5	+11	+110	1210
	n = 250			+674	6058
				Σfx =	Σfx^2 =

$$\bar{x} = \frac{\Sigma fx}{n} \times \frac{1}{2} = \frac{674}{250} \times \frac{1}{2} = 2.696 \times \frac{1}{2} = \mathbf{1.348} \qquad \therefore \text{ Rs. } 1{,}348$$

$$\sigma = \sqrt{\frac{\Sigma fx^2}{n} - \left(\frac{\Sigma fx}{n}\right)^2} \times \frac{1}{2} = \sqrt{\frac{6058}{250} - \left(\frac{-674}{250}\right)^2} \times \frac{1}{2}$$

$$= \sqrt{24.232 - (-2.696)^2} \times \frac{1}{2} = \sqrt{24.232 - 7.2684} \times \frac{1}{2}$$

$$= \sqrt{16.96} \times \frac{1}{2} = 4.1187 \times \frac{1}{2} = \mathbf{2.059}$$

$$\text{c.v.} = \frac{\sigma}{\bar{x}} \times 100 = \frac{2.059}{1.348} \times 100 = \mathbf{152.745\%}$$

Example 10.29 *A factory produces two types of tyres. In an experiment in the working life of these tyres the following results are obtained :*

(BU – N89)

Length of life in '00' hours:	*15-17*	*17-19*	*19-21*	*21-23*	*23-25*
Type A	*50*	*110*	*260*	*100*	*80*
Type B	*40*	*300*	*120*	*80*	*60*

State which type of tyres are more stable.

Solution : **Computation of Standard Deviation**

Length of life in '00' hours C.I	x	(x – 20)/2 d'	A type			B type		
			f	fd'	fd'²	f	fd'	fd'²
15 – 17	16	-2	50	-100	200	40	- 80	160
17 – 19	18	-1	100	-110	110	300	-300	300
19 – 22	20	0	260	0	0	120	0	0
21 – 23	22	+1	100	+100	100	80	+ 80	80
23 – 25	24	+2	80	+160	320	60	+120	240
		Σd = C	600 n =	50 Σfd'=	730 Σfd'² =	60 n =	180 Σfd'=	780 Σfd'² =

$$\bar{x}_A = A + \frac{\Sigma fd'}{n} \times c = 20 + \frac{50}{600} \times 2 = 20 + 0.1667 = \mathbf{20.1667}$$

$$\bar{x}_B = A + \frac{\Sigma fd'}{n} \times c = 20 + \frac{-180}{600} \times 2 = 20 - 0.6 = \mathbf{19.4}$$

$$\sigma_A = \sqrt{\frac{\Sigma fd'^2}{n} - \left(\frac{\Sigma fd'}{n}\right)^2} \times c = \sqrt{\frac{730}{600} - \left(\frac{50}{600}\right)^2} \times 2$$

$$= \sqrt{1.2167 - (0.083)^2} \times 2 = \sqrt{1.2167 - 0.00694} \times 2$$

$$= \sqrt{1.20976} \times 2 = 1.099891 \times 2 = \mathbf{2.1998}$$

$$\text{c.v.} = \frac{\sigma}{\bar{x}} \times 100 = \frac{2.1998}{20.1667} \times 100 = \mathbf{10.91\%}$$

$$\sigma_B = \sqrt{\frac{\Sigma fd'^2}{n} - \left(\frac{\Sigma fd'}{n}\right)^2} \times c = \sqrt{\frac{780}{600} - \left(\frac{-180}{600}\right)^2} \times 2$$

$$= \sqrt{1.3 - (-0.3)^2} \times 2 = \sqrt{1.3 - 0.09} \times 2$$

$$= \sqrt{1.21} \times 2 = 1.1 \times 2 = \mathbf{2.2}$$

$$\text{c.v.} = \frac{\sigma}{\bar{x}} \times 100 = \frac{2.2}{19.4} \times 100 = \mathbf{11.34\%}$$

Type **'A'** tyres are more stable as their variation is less than **'B'** tyres.

Example 10.30. *An agent obtained samples of bulbs from the 2 companies. He had them tested for durability and got the following results :*

Durability in '00' hr.	*Company A*	*Company B*
17 – 19	*100*	*30*
19 – 21	*160*	*420*
21 – 23	*260*	*120*
23 – 25	*80*	*30*

Which company bulbs are more uniform? *(BU – A91)*

Solution : Computation of Standard Deviation

Durability in '00' hours C.I.	x	(x – 20)/2 d'	A Company f	A Company fd'	A Company fd'²	B Company f	B Company fd'	B Company fd'²
17 – 19	18	-1	100	-100	100	30	- 30	30
19 – 21	20	0	160	0	0	420	0	0
21 – 23	22	+1	260	+260	260	120	+120	120
23 – 25	24	+2	80	+160	320	80	+60	120
			600 n =	320 Σfd'=	680 Σfd'² =	600 n =	150 Σfd'=	270 Σfd'² =

$$\bar{x}_A = A + \frac{\Sigma fd'}{n} \times c = 20 + \frac{320}{600} \times 2 = 20 + 1.0667 = \mathbf{21.0667}$$

$$\bar{x}_B = A + \frac{\Sigma fd'}{n} \times c = 20 + \frac{150}{600} \times 2 = 20 + 0.5 = \mathbf{20.5}$$

$$\sigma_A = \sqrt{\frac{\Sigma fd'^2}{n} - \left(\frac{\Sigma fd'}{n}\right)^2} \times 2 = \sqrt{\frac{680}{600} - \left(\frac{320}{600}\right)^2} \times 2$$

$$= \sqrt{1.1333 - (0.533)^2} \times 2 = \sqrt{1.1333 - 0.2844} \times 2$$

$$= \sqrt{0.84885} \times 2 = 0.92136 \times 2 = \mathbf{1.8427}$$

$$\text{c.v.} = \frac{\sigma}{\bar{x}} \times 100 = \frac{184.27}{2106.67} \times 100 = \mathbf{8.747\%}$$

$$\sigma_B = \sqrt{\frac{\Sigma fd'^2}{n} - \left(\frac{\Sigma fd'}{n}\right)^2} \times c = \sqrt{\frac{270}{600} - \left(\frac{150}{600}\right)^2} \times 2$$

$$= \sqrt{0.45 - (-0.25)^2} \times 2 = \sqrt{0.45 - 0.0625} \times 2$$

$$= \sqrt{0.3875} \times 2 = 0.622495 \times 2 = \mathbf{1.245}$$

$$\text{c.v.} = \frac{\sigma}{\bar{x}} \times 100 = \frac{1.245}{20.5} \times 100 = \mathbf{6.073\%}$$

The Bulbs of **'B'** company are more uniform and durable than the bulbs of **'A'** company as the variation in B bulbs is less.

Example 10.31. Find which of the two classes is more consistent in scoring marks from the following table: (BU- A92)

Marks	:	20-30	30-40	40-50	50-60	60-70
Class A	:	7	10	20	18	7
Class B	:	5	9	21	15	6

Solution : **Computation of Standard Deviation**

Marks Class	x	(x – 45)/10 d'	A Class f	A Class fd'	A Class fd'²	B Class f	B Class fd'	B Class fd'²
20 – 30	25	-2	7	-14	28	5	-10	20
30 – 40	35	-1	10	-10	10	9	-9	9
40 – 50	45	0	20	0	0	21	0	0
50 – 60	55	+1	18	+18	18	15	+15	15
60 – 70	65	+2	7	+14	28	6	+12	24
			n = 62	Σfd' = 8	Σfd'² = 84	n = 56	Σfd' = 8	Σfd'² = 68

$$\bar{x}_A = A + \frac{\Sigma fd'}{n} \times c = 45 + \frac{8}{62} \times 10 = 45 + 1.29 = \mathbf{46.29}$$

$$\bar{x}_B = A + \frac{\Sigma fd'}{n} \times c = 45 + \frac{8}{56} \times 10 = 45 + 1.429 = \mathbf{46.43}$$

$$\sigma_A = \sqrt{\frac{\Sigma fd'^2}{n} - \left(\frac{\Sigma fd'}{n}\right)^2} \times c = \sqrt{\frac{84}{62} - \left(\frac{8}{62}\right)^2} \times 10$$

$$= \sqrt{1.3548 - (0.129)^2} \times 10 = \sqrt{1.3548 - 0.01665} \times 10$$

$$= \sqrt{1.33815} \times 10 = \mathbf{11.568}$$

$$\text{c.v.} = \frac{\sigma}{\bar{x}} \times 100 = \frac{11.568}{46.29} \times 100 = \mathbf{24.99\%}$$

$$\sigma_B = \sqrt{\frac{\Sigma fd'^2}{n} - \left(\frac{\Sigma fd'}{n}\right)^2} \times c = \sqrt{\frac{68}{56} - \left(\frac{8}{56}\right)^2} \times 10$$

$$= \sqrt{1.2143 - (-0.1429)^2} \times 10 = \sqrt{1.2143 - 0.0204} \times 10$$

$$= \sqrt{1.9939} \times 10 = \mathbf{10.927}$$

$$\text{c.v.} = \frac{\sigma}{\bar{x}} \times 100 = \frac{10.927}{46.43} \times 100 = \mathbf{23.53\%}$$

Class **'B'** students are more consistent as their variation is less.

Example 10.32. Two brands of Tyres are tested for their life and the following results were obtained:

Life (in months)	:	20-25	25-30	30-35	35-40	40-45
No. of Tyres `X'	:	1	22	64	10	3
No. of Tyres `Y'	:	3	21	74	1	1

If consistency is the criterion which brand of tyres would you prefer? (BU – N92)

Solution : Computation of Standard Deviation

Life (in months) C.I.	x	$(x-32)/5$ d'	X Brand			Y Brand		
			f	fd'	fd'^{2}	f	fd'	fd'^{2}
20 – 25	22.5	-2	1	-2	4	3	-6	12
25 – 30	27.5	-1	22	-22	22	21	-21	21
30 – 35	32.5	0	64	0	0	74	0	0
35 – 40	37.5	+1	10	+10	10	1	+1	1
40 – 45	42.5	+2	3	+6	12	1	+2	4
		$\Sigma d' = 0$	n = 100	$\Sigma fd' = -8$	$\Sigma fd'^2 = 48$	n = 100	$\Sigma fd' = -24$	$\Sigma fd'^2 = 38$

$$\overline{x} = A + \frac{\Sigma fd'}{n} \times c = 32.5 + \frac{-8}{100} \times 5 = 32.5 - 0.4 = \mathbf{32.1}$$

$$\overline{y} = A + \frac{\Sigma fd'}{n} \times c = 32.5 + \frac{-24}{100} \times 5 = 32.5 + 1.2 = \mathbf{31.3}$$

$$\sigma_x = \sqrt{\frac{\Sigma fd'^2}{n} - \left(\frac{\Sigma fd'}{n}\right)^2} \times c = \sqrt{\frac{48}{100} - \left(\frac{-8}{100}\right)^2} \times 5$$

$$= \sqrt{0.48 - (-0.08)^2} \times 5 = \sqrt{0.48 - 0.0064} \times 5$$

$$= \sqrt{0.4736} \times 5 = 0.6882 \times 5 = \mathbf{3.44}$$

$$c.v = \frac{\sigma}{\overline{x}} \times 100 = \frac{3.44}{32.1} \times 100 = \mathbf{10.72\%}$$

$$\sigma_y = \sqrt{\frac{\Sigma fd'^2}{n} - \left(\frac{\Sigma fd'}{n}\right)^2} \times c = \sqrt{\frac{38}{100} - \left(\frac{-24}{100}\right)^2} \times 5$$

$$= \sqrt{0.38 - (-0.24)^2} \times 5 = \sqrt{0.38 - 0.0576} \times 5$$

$$= \sqrt{0.3224} \times 5 = 0.5678 \times 5 = \mathbf{2.839}$$

$$\text{c.v.} = \frac{\sigma}{\bar{x}} \times 100 = \frac{2.839}{31.3} \times 100 = \mathbf{9.07\%}$$

'Y' Brand Tyres are more consistent than 'X' Brand Tyres.

Example 10.33. *A purchasing agent obtained samples of lamps from two suppliers 'A' and 'B' with the following information:*

Length of the Life (in hours) :	*500-700*	*700-900*	*900-1100*	*1100-1300*
Supplier 'A' :	*10*	*16*	*30*	*8*
Supplier 'B' :	*3*	*42*	*12*	*4*

Which supplier's lamps are more uniform? (BU-A93)

Solution : Computation of Standard Deviation

Length of life (in hours) C.I.	x	$\frac{(x-20)}{2}$ d'	Supplier A f	Supplier A fd'	Supplier A fd'²	Supplier B f	Supplier B fd'	Supplier B fd'²
500 – 700	600	-1	10	-10	10	3	-3	3
700 - 900	800	0	16	0	0	42	0	0
900- 1100	1000	+1	30	+30	30	12	+12	12
1100-1300	1200	+2	8	+16	32	4	+8	16
		Σd'= +1	n = 64	Σfd'= 36	Σfd'² = 72	n = 61	Σfd'= 17	Σfd'² = 31

$$\bar{x}_A = A + \frac{\Sigma fd'}{n} \times c = 800 + \frac{36}{64} \times 200 = 800 + 112.5 = \mathbf{912.5}$$

$$\bar{x}_B = A + \frac{\Sigma fd'}{n} \times c = 800 + \frac{17}{61} \times 200 = 800 + 55.7377 = \mathbf{855.74}$$

$$\sigma_A = \sqrt{\frac{\Sigma fd'^2}{n} - \left(\frac{\Sigma fd'}{n}\right)^2} \times c = \sqrt{\frac{72}{64} - \left(\frac{36}{64}\right)^2} \times 200$$

$$= \sqrt{1.125 - (0.5625)^2} \times 200 = \sqrt{1.125 - 0.31641} \times 200$$

$$= \sqrt{0.80859} \times 200 = 0.89922 \times 200 = \mathbf{179.84}$$

$$\text{c.v.} = \frac{\sigma}{\bar{x}} \times 100 = \frac{179.84}{912.5} \times 100 = \mathbf{19.71\%}$$

$$\sigma_B = \sqrt{\frac{\Sigma fd'^2}{n} - \left(\frac{\Sigma fd'}{n}\right)^2} \times c = \sqrt{\frac{31}{61} - \left(\frac{17}{61}\right)^2} \times 200$$

$$= \sqrt{0.5082 - (-0.2787)^2} \times 200 = \sqrt{0.5082 - 0.07767} \times 200$$

$$= \sqrt{0.43053} \times 200 = 0.65615 \times 200 = \mathbf{131.23}$$

$$\text{c.v.} = \frac{\sigma}{\bar{x}} \times 100 = \frac{131.23}{855.74} \times 100 = \mathbf{15.34\%}$$

'B' Supplier's lamps are uniform as their variation is less than the **'A'** supplier`s lamps.

Example 10.34. *A factory produces two types of electric lamps `A' and `B' Details regarding their life were as follows:*

Length of Life (in hours)	*: 500-700*	*700-900*	*900-1100*	*1100-1300*	*1300-1500*
No of Lamps`A' :	*5*	*11*	*26*	*10*	*8*
No of Lamps`B' :	*4*	*30*	*12*	*8*	*6*

Compare the variability of life of the two lamps *(BU-A96)*

Solution : **Computation of Standard Deviation**

Length of life (in hours) C.I.	x	$\frac{(x-1000)}{200}$ d'	A Lamps			B Lamps		
			f	fd'	fd'²	f	fd'	fd'²
500–700	600	-2	5	-10	20	4	-8	16
700-900	800	-1	11	-11	11	30	-30	30
900-1100	1000	0	26	0	0	12	0	0
1100-1300	1200	+1	10	+10	10	8	+8	8
1200-1500	1400	+2	8	+16	32	6	+12	24
		$\Sigma d' = 0$	n = 60	$\Sigma fd' = 36$	$\Sigma fd'^2 = 5$	n = 60	$\Sigma fd' = -18$	$\Sigma fd'^2 = 78$

$$\bar{x}_A = A + \frac{\Sigma fd'}{n} \times c = 1000 + \frac{5}{60} \times 200 = 1000 + 16.667 = \mathbf{1016.667}$$

$$\bar{x}_B = A + \frac{\Sigma fd'}{n} \times c = 1000 + \frac{-18}{60} \times 200 = 1000 - 60 = \mathbf{940}$$

$$\sigma_A = \sqrt{\frac{\Sigma fd'^2}{n} - \left(\frac{\Sigma fd'}{n}\right)^2} \times c = \sqrt{\frac{73}{60} - \left(\frac{5}{60}\right)^2} \times 200$$

$$= \sqrt{1.21667 - (0.0833)^2} \times 200 = \sqrt{1.21667 - 0.00694} \times 200$$

$$= \sqrt{1.20973} \times 200 = 1.09988 \times 200 = \mathbf{219.975}$$

$$\text{c.v.} = \frac{\sigma}{\bar{x}} \times 100 = \frac{219.975}{1016.667} \times 100 = \mathbf{21.637\%}$$

$$\sigma_B = \sqrt{\frac{\Sigma fd'^2}{n} - \left(\frac{\Sigma fd'}{n}\right)^2} \times c = \sqrt{\frac{78}{60} - \left(\frac{-18}{60}\right)^2} \times 200$$

$$= \sqrt{1.30 - (0.3)^2} \times 200 = \sqrt{1.30 - 0.09} \times 200$$

$$= \sqrt{1.21} \times 200 = 1.1 \times 200 = \mathbf{220.00}$$

$$\text{c.v.} = \frac{\sigma}{\bar{x}} \times 100 = \frac{220}{940} \times 100 = \mathbf{23.40\%}$$

Variability of life of the **'A'** bulb is less and it is more durable than the **'B'** bulb.

Example 10.35. *The following data relates to the wages of workers in two factories 'A' and 'B'. Which factory wages are more variable?* *(BU-N96)*

Wages (Rs) :	*Less than 5*	*5-10*	*10-15*	*15-20*	*20-25*	*25-30*
No. of workers 'A' :	*20*	*18*	*30*	*25*	*20*	*15*
No. of workers 'B' :	*15*	*20*	*35*	*30*	*18*	*17*

Solution : Computation of Standard Deviation

Wages (Rs.) C.I.	x	$(x-12.5)/5$ d'	A Factory f	A Factory fd'	A Factory fd'²	B Factory f	B Factory fd'	B Factory fd'²
0 – 5	2.5	-2	20	-40	80	15	-30	60
5 – 10	7.5	-1	18	-18	18	20	-20	20
10 – 15	12.5	0	30	0	0	35	0	0
15 - 20	17.5	+1	25	+25	25	30	+30	30
20 – 25	22.5	+2	20	+40	80	18	+36	72
25 - 30	27.5	+3	15	+45	135	17	+51	153
		$\Sigma d' = +3$	n = 128	$\Sigma fd' = 52$	338 $\Sigma fd'^2 =$	n = 135	67 $\Sigma fd' =$	335 $\Sigma fd'^2 =$

$$\bar{x}_A = A + \frac{\Sigma fd'}{n} \times c = 12.5 + \frac{52}{128} \times 5 = 12.5 + 2.031 = \mathbf{14.531}$$

$$\bar{x}_B = A + \frac{\Sigma fd'}{n} \times c = 12.5 + \frac{67}{135} \times 5 = 12.5 + 2.482 = \mathbf{14.982}$$

$$\sigma_A = \sqrt{\frac{\Sigma fd'^2}{n} - \left(\frac{\Sigma fd'}{n}\right)^2} \times c = \sqrt{\frac{338}{128} - \left(\frac{52}{128}\right)^2} \times 5$$

$$= \sqrt{2.6406 - (0.4063)^2} \times 5 = \sqrt{2.6406 - 0.16504} \times 5$$

$$= \sqrt{2.47556} \times 5 = 1.5733912 \times 5 = \mathbf{7.8669}$$

$$\text{c.v.} = \frac{\sigma}{\bar{x}} \times 100 = \frac{7.8669}{14.531} \times 100 = \mathbf{54.14\%}$$

$$\sigma_B = \sqrt{\frac{\Sigma fd'^2}{n} - \left(\frac{\Sigma fd'}{n}\right)^2} \times c = \sqrt{\frac{335}{135} - \left(\frac{67}{135}\right)^2} \times 5$$

$$= \sqrt{2.4815 - (0.4963)^2} \times 5 = \sqrt{2.4815 - 0.24631} \times 5$$

$$= \sqrt{2.23519} \times 5 = 1.4951 \times 5 = \mathbf{7.475}$$

$$\text{c.v.} = \frac{\sigma}{\bar{x}} \times 100 = \frac{7.475}{14.982} \times 100 = \mathbf{49.89\%}$$

Wages of the workers of factory **A** are more variable as their variation is more than the variance of the workers of factory **B**.

Example 10.36. *From the data given below state which of the two series is more variable:* *(BU-A97)*

Variable	:	*10-20*	*20-30*	*30-40*	*40-50*	*50-60*	*60-70*
frequency`A'	:	*10*	*18*	*32*	*40*	*22*	*18*
frequency`B'	:	*18*	*22*	*40*	*32*	*18*	*10*

Solution : Computation of Standard Deviation

Variable C.I.	x	(x – 35)/10 d'	A f	A fd'	A fd'^{2}	B f	B fd'	B fd'^{2}
10 – 20	15	-2	10	-20	40	18	-36	72
20 – 30	25	-1	18	-18	18	22	-22	22
30 – 40	35	0	32	0	0	40	0	0
40 – 50	45	+1	40	+40	40	32	+32	32
50 – 60	55	+2	22	+44	88	18	+36	72
60 – 70	65	+3	18	+54	162	10	+30	90
		Σd'= +3	n = 140	100 Σfd'=	348 Σfd^2 =	n = 140	40 Σfd'=	288 Σfd^2 =

$$\bar{x}_A = A + \frac{\Sigma fd'}{n} \times c = 35 + \frac{100}{140} \times 10 = 35 + 7.1429 = \mathbf{42.1429}$$

$$\bar{x}_B = A + \frac{\Sigma fd'}{n} \times c = 35 + \frac{40}{140} \times 10 = 35 + 2.8571 = \mathbf{37.8571}$$

$$\sigma_A = \sqrt{\frac{\Sigma fd'^2}{n} - \left(\frac{\Sigma fd'}{n}\right)^2} \times c = \sqrt{\frac{348}{140} - \left(\frac{100}{140}\right)^2} \times 10$$

$$= \sqrt{2.4857 - (0.714285)^2} \times 10 = \sqrt{2.4857 - 0.5102} \times 10$$

$$= \sqrt{1.9755} \times 10 = 1.405525 \times 10 = \mathbf{14.055}$$

$$\text{c.v.} = \frac{\sigma}{\bar{x}} \times 100 = \frac{14.055}{42.1429} \times 100 = \mathbf{33.351\%}$$

$$\sigma_B = \sqrt{\frac{\Sigma fd'^2}{n} - \left(\frac{\Sigma fd'}{n}\right)^2} \times c = \sqrt{\frac{288}{140} - \left(\frac{40}{140}\right)^2} \times 10$$

$$= \sqrt{2.05714 - (0.28571)^2} \times 10 = \sqrt{2.05714 - 0.081633} \times 10$$

$$= \sqrt{1.97551} \times 10 = 1.405527 \times 10 = \mathbf{14.055}$$

$$\text{`c.v.} = \frac{\sigma}{\bar{x}} \times 100 = \frac{14.055}{37.8571} \times 100 = \mathbf{37.127\%}$$

Series 'B' is more variable.

Example 10.37. *Two brands of tyres are tested with the following results:*

Life in ('000' miles)	:	*20-25*	*25-30*	*30-35*	*35-40*	*40-45*
No. of Tyres 'X'	:	*1*	*22*	*64*	*10*	*3*
No. of Tyres 'Y'	:	*0*	*24*	*76*	*0*	*0*

Compare the variability and state which brand of tyres would you use on your fleet of trucks? *(BU-N97)*

Solution : **Computation of Standard Deviation**

Life in '000' miles	x	(x − 32.5)/ d'	X type			Y type		
			f	fd'	fd'^{2}	f	fd'	fd'^{2}
20 – 25	22.5	-2	1	-2	4	0	0	0
25 – 30	27.5	-1	22	-22	22	24	-24	+24
30 – 35	32.5	0	64	0	0	76	0	0
35 – 40	37.5	+1	10	+10	10	0	0	0
40 - 45	42.5	+2	3	+6	12	0	0	0
		Σd' = 0	n = 100	− 8 Σfd' =	48 Σfd'^{2} =	n = 100	−24 Σfd' =	+ 24 Σfd'^{2} =

$$\bar{x}_A = A + \frac{\Sigma fd'}{n} \times c = 32.5 + \frac{-8}{100} \times 5 = 32.5 - 0.4 = \mathbf{32.1}$$

$$\bar{x}_B = A + \frac{\Sigma fd'}{n} \times c = 32.5 + \frac{-24}{100} \times 5 = 32.5 - 1.2 = \mathbf{31.3}$$

$$\sigma_A = \sqrt{\frac{\Sigma fd'^2}{n} - \left(\frac{\Sigma fd'}{n}\right)^2} \times c = \sqrt{\frac{48}{100} - \left(\frac{-8}{100}\right)^2} \times 5$$

$$= \sqrt{0.48 - (-0.08)^2} \times 5 = \sqrt{0.48 - 0.0064} \times 5$$

$$= \sqrt{0.4736} \times 5 = 0.6882 \times 5 = \mathbf{3.44}$$

$$\text{c.v.} = \frac{\sigma}{\bar{x}} \times 100 = \frac{3.44}{32.1} \times 100 = \mathbf{10.72\%}$$

$$\sigma_B = \sqrt{\frac{\Sigma fd'^2}{n}\left(\frac{\Sigma fd'}{n}\right)^2} \times c = \sqrt{\frac{24}{100} - \left(\frac{-24}{100}\right)^2} \times 5$$

$$= \sqrt{0.24 - (-0.24)^2} \times 5 = \sqrt{0.24 - 0.0576} \times 5$$

$$= \sqrt{0.1824} \times 5 = 0.42708 \times 5 = \mathbf{2.14}$$

$$\text{c.v.} = \frac{\sigma}{\overline{x}} \times 100 = \frac{2.14}{31.3} \times 100 = \mathbf{6.837\%}$$

We can use `Y' brand types as their variation is less than the `x' brand tyres.

Example 10.38. *Mean and Standard Deviation of the following continuous series are 31 and 15.9 respectively. The distribution, after taking step deviations is follows:* ***(BU-N93)***

dx	:	*-3*	*-2*	*-1*	*0*	*+1*	*+2*	*+3*
f	:	*10*	*15*	*25*	*25*	*10*	*10*	*5*

Determine the actual classes.

Solution : To determine the classes, we need two values-class interval and assumed mean as under:

d'	f	fd'	fd'²
-3	10	-30	90
-2	15	-30	60
-1	25	-25	25
0	25	0	0
1	10	+10	10
2	10	+20	40
3	5	+15	45
	n = 100	$\Sigma fd' = -40$	$\Sigma fd'^2 = 270$

$$\sigma = \sqrt{\frac{\Sigma fd'}{n} - \left(\frac{\Sigma fd}{n}\right)^2} \times c \qquad 15.9 = \sqrt{\frac{270}{100} - \left(\frac{-40}{100}\right)^2} \times c$$

$$15.9 = \sqrt{2.7 - (0.4)^2} \times c \qquad 15.9 = \sqrt{2.7 - 0.16} \times c$$

$$15.9 = \sqrt{2.54} \times c \qquad \overline{x} = A + \frac{\Sigma fd'}{n} \times c$$

$$15.9 = 1.5937 \times c \qquad 31 = A + \frac{-40}{100} \times 10$$

$$c = \frac{1.59}{1.59} = 10 \qquad 31 = A - 4$$

$$A = 35$$

The variable under study is a continuous series . The d = 0 class refers to 35 and its class is $\left(35 - \frac{c}{2}\right)$ and $\left(35 + \frac{c}{2}\right)$ i.e., 30 - 40.

Take the remaining classes on both the sides as under,

Class : 0-10 10-20 20-30 ←30-40→ 40-50 50-60 60-70

Characteristics of Standard Deviation

Standard Deviation and Coefficient of Variation possess all those properties, which a good measure of dispersion should possess. The process of squaring the deviations eliminates negative sins, and thus makes the mathematical manipulation of figures easy.

Merits of Standard Deviation : Following are the merits of standard deviations.

i) It is based on all the observations given.

ii) It can be smoothly handled algebraically.

iii) It is a well defined and definite measure of dispersion

iv) It is of great importance, when we are making comparison between variability of two series.

Demerits of Standards Deviations : In spite of its merits the standard deviation suffers from the following limitations:

i) It is difficult to calculate and understand.

ii) It gives more weight to extreme values as the deviations are squared.

iii) It is not useful in economic studies.

Questions

1. What are the objects of measuring dispersion?(BU-A83, N86)
2. State the limitations of range method of dispersion. (BU-N83,N87,A90)
3. State demerits of Mean Deviation. (BU-A85,N89)
4. "Dispersion is known as the average of the second order" Give reasons. (BU-A86,A93)
5. What is Mean Deviation? What are its merits? (BU-A88)
6. What are the uses of range as a method of dispersion? (BU-A89)
7. Define Standard Deviation. (BU-N90,N95)
8. Name the various measures of dispersions. (BU-A91)
9. What is dispersion? What are its objects? (BU-N93)
10. What are the merits and demerits of Mean Deviation? (BU-A93)
11. Give two merits of Quartile Deviation. (BU-A95)
12. What is Range? State its limitations. (BU-N97)
13. The upper and the lower quartile income of a group of workers are Rs.8. and Rs.3. per day respectively. Calculate the Quartile Deviations and its Coefficient.

    (Q.D.=25. Coefficient of Q.D.=0.4545)
14. In a distribution the following results are given:

    Maximum Value = 60, Coefficient of Range = 0.6.

    Find the Range and minimum value. (minimum value = 15. Range = 45)
15. Calculate the value of Mean Deviation from Mean, Median and Mode and their coefficients from the following distribution:

Monthly Rent in Rs.	No. of houses	Monthly Rent in Rs.	No of houses
Less than 10	3	Less than 50	37
Less than 20	8	Less than 60	50
Less than 30	16	Less than 70	56
Less than 40	26	Less than 80	60

M.D. from $\bar{x}$ = 15.36- Coefficient of M.D. = 0.3628	$\bar{x}$ = 42.3333
M.D.from me =15.18- Coefficient of M.D. = 0.3479	me = 43.6363
M.D. from z = 15.22- Coefficient of M.D.= 0.3512	z = 43.3333

16. The coefficient of variation of two series are 66% and 80% and their Standard Deviation are 20 and 16 respectively. Find their arithmetic means. ($\bar{x}$ = 30.3 and $\bar{x}$ = 20)

17. Compute the Mean Deviation from Mean from the following data:

C.I:	140–150	150–160	160–170	170–180	180–190	190-100
f :	4	6	10	18	9	3

(M.D. = 10.56)

18. Calculate Quartile Deviation and its Coefficient from the following data:

Marks more than :	0	10	20	30	40	50	60	70
No of students :	150	142	130	100	72	30	12	4

(Q.D. = 11.9 Coefficient of Q.D. = 0.3)

19. Calculate the Mean Deviation and Standard Deviation from the following data:

Value :	90–99	80–89	70–79	60–69	50–59	40–49	30–39
Frequencies :	2	12	22	20	14	4	1

(M.D. = 10.25, S.D. = 12.5)

11

Skewness

'Skewness' means a tendency of **'Twist'** or **'Turn'** or **'Not Being Straight'.** Skewness is a refined measure of dispersion. This measure gives a degree of twist by which we can have the clear picture of the formation of the distribution. It provides the basis upon which different distributions can be distinguished. It is concerned with the direction of variation and tells how far the distribution departs from the symmetry (Bell shaped) or uniformity or similarity. It is a lack of symmetry.

Skewness denotes the opposite of symmetry and relates to the shape of the curve of a distribution. It means all the asymmetrical distributions are skewed which protuberate on one side more as compared to the other side. Measures of skewness not only indicate the extent of skewness but also the direction. Skewness may be positive or negative.

In a positively skewed distribution, the tail of the curve slopes down from the left to the right in a graph. In a negatively skewed distribution, the tail of the curve slopes down from the right to the left of a graph.

I. Analysis of Skewness

Skewness can be determined by two ways :

(a) By Tests and

(b) By Extent of Skewness.

(a) Tests of Skewness : The existence of skewness in any distribution can be confirmed if the distribution is asymmetrical (i.e., Not Bell Shaped). In a skewed distribution the **Mean**, the **Median** and the **Mode** do not coincide. Let us study the distributions :

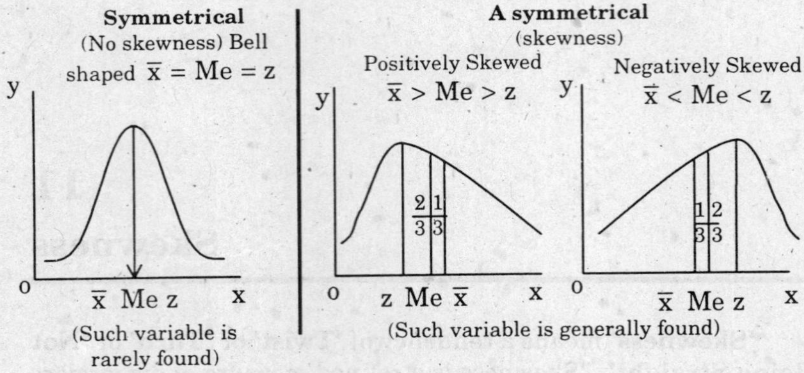

From the above analysis of three types of distributions, the following tests can be applied to know the presence or absence of skewness :

(i) ***Relationship Among Averages :*** All the averages do not coincide (i.e., $\bar{x}$ > Me > Z or $\bar{x}$ < Me < Z). $\bar{x}$ and Z are pulled wide apart, and Me lies in between the two.

(ii) ***Graphic View :*** In a graph, the curve is not in a bell shaped view. If the curve is vertically divided at the centre, the two parts do not result into two halves.

(iii) ***Relationship Among Quartiles :*** In an asymmetrical distribution (skewed) Q_1 and Q_3 are not equidistant from Median. It means,

(iv) $Q_3 - Me \neq Me - Q_1$

(v) ***Sum of the Deviations :*** In an asymmetrical distribution (skewed) the sum of the positive deviations from the Median (or Mode) is not equal to the sum of the negative deviations from the Median (or Mode).

(vi) ***Frequencies of Mode :*** The frequencies are not equally distributed on either side of the Mode.

(b) Extent of Skewness (Measurement) : The skewness can be determined by the statistical measurements which may be absolute or relative. Absolute measures of skewness tell us the extent of asymmetry and the direction (positive or negative). Relative measures of skewness are useful when we study the two series comparatively. Skewness is denoted symbolically by **'Sk'**.

(i) Absolute Measures of Skewness :

$$Sk = (\overline{x} - Me),\ Sk = (Me - z) \text{ or } Sk = (\overline{x} - z)$$

(Note : The positive or negative answers state that the skewness is positive or negative).

The absolute measures of skewness are not of much practicable utility. They are not at all considered as useful devices in regular day to day activities concerning with the study of quantitive data.

(ii) Relative Measures of Skewness : The absolute measures of skewness are not satisfactory. They are to be changed to relative measures. The relative measures of skewness are called "Coefficient of Skewness". They are of two types as under:

(a) Karl Pearson's Coefficient of Skewness and
(b) Bowley's Coefficient of Skewness.

II. Karl Pearson's Coefficient of Skewness

Karl Pearson has stated a formula for relative measure of skewness. That is why, the formula is known as "Karl Pearson's Coefficient of Skewness". It is based on the difference between the Mean and Mode of the distribution which is divided by the standard deviation. It is denoted symbolically by **'Skp'**.

(i) $Skp = \dfrac{\overline{x} - z}{\sigma}$ ... when z is clearly defined or

(ii) $Skp = \dfrac{\overline{x} - (3\,Me - 2\overline{x})}{\sigma} = \dfrac{\overline{x} - 3Me + 2\overline{x}}{\sigma}$

$$= \frac{3\,(\text{Mean} - \text{Median})}{\sigma} = \frac{3\,(\overline{x} - Me)}{\sigma} \text{ .... when z is ill - defined.}$$

Note :

(a) When the z is clearly defined, as in the case of (i) fromula, the answers generally fall between **–1** and **+1**.

(b) When the z is ill-defined, as in the case of (ii) formula, the answers may fall in between **–3** and **+3**.

Example 11.1. From the following information relating to the marks of 40 students in Statistics, find out the Karl Pearson's Coefficient of Skewness. Divide the data into ten strata having marks range of 0 – 10, 10 – 20, 20 – 30 and so on. (BU-A92)

30	20	18	15	10	22	25	17	41	48
56	91	73	84	75	99	08	35	69	07
00	13	21	33	44	55	66	77	88	27
96	20	40	50	60	70	80	90	38	54

Solution : Let us have the observations grouped into classes as under.

Computation of Coefficient of Skewness

Marks C.I.	Tally Marks	f	MV x	$\left(\frac{x-45}{10}\right)$ d'	fd'	fd'^{2}
0 – 10	III	3	5	-4	-12	48
10 – 20	~~IIII~~	5 f_0	15	-3	-15	45
20 – 30	~~IIII~~ I	6 f_1	25	-2	-12	24
30 – 40	IIII	4 f_2	35	-1	- 4	4
40 – 50	IIII	4	45	0	0	0
50 – 60	IIII	4	55	+1	+ 4	4
60 – 70	III	3	65	+2	+ 6	12
70 – 80	IIII	4	75	+3	+12	36
80 – 90	III	3	85	+4	+12	48
90 – 100	IIII	4	95	+5	+20	100
		n = 40			Σfd' = 11	Σfd'^{2} = 321

$$z = l + \frac{(f_1 - f_0)}{(f_1 - f_0) + (f_1 - f_2)} \times c$$

$$= 20 + \frac{(6-4)}{(6-4)+(6 \ \text{-} 5)}$$

$$= 20 + \frac{1}{2+1} \times 10$$

$$= 20 + 3.3333 = \mathbf{23.3333}$$

$$\bar{x} = A + \frac{\Sigma fd'}{n} \times c$$

$$= 45 + \frac{11}{40} \times 10$$

$$= 45 + 2.75$$

$$= \mathbf{47.75}$$

$$\sigma = \sqrt{\frac{\Sigma fd'}{n} - \left(\frac{\Sigma fd'}{n}\right)^2} \times c$$

$$= \sqrt{\frac{321}{40} - \left(\frac{11}{40}\right)^2} \times 10$$

$$= \sqrt{8.025 - (0.275)^2} \times 10$$

$$= \sqrt{8.025 - 0.075625} \times 10$$

$$= \sqrt{7.949375} \times 10 = 2.8195 \times 10$$

$$= \mathbf{28.195}$$

$$Skp = \frac{\overline{x} - z}{\sigma}$$

$$= \frac{47.75 - 23.3333}{28.195}$$

$$= \frac{24.4167}{28.195}$$

$$= \mathbf{0.866}$$

Example 11.2. Calculate Karl Pearson's Coefficient of Skewness from the following data : (BU-N93, A94)

Marks Above :	0	10	20	30	40	50	60	70	80
No. of Students :	150	140	100	80	80	70	30	14	0

Solution : Let us convert the cumulative series into class interval.

Computation of Coefficient of Skewness

Marks C.I.	c.f.	f	MV x	$\left(\frac{x-35}{10}\right)$ d'	fd'	fd'²
0 – 10	10	10	5	- 3	- 30	90
10 – 20	50	40	15	- 2	- 80	160
20 – 30	70	20	25	- 1	- 20	20
30 – 40	70	0	35	0	0	0
40 – 50	80	10	45	+1	+10	10
50 – 60	120	40	55	+2	+80	160
60 – 70	136	16	65	+3	+48	144
70 – 80	150	14	75	+4	+56	224
		n = 150			$\Sigma fd'$ = 64	$\Sigma fd'^2$ = 808

$$\bar{x} = A + \frac{\Sigma fd'}{n} \times c \qquad \sigma = \sqrt{\frac{\Sigma fd'^2}{n} - \left(\frac{\Sigma fd'}{n}\right)^2} \times c$$

$$= 35 + \frac{64}{150} \times 10 \qquad = \sqrt{\frac{808}{150} - \left(\frac{64}{150}\right)^2} \times 10$$

$$= 35 + 4.2667 \qquad = \sqrt{5.38667 - (0.42667)^2} \times 100$$

$$= \mathbf{39.2667} \qquad = \sqrt{5.38667 - 0.18201} \times 10$$

$$= \sqrt{5.20466} \times 10 = 2.2813723 \times 10 = \mathbf{22.814}$$

Median is the size of $\frac{n}{2}$th item. $\therefore$ $\frac{150}{2}$th = 75th item .

It lies in 80 c.f..

Against 80 c.f.. Median class is (40 – 50).

$$Me = l + \frac{\frac{n}{2} - m}{f} \times c$$

$$= 40 + \frac{75 - 70}{10} \times 10 = 40 + \frac{50}{10} = 40 + 5 = \mathbf{45}$$

Determination of Modal Class (Grouping)

C.I.	f_1	f_2	f_3	f_4	f_5	f_6
0 – 10	10	(50)				
10 – 20	(40)		(60)	(70)		
20 – 30	20	20			60	
30 – 40	0		10			30
40 – 50	10	(50)		50		
50 – 60	(40)		56		(66)	
60 – 70	16	30				(70)
70 – 80	14					

Analysis

C.I. / f	0 – 10	10 – 20	20 – 30	30 – 40	40 – 50	50 – 60	60 – 70	70 – 80
f_1		I				I		
f_2	I	I			I	I		
f_3		I	I					
f_4	I	I	I					
f_5					I	I	I	
f_6						I	I	I
Total	2	4	2		2	4	2	1

Note : Mode is ill-defined. We are using the empirical formula to determine the Mode, and to find the value of Karl Person's Coefficient of Skewness.

There are two model classes i.e., (10 – 20) and (50 – 60). It is a bimodal distribution. So we shall apply the formula based on empirical relationship among the averages.

$$Skp = \frac{3(\text{Mean - Median})}{\sigma}$$

$$= \frac{3(39.2667 - 45)}{22.814} = \frac{3(-5.7333)}{22.814} = \frac{17.1999}{22.814} = \mathbf{-0.75392}$$

Example 11.3. Calculate Karl Pearson's Coefficient of Skewness from the following information given when its Mode is 54.

Marks	0 – 20	20 – 40	40 – 60	60 – 80	80 – 100	
No. of Students	10	--	30	--	14	= 94

Find the missing frequencies (BU-A95)

Solution : Let us assume that the missing frequencies are A and B respectively.

$$10 + A + 30 + B + 14 = 94$$

$$A = B = 94 - 54$$

$$\mathbf{A + B = 40}$$

Further,

(B = 40 – A)

Computation of Coefficient of Skewness

Marks C.I.	f	f	x	$\left(\frac{x-50}{30}\right)$ d'	fd'	fd'²
0 – 20	10	10	10	-2	-20	40
20 – 40	(A)	16 •	30	-1	-16	16
40 – 60 *	30	30	50	0	0	0
60 – 80	(40 – A)	24	70	+1	+24	24
80 – 100	14	14	90	+2	+28	56
	n - 94	94			Σfd' = 16	Σfd'² = 136

$$\bar{x} = A + \frac{\Sigma fd'}{n} \times c$$

$$= 50 + \frac{16}{94} \times 20 = 50 + \frac{320}{94} = 50 + 3.404 = \mathbf{53.404}$$

Mode is 54 and it lies in 40 – 60 class. So, $f_0 = A$, $f_1 = 30$ and $f_2 = (40 - A)$.

$$* z = l + \frac{(f_1 - f_0)}{(f_1 - f_0) + (f_1 - f_2)} \times c$$

$$54 = 40 + \frac{(30 - A)}{(30 - A) + [30 - (40 - A)]} \times 20$$

$$14 = \frac{30 - A}{30 - A + 30 - 40 + A} \times 20$$

$$14 = \frac{30 - A}{30 + 30 - 40} \times 20$$

$$14 = \frac{30 - A}{20} \times 20$$

$$14 = 30 - A$$

$A = \mathbf{16}$ •

$A + B = 40$

$16 + B = 40 \qquad B = \mathbf{24}$

$$\sigma = \sqrt{\frac{\Sigma fd'^2}{n} - \left(\frac{\Sigma fd'}{n}\right)^2} \times 20$$

$$= \sqrt{\frac{136}{94} - \left(\frac{16}{94}\right)^2} \times 20$$

$$= \sqrt{1.4468 - (0.17)^2} \times 20$$

$$= \sqrt{1.4468 - 0.029} \times 20$$

$$= \sqrt{1.4178} \times 20$$

$$= 1.1907 \times 20$$

$$= \mathbf{23.8143}$$

$$Skp = \frac{\overline{x} - z}{\sigma}$$

$$= \frac{53.404 - 54}{23.8143} = \frac{-0.596}{23.8143} = \mathbf{-0.0250}$$

Example 11.4. Calculate the Pearson's Coefficient of Skewness from the followng : (BU-A96)

Age :	0 – 10	10 – 20	20 – 30	30 – 40	40 – 50	50 – 60	60 – 70
No. of Persons :	10	12	24	32	28	11	3

Solution : Computation of Coefficient of Skewness

Age C.I.	No. of Persons f	MV x	$\left(\frac{x-35}{10}\right)$ d'	fd'	fd'^{2}
0 – 10	10	5	-3	-30	90
10 – 20	12	15	-2	-24	48
20 – 30	24 f_0	25	-1	-24	24
30 – 40	32 f_1	35	0	0	0
40 – 50	28 f_2	45	+1	+28	28
50 – 60	11	55	+2	+22	44
60 – 70	3	65	+3	+9	27
	n = 120			Σfd' = −19	Σfd'^{2} = 261

$$\overline{x} = A + \frac{\Sigma fd'}{n} \times c$$

$$= 35 + \frac{-19}{120} \times 100 = 35 - 1.58333 = \mathbf{33.4167}$$

$$\sigma = \sqrt{\frac{\Sigma fd'^2}{n} - \left(\frac{\Sigma fd'}{n}\right)^2} \times c$$

$$= \sqrt{\frac{261}{120} - \left(\frac{-19}{120}\right)} \times 10$$

$$= \sqrt{2.175 - (0.15833)^2} \times 10$$

$$= \sqrt{2.175 - 0.02507} \times 10$$

$$= \sqrt{2.14993} \times 10$$

$$= 1.4663 \times 10$$

$$= \mathbf{14.663}$$

$$z = l + \frac{(f_1 - f_0)}{(f_1 - f_0) + (f_1 - f_2)} \times c$$

$$= 30 + \frac{(32 - 24)}{(32 - 24) + (32 - 28)} \times 10$$

$$= 30 + \frac{8}{8 + 4} \times 10$$

$$= 30 + \frac{80}{12} = 30 + 6.6667$$

$$= \mathbf{36.667}$$

$$Skp = \frac{\overline{x} - z}{\sigma} = \frac{33.4167 - 36.667}{15.663} = \frac{-3.2503}{14.663} = \mathbf{-0.22167}$$

Example 11.5. Compute the Pearson's Coefficient of Skewness from the following : (BU-N96)

Age :	0 – 10	10 – 20	20 – 30	30 – 40	40 – 50	50 – 60	60 – 70
No. of Persons :	15	10	18	12	10	5	2

Solution : Computation of Coefficient of Skewness

Marks C.I.	No. of Persons f	MV x	$\left(\frac{x - 25}{10}\right)$ d'	fd'	fd'^{2}
0 – 10	15	5	- 3	-30	60
10 – 20	10 f_0	15	- 2	-10	10
20 – 30	18 f_1	25	0	0	0
30 – 40	12 f_2	35	+1	+12	12
40 – 50	10	45	+2	+20	40
50 – 60	5	55	+3	+15	45
60 – 70	2	65	+4	+ 8	32
		n = 72		$\Sigma fd'$ = 15	$\Sigma fd'^2$ = 199

$$\bar{x} = A + \frac{\Sigma fd'}{n} \times c$$

$$= 25 + \frac{15}{72} \times 10 = 25 + \frac{150}{72} = 25 + 2.0833 = \mathbf{27.0833}$$

$$\sigma = \sqrt{\frac{\Sigma fd'^2}{n} - \left(\frac{\Sigma fd'}{n}\right)^2} \times c$$

$$= \sqrt{\frac{199}{72} - \left(\frac{15}{72}\right)^2} \times 10$$

$$= \sqrt{2.7639 - (0.2083)^2} \times 10$$

$$= \sqrt{2.7639 - 0.04339} \times 10$$

$$= \sqrt{2.7205} \times 10$$

$$= 1.6494 \times 10$$

$$= \mathbf{16.494}$$

$$z = l + \frac{(f_1 - f_0)}{(f_1 - f_0) + (f_1 - f_2)} \times c$$

$$= 20 + \frac{(18 - 10)}{(18 - 10) + (18 - 12)} \times 10$$

$$= 20 + \frac{8}{8 + 6} \times 10$$

$$= 20 + \frac{80}{14} = 20 + 5.7143$$

$$= \mathbf{25.7143}$$

$$Skp = \frac{\bar{x} - z}{\sigma} = \frac{27.0833 - 25.7143}{16.494} = \frac{1.369}{16.494} = \mathbf{0.083}$$

Example 11.6. Find out Pearson's coefficient of Skewness from the following data : (BU-A97)

Wages Rs. :	270–280	280–290	290–300	300–310	310–320	320–330	330–340	340–350
No. of Persons :	12	18	35	42	50	45	20	8

Solution : Computation of Coefficient of Skewness

C.I.	MV x	$\left(\frac{x - 305}{10}\right)$ d'	f	fd'	fd'^2
270 – 280	275	- 3	12	- 36	108
280 – 290	285	- 2	18	- 36	72
290 – 300	295	- 1	35 f_0	- 35	35
300 – 310	305	0	42 f_1	0	0
310 – 320	315	+1	50 f_2	+50	50
320 – 330	325	+2	45	+90	180
330 – 340	335	+3	20	+60	180
340 – 350	345	+4	8	+32	128
			n = 230	Σfd' = 125	$\Sigma fd'^2$ = 753

$$\bar{x} = A + \frac{\Sigma fd'}{n} \times c$$

$$= 305 + \frac{125}{230} \times 10 = 350 + \frac{1250}{230} = 305 + 5.4348 = \mathbf{310.4348}$$

$$\sigma = \sqrt{\frac{\Sigma fd'^2}{n} - \left(\frac{\Sigma fd'}{n}\right)^2} \times c$$

$$= \sqrt{\frac{753}{230} - \left(\frac{125}{230}\right)^2} \times 10$$

$$= \sqrt{3.273913 - (0.54348)^2} \times 10$$

$$= \sqrt{3.273913 - 0.29537} \times 10$$

$$= \sqrt{2.9785} \times 10 = 1.72585 \times 10$$

$$= \mathbf{17.2585}$$

$$z = l + \frac{(f_1 - f_0)}{(f_1 - f_0) + (f_1 - f_2)} \times c$$

$$= 310 + \frac{(50 - 42)}{(40 - 42) + (50 - 45)} \times 10$$

$$= 310 + \frac{80}{8 + 5}$$

$$= 310 + \frac{80}{13}$$

$$= 310 + 6.15385$$

$$= \mathbf{316.15385}$$

$$Skp = \frac{\bar{x} - z}{\sigma} = \frac{310.4348 - 316.15385}{17.2585} = \frac{-5.7191}{17.2585} = \mathbf{-0.3314}$$

Example 11.7. Calculate the coefficient of variation and Karl Pearson's Coefficient of Skewness from the following age distribution of 125 persons : (BU-A87)

Age (in years) C.I. :	10	20	30	40	50	60	70	80
No. of Persons :	5	15	30	55	81	100	120	125

Solution : Computation of Coefficient of Skewness

Age (in years) C.I.	No. of Persons	x	$(x-45)/10$ d'	fd'	fd'^2
0 – 10	5	5	- 4	- 20	80
10 – 20	10	15	- 3	- 30	90
20 – 30	15	25	- 2	- 30	60
30 – 40	25 f_0	35	- 1	- 25	25
40 – 50	26 f_1	45	0	0	0
50 – 60	19 f_2	55	+1	+19	19
60 – 70	20	65	+2	+40	80
70 – 80	5	75	+3	+15	45
	n = 125			$\Sigma fd' = -31$	$\Sigma fd'^2 = 399$

$$\bar{x} = A + \frac{\Sigma fd'}{n} \times c$$
$$= 45 + \frac{-31}{125} \times 10$$
$$= 45 - 2.48 = \mathbf{42.52}$$

$$c.v. = \frac{\sigma}{\bar{x}} \times 100$$
$$= \frac{17.6932}{42.52} \times 100$$
$$= 41.61\%$$

$$\sigma = \sqrt{\frac{\Sigma fd'^2}{n} - \left(\frac{\Sigma fd'}{n}\right)^2} \times c$$
$$= \sqrt{\frac{399}{125} - \left(\frac{-31}{125}\right)^2} \times 10$$
$$= \sqrt{3.192 - (-2.48)^2} \times 10$$
$$= \sqrt{3.192 - 0.0615} \times 10$$
$$= \sqrt{3.1305} \times 10$$
$$= 1.76932 \times 10$$
$$= \mathbf{17.6932}$$

$$z = l + \frac{(f_1 - f_0)}{(f_1 - f_0) + (f_1 - f_2)} \times c$$
$$= 40 + \frac{(26 - 25)}{(26 - 25) + (26 - 19)} \times 10$$
$$= 40 + \frac{1}{1 + 7} \times 10$$
$$= 40 + \frac{10}{8}$$
$$= 40 + 1.25$$
$$= \mathbf{41.25}$$

Example 11.8. Calculate Pearson's Coefficient of Skewness for the following data : (BU-N97)

Age Under (in years) :	10	20	30	40	50	60	70	80
No. of Persons :	5	15	30	60	80	90	96	100

Solution : Let us convert the series from cumulative to class interval.

Computation of Coefficient of Skewness

Age (in years) C.I.	M.V. x	No. of Persons f	$(x - 35)/10$ d'	fd'	fd'^2
0 – 10	5	5	- 3	- 15	45
10 – 20	15	10	- 2	- 20	40
20 – 30	25	15	- 1	- 15	15
30 – 40	35	30	0	0	0
40 – 50	45	20	+1	+20	20
50 - 60	55	10	+2	+20	40
60 – 70	65	6	+3	+18	54
70 – 80	75	4	+4	+16	64
		n = 100		Σfd' = 24	$\Sigma fd'^2$ = 278

$$\bar{x} = A + \frac{\Sigma fd'}{n} \times c$$

$$= 35 + \frac{24}{100} \times 10 = 35 + \frac{240}{100} = 35 + 2.4 = \mathbf{37.4}$$

$$\sigma = \sqrt{\frac{\Sigma fd'^2}{n} - \left(\frac{\Sigma fd'}{n}\right)^2} \times c$$

$$= \sqrt{\frac{278}{100} - \left(\frac{24}{100}\right)^2} \times 10$$

$$= \sqrt{2.78 - (0.24)^2} \times 10$$

$$= \sqrt{2.78 - 0.0576} \times 10$$

$$= \sqrt{2.7224} \times 10$$

$$= 1.64999 \times 10$$

$$= \mathbf{16.50}$$

$$z = l + \frac{(f_1 - f_0)}{(f_1 - f_0) + (f_1 - f_2)} \times c$$

$$= 30 + \frac{(30 - 15)}{(30 - 15) + (30 - 20)} \times 10$$

$$= 30 + \frac{15}{15 + 10} \times 10 = 30 + \frac{150}{25}$$

$$= 30 + 6 = \mathbf{36}$$

$$Skp = \frac{\bar{x} - x}{\sigma} = \frac{37.4 - 36}{16.50}$$

$$= \frac{1.4}{16.50}$$

$$= \mathbf{0.08485}$$

Example 11.9. In a certain distribution, the following results were established :

Mean = 45, Median = 48 and Skp = - 0.4

Find the Standard Deviation. (BU-N83, A86)

Solution :

$$Skp = \frac{3(\text{Mean} - \text{Median})}{\sigma}$$

$$= -0.4 = \frac{3(45 - 48)}{\sigma} = -0.4 = \frac{3(-3)}{\sigma} =$$

$$\sigma = \frac{-9}{-0.4}$$

$$\sigma = \mathbf{22.5}$$

Example 11.10. Compute the Coefficient of Skewness from the following :

Mean Wages (in Rs.) = 59.50 Median Wages (in Rs.) = 55.70

Variance of Wages (in Rs.) = 110 (BU – A85)

Solution :

$$\sigma = \sqrt{\text{Variance}} = \sqrt{110} = \mathbf{10.488}$$

$$Skp = \frac{3(\overline{x} - Me)}{\sigma} = \frac{3(59.50 - 55.70)}{10.488} = \frac{3(3.8)}{10.488} = \frac{11.4}{10.488} = \mathbf{1.08696}$$

Example 11.11. In a certain distribution, the following results were obtained : (BU-N85)

c.v. = 40%, $\overline{x} = 25$, $z = 20$. Find the Coefficient of Skewness.

Solution :

$$c.v. = \frac{\sigma}{\overline{x}} \times 100$$

$$40\% = \frac{\sigma}{25} \times 100$$

$$0.4 = \frac{\sigma}{25}$$

$$\sigma = \mathbf{10}$$

$$Skp = \frac{\overline{x} - z}{\sigma} = \frac{25 - 20}{10} = \frac{5}{10} = \mathbf{0.5}$$

Example 11.12 : Calculate Coefficient of Skewness if, $\Sigma fx = 350$, n = 10, Median = 38 and Variance = 49. (BU-N94)

Solution :

$$\sigma = \sqrt{\text{Variance}} = \sqrt{49} = \mathbf{7}$$

$$\overline{x} = \frac{\Sigma fx}{n} = \frac{350}{10} = \mathbf{35}$$

$$Skp = \frac{3(\overline{x} - Me)}{\sigma} = \frac{3(35 - 38)}{7} = \frac{3(-3)}{7} = \frac{-9}{7} = \mathbf{-1.2857}$$

Example 11.13 : The following facts are gathered before and after the settlement of an industrial dispute :

		Before	After
Number of Workers	...	515	509
Mean Wages (Rs.)	...	49.50	52.75
Median Wages (Rs.)	...	52.80	50.00
Variance of Wages (Rs.)	...	121	144

Compare the position before and after the settlement of dispute in respect of (a) Total Wages : (b) Modal Wages : (c) Dispersion (d) C. V. and (e) Skewness.

Solution :

Before Dispute

(a) Total Wages

$$\Sigma x = \overline{x} \times n$$
$$= 49.50 \times 515$$
$$= \textbf{Rs. 25,492.50}$$

(b) Modal Wages

$$z = 3Me - 2\overline{x}$$
$$= 3(52.80) - 2(49.50)$$
$$= 158.4 - 99$$
$$= \mathbf{59.4}$$

(c) Dispersion (σ)

$$\sigma = \sqrt{\text{Variance}}$$
$$= \sqrt{121}$$
$$= \mathbf{11}$$

(d) Coefficient of Variation

$$\text{C.V.} = \frac{\sigma}{\overline{x}} \times 100$$
$$= \frac{11}{49.50} \times 100$$
$$= \mathbf{22.22\%}$$

After Dispute

(a) Total Wages

$$\Sigma x = \overline{x} \times n$$
$$= 52.75 \times 509$$
$$= \textbf{Rs.26,849.75}$$

(b) Modal Wages

$$z = 3Me - 2\overline{x}$$
$$= 3(50) - 2(52.75)$$
$$= 150 - 105.50$$
$$= \mathbf{44.5}$$

(c) Dispersion (σ)

$$\sigma = \sqrt{\text{Variance}}$$
$$= \sqrt{144}$$
$$= \mathbf{12}$$

(d) Coefficient of Variation

$$\text{C.V.} = \frac{\sigma}{\overline{x}} \times 100$$
$$= \frac{12}{52.75} \times 100$$
$$= \mathbf{22.75\%}$$

(e) Skewness

$$Skp = \frac{3(\overline{x} - Me)}{\sigma}$$

$$= \frac{3(49.50 - 52.80)}{11}$$

$$= \frac{3(-3.3)}{11} = \frac{-9.9}{11}$$

$$= \mathbf{-0.9}$$

(e) Skewness

$$Skp = \frac{3(\overline{x} - Me)}{\sigma}$$

$$= \frac{3(52.75 - 50.00)}{12}$$

$$= \frac{3(2.75)}{12} - \frac{8.25}{12}$$

$$= \mathbf{0.6875}$$

Example 11.14. Calculate the Karl Pearson's Coefficient of Skewness from the following : (BU-N90)

Age in Years Over :	55	50	45	40	35	30	25	20
No. of Persons :	32	78	144	259	363	449	494	525

Solution : Let us convert the cumulative distribution into class interval.

Computation of Coefficient of Skewness

Age in Years C.I.	No. of Persons f	x	$(x - 37.5)/5$ d'	fd'	fd'^{2}
20 – 25	31	22.5	- 3	- 93	279
25 – 30	45	27.5	- 2	- 90	180
30 – 35	86 f_0	32.5	- 1	- 86	86
35 – 40	104 f_1	37.5	0	0	0
40 – 45	115 f_2	42.5	+1	+115	115
45 – 50	660	47.5	+2	+132	264
50 – 55	46	52.5	+3	+138	414
55 – 60	32	57.5	+4	+128	512
	n = 525			Σfd' = 244	Σfd'^{2} = 1850

$$\overline{x} = A + \frac{\Sigma fd'}{n} \times c$$

$$= 37.5 + \frac{244}{525} \times 5 = 37.5 + 2.3238 = \mathbf{39.8238}$$

To Determine the Modal Class Grouping is Adopted

C.I.	f_1	f_2	f_3	f_4	f_5	f_6
20 – 25	31					
		76				
25 – 30	45			162		
			131			
30 – 35	86				(235)	
		(190)				
35 – 40	104					(305)
			(219)			
40 – 45	(115)			(285)		
		181				
45 – 50	66				227	
			112			
50 – 55	46					144
		78				
55 – 60	32					

Analysis

x / f	20 – 25	25 - 30	30 - 35	35 – 40	40 – 45	45 – 50	50 – 55	55 – 60
1					I			
f_2			I	I				
f_3				I	I			
f_4				I	I	I		
f_5		I	I	I				
f_6			I	I	I			
Total		1	3	5	4	1		

So Modal Class is 35 – 40.

$$z = l + \frac{(f_1 - f_0)}{(f_1 - f_0) + (f_1 - f_2)} \times c$$

$$= 35 + \frac{(104 - 86)}{(104 - 86) + (104 - 115)} \times 5 = 35 + \frac{18}{18 + 11} \times 5$$

$$= 35 + \frac{90}{29} = 35 + 3.103 = \mathbf{38.103}$$

$$\sigma = \sqrt{\frac{\Sigma fd'^2}{n} - \left(\frac{\Sigma fd'}{n}\right)^2} \times c$$

$$= \sqrt{\frac{1850}{525} - \left(\frac{244}{525}\right)^2} \times 5 = \sqrt{3.52381 - (0.46476)^2} \times 5$$

$$= \sqrt{3.52381 - 0.216} \times 5 = \sqrt{3.30781} \times 5$$

$$= 1.81874 \times 5 = \mathbf{9.09369}$$

$$Skp = \frac{\bar{x} - z}{\sigma}$$

$$= \frac{39.8238 - 38.103}{9.09369} = \frac{1.7208}{9.09369} = \mathbf{0.18923}$$

Example 11.15. Calculate Karl Pearson's Coefficient of Skewness for the following distribution : (BU-A91)

Monthly Salary 400, but less than :	600	800	1000	1200	1400	1600
No. of Salesmen :	4	14	33	45	49	50

Solution : Let us convert the cumulative distribution into class interval.

Computation of Coefficient of Skewness

Salary Monthly C.I.	No. of Persons f	x	$\left(\frac{x-900}{200}\right)$ d'	fd'	fd'^2
400 – 600	4	500	- 2	- 8	16
600 – 800	10 f_0	700	- 1	-10	10
800 – 1000	19 f_1	900	0	0	0
1000 – 1200	12 f_2	1100	+ 1	+12	12
1200 – 1400	4	1300	+ 2	+ 8	16
1400 – 1600	1	1500	+ 3	+ 3	9
	n = 50			$\Sigma fd'$ = 5	$\Sigma fd'^2$ = 63

$$\bar{x} = A + \frac{\Sigma fd'}{n} \times c$$

$$= 900 + \frac{5}{50} \times 200 = 900 + 20 = \mathbf{920}$$

$$z = l + \frac{(f_1 - f_0)}{(f_1 - f_0) + (f_1 - f_2)} \times c$$

$$= 800 + \frac{(19-10)}{(19-10)+(19-12)} \times 200$$

$$= 800 + \frac{9}{9+7} \times 200$$

$$= 800 + \frac{1800}{16}$$

$$= 800 + 112.5$$

$$= \mathbf{912.5}$$

$$\sigma = \sqrt{\frac{\Sigma fd'^2}{n} - \left(\frac{\Sigma fd'}{n}\right)^2} \times c$$

$$= \sqrt{\frac{63}{50} - \left(\frac{5}{50}\right)^2} \times 200$$

$$= \sqrt{1.26 - (0.1)^2} \times 200$$

$$= \sqrt{1.26 - 0.01} \times 200$$

$$= \sqrt{1.25} \times 200 = 1.118 \times 200$$

$$= \mathbf{233.61}$$

$$Skp = \frac{\bar{x} - z}{\sigma}$$

$$= \frac{920 - 912.5}{233.61} = \frac{7.5}{223.61} = \mathbf{0.03354}$$

III. Bowley's Coefficient of Skewness

As the Pearsonian Coefficient of Skewness involves a tedious job in calculation, **Prof. Bowley** has introduced a Coefficient of Skewness based on quartiles. This measure is also called "Quartile Coefficient of Skewness". It is a known fact that,

$Q_3 - Me \neq Me - Q_1$ or $Q_3 - Q_1 - 2Me \neq 0 \ldots$ signifies the existence of skewness in the distribution. So Bowley's Coefficient of Skewness is denoted symbolically by **Skb**.

$$Skb = \frac{Q_3 + Q_1 - 2Me}{Q_3 - Q_1}$$

Bowley's formula is useful when, **(i)** 'z' is ill-defined, **(ii)** there are open end class intervals and **(iii)** there are unequal class intervals.

Example 11.16. Find out Karl Pearson's Coefficient of Skewness and Bowley's Coefficient of Skewness from the following data of monthly sales in two departments A and B.

(BU-N92)

Months .. Sales (in '000' tonnes)	Jan.	Feb.	Mar.	Apr.	May	June	July	Aug.	Sept.	Oct.	Nov.	Dec.
A :	3	5	10	16	17	18	12	10	7	5	3	2
B :	20	14	8	4	3	1	2	5	7	10	16	18

Solution : Computation of Coefficient of Skewness

S. No.	A Series x	$(x-\bar{x})$ d	d^2
1	2	- 7	49
2	3	- 6	36
3	3	- 6	36
4	5	- 4	16
5	5	- 4	16
6	7	- 2	4
7	10	+1	1
8	10	+1	1
9	12	+3	9
10	16	+7	49
11	17	+8	64
12	18	+9	81
	$\Sigma x = 108$	$\Sigma d = 0$	$\Sigma d^2 = 362$

$$\bar{x} = \frac{108}{12} = 9$$

$$\sigma = \sqrt{\frac{\Sigma d^2}{n}} = \sqrt{\frac{362}{12}} = \sqrt{30.1667} = \mathbf{5.4924}$$

(a) Q_1 is the size of $\frac{n+1}{4}$th item

$$\therefore \quad \frac{12+1}{4}\text{th} = 3.25\text{th item}$$

$$Q_1 = 3\text{rd item} + 0.25(5-3)$$
$$= 3 + 0.5 = \mathbf{3.5}$$

(b) Me is the size of $\frac{n+1}{2}$th item.

$$\therefore \quad \frac{12+1}{2}\text{th} = 6.5\text{th item}$$

$$Me = 6\text{th item} + 0.5(10-7)$$
$$= 7 + 1.5 = \mathbf{8.5}$$

(b) Q_3 is the size of $\frac{3(n+1)}{4}$ th item

$$\therefore \quad \frac{3(12+1)}{4}\text{th} = 9.75\text{th item}$$

$$Q_3 = 9\text{th item} + 0.75(16-12)$$
$$= 12 + 3 = \mathbf{15}$$

$$Skp = \frac{3(\overline{x} - Me)}{\sigma} = \frac{3(9-8.5)}{5.4924} = \frac{1.5}{5.4924} = \mathbf{0.273}$$

$$Skb = \frac{Q_3 + Q_1 - 2Me}{Q_3 - Q_1} = \frac{15 + 3.5 - 2(8.5)}{15 - 3.5}$$

$$= \frac{18.5 - 17}{11.5} = \frac{1.5}{11.5} = \mathbf{0.1304}$$ (Note : Mode is ill-defined)

B Series

S. No.	x	$(x-\overline{x})$ d	d^2
1	1	- 8	64
2	2	- 7	49
3	3	- 6	36
4	4	- 5	25
5	5	- 4	16
6	7	- 2	4
7	8	- 1	1
8	10	+ 1	1
9	14	+ 5	25
10	16	+ 7	49
11	18	+ 9	81
12	20	+11	121
	$\Sigma x = 108$	$\Sigma d = 0$	$\Sigma d^2 = 472$

$$x = \frac{108}{12} = 9$$

$$\sigma = \sqrt{\frac{\Sigma d^2}{n}} = \sqrt{\frac{472}{12}} = \sqrt{39.3333} = \mathbf{6.2716}$$

(a) Q_1 is the size of $\frac{n+1}{4}$th item

$$\therefore \frac{12+1}{4}\text{th} = 3.25\text{th item}$$

$$Q_1 = 3\text{rd item} + 0.25(4-3)$$
$$= 3 + 0.25(1) = \mathbf{3.25}$$

(b) Me is the size of $\frac{n+1}{2}$th item.

$$\therefore \frac{12+1}{2}\text{th} = 6.5\text{th item}$$

$$Me = 6\text{th item} + 0.5(8-7)$$
$$= 7 + 0.5(1) = 7 + 0.5 = \mathbf{7.5}$$

(c) Q_3 is the size of $\frac{3(n+1)}{4}$th item

$$\therefore \frac{3(12+1)}{4}\text{th} = 9.75\text{th item}$$

$$Q_3 = 9\text{th item} + 0.75(16-14)$$
$$= 14 + 0.75(2) = 14 + 1.5 = \mathbf{15.5}$$

$$Skp = \frac{3(\overline{x} - Me)}{\sigma} = \frac{3(9-7.5)}{6.2716} = \frac{3(1.5)}{6.2716} = \frac{4.5}{6.2716} = \mathbf{0.7175}$$

$$Skb = \frac{Q_3 + Q_1 - 2Me}{Q_3 - Q_1} = \frac{15.5 + 3.25 - 2(7.5)}{15.5 - 3.25} = \frac{18.75 - 15}{12.25}$$

$$= \frac{3.75}{12.25} = \mathbf{0.306}$$ (Note : Mode is ill-defined)

Example 11.17. From the following compute Quartile Deviation and the Coefficient of Skewness : (BU-A86)

Weekly Wages Rs. :	4 – 8	8 – 12	12 – 16	16 – 20	20 – 24	24 – 28	28 – 32	32 – 36	36 – 40
No. of Workers :	6	10	18	30	15	12	10	6	2

Solution : Computation of Coefficient of Skewness

	Weekly Wages C.I.	No. of Workers f	c.f.
	4 – 8	6	6
	8 – 12	10	16
(l)	12 – 16	18(f)	34(m)
(l)	16 – 20	30(f)	64(m) ←
	20 – 24	15	79
(l)	24 – 28	12(f)	91(m) ←
	28 – 32	10	101
	32 – 36	6	108
	36 – 40	2	109
		n = 109	

(a) Q_1 is the size of $\frac{n}{4}$ th item.

$\therefore \frac{109}{4}$ th item = 27.25 th item.

It lies in 34 c.f..

Against 34 c.f. (12 – 16) is the Q_1 class

$$Q_1 = l + \frac{\frac{n}{2} - m}{f} \times c$$

$$= 12 + \frac{27.25 - 16}{18} \times 4$$

$$= 12 + \frac{11.25}{18} \times 4 = 12 + \frac{45}{18}$$

$$= 12 + 2.5 = \mathbf{14.5}$$

(b) Me is the size of $\frac{n}{2}$ th item

$\therefore \frac{109}{2}$ th item = 54.5 th item. It lies in 64 c.f..

Against 64 c.f. (16 – 20) is the Median class

$$Me = l + \frac{\frac{n}{2} - m}{f} \times c$$

$$= 16 + \frac{54.5 - 34}{30} \times 4 = 16 + \frac{20.5}{30} \times 4 = 16 + \frac{82}{30} = 16 + 2.733$$

$$= \mathbf{18.733}$$

(c) Q_3 is the size of $\frac{3n}{4}$ th item.

$\therefore \frac{3(109)}{4}$ th item = 81.75th item. It lies in 91 c.f..

Against 91 c.f. (24 – 28) is the Q_3 class.

$$Q_3 = l + \frac{\frac{3n}{4} - m}{f} \times c$$

$$= 24 + \frac{81.75 - 79}{12} \times 4 = 24 + \frac{2.75}{12} \times 4 = 24 + \frac{11}{12} = 24 + 0.9167$$

$$= \mathbf{24.9167}$$

(1) Quartile Deviation

$$Q.D = \frac{Q_3 - Q_1}{2}$$

$$= \frac{24.9167 - 14.5}{2}$$

$$= \frac{10.4167}{2}$$

$$= \mathbf{5.2084}$$

(2) Coefficient of Skewness

$$Skb = \frac{Q_3 + Q_1 - 2Me}{Q_3 - Q_1}$$

$$= \frac{24.9167 + 14.5 - 2(18.733)}{24.9167 - 14.5}$$

$$= \frac{39.4167 - 37.466}{10.4167} = \frac{1.9507}{10.4167}$$

$$= \mathbf{0.18727}$$

Example 11.18. Calculate Bowley's Coefficient of Skewness from the data given below : (BU-A-88)

Mid – Points :	35	45	55	65	75	85	95
Frequency :	1	3	11	21	43	32	9

Solution : Mid-points are converted into class intervals by adding and substracting the ½ of the existing interval between the two mid-points.

$$\left[35 - \frac{1}{2}(10)\right] \text{to} \left[35 + \frac{1}{2}(10)\right] \ldots 30 - 40 \ldots 40 - 50 \ldots 50 - 60 \ldots \text{ so on.}$$

Computation of Coefficient of Skewness

C.I.	f	c.f.
30 – 40	1	1
40 – 50	3	4
50 – 60	11	15(m)
(l) 60 – 70	21(f)	36(m) ←
(l) 70 – 80	43(f)	79(m) ←
(l) 80 – 90	32(f)	111 ←
90 – 100	9	120
	n = 120	

(a) Q_1 is the size of $\frac{n}{4}$ th item.

$\therefore \frac{120}{4}$ th item = 30 th item.

It lies in 36 c.f..

Against 36 c.f. (60 – 70) is the Q_1 class

$$Q_1 = l + \frac{\frac{n}{4} - m}{f} \times c$$

$$= 60 + \frac{\frac{120}{4} - 15}{21} \times 10 = 60 + \frac{30 - 15}{21} \times 10 = 60 + \frac{15}{21} \times 10$$

$$= 60 + \frac{150}{21} = 60 + 7.1429 = \mathbf{67.1429}$$

(b) Me is the size of $\frac{n}{2}$ th item

$\therefore \quad \frac{120}{2}$ th item = 60 th item. It lies in 79 c.f..

Against 79 c.f. (70 – 80) is the Median class

$$Me = l + \frac{\frac{n}{2} - m}{f} \times c$$

$$= 70 + \frac{\frac{120}{2} - 36}{43} \times 10 = 70 + \frac{60 - 36}{43} \times 10 = 70 + \frac{24}{43} \times 10$$

$$= 70 + \frac{240}{43} = 70 + 5.5814 = \mathbf{75.5814}$$

(c) Q_3 is the size of $\frac{3n}{4}$ th item.

$\therefore \quad \frac{3(120)}{4}$ th item = 90th item. It lies in 111 c.f..

Against 11 c.f. (80 – 90) is the Q_3 class.

$$Q_3 = l + \frac{\frac{3n}{4} - m}{f} \times c$$

$$= 80 + \frac{\frac{3(120)}{4} - 79}{32} \times 10 = 80 + \frac{90 + 79}{32} \times 10 = 80 + \frac{11}{32} \times 10$$

$$= 80 + \frac{110}{32} = 80 + 3.4375 = \mathbf{83.4375}$$

(d) Coefficient of Skewness

$$Skb = \frac{Q_3 + Q_1 - 2Me}{Q_3 - Q_1}$$

$$= \frac{83.4375 + 67.1429 - 2(75.5814)}{83.4375 - 67.1429} = \frac{150.58 - 151.1628}{16.2946}$$

$$= \frac{-0.5828}{16.2946} = \mathbf{-0.03577}$$

Example 11.19. Calculate Bowley's Coefficient of Skewness from the following distribution. (BU-N89)

Marks :	Less than 10	20	30	40	50	60
No. of Students :	5	12	22	36	12	4

Solution : Let us convert the cumulative distribution into class interval.

Computation of Coefficient of Skewness

Marks C.I.	No. of Students f	c.f.
Less	5	5
than 10	7	12
10 – 20	10	22 (m)
(l) 20 – 30	14(f)	36 (m) ←
(l) 30 – 40	12(f)	48(m) ←
(l) 50 – 60	4(f)	52 ←
	n = 52	

(a) Q_1 is the size of $\frac{n}{4}$ th item.

$\therefore \frac{52}{4}$ th item = 13 th item.

It lies in 22 c.f..

Against 22 c.f. (20 – 30) is the Q_1 class

$$Q_1 = l + \frac{\frac{n}{4} - m}{f} \times 10$$

$$= 20 + \frac{\frac{52}{4} - 12}{10} \times 10 = 20 + \frac{13 - 12}{10} \times 10 = 20 + \frac{10}{10} = 20 + 1 = \mathbf{21}$$

(b) Me is the size of $\frac{n}{2}$ th item.

$\therefore \quad \frac{52}{2}$ th item = 26th item. It lies in 36 c.f..

Against 36 c.f. (30 – 40) is the Median Class

$$Me = l + \frac{\frac{n}{2} - m}{f} \times c$$

$$= 30 + \frac{\frac{52}{2} - 22}{14} \times 10 = 30 + \frac{26 - 22}{14} \times 10 = 30 + \frac{4}{14} \times 10$$

$$= 30 + \frac{40}{14} = 30 + 2.8571 = \mathbf{32.8571}$$

(c) Q_3 is the size of $\frac{3n}{4}$ th item

$\therefore \quad \frac{3(52)}{4}$ th = 39th item . It lies in 48 c.f..

Against 48 c.f. (40 – 50) is the Q_3 class.

$$Q_3 = l + \frac{\frac{3n}{4} - m}{f} \times c$$

$$= 40 + \frac{\frac{3(52)}{4} - 36}{12} \times 10 = 40 + \frac{39 - 36}{12} \times 10 = 40 + \frac{3}{12} \times 10$$

$$= 40 + \frac{30}{12} = 40 + 2.5 = \mathbf{42.5}$$

(d) $Skb = \frac{Q_3 + Q_1 - 2Me}{Q_3 - Q_1}$

$$= \frac{42.5 + 21 - 2(32.8571)}{42.5 - 21} = \frac{63.5 - 65.7142}{21.5}$$

$$= \frac{-2.2142}{21.5} = \mathbf{-0.10299}$$

Example 11.20. Find the appropriate measure of Skewness from the following data : (BU – N91)

Age :	Below 10	10 – 15	15 – 20	20 – 25	25 – 30	30 – 35	35 – 40	40 & above
Employees :	15	28	39	95	50	24	16	8

Solution : Class intervals are open end. So we should use Bowley's Coefficient of Skewness.

Computation of Coefficient of Skewness

Age C.I.	Employees f	c.f.
Below 10	15	15
10 – 15	28	43(m)
(l) 15 – 20	39(f)	82(m) ←
(l) 20 – 25	95(f)	177(m) ←
(l) 25 – 30	50(f)	227 ←
30 – 35	24	251
35 – 40	16	267
40 & above	8	275
	n = 275	

(a) Q_1 is the size of $\frac{n}{4}$th item.

$\therefore \frac{275}{4}$th item = 68.75 th item.

It lies in 82 c.f..

Against 82 c.f. (15 – 20) is the Q_1 class

$$Q_{139} = l + \frac{\frac{n}{4} - m}{f} \times c$$

$$= 15 + \frac{\frac{275}{4} - 43}{39} \times 5 = 15 + \frac{68.75 - 43}{39} \times 5 = 15 + \frac{25.75}{39} \times 5$$

$$= 15 + \frac{128.75}{39} = 15 + 3.3013 = \mathbf{18.3013}$$

(b) Me is the size of $\frac{n}{2}$th item.

$\therefore \frac{275}{2}$th item = 137.50th item. It lies in 177 c.f..

Against 177 c.f. (20 – 25) is the Me class.

$$Me = l + \frac{\frac{n}{2} - m}{f} \times c$$

$$= 20 + \frac{\frac{275}{2} - m}{95} \times 5 = 20 + \frac{137.50 - 82}{95} \times 5 = 20 + \frac{55.5}{95} \times 5$$

$$= 20 + \frac{277.5}{95} = 20 + 2.9211 = \mathbf{22.9211}$$

(c) Q_3 is the size $\frac{3n}{4}$ th item.

$\therefore \quad \frac{3(275)}{4}$ th item = 206.25th item. It lies in 227 c.f..

Against 227 c.f. (25 – 30) is the Q_3 class.

$$Q_3 = l + \frac{\frac{3n}{4} - m}{f} \times c$$

$$= 25 + \frac{\frac{3(275)}{4} - 177}{50} \times 5 = 25 + \frac{206.25 - 177}{50} \times 5$$

$$= 25 + \frac{29.25}{50} \times 5 = 25 + \frac{29.25}{10} = 25 + 2.925 = \mathbf{27.925}$$

(d) $Skb = \frac{Q_3 + Q_1 - 2Me}{Q_3 - Q_1}$

$$= \frac{27.925 + 18.3013 - 2(22.9211)}{27.925 - 18.3013} = \frac{46.2263 - 45.8422}{9.6237}$$

$$= \frac{0.3841}{9.6237} = \mathbf{0.03991}$$

Example 11.21. Calculate the appropriate measure of Skewness from the following distribution. (BU-A93)

Monthly Income Rs. :	Up to 100	101 – 150	151 – 200	201 – 300	301 – 500	501 – 750	751 – 1000	1000 & above
Frequency :	9	51	120	240	136	33	9	2

Solution : The class intervals are open end and unequal. So the Bowley's Coefficient of Skewness is the appropriate measure. Inclusive class intervals are converted into exclusive class interval.

Computation of Coefficient of Skewness

Monthly Income (Rs.) C. I.	Frequency f	c.f.
Up to 100	9	9
100.5 – 150.5	51	60(m)
(l) 150.5 – 200.5	(f) 120	180(m) ←
(l) 200.5 – 300.5	(f) 240	420 (m) ←
(l) 300.5 – 500.5	(f) 136	556 ←
500.5 – 750.5	33	589
750.5 – 1000.5	9	598
1000.5 & above	2	600
	n = 600	

(a) Q_1 is the size of $\frac{n}{4}$th item.

$\therefore\ \frac{600}{4}$th item = 150th item. It lies in 180 c.f..

Against 180 c.f. (150.5 – 200.5) is the Q_1 class.

$$Q_1 = l + \frac{\frac{n}{4} - m}{f} \times c$$

$$= 150.5 + \frac{\frac{600}{4} - 60}{120} \times 150 = 150.5 + \frac{150 - 60}{120} \times 50$$

$$= 150.5 + \frac{90}{120} \times 50 = 150.5 + \frac{4500}{120} = 150.5 + 37.5 = \mathbf{188}$$

(b) Me is the size of $\frac{n}{2}$th item.

$\therefore\ \frac{600}{2}$th item = 300th item. It lies in 420 c.f...

Against 420 c.f. (200.5 – 300.5) is the Median Class.

$$Me = l + \frac{\frac{n}{2} - m}{f} \times c$$

$$= 200.5 + \frac{\frac{600}{2} - 180}{240} \times 100 = 200.5 + \frac{300 - 180}{240} \times 100$$

$$= 200.5 + \frac{120}{240} \times 100 = 200.5 + \frac{12000}{240} = 200.5 + 50 = \mathbf{250.5}$$

(c) Q_3 is the size of $\frac{3n}{4}$ th item.

$\therefore \quad \frac{3(600)}{4}$ th item = 450 th item. It lies in 556 c.f..

Against 556 c.f. (300.5 – 500.5) is the Q_3 class.

$$Q_3 = l + \frac{\frac{3n}{4} - m}{f} \times c$$

$$= 300.5 + \frac{\frac{3(600)}{4} - 420}{136} \times 200 = 300.5 + \frac{450 - 420}{136} \times 200$$

$$= 300.5 + \frac{30}{136} \times 200 = 300.5 + \frac{6000}{136}$$

$$= 300.5 + 44.11765 = \mathbf{344.6177}$$

(d) $$Skb = \frac{Q_3 + Q_1 - 2Me}{Q_3 - Q_1}$$

$$= \frac{344.6177 + 188 - 2(250.5)}{344.6177 - 188} = \frac{532.6177 - 501}{156.6177}$$

$$= \frac{31.6177}{56.6177} = \mathbf{0.20188}$$

Example 11.22. Find the appropriate measure of Skewness from the following distribution. (BU – N94)

Age (in years) :	Below 20	20 – 25	25 – 30	30 – 35	35 – 40	40 – 45	45 – 50	50 & above
No. of Employees :	113	129	146	160	212	194	145	121

Solution : The class intervals are open end. So the Bowley's Coefficient of Skewness is the appropriate measure.

Computation of Coefficient of Skewness

Age (in years) C.I.	Employees (f)	C.f.
Below 20	113	113
20 – 25	129	242 (m)
(l) 25 – 30	146 (f)	388 ←
30 – 35	160	548 (m)
(l) 35 – 40	212 (f)	760 (m) ←
(l) 40 – 45	194 (f)	954 ←
45 – 50	145	1099
50 & above	121	1220
	n = 1220	

(a) Q_1 is the size of $\frac{n}{4}$th item.

$\therefore \quad \frac{1220}{4}$ th item = 305th item. It lies in 388 c.f..

Against 388 c.f. (25 – 30) is the Q_1 class.

$$Q_1 = l + \frac{\frac{n}{4} - m}{f} \times c$$

$$= 25 + \frac{\frac{1220}{4} - 242}{146} \times 5 = 25 + \frac{305 - 242}{146} \times 5 = 25 + \frac{63}{146} \times 5$$

$$= 25 + \frac{315}{146} = 25 + 2.1575 = \mathbf{27.1575}$$

(b) Me is the size of $\frac{n}{2}$th item.

$\therefore \quad \frac{1220}{2}$ th item = 610th item. It lies in 760 c.f.

Against 760 c.f. (35 – 40) is the Median class.

$$Me = l + \frac{\frac{n}{2} - m}{f} \times c$$

$$= 35 + \frac{\frac{1220}{2} - 548}{212} \times 5 = 35 + \frac{610 - 548}{212} \times 5 = 35 + \frac{62}{212} \times 5$$

$$= 35 + \frac{310}{212} = 35 + 1.4623 = \mathbf{36.4623}$$

(c) Q_3 is the size of $\frac{3n}{4}$ th item.

$\therefore \quad \frac{3(1220)}{4}$ th item = 915th item. It lies in 954 c.f..

Against 954 c.f. (40 – 45) is the Q_3 class.

$$Q_3 = l + \frac{\frac{3n}{4} - m}{f} \times c$$

$$= 40 + \frac{\frac{3(1220)}{4} - 760}{194} \times 5 = 40 + \frac{915 - 760}{194} \times 5$$

$$= 40 + \frac{155}{194} \times 5 = 40 + \frac{775}{194} = 40 + 3.9948 = \mathbf{43.9948}$$

(d) $Skb = \frac{Q_3 + Q_1 - 2Me}{Q_3 - Q_1}$

$$= \frac{43.9948 + 27.1575 - 2(36.4623)}{43.9948 - 27.1575} = \frac{71.1523 - 72.9246}{16.8373}$$

$$= \frac{1.7723}{16.8373} = \mathbf{0.10526}$$

Example 11.23. Calculate the Quartile Coefficient of Skewness of the following. (BU – N95)

Central Point :	10	20	30	40	50	60	70	80	90	100
Frequency :	2	9	11	14	20	24	20	16	5	2

Solution : Mid-points are converted into class intervals by adding and substracting the ½ of the existing interval between the two mid-points.

$\left[10 - \frac{1}{2}(10)\right]$ to $\left[10 + \frac{1}{2}(10)\right]$..**5 – 15...15 – 25....25 – 35...so on.**

Computation of Coefficient of Skewness

C.I.	f	c.f
5 – 15	2	2
15 – 25	9	11
25 – 35	11	22 (m)
(l) 35 – 45	14 (f)	36 ←
45 – 55	20	56 (m)
(l) 55 – 65	24 (f)	80 (m) ←
(l) 65 – 75	20 (f)	100 ←
75 – 85	16	116
85 – 95	5	121
95 – 100	2	123
	n = 123	

(a) Q_1 is the size of $\frac{n}{4}$ th item.

$\therefore \quad \frac{123}{4}$ th item = 30.75th item. It lies in 36 c.f..

Against 36 c.f. (35 – 45) is the Q_1 class.

$$Q_1 = l + \frac{\frac{n}{4} - m}{f} \times c$$

$$= 35 + \frac{\frac{123}{4} - 22}{14} \times 10 = 35 + \frac{30.75 - 22}{14} \times 10 = 35 + \frac{8}{14} \times 10$$

$$= 35 + \frac{80}{14} = 35 + 5.7143 = \mathbf{40.7143}$$

(b) Me is the size of $\frac{n}{2}$ th item.

$\therefore \quad \frac{123}{2}$ th item = 61.50 th item. It lies in 80 c.f..

Against 80 c.f. (55 – 65) is the Median Class.

$$Me = l + \frac{\frac{n}{2} - m}{f} \times c$$

$$= 55 + \frac{\frac{123}{2} - 56}{24} \times 10 = 55 + \frac{61.5 - 56}{24} \times 10 = 55 + \frac{5.5}{24} \times 10$$

$$= 55 + \frac{55}{24} = 55 + 2.2917 = \mathbf{57.2917}$$

(c) Q_3 is the size of $\frac{3n}{4}$ th item.

$\therefore \quad \frac{3(123)}{4}$ th item = 92.25[th] item. It lies in 100 c.f..

Against 100 c.f. (65 – 75) is the Q_3 class.

$$Q_3 = l + \frac{\frac{3n}{4} - m}{f} \times c$$

$$= 65 + \frac{\frac{3(123)}{4} - 80}{20} \times 10 = 65 + \frac{92.25 - 80}{20} \times 10$$

$$= 65 + \frac{12.25}{20} \times 10 = 65 + \frac{122.5}{20} = 65 + 6.125 = \mathbf{71.125}$$

(d) $Skb = \frac{Q_3 + Q_1 - 2Me}{Q_3 - Q_1}$

$$= \frac{71.125 + 40.7143 - 2(57.2197)}{71.125 - 40.7143} = \frac{111.8393 - 114.5834}{30.4107}$$

$$= \frac{2.7441}{30.4107} = \mathbf{-0.0902}$$

Example 11.24. By using the Quartiles, find the measure of Skewness for the following distribution. (BU – A98)

Annual Sales Rs. ('000')	No. of Firms	Annual Sales Rs. ('000')	No. of Firms
Less than 20	30	Less than 70	644
Less than 30	225	Less than 80	650
Less than 40	465	Less than 90	665
Less than 50	580	Less than 100	680
Less than 60	634	--	--

Solution : Since there is an equal class interval of 10 throughout the series, the first class interval should be taken as 10 – 20. Let us convert the 'Less Than' frequencies into frequencies.

Computation of Coefficient of Skewness

Annual Sales Rs.('000') C.I.	No. of firms (f)	C.f.
10 – 20	30	30 (m)
(l) 20 – 30	195 (f)	225 (m) ←
(l) 30 – 40	240 (f)	465 (m) ←
(l) 40 – 50	115 (f)	580 ←
50 – 60	54	634
60 – 70	10	644
70 – 80	6	650
80 – 90	15	665
90 – 100	15	680
	n = 680	

(a) Q_1 is the size of $\frac{n}{4}$ th item.

$\therefore \quad \frac{680}{4}$ th item = 170th item. It lies in 225 c.f..

Against 225 c.f. (20 – 30) is the Q_1 class.

$$Q_1 = l + \frac{\frac{n}{4} - m}{f} \times c$$

$$= 20 + \frac{\frac{680}{4} - 30}{195} \times 10 = 20 + \frac{170 - 30}{195} \times 10 = 20 + \frac{140}{195} \times 10$$

$$= 20 + \frac{1400}{195} = 20 + 7.179487 = \mathbf{27.179487}$$

(b) Median is the size of $\frac{n}{2}$ th item.

$\therefore \quad \frac{680}{2}$ th item = **340th item.** It lies in 465 c.f..

Against 465 c.f. (30 – 40) is the Median Class.

$$Me = l + \frac{\frac{n}{2} - m}{f} \times c$$

$$= 30 + \frac{\frac{680}{2} - 225}{240} \times 10 = 30 + \frac{340 - 225}{240} \times 10 = 30 + \frac{115}{240} \times 10$$

$$= 30 + \frac{1150}{240} = 30 + 4.79167 = \mathbf{34.79167}$$

(c) Q_3 is the size of $\frac{3n}{4}$ th item.

$\therefore \quad \frac{3(680)}{4}$ th item = 510th item. It lies in 580 c.f..

Against 580 c.f. (40 – 50) is the Q_3 class.

$$Q_3 = l + \frac{\frac{3n}{4} - m}{f} \times c$$

$$= 40 + \frac{\frac{3(680)}{4} - 465}{115} \times 10 = 40 + \frac{510 - 465}{115} \times 10$$

$$= 40 + \frac{45}{115} \times 10 = 40 + \frac{450}{115} = 40 + 3.913 = \mathbf{43.913}$$

(d) $$Skb = \frac{Q_3 + Q_1 - 2Me}{Q_3 - Q_1}$$

$$= \frac{43.913 + 27.179487 - 2(34.79167)}{43.913 - 27.179487}$$

$$= \frac{71.092487 - 69.58334}{16.733513} = \frac{1.509147}{16.733513} = \mathbf{0.090187}$$

Example 11.25. In a frequency distribution, the Coefficient of Skewness, based on quartiles is 0.6. If the sum of the upper and lower quartiles is 100 and Median is 38, find the values of upper quartile and lower quartile. (BU-N83, N85, A93)

Solution : Computation of Coefficient of Skewness

$$Skb = \frac{Q_3 + Q_1 - 2Me}{Q_3 - Q_1}$$

$$0.6 = \frac{100 - 2(38)}{Q_3 - Q_1}$$

$$Q_3 - Q_1 = \frac{100 - 2(38)}{0.6}$$

$$= \frac{100 - 76}{0.6} = \frac{24}{0.6} = \mathbf{40}$$

$$\begin{aligned} Q_3 + Q_1 &= 100 \\ Q_3 - Q_1 &= 40 \\ \hline 2Q_3 &= 140 \\ Q_3 &= \mathbf{70} \end{aligned}$$

Substitute Q_3 Value

$$\begin{aligned} Q_3 + Q_1 &= 100 \\ 70 + Q_1 &= 100 \\ Q_1 &= 100 - 70 \\ Q_1 &= \mathbf{30} \end{aligned}$$

Upper Quartile = **70**

Lower Quartile = **30**.

Example 11.26. In a distribution the difference between the two quartiles is 8, and their sum is 22 and the Median is 10.5. Find the Coefficient of Skewness. (BU – N86)

Solution : Computation of Coefficient of Skewness

$$\begin{aligned} Q_3 + Q_1 &= 22 \\ Q_3 - Q_1 &= 8 \\ \hline 2Q_3 &= 30 \\ Q_3 &= \mathbf{15} \end{aligned}$$

Substitute Q_3 Value

$$\begin{aligned} Q_3 + Q_1 &= 22 \\ 70 + Q_1 &= 22 \\ Q_1 &= 22 - 15 \\ Q_1 &= \mathbf{7} \end{aligned}$$

$$Skb = \frac{Q_3 + Q_1 - 2Me}{Q_3 - Q_1}$$

$$= \frac{15 + 7 - 2(10.5)}{15 - 7}$$

$$= \frac{22 - 21}{8} = \frac{1}{8} = \mathbf{0.125}$$

Example 11.27. For a distribution Bowley's Coefficient of Skewness is –0.36, Q_1 is 8.6 and Median is 12.3. Find the value of upper quartile. (BU-A90)

Solution :

$$Skb = \frac{Q_3 + Q_1 - 2Me}{Q_3 - Q_1}$$

$$-0.36 = \frac{Q_3 + 8.6 - 2(12.3)}{Q_3 - 8.6}$$

$$-0.36(Q_3 - 8.6) = Q_3 + 8.6 - 24.6$$

$$-0.36\,Q_3 + 3.096 = Q_3 + 8.6 - 24.6$$

$$-1.36Q_3 = 8.6 - 24.6 - 3.096$$

$$-1.36\,Q_3 = 8.6 - 27.696$$

$$-1.36\,Q_3 = -19.096$$

$$Q_3 = \mathbf{14.04}$$

Questions

1. What is Skewness? (BU - N84)
2. State any four tests of Skewness.

   (BU – N85, N87, A88, N90, N92, N96, A97, A98).
3. In a negatively skewed distribution which avegages are the maximum and the least? (BU-A85, N94)
4. Indicate what you know about Skewness in the following cases :

   (i) A distribution in which $Me = \frac{Q_3 + Q_1}{2}$, and

   (ii) A distribution in which $\overline{x} > Me > z$. (BU – A87)
5. State the nature of symmetry in the following cases.

   (i) When Median is greater than mean, and

   (ii) When Mean is greater than Median (BU – A89)
6. In a positively skewed distribution, which averages are the maximum and the least? (BU – A91)
7. Distinguish between dispersion and skewness. (BU – A92, A94)
8. When is Skewness present in a series? (BU – N93, A96)
9. Calculate the KarlPearson's Coefficient of Skewness from the following data :

   25 15 23 40 27 25 23 25 20

   (Skp = – 0.03)

10. Compute the quartile deviation and coefficient of Skewness from the following data :

Size	: 5 – 7	8 – 10	11 – 13	14 – 16	17 – 19
Frequency	: 14	24	38	20	4

$(Q_1 = 8.88,\ Me = 11.447,\ Q_3 = 13.42, Q.D. = 2.27,\ Skb = -0.13)$

11. Find the Standard Deviation and Coefficient of Skewness from the following distribution.

C.I. :	0 – 5	5 – 10	10 – 15	15 – 20	20 – 25	25 – 30	30 – 35	35 – 40
f :	2	5	7	13	21	16	8	3

$(\sigma = 7.99,\ \overline{x} = 21.9,\ z = 23.08,\ Skp = -148)$

12. Consider the following distribution :

		Distribution A	Distribution B
Mean	...	100	90
Median	...	90	80
Standard Deviation	...	10	10

(a) Both the distribution have the same degree of variation, and (b) Both the distribution have the same degree of skewness. State that these statements are ture or false. [(a) False and (b) True.]

13. From the following data find the Coefficient of Skewness :

Mean = 56.8, Me = 59.5 σ = 12.4 (Skp = -0.65)

14. Find the coefficient of quartile measure of Skewness for the following :

Mid-value :	15	20	25	30	35	40
Frequency :	30	28	25	24	20	21

(Skb = 0.058)

15. From a moderately skewed distribution following figures are obtained :

$\overline{x} = 20$; Me = 17 and C.V. = 20%. Find the Pearsonian Coefficient of Skewness. (Skp = 2.25)

16. From the following distribution, find out the quartiles and Coefficient of Skewness :

Marks	:	0 – 10	10 – 20	20 – 30	30 – 40	40 – 50	50 – 60
Frequency	:	3	9	15	30	18	5

($Skb = -0.02,\ Q_1 = 25.33,\ Me = 34.33,\ Q_3 = 41.67$)

17. From the marks secured by 120 students in the two sections – A and B, the following information is obtained :

	$\bar{x}$	σ	z
Section A ...	42.32	15	47.28
Section B ...	58.37	15	57.62

Determine which distribution is more skewed.

($Skp_A = -0.33$, $Skp_B = +0.05$, A is more skewed)

18. From the following series find out the Karl Pearson's Coefficient of Skewness :

Measurement :	11	12	13	14	15
Frequency :	3	9	6	4	3

($\bar{x} - 12.8,\ z = 12,\ \sigma = 1.2,\ Skp = 0.667$)

19. From the following available figures find the Coefficient of Variation and Coefficient of Skewness :

$n = 20,\ \Sigma x = 300,\ \Sigma x^2 = 5000,\ Me = 15$ (Skp = 0)

20. In a moderately skewed distribution the Mean is Rs.15 and the Median is Rs.14. If the coefficient of variation is 30%, find the Pearsonian Coefficient of Skewness. (Skp = 0.67)

21. From the data given below, calculate Karl Pearson's and Bowley's Coefficient of Skewness and comment on the values :

Income Rs. Less Than :	500	600	700	800	900
No. of Persons :	6	13	20	12	9

($\bar{x} = 658.33,\ Me = 655,\ z = 646.67,\ Q_1 = 569.23,\ \sigma = 118.74$
$Q_3 = 750$, Skp = 0.098 and Skb = 0.051)

22. For a distribution, Bowley's Coefficient of Skewness is –0.56, Q1 is 16.4 and Median is 24.2. Find the Quartile Deviation. ($Q_3 = 26.4$ and Q.D. = 5)

23. If Pearsonian Coefficient of correlation is 0.2, arithmetic mean is 100 and coefficient of variation is 35, find the Mode and Median. (z = 93 and Me = 97.67)

12

Correlation (I)

"Correlation" means a possible connection or relationship or interdependence between the values of two or more variables of the same phenomenon or individual series. It indicates the strength of the relationship. If we measure the heights and weights of 'n' individuals, we assume two values - one relating to heights and the other relating to weights. Such distributions, in which each unit of the series assumes two values, are called "Bivariate Distributions." If there are more than two variables in each unit, such distributions are called "Multivariate Distributions."

We can establish the relationship between the two or more values of the same series for the purpose of a comparative study. Such a relationship can be established logically with some beliefs or assumptions or notions. It is purely a guess work. It does not relate to the establishment of cause and effect. However, there may or may not be the factor of causation. There may be third group of influencing factors of the changes in the values of variables. Thus, sometimes, the existence of the relationship is just purely a chance or accidental event.

Increase or decrease in one set of values of variables of the series may influence the increase or decrease in the other set of values of variable of the same series. In some of the series we find a definite relationship between their values of variables and in some other series we cannot. We are more concerned with the relationship rather than causes.

In natural sciences correlation can be reduced to absolute mathematical terms. Heat always increases with light and an electric current is always associated with magnetic field. These instances suggest a high degree of correlation. But in social sciences it is seldom found. The laws of demand and supply suggest correlation, but not the high degree or perfect correlation.

In social sciences, We must take the correlation granted, if in a large number of cases two variables always tend to move either in the same direction or opposite direction. Such phenomena are not uncommon in the social and economic sphere. For example we may have:

(i) The series of marks of individuals in two subjects in an examination-Accountancy and Statistics.

(ii) The series of 'sales revenue' and 'advertising expenditure' of different companies in a particular year

(iii) The series of 'exports' of raw cotton in crores of rupees and 'imports' of finished goods in crores of rupees for the two years.

(iv) The series of ages of 'husbands' and 'wives' in a sample of selected married couples and so on.

Thus, two variables are said to be correlated if the change in one variable results in a corresponding change in the other variable. This type of relationship can be measured mathematically. The correlation measure is a statistical tool which studies the relationship between the two variables. It helps to find out the degree of association between the two or more variables.

I. Types of Correlation

Correlation is classified, on the basis of its nature, into the following ways:

Types of Correlation on the basis of

- Direction
  - Same (Positive or Direct)
  - Opp. (Negative or Indirect)
  - Partial (One depending on other)
- Number of Sets
  - Only Two Sets (Simple)
  - More than two sets (Multiple)
- Change
  - Linear (Straight Line)
  - Non-Linear (curve type)

If the values of the two variables deviate in the same direction, correlation is said to be **'positive'** or **'direct'**. It means the increase in the values of one variable results, on an average, in a corresponding increase in the values of other variable.

If the values of the two variables deviate in the opposite direction, correlation is said to be **'negative'** or **'indirect'**. It means the increase in the values of one variable results, on an average, in a corresponding decrease in the values of other variable.

When one variable is independent and the other variable is dependent on the former, it is the case of a **'partial correlation'**.

When only two variables are studied, it is called a **'simple correlation'**. It means the study involves only two variables which are changing either in the same or opposite direction.

When three or more variables are studied, it is called a **"multiple correlation"**. It means the study involves three or more variables which are changing either in the same direction or in the different directions.

If for corresponding to a unit change in one variable, there is a constant change in the other variable over the entire range of the values, it is said to be a **'linear correlation'**. It is the consistency of the ratio of change between the two variables. It means the amount of change in one variable tends to bear a constant ratio to the amount of the change in the other variable. For example:

variable 'X' :	2	4	6	8	10	12	14	16
variable 'Y' :	3	6	9	12	15	18	21	24

Thus for a unit change in the value of **'X'** there is a constant change viz. 1.5 in the corresponding values of **'Y'**. Mathematically, the above calculation can be expressed by the relation as under:

$Y= a + bx$ 'a' is the intercept. (here it is zero)

$Y= o + 1.5x$ 'b' is the constant ($b = 1.5$)

This type of relationship (or equation) exists only in the natural sciences. It does not exist in the social sciences, as the values of variables under study are affected simultaneously by multiplicity of factors. However, we can estimate the most probable values of **'Y'** with the help of mathematical analysis.

If the variables under study are graphed and the plotted points do not form a straight line, it is said to be a **'non-linear correlation' or 'curvi-linear correlation'**. The amount of change in one variable does not bear a constant change in the other variable.

II. Methods of Determining Correlation (Interpretation)

The degree of correlation between the two variables can be determined by the quantitative value of coefficient of correlation. On the basis of the formula given by Karl Pearson, we can state approximately the degree of correlation as under:

Degree of Correlation	Positive		Negative	
Correlation lies between +1 and –1 (Approximation)	Range		Range	
	From	To	From	To
	+1	0.00	0.00	-1.00
1. Perfect	+1		-1	
2. Very High Degree	+1.00	+0.90	-0.90	-1.00
3. High Degree	+0.90	+0.75	-0.75	-0.90
4. Moderate Degree	+0.75	+0.60	-0.60	-0.75
5. Low Degree	+0.60	+0.30	-0.30	-0.60
6. Very Low Degree	+0.30	+0.00	-0.00	-0.30
7. No Correlation	0		0	

In correlation, we are required to know the relationship and to measure the extent of relationship. There are two steps in studying the correlation- Graphic and Mathematical.

Methods of Studying Correlation

- Graphic
  - Scatter Diagram (Dotogram)
  - Simple Graph (Correlogram)
- Mathematical
  - Karl Pearson's Cofficient of Correlation
  - Spearman's Rank Coefficient of Correlation
  - Concurrent Deviation Method
  - Least Square Method

(i) Scatter Diagram Method : It is a simple way of diagrammatic representation of a bivariate distribution by which we can ascertain the correlation between the two variables. It tells us how closely the two variables are related and indicates the direction of the changes in respective variables. In this method, the given **X** and **Y** variables are shown in a graph paper and the respective-values are plotted in the **XY** plane. The points plotted will show the degree of correlation. The following diagrams will show the different types of correlation:

Positive Correlation | Negative Correlation

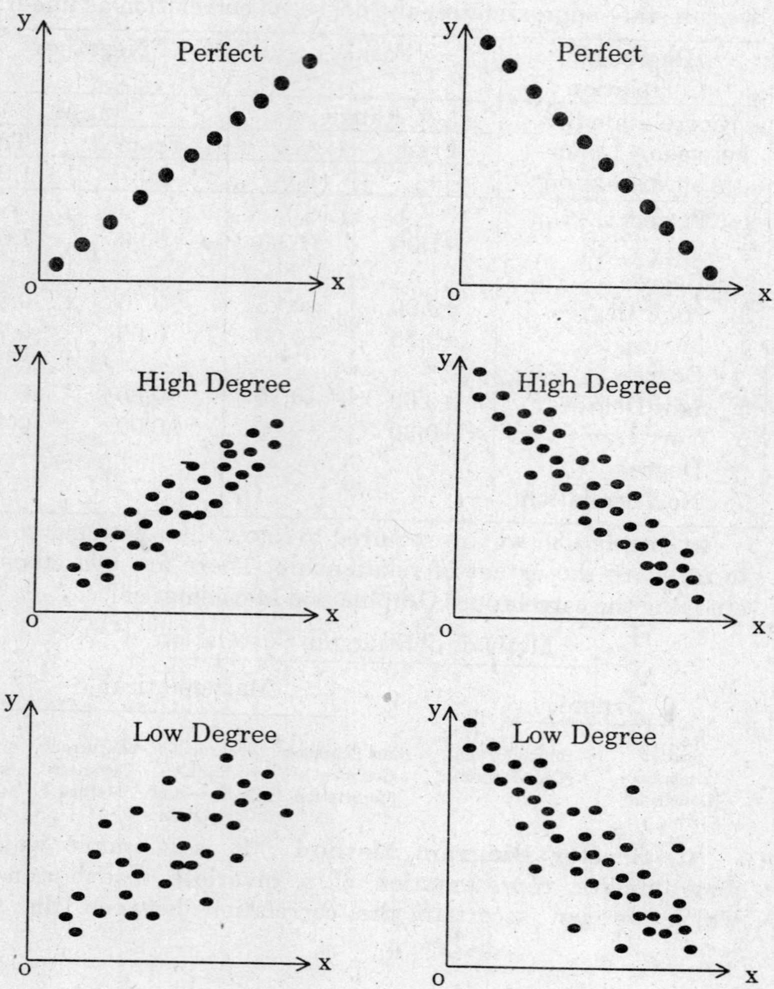

No Correlation

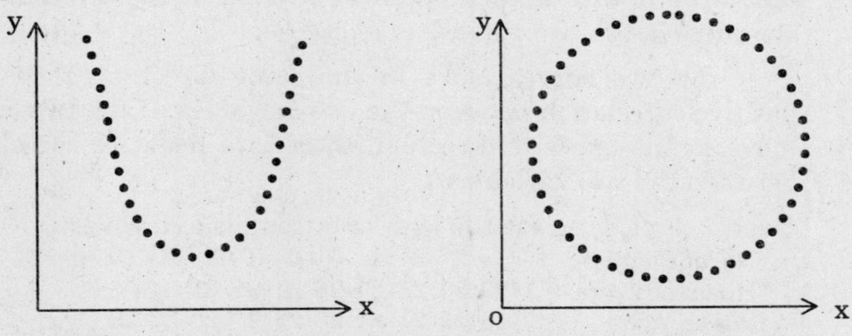

The method of scatter diagram is readily comprehensible and enables us to form a rough idea of the nature of the relationship between the two variables. It also enables us to obtain an approximate line of best fit (estimating line) by free hand method. It consists in stretching a piece of thread through the plotted points to locate the best possible line.

However, the method of scatter diagram is not suitable if the number of observations is fairly large. It does not provide us an exact measure between the two variables.

Case1. Following are the marks, in a class test in Mathematics and Statistics, secured by 12 students. Draw a scatter diagram and show the line of best fit (estimating line).

Sl.No.	Maths	Statistics
1.	55	60
2.	70	65
3.	35	50
4.	40	60
5.	65	75
6.	40	70
7.	60	50
8.	20	40
9.	30	60
10.	50	30
11.	10	30
12.	20	10

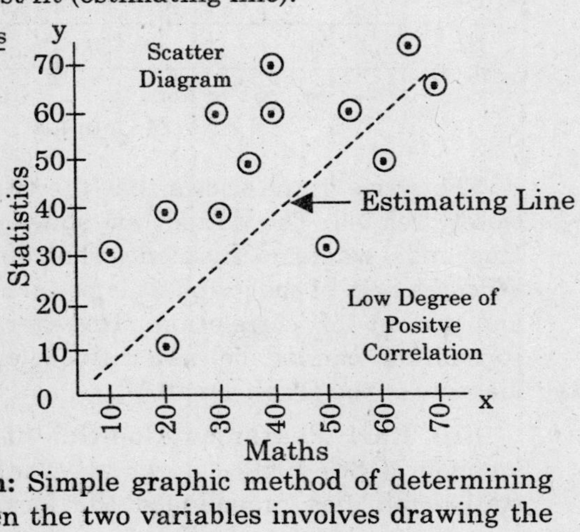

(ii) Simple Graph: Simple graphic method of determining the correlation between the two variables involves drawing the two curves **X** curve and **Y** curve-on a graph paper. We can study the nature of correlation by looking at the direction and closeness of the two curves.

If the two curves move in the same direction, there is a positive correlation between the two variables. If the two curves move in the opposite direction, there is a negative correlation between the two variables.

Case 2. Following are the ages of husbands and wives:

No. of Couples	:	1	2	3	4	5	6	7	8	9	10
Husbands' Age	:	23	27	28	25	26	34	32	31	34	33.5
Wives' Age	:	18	22	21	24	26	28	27	28	27	29

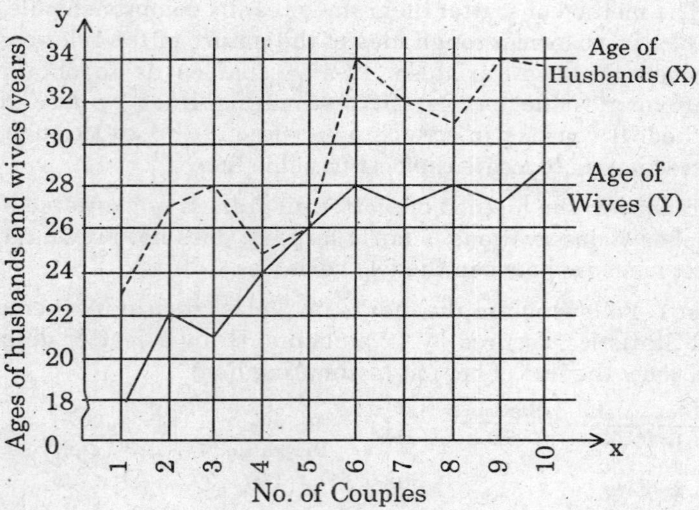

The above graph shows that the two variables **X** and **Y** are closely related. The dotted line shows the X variable (Ages of Husbands) where as thick lines shows Y variable (Age of wives). With the help of the graph, it is possible to ascertain the nature and extent of correlation. However, the exact degree of correlation cannot be ascertained either from the scatter diagram or the graphic method.

(iii) Karl Pearson;s Coefficient of Correlation: Karl Pearson (1867-1936), a great British Bio-metrician and statistician, has propounded the formula for calculating the coefficient of correlation. The formula is based on arithmetic mean and standard deviation and it is most widely used. Following are the some assumptions on which the formula is based:

(a) The two variables are affected by a large number of independent causes.

(b) The forces affecting the distribution of items in two variables are related to each other in relationship of cause and effect.

(c) There is a possibility of linear relationship between the two variables.

The formula indicates whether the correlation is positive or negative. The answer lies between +1 and -1 (Perfect Positive and Negative correlation respectively). Zero represents the absence of correlation. The formula is subject to algebraic manipulations and it is based on covariance which is the arithmetic mean of cross-products. Covariance is a highly useful concept in the statistical anaylsis. Karl Pearson's coefficient of correlation is also known as the **"Product Moment Coefficient"**. It is denoted by **'r'** which is the symbol of the degree of correlation between the two variables. It is a measure of association.

"Coefficient of Correlation" is the numerical measure of the amount of correlation existing between the two variables **X** and **Y** - the subject and the relative respectively. The variable which is used as the standard is called the **subject**, and the variable which is compared with the subject (measured in terms of the subject) is called the **relative**. The coefficient is calculated by *"dividing the product of all the deviations of each pair of observations from their respective means by the product of the standard deviations of the two variables multiplied by the number of items"*. So the Pearsonian coefficient of correlation will be:

$$r = \frac{\Sigma xy}{n\sigma x\ \sigma y}$$

Where, $x = (x - \bar{x}) = dx$

$y = (y - \bar{y}) = dy$

dx = Deviation of 'x' values of variable from there $\bar{x}$ i.e. $(x - \bar{x})$.

dy = Deviation of 'y' values of variable from there $\bar{y}$ i.e. $(y - \bar{y})$

σ_x = Standard Deviation of 'X' variable.

σ_y = Standard Deviation of 'Y' variable.

n = Number of items paired.

The formula may be presented as under,

$$r = \frac{\Sigma dxdy}{n\sigma x\sigma y} \quad \text{(Note : Deviations are taken from actual mean)}$$

The above formula can be simplified mathematically as under.

$$r = \frac{\Sigma dxdy}{n \times \sqrt{\frac{\Sigma dx^2}{n}} \times \sqrt{\frac{\Sigma dy^2}{n}}} = r = \frac{\Sigma dxdy}{\sqrt{\Sigma dx^2}\ \sqrt{\Sigma dy^2}}$$

(Note : No need to Compute Standard Deviation)

These above formula are quite conveniently applied, if the $\bar{x}$ and $\bar{y}$ of the variables are integers or whole numbers.

When the $\bar{x}$ and $\bar{y}$ of the variables are fractional figures, the computation will be a tedious job. Under such circumstances, we can take the deviations from the assumed means for the two variables (the next nearest whole number to the actual mean preferably). Then we can have the "Short-cut" formula as under:

$$r = \frac{\Sigma dxdy - \frac{(\Sigma dx)(\Sigma dy)}{n}}{\sqrt{\Sigma dx^2 - \frac{(\Sigma dx)^2}{n}}\ \sqrt{\Sigma dy^2 - \frac{(\Sigma dy)^2}{n}}}$$

(Note: Though the formula seems to be lengthy, the calculations are amazingly simplified.)

(a) Refer ... $\frac{(\Sigma dx)(\Sigma dy)}{n} = n(\bar{x} - Ax)(\bar{y} = Ay)$

$\bar{x}$ = Actual Mean of x	$\bar{y}$ = Actual Mean of y
Ax = Assumed Mean of x	Ay = Assume Mean of y

(b) Refer ... $\text{Covariance} = \dfrac{\Sigma dxdy}{n}$

(c) Refer ... $r = \dfrac{\text{covariance}}{\sigma x\, \sigma y} = \dfrac{\dfrac{\Sigma dxdy}{n}}{\sigma x\, \sigma y}$

Probable Error: It is a difference resulting due to taking samples from the mass or population. It is not possible to consider the entire population (census method) in statistical analysis and arrive true or actual results. So there lies error in the sampling result as compared to the actual result obtained in the census method.

Generally samples are taken and results are arrived at from the samples. Naturally such results differ from that of the census method. Any number of series of samples taken from the same population may give different answers, All these answers, based on the same population, vary in a particular range. **"Probable Error"** is a measure (a single fractional figure) which when 'added to' and 'substracted from', gives us the two limits, within these two limits, it is probable that all the results or answers (coefficients of correlation) of the sample pairs, selected from the same population, will fall. Thus the probable error is a statistical measure which provides for two limits within which all the answers, obtained from different sample pairs of the population, will fall.

According to **Secrist**, *"The probable error of the correlation coefficient is an amount, which if added to and substracted from the average correlation coefficient, produces amounts within which the chances are even that a coefficient of correlations from a series selected at random will fall"*.

With the help of probable error, it is possible to determine the reliability of the value of the coefficient in so far as it depends on the conditions of random sampling. It is a old measure of testing the reliability of an observed value of correlation coefficient. It is based on the standard errors multiplied by the probable factor. It is obtained by the formula:

$$P.E = \text{Probable factor x Standard Error} = 0.6745\frac{1-r^2}{\sqrt{n}}$$

Reason for taking the factor 0.6745 is that in a normal distribution 50% of the observations lie in the range, $\mu \pm 0.6745\ \sigma$ where μ is the mean and σ is the standard deviation.

Uses of Probable Error : Following are the some of the uses of Probable Error.

(i) It is used to determine the limits within which the population correlation coefficient may be expected to lie.

(ii) It may be used to test if an observed value of sample correlation coefficient is significant of any correlation in population.

Conditions for the use of Probable Error:

The measure of probable error can be properly used only when the following three conditions exist:

(i) The data must have been drawn from a normal population

(ii) The conditions of random sampling should prevail in selecting the samples from the population

(iii) The coefficient of correlation must have been computed from the sample.

However, the P.E. may lead to fallacious conclusions particularly when 'n' (the number of pairs of observations) is small. In order to use the P.E. effectively, 'n' should be fairly large. If 'r' is less than six times of its P.E. (r < 6. P.E.), then correlation is not at all significant. If 'r' is greater than six times of its P.E. (r > 6. P.E.), then 'r' is definitely significant. In all other cases, nothing can be concluded with certainty.

Example 12.1. *From the following table calculate the coefficient of correlation by Karl Pearson's method. Arithmetic means of X and Y variables are 6 and 8 respectively.*

X :	6	2	10	-	8
Y :	9	11	-	8	7

(BU-N87)

Solution : Let us find out the missing figures in X and Y variables.

X variable

$$\bar{x} = \frac{\Sigma x}{n}$$

$$6 = \frac{6+2+10+A+8}{5}$$

$$6 = \frac{26+A}{5}$$

$$30 = 26 + A$$

$$A = \mathbf{4}$$

Y variable

$$\bar{y} = \frac{\Sigma y}{n}$$

$$8 = \frac{9+11+B+8+7}{5}$$

$$8 = \frac{35+B}{5}$$

$$40 = 35 + B$$

$$B = \mathbf{5}$$

Computation of Coefficient of Correlation

x	y	(x − 6) dx	dx^2	(y − 8) dy	dy^2	dxdy
6	9	0	0	+1	1	0
2	11	-4	16	+3	9	-12
10	5	+4	16	−3	9	-12
4	8	-2	4	0	0	0
8	7	+2	4	-1	1	-2
30	40	0	40	0	20	−26
Σx =	Σy =	Σdx =	Σdx^2 =	Σdy =	Σdy^2 =	Σdxdy =

$$r = \frac{\Sigma dxdy}{\sqrt{\Sigma x^2 \times \Sigma dy^2}} = \frac{-26}{\sqrt{40 \times 20}} = \frac{-26}{\sqrt{800}} = \frac{-26}{28.28472} = \mathbf{-0.9192388}$$

High Degree of Negative Correlation

$$\text{P.E.} = 0.6745\frac{1-r^2}{\sqrt{n}} = 0.6745\frac{1-(-0.9193)^2}{\sqrt{5}} = 0.6745\frac{1-0.8451}{\sqrt{5}}$$

$$= 0.6745\frac{0.1549}{2.2361} = 0.6745 \times 0.06927 = \mathbf{0.04672}$$

Example 12.2. *Find the coefficient of correlation between the following two variables. Comment on the result through the Probable Error.* (BU – A94)

X : 6 8 12 15 18 20 24 28 31

Y : 10 12 15 15 18 25 22 26 28

Solution : Computation of Coefficient of Correlation

x	y	$(x-18)dx$	dx^2	$(y-19)dy$	dy^2	$dxdy$
6	10	-12	144	-9	81	+108
8	12	-10	100	-7	49	+70
12	15	- 6	36	-4	16	+24
15	15	- 3	9	-4	16	+12
18	18	0	0	-1	1	0
20	25	+ 2	4	+6	36	+12
24	22	+ 6	36	+3	9	+18
28	26	+10	100	+7	49	+70
31	28	+13	169	+9	81	+117
162	171	0	598	0	338	431
$\Sigma x =$	$\Sigma y =$	$\Sigma dx =$	$\Sigma dx^2 =$	$\Sigma dy =$	$\Sigma dy^2 =$	$\Sigma dxdy =$

$$\bar{x} = \frac{\Sigma x}{n} = \frac{162}{9} = \mathbf{18} \qquad \bar{y} = \frac{\Sigma y}{n} = \frac{171}{9} = \mathbf{19}$$

$$r = \frac{\Sigma dxdy}{\sqrt{\Sigma dx^2}\sqrt{\Sigma dy^2}} = \frac{431}{\sqrt{598 \times 338}} = \frac{431}{\sqrt{20212.4}}$$

$$= \frac{431}{449.582} = 0.958668 = \mathbf{0.9587}$$

(High Degree of Positive correlation)

$$P.E. = 0.6745\,\frac{1-r^2}{\sqrt{n}} = 0.6745\,\frac{1-(0.9587)^2}{\sqrt{9}} = 0.6745\,\frac{1-0.9191}{3}$$

$$= 0.6745\,\frac{0.0809}{3} = 0.6745 \times 0.02697 = 0.018192$$

$$r = 0.9587 \quad \text{and} \quad 6 \times 0.018192 = \mathbf{0.109152}$$

Since 'r' is more than six times of the P.E., r is significant.

Example 12.3. *Calculate the coefficient of correlation from the following data and calculate its Probable Error.*

Marks in

Statistics (X) : 30, 60, 30, 66, 72, 24, 18, 12, 42, 06

Accountancy (Y) : 06, 36, 12, 48, 30, 06, 24, 36, 30, 12

Solution: Computation of Coefficient of Corrolation

x	y	$(x-36)/6$ dx	dx^2	$(y-24)/6$ dy	dy^2	dxdy
30	06	-1	1	-3	9	+3
60	36	+4	16	+2	4	+8
30	12	-1	1	-2	4	+2
66	48	+5	25	+4	16	+20
72	30	+6	36	+1	1	+6
24	06	-2	4	-3	9	+6
18	24	-3	9	0	0	0
12	36	-4	16	+2	4	- 8
42	30	+1	1	+1	1	+ 1
06	12	-5	25	-2	4	+10
360	240	0	134	0	52	+ 48
$\Sigma x =$	$\Sigma y =$	$\Sigma dx =$	$\Sigma dx^2 =$	$\Sigma dy =$	$\Sigma dy^2 =$	$\Sigma dxdy =$

$$\bar{x} = \frac{\Sigma x}{n} = \frac{360}{10} = \mathbf{36} \qquad \bar{y} = \frac{\Sigma y}{n} = \frac{240}{10} = \mathbf{24}$$

$$r = \frac{\Sigma dxdy}{\sqrt{\Sigma dx^2}\ \sqrt{\Sigma dy^2}} = \frac{48}{\sqrt{134}\ \sqrt{52}} = \frac{48}{11.5758 \times 7.2111}$$

$$= \frac{48}{83.4743} = \mathbf{0.575}$$

$$P.E = 0.6745\,\frac{1-r^2}{\sqrt{n}} = 0.6745\,\frac{1-(0.575)^2}{\sqrt{10}} = 0.6745\,\frac{1-0.330625}{3.1622776}$$

$$= 0.6745\,\frac{0.669375}{3.1622776} = 0.6745 \times 0.2116749 = 0.14277$$

The two limits, within which all the 'r's of different samples fall, are

0.575	0.575
+ 0.143	- 0.143
0.718	0.432

'r' answers fall within '0.718 to 0.432' (positive range)

Example 12.4. *Calculate the coefficient of correlation between income and weight from the following data. Comment on the result.* (BU-A89)

Income (Rs) :	100	200	300	400	500	600
Weight (lbs) :	120	130	140	150	160	170

Solution: Computation of Coefficient of Correlation

x	y	$(x-350)/50$ dx	dx^2	$(y-145)/5$ dy	dy^2	dxdy
100	120	-5	25	-5	25	25
200	130	-3	9	-3	9	9
300	140	-1	1	-1	1	1
400	150	+1	1	+1	1	1
500	160	+3	9	+2	9	9
600	170	+5	25	+3	25	25
2100	870	0	70	0	70	70
$\Sigma x =$	$\Sigma y =$	$\Sigma dx =$	$\Sigma dx^2 =$	$\Sigma dy =$	$\Sigma dy^2 =$	$\Sigma dxdy =$

$$\bar{x} = \frac{\Sigma x}{n} = \frac{2100}{6} = \mathbf{350} \qquad \bar{y} = \frac{\Sigma y}{n} = \frac{70}{6} = \mathbf{145}$$

The deviations are divided by the common factor and short-cut method is adopted.

$$r = \frac{\Sigma dxdy}{\sqrt{\Sigma dx^2 \times \Sigma dy^2}} = \frac{70}{\sqrt{70 \times 70}} = \frac{70}{70} = +1$$ (There is a perfect positive correlation.)

Example 12.5. *Calculate Karl Pearson's coefficient of correlation between percentages of pass and failure from the following data.* (BU-A92)

No.of Students :	800	600	900	700	500	400
No. passed :	480	300	450	560	450	300

Solution : Let us convert the data into the number of students passed and failed.

No. of students passed (X) :	480	300	450	560	450	300
Failed (Y) :	320	300	450	140	50	100
% (X) :	60	50	50	80	90	75
% (Y) :	40	50	50	20	10	25

Computation of Coefficient of Correlation

x	y	$(x-60)$ dx	dx^2	$(y-35)$ dy	dy^2	dxdy
60	40	0	0	+ 5	25	0
50	50	-10	100	+15	225	-150
50	50	-10	100	+15	225	-150
80	20	+20	400	-15	225	-300
90	10	+30	900	-15	625	-750
75	25	+15	225	-10	100	-150
405	195	+ 45	1725	–15	1425	–1500
$\Sigma x =$	$\Sigma y =$	$\Sigma dx =$	$\Sigma dx^2 =$	$\Sigma dy =$	$\Sigma dy^2 =$	$\Sigma dxdy =$

$$\bar{x} = \frac{\Sigma x}{n} = \frac{405}{6} = \mathbf{67.5} \qquad \bar{y} = \frac{\Sigma x}{n} = \frac{195}{6} = \mathbf{32.5}$$

$$r = \frac{\Sigma dxdy - \frac{(\Sigma dx)(\Sigma dy)}{n}}{\sqrt{\Sigma dx^2 - \frac{(\Sigma dx)^2}{n}}\sqrt{\Sigma dy^2 - \frac{(\Sigma dy)^2}{n}}} = \frac{-1500 - \frac{(45)(-15)}{6}}{\sqrt{1725 - \frac{(45)^2}{6}}\sqrt{1425 - \frac{(-15)^2}{6}}}$$

$$= \frac{-1500 + 112.5}{\sqrt{1725 - 337.5}\sqrt{1425 - 37.5}} = \frac{-1387.5}{\sqrt{1387.5}\sqrt{1387.5}}$$

$$= \frac{-1387.5}{1387.5 \times 1387.5} = \frac{-1387.5}{1387.5} = \mathbf{-1}$$

(A perfect negative correlation)

(**Note:** Deviations are taken from the assumed means and the short-cut formula is used. Because actual means- 67.5 and 32.5 -are in fractions.)

Example 12.6. *Following are the results of B.Com. Examination in a college. Compute coefficient of correlation between age and success in the examination and interpret the result.* (BU-N90)

Age of Candidates :	20-21	21-22	22-23	23-24	24-25	25-26
Candidates Appeared :	120	100	70	40	10	5
Successful Candidates :	72	55	35	18	4	1

Solution : Let us obtain the Mid-values of age group and convert the successful candidates into percentages.

Computation of Coefficient of Correlation

Age (C.I)	M.V. x	(x–23.5) dx	dx^2	% of passing y	$(y-50)/5$ dy	dy^2	dxdy
20-21	20.5	-3	9	60	+2	4	-6
21-22	21.5	-2	4	55	+1	1	-2
22-23	22.5	-1	1	50	0	0	0
23-24	23.5	0	0	45	-1	1	0
24-25	24.5	+1	1	40	-2	4	-2
25-26	25.5	+2	4	20	-6	36	-12
		-3	19		-6	46	-22
		Σdx =	Σdx^2 =		Σdy =	Σdy^2 =	Σdxdy

We are taking assumed means. In Y variable we are dividing the deviations by the common factor. So a short-cut formula is used.

$$r = \frac{\Sigma dxdy - \frac{(\Sigma dx)(\Sigma dy)}{n}}{\sqrt{\Sigma dx^2 - \frac{(\Sigma dx)^2}{n}}\sqrt{\Sigma dy^2 - \frac{(\Sigma dy)^2}{n}}} = \frac{-22 - \frac{(-3)(-6)}{6}}{\sqrt{19 - \frac{(-3)^2}{6}}\sqrt{46 - \frac{(-6)^2}{6}}}$$

$$= \frac{-22 - \frac{18}{6}}{\sqrt{19 - \frac{9}{6}}\sqrt{46 - \frac{36}{6}}} = \frac{-22-3}{\sqrt{19-1.5}\sqrt{46-6}} = \frac{-25}{\sqrt{17.5}\sqrt{40}}$$

$$= \frac{-25}{4.1833 \times 6.3245} = \frac{-2.5}{26.457} = \mathbf{-0.94492}$$

Example 12.7. *Calculate coefficient of correlation between age and playing habit from the following data.* (BU-N89)

Age in Years	:	15-20	20-25	25-30	30-35	35-40	40-45	45-50	50-55	55-60
Population	:	1500	2000	4000	3000	2500	1000	800	500	200
No. of Players	:	1200	1560	2280	1500	1000	300	200	50	6

Solution: Let us obtain the Mid-values of age group and playing habit in percentages before computing the coefficient of correlation.

Population	: 1500	2000	4000	3000	2500	1000	800	500	200
No of players	: 1200	1560	2280	1500	1000	300	200	50	6
Percentage	: 80	78	57	50	40	30	25	10	3

Computaion of Coefficient of Correlation

Age in years	M.V . x	$(x-375)/5$ dx	dx^2	% of y	$(y-40)$ dy	dy^2	dxdy
15-20	17.5	-4	16	80	+40	1600	-160
20-25	22.5	-3	9	78	+38	1444	-114
25-30	27.5	-2	4	57	+17	289	- 34
30-35	32.5	-1	1	50	+10	100	- 10
35-40	37.5	0	0	40	0	0	0
40-45	42.5	+1	1	30	-10	100	- 10
45-50	47.5	+2	4	25	-15	225	- 30
50-55	52.5	+3	9	10	-30	900	- 90
55-60	57.5	+4	16	3	-37	1369	-148
		0	60		13	6027	−596
		$\Sigma dx =$	$\Sigma dx^2 =$		$\Sigma dy =$	$\Sigma dy^2 =$	$\Sigma dxdy =$

$$r = \frac{\Sigma dxdy - \frac{(\Sigma dx)(\Sigma dy)}{n}}{\sqrt{\Sigma dx^2 - \frac{(\Sigma dx)^2}{n}}\sqrt{\Sigma dy^2 - \frac{(\Sigma dy)^2}{n}}}$$

$$= \frac{-596 - \frac{(0)(13)}{9}}{\sqrt{60 - \frac{(0)^2}{9}}\sqrt{6027 - \frac{(13)^2}{9}}} = \frac{-596}{\sqrt{60}\ \sqrt{6027 - 18.7778}}$$

$$= \frac{-596}{\sqrt{60}\ \sqrt{6008.2222}} = \frac{-596}{7.746 \times 77.5127} = \frac{-596}{600.411} = \mathbf{-0.99265}$$

Example 12.8. *Find Pearsonian coefficient of correlation between average profits and average advertisement expenditure per shop and interpret.* (BU-A93,N93)

No. of shops	:	*12*	*18*	*25*	*20*	*10*
Total Profits(Rs)	:	*7,200*	*5,400*	*10.000*	*3,000*	*1,800*
Total Advertisement Expenses (Rs)	:	*1,200*	*3,600*	*7,500*	*1,000*	*600*

Solution: Let us obtain the average profits and average advertisement expenses-x and y.

$$\text{Average profits} = \frac{\text{Profits}}{\text{No. of shops}} \text{ \& Average A.E} = \frac{\text{Advertisement Exp}}{\text{No. of shops}}$$

Compuation of Coefficient of Corrolation

x	y	$(x-320)/10$ dx	dx^2	$(y-140)/10$ dy	dy^2	dxdy
600	100	+28	784	-4	16	-112
300	200	- 2	4	+6	36	- 12
400	300	+ 8	64	+16	256	+128
150	50	-17	289	-9	81	+153
180	60	-14	196	-8	64	+112
1630	710	+ 3	1337	+ 1	453	269
$\Sigma x =$	$\Sigma y =$	$\Sigma dx =$	$\Sigma dx^2 =$	$\Sigma dy =$	$\Sigma dy^2 =$	$\Sigma dxdy$

(Note : Deviations are taken from the assumed means)

$$r = \frac{\Sigma dxdy - \frac{(\Sigma dx)(\Sigma dy)}{n}}{\sqrt{\Sigma dx^2 - \frac{(\Sigma dx)^2}{n}}\sqrt{\Sigma dy^2 - \frac{(\Sigma dy)^2}{n}}}$$

$$= \frac{269 - \frac{(3)(1)}{5}}{\sqrt{1337 - \frac{(3)^2}{5}}\sqrt{453 - \frac{(1)^2}{5}}} = \frac{269 - 0.6}{\sqrt{1337 - 1.8}\sqrt{453 - 0.2}}$$

$$= \frac{268.4}{\sqrt{1335.2}\sqrt{452.8}} = \frac{268.4}{36.54 \times 21.2791} = \frac{268.4}{777.5382} = \mathbf{+0.345192}$$

(There is a possibility of 'r')

Example 12.9. *Following are the results of B.Com examination.*

Age of Candidates	*13-14*	*14-15*	*15-16*	*16-17*	*17-18*	*18-19*	*19-20*	*20-21*	*21-22*	*22-23*
Candidates Appeared	*200*	*300*	*100*	*50*	*150*	*400*	*250*	*150*	*25*	*75*
Passed	*124*	*180*	*65*	*34*	*99*	*252*	*145*	*81*	*12*	*33*

Solution : Let us obtain the Mid-values of age group and convert the successful candidates into percentages.

Computation of Coefficient of Corrolation

Age in C.I	M.V. x	$(x-18.5)$ dx	dx^2	% of y	$(y-58)$ dy	dy^2	$dxdy$
13-14	13.5	-5	25	62	+ 4	16	-20
14-15	14.5	-4	16	60	+ 2	4	- 8
15-16	15.5	-3	9	65	+ 7	49	-21
16-17	16.5	-2	4	68	+10	100	-20
17-18	17.5	-1	1	66	+ 8	64	- 8
18-19	18.5	0	0	63	+ 5	25	0
19-20	19.5	+1	1	58	0	0	0
20-21	20.5	+2	4	54	- 4	16	- 8
21-22	21.5	+3	9	48	-10	100	-30
22-23	22.5	+4	16	44	-14	196	-56
		-5	85		8	570	-171
		$\Sigma dx =$	$\Sigma dx^2 =$		$\Sigma dy =$	$\Sigma dy^2 =$	$\Sigma dxdy =$

$$r = \frac{\Sigma dxdy - \frac{(\Sigma dx)(\Sigma dy)}{n}}{\sqrt{\Sigma dx^2 - \frac{(\Sigma dx)^2}{n}}\sqrt{\Sigma dy^2 - \frac{(\Sigma dy)^2}{n}}}$$

$$= \frac{-171 - \frac{(-5)(8)}{10}}{\sqrt{85 - \frac{(-5)^2}{10}}\sqrt{570 - \frac{(8)^2}{10}}} = \frac{-171+4}{\sqrt{85-2.5}\sqrt{570-6.4}}$$

$$= \frac{-167}{\sqrt{82.5}\sqrt{563.6}} = \frac{-167}{9.08295 \times 23.74026} = \frac{-167}{215.6316} = \mathbf{-0.774469}$$

Example 12.10. *With the following data in six cities calculate the coefficient of correlation by pearson's method between the density of population and death rate.* (BU-A85,N96)

City	:	*A*	*B*	*C*	*D*	*E*	*F*
Density of population	:	*200*	*500*	*400*	*700*	*600*	*300*
Population (in'000')	:	*30*	*90*	*40*	*42*	*72*	*24*
No. of Deaths	:	*300*	*1440*	*560*	*840*	*1224*	*312*

Solution: Let us obtain the death rate as under

$$\text{Death Rate} = \frac{\text{No. of Deaths}}{\text{Population}}$$

Computation of Coefficient of Correlation

x	y	$(x-450)/50$ dx	dx^2	$(y-15)$ dy	dy^2	$dxdy$
200	10	- 5	25	- 5	25	+25
500	16	+1	1	+1	1	+ 1
400	14	- 1	1	- 1	1	+ 1
700	20	+5	25	+5	25	+25
600	17	+3	9	+2	4	+ 6
300	13	- 3	9	- 2	4	+ 6
2700	90	0	70	0	60	64
$\Sigma x =$	$\Sigma y =$	$\Sigma dx =$	$\Sigma dx^2 =$	$\Sigma dy =$	$\Sigma dy^2 =$	$\Sigma dxdy =$

$$r = \frac{\Sigma dxdy}{\sqrt{\Sigma dx^2}\ \sqrt{\Sigma dy^2}} = \frac{64}{\sqrt{70}\ \sqrt{60}} = \frac{64}{8.36666 \times 7.74597}$$

$$= \frac{64}{64.807868} = .9875344 = \mathbf{.9875}$$

Example 12.11. *From the following data find out if there is any relationship between density of population and death rates.* (BU-A83)

Districts	:	A	B	C	D	E
Area in Kilometers	:	120	150	80	50	200
Population	:	24,000	75,000	48,000	40,000	50,000
No. of Deaths	:	288	1,125	768	720	650

Solution: Let us obtain the density of population and death rate in each districts.

$$\text{Density} = \frac{\text{Population}}{\text{Area}}$$

$$\text{Death Rate} = \frac{\text{No. of Deaths}}{\text{Population}} \times 100$$

Computaion of Coefficient of Correlation

Density x	$(x-470)/$ dx	dx^2	y	$(y-15)$ dy	dy^2	dxdy
200	- 27	729	12	- 3	9	81
500	+ 3	9	15	0	0	0
600	+13	169	16	+1	1	13
800	+33	1089	18	+3	9	99
250	-22	484	13	- 2	4	44
2350	0	2480	74	-1	23	237
$\Sigma x =$	$\Sigma dx =$	$\Sigma dx^2 =$	$\Sigma y =$	$\Sigma dy =$	$\Sigma dy^2 =$	$\Sigma dx\,dy =$

$$r = \frac{\Sigma dxdy - \frac{(\Sigma dx)(\Sigma dy)}{n}}{\sqrt{\Sigma dx^2 - \frac{(\Sigma dx)^2}{n}}\sqrt{\Sigma dy^2 - \frac{(\Sigma dy)^2}{n}}}$$

$$= \frac{237 - \frac{(0)(-1)}{5}}{\sqrt{2480 - \frac{(0)^2}{5}}\sqrt{23 - \frac{(-1)^2}{5}}} = \frac{237}{\sqrt{2480}\sqrt{23 - 0.2}}$$

$$= \frac{237}{\sqrt{2480}\sqrt{22.8}} = \frac{237}{49.799598 \times 4.7749} = \frac{237}{237.78981} = \mathbf{0.9966785}$$

Example 12.12. *The following table gives the distribution of the total population and those who are totally or partially blind among them. Find out if there is any relation between age and blindness.* (BU-A97)

Age in years :	*0-10*	*10-20*	*20-30*	*30-40*	*40-50*	*50-60*	*60-70*	*70-80*
No. of Persons (000's) :	*100*	*60*	*40*	*36*	*24*	*11*	*6*	*3*
Blind :	*55*	*40*	*40*	*40*	*36*	*22*	*18*	*15*

Solution: Let us obtain the Mid-values of age groups and blind men per one lakh persons.

Computation of Coefficient of Corrleation

Age x	Per lakh y	$(x-40)/5$ dx	dx^2	$(y-185)$dy	dy^2	dxdy
5	55.00	- 7	49	-130.00	16900	+910.00
15	66.67	- 5	25	-118.33	14002	+591.65
25	100.00	- 3	9	- 85.00	7225	+255.00
35	111.11	- 1	1	- 73.89	5460	+ 73.89
45	150.00	+1	1	- 35.00	1225*	- 35.00
55	200.00	+3	9	+ 15.00	225	+ 45.00
65	300.00	+5	25	+115.00	13225	+ 575.00
75	500.00	+7	49	+315.00	99225	+2205.00
320	1482.78	0	168	+ 2.78	157487	4620.54
$\Sigma x =$	$\Sigma y =$	$\Sigma dx =$	$\Sigma dx^2 =$	$\Sigma dy =$	$\Sigma dy^2 =$	$\Sigma dxdy =$

* negative

$$r = \frac{\Sigma dxdy - \frac{(\Sigma dx)(\Sigma dy)}{n}}{\sqrt{\Sigma dx^2 - \frac{(\Sigma dx)^2}{n}}\sqrt{\Sigma dy^2 - \frac{(\Sigma dy)^2}{n}}}$$

$$= \frac{4620.54 - \frac{(0)(2.78)}{8}}{\sqrt{168 - \frac{(0)^2}{8}}\sqrt{157487 - \frac{(2.78)^2}{8}}} = \frac{4620.54}{\sqrt{168}\ \sqrt{157487 - 0.9661}}$$

$$= \frac{4620.54}{\sqrt{168}\ \sqrt{157486.04}} = \frac{4620.54}{12.96148 \times 396.8451} = \frac{4620.54}{5154.6998} = \mathbf{0.898}$$

Example 12.13. *The following are the monthly figures of advertising expenditure and sales of a firm. It is generally found that advertising expenditure has its impact on sales generally after two months. Allowing this time lag, calculate coefficient of correlation.* (BU - A95)

Months	Advertising Expenses Rs.	Sales Rs.	Month	Advertising Expenses Rs.	Sales Rs.
Jan	50	1200	July	140	2400
Feb	60	1500	Aug	160	2600
Mar	70	1600	Sept.	170	2800
April	90	2000	Oct	190	2900
May	120	2200	Nov	200	3100
June	150	2500	Dec	250	3900

Solution: Let us allow a time lag of two months by linking the January Advertising Expenses to the March Sales, February Advertising Expenses to the April sales and so on.

Computation of Coefficient of Corrleation

x	y	$\frac{(x-120)}{10}$ dx	dx^2	$\frac{(y-2600)}{100}$ dy	dy^2	dxdy
50	1600	- 7	49	-10	100	+70
60	2000	- 6	36	- 6	36	+36
70	2200	- 5	25	- 4	16	+20
90	2500	- 3	9	- 1	1	+ 3
120	2400	0	0	- 2	4	0
150	2600	+3	9	0	0	0
140	2800	+2	4	+ 2	4	+ 4
160	2900	+4	16	+ 3	9	+12
170	3100	+5	25	+ 5	25	+25
190	3900	+7	49	+13	169	+91
1200	26000	0	222	0	364	+261
$\Sigma x =$	$\Sigma y =$	$\Sigma dx =$	$\Sigma dx^2 =$	$\Sigma dy =$	$\Sigma dy^2 =$	$\Sigma dxdy =$

$$r = \frac{\Sigma dxdy}{\sqrt{\Sigma dx^2}\ \sqrt{\Sigma dy^2}} = \frac{261}{\sqrt{222}\ \sqrt{364}} = \frac{261}{14.8997 \times 98.07878}$$

$$= \frac{261}{284.2682} = \mathbf{0.918147}$$ (very high degree of 'r')

Example 12.14. *From the following table, find correlation coefficient between age and playing habit of students:* (BU-A87)

Age (years)	:	*15*	*16*	*17*	*18*	*19*	*20*
No. of Students	:	*250*	*200*	*150*	*120*	*100*	*80*
Regular Players	:	*200*	*150*	*90*	*48*	*30*	*12*

Solution : Let us obtain the percentage of regular players and then calculate coefficient of correlation between age and percentage.

Computation of Coefficient of Correlation

Age x	% of R.Play y	$(x-17)$ dx	dx^2	$\frac{(y-50)}{10}$ dy	dy^2	Dxdy
15	80	- 2	4	+3.00	9.00	- 6.00
16	75	- 1	1	+2.50	6.25	- 2.50
17	60	0	0	+1.00	1.00	0
18	40	+1	1	-1.00	1.00	- 1.00
19	30	+2	4	-2.00	4.00	- 4.00
20	15	+3	9	-3.50	12.25	-10.50
105	300	+ 3	19	0	33.50	24.00
$\Sigma x =$	$\Sigma y =$	$\Sigma dx =$	$\Sigma dx^2 =$	$\Sigma dy =$	$\Sigma dy^2 =$	$\Sigma dxdy =$

$$r = \frac{\Sigma dxdy - \frac{(\Sigma dx)(\Sigma dy)}{n}}{\sqrt{\Sigma dx^2 - \frac{(\Sigma dx)^2}{n}}\sqrt{\Sigma dy^2 - \frac{(\Sigma dy)^2}{n}}}$$

$$= \frac{24 - \frac{(+3)(0)}{6}}{\sqrt{19 - \frac{(3)^2}{6}}\sqrt{33.50 - \frac{(0)^2}{6}}} = \frac{24}{\sqrt{19-1.5}\ \sqrt{33.50}} = \frac{24}{\sqrt{17.5}\ \sqrt{33.50}}$$

$$= \frac{24}{4.1833 \times 5.78792} = \frac{24}{24.21261} = 0.991219 = +\mathbf{0.991}$$

Example 12.15. Compute Karl Person's coefficient of correlation between per capita National Income and per capita Consumer Expenditure from the data given below :

Year :	1978	1979	1980	1981	1982	1983	1984	1985	1986	1987
Per Capita N. I :	249	251	248	252	258	269	271	272	280	275
Per Capita Con. Exp :	237	238	236	240	245	255	254	252	258	251

Also calculate Probable Error (BỤ – A98)

Solution : Computation of Coefficient of Correlation

x	y	(x–262) dx	(y- 246) dy	dx^2	dy^2	dxdy
249	237	- 13	- 9	169	81	+117
251	238	- 11	- 8	121	64	+ 88
248	236	- 14	-10	196	100	+140
252	240	- 10	- 6	100	36	+ 60
258	245	- 4	- 1	16	1	+ 4
269	255	+ 7	+ 9	49	81	+ 63
271	254	+ 9	+ 8	81	64	+ 72
272	252	+10	+ 6	100	36	+ 60
280	258	+18	+12	323	144	+216
275	251	+13	+ 5	169	25	+ 65
2615	2466	+ 5	+ 6	1325	632	885
Σx =	Σy =	Σdx =	Σdy =	Σdx^2 =	Σdy^2 =	Σdxdy =

$$r = \frac{\Sigma dxy - \frac{(\Sigma dx)(\Sigma dy)}{n}}{\sqrt{\Sigma dx^2 - \frac{(\Sigma dx)^2}{n}}\sqrt{\Sigma dy^2 - \frac{(\Sigma dy)^2}{n}}}$$

$$= \frac{885 - \frac{(5)(6)}{10}}{\sqrt{1325 - \frac{(5)^2}{10}}\sqrt{632 - \frac{(6)^2}{10}}} = \frac{885 - 3}{\sqrt{1325 - 2.5}\ \sqrt{632 - 3.6}}$$

$$= \frac{882}{\sqrt{1322}\ \sqrt{628.4}} = \frac{882}{36.3662 \times 25.0679} = \frac{882}{911.6244} = \mathbf{+0.9675}$$

$$\text{Parabola Error} = 0.6745\ \frac{1 - r^2}{\sqrt{n}}$$

$$= 0.6745\ \frac{1 - (0.9675)^2}{\sqrt{10}} = 0.675\ \frac{1 - 0.9361}{3.16228}$$

$$= 0.6745\ \frac{0.0639}{3.16228} = 0.6745 \times 0.02021 = \mathbf{0.01363}$$

Example 12.16. *Calculate the coefficient of correlation between X and Y series from the following data:* *(BU – A90)*

	Series A	Series B
No. of Pairs	**15**	**15**
Variance	**10**	**12**

Summation of products of deviations of x and y series from their respective means is **122**.

Solution:

$$r = \frac{\Sigma dxdy}{n\,\sigma x\,\sigma y} = \frac{122}{15 \times \sqrt{10} \times \sqrt{12}} = \frac{122}{15 \times 3.162 \times 3.464}$$

$$= \frac{122}{164.3} = \mathbf{0.7425}$$

Example 12.17. *Calculate the correlation coefficient between the variables X and Y from the following figures:*

$\Sigma x = \mathbf{118}$ $\quad \Sigma x^2 = \mathbf{556}$ $\quad \Sigma xy = \mathbf{368}$

$\Sigma y = \mathbf{93}$ $\quad \Sigma y^2 = \mathbf{309}$ $\quad n = \mathbf{30}$

Solution:

$$r = \frac{\Sigma xy - \frac{(\Sigma x)(\Sigma y)}{n}}{\sqrt{\Sigma x^2 - \frac{(\Sigma x)^2}{n}}\sqrt{\Sigma y^2 - \frac{(\Sigma y)^2}{n}}}$$

$$= \frac{368 - \frac{(118)(93)}{30}}{\sqrt{556 - \frac{(118)^2}{30}}\sqrt{309 - \frac{(-93)^2}{30}}} = \frac{368 - \frac{10974}{30}}{\sqrt{556 - \frac{13924}{30}}\sqrt{309 - \frac{8649}{30}}}$$

$$= \frac{368 - 365.8}{\sqrt{556 - 464.13}\ \sqrt{309 - 288.3}} = \frac{2.2}{\sqrt{91.87}\ \sqrt{20.7}}$$

$$= \frac{2.2}{9.5849 \times 4.5498} = \frac{2.2}{43.609} = \mathbf{0.0505}$$

Example 12.18. *What inference do you draw when the correlation coefficient between the two variables is* (BU-A87,N89)

*(i) Equal to **zero** and (ii) Equal to **-1***

Solution:

(i) No correlation.

(ii) Perfect Negative correlation.

Example 12.19. *Interprete `r' in the following case:* (BU-A91)
(i) when = -0.87 and (ii) when r = +0.25

Solution:

(i) High Degree of Negative Correlation.

(ii) Very Low Degree of Positive Correlation.

Example 12.20. *Calculate the coefficient of correlation between the X and Y series from the following data:*

	X	Y
Arithmetic Mean	74.5	125.5
Assumed Mean	69.0	112.0
Standard Deviation	13.07	15.85

Sum of the products of deviations of **X** and **Y** from their assumed means + 2176

No. of pairs of observations 8

Solution:

$$r = \frac{\Sigma dxdy - n(\bar{x} - A_x)(\bar{y} - A_y)}{n \times \sigma_x \times \sigma_y}$$

$$= \frac{2176 - 8(74.5 - 69.0)(125.5 - 112.0)}{8 \times 13.07 \times 15.85}$$

$$= \frac{2176 - 8(5.5)(13.5)}{1657.276} = \frac{2176 - 594}{1657\ 276} = \frac{1582}{1657.276} = 0.9546$$

Example 12.21. Given n = **25**, **Σx = 125**, Σy = **100**, Σx² = **650**, Σy² = **460** and Σxy = **508**, calculate **the coefficient** of correlation.

Solution:

$$r = \frac{\Sigma xy - \frac{(\Sigma x)(\Sigma y)}{n}}{\sqrt{\Sigma x^2 - \frac{(\Sigma x)^2}{n}}\sqrt{\Sigma y^2 - \frac{(\Sigma y)^2}{n}}}$$

$$= \frac{508 - \frac{(125)(100)}{25}}{\sqrt{650 - \frac{(125)^2}{25}}\sqrt{460 - \frac{(100)^2}{25}}} = \frac{508 - 500}{\sqrt{650 - 625}\ \sqrt{460 - 400}}$$

$$= \frac{8}{\sqrt{25}\ \sqrt{60}} = \frac{8}{5 \times 7.746} = \frac{8}{38.73} = \mathbf{0.2066}$$

Example 12.22. *Given the following, calculate Karl Pearson's coefficient of correlation between X and Y series.*

	X	Y
Sum of the deviations from assumed mean	**-14**	**18**
Sum of squares of deviations from assumed mean	**4304**	**6308**
Sum of products of deviations from their respective assumed means.		**1510**
No. of pairs of observations		**12**

Solution:

$$r = \frac{\Sigma dx dx - \frac{(\Sigma dx)(\Sigma dy)}{n}}{\sqrt{\Sigma dx^2 - \frac{(\Sigma dx)^2}{n}} - \sqrt{\Sigma dy^2 - \frac{(\Sigma dy)^2}{n}}}$$

$$= \frac{1510 - \frac{(-14)\,(18)}{12}}{\sqrt{4304 - \frac{(-14)^2}{12}}\ \sqrt{6308 - \frac{(18)^2}{12}}} = \frac{1510 + 21}{\sqrt{4304 - 16.33}\ \sqrt{6308 - 27}}$$

$$= \frac{1531}{\sqrt{4287.67}\ \sqrt{6281}} = \frac{1531}{65.48 \times 79.253} = \frac{1531}{5189.51} = \mathbf{0.295}$$

Example 12.23. Coefficient of correlation between two variates x and y is **0.8**. Their covariance is **20**. The variance of x is **16**. find the standard deviation of y series.

$$r = \frac{\Sigma xy}{n \sigma_x\ \sigma_y}$$

$$0.8 = \frac{\Sigma xy}{n} \times \frac{1}{\sigma_x\ \sigma_y}$$

$$0.8 = 20 \times \frac{1}{\sqrt{16} \times \sigma_y}$$

$$0.8 = 20 \times \frac{1}{4 \times \sigma_y}$$

$$3.2 = 20 \frac{1}{\sigma_y}$$

$$\sigma_y = \frac{20}{3.2}$$

$$\sigma_y = \mathbf{6.25}$$

Example 12.24. *In a distribution **n** is **5** and **r** is **0.7**, comment.*
Solution:

$$P.E = 0.6745\frac{1-r^2}{\sqrt{n}} = 0.6745\frac{1-(0.7)^2}{\sqrt{5}} = 0.6745\frac{1-0.49}{2.2361}$$

$$= 0.6745\frac{0.51}{2.2361} = 00.6745 \times 0.2281 = 0.15384$$

$r = \mathbf{0.7}$ and $6 \times .15384 = \mathbf{0.92304}$

"Since 'r' is less than six times of the P.E., **r is not significant.**"

Example 12.25. *From the following figures in two cases, which value of 'r' is more significant.*

(a) r = 0.6 & P.E. = 0.05
(b) r = 0.9 & P.E. = 0.09

Solution :

(a) r = 0.6   b) r = 0.9
6 x 0.05 = 0.3   6 x 0.09 = 0.54   Both the 'r' values are significant

(a) $\frac{0.6}{0.05} = 12$ b) $\frac{0.9}{0.09} = 10$ (a) 'r' is more significant

Example 12.26. *Answer the following:*

(a) r = **0.48**, covariance = **36**, variance of x = **16** find the σy and

(b) n = **25**, P.E. = **0.045**, find the 'r'

Solution:

a) Covariance = $r \times \sigma_x \times \sigma_y$

$36 = 0.48 \times \sqrt{16} \times \sigma_y$

$36 = 0.48 \times 4 \times \sigma_y$

$36 = 1.92 \times \sigma_y$

$\sigma_y = \mathbf{18.75}$

b) $0.045 = 0.6745\frac{1-r^2}{\sqrt{n}}$

$0.045 = 0.6745\frac{1-r^2}{\sqrt{25}}$

$0.045 = 0.6745\frac{1-r^2}{5}$

$0.225 = 0.6745(1-r^2)$

$\frac{0.225}{0.6745} = 1-r^2$

$0.33358 = 1-r^2$

$r^2 = 1-0.33358 = 0.66642$

$r = \sqrt{0.66642} = \mathbf{0.81634}$

Karl Pearson's coefficient of correlation method gives a precise and summary quantitative figure which can be meaningfully interpreted. It gives either positive or negative direction or degree of the relationship between the two variables. However following are the **limitations** of the method:

(i) It is based on a linear relationship which may or may not exist.

(ii) The coefficient value is affected by the extreme items.

(iii)The answer following between **+1** and **-1** requires to be interpreted carefully.

(iv) It involves a tedious job of computation.

Questions

1. State the types of correlation. (BU-N84)
2. State the assumption of Karl Perason's coefficient of correlation. (BU-N85,N93,N95)
3. What is a probable error? What are its uses? (BU-A90, A91, N96, A97)
4. What is a linear correlation? (BU-A91)
5. What is a meant by coefficient of correlation? (BU-A94)
6. Mention the uses of correlation. (BU-N94, A96)
7. What is a "Scatter Diagram"? (BU-N94)
8. Calculate the coefficient of correlation between x and y variables given below:

X :	15	18	30	27	25	23	30
Y :	7	10	17	16	12	13	9

(r = 0.63)

9. **The corresponding** values of two series are given in the **following** table:

X :	42	44	58	55	89	98	66
Y :	56	49	53	58	65	76	58

Find out coefficient of correlation and probable error.

(r = 0.904 and P.E. = 0.047).

10. Calculate Karl Pearson's coefficient of correlation for the following data:

Heights (in inches)								
of Husbands (x)	:	60	62	64	66	68	70	72
of Wives (y)	:	61	63	63	63	64	65	67

(r = 0.939)

11. From the following data find the Karl Pearson's coefficient : $\Sigma dx = \mathbf{5}$, $\Sigma dy = \mathbf{4}$, $\Sigma dx^2 = \mathbf{40}$, $\Sigma dy^2 = \mathbf{50}$, $\Sigma dxdy = \mathbf{32}$, $n = \mathbf{10}$. (r = 0.704)

12. In a question on correlation the value of r is **0.64** and its P.E.= **0.13274**. What was the value of 'n'? (n = 9)

13. Calculate the coefficient of correlation from the following data shown:

X :	12	9	8	10	11	13	7
Y :	14	8	6	9	11	12	3

(r = 0.9486)

14. Find the correlation coefficient between the production items and defective items among them and the probable error.

Size	:	15-16	16-17	17-18	18-19	19-20	20-21
Production Items	:	200	270	340	360	400	300
Detective Items	:	150	162	170	180	180	114

(Hints: x = Mid-point. Y = % of defective items. 'r' = 0.949 P.E. = 0.027)

15. Find the number of items if $r = 0.5$, $\Sigma xy = 120$, $\Sigma x^2 = 90$, $\sigma y = 8$. (n = 10)

16. Find out the correlation coefficient from the following data

X :	3	5	6	7	9	12
Y :	20	14	12	10	9	7

(r= -0.9203)

17. Calculate the coefficient of correlation for the ages of husbandand wives :

Ages of Husbands :	23	27	28	29	30	31	33	35	36	39
Ages of Wives :	18	22	23	24	25	26	28	29	30	32

(r = +0.995)

18. Calculate Pearson's coefficient of correlation between Advertisement cost and Sales as per the data given below:

Cost in '000' Rs :	39	65	62	90	82	75	25	98	36	78
Sales in lakhs Rs :	47	53	58	86	62	68	60	91	51	84

(r = +0.78)

19. A student calculates the value of 'r' as +**0.5** when the value of '**n**' is **16** and comments that 'r' is significant. Is he correct?
(P.E. = 0.126 r < 6 P.E. so he is not correct)

20. From the following data calculate the correlation coefficient:
$\Sigma x = \mathbf{28}$, $\Sigma y = \mathbf{38}$, $\Sigma x^2 = \mathbf{208}$, $\Sigma y^2 = \mathbf{312}$, $\Sigma xy = \mathbf{194}$ & n = **5**. (r = -0.545)

21. Given the following details, find the value of σy.
r = **0.6**, covariance = **12** and σx = **5**

(Hint : $\text{Covariance} = \frac{\Sigma xy}{n}$, $r = \frac{\text{Covariance}}{\sigma_x\ \sigma_y}$, $\sigma_y = 4$)

22. From the following summarized details, find the correlation coefficient for (i) and σy for (ii)
(i) Covariance = **488**, variance of x = **824** and variance of y = **325**.
(ii) r = **-0.75**, covariance = **-15**, σx = **5**

$$\left[r = \frac{\text{Covariance}}{\sqrt{\text{Variance X}}\sqrt{\text{Variance Y}}},\ r = 0.9428\right]$$

23. Answer the following questions:
(i) n = **50**, $\sigma_x = \mathbf{4.5}$, $\sigma_y = \mathbf{3.5}$ and $\Sigma xy = \mathbf{420}$
Find the coefficient correlation. (r = 0.533)
(ii) r = **0.5212** covariance = **7.8** and 'X' variance = **16**. Find the 'Y' variance. (covariance of y = 14)

24. State in each of the following cases whether you would expect to find a positive or negative or no correlation.
(i) Ages of Husbands and Wives (+)
(ii) Shoe sizes and Intelligence (o)
(iii) Educational Qualification and Income (+)
(iv) Insurance Company's Profit and Claims (-)
(v) Rainfall and yield (+)
(vi) Increase in price and sales (-)
(vii) Cricket Players and Blind Persons (o)
(viii) Heights and Weights (+)

13

Correlation (II)

(iv) Spearman's Rank Correlation Coefficient

Charles Edward Spearman, a British Psychologist, developed a formula to obtain the rank correlation coefficient in 1904. He has tried to establish the rank correlation coefficient between the **'Ranks'** of **'n'** individuals in the two or more variables. Accordingly, it is possible for a class teacher to arrange his students in an ascending or descending order of intelligence though intelligence cannot be measured quantitatively. In a similar way, ranking can be made in a beauty contest and correlation can be established among the scores given by the different judges or selectors.

It is, however, possible to measure the degree of correlation between two sets of observations or between paired values when only the relative order of magnitude is given for each series. For example, suppose 10 students have appeared for two papers in a test and from actual marks obtained by them their rankings can be determined. If we want to know whether their performances are correlated, we can use the **Spearman's Rank Correlation Coefficient** method. The formula is based on the ranks of the variables according to their sizes. Following are the circumstances when the Rank Correlation coefficient is used,

(i) In a beauty contest, cooking contest, flower show contest and interview involving selections, we can use the rank correlation coefficient.

(ii) If the data are irregular or extreme items are erratic or inaccurate, we can use the rank correlation coefficient.

Under this method of rank correlation coefficient, the individual items of variables(x and y) are arranged in order of their ranks. We can apply this method only to individual observations, but not to frequency distributions. In the process of ranking, the original values are not taken into account, but only the ranks are assigned on the basis of original values. The Rank Correlation Coefficient is denoted symbolically **'r_s'**.

$$'r_s' = 1 - \frac{6 \sum d^2}{n(n^2 - 1)} \quad \text{or} \quad 1 - \frac{6 \sum d^2}{n^3 - n}$$

where,

6 = The number six

d = The numerical difference between corresponding pairs of ranks

n = The number of pairs

Σd^2 = The sum of squares of 'd'

In the ranking systems, the biggest item gets the first rank, the next to it gets the second rank and so on.

The value of 'r_s' will be interpreted in the same way as that of the Karl Pearson's correlation coefficient. Its value also ranges between **+1** and **-1**. Where 'r_s' is **+1**, it indicates the perfect agreement in the order of ranking or selection or judging, where 'r_s' is **-1**, it indicates the perfect disagreement in the order of ranking or selection or judging. There are two types of distribution,

(i) Only values are given(i.e. ranking should be given on the basis of values).

(ii) Only Ranks are given(i.e. there is no need to give ranks).

Common Ranks: Sometimes, we may come across with the equal ranks. There may be more than one items with the same value. For such items we have to give common ranks. The common rank is given to all the items having the same value by averaging the normal ranks which the items would have got if they have differed slightly from each other. For example:

x:	35	60	20	35	35	4	15	35	7	2
Ranks:	3.5	1	6	3.5	3.5	9	7	3.5	8	10

The item 35 is repeated four times. Against these items there are four ranks i.e. 2, 3, 4 and 5. If we take the average of these four ranks, we get the common rank 3.5 as under,

$$\text{Common Rank} = \frac{\text{Normal Ranks}}{\text{No. of Ranks Pooled}} = \frac{2 + 3 + 4 + 5}{4} = 3.5$$

When there are common ranks in the series, the rank correlation coefficient formula is modified with some adjustment to the Σd^2.

Suppose there are **'m'** items in the series and their ranks are common. Then a correction is to be made to the value of **'Σd^2'**

as under :

$$\Sigma d^2 + \frac{1}{12}(m^3 - m).$$

If there are more than one such groups of items with the common rank, again the above value is added as many times as the number of such groups. For example, in **X** series there are two items having the same value and a common rank is 6.5 (i.e. average of 6th and 7th rank), and in **Y** series there are three items with rank 3 (i.e. 2,3 and 4 rank) and four items with rank 8.5 (i.e. 7,8,9 and 10), we have to add to the value of Σd^2 three times as under:

$$\Sigma d^2 + \frac{1}{12}(2^3 - 2) + \frac{1}{12}(3^3 - 3) + \frac{1}{12}(4^3 - 4)$$

Thus for two items **m=2**, for 3 items **m =3** and for four items **m =4.** For each group of tied ranks, the adjustment is made to Σd^2. The **'m'** represents the number of items having tied ranks.

Example 13.1. *Calculate the rank correlation coefficient for the following data:*

x :	60	34	40	50	45	41	22	43	42	66	64	46
y :	75	32	35	40	45	33	12	30	36	72	41	57

(BU - N86)

Solution:

Values are given . Ranks are to be assigned.

x	y	Rx	Ry	d	d2
60	75	3	1	+2	4
34	32	11	10	+1	1
40	35	10	8	+2	4
50	40	4	6	-2	4
45	45	6	4	+2	4
41	33	9	9	0	0
22	12	12	12	0	0
43	30	7	11	-4	16
42	36	8	7	+1	1
66	72	1	2	-1	1
64	41	2	5	-3	9
46	57	5	3	+2	4
				$\Sigma d=0$	$\Sigma d^2=48$

$$r_s = 1 - \frac{6\,\Sigma d^2}{n^3 - n}$$

$$= 1 - \frac{6 \times 48}{12^3 - 1}$$

$$= 1 - \frac{6 \times 48}{12^3 - 12}$$

$$= 1 - \frac{288}{1716}$$

$$= 1 - 0.16783$$

$$= \mathbf{0.83217}$$

Example 13.2. *The competitors in a beauty contest were ranked by three judges as follows:*

Judge A:	3	5	4	10	8	8	1	6	8	2
Judge B:	5.5	5.5	1	8.5	4	10	2	7	8.5	3
Judge C:	9	9	7	5	2	2	2	5	5	9

Which pair of judges has the nearest approach to common taste in beauty? (BU-88)

Solution:

Ranks are already given.

			$(R_A - R_B)$		$(R_B - R_C)$		$(R_A - R_C)$	
R_A	R_B	R_C	d	d^2	d	d^2	d	d^2
3	5.5	9	-2.5	6.25	-3.5	12.25	-6	36
5	5.5	9	-0.5	0.25	-3.5	12.25	-4	16
4	1	7	+3	9.00	-6	36.00	-3	9
10	8.5	5	+1.5	2.25	+3.5	12.25	+5	25
8	4	2	+4	16.00	+2	4.00	+6	36
8	10	2	-2	4.00	+8	64.00	+6	36
1	2	2	-1	1.00	0	0	-1	1
6	7	5	-1	1.00	+2	4.00	+1	1
8	8.5	5	-0.5	0.25	+3.5	12.25	+3	9
2	3	9	-1	1.00	-6	36.00	-7	49
			$\Sigma d=0$	$\Sigma d^2=41$	$\Sigma d=0$	$\Sigma d^2 =193$	$\Sigma d =0$	$\Sigma d^2 =218$

(I) When we compare Judge A and Judge B we find that,

(i) in **A** series three ranks (7th,8th and 9th)are tied. and

(ii) in **B** series, (a) two ranks (5th and 6th) and (b) two ranks (8th and 9th)are tied.

$$r_s = 1 - \frac{6\left[\Sigma d^2 + \frac{1}{12}(3^3 - 3) + \frac{1}{12}(2^3 - 2) + \frac{1}{12}(2^3 - 2)\right]}{n^3 - n}$$

$$= 1 - \frac{6\,[41 + 2 + 0.5 + 0.5]}{10^3 - 10} = 1 - \frac{6\,(44)}{990}$$

$$= 1 - \frac{264}{990} = 1 - 0.26667 = \mathbf{0.7333}$$

(II) When we compare Judge B and Judge C, we find that

(i) In **B** series, (a) two ranks (5th and 6th) and

(b) two ranks (8th and 9th) are tied, and

(ii) In **C** series, (a) three ranks (1st,2nd and 3rd),

(b) three ranks (4th,5th and 6th) and

(c) three ranks (8th,9th and 10th) are tied.

$$r_s = 1 - \frac{6\left[\Sigma d^2 + \frac{1}{12}(2^3 - 2) + \frac{1}{12}(2^3 - 2) + \frac{1}{12}(3^3 - 3) + \frac{1}{12}(3^3 - 3) + \frac{1}{12}(3^3 - 3)\right]}{n^3 - n}$$

$$= 1 - \frac{6\,[193 + 0.5 + 0.5 + 2 + 2 + 2]}{10^3 - 10}$$

$$= 1 - \frac{6\,(200)}{990} = 1 - \frac{1200}{990} = 1 - 1.2121 = \mathbf{-\,0.2121}$$

(III) When we compare Judge A and Judge C, we find that,

(i) In **A** series, three ranks (7th, 8th and 9th) and

(ii) In **C** series,(a) three ranks (1st, 2nd and 3rd),

(b) three ranks (4th, 5th and 6th)and

(c) three ranks (8th, 9th and 10th) are tied.

$$r_s = 1 - \frac{6\left[\Sigma d^2 + \frac{1}{12}(3^3 - 3) + \frac{1}{12}(3^3 - 3) + \frac{1}{12}(3^3 - 3) + \frac{1}{12}(3^3 - 3)\right]}{n^3 - n}$$

$$= 1 - \frac{6\,(128 + 2 + 2 + 2 + 2]}{10^3 - 10}$$

$$= 1 - \frac{6\,(216)}{990} = 1 - \frac{1296}{990} = 1 - 1.3091 = \mathbf{-\,0.3091}$$

Thus, A & B Judges = **0.7333**

B & C Judges = **-0.2121**

A & C Judges = **-0.3091**

So A & B pair of judges has the nearest approach to common taste in beauty, since the rank correlation is the maximum (and positive) between their judgement.

Example 13.3. *From the marks obtained by 8 students in Accountancy and statistics, compute coefficient of correlation by rank difference method.* (BU.N89)

Marks in Accountancy:	60	15	20	28	12	40	80	20
Statistics:	10	40	30	50	30	20	60	30

Solution: The values are given. So ranks must be assigned.

Acct. x	Stat. y	Rx	Ry	Rx - Ry d	d2
60	10	2	8	-6	36
15	40	7	3	+4	16
20	30	5.5	5	+0.5	0.25
28	50	4	2	+2	4
12	30	8	5	+3	9
40	20	3	7	-4	16
80	60	1	1	0	0
20	30	5.5	5	+0.5	0.25
				Σd=0	Σd^2=81.50

Tied Ranks

(i) In X series 5th & 6th.

(ii) In Y series 4th, 5th & 6th.

$$r_s = 1 - \frac{6\,[\Sigma d^2 + \frac{1}{12}(2^3 - 2) + \frac{1}{12}(3^3 - 3)]}{n^3 - n}$$

$$= 1 - \frac{6\,[81.50 + 0.5 + 2]}{8^3 - 8} = 1 - \frac{6\,(84)}{504}$$

$$= 1 - \frac{504}{504} = 1 - 1 = \mathbf{0}$$

Example 13.4. *Calculate the rank correlation between the length of service and order of merit from the following data:*

Employee:	A	B	C	D	E	F	G	H	I	J	K	L
Years of Service :	5	2	10	8	6	4	12	2	7	5	9	3
Order of Merit (Efficiency):	6	12	1	9	8	5	2	10	3	7	4	11

(BU-A91)

Solution: Years of service should be ranked, whereas the order of merit (efficiency) not.

Years of Service x	Rx	Merit Ry	Rx - Ry d	d2
5	7.5	6	+1.5	2.25
2	11.5	12	-0.5	0.25
10	2	1	+1	1
8	4	9	-5	25
6	6	8	-2	4
4	9	5	+4	16
12	1	2	-1	1
2	11.5	10	+1.5	2.25
7	5	3	+2	4
5	7.5	7	+0.5	0.25
9	3	4	-1	1
3	10	11	-1	1
			Σd=0	Σd^2=58.00

Tied Ranks

(i) In x series (a)7th & 8th and (b) 11th &12th.

(ii) In y series No tied ranks.

$$r_s = 1 - \frac{6\left[\Sigma d^2 + \frac{1}{12}(2^3 - 2) + \frac{1}{12}(2^3 - 2)\right]}{n^3 - n}$$

$$= 1 - \frac{6\,[58 + 0.5 + 0.5]}{12^3 - 12} = 1 - \frac{6\,(59)}{1716}$$

$$= 1 - \frac{354}{1716} = 1 - 0.2063 = \mathbf{0.7937}$$

Example 13.5. *10 students obtained the following marks in Statistics and Accountancy:*

Students	A	B	C	D	E	F	G	H	I	J
Statistics	115	109	112	87	98	120	98	100	98	118
Accountancy	75	73	85	70	76	82	65	73	68	80

(BU-N94)

Solution:

Values are given. So ranks are to be allotted.

Statistics x	Accountancy y	Rx	Ry	Rx - Ry d	d^2
115	75	3	5	-2	4
109	73	5	6.5	-1.5	2.25
112	85	4	1	+3	9
87	70	10	8	+2	4
98	76	8	4	+4	16
120	82	1	2	-1	1
98	65	8	10	-2	4
100	73	6	6.5	-0.5	0.25
98	68	8	9	-1	1
118	80	2	3	-1	1
				$\Sigma d=0$	$\Sigma d^2= 42.50$

Tied Ranks

(i) In **X** series, 7th, 8th and 9th are tied.

(ii) In **Y** series, 6th and 7th are tied.

$$r_s = 1 - \frac{6\left[\Sigma d^2 + \frac{1}{12}(3^3 - 3) + \frac{1}{12}(2^3 - 2)\right]}{n^3 - n}$$

$$= 1 - \frac{6\,[42.50 + 2 + 0.5]}{10^3 - 10} = 1 - \frac{6\,(45)}{990}$$

$$= 1 - \frac{270}{990} = 1 - 0.27273 = \mathbf{0.7273}$$

Example 13.6 . *Calculate the coefficient of rank correlation from the following:*

X:	48	33	40	9	16	16	65	24	16	57
Y:	13	13	24	6	15	4	20	9	6	19

(BU-N95)

Solution:

Values are given. So ranks are to be allotted.

x	y	Rx	Ry	d (Rx - Ry)	d^2
48	13	3	5.5	-2.5	6.25
33	13	5	5.5	-0.5	0.25
40	24	4	1	+3	9.00
9	6	10	8.5	+1.5	2.25
16	15	8	4	+4	16.00
16	4	8	10	-2	4.00
65	20	1	2	-1	1.00
24	9	6	7	-1	1.00
16	6	8	8.5	-0.5	0.25
57	19	2	3	-1	1.00
				$\Sigma d = 0$	$\Sigma d^2 = 41.00$

Tied Ranks **(i)** In **X** series, 7th, 8th and 9th .

(ii) In **Y** series (a) 5th and 6th (b) 8th and 9th.

$$r_s = 1 - \frac{6\left[\Sigma d^2 + \frac{1}{12}(3^3 - 3) + \frac{1}{12}(2^3 - 2) + \frac{1}{12}(2^3 - 2)\right]}{n^3 - n}$$

$$= 1 - \frac{6\,[41 + 2 + 0.5 + 0.5]}{10^3 - 10} = 1 - \frac{6\,(44)}{990}$$

$$= 1 - \frac{264}{990} = 1 - 0.2667 = \mathbf{0.7333}$$

Example 13.7. *Ten competitors in a voice contest are ranked by three judges in the following order:*

Judge 1 : 1 6 5 10 3 2 4 9 7 8

Judge 2 : 3 5 8 4 7 10 2 1 6 9

Judge 3 : 6 4 9 8 1 2 3 10 5 7

Solution:

Ranks are already given.

			$R_1 - R_2$		$R_2 - R_3$		$R_1 - R_3$	
R_1	R_2	R_3	d	d^2	d	d^2	d	d^2
1	3	6	-2	4	-3	9	-5	25
6	5	4	+1	1	+1	1	+2	4
5	8	9	-3	9	-1	1	-4	16
10	4	8	+6	36	-4	16	+2	4
3	7	1	-4	16	+6	36	+2	4
2	10	2	-8	64	+8	64	0	0
4	2	3	+2	4	-1	1	+1	1
9	1	10	+8	64	-9	81	-1	1
7	6	5	+1	1	+1	1	+2	4
8	9	7	-1	1	+2	4	+1	1
			$\Sigma d=0$	$\Sigma d^2=200$	$\Sigma d=0$	$\Sigma d^2=214$	$\Sigma d=0$	$\Sigma d^2=60$

Correlation Based on the,

(i) Ranks of 1st and 2nd Judge:-

$$r_s = 1 - \frac{6\sum d^2}{n^3 - n} = 1 - \frac{6 \times 200}{10^3 - 10} = 1 - \frac{1200}{990}$$

$$= 1 - 1.2121 = \mathbf{-0.2121}$$

(ii) Ranks of 2nd and 3rd Judge:-

$$r_s = 1 - \frac{6\sum d^2}{n^3 - n} = 1 - \frac{6 \times 214}{10^3 - 10} = 1 - \frac{1284}{990}$$

$$= 1 - 1.29696 = \mathbf{-0.29697}$$

(iii) Ranks of 1st and 3rd Judge:-

$$r_s = 1 - \frac{6\sum d^2}{n^3 - n} = 1 - \frac{6 \times 60}{10^3 - 10} = 1 - \frac{360}{990}$$

$$= 1 - 0.3639 = \mathbf{+0.6361}$$

Thus, the **first** and the **third** judges **have the nearest** approach to common likings in voice as the rank **correlation is positive** and the highest.

Example 13.8. *The coefficient of rank correlation between marks in Statistics and in Accountancy obtained by a certain group of students is 0.8. If the sum of the squares of the differences in ranks is given to be 33, find the number of students in the group.*

(BU-N83)

Solution:

$$r_s = 1 - \frac{6\sum d^2}{n^2(n-1)}$$

$$0.8 = 1 - \frac{6 \times 33}{n^2(n-1)}$$

$$0.8 = 1 - \frac{198}{n^2(n-1)}$$

$$\frac{198}{n^2(n-1)} = 1 - 0.8$$

$$\frac{198}{n^2(n-1)} = 0.2$$

$$198 = 0.2\ (n^3 - n)$$

$$\frac{198}{0.2} = (n^3 - n)$$

$$990 = (n^3 - n)$$

$$n^3 - n - 990 = 0$$

$$n^3 - n - 1000 + 10 = 0$$

$$n^3 - n - 10^3 - 10 = 0$$

$$n^3 - 10^3 - (n - 10) = 0$$

$$(n - 10)(n^2 + 100 + 10n) - (n - 10) = 0$$

Thus, in the above equation, (n+100+10n) is a positive sum. So it cannot be zero. Then naturally (n-10) must be Zero.

$\therefore$ n - 10 = 0; n = **10**

i.e. the number of students is 10.

Example 13.9. *If $\Sigma d^2 = 80$ and n=9 find the Rank correlation coefficient.*

Solution:

$$r_s = 1 - \frac{6\sum d^2}{n^3 - n} = 1 - \frac{6 \times 80}{9^3 - 9} = 1 - \frac{480}{720}$$

$$= 1 - 0.66667 = \mathbf{0.3333}$$

Example 13.10. *In a beauty competition, two judges ranked 12 participants as follows:*

Judge 1 :	3	4	1	5	2	10	6	9	8	7	12	11
Judge 2 :	6	10	12	3	9	2	5	8	7	4	1	11

What is the degree of agreement between the judgement of two judges?

Solution:

Ranks are already given.

R1	R2	d	d2
3	6	- 3	9
4	10	- 6	36
1	12	-11	121
5	3	+ 2	4
2	9	- 7	49
10	2	+ 8	64
6	5	+ 1	1
9	8	+ 1	1
8	7	+ 1	1
7	4	+ 3	9
12	1	+11	121
11	11	0	0
		$\Sigma d = 0$	$\Sigma d^2 = 416$

$$r_s = 1 - \frac{6\Sigma d^2}{n^3 - n}$$

$$= 1 - \frac{6\,(416)}{12^3 - 12}$$

$$= 1 - \frac{2496}{1728 - 12}$$

$$= 1 - \frac{2496}{1716}$$

$$= 1 - 1.454545$$

$$= \mathbf{-0.45455}$$

"The agreement between the two judges is in the opposite direction, as the r_s is negative"

Example 13.11. *Two ladies were asked to rank seven different brands of lipsticks as listed below:*

Brands :	A	B	C	D	E	F	G
Lady 1 :	1	3	2	7	6	4	5
Lady 2 :	2	1	4	6	7	3	5

Calculate the rank correlation coefficient.

Solution:

Ranks are given already.

R_1	R_2	d	d^2
1	2	- 1	1
3	1	+ 2	4
2	4	- 2	4
7	6	+ 1	1
6	7	- 1	1
4	3	+ 1	1
5	5	0	0
		$\Sigma d = 0$	$\Sigma d^2 = 12$

$$r_s = 1 - \frac{6\Sigma d^2}{n^3 - n}$$

$$= 1 - \frac{6 \times 12}{7^3 - 7}$$

$$= 1 - \frac{72}{343 - 7}$$

$$= 1 - 0.2143$$

$$= \mathbf{0.786}$$

Example 13.12. *Ten participants in a beauty contest were ranked by three judges in the following order:*

Judge 1.	8	1	2	10	3	7	5	9	4	6
Judge 2.	4	7	10	1	2	9	6	8	5	3
Judge 3.	10	3	2	9	4	8	7	5	6	1

Using rank correlation, determine which pair of judges have the nearest approach to common tastes in beauty.

Solution:

Ranks are given already.

			$R_1 - R_2$		$R_2 - R_3$		$R_1 - R_3$	
R_1	R_2	R_3	d	d^2	d	d^2	d	d^2
8	4	10	+4	16	-6	36	-2	4
1	7	3	-6	36	+4	16	-2	4
2	10	2	-8	64	+8	64	0	0
10	1	9	+9	81	-8	64	+1	1
3	2	4	+1	1	-2	4	-1	1
7	9	8	-2	4	+1	1	-1	1
5	6	7	-1	1	-1	1	-2	4
9	8	5	+1	1	+3	9	+4	16
4	5	6	-1	1	-1	1	-2	4
6	3	1	+3	9	+2	4	+5	25
			$\Sigma d=0$	$\Sigma d^2=214$	$\Sigma d=0$	$\Sigma d^2=200$	$\Sigma d=0$	$\Sigma d^2=60$

<u>Judge 1 & Judge 2</u>

$$r_s = 1 - \frac{6\Sigma d^2}{n^3 - n} = 1 - \frac{6\,(214)}{10^3 - 10} = 1 - \frac{1284}{990} = 1 - 1.29697 = \mathbf{-\,0.29697}$$

<u>Judge 2 & Judge 3</u>

$$r_s = 1 - \frac{6\Sigma d^2}{n^3 - n} = 1 - \frac{6\,(200)}{10^3 - 10} = 1 - \frac{1200}{990} = 1 - 1.21212 = \mathbf{-\,0.21212}$$

<u>Judge 1 & Judge 3</u>

$$r_s = 1 - \frac{6\Sigma d^2}{n^3 - n} = 1 - \frac{6\,(60)}{10^3 - 10} = 1 - \frac{360}{990} = 1 - 0.36364 = \mathbf{+\,0.6364}$$

As the rank correlation coefficient is positive in case of Judge 1 and Judge 3, they have the nearest approach to common tastes in beauty.

Example 13.13. *Determine the Spearman's rank correlation coefficient from the following data:*

$\Sigma d^2 = 30$ and $n = 10$.

Solution:

$$r_s = 1 - \frac{6\Sigma d^2}{n^3 - n} = 1 - \frac{6(30)}{10^3 - 10} = 1 - \frac{180}{990} = 1 - 0.18182.$$

$= \mathbf{+0.8182.}$

Merits of Rank Coefficient Correlation.

Spearman's Rank coefficient correlation is very much in use when we are studying the qualitative data that can be expressed in ranks. Following are the merits of this method:

(i) It is very simple to compute and understand.

(ii) When only ranks are available (but not the values), this is the only coefficient correlation.

(iii) Giving ranks is very simple which makes the fluctuations in the values of variables simple.

(iv) It is the only method adopted in case of all the competition, interviews or contests.

Demerits of Rank Coefficient Correlation.

In spite of the merits of rank method, the method is suffering from certain limitations as under:

(i) It is not suitably applicable to frequency distribution.

(ii) It is difficult to compute when the items increase from 20 to 30 or 50 or 60.

(iii)It lacks precision in results as compared to pearson's method since values are not at all taken into account.

Questions

1. Define rank correlation?
2. Write down Spearman's formula for rank correlation coefficient?
3. What are the uses of spearman's rank correlation coefficient?
4. What are the limits of 'r'?
5. Define positive and negative correlation.
6. Answer the following:

   (i) $n = 6$ and 'r_s' = 0.42857, find Σd^2.... ($\Sigma d^2 = 20$)

   (ii) $\Sigma d^2 = 23.50$ and 'r_s' = 0.32857, find 'n'.... ($n = 6$)

(iii) n = 10 and Σd^2 = 200, find 'r$_s$'... ('r$_s$'= -0.21)

(iv) Σd^2 = 60 and n = 10, find "r$_s$'.. ('r$_s$'= 0.636)

(v) "r$_s$' =- 0.2969 and n = 10, find Σd^2.... (Σd^2 = 214)

(vi) n = 10 and Σd^2 = 122.5, find 'r$_s$'... ('r$_s$'=0.2576)

(vii) Σd^2 = 204 and n = 15, find 'r$_s$'... ("r$_s$'=0.64)

(viii) n = 8 and Σd^2 = 4, find 'r$_s$'... ('r$_s$'=0.95)

7. In a contest, two judges ranked eight candidates in order of their performance as follows:

First Judge :	5	2	8	1	4	6	3	7
Second Judge:	4	5	7	3	2	8	1	6 (r=0.099)

8. Answer the following:

(i) If n=10 and Σd^2=280, find the r_s (r_s = -0.7)

(ii) If r_s =0.6 and n=10, find the Σd^2. (Σd^2=66)

(iii)If n=10 and Σd^2=122.5, find the r_s (r_s =-0.288)

9. Ten competitors in a beauty contest are ranked by three judges in the following order:

First Judge :	1	5	4	8	9	6	10	7	3	2
Second Judge :	4	8	7	6	5	9	10	3	2	1
Third Judge :	6	7	8	1	5	10	9	2	3	4

Use the rank correlation coefficient to discuss which pair of judges have the nearest approach to common tastes in beauty.

(1st & 2nd = +0.552, 2nd & 3rd = +0.733 and 1st & 3rd=+0.055 ∴ 2nd & 3rd Judges have the nearest approach to common tastes in beauty)

10. Eight students have obtained the following marks in Economics and Statistics. Calculate the Rank coefficient Correlation.

Economics :	50	40	60	40	30	20	40	70
Accountancy:	25	30	38	22	50	70	30	90

(rs=0)

11. The personnel department of a large company is investigating the possibility of assessing the suitability of applicants by two procedures as under:

Applicants:	A	B	C	D	E	F	G
Ranking by Interview:	4	1	7	6	2	3	5
Ranking by Written Test:	5	2	7	4	1	3	6

Calculate the rank coefficient correlation. ("r$_s$'=0.86)

12. Quotations of index number of security prices of a certain joint stock company are given below:

Preference share prices:	73.2	85.8	78.9	75.8	77.2	81.2	83.8
Debenture Prices:	97.8	99.2	98.8	98.3	98.3	96.7	97.1

Using the method of rank correlation coefficient determine the relationship between the security prices. ("r_s'=0.125)

13. Calculate the rank coefficient of correlation from the following data:

X:	80	78	75	75	68	67	60	59
Y:	12	13	14	14	14	16	15	17

(r_s=-0.929)

14. Apply rank method to find out correlation between X and Y from the following data:

X:	10	12	60	60	70
Y:	15	20	20	20	50

("r_s'=+0.8)

15. The table below shows the respective I.Q.s of 10 fathers and their eldest sons:

Father's I.Q.:	91	97	102	103	103	105	110	114	116	124
Son's I.Q.:	102	94	105	115	113	99	98	112	120	108

Calculate the rank correlation coefficient for the above statistics.

("r_s'= 0.4)

16. Two coaches are asked to rate the 11 players of a football team. X and Y are the ranks assigned by coaches I and II respectively. Find rank correlation coefficient.

Players:	A	B	C	D	E	F	G	H	I	J	K
Rank X:	1	2	3	4	5	6	7	8	9	10	11
Rank Y:	3	5	1	2	6	4	9	10	7	8	11

("r_s'=0.81)

17. Calculate Rank Correlation coefficient between the ranks given for X and Y variables:

X:	6	4	5	3	1	2
Y:	5	6	3	4	1	2

("r_s'=0.714)

14
Regression

"Regression" means returning or stepping back to the average value. With the help of values of one variable (independent) we can establish most likely values of other variable (dependent). On the basis of two available correlated variables, we can forecast the future data or events or values.

In statistics, the term **"Regression"** means simply the "Average Relationship." We can predict or estimate the values of dependent variable from the given related values of independent variable with the help of a Regression Technique. The Measure of Regression studies the nature of correlationship to estimate the most probable values. It establishes a functional relationship between the *`Independent'* and *`Dependent'* variables.

The "Regression" succeeds the "Correlation". Once the correlationship between the two variables is established, the regression analysis proceeds with the estimation of probable values. **Sir Francis Galton,** a British biometrician, introduced the concept "Regression" for the first time in 1877, while studying the correlation between the `heights' of sons and their fathers. He concluded in his studies,"Tall fathers tend to have tall sons and short fathers short sons. The average height of the sons of a group of tall fathers is less than that of the fathers, while the average height of the sons of a group of short fathers is greater than that of the fathers." It means the coming generations of tall or short parents tend to step back to `average height of population. The line showing this tendency was called by Galton a "Regression Line."

Nowadays, a modern statistician prefers to use the term **"Regression"** in the sense of **"Estimation"** which is an important statistical tool in economics and business. Estimation or prediction of economic activities is very essential in planning. Estimating the relationship among the economic variables constitutes the essence of modern business management. That is why the term **'estimating line'** is used instead of 'regression line' by the modern statisticians. Today, the term `Regression' is used in a much broader sense to imply **'functional relationships.'** It means the estimation or prediction of the unknown value of one variable from the known value of the other variable. The closer the relationship between the two variables, the greater the confidence may be placed in the estimates.

Distinction Between Correlation and Regression

The correlation and the regression analysis help us in studying the relationship between the two variables, yet they differ in their approach and objectives.

Correlation	Regression
1. It preceds regression.	1. It succeeds correlation.
2. It tests the closeness between the two variables.	2. It studies the closeness between the two variables and estimates the values.
3. It measures the degree of covariation.	3. It measures the nature of covariation.
4. It is merely a tool of ascertaining the degree of relationship.	4. It is also a tool of studying cause and effect of relationship.
5. The relationship may be purely a chance and it may not have practical relevance.	5. There is a perfect relationship and it has practical relevance.
6. There is no question of independent and dependent variables.	6. There is an identification of independent and dependent variables.
7. It is a two-way average of relationship.	7. It is a directional relationship with cause and effect.
8. It establishes just a relationship.	8. It studies the functional relationship with the two equations of lines.

Both the techniques are based on different sets of assumptions. In practice, the choice between the two techniques depends upon the purpose of investigation. The presence of correlationship does not imply causation, but the presence of causation certainly implies correlationship. The association (correlation) need not imply causation (regression) because a close association may be the result of pure chance. The causation (regression) definitely implies association (correlation), because cause and effect are based on relationship.

I. Regression Analysis

Regression Analysis refers to the methods by which estimates are made of the values of a dependent variable from the values of an independent variable. It is a technique of predicting the unknown values on the basis of the *"average relationship"*. It studies the pattern of relationship and the closeness of the relationship in 'absolute terms'. Thus it is a statistical tool to deal with the formulation of mathematical models depicting relationships between the two variables. In the words of **M.M.Blair**.

"Regression analysis is a mathematical measure of the average relationship between two or more variables in terms of the original units of data."

In regression analysis we deal with two types of variables Independent and Dependent.

(i) Independent Variable :- It is the variable whose value influences the values of other (dependent) variable. It is called "Regressor or Predictor or Explanator".

(ii) Dependent Variable :- It is the variable whose values are influenced by the values of other (independent) variable. It is called "Regressed or Predicted or Explained."

II. Two Lines of Regression

Let us confine our study to only two variables involving simple regression. Then we shall have "two regression lines",

Y on X .... and .... **X on Y**

(i) Line of regression of **"Y on X"** is the line which gives the best estimate for the value of Y for any specified value of X.

(ii) Line of regression of **"X on Y"** is the line which gives the best estimate for the value of X for any specified value of Y.

While studying these two variables, we find that they are more statistically related than mathematically. However, we can establish a mathematical relationship between the two variables and algebraic equations are obtained to represent the relative movements of both the variables. The two regression lines show the average relationship between the two variables based on the two equations known as **"Regression Equations."**

The two regression equations -- Y on X and X on Y -- give the best estimate of one variable for the known value of the other. The equations are representing the mathematical equation of the regression curve.

If the given bivariate data are plotted on a graph, the points so obtained on the scatter diagram, will more or less concentrate round a curve, called the **"curve of regression"**. When the regression curve is a straight line, it is called a **"linear regression"**. The equation of such a curve is the equation of a straight line, i.e., a first degree equation.

In case of linear regression, the values of the dependent variable increase by a constant absolute amount for a unit change in the value of the independent variable. Otherwise, there will be non-linear or curved regression. Now the linear regression equations are

(i) y on x .... $y = a + bx$

y, being dependent on x will be the Best Estimate.

(ii) x on y......... $x = a + by$

x, being dependent on y, will be the Best Estimate.

'a' and **'b'** are called constants.

It is important to note that the regression lines are drawn on least squares assumption. The principles of **"least squares"** provides a convenient device to obtain the straight line of **"Best Fit"** curve. It stipulates that the sum of the squares of the deviations of the observed values of variable from the fitted line shall be the minimum. A line fitted by the method of least squares is known as the line of best fit.

Least Squares Method: It states that the line should be drawn through the plotted points in such a way that the sum of the squares of the deviations of the actual Y (or X) values from the computed X (or Y) values is minimum or least.

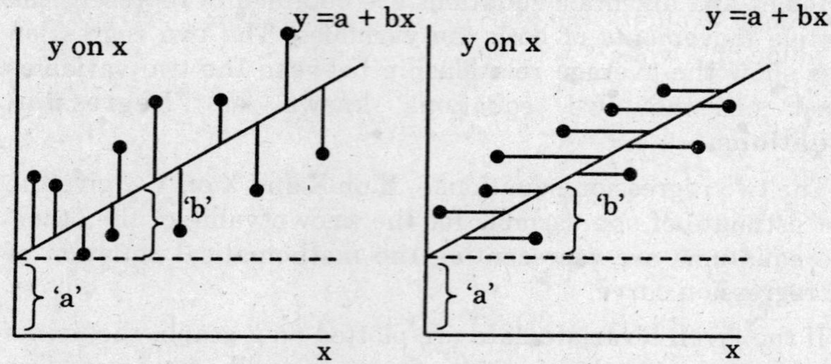

The line which fits the points in the best manner should have $\Sigma(y - y_c)^2$ be the minimum. [or $\Sigma(x - x_c)^2$ is the minimum]. It implies that the deviations above the line are equal to the deviations below the line. The best fit or the straight line goes through the mean of the data (i.e. $\bar{x}$ or $\bar{y}$).

The least squares method consists in minimising the sum of the squares of the residuals or the errors of estimates. We will have such errors for all the points on scatter diagram. For the points which lie above the line, the error would be positive and for the points which lie below the line, the error would be negative. The only thing we have to determine is the values of the constants **'a'** and **'b'**.

The algebraic sum of the deviations in the individual observations from the mean is equal to zero. it means,

$$\Sigma(x - \bar{x}) = 0 \quad \text{or} \quad \Sigma(y - \bar{y}) = 0$$

The sum of the squares of the deviations from the means is less than the sum of the squares of deviations from any other value (other than mean).

Regression Equation of Y on X :- It is the equation which gives the best estimate of Y for the known value of X. It is expressed as follows:

$$\mathbf{Y = a + bX} \quad \text{..... (Basic Equation)}$$

The constant **'a'** is the **y** intercept or catch which is the difference between the point of origin (o) and the point when the trend (straight) line and Y - axis intersect in a graph. It is the value of Y when X = 0.

The constant **'b'** indicates the slope of the trend line which signifies the change in Y for each unit of change in X. It is the amount by which the computed value of Y changes with each unit of change in X..

The numerical constants of 'a' and 'b' does not change for any given straight line in the equation. To obtain the values of **'a'** and 'b' we can use the secondary equations as under,

$$\mathbf{\Sigma y = na + b\Sigma x}$$

$$\mathbf{\Sigma xy = a\Sigma x + b\Sigma x^2} \quad \text{... (Secondary Equations)}$$

with the help of algebra and differential calculus, the above equations can be solved simultaneously to yield the values of '**a**' and '**b**'.

Regression Equation of X on Y:- It is the equation which gives the best estimate of X for the known value of Y. It is expressed as follows:

$$\mathbf{X = a + bY} \quad \text{... (Basic Equation)}$$

The constant **'a'** is the **y** intercept or catch which is the difference between the point of origin (o) and the point when the trend (straight) line and Y-axis intersect in a graph. It is the value of X when Y = 0.

The constant **'b'** indicates the slope of the trend line which signifies the change in X for each unit of change in Y. It is the amount by which the computed value of X changes with each unit of change in Y.

The numerical constants of `a' and `b' do not change for any given straight line in the equation. To obtain the values of `a' and `b', we can use the secondary equations as under,

$$\Sigma x = na + b\Sigma y$$

$$\Sigma xy = a\Sigma y + b\Sigma y^2 \text{ .... (Secondary Equations)}$$

With the help of algebra and differential calculus, the above equations can be solved simultaneously to yield the values of **'a'** and **'b'**.

Let us analyse the following variables and represent them in a graph :

x	y	x^2	xy
2	8	4	16
4	5	16	20
6	6	36	36
8	10	64	80
10	11	100	110
$\Sigma x = 30$	$\Sigma y = 40$	$\Sigma x^2 = 220$	$\Sigma xy = 262$

"Linear equation is absolutely based on the assumption that the independent values of variable changes at constant interval"

$$\Sigma y = na + b\Sigma x$$

$$\Sigma xy = a\Sigma x + b\Sigma x^2$$

$$40 = 5a + 30b \text{ ... (i) ... } \times 6$$

$$262 = 30a + 220b \text{ ..... (ii)}$$

$$\begin{aligned} 262 &= 30a + 220b \\ (-)240 &= 30a + 180b \\ 22 &= 40b \end{aligned}$$

$$b = \frac{22}{40} = \mathbf{0.55}$$

Substitute 'b' in (i)

$$40 = 5a + 30(0.55)$$

$$40 = 5a + 16.5$$

$$5a = 40 - 16.5$$

$$5a = 23.5$$

$$a = \mathbf{4.7}$$

Linear Equation y on x

$$y = a + bx$$

$$\mathbf{y = 4.7 + 0.55x}$$

Best Estimates of Y_c

$$\begin{aligned}
&\text{(i) } y_1 = 4.7 + 0.55(2) = 4.7 + 1.1 = 5.8 \\
&\text{(ii) } y_2 = 4.7 + 0.55(4) = 4.7 + 2.2 = 6.9 \\
&\text{(iii) } y_3 = 4.7 + 0.55(6) = 4.7 + 3.3 = 8.0 \\
&\text{(iv) } y_4 = 4.7 + 0.55(8) = 4.7 + 4.4 = 9.1 \\
&\text{(v) } y_5 = 4.7 + 0.55(10) = 4.7 + 5.5 = 10.2 \\
&\Sigma y_c = 40.0
\end{aligned}$$

Elimination of Trend Values

x	y	y_c	$(y - y_c)$
2	8	5.8	+2.2
4	5	6.9	-1.9
6	6	8.0	-2.0
8	10	9.1	+0.9
10	11	10.2	+0.8
$\Sigma x = 30$	$\Sigma y = 40$	$\Sigma y_c = 40.0$	$\Sigma(y - y_c) = 0$

Graphic Presentation

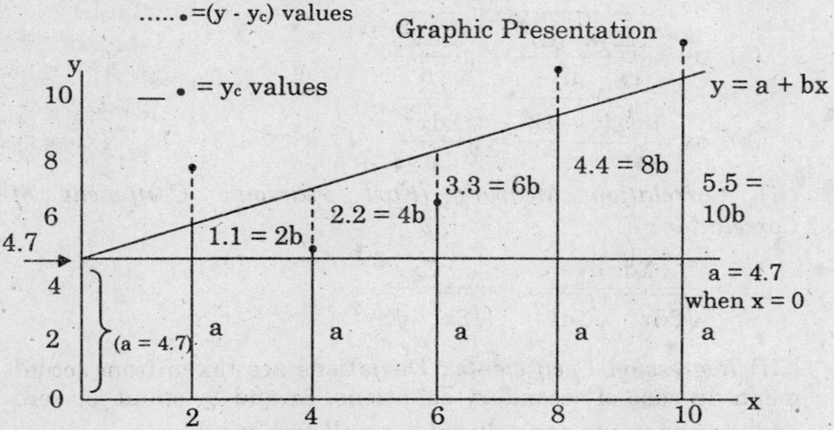

Thus, the constant 'b' is called a **"Regression Coefficient"**. It indicates the slope which signifies the slope of the line. The constant 'a' is the Y – intercept or catch. It shows the value of Y, when X = 0.

The straight line ascends from the left to the right when 'b' is positive; it descends from the left to right when 'b' is negative. Such a linear straight line is possible only when the values of independent variable increase or decrease at a constant or equal ratio. Otherwise, the distribution would be a *'Non-linear'* one. However, we can have the same process of algebraic calculations in those distributions which are non-linear. (i.e., independent values of variables change without any constant ratio). The similar procedure is also followed when we come across with the X on Y equation.

III. Relationship Between 'σ', 'b' and 'r'

There exists a close mathematical relationship among the five measures.

(i) σ_x (ii) σ_y (iii) 'r' (iv) b_{yx} (v) b_{xy}

***(i)** Standard Deviation Measures :*

Deviations are taken from actual mean

We can use x for $(x - \bar{x}) = dx$

y for $(y - \bar{y}) = dy$

$$\text{(a)} \quad \sigma y = \sqrt{\frac{\Sigma(x-\bar{x})^2}{n}} = \sqrt{\frac{\Sigma dx^2}{n}}$$

$$\text{(b)} \quad \sigma y = \sqrt{\frac{\Sigma(y-\bar{y})^2}{n}} = \sqrt{\frac{\Sigma dx^2}{n}}$$

***(ii)** Correlation Measure (Karl Pearson's Coefficient of Correlation):*

$$'r' = \frac{\Sigma dx\, dy}{\sqrt{\Sigma dx^2}\,\sqrt{\Sigma dy^2}} = \frac{\Sigma xy}{\sqrt{\Sigma x^2}\,\sqrt{\Sigma y^2}}$$

***(iii)** Regression Coefficients :* Deviations are taken from actual mean. In case of secondary equations, Σx and Σy stand for zero and the equations are reduced to small size as under,

$\Sigma y = na + b\Sigma x$	$\Sigma x = na + b\Sigma y$
$0 = na + b(0)$	$0 = na + b(0)$
$0 = na + 0$	$0 = na + 0$
$0 = 0 + 0$	$0 = 0 + 0$
The first equation disappears.	The first equation disappears.
$\Sigma xy = a\Sigma x + b\Sigma x^2$	$\Sigma xy = a\Sigma y + b\Sigma y^2$
$\Sigma xy = a(0) + b\Sigma x^2$	$\Sigma xy = a(0) + b\Sigma y^2$
$\Sigma xy = b\Sigma x^2$	$\Sigma xy = b\Sigma y^2$
$b_{yx} = \frac{\Sigma xy}{\Sigma x^2}$	$b_{xy} = \frac{\Sigma xy}{\Sigma y^2}$

In the above mathematical simplication, the constant 'a' disappears from the calculations and the basic formulas are changed to,

$$y = bx \qquad\qquad x = by$$

$$(y - \bar{y}) = b_{yx}(x - \bar{x}) \quad \text{and} \quad (x - \bar{x}) = b_{xy}(y - \bar{y})$$

$$y = (y - \bar{y}) \qquad\qquad x = (x - \bar{x})$$

(iv) Standard Deviations, Correlation and Regression Coefficients:

$$r = \frac{\Sigma xy}{\sqrt{\Sigma x^2}\,\sqrt{\Sigma y^2}}$$

$$r\frac{\sigma y}{\sigma x} = \frac{\Sigma xy}{\sqrt{\Sigma x^2}\,\sqrt{\Sigma y^2}} \times \frac{\sqrt{\dfrac{\Sigma y^2}{n^*}}}{\sqrt{\dfrac{\Sigma x^2}{n^*}}} = \frac{\Sigma xy}{\sqrt{\Sigma x^2}\,\sqrt{\Sigma y^2}} \times \frac{\sqrt{\Sigma y^2}}{\sqrt{\Sigma x^2}}$$

$$= \frac{\Sigma xy}{\sqrt{\Sigma x^2}\,\sqrt{\Sigma x^2}} = \frac{\Sigma xy}{\Sigma x^2} = byx \;\ldots\ldots \quad \therefore \quad byx = r\frac{\sigma_y}{\sigma_x}$$

$$r = \frac{\Sigma xy}{\sqrt{\Sigma x^2}\,\sqrt{\Sigma y^2}}$$

$$r\frac{\sigma x}{\sigma y} = \frac{\Sigma xy}{\sqrt{\Sigma x^2}\,\sqrt{\Sigma y^2}} \times \frac{\sqrt{\dfrac{\Sigma x^2}{n^*}}}{\sqrt{\dfrac{\Sigma y^2}{n^*}}} = \frac{\Sigma xy}{\sqrt{\Sigma x^2}\,\sqrt{\Sigma y^2}} \times \frac{\sqrt{\Sigma x^2}}{\sqrt{\Sigma y^2}}$$

$$= \frac{\Sigma xy}{\sqrt{\Sigma y^2}\,\sqrt{\Sigma y^2}} = \frac{\Sigma xy}{\Sigma y^2} = byx \;\ldots\ldots \quad \therefore \quad byx = r\frac{\sigma_x}{\sigma_y}$$

(* common 'n' goes out of the process)

Thus, we can have the revised regression equations as under:

y on x	**x on y**
$y = bx$	$x = by$
$(y - \bar{y}) = byx\,(x - \bar{x})$	$(x - \bar{x}) = bxy\,(y - \bar{y})$
$(y - \bar{y}) = r\dfrac{\sigma_y}{\sigma_x}(x - \bar{x})$	$(x - \bar{x}) = r\dfrac{\sigma_x}{\sigma_y}(y - \bar{y})$

The actual values of `x' and `y' are not considered. The deviations are taken from actual means. This process reduces the tedious job of calculations and it makes the method of obtaining regression equations more simple. The regression coefficients (b_{yx} and b_{xy}) possess some important mathematical properties as under,

$$b_{yx} = r\frac{\sigma_y}{\sigma_x} = \frac{\Sigma xy}{\Sigma x^2} \qquad b_{xy} = r\frac{\sigma_x}{\sigma_y} = \frac{\Sigma xy}{\Sigma y^2}$$

$$b_{yx} \times b_{xy} = r\frac{\sigma_y}{\sigma_x} \times r\frac{\sigma_x}{\sigma_y} = r \times r = r^2$$

$$\therefore \quad r^2 = b_{yx} \times b_{xy}$$

$$r = \sqrt{b_{yx} \times b_{xy}}$$

The values of b_{yx} and b_{xy} individually both cannot be more than **1**. If one is more than **1**, the other must be less than **1**. When we take the product of the both, and root of it the resultant will always be correlation. Both the regression coefficients will have the same algebraic signs. Either both of them would be positive or both of them would be negative. It is not possible that one has a positive sign and the other a negative sign. The reason is that the standard deviations are always positive. Only the coefficient of correlation can be either positive or negative.

Example. *$b_{yx} = 3.5$ and $b_{xy} = 0.5$*

$$r = \sqrt{3.5 \times 0.5} = \sqrt{1.75} = 1.3228$$

"The coefficients are not correct as 'r' is more than **1**."

When the Actual Means are in fraction :

Sometimes we find the means are in fractions. This makes the deviations and their squares are also in fractions. To avoid the tedious calculations, we can have the assumed means in round figures. Then, to find the regression coefficients we can use the following procedure:

$$b_{xy} = \frac{n\Sigma dxdy - (\Sigma dx)(\Sigma dy)}{n\Sigma dx^2 - (\Sigma dx)^2}$$

$$\text{and } b_{xy} = \frac{n\Sigma dxdy - (\Sigma dx)(\Sigma dy)}{n\Sigma dy^2 - (\Sigma dy)^2}$$

Let us take the following data,

x	y	(x–11) dx	(y-12) dy	dx^2	dy^2	dxdy
8	4	-3	-8	9	64	+24
9	6	-2	-6	4	36	+12
10	8	-1	-4	1	16	+4
10	12	-1	0	1	0	0
11	13	0	+1	0	1	0
13	15	+2	+3	4	9	+6
14	17	+3	+5	9	25	+15
16	28	+5	+16	25	256	+8
Σx = 9	Σy = 103	= +3 Σdx	= +7 Σdy	=53 Σdx^2	= 407 Σdy^2	=141 Σdxdy

$$\bar{x} = \frac{\Sigma x}{n} = \frac{91}{8} = \mathbf{11.375} \qquad \bar{y} = \frac{\Sigma x}{n} = \frac{103}{8} = \mathbf{12.875}$$

$$b_{yx} = \frac{n\,\Sigma dxdy - (\Sigma dx)(\Sigma dy)}{n\,\Sigma dx^2 - (\Sigma dx)^2} = \frac{8(141) - (3)(7)}{8(53) - (3)^2}$$

$$= \frac{1128 - 21}{424 - 9} = \frac{1107}{415} = \mathbf{2.66747}$$

$$b_{xy} = \frac{n\Sigma dxdy - (\Sigma dx)(\Sigma dy)}{n\Sigma dy^2 - (\Sigma dy)^2} = \frac{8(141) - (3)(7)}{8(407) - (7)^2}$$

$$= \frac{1128 - 21}{3256 - 49} = \frac{1107}{3207} = \mathbf{0.34518}$$

Now let us consider the deviations from actual means and see that how tedious the calculation would be.

(x-11.375) X	(y-12.875) Y	x^2	y^2	xy
-3.375	-8.875	11.3906	78.7656	+29.9531
-2.375	-6.875	5.6406	47.2656	+16.3281
-1.375	-4.875	1.8906	23.7656	+6.7031
-1.375	-0.875	1.8906	0.7656	+1.2031
-0.375	+0.125	0.1406	0.0156	(-0.0469)
+1.625	+2.125	2.6406	4.5156	+3.4531
+2.625	+4.125	6.8906	17.0156	+10.8281
+4.625	+15.125	21.3906	228.7656	+69.9531
$\Sigma x = 0$	$\Sigma y = 0$	51.8748	400.8748	138.3748
		$\Sigma x^2 =$	$\Sigma y^2 =$	$\Sigma xy =$

$$b_{xy} = \frac{\Sigma xy}{\Sigma x^2} = \frac{138.3748}{51.8748} = \mathbf{2.667463}$$

$$b_{yx} = \frac{\Sigma xy}{\Sigma y^2} = \frac{138.3748}{400.8748} = \mathbf{0.345182}$$

Thus, to avoid tedious the task of calculations, we should use the assumed mean (when the actual means are in fraction) and obtain the Regression Coefficients. Then we have to apply the normal procedure as under,

y on x	**x on y**
$y = bx$	$x = by$
$(y - \bar{y}) = b_{yx}(x - \bar{x})$	$(x - \bar{x}) = b_{xy}(y - \bar{y})$
$y - 12.875 = 2.6675(x - 11.375)$	$(x - 11.375) = 0.3452(y - 12.875)$
$y - 12.875 = 2.6675x - 30.3428$	$(x - 11.375) = 0.3452y - 4.4445$
$y = 2.6675x - 30.3428 + 12.875$	$x = 0.3452y - 4.4445 + 11.375$
$\mathbf{y = 2.6675x - 17.4678}$	$\mathbf{x = 0.3452y + 6.9306}$

Example 14.1. *By using the simultaneous equations method, find out the most probable value of y, when x =15*

x	:	1	2	3	4	5	
y	:	2	5	3	8	7	(BU-A83)

Solution:

X	y	x^2	xy
1	2	1	2
2	5	4	10
3	3	9	9
4	8	16	32
5	7	25	35
$\Sigma x = 15$	$\Sigma y = 25$	$\Sigma x^2 = 55$	$\Sigma xy = 88$

y on x

$y = a + bx$

To obtain 'a' and 'b' values,

$$\Sigma y = na + b\Sigma x$$

$$\Sigma xy = a\Sigma x + b\Sigma x^2$$

$$25 = 5a + 15b....(i)\times 3$$

$$88 = 15a + 55b....(ii)$$

$$88 = 15a + 55b$$

$$(-)75 = 5a + 45b$$

$$13 = 10b$$

$$b = 1.3$$

Substitute 'b' in (i)

$$25 = 5a + 15(1.3)$$

$$25 = 5a + 19.95$$

$$5a = 5.5$$

$$a = 1.1$$

$$y = a + bx$$

$$\mathbf{y = 1.1 + 1.3x}$$

If $x = 15$,

$$y = 1.1 + 1.3(15)$$

$$= 1.1 + 19.5 = 20.6$$

Other Alternative Method.

x	y	$(x-\bar{x})$ x	$(y-\bar{y})$ y	x^2	xy
1	2	- 2	- 3	4	6
2	5	- 1	0	1	0
3	3	0	- 2	0	0
4	8	+1	+ 3	1	3
5	7	+2	+ 2	4	4
$\Sigma x = 15$	$\Sigma y = 25$	$\Sigma x = 0$	$\Sigma y = 0$	$\Sigma x^2 = 10$	$\Sigma xy = 13$

$$\bar{x} = \frac{\Sigma x}{n} = \frac{15}{5} = 3 \qquad \bar{y} = \frac{\Sigma y}{n} = \frac{25}{5} = 5$$

$$b_{xy} = \frac{\Sigma xy}{\Sigma x^2}$$

y on x

$y = bx$

$(y - \bar{y}) = b_{yx}(x - \bar{x})$

$(y - 5) = \frac{13}{10}(x - 3)$

$y - 5 = 1.3x - 3.9$

$\mathbf{y = 1.3x + 1.1}$

If $x = 15$

$y = 1.3(15) + 1.1$

$= 19.5 + 1.1$

$= \mathbf{20.6}$

Example 14.2. *The following data relate to the ages of husbands and wives:*

Ages of Husbands		25	28	30	32	35	36	38	39	42	55
Wives	:	20	26	29	30	25	18	26	35	35	46

Obtain the two regression equations and determine the most likely age of husband for the age of wife 25 years. (BU-N87)

Solution:

Husbands' Ages (x)	Wives Age (y)	$(\bar{x} - x)$ x	$(y - \bar{y})$ y	x^2	y^2	xy
25	20	-11	-9	121	81	+ 99
28	26	-8	-3	64	9	+ 24
30	29	-6	0	36	0	0
32	30	-4	+1	16	1	- 4
35	25	-1	-4	1	16	+ 4
36	18	0	-11	0	121	0
38	26	+2	-3	4	9	- 6
39	35	+3	+6	9	36	+ 18
42	35	+6	+6	36	36	+ 36
55	46	+19	+17	361	289	+323
$\Sigma x = 360$	$= 290$ Σy	$\Sigma x = 0$	$\Sigma y = 0$	$= 648$ Σx^2	$= 598$ Σy^2	$= 494$ Σxy

$\bar{x} = \frac{\Sigma x}{n} = \frac{360}{10} = \mathbf{36}$

$\bar{y} = \frac{\Sigma y}{n} = \frac{290}{10} = \mathbf{29}$

y on x

$y = bx$

$(y - \bar{y}) = \frac{\Sigma xy}{\Sigma x^2}(x - \bar{x})$

$(y - 29) = \frac{494}{648}(x - 36)$

$y - 29 = 0.7624\ (x - 36)$

$y - 29 = 0.7624x - 27.4464$

$y = 0.7624x - 27.4464 + 29$

$\mathbf{y = 0.7624x + 1.5536}$

x on y

$x = by$

$(x - \bar{x}) = \frac{\Sigma xy}{\Sigma y^2}(y - \bar{y})$

$(x - 36) = \frac{494}{598}(y - 29)$

$x - 36 = 0.8261(y - 29)$

$x - 36 = 0.8261y - 23.9569$

$x = 0.8261y - 23.9569 + 36$

$\mathbf{x = 0.8261y + 12.0431}$

If a wife's age is 25,

$x = 0.8261(25) + 12.0431$

$x = 20.6525 + 12.0431$

$\mathbf{x = 32.6956}$

= 32.7years = **32** years 8 monts 12 days

Example 14.3. *From the following data:*

(a) Calculate the two regression equations.

(b) Estimate the value of x when y is 20. and

(c) Determine the value of coefficient of correlation through regression coefficients.

x :	10	12	13	17	18
y :	5	6	7	9	13

(BU-A90)

Solution:

x	y	$(x-\bar{x})$ x	$(y-\bar{y})$ y	x^2	y^2	xy
10	5	-4	-3	16	9	+12
12	6	-2	-2	4	4	+4
13	7	-1	-1	1	1	+1
17	9	+3	+1	9	1	+3
18	13	+4	+5	16	25	+20
Σx = 70	Σy = 40	Σ*x* = 0	Σ*y* = 0	= 46 Σx^2	= 40 Σy^2	= 40 Σxy

$\bar{x} = \frac{\Sigma x}{n} = \frac{70}{5} = \mathbf{14}$

$\bar{y} = \frac{\Sigma y}{n} = \frac{40}{5} = \mathbf{8}$

(a) **y on x**

$y = bx$

$(y - \bar{y}) = b_{yx}(x - \bar{x})$

$(y - \bar{y}) = \frac{\Sigma xy}{\Sigma x^2}(x - \bar{x})$

$(y - 8) = \frac{40}{46}(x - 14)$

$y - 8 = 0.8696(x - 14)$

$y - 8 = 0.8696x - 12.1739$

$\mathbf{y = 0.8696x - 4.1739}$

x on y

$x = by$

$(x - \bar{x}) = b_{xy}(y - \bar{y})$

$(x - 14) = \frac{\Sigma xy}{\Sigma y^2}(y - 8)$

$x - 14 = \frac{40}{40}(y - 8)$

$x - 14 = 1(y - 8)$

$x = y - 8 + 14$

$\mathbf{x = y + 6}$

(b) when $y = 20$,

$x = y + 6$

$x = 20 + 6$

$x = \mathbf{26}$

(c) $r = \sqrt{b_{yx} \times b_{xy}}$

$= \sqrt{0.8696 \times 1}$

$= \sqrt{0.8696} = \mathbf{+0.9325}$

Example 14.4. *From the following data:*

(a) Calculate the two regression equations.

(b) Estimate the value of x when y = 40.

(c) Determine the value of correlation coefficient through regression coefficients.

x :	20	24	26	34	36
y :	10	12	14	18	26

(BU- N95)

Solution:

x	y	$(x - \bar{x})$ x	$(y - \bar{y})$ y	x^2	y^2	xy
20	10	-8	-6	64	36	+48
24	12	-4	-4	16	16	+16
26	14	-2	-2	4	4	+4
34	18	+6	+2	36	4	+12
36	26	+8	+10	64	100	+80
140 $\Sigma x =$	$\Sigma y = 80$	$\Sigma x = 0$	$\Sigma y = 0$	184 $\Sigma x^2 =$	160 $\Sigma y^2 =$	160 $\Sigma xy =$

$\bar{x} = \frac{\Sigma x}{n} = \frac{140}{5} = \mathbf{28}$

$\bar{y} = \frac{\Sigma y}{n} = \frac{80}{5} = \mathbf{16}$

(a) **y on x**

$y = bx$

$(y - \bar{y}) = b_{yx}(x - \bar{x})$

$(y - 16) = \frac{\Sigma xy}{\Sigma x^2}(x - 28)$

$(y - 16) = \frac{160}{184}(x - 28)$

$y - 16 = 0.8696(x - 28)$

$y - 16 = 0.8696x - 24.3478$

$y = 0.8696x - 24.3478 + 16$

$y = 0.8696x - 8.3478$

x on y

$x = by$

$(x - \bar{x}) = b_{xy}(y - \bar{y})$

$(x - 28) = \frac{\Sigma xy}{\Sigma y^2}(y - 16)$

$x - 28 = \frac{160}{160}(y - 16)$

$x - 28 = 1(y - 16)$

$x - 28 = y - 16$

$\mathbf{x = y + 12}$

(b) when $y = 40$

$x = y + 12$

$x = 40 + 12$

$x = \mathbf{52}$

$r = \sqrt{b_{yx} \times b_{xy}}$

$= \sqrt{0.8696 \times 1}$

$= \sqrt{0.8696} = \mathbf{+0.9325}$

Example 14.5. *Find the Regression Equations for the following data and also predict the average value of Y when X is 9.*

X :	3	6	5	4	7	2	8	1
Y :	3	2	3	5	3	6	6	4 (BU-A96)

Solution:

x	y	$(x - \bar{x})$ x	$(y - \bar{y})$ y	x^2	y^2	xy
3	3	-1.5	-1	2.25	1	+1.5
6	2	+1.5	-2	2.25	4	-3.0
5	3	+0.5	-1	0.25	1	-0.5
4	5	-0.5	+1	0.25	1	-0.5
7	3	+2.5	-1	6.25	1	-2.5
2	6	-2.5	+2	6.25	4	-5.0
8	6	+3.5	+2	12.25	4	+7.0
1	4	-3.5	0	12.25	0	0
36 $\Sigma x =$	$\Sigma y = 32$	$\Sigma x = 0$	$\Sigma y = 0$	42.00 $\Sigma x^2 =$	16 $\Sigma y^2 =$	– 3.0 $\Sigma xy =$

$\bar{x} = \frac{\Sigma x}{n} = \frac{36}{8} = \mathbf{4.5}$

$\bar{y} = \frac{\Sigma y}{n} = \frac{32}{8} = \mathbf{4}$

y on x

$y = bx$

$(y - \bar{y}) = b_{yx}(x - \bar{x})$

$(y - 4) = \frac{\Sigma xy}{\Sigma x^2}(x - 4.5)$

$(y - 4) = \frac{-3}{42}(x - 4.5)$

$y - 4 = -0.0714(x - 4.5)$

$y - 4 = -0.0714x + 0.3214$

$\mathbf{y = -0.0714x + 4.3214}$

x on y

$x = by$

$(x - \bar{x}) = b_{xy}(y - \bar{y})$

$(x - 4.5) = \frac{\Sigma xy}{\Sigma y^2}(y - 4)$

$x - 4.5 = \frac{-3}{16}(y - 4)$

$x - 4.5 = -0.1875(y - 4)$

$x - 4.5 = y - 0.1875y + 0.75$

$\mathbf{x = -0.1875y + 5.25}$

when $x = 9$

$y = -0.0714x + 4.3214 = -0.0714(9) + 4.3214$

$= -0.6426 + 4.3214 = \mathbf{3.6788}$

Example 14.6. *Following data relate to years of service in a factory of seven persons in a specialised field and their monthly income.*

Years of Service	:	11	7	9	5	8	6	10
Income (in'00'Rs)	:	7	5	3	2	6	4	8

Find the two regression equations and also estimate the income of a person of 12 years service. (BU-N96)

Solution:

x	y	$(x - \bar{x})$ x	$(y - \bar{y})$ y	x^2	y^2	xy
11	7	+3	+2	9	4	+6
7	5	-1	0	1	0	0
9	3	+1	-2	1	4	- 2
5	2	-3	-3	9	9	+ 9
8	6	0	+1	0	1	0
6	4	-2	-1	4	1	+ 2
10	8	+2	+3	4	9	+ 6
56 $\Sigma x =$	$\Sigma y = 35$	$\Sigma x = 0$	$\Sigma y = 0$	28 $\Sigma x^2 =$	28 $\Sigma y^2 =$	21 $\Sigma xy =$

$\bar{x} = \frac{\Sigma x}{n} = \frac{56}{7} = \mathbf{8}$ $\bar{y} = \frac{\Sigma y}{n} = \frac{35}{7} = \mathbf{5}$

y on x

$y = bx$

$(y - \bar{y}) = b_{yx}(x - \bar{x})$

$(y - 5) = \dfrac{\Sigma xy}{\Sigma x^2}(x - 8)$

$(y - 5) = \dfrac{21}{28}(x - 8)$

$y - 5 = 0.75(x - 8)$

$y - 5 = 0.75x - 6$

$y = 0.75x - 6 + 5$

$\mathbf{y = 0.75x - 1}$

x on y

$x = by$

$(x - \bar{x}) = b_{xy}(y - \bar{y})$

$(x - 8) = \dfrac{\Sigma xy}{\Sigma y^2}(y - 5)$

$(x - 8) = \dfrac{21}{28}(y - 5)$

$x - 8 = 0.75(y - 5)$

$x - 8 = 0.75y - 3.75$

$x = 0.75y - 3.75 + 8$

$\mathbf{x = 0.75y + 4.25}$

If a person has completed 12 years of his service, his income would be,

$y = 0.75x - 1$

$y = 0.75(12) - 1 = 9 - 1 = 8(\text{in '00'})$

$\therefore$ Rs. **800**

Example 14.7. *Find the Regression Equations from the following and estimate the yield for 10 inches rainfall.*

Rainfall (in inches) :	1	2	3	4	5	6	7	8	9
Yield (tons) :	1	3	2	5	5	7	6	9	8 (BU-A97)

Solution:

x	y	$(x - \bar{x})$ x	$(y - 5)$ y	x^2	y^2	xy
1	1	-4	-4	16	16	+16
2	3	-3	-2	9	4	+6
3	2	-2	-3	4	9	+6
4	5	-1	0	1	0	+0
5	5	0	0	0	0	+0
6	7	+1	+2	1	4	+2
7	6	+2	+1	4	1	+2
8	9	+3	+4	9	16	+12
9	8	+4	+3	16	9	+12
45 $\Sigma x =$	$\Sigma y = 46$	$\Sigma x = 0$	$\Sigma y = 1$	60 $\Sigma x^2 =$	59 $\Sigma y^2 =$	56 $\Sigma xy =$

$\bar{x} = \dfrac{\Sigma x}{n} = \dfrac{45}{9} = 5$ $\qquad$ $\bar{y} = \dfrac{\Sigma y}{n} = \dfrac{46}{9} = \mathbf{5.1111}$

$$b_{yx} = \frac{n\Sigma dxdy - (\Sigma dx)(\Sigma dy)}{n\Sigma dx^2 - (\Sigma dx)^2} = \frac{9(56) - (0)(1)}{9(60) - (0)^2} = \frac{504}{540} = \mathbf{0.9333}$$

$$b_{xy} = \frac{n\Sigma dxdy - (\Sigma dx)(\Sigma dy)}{n\Sigma dy^2 - (\Sigma dy)^2} = \frac{9(56) - (0)(1)}{9(59) - (1)^2} = \frac{504}{531 - 1} = \frac{504}{530} = \mathbf{0.9509}$$

y on x	**x on y**
$Y = bX$	$x = by$
$(y - \bar{y}) = b_{yx}(x - \bar{x})$	$(x - \bar{x}) = b_{xy}(y - \bar{y})$
$(y - 5.1111) = 0.9333(x - 5)$	$(x - 5) = 0.9509(y - 5.1111)$
$(y - 5.1111) = 0.9333x - 4.6665$	$x - 5 = 0.9509y - 4.86$
$y = 0.9333x + 4.6665 + 5.1111$	$x = 0.9509y - 4.86 + 5$
$\mathbf{y = 0.9333x + 0.4446}$	$\mathbf{x = 0.9509y + 0.14}$

Yield for 10" Rainfall would be,

$$y = 0.9333(10) + 0.4446$$

$$y = 9.333 + 0.4446 = 9.7776 \text{ tonnes}$$

Example 14.8. *Obtain the two Regression Equations by taking deviations from actual means of x and y series.*

X :	2	4	6	8	10
Y :	5	7	9	8	11

(BU-A88)

Solution:

x	y	$(x-6)$ x	$(y-8)$ y	x^2	y^2	xy
2	5	-4	-3	16	9	12
4	7	-2	-1	4	1	2
6	9	0	+1	0	1	0
8	8	+2	0	4	0	0
10	11	+4	+3	16	9	12
$=30$ Σx	$\Sigma y = 40$	$\Sigma x = 0$	$\Sigma y = 0$	$=40$ Σx^2	$=20$ Σy^2	$=26$ Σxy

$$\bar{x} = \frac{\Sigma x}{n} = \frac{30}{5} = \mathbf{6} \qquad \bar{y} = \frac{\Sigma y}{n} = \frac{40}{5} = \mathbf{8}$$

y on x

$x = by$

$$(y - \bar{y}) = \frac{\Sigma xy}{\Sigma x^2}(x - \bar{x})$$

$$(y - 8) = \frac{26}{40}(x - 6)$$

$$(y - 8) = 0.65(x - 6)$$

$$y - 8 = 0.65x - 3.9$$

$$y = 0.65x - 3.9 + 8$$

$$\mathbf{y = 0.65x + 4.1}$$

x on y

$x = by$

$$(x - \bar{x}) = \frac{\Sigma xy}{\Sigma y^2}(y - \bar{y})$$

$$(x - 6) = \frac{26}{20}(y - 8)$$

$$(x - 6) = 1.3(y - 8)$$

$$x - 6 = 1.3y - 10.4$$

$$x = 1.3y - 10.4 + 6$$

$$\mathbf{x = 1.3y - 4.4}$$

Example 14.9. *Karl Pearson's Coefficient of Correlation between the ages of brother's and sisters in a community was found to be 0.8.*

Average of the brother's ages was 25 years and that of sister's was 22 years. Their standard deviations were 4 and 5 respectively. Find,

(a) The expected age of brother when the sister's age is 12 years and

(b) The expected age of sister when the brother's age is 33 years .

(BU-N83)

Solution:

Given		Brothers x	Sisters y
Mean age	...	25	22
Standard Deviation	...	4	5
Correlation.	...	+0.8	

y on x

$$(y - \bar{y}) = r\frac{\sigma y}{\sigma x}(x - \bar{x})$$

$$(y - 22) = 0.8\frac{5}{4}(x - 25)$$

$$y - 22 = (1)(x - 25)$$

$$y = x - 25 + 22$$

$$\mathbf{y = x - 3}$$

x on y

$$(x - \bar{x}) = r\frac{\sigma x}{\sigma y}(y - \bar{y})$$

$$(x - 25) = 0.8\frac{4}{5}(y - 22)$$

$$x - 25 = 0.64(y - 22)$$

$$x - 25 = 0.64y - 14.08$$

$$x = 0.64y - 14.08 + 25$$

$$\mathbf{x = 0.64y + 10.92}$$

when brothers age is 33,	when sisters age is 12,
$y = x - 3$	$x = 0.64(12) + 10.92$
$y = 33 - 3$	$x = 7.68 + 10.92$
$y = \mathbf{30}$ (sister's age)	$x = \mathbf{18.6}$ (Brothers age)

Example 14.10. *You are given below the information about advertising and sales of a company:*

	Advertising expenses (x) (Rs. in lakhs)	Sales (y) (Rs. in lakhs)
Mean	*10*	*90*
Variance	*9*	*144*
Correlation	*0.8*	

(a) Calculate the two regression lines.

(b) Find the likely sales when advertising expenses are Rs.15 and Rs.20.

(c) *What should be the advertising expenses when the company wants to attain a sales target of Rs.140 lakhs and Rs. 190 lakhs.* (BU-A84, N85)

Solution:

(a) Calculation of Two Regression Lines

$\sigma_x = \sqrt{\text{variance}} = \sqrt{9} = \mathbf{3}, \ \sigma_y = \sqrt{\text{variance}} = \sqrt{144} = \mathbf{12}$

y on x	**x on y**
$y = bx$	$x = by$
$(y - \bar{y}) = b_{yx}(x - \bar{x})$	$(x - \bar{x}) = b_{xy}(y - \bar{y})$
$(y - 90) = r\frac{\sigma y}{\sigma x}(x - 10)$	$(x - 10) = r\frac{\sigma x}{\sigma y}(y - 90)$
$(y - 90) = 0.8\frac{12}{3}(x - 10)$	$(x - 10) = 0.8\frac{3}{12}(y - 90)$
$y - 90 = 3.2(x - 10)$	$(x - 10) = 0.2(y - 90)$
$y - 90 = 3.2x - 32$	$x - 10 = 0.2y - 18$
$y = 3.2x - 32 + 90$	$x = 0.2y - 18 + 10$
$\mathbf{y = 3.2x + 58}$	$\mathbf{x = 0.2y - 8}$

(b) If Advertising expenses are, Rs.15 lakhs, sales would be

$y = 3.2(15) + 58 = 48 + 58$

Sales = **Rs.106 lakhs**

Rs.20 lakhs, sales would be,

$y = 3.2(20) + 58$

$y = 64 + 58$

Sales = **Rs.122 lakhs**

(c) If expected sales are, Rs.140, Advt. exp. would be

$x = 0.2(140) - 8 = 28 - 8$

Advt. exp. = **Rs.20 lakhs**

Rs.190, Advt. exp would be

$x = 0.2(190) - 8$

$x = 38 - 8$

Advt. exp. = **Rs.30 lakhs.**

Example 14.11. *From the following data find:*

(a) The most probable value of y, when x is 60 and

(b) The most probable value of x, when y is 40 and

(c) The coefficient of correlation.

$\bar{x} = 53.2,\ \bar{y} = 27.9,\ b_{yx} = -1.5$ *and* $b_{xy} = -0.2$ *(BU-A85)*

Solution:

y on x

$y = bx$

$(y - \bar{y}) = b_{yx}(x - \bar{x})$

$(y - 27.9) = -1.5(x - 53.2)$

$(y - 27.9) = -1.5x + 79.8$

$y = -1.5x + 79.8 + 27.9$

$\mathbf{y = -1.5x + 107.7}$

If x is 60,

$y = -1.5(60) + 107.7$

$= -90 + 107.7$

$= \mathbf{17.7}$

x on y

$x = by$

$(x - \bar{x}) = b_{xy}(y - \bar{y})$

$(x - 53.2) = -0.2(y - 27.9)$

$x - 53.2 = -0.2y + 5.58$

$x = -0.2y + 5.58 + 53.2$

$\mathbf{x = -0.2y + 58.78}$

If y is 40,

$x = -0.2(40) + 58.78$

$= -8 + 58.78$

$= \mathbf{50.78}$

Coefficient correlation will be,

$'r' = \sqrt{b_{yx} \times b_{xy}} = \sqrt{-1.5 \times -0.2} = \sqrt{0.3} = \mathbf{0.5477}$

Example 14.12. *(a) Given the following data, estimate*

(i) The value of y, when x = 70 and

(ii) The value of x when y = 90

(b) If two regression coefficients are 0.8 and 0.6, what would be the value of coefficient of correlation? (BU-A86)

	x	*y*
Mean	*18*	*100*
Standard Deviation	*14*	*20*
Coefficient Correlation	*+0.8*	

Solution:

(a) **y on x**

$y = bx$

$(y - \bar{y}) = r\frac{\sigma y}{\sigma x}(x - \bar{x})$

$(y - 100) = 0.8\frac{20}{14}(x - 18)$

$(y - 100) = 1.1429(x - 18)$

$y - 100 = 1.1429x - 20.57$

$y = 1.1429x - 20.57 + 100$

$\mathbf{y = 1.1429x + 79.43}$

If x is 70,

$y = 1.1429(70) + 79.43$

$y = 80 + 79.43$

$\mathbf{y = 159.43}$

x on y

$x = by$

$(x - \bar{x}) = r\frac{\sigma x}{\sigma y}(y - \bar{y})$

$(x - 18) = 0.8\frac{14}{20}(y - 100)$

$(x - 18) = 0.56(y - 100)$

$x - 18 = 0.56y - 56$

$x = 0.56y - 56 + 18$

$\mathbf{x = 0.56y - 38}$

If y is 90,

$x = 0.56(90) - 38$

$x = 50.4 - 38$

$\mathbf{x = 12.4}$

(b) Coefficient correlation would be, (If $b_{yx} = 0.8$ & $b_{xy} = 0.6$)

$r = \sqrt{b_{yx} \times b_{xy}} = \sqrt{0.8 \times 0.6} = \sqrt{0.48} = \mathbf{0.6928}$

Example 14.13. *The following data based on 450 students, are given for marks in Statistics and Economics at a certain examination:*

	Statistics	*Economics*
Mean Marks ...	*40*	*48*
Standard Deviation ...	*12*	*16*
Sum of the products of deviations of marks from their respective means	*42,075*	

(a) Give the equations to the two lines of regressions.

(b)Estimate the average marks in Economics of the candidate who obtained 50 marks in statistics. (BU-N86, N91)

Solution: x = Statistics and y = Economics

$$'r' = \frac{\Sigma dxdy}{n \times \sigma x \times \sigma y} = \frac{42{,}075}{450 \times 12 \times 16} = \frac{42{,}075}{86{,}400} = \mathbf{0.48698}$$

y on x

$$y = bx$$
$$(y - \bar{y}) = b(x - \bar{x})$$
$$(y - 48) = r\frac{\sigma y}{\sigma x}(x - 40)$$
$$(y - 48) = 0.487\frac{16}{12}(x - 40)$$
$$(y - 48) = 0.649(x - 40)$$
$$y - 48 = 0.649x - 25.97$$
$$y = 0.649x - 25.97 + 48$$
$$\mathbf{y = 0.649x + 22.03}$$

x on y

$$x = by$$
$$(x - \bar{x}) = b_{xy}(y - \bar{y})$$
$$(x - 40) = r\frac{\sigma x}{\sigma y}(y - 48)$$
$$(x - 40) = 0.487\frac{12}{16}(y - 48)$$
$$x - 40 = 0.3653(y - 48)$$
$$x - 40 = 0.3653y - 17.532$$
$$x = 0.3653y - 17.532 + 40$$
$$\mathbf{x = 0.3653y + 22.468}$$

If a student obtains 50 marks in Statistics, the average marks in Economics are.,

$$y = 0.649(50) + 22.03$$
$$y = 32.45 + 22.03 = \mathbf{54.48}$$

Example 14.14. *To study the relationship between expenditure on accommodation (x) and expenditure on food and entertainment (y), an enquiry into 50 families gave the following results:*

$$\Sigma x = 8500,\ \Sigma y = 9600,\ \sigma x = 60,\ \sigma y = 20 \text{ and } r = 0.6$$

Estimate the expenditure on food and entertainment when expenditure on accommodation is Rs.200. (BU-A89,A95)

Solution: For estimating expenditure on food and entertainment (y), we should obtain y on x equation.

y on x

$y = bx$

$(y - \bar{y}) = b_{xy}(x - \bar{x})$

$(y - 192) = r\frac{\sigma y}{\sigma x}(x - 170)$

$(y - 192) = 0.6\frac{20}{60}(x - 170)$

$(y - 192) = 0.1999(x - 170)$

$y - 192 = 0.1999x - 33.9999$

$y = 0.1999x - 33.9999 + 192$

$\mathbf{y = 0.1999x + 158}$

$\bar{x} = \frac{\Sigma x}{n} = \frac{8500}{50} = \mathbf{170}$

$\bar{y} = \frac{\Sigma y}{n} = \frac{9600}{50} = \mathbf{192}$

If Rs.200 is spent on accommodation,

$y = 0.1999(200) + 158$

$= 39.98 + 158$

= Rs.**197.98** is spent on food and entertainment.

Example 14.15. *Find the most likely production corresponding to a rain fall 40" from the following data:* (BU-N89)

		Rainfall	Production
Average	...	30"	500kg
Standard deviation	...	5"	100kg
Coefficient or Correlation	...	0.8	

Solution: Rainfall = x and Productivity y

To estimate production we require y on x.

y on x

$y = bx$

$(y - \bar{y}) = b_{yx}(x - \bar{x})$

$(y - 500) = r\frac{\sigma y}{\sigma x}(x - 30)$

$(y - 500) = 0.8\frac{100}{5}(x - 30)$

$(y - 500) = 16(x - 30)$

$y - 500 = 16x - 480$

$y = 16x - 480 + 500$

$\mathbf{y = 16x + 20}$

To estimate production when rainfall is 40",

$y = 16(40) + 20$

$= 640 + 20$

$= \mathbf{660}$ kg.

Example 14.16. *Obtain the two Regression Equations from the following:* (BU-N90)

		x – series	y – series
Mean	...	20	25
Variance	...	4	9
Coefficient of correlation	...	0.75	

Solution:

$\sigma x = \sqrt{\text{Variance}} = \sqrt{4} = \mathbf{2}$ $\sigma y = \sqrt{\text{Variance}} = \sqrt{9} = \mathbf{3}$

y on x

$y = bx$

$(y - \bar{y}) = b_{yx}(x - \bar{x})$

$(y - 25) = r\dfrac{\sigma y}{\sigma x}(x - 20)$

$(y - 25) = 0.75\dfrac{3}{2}(x - 20)$

$(y - 25) = 1.125 \times (x - 20)$

$y - 25 = 1.125x - 22.5$

$y = 1.125x - 22.5 + 25$

$\mathbf{y = 1.125x + 2.5}$

x on y

$x = by$

$(x - \bar{x}) = b_{xy}(y - \bar{y})$

$(x - 20) = r\dfrac{\sigma x}{\sigma y}(y - 25)$

$(x - 20) = 0.75\dfrac{2}{3}(y - 25)$

$(x - 20) = 0.4999(y - 25)$

$x - 20 = 0.4999y - 12.4999$

$x = 0.4999y - 12.4999 + 20$

$\mathbf{x = 0.49999y + 7.5}$

Example 14.17. *Given the following information:*

$\bar{x} = 65$, $\bar{y} = 67$, $\sigma x = 2.5$, *variance of* $y = 12.25$ *and correlation coefficient = 0.8. Obtain (i) the two regression lines, and (ii) the estimate of x when x = 70 and of y when x = 58.*

(BU – A92)

Solution: $\sigma y = \sqrt{\text{Variance}} = \sqrt{12.25} = \mathbf{3.5}$

y on x

$y = bx$

$(y - \bar{y}) = b_{yx}(x - \bar{x})$

$(y - 67) = r\dfrac{\sigma y}{\sigma x}(x - 65)$

$(y - 67) = 0.8\dfrac{3.5}{2.5}(x - 65)$

$(y - 67) = 1.12(x - 65)$

$(y - 67) = 1.12x - 72.8$

$y = 1.12x - 72.8 + 67$

$\mathbf{y = 1.12x - 5.8}$

x on y

$x = by$

$(x - \bar{x}) = b_{xy}(y - \bar{y})$

$(x - 65) = r\dfrac{\sigma x}{\sigma y}(y - 67)$

$(x - 65) = 0.8\dfrac{2.5}{3.5}(y - 67)$

$(x - 65) = 0.5714(y - 67)$

$(x - 65) = 0.5714y - 38.2857$

$x = 0.5714y - 38.2857 + 65$

$\mathbf{x = 0.5714y + 26.7143}$

(ii) Estimation of y when x = 58,

$y = 1.12(58) - 5.8$

$y = 64.96 - 5.8$

$y = \mathbf{59.16}$

Estimation of x when y = 70,

$x = 0.5714(70) + 26.7143$

$= 39.998 + 26.7143$

$= \mathbf{66.7123}$

Example 14.18. You are given the following data:

Variables		x	y
Mean	...	47	96
Variance	...	64	81
Correlation coefficient between x and y	...	0.36	

Calculate y when x is 50, and x when y is 88. (BU-N92)

Solution:

$\sigma_x = \sqrt{\text{Variance}} = \sqrt{64} = 8$ & $\sigma_y = \sqrt{\text{Variance}} = \sqrt{81} = \mathbf{9}$

y on x

$y = bx$

$(y - \bar{y}) = b_{yx}(x - \bar{x})$

$(y - 96) = r\dfrac{\sigma y}{\sigma x}(x - 47)$

$(y - 96) = 0.36\dfrac{9}{8}(x - 47)$

$(y - 96) = 0.405(x - 47)$

$(y - 96) = 0.405x - 19.035$

$y = 0.405x - 19.035 + 96$

$\mathbf{y = 0.405x + 76.965}$

Estimation of y when x = 50,

$y = 0.405(50) + 76.965$

$y = 20.25 + 76.965$

$y = \mathbf{97.215}$

x on y

$x = by$

$(x - \bar{x}) = b_{xy}(y - \bar{y})$

$(x - 47) = r\dfrac{\sigma x}{\sigma y}(y - 96)$

$(x - 47) = 0.36\dfrac{8}{9}(y - 96)$

$(x - 47) = 0.3199(y - 96)$

$(x - 47) = 0.3199y - 30.7199$

$x = 0.3199y - 30.7199 + 47$

$\mathbf{x = 0.3199y + 16.28}$

Estimation of x when y = 88,

$x = 0.3199(88) + 16.28$

$= 28.1512 + 16.28$

$= \mathbf{44.4312}$

Example 14.19. *The following results for heights and weights of 100 men were calculated:*

	Mean	*Standard Deviation*	*Coefficient of correlation*
Weights :	*150 lbs*	*20 lbs*	
Heights :	*68"*	*2.5"*	*0.6*

Find an estimate,

(i) the weight of a man whose height is 5', and

(ii) height of a man whose weight is 200 lbs. (BU-N93)

Solution: Weight = x and Height = y

y on x

$$y = bx$$
$$(y-\bar{y}) = b_{yx}(x-\bar{x})$$
$$(y-68) = r\frac{\sigma y}{\sigma x}(x-150)$$
$$(y-68) = 0.6\frac{2.5}{20}(x-150)$$
$$(y-68) = 0.075(x-150)$$
$$(y-68) = 0.075x-11.25$$
$$y = 0.75x-11.25+68$$
$$\mathbf{y = 0.75x+56.75}$$

x on y

$$x = by$$
$$(x-\bar{x}) = b_{xy}(y-\bar{y})$$
$$(x-150) = r\frac{\sigma x}{\sigma y}(y-68)$$
$$(x-150) = 0.6\frac{20}{2.5}(y-68)$$
$$(x-150) = 4.8(y-68)$$
$$(x-150) = 4.8y-326.4$$
$$x = 4.8y-326.4+150$$
$$\mathbf{x = 4.8y-176.4}$$

(i) Estimation of weight when height 5' = 60",

$$x = 4.8(60)-176.4$$
$$= 288-176.4$$
$$= 111.6"$$
$$= \mathbf{9'\text{-}3.6"}$$

(ii) Estimation of Height when x = 200 lbs,

$$y = 0.75(200)+56.75$$
$$y = 15+56.75$$
$$y = 71.75"$$
$$= \mathbf{5'\text{-}11.75"}$$

Example 14.20. *A study of wheat prices at Mysore and Bangalore yields the following data:*

	Mysore	*Bangalore*
Average Price ...	*Rs.2.463*	*Rs.2.797*
Standard Deviation ...	*Rs.0.326*	*Rs.0.207*
Correlation Coefficient ...	*0.774*	

Estimate from the above data the most likely,

(a) Price of wheat at Mysore corresponding to the price of Rs.2.354 per kg at Bangalore. and (b) Price of wheat at Bangalore corresponding to the price of Rs.3.05 per kg at Mysore. (BU-N94)

Solution:

X = Mysore Prices, and Y = Bangalore Price

y on x

$y = bx$

$(y - \bar{y}) = b_{yx}(x - \bar{x})$

$(y - 2.797) = r\frac{\sigma y}{\sigma x}(x - 2.463)$

$(y - 2.797) = 0.774\frac{0.207}{0.326}(x - 2.463)$

$(y - 2.797) = 0.4915(x - 2.463)$

$y - 2.797 = 0.4915x - 1.2105$

$y = 0.4915x - 1.2105 + 2.797$

$\mathbf{y = 0.4915x + 1.5865}$

x on y

$x = by$

$(x - \bar{x}) = b_{xy}(y - \bar{y})$

$(x - 2.463) = r\frac{\sigma x}{\sigma y}(y - 2.797)$

$(x - 2.463) = 0.774\frac{0.326}{0.207}(y - 2.797)$

$(x - 2.463) = 1.219(y - 2.797)$

$(x - 2.463) = 1.219y - 3.409$

$x = 1.219y - 3.409 + 2.463$

$\mathbf{x = 1.219y - 0.946}$

(a) Estimation of price at Mysore, when the wheat Price at Bangalore is Rs.2.354 per kg,

$x = 1.219(2.354) - 0.946$

$= 2.8695 - 0.946$

$=$ **Rs.1.9235** per kg.

(b) Estimation of price at Bangalore, when the wheat Price at Mysore is Rs.3.05 per kg,

$y = 0.4915(3.05) + 1.5865$

$y = 1.4991 + 1.5865$

$y =$ **Rs.3.0856** per kg.

Example 14.21. *Obtain the two Regression Equations from the following data, where the deviations were obtained from mean:*

$n = 20,\ \bar{x} = 4,\ \bar{y} = 2,\ \Sigma x^2 = 1680,\ \Sigma y^2 = 320,\ \Sigma xy = 480$ *(BU-N97)*

Solution:

y on x	x on y
$y = b_{yx}\,x$	$x = b_{xy}\,y$
$(y-2) = \frac{\Sigma xy}{\Sigma x^2}(x-4)$	$(x-4) = \frac{\Sigma xy}{\Sigma y^2}(y-2)$
$(y-2) = \frac{480}{1680}(x-4)$	$(x-4) = \frac{480}{320}(y-2)$
$(y-2) = 0.2857(x-4)$	$(x-4) = 1.5(y-2)$
$(y-2) = 0.2857x - 1.1429$	$(x-4) = 1.5y - 3$
$y = 0.2857x - 1.1429 + 2$	$x = 1.5y - 3 + 4$
$\mathbf{y = 0.2857x + 0.8571}$	$\mathbf{x = 1.5y + 1}$

Example 14.22. *Answer the following: If r = 0.5, $\Sigma xy = 27$, $\sigma x = 3$, $\Sigma y^2 = 36$ find the value of n and Regression Coefficients. (Deviations are taken from means).*

Solution:

$$r = \frac{\Sigma xy}{n \times \sigma x \times \sigma y}$$

$$0.5 = \frac{27}{n \times 3 \times \sqrt{\frac{36}{n}}}$$

$$n \times \sqrt{\frac{36}{n}} \times 0.5 = \frac{27}{3} = 9$$

$$n \times \sqrt{\frac{36}{n}} = \frac{9}{0.5}$$

$$n \times \sqrt{\frac{36}{n}} = 18$$

$$n^2 \times \sqrt{\frac{36}{n}} = 18^2 = 324$$

$$36n = 324$$

$$n = \frac{324}{36} = \mathbf{9}$$

$$b_{yx} = r\frac{\sigma y}{\sigma x}$$

$$= 0.5\frac{2}{3} = \mathbf{0.3333}$$

$$b_{xy} = r\frac{\sigma x}{\sigma y}$$

$$= 0.5\frac{3}{2} = \mathbf{0.75}$$

Confirmation of computation

$$r = \sqrt{b_{yx} \times b_{xy}}$$

$$= \sqrt{0.3333 \times 0.75}$$

$$= \sqrt{0.249975} = 0.4999$$

$$= \mathbf{0.5}$$

No. of observations = **9**

$$\sigma y = \sqrt{\frac{36}{9}} = \sqrt{4} = \mathbf{2}$$

Example 14.23. Find the Regression Equation y on x from the following information: $\Sigma x = 130$, $\Sigma y = 220$, $\Sigma \mathbf{x}^2 = 2288$, $\Sigma \mathbf{xy} = 3459$ and n = 10. (x and y denote variables but not derivations).

Solution :

y on x

$$\Sigma y = na + b\Sigma x$$

$$\Sigma xy = a\Sigma x + b\Sigma x^2$$

$$220 = 10a + 130b \quad (i) \times 13$$

$$3459 = 130a + 2288b$$

$$3459 = 130a + 2288\ b$$

$$(-)\ 2860 = 130a\ 1690\ b$$

$$599 = 598\ b$$

$$b = \mathbf{1.00167}$$

Substitute the value of 'b' in (i) Eq.

$$220 = 10a + 130(1.00167)$$

$$220 = 10a + 130.2174$$

$$10a = 130.2174 - 220$$

$$10a = -89.7826$$

$$a = \mathbf{8.978}$$

$$y = a + bx$$

$$\mathbf{y = 8.978 + 1.0017x}$$

Example 14.24. A survey was conducted to study the relationship between expenditure on accommodation (x) and expenditure on food and entertainment (y) and the following results were obtained :

		Mean	Standard Deviation
Expenditure on Accommodation	Rs.	... 173	63.15
Expenditure on Food and Entertatinment	Rs.	... 47.8	22.98
Coefficient of Corroleation ...		+0.5	

Write down the regression equation and estimate the expenditure on food and entertainment, if the expenditure on accommodation is Rs.200. (BU-A98)

Solution : For estimating the expenditure on food and entertainment we require y on x equation.

y on x

$y = bx$

$(y - \bar{y}) = b_{xy}(x - \bar{x})$

$(y - 47.8) = 0.57\dfrac{22.98}{47.8}(x - 173)$

$(y - 47.8) = 0.2074(x - 173)$

$(y - 47.8) = 0.2074x - 35.8837$

$y = 0.2074x - 35.8837 + 47.8$

$\mathbf{y = 0.2074x + 11.9163}$

Estimation of Y when x is 200

$y = 0.2074x + 11.9163$

$= 0.2074(200) + 11.9163$

$= 41.48 \ 11.9163$

$= 53.3963$

∴ The expenditure on Food & Entertainment is extimated to be **Rs.53.40 ps**

Questions

1. Define the term "Regression". (BU-A84,A85,N85)
2. State any two merits of the method of the least square. (BU-A84)
3. "Y=a+bx" where it is used? (BU-A86,A89)
4. What do you mean by "Regression Coefficients? (BU-N87,A94)
5. What are the "Regression Lines"? (BU-A90)
6. A computer obtained the Regression Coefficients, $b_{yx} = 3.5$ and $b_{xy} = 0.5$ comment on the values. (BU-N90)
7. Calculate two regression coefficients when, $r = 0.8$, $\sigma x = 5$ and $\sigma y = 7$. (BU-N91)
   (Ans : $b_{yx} = 1.12$ and $b_{xy} = 0.5714$)
8. Calculate two regression coefficients when $r = 0.99$, $\sigma x = 10$ and $\sigma y = 12$. (Ans : $b_{xy} = 1.88$ & $b_{xy} = 0.825$) (BU-A94)
9. What is the utility of Regression? (BU-A95,N97)
10. Calculate the two regression equations from the following marks of Statistics (x) and Mathematics (y) :

Marks in Statistics (x) :	40	38	35	42	30
Marks in Mathematics :	30	35	40	36	29

11. You are given below the information:

	x	y
Mean ...	20	120
S.D ...	5	25
Correlation Coefficient	0.8	

(i) Calculate the two Regression equations.

(ii) Find y when x is 25, and x when y is 150.

(y = 4x + 40, x = 0.16y + 16.8, y = 140 & x = 40.8)

12. If $\overline{x} = 35$, $\overline{y} = 50$, $\sigma x = 5$, $\sigma y = 8$ and r = 0.8 find the y on x equation and estimate y if x =40 (Ans : y = 1.28x + 5.2 & y = 56.4)

13. From the data given below find the number of items:

$r = 0.5$, $\Sigma xy = 120$, $\sigma y = 8$ $\Sigma x^2 = 90$ where deviations are taken from means. (N = 10)

14. With the help of the following data, find out 'r' and σy :

$b_{yx} = 0.85$, $b_{xy} = 0.89$ and $\sigma x = 3$ (Ans : σx = 3.07 & r = 0.869)

15. From the following information obtain the regression equation for estimating the value of sales for the advertising expenses of Rs.100 lakhs, and value of advertising expenses for the sales Rs.150 crores.

		Advertising Expenses (in lakhs) (x)	Sales Rs. (in crores) y
Mean	...	120	115
σ	...	15	10
Correlation coefficient	...	0.75	

(y = 0.5 x + 55, x = 1.125 y – 9.375, sales Rs.105 crores and Advertising Expenses Rs.159.375 lakhs).

16. Find the two regression equations, regression coefficients and coefficient of correlation from the following figures:

$\Sigma x = 120$, $\Sigma y = 432$, $\Sigma xy = 4992$, $\Sigma x^2 = 1392$, $\Sigma y^2 = 18{,}252$ and $n = 12$. [Ans : y = 3.5x +1, x = 0.2489 + 1.04]

17. You are given the following observations of x and y. Find the y on x equation.

x	:	2	4	6	8
y	:	10	20	25	30

(y = 3.25 x + 5)

18. From the following information find the two regression equations:

		x	y
Arithmetic Mean	...	36	85
Standard Deviation	...	11	8
Coefficient of correlation	...	+0.66	

Estimate the value of x when y = 75.

(y = 0.48x + 67.72, x = 0.908y – 41.318, x_{15} = 26.92)

19. Calculate the regression coefficients for the following data.

x :	8	6	4	7	5
y :	9	8	5	6	2

(b_{yx} = 1.2 and b_{xy} = 0.4)

20. Find out the two Regression Equations.

x :	6	2	10	4	8
y :	9	11	5	8	7

(y = 11.9 – 0.65x and x = 16.4 – 1.3y)

21. Given the following data, find the Regression Equations:

	x	y
Mean ...	40	50
Standard Deviation	10	16
'r'	= +0.5	

(y = 0.8x + 18 and x = 0.32y + 14)

23. From the data given below, find the Regression Equations:

x :	1	5	3	2	1	1	7	3
y :	6	1	0	0	1	2	1	5

(i) Estimate y, when x = 10

(ii) Estimate x, when y = 13 and

(iii) Obtain Karl Pearson's Coefficient Correlation.

[Ans : -0.304x + 2.874, y = -0.13, x = 0.278y + 3.431, x = 2.62 and r = 0.29]

24. Calculate the two regression equations from the data given below:

Price (Rs) :	10	12	13	12	16	15
Demand (units) :	40	38	43	45	37	43

(y = -0.25x + 44.25 and x = -0.12y + 17.92)

25. Correlation Coefficient between the x and y variables is 0.60 σx = 1.50 σy = 2.00 $\overline{x}$ = 10 and $\overline{y}$ = 20 find the two regression equations.

(x = 0.45y +1 & y = 0.8x + 12)

26. Answer the following:

(a) If two regression coefficients are 1.1 and 0.5, what would be the value of 'r'?

(b) If two regression coefficients are 1.2 and 0.8, find the coefficients of correlation.

(c) Given $b_{yx} = -0.47$ and $b_{xy} = -1.01$ find the value of 'r'

(d) With $b_{xy} = 0.5$, $r = 0.8$ and variance of y = 16 find the σx.

(a = 0.7416, b = 0.9798, c = 0.6889 and d = 2.5)

26. Given the following data of heights (x) and weights (y) of 1000 students find the Regression Equations :

$$\bar{x} = 68,\ \bar{y} = 150,\ \sigma x = 2.5,\ \sigma y = 20 \text{ and } r = 0.60$$

$$(y = 4.8x - 176.4 \ \&\ x = 0.75y + 56.75)$$

27. Find the two regression equations from the following data :

$$\Sigma x = 23,\ \Sigma y = 16,\ \Sigma x^2 = 99,\ \Sigma y^2 = 68,\ \Sigma xy = 36 \text{ and } n = 8$$

$$(y - 0.3042x + 2.8745 \text{ and } x = -0.2778y + 3.431)$$

28. Find the two regression equations from the following data :

$$n = 20,\ \Sigma x = 80,\ \Sigma y = 40,\ \Sigma x^2 = 1680,\ \Sigma y^2 = 320 \text{ and } \Sigma xy = 48$$

$$(y = 0.2353x + 1.0588 \text{ and } x = 1.333y + 1.3334)$$

15
Time Series

A **'Time Series'** is a series of numerical data, which have been recorded at different intervals of time. It is a record of changes in variables over a period of time. In this series, the observations are arranged in a chronological order. Statistical techniques analyse the time series and isolate the factors that determine the forms of series. A variable which depends upon time factor will give rise to a time series.

I. Significance of Time Series

A study of time series throws light on the future economic behaviour of a certain variable. Forecasting with reasonable accuracy of the future economic conditions is an indespensable need for all successful planning. The analysis of time series helps to study the factors or forces that influence the changes in economic activities and predict the future variations in them with certain limitations.

The analysis of time series reflects the dynamic pace of movements of a phenomenon over a period of time. It has an important and significant place in business and economics. It is also helpful to sociologists, biologists, doctors and workers. It determines the pattern of data collected over a period of time, helps in understanding the past behaviour of data and guides in predicting the future behaviour of the same. It is also of much importance in evaluating the current performance of the data and in comparing the actual performance with the predicted performance.

II. Components of Time Series

The changes or variations in the values of any phenomenon over a period of time are due to a number of forces or factors or components and their cumulative effects. The forces or factors, due to which the values of phenomenon over a period of time change, are called the **"Components of Time Series."**

If the values of the phenomenon are plotted on a graph and the plotted points fall more or less in the pattern around a straight line, it is called a **"Linear Trend"**. If the values of the phenomenon do not fall in the pattern of a straight line, it is called a **"Non-linear"** or **"Curvilinear Trend"**. In a linear trend, the values increase or decrease by a constant absolute amount. In a non-linear trend, the values have no particular trend in their changes.

Thus the values of phenomenon or variable change due to the interaction of a number of forces or components or factors which are complex and dynamic in nature. The components of time series are classified as under:

Components of Time Series

Long-term	Medium–term	Short term	Residual
SECULAR	CYCLICAL	SEASONAL	RANDOM

(i) Secular Fluctuations : The values of variables tend to increase or decrease (not both) over a period of 6 to 7 years. Though there are upward and downward changes in the trend, we find in general, only one trend over a period of time i.e. either an upward trend or a downward trend or sometimes constant trend. The fluctuations indicate a simple or secular trend, which depicts the smooth regular and slow movement in the changes in one direction.

The term **'long term'** is a relative term, which cannot be defined precisely. It is interpreted with reference to the nature of data and changes in the technology, institutions and culture. There will be an overall general tendency in the phenomenon. It is all due to the tastes, habits and customs of the people. It may also be due to new techniques, new products and new substitutes that the changes take place. Steady growth in the population, gradual decline in the death rate and slow increase in the demand for electronic goods are the examples involving secular forces or components. Secular trend or change is the basic tendency of time series with which a statistician is more concerned.

(ii) Cyclical Fluctuations: The values of variables change in a rhythmic pattern over a period of time from 2 to 6 years extending even upto 8 years. There are oscillatory movements in the economic activities, which are complex, less regular and less uniform. They are the outcome of the business cycles-- **Boom** period (prosperity), **Recession** (Downward movement), **Depression** (Reaching a rock bottom) and **Recovery** (picking up again), and again Boom period. These phases of trade cycle follow each other in a cyclic order. They generally relate to the economic activities. The fluctuations are not necessarily regular, uniform or even. They may or may not follow a similar pattern.

In practice, for the purpose of effective economic offsetting action, anticipation of cyclical fluctuations is very essential. There are waves like movements in economic activities.

(iii) Seasonal Fluctuations: The values of variables change in a regular, periodic and rhythmic order according to season covering a period of time not exceeding 12 months. Every year the fluctuations are noticed regularly influencing the economic activities. Most of the time series are influenced by the seasonal forces. They can be predicted accurately.

The seasonal factors or forces may be 'natural components' -- whether condition, climatic changes, rainfalls and sunlight, or man made coventions -- habits, customs, fashions, marriages, traditions and festivals. All these components occur at regular intervals during the year. A study of seasonal fluctuations is of utmost importance to the business men in framing the policies.

(iv) Random Fluctuations: The values of variables change suddenly or unexpectedly. The influencing factors are unforeseen and unpredictable. They are generally mixed up with the seasonal and cyclical fluctuations. They are irregular, erratic and accidental; they do not have repetitive tendency. They do not show any definite pattern or period. They are caused by non-recurring factors like strike, lock-outs, floods, famines, wars, earthquakes, epidemics, revolutions and storms.

Normally the random components play their role for a few days or months but their effects are so intense that they may give rise to new cyclical movements which are abnormal in nature. It is very difficult to study them exclusively and isolate them.

III. Analysis of Time Series

The various factors which influence the time series are identified or determined. In order to study any one of the factors, it is desirable to isolate it from all other factors. If we are studying the long term fluctuations, we should remove the short term fluctuations from the field of study. If we are interested in short-term oscillations only, we should eliminate random fluctuations from the study. So by isolating the factors, we can analyse the time series. We are more concerned with the effects rather than the causes.

The analysis of time series involves the study of past behaviour of data, the prediction of the future data and the comparison of the actual performance with the predicted performance. It aims at separating the components from each other in the study which is known as 'isolating the factors or forces'. Thus the study of time series is very often highly complicated and remains the preserve of the experts.

IV. Computation of Trend Values

The collected data is vast and complex. It is the composition of several forces, which may be pulling together the trend in different directions. The problem is solved by statisticians by decomposing the time series to understand the historical past and to give insight in to the future. There are four methods commonly used in measuring the trend values,

(A) Graphic (Freehand Curve Fitting) Method.

(B) Method of Semi-Average.

(C) Method of Moving Averages and

(D) Least - squares Method.

(A) Freehand Curve Method: A trend is determined by just inspecting the plotted points on a graph sheet. Observe the up and down movements of the points. Smooth out the irregularities by drawing a freehand curve or line through the scatter points. The curve so drawn would give a general notion of the direction of the change. Such a freehand smoothed curve eliminates the short-time swings and shows the long period general tendency of the changes in the data.

Drawing a smooth freehand curve requires a personal skill and judgement. The drawn curve should pass through the plotted points in such a manner that the variations in one direction are approximately equal to the variations in other direction. Different persons, however, draw different curves at different directions, with different slopes and in different styles. This may lead to different conclusions. To overcome these limitations, we can use the semi-average method of measuring the trend.

(B) Semi-Average Method : Under this method there are three procedures to be followed according to the data available and growth rate.

(a) Simple semi-Average method: Divide the series into two equal halves. If the items are odd in number, the middle item is left out and kept isolated. If the items are even, we will have two equal parts with no middle item. For example.

Years	x		Year	
1992	20	Part I	1992	Part I
1993	18		1993	
1994	22	→ Left out	1994	
				→ No. Middle Item
1995	25		1995	
1996	28	Part II	1996	Part II
			1997	

The total of the values in each part is divided by the total number of the items of that part. This gives us the mean value for each part. Each average is then centred in the period of time from which we have to plot the two points on the graph i.e. "Two Average Values are plotted". Then both these two points are joined by a straight line which gives the simple semi-average trend.

Example 15.1. *Using the method of simple semi-average determine the trend of the following data:*

Year	:	*1990*	*1991*	*1992*	*1993*	*1994*	*1995*	*1996*	*1997*
Sugar Production (in '000' tonnes)	:	*16*	*14*	*20*	*18*	*12*	*23*	*28*	*28*

Solution: The number of observations are even i.e. 8. The two middle parts will be 1989 to 1993 and 1994 to 1998.

Year	Actual values	4 yearly total and average	Semi-average
1990	16		
1991	14	$\frac{16+14+20+18}{4}$	$\frac{68}{4} = 17....\bar{x}_1$
1992	20		
1993	18		
1994	12	$\frac{12+23+28+25}{4}$	$\frac{88}{4} = 22......\bar{x}_2$
1995	23		
1996	28		
1997	25		

The value 17 is plotted against the middle of the first four years i.e. 1990-1993. The value 22 is plotted against the middle of the last four years i.e. 1994-1997. Then both the points are joined by a straight line as under,

Graph Showing Sugar Production (in '000' tonnes) With Trend Line

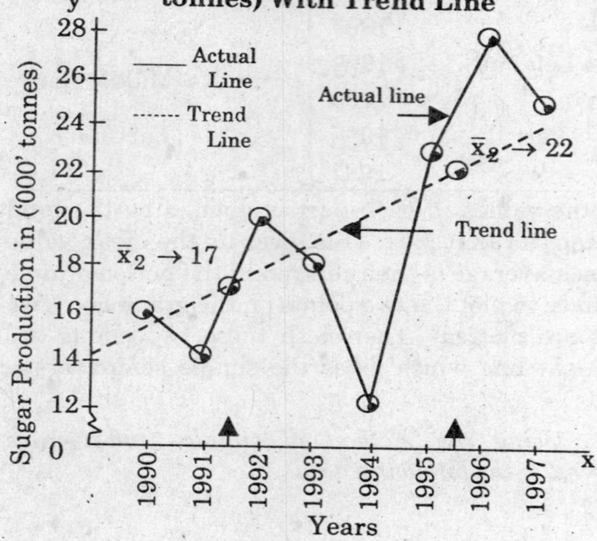

(b) Annual Increment Semi-Average Method: Under this method, the data are divided into the two equal haves. For each half, a simple arithmetic mean is obtained i.e. $\overline{x}_1$ and $\overline{x}_2$.

The difference between the two means is divided by the number of items in each part (i.e. items in one section). This gives us the `Annual Increment'.

$$\text{Annual Increment} = \frac{\overline{x}_2 - \overline{x}_1}{n}$$

The means will be placed against, the respective years with the adjustment by the `Annual increment'. Let us consider the Example 15.1 figures for finding the trend values as under,

Year	Actual valus		(Adjustment to Averages)	Trend Values	
1990	16		16.375 – 1.250	15.125	
1991	14	$\overline{x}_1$ → 17	17.000 – 0.625	16.375	→ 17
1992	20		17.000 + 0.625	17.625	
1993	18		17.625 + 1.250	18.875	
1994	12		21.375 – 1.250	20.125	
1995	23	$\overline{x}_2$ → 22	22.000 – 0.625	21.375	→ 22
1996	28		22.000 + 0.625	22.625	
1997	25		22.625 + 1.250	23.875	
	156		156.000	156.000	

$$\text{Annual Increment} = \frac{22-17}{4} = \frac{5}{4} = \mathbf{1.25}$$

$$\text{Half yearly Increment} = \frac{1}{2} \times \text{A.I} = \mathbf{0.625}$$

Annual increment = 1.25 and half yearly increment = 0.625

Graph Showing Sugar Production (in '000' tonnes)

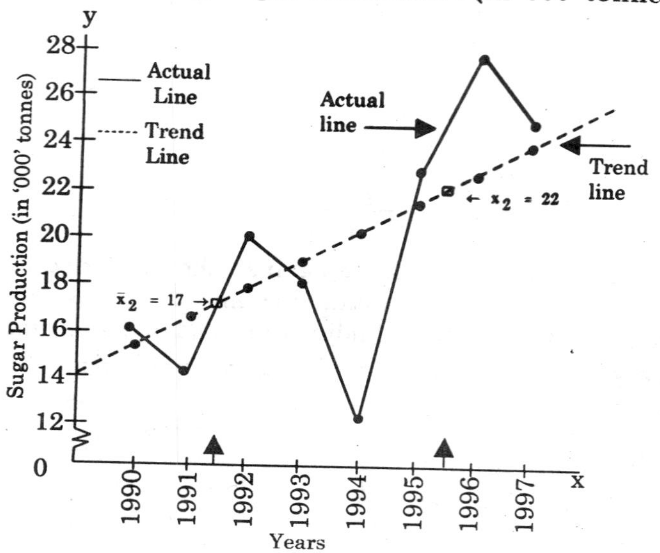

(c) Annual Growth Rate Semi-Average Method : Under this method, the data are divided into the two equal halves. For each half, a simple arithmetic mean is obtained, i.e. $\bar{x}_1$ and $\bar{x}_2$.

The average of the whole series is centred and annual growth rate is calculated with the help of the following formula:

$$\bar{y} = \frac{\Sigma y}{n} \text{ and Annual growth rate } = \frac{\Sigma y_2 - \Sigma y_1}{n'(n - n')}$$

n' = number of items for computing semi – average

n = number of items in the series as a whole

The $\bar{y}$ will be centred and below it the negative signs and above it the positive signs for `x' are considered for deviations of serial number of years. Then the product of the deviation dx and annual growth are adjusted to the $\bar{y}$. *Let us consider the Example 15.1 figures for finding the trend values as under:*

Years (x)	Actual Value (y)	x		'a'	xa	$\bar{y} = xa$ y_c
1990	16	-3.5	Σy_1	1.25	-4.375	15.125
1991	14	-2.5	= 68	1.25	-3.125	16.375
1992	20	-1.5		1.25	-1.875	17.625
1993	18	-0.5		1.25	-0.625	18.875
		0		(Centrend19.5)		
1994	12	+0.5	Σy_2	1.25	+0.625	20.125
1995	23	+1.5	= 88	1.25	+1.875	21.375
1996	28	+2.5		1.25	+3.125	22.625
1997	25	+3.5		1.25	+4.375	23.875
	156 $\Sigma y =$					156.000 $\Sigma y_c =$

$$\bar{y} = \frac{\Sigma y}{n} = \frac{156}{8} = 19.5$$

$$\text{Annual Growth Rate} = \frac{\Sigma y_2 - \Sigma y_1}{n(n - n')} = \frac{88 - 68}{4(8-4)} = \frac{20}{16} = 1.25$$

(Note : The same values are shown on a graph sheet already.)

Thus, the trend values are computed and presented in the graph by three ways - Simple, Annual Increment and Annual Growth Methods - by semi-average method. All the ways are giving the same results.

Example 15.2. *Using the method of simple semi-average determine the trend of the following data:*

Year :	*1990*	*1991*	*1992*	*1993*	*1994*	*1995*	*1996*	*1997*	*1998*
Population : (in crores)	*16*	*14*	*20*	*18*	*19.5*	*12*	*23*	*28*	*25*

Solution: The number of observations are odd i.e. 9. The two middle parts will be 1990-1993 and 1995-1998.

The value 17 will be plotted in the middle of the two years i.e. 1991 and 1992(against the first four years). The value 22 will be plotted in the middle of the two years i.e. 1996 and 1997 (against the last four years). The year 1994 and the item 19.5 are left out.

Year	Population in Crores	4 yearly total and average	Semi-average
1990	16		
1991	14	$\frac{16+14+20+18}{4}$	$\frac{68}{4}$ 17....$\bar{x}_1$
1992	20		
1993	18		
1994	19.5 (left out)		$\frac{88}{4} = 22......\bar{x}_2$
1995	12	$\frac{12+23+28+25}{4}$	
1996	23		
1997	28		
1998	25		
	=175.5		

Graph Showing Population Growth and Trend Line

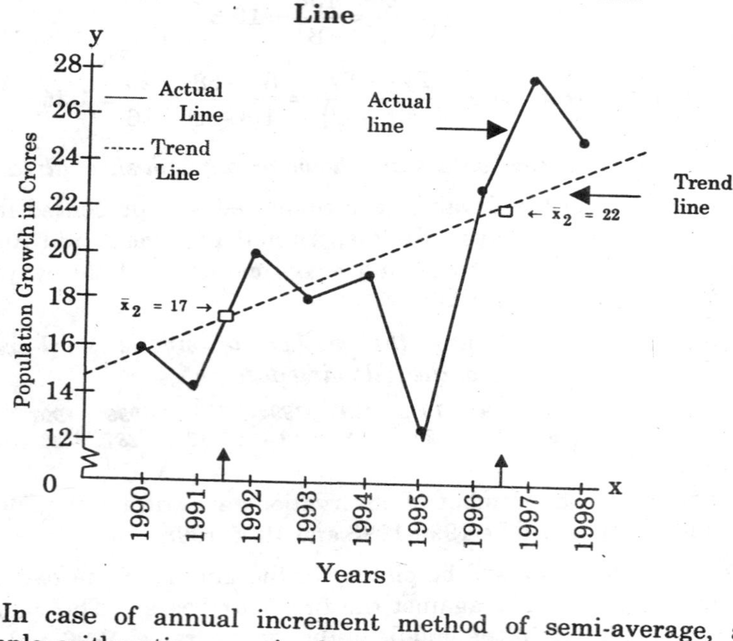

In case of annual increment method of semi-average, a simple arithmetic mean is obtained for each section as usual. The difference between the two means is divided by the number of items in each part (i.e. items of one section). This gives us the 'Annual Increment'.

$$\text{Annual Increment} = \frac{\bar{x}_2 - \bar{x}_1}{n}$$

The means will be placed against the respective years with the adjustment by the 'Annual Increment'. Let us consider the Example 15.2 figures for finding the trend values as under,

Year	Actual Values		Adjustment to Averages	
1990	16	$\bar{x}_1$ → 17	16.50 – 1.0 = 15.5	→17
1991	14		17.00 – 0.5 = 16.5	
1992	20		17.00 + 0.5 = 17.5	
1993	18		17.50 + 1.0 = 18.5	
1994	19.5		Centred = 19.5	
1995	12	$\bar{x}_1$ → 22	21.50 – 1.0 = 20.5	→ 22
1996	23		22.00 – 0.5 = 21.5	
1997	28		22.00 + 0.5 = 22.5	
1998	25		22.50 + 1.0 = 23.5	
	175.5 Σy		Σy = 175.5	

Annual Increment $= \frac{22-17}{5} = \frac{5}{5} =$

Half yearly A.I $= \frac{1}{2} = \mathbf{0.5}$

Graph Showing Population Growth and Trend Line

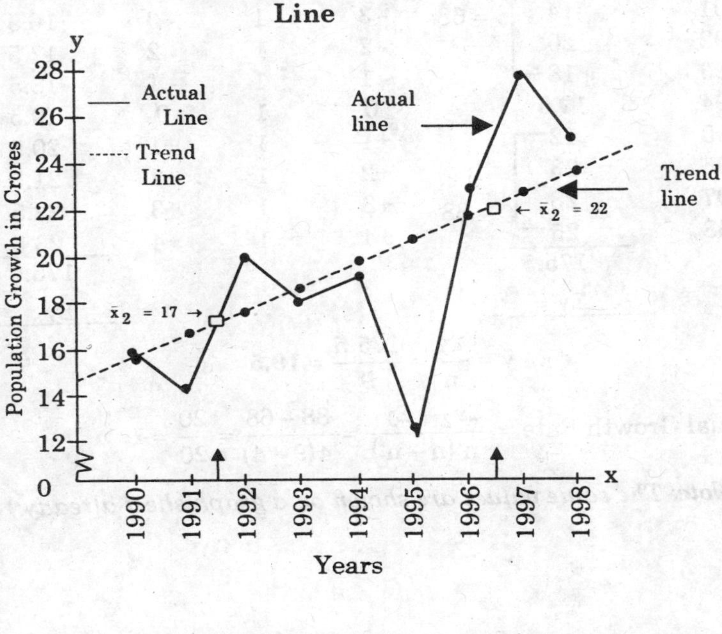

[Note: Annual Increment is arrived at by dividing the difference between the two semi-averages by 5 (not by 4), because the averages cover the period from 1991-1992 to 1996-1997. It is so because we have ignored the year 1994.]

In case of annual growth semi-average method, the data are divided into the two equal halves. For each half; a simple arithmetic mean is obtained i.e. $\bar{x}_1$ and $\bar{x}_2$. The average of the whole series is centered and annual growth rate is calculated with the help of the following formula.

$$\bar{y} = \frac{\Sigma y}{n} \text{ and Annual growth rate} = \frac{\Sigma y_2 - \Sigma y_1}{n'(n - n')}$$

n' = No. of items for computing semi average.

n = No. of items in the entire series.

The $\bar{y}$ will be centered and below it the negative signs and above it the positive signs for `x' are considered for deviations of serial number of years. Then the product of the deviation of x and annual growth are adjusted to the $\bar{y}$. *Let us consider the Example 15.2 figures for finding the trend values as under;*

Years (x)	Actual value (y)		*x*	'a'	*xa*	$\bar{y}$ = *xa* y_c
1990	16	Σy_1	- 4	1	- 4	15.5
1991	14	= 68	- 3	1	- 3	16.5
1992	20		- 2	1	- 2	17.5
1993	18		- 1	1	- 1	18.5
1994	19.5		0	1	0	19.5
1995	12		+1	1	+1	20.5
1996	23	Σy_2	+2	1	+2	21.5
1997	28	= 88	+3	1	+3	22.5
1998	25		+4	1	+4	23.5
	175.5 Σy =					175.5 Σy_c =

$$\bar{y} = \frac{\Sigma y}{n} = \frac{175.5}{9} = \mathbf{19.5}$$

$$\text{Annual Growth Rate} = \frac{\Sigma y_2 - \Sigma y_1}{n'(n - n')} = \frac{88 - 68}{4(9 - 4)} = \frac{20}{20} = \mathbf{1}$$

***(Note:** The same values are shown on a graph sheet already.)*

xample 15.3. *Draw a trend by the method of semi-average om the following data :*

Year	*1977*	*1978*	*1979*	*1980*	*1981*	*1982*	*1983*	*1984*
Sales ('000' units)	*200*	*105*	*109*	*96*	*102*	*108*	*112*	*114*

(BU – N84)

Also predict the sales for the year 1981 from the graph.

olution :

Year	Y	Semi-Average
1977	200	
1978	105	
1979	109	$\frac{510}{4} = \mathbf{127.5}\ \bar{x}_1$
1980	96	
1981	102	
1982	108	
1983	112	$\frac{436}{4} = \mathbf{109}\ \bar{x}_2$
1984	114	

Graph showing sales ('000' units)

ales : 2 cm. = 1 year
1 cm. = 1,00,000 units

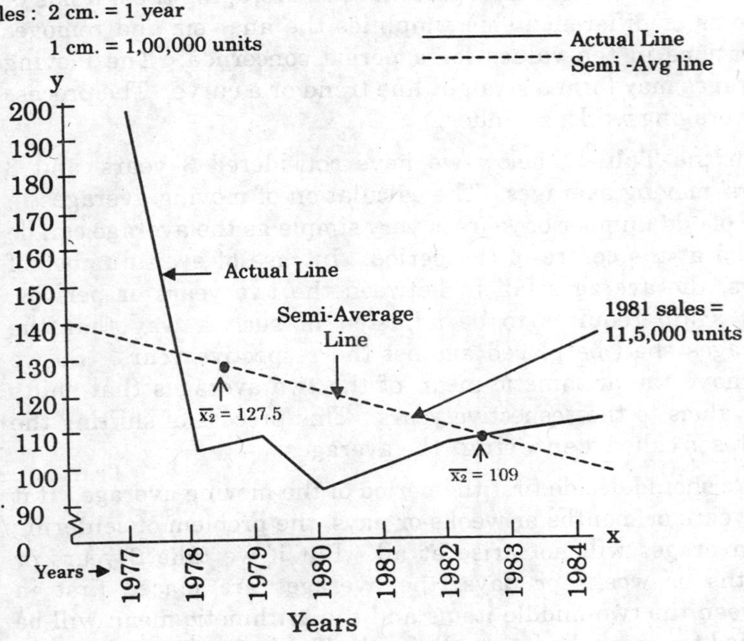

Merits of Semi-Average Method:

(i) The method is simple to follow and compute.

(ii) The method is an objective one; there will not be variations in the answers, if trend values are calculated by two or more persons. It is not depending upon the personal judgement like freehand smoothed curve drawing.

Limitations of Semi-Average Method:

(i) The method is based on the assumption that there is a linear trend which may not be true in all the cases.

(ii) Under this method, the trend is greatly affected by the extreme values as it is based on the arithmetic mean.

(iii) This method is not suitable when time period represented by average is small.

(C) Method of Moving Averages: Under this method, the trend values can be obtained by employing arithmetic means of the series except at the two ends of the series. We can have the moving averages for 3, 4, 5, 6, 7, 8 or 9 years depending upon the size of the items. The procedure of averaging the 3 items or 4 items or different items simplifies the analysis and removes variations in the values for a period concerned. The moving averages may form a straight line trend or a curve. The process of averaging works as under,

In the **Table.1** below we have considered 3 years' and 8 years' moving averages. The calculation of moving averages in case of odd number of years is very simple as the average can be placed at the centre of the period. In case of even number of years, the averages fall in between the two years or periods. This again requires to be adjusted in such a way that the averages shall be placed against the respective years. So we can have the arithmetic mean of the two averages that shifts the values to the respective years. This process of shifting the figures is called **'centering'** the averages.

We should decide first the period of the moving average. If it is 3 years or months or weeks or days, the problem of centering the averages will not arise at all. But if we take 6 years or months or weeks or days, the averages are placed first in between the two middle items and the arithmetic mean will be applied to center the items. (Refer the **Table.2** below)

Table 1.

Years	Values	3 Yearly Mov. total	3 yearly Mov Av.	8 yearly Mov. Total	8 yearly Mov. Av.	8 yearly Mov. Av
1976	330	--	--	--	--	--
1977	340	1044	348	Not Centred		Centered
1978	374	1047	349	--	--	($\bar{x}$ of
1979	333	1050	350	--	--	two)
1980	343	1053	351	2791	348.875	352.000
1981	377	1068	356	2841	355.125	356.375
1982	348	1071	357	2861	375.635	357.750
1983	346	1074	358	2839	354.875	358.375
1984	380	1086	362	2895	361.875	363.313
1985	360	1092	364	2918	364.750	363.938
1986	352	1101	367	2905	363.125	366.438
1987	389	1107	369	2958	369.750	370.813
1988	366	1119	373	2975	371.875	371.438
1989	364	1131	377	2968	371.000	374.125
1990	401	1128	376	3018	377.250	379.063
1991	363	1137	379	3047	380.875	380.625
1992	373	1146	382	3043	380.375	383.688
1993	410	1164	388	3096	387.000	388.250
1994	381	1176	392	3116	389.500	389.250
1995	385	1185	395	3112	389.000	--
1996	419	1188	396	--	--	--
1997	384	1200	400	-- Not Centred		Centred
1998	397	--	--	--	--	--

Table 2.

Year	Values	5.y.T	5.y.A	6.y.T	6.y.A	6.y.Centered. A.
1991	52					
1992	50					
1993	55	280	56			
1994	59	295	59	347	57.83	59.250
1995	64	314	62.8	364	60.67	62.335
1996	67	329	65.8	384	64	
1997	69					
1998	70					

Thus, 5 years' moving averages are placed against 1993, 1994, 1995 and 1996, whereas 6 year's moving averages (after using arithmetic mean and centering the averages) are placed against 1994 and 1995.

In case of 3 years' moving averages, take the totals of first three items (1st, 2nd and 3rd) and put the total and average against the 2nd item. Then take the total of next three items (2nd, 3rd and 4th) and put the total and average against the 3rd item. This procedure is continued till the end. The first and the last items remain without the average figures.

In case of 4 years' moving averages, take the totals of first four items (1st, 2nd, 3rd and 4th) and put the total and average in between the 2nd and 3rd item. Then continuing the next process, put the total and average in between the 3rd and 4th item. In this way we have the 4 years' moving averages which are laying between the two periods. This needs the procedure of shifting or centering the averages. If we simply obtain the means of the two averages, the new averages will be centered exactly against the periods mentioned.

The moving averages can be neatly presented in the form of a graph. If a series contains no fluctuations, the values plotted on a graph give a straight line trend to some extent. Let us represent the moving averages of 5 and 6 years' period, as illustrated above, on a graph sheet as under.

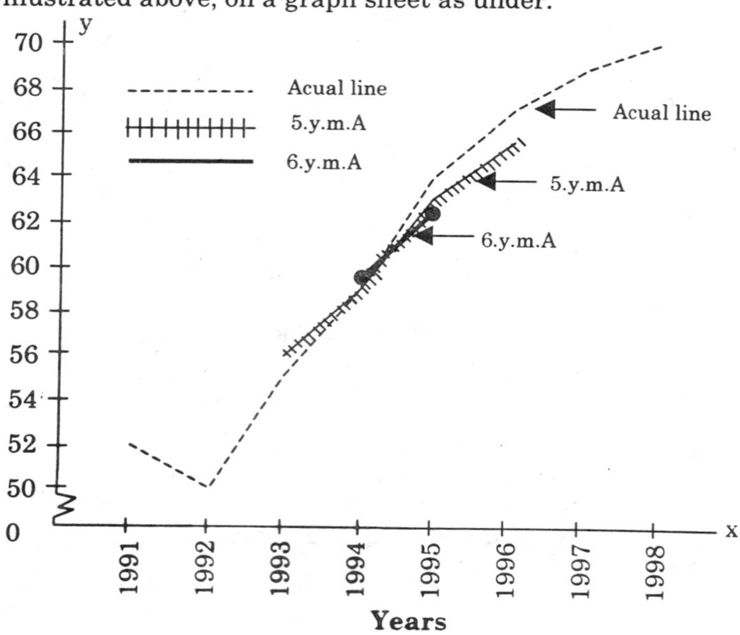

xample 15.4. *Calculate the trend values by five yearly moving erage method and plot the same on a graph from the llowing:* (BU-N83)

ar :	1965	1966	1967	1968	1969	1970	1971	1972	1973	1974	1975
nsumption `000' its :	12	14	18	24	22	20	16	25	26	34	31

olution : Computation of Trend Values

ear	Values	5. y.T	5.y.M.A	Year
965	12	--	--	--
966	14	--	--	--
967	18	90	18.0	1967
968	24	98	19.6	1968
969	22	100	20.0	1969
970	20	107	21.4	1970
971	16	109	21.8	1971
972	25	121	24.2	1972
973	26	132	26.4	1973
974	34	--	--	--
975	31	--	--	--

Note : The two items in the opening and the two items in the ending are left out in the 5 yearly moving average

Graph Showing Consumption of Units for 11 year's and 5 year's Trend Lines

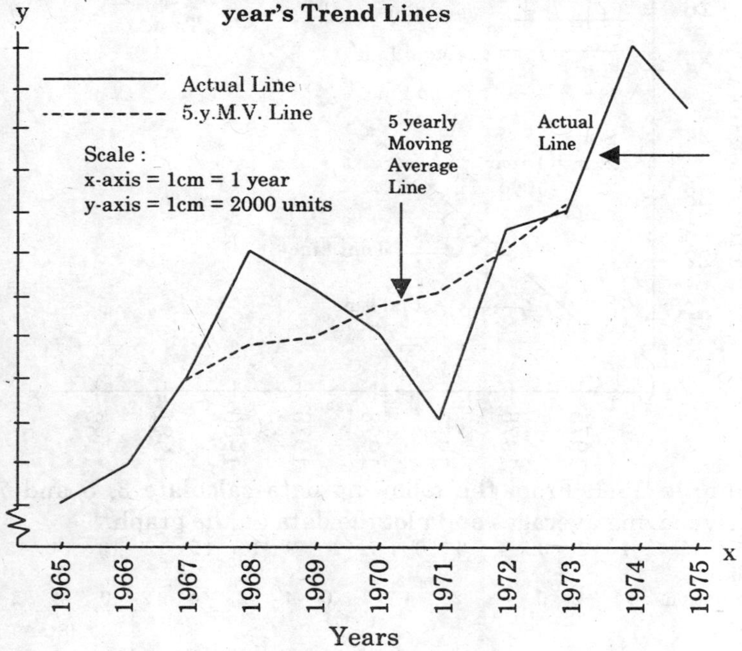

Example 15.5. *Using the three yearly moving averages determine the trend and plot the original and trend values on a graph* *(BU – A85)*

Year	: *1975*	*1976*	*1977*	*1978*	*1979*	*1980*	*1981*	*1982.*
Production (in 000 units)	: *21*	*22*	*23*	*24*	*25*	*26*	*27*	*26*

Solution : Computation of Trend Values

Year	Production	3.y.Total	3.y.M.A
1975	21	--	--
1976	22	66	22
1977	23	69	23
1978	24	72	24
1979	25	75	25
1980	26	78	26
1981	27	79	26.33
1982	26	--	--

Note : One item in the opening and one item in the ending are left out in the 3 yearly moving averages

Graph Showing Production (in 000 units) for the Period 1975-1982

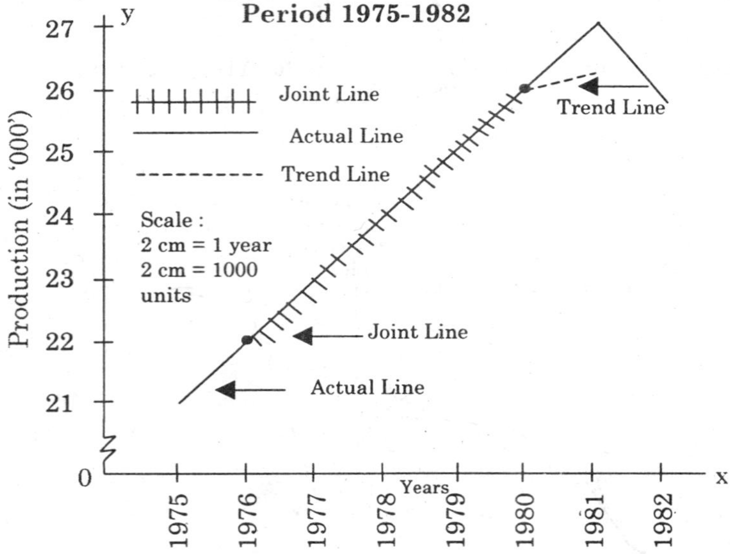

Example 15.6. From the following data calculate 3, 5 and 7 yearly moving averages and plot the data on the graph.

Year	: 1	2	3	4	5	6	7	8	9	10	11	12	13	14	15
Cyclical Fluctuations	: +4	+2	0	-4	-2	+4	+2	0	-4	-2	+4	+2	0	-4	-2

(BU-A91)

Solution : Computation of Trend Values

Year	Cy. Flu	3. y.T	3.y.MA	5.y.T	7.y.T	7.MA	Year
1	+4						
2	+2	+6	+2.000				
3	0	- 2	-0.667	0			
4	- 4	- 6	-2.000	0	+6	+0.8571	4
5	- 2	- 2	-0.667	0	+2	+0.2857	5
6	+4	+4	+1.333	0	- 4	- 0.5714	6
7	+2	+6	+2.000	0	- 6	- 0.8571	7
8	0	- 2	-0.667	0	+2	+0.2857	8
9	- 4	- 6	-2.000	0	+6	+0.8571	9
10	- 2	- 2	-0.667	0	- 4	+0.2857	10
11	+4	+4	+1.333	0	- 6	- 0.5714	11
12	+2	+6	+2.000	0		- 0.8571	12
13	0	- 2	-0.667	0			
14	- 4	- 6	-2.000				
15	- 2						

Graph Showing Cyclical Fluctuations for 15 years

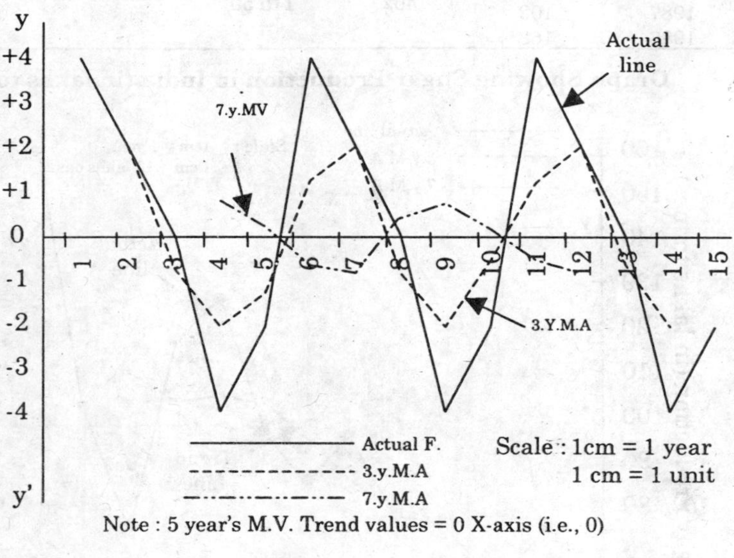

Note : 5 year's M.V. Trend values = 0 X-axis (i.e., 0)

Example 15.7. *Calculate the trend values by the method of moving averages assuming a four yearly cycle from the following data relating to sugar production in India. Also plot the actual and trend values on a graph.* *(BU – N89)*

Year :	1977	1978	1979	1980	1981	1982	1983	1984	1985	1986	1987	19
Sugar Production (in lakhs tons.) :	75	62	76	78	94	84	96	128	116	76	102	

Solution : Computation of Trend Values

Year	Sales (in lakhs tons)	4. y. T	4.M.A	Centred	Year
1977	75				
1978	62				
1979	76	291	72.75	75.125	1979
1980	78	310	77.70	80.250	1980
1981	94	332	83.00	85.500	1981
1982	84	352	88.00	94.250	1982
1983	96	402	100.50	103.250	1983
1984	128	424	106.00	105.000	1984
1985	116	416	104.00	104.750	1985
1986	76	422	105.50	110.500	1986
1987	102	462	115.50		
1988	168				

Graph Showing Sugar Production in India (in lakhs tons

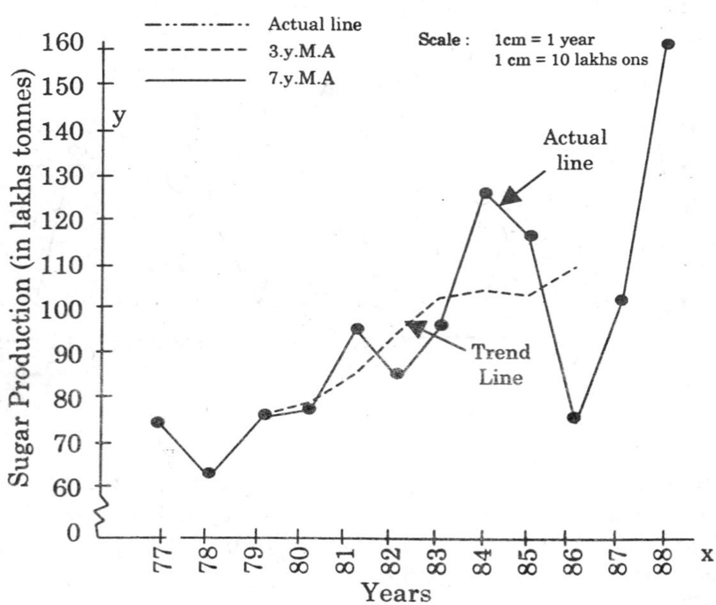

Example 15.8. *Calculate trend values from the following data using three yearly moving averages and show the trend line on the graph :*

Year :	*1967*	*1968*	*1969*	*1970*	*1971*	*1972*	*1973*	*1974*	*1975*	*1976*	*1977*	*1978*
Price Rs. :	*30*	*45*	*35*	*41*	*42*	*47*	*48*	*46*	*40*	*50*	*55*	*52*

Solution : Computation of Trend Values

Year	Price (Rs.)	3. y. T	3. y. M.A
1967	30		
1968	45	110	36.667
1969	35	121	40.333
1970	41	118	39.333
1971	42	130	43.333
1972	47	137	45.667
1973	48	141	47.000
1974	46	134	44.667
1975	40	136	45.333
1976	50	145	48.333
1977	55	157	52.333
1978	52		

Scale : 1 cm = Rs. 2
1 cm = 1 year

Graph Showing Price For 12 years

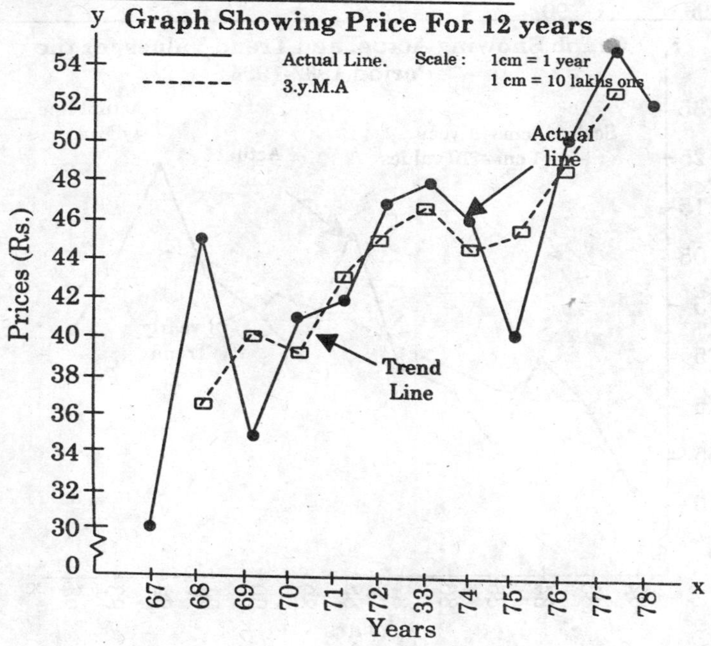

Example 15.9. Estimate the trend values using the data given below by taking four yearly moving average and show the actual values as well as trend values on a graph.

Year :	1982	1983	1984	1985	1986	1987	1988	1989	1990	1991	1992	1993	1994
Values :	8	74	86	68	80	84	110	86	94	102	126	106	106

(BU-A95)

Solution :

Year	Values	4.y.T	4.M.A	Centered	Year
1982	58				
1983	74				
		286	71.5		
1984	86			74.25	1984
		308	77.0		
1985	68			78.25	1985
		318	79.5		
1986	80			82.50	1986
		342	85.5		
1987	84			87.75	1987
		360	90.0		
1988	110			91.75	1988
		374	93.5		
1989	86			95.75	1899
		392	98.0		
1990	94			100.00	1990
		408	102.0		
1991	102			104.45	1991
		428	107.0		
1992	126			106.50	1992
		424	106.0		
1993	106				
1994	90				

Graph Showing Actual and Trend Values for the Period 1982-1994

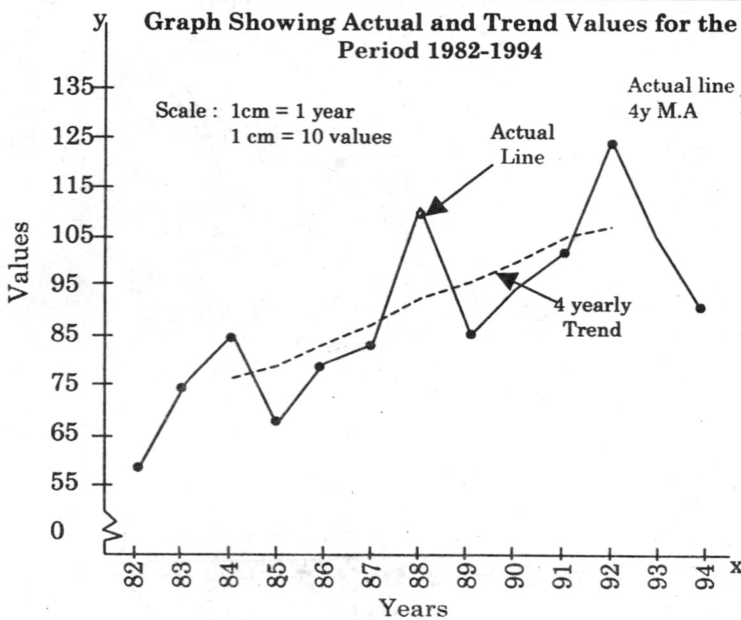

Method of moving averages just reduces the irregular fluctuations in the values over a period of time. As the period covered is longer the degree of reduction in irregularities will be greater. It reproduces the linear trend, if the period covered is long. However, too long a period of time, sometimes, is likely to lead further fluctuations in the averaged values. That is why the period covered should neither be too long nor too short.

Following are the merits and limitations of the moving average method,

Merits:

(i) It is very simple in calculation. There are no higher degree mathematical calculations.

(ii) It is objective method; there will not be variations in the answers, if trend values are calculated by two or more persons. It is not depending upon the personal judgement like freehand smoothed curve drawing.

(iii) It considers all the values in the series. The extreme values are also included in the process of calculating averages.

(iv) It not only determines the trend values but also reflects light on the seasonal, cyclical and irregular variations.

(v) It tries to eliminate the oscillatory movements in the time series by selecting a proper period for averages.

(vi) It is a flexible method as we can add a few more items to the given data without disturbing the trend values already calculated.

Limitations:

(i) This method fails to provide trend values for the early part and the last part of the series. We have to leave out the trend values for both the end of the series.

(ii) It does not establish functional relationship between the period (x) and the values of variable (y).

(iii) The averages obtained in case of non-linear trend are biased and the lie either above or below the true sweep of the data.

(iv) When a period selected is not appropriate, the moving averages fail to represent a true picture of the real trend. So it is difficult to select the suitable period.

(D) Least-Squares Method:- This is the most accurate method of finding the trend values with the help of a mathematical technique,which gives us a straight line trend. A line of the `Best Fit' can be obtained by the regression equation Y on X. It is a line from which the actual values deviate on either sides. The sum of the deviations taken from the arithmetic mean will be zero. Consequently, the sum of squares of deviations will be least, as compared to the other alternatives. That is why this method is called the "**Method of Least-Squares**".

The trend line, the line of **'Best Fit'**, will be drawn under the least squares method. It is the line from which the sum of the squares of the items, measured parallel to the Y axis, is the least. This can be represented by an equation,

Y on X .... **Y= a + bX**

To obtain the values of `**a**' and `**b**' constants, we have the following two secondary equations,

$\Sigma y = na + b\Sigma x$

$\Sigma xy = a\Sigma x + b\Sigma x^2$

Considering the y on x equation, as already studied in the Regress Analysis, we should take the period as x and values as y--one variable independent and another dependent (respectively). *Generally, the time factor changes at regular intervals.*

A linear trend values are obtained by the y on x equation which form a series in arithmetic progression, the constant difference being the value of `b' representing the slope. Following are the notations,

'x' = Independent variable

'y' = Dependent variable on `x'

'a' = The `y' intercept or catch --- constant

'b' = Indicates slope and signifies the change in x -- constant

Σ **y** = Sum of `y' values

Σ **x** = Sum of `x' values

n =Number of observations

Σ $\mathbf{x^2}$ = Sum of the squares

Σ **xy** = Sum of the products of x and y

A mathematical functional relationship is established between the two variables in the least squares method of finding the trend line. It satisfies the following two conditions:

(i) The sum of deviations of the `Y' (actual values) from the Y_c (computed values) is equal to zero.

Y = actual values ... $\Sigma (Y - Y_c) = 0$

Y_c = trend values ...

(ii) The sum of the squares of the x values is minimum.

In time series, the variable `x' can be measured from any point of origin period as first year or starting point. *It is always better to select the point of origin in the middle of the `x' series (i.e., $\Sigma x = 0$).* This brings balance between the negative and positive values. The period indicating the higher values can be reduced to the minimum symbolically as under,

(A) Year(x)	$(x - \bar{x})dx$	(B) Year (x)	$(x - \bar{x})dx$	dx
1991	- 3	1991	- 3.5	- 7
1992	- 2	1992	- 2.5	- 5
1993	- 1	1993	- 1.5	- 3
1994	0	1994	-0.5 (or)	- 1
1995	+1	1995	+0.5	+1
1996	+2	1996	+1.5	+3
1997	+3	1997	+2.5	+5
		1998	+3.5	+7

Thus, $\Sigma x = 0$ (as the deviations are calculated from mean). With the application of the above procedure, we can consider the years symbolically as under,

(A) 1991 as (-3), 1994 as (0), 1996 as (+2) and 1999 as (+5)

(B) 1993 as (-1.5) or (-3), 1997 as (+3.5) or (+7) and 2002 as (+7.5) or (+15).

As Σx or $\Sigma(x - \bar{x})$ or Σdx = zero, the secondary equations (as explained already) can be reduced to the minimum. Then we can get the **'a'** and **'b'** values easily as under,

$$a = \frac{\Sigma y}{n} \text{ and } b = \frac{\Sigma xy}{\Sigma x^2}$$

Illustration 1. *Let us obtain the straight line trend for the values given in the Example 15.1.*

x	y	x	x^2	xy	Trend Values (Straight Line)
1990	16	- 7	+49	-112	$y_c = 19.5 + 0.8096(-7) = 13.8328$
1991	14	- 5	25	-70	$y_c = 19.5 + 0.8096(-5) = 15.4520$
1992	20	- 3	9	-60	$y_c = 19.5 + 0.8096(-3) = 17.0712$
1993	18	- 1	1	-18	$y_c = 19.5 + 0.8096(-1) = 18.6904$
1994	12	+1	1	+12	$y_c = 19.5 + 0.8096(+1) = 20.3096$
1995	23	+3	9	+69	$y_c = 19.5 + 0.8096(+3) = 21.9288$
1996	28	+5	25	+140	$y_c = 19.5 + 0.8096(+5) = 23.5480$
1997	25	+7	49	+175	$y_c = 19.5 + 0.8096(+7) = 25.1672$
	156 $\Sigma y =$	0 $\Sigma x =$	168 $\Sigma x^2 =$	+136 $\Sigma xy =$	$\Sigma y_c = 156.000$

$$'a' = \frac{\Sigma y}{n} = \frac{156}{8} = \mathbf{19.5} \qquad 'b' = \frac{\Sigma xy}{\Sigma x^2} = \frac{136}{168} = \mathbf{0.8096}$$

$y = a + bx$

$$\mathbf{y_c = 19.5 + 0.8096x}$$

Illustration 2. *Let us obtain the straight line trend increasing one more observation in the series making the whole observation odd number of items.*

x	y	x	x^2	Xy	Trend Values (Straight Line)
1990	16	-4	16	-64	$y_c = 19.5 + 1.3(-4) = 14.3$
1991	14	-3	9	-42	$y_c = 19.5 + 1.3(-3) = 15.6$
1992	20	-2	4	-40	$y_c = 19.5 + 1.3(-2) = 16.9$
1993	18	-1	1	-18	$y_c = 19.5 + 1.3(-1) = 18.2$
1994	19.5	0	0	0	$y_c = 19.5 + 1.3(0) = 19.5$
1995	12	+1	1	+12	$y_c = 19.5 + 1.3(+1) = 20.8$
1996	23	+2	4	+ 4	$y_c = 19.5 + 1.3(+2) = 22.1$
1997	28	+3	9	+ 84	$y_c = 19.5 + 1.3(+3) = 23.4$
1998	25	+4	16	+100	$y_c = 19.5 + 1.3(+4) = 24.7$
	175.5 $\Sigma y =$	0 = Σx	60 = Σx^2	+78 $\Sigma xy =$	$\Sigma y_c = 175.5$

$$'a' = \frac{\Sigma y}{n} = \frac{175.5}{9} = \mathbf{19.5} \qquad 'b' = \frac{\Sigma xy}{\Sigma x^2} = \frac{78}{60} = \mathbf{1.3}$$

$y = a + bx$

$$\mathbf{y_c = 19.5 + 1.3x}$$

When the trend values are plotted on a graph, we have a straight line sloping from one end to the other end. It is needless to say that the values obtained by a straight line method (Least Squares) are mathematically accurate and tend to differ from the 'semi-average' method trend values as discussed earlier.

Example 15.10. *Obtain the straight line trend equation and tabulate against each year the trend values:* (BU-N85)

Year :	*1972*	*1973*	*1974*	*1975*	*1976*	*1977*	*1978*	*1979*	*1980*
Values :	*380*	*400*	*650*	*720*	*690*	*620*	*670*	*950*	*1040*

Solution: Computation of Trend Values

Years	Values (y)	x	x^2	xy	Trend Values (Straight Line)
1972	380	-4	16	-1520	$y_c = 680 + 70.5(-4) = 398.00$
1973	400	-3	9	-1200	$y_c = 680 + 70.5(-3) = 468.50$
1974	650	-2	4	-1300	$y_c = 680 + 70.5(-2) = 539.00$
1975	720	-1	1	-720	$y_c = 680 + 70.5(-1) = 609.50$
1976	690	0	0	0	$y_c = 680 + 70.5(0) = 680.00$
1977	620	+1	1	+620	$y_c = 680 + 70.5(+1) = 750.50$
1978	670	+2	4	+1340	$y_c = 680 + 70.5(+2) = 821.00$
1979	950	+3	9	+2850	$y_c = 680 + 70.5(+3) = 891.50$
1980	1040	+4	16	+4160	$y_c = 680 + 70.5(+4) = 962.00$
	6120 $\Sigma y =$	0 $\Sigma x =$	60 $\Sigma x^2 =$	+4230 $\Sigma xy =$	$\Sigma y_c = 6120.00$

$$'a' = \frac{\Sigma y}{n} = \frac{6120}{9} = \mathbf{680} \qquad 'b' = \frac{\Sigma xy}{\Sigma x^2} = \frac{420}{60} = \mathbf{70.5}$$

$$y = a + bx \qquad \mathbf{y_c = 680 + 70.5x}$$

Example 15.11. *Calculate the trend values by the method of least squares and prove that* $\Sigma(y - y_c) = 0$. (BU-A88)

Year	:	*1982*	*1983*	*1984*	*1985*
Sales (Rs. in `000')	:	*10*	*13*	*15*	*02*

Solution: Computation of Trend Values

Years	Sales ('000' Rs.) (y)	x	x^2	xy	Trend Values (Straight Line)	
1982	10	-3	9	-30	$12.5 + 0.4(-3) = 11.3$	-1.3
1983	13	-1	1	-13	$12.5 + 0.4(-1) = 12.1$	+0.9
1984	15	+1	1	+15	$12.5 + 0.4(+1) = 12.9$	+2.1
1985	12	+3	9	+36	$12.5 + 0.4(+3) = 13.7$	-1.7
	50 = Σy	0 $\Sigma x =$	20 = Σx^2	+8 = Σxy	$\Sigma y_c = 50.0$	$\Sigma(y + y_c) = 0$

$$'a' = \frac{\Sigma y}{n} = \frac{50}{4} = \mathbf{12.5} \qquad 'b' = \frac{\Sigma xy}{\Sigma x^2} = \frac{8}{20} = \mathbf{0.4}$$

$$y = a + bx \qquad \mathbf{y_c = 12.5 + 0.4x}$$

Example 15.12. *Fit a straight line trend by the method of least squares from the following data:* (BU-A89)

Year :	1979	1980	1981	1982	1983	1984	1985
Sales (in `000' units) :	100	105	109	96	102	108	112

Solution: Computation of Trend Values

Year	Sales (y)	x	x^2	xy	Trend Values (Straight Line)
1979	100	-3	9	-300	$y_c = 104.57 + 1.25(-3) = 100.82$
1980	105	-2	4	-210	$y_c = 104.57 + 1.25(-2) = 102.07$
1981	109	-1	1	-109	$y_c = 104.57 + 1.25(-1) = 103.32$
1982	96	0	0	0	$y_c = 104.57 + 1.25(0) = 104.57$
1983	102	+1	1	+102	$y_c = 104.57 + 1.25(+1) = 105.82$
1984	108	+2	4	+216	$y_c = 104.57 + 1.25(+2) = 107.07$
1985	112	+3	9	+336	$y_c = 104.57 + 1.25(+3) = 108.32$
	732 = Σy	0 = Σx	28 = Σx^2	+35 = Σxy	$\Sigma y_c = 731.99$

$$'a' = \frac{\Sigma y}{n} = \frac{732}{7} = \mathbf{104.57} \qquad 'b' = \frac{\Sigma xy}{\Sigma x^2} = \frac{35}{28} = \mathbf{1.25}$$

$$y = a + bx \qquad \mathbf{y_c = 104.57 + 1.25x}$$

Example 15.13. *The number of units of a product exported during 1985-1992 are given below. Compute the trend values by the method of least squares and prove that $\Sigma(y - y_c) = 0$.* (BU-N93)

Year :	*1985*	*1986*	*1987*	*1988*	*1989*	*1990*	*1991*	*1992*
Export :	*12*	*13*	*13*	*16*	*19*	*23*	*21*	*23*

Solution: Components of Trend Value

Year	Export units (y)	x	x^2	xy	Trend Values	$(y - y_c)$
1985	12	- 7	49	- 84	$y_c = 17.5 + 0.893(-7) = 11.249$	+0.751
1986	13	- 5	25	- 65	$y_c = 17.5 + 0.893(-5) = 13.035$	- 0.035
1987	13	- 3	9	- 39	$y_c = 17.5 + 0.893(-3) = 14.821$	- 1.821
1988	16	- 1	1	- 16	$y_c = 17.5 + 0.893(-1) = 16.607$	- 0.607
1989	19	+1	1	+ 19	$y_c = 17.5 + 0.893(+1) = 18.393$	+ 0.607
1990	23	+3	9	+ 69	$y_c = 17.5 + 0.893(+3) = 20.179$	+ 2.821
1991	21	+5	25	+105	$y_c = 17.5 + 0.893(+5) = 21.965$	- 0.965
1992	23	+7	49	+161	$y_c = 17.5 + 0.893(+7) = 23.751$	- 0.751
	140 Σy =	0 Σx=	168 Σx^2 =	+150 Σxy =	$y_c = 140.000$	$\Sigma(y - y_c) = 0$

$$'a' = \frac{\Sigma y}{n} = \frac{140}{8} = \mathbf{17.5} \qquad 'b' = \frac{\Sigma xy}{\Sigma x^2} = \frac{150}{168} = \mathbf{0.893}$$

$y = a + bx$

$\mathbf{y_c = 17.5 + 0.893x}$

Example 15.14. *Calculate the trend values by the least squares method for the following data:* (BU-N95)

Year :	*1986*	*1987*	*1988*	*1989*	*1990*	*1991*	*1992*	*1993*	*1994*
Values (Rs) :	*1900*	*2000*	*3250*	*3600*	*3450*	*3100*	*3350*	*4750*	*5200*

Solution: **Components of Trend Value**

Year	Values (Rs.) (y)	x	x^2	xy	Trend Values (y_c)
1986	1900	- 4	16	-7600	$y_c = 3400 + 389.1667(-4) = 1843.3332$
1987	2000	- 3	9	-6000	$y_c = 3400 + 389.1667(-3) = 2232.4999$
1988	3250	- 2	4	-6500	$y_c = 3400 + 389.1667(-2) = 2621.6666$
1989	3600	- 1	1	-3600	$y_c = 3400 + 389.1667(-1) = 3010.8333$
1990	3450	0	0	0	$y_c = 3400 + 389.1667(0) = 3400.0000$
1991	3100	+1	1	+3100	$y_c = 3400 + 389.1667(+1) = 3789.1667$
1992	3350	+2	4	+6700	$y_c = 3400 + 389.1667(+2) = 4178.3334$
1993	4750	+3	9	+14250	$y_c = 3400 + 389.1667(+3) = 4567.5001$
1994	5200	+4	16	+26000	$y_c = 3400 + 389.1667(+4) = 4956.6668$
	30600 $\Sigma y =$	0 $\Sigma x =$	60 $\Sigma x^2 =$	$\Sigma xy =$ +23350	$\Sigma y_c = 30{,}600.0000$

$$'a' = \frac{\Sigma y}{n} = \frac{30{,}600}{9} = \mathbf{3{,}400} \qquad 'b' = \frac{\Sigma xy}{\Sigma x^2} = \frac{23{,}350}{60} = \mathbf{389.1667x}$$

$y = a + bx$

$\mathbf{y_c = 3400 + 389.1667x}$

Example 15.15. *Fit a straight line trend by the method of least squares for the following and tabulate the trend values.* (BU-A96)

Years :	*1989*	*1990*	*1991*	*1992*	*1993*	*1994*	*1995*
Sales :	*20*	*24*	*22*	*30*	*28*	*32*	*30*

Solution: Computation of Trend Values

Year	Sales (y)	x	x^2	xy	Trend Values Table
1989	20	-3	9	-60	$y_c = 26.5714 + 1.8571(-3) = 21.0001$
1990	24	-2	4	-48	$y_c = 26.5714 + 1.8571(-2) = 22.8572$
1991	22	-1	1	-22	$y_c = 26.5714 + 1.8571(-1) = 24.7143$
1992	30	0	0	0	$y_c = 26.5714 + 1.8571(0) = 26.5714$
1993	28	+1	1	+28	$y_c = 26.5714 + 1.8571(+1) = 28.4285$
1994	32	+2	4	+64	$y_c = 26.5714 + 1.8571(+2) = 30.2856$
1995	30	+3	9	+90	$y_c = 26.5714 + 1.8571(+3) = 32.1427$
	= 186 Σy	= 0 Σx	= 28 Σx^2	= +52 Σxy	$\Sigma y_c = 185.9998$

$$'a' = \frac{\Sigma y}{n} = \frac{186}{7} = \mathbf{26.5714} \qquad 'b' = \frac{\Sigma xy}{\Sigma x^2} = \frac{52}{28} = \mathbf{1.8571}$$

$$y = a + bx \qquad \mathbf{y_c = 26.5714 + 1.8571x}$$

Example 15.16. *Below are given figures of production of a cement factory. Fit a straight line trend by the least squares method and tabulate the trend values and find the monthly increase in production.* (BU-A83, A92, N96)

Years :	*1985*	*1986*	*1987*	*1988*	*1989*	*1990*	*1991*
Prod. ('000' tons.) :	*77*	*88*	*94*	*85*	*91*	*98*	*90*

Solution: Computation of Trend Values

Year	Production (000 tons (y))	x	x^2	xy	Trend Values Table
1985	77	- 3	9	-231	$y_c = 89 + 2(-3) = 83$
1986	88	- 2	4	-176	$y_c = 89 + 2(-2) = 85$
1987	94	- 1	1	-94	$y_c = 89 + 2(-1) = 87$
1988	85	0	0	0	$y_c = 89 + 2(0) = 89$
1989	91	+1	1	+91	$y_c = 89 + 2(+1) = 91$
1990	98	+2	4	+196	$y_c = 89 + 2(+2) = 93$
1991	90	+3	9	+270	$y_c = 89 + 2(+3) = 95$
	623 $\Sigma y =$	$\Sigma x = 0$	28 $\Sigma x^2 =$	$\Sigma xy = +56$	$\Sigma y_c = 623$

$$'a' = \frac{\Sigma y}{n} = \frac{623}{7} = \mathbf{89} \qquad 'b' = \frac{\Sigma xy}{\Sigma x^2} = \frac{56}{28} = \mathbf{2}$$

$$y = a + bx$$

$$\mathbf{y_c = 89 + 2x}$$

Monthly increase of production,

$$\frac{b}{12} = \frac{2}{12} = \mathbf{1.667} \text{ tonnes.}$$

Example 15.17. *Fit a straight line trend by the method of least squares, tabulate the trend values and show the values on a graph from the following figures of production of sugar factory:*

(BU-N86,A93,A97, A98)

Year	:	*1981*	*1982*	*1983*	*1984*	*1985*	*1986*	*1987*
Production ('000' tons)	:	*80*	*90*	*92*	*83*	*94*	*99*	*92*

Solution: Computation of Trend Values

Year	Production (000 tons. y)	x	x^2	xy	Trend Values Table
1981	80	-3	9	-240	$y_c = 90 + 2(-3) = 84$
1982	90	-2	4	-180	$y_c = 90 + 2(-2) = 86$
1983	92	-1	1	-92	$y_c = 90 + 2(-1) = 88$
1984	83	0	0	0	$y_c = 90 + 2(0) = 90$
1985	94	+1	1	+94	$y_c = 90 + 2(+1) = 92$
1986	99	+2	4	+198	$y_c = 90 + 2(+2) = 94$
1987	92	+3	9	+276	$y_c = 90 + 2(+3) = 96$
	$\Sigma y = 630$	$= 0$ Σx	$= 28$ Σx^2	$= +56$ Σxy	$\Sigma y_c = 630$

$$'a' = \frac{\Sigma y}{n} = \frac{630}{7} = \mathbf{90} \qquad 'b' = \frac{\Sigma xy}{\Sigma x^2} = \frac{56}{28} = \mathbf{2}$$

$y = a + bx$

$\mathbf{y_c = 90 + 2x}$

Estimation of production for 1989

$\mathbf{y = 90 + 2(+6) = 90 + 12 = 102}$ **('000' tonnes.)**

Graph Showing for the Period 1981 – 1887

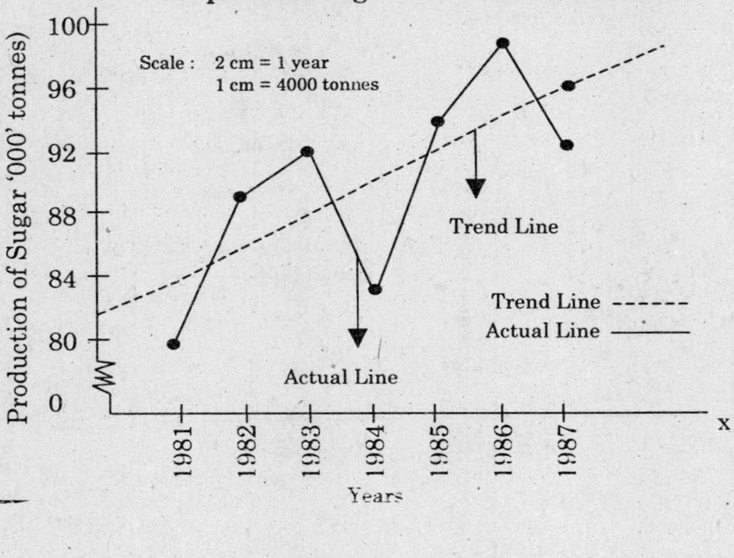

Example 15.18. *Below are given the figures of production ('000' tonnes) of a sugar factory. Fit a straight line trend by the method of least squares and obtain trend values.*

Show the trend line on a graph. (BU-A86,N97)

Year	:	*1990*	*1991*	*1992*	*1993*	*1994*	*1995*	*1996*
Prod.('000' tons)	:	*12*	*10*	*14*	*11*	*13*	*15*	*16*

Solution : Computation of Trend Values

Year	Production (000 tons y)	x	x^2	xy	Trend Values Table
1990	12	-3	9	-36	$y_c = 13 + 0.75(-3) = 10.75$
1991	10	-2	4	-20	$y_c = 13 + 0.75(-2) = 11.50$
1992	14	-1	1	-14	$y_c = 13 + 0.75(-1) = 12.25$
1993	11	0	0	0	$y_c = 13 + 0.75(0) = 13.00$
1994	13	+1	1	+13	$y_c = 13 + 0.75(+1) = 13.75$
1995	15	+2	4	+30	$y_c = 13 + 0.75(+2) = 14.50$
1996	16	+3	9	+48	$y_c = 13 + 0.75(+3) = 15.25$
	$\Sigma y = 91$	$= 0$ Σx	$= 28$ Σx^2	$= +21$ Σxy	$\Sigma y_c = 91.00$

$$'a' = \frac{\Sigma y}{n} = \frac{91}{7} = \mathbf{13} \qquad 'b' = \frac{\Sigma xy}{\Sigma x^2} = \frac{21}{28} = \mathbf{0.75}$$

$$y = a + bx$$

$$y_c = \mathbf{13 + 0.75x}$$

Graph Showing Sugar Production for the period 1990 - 1996

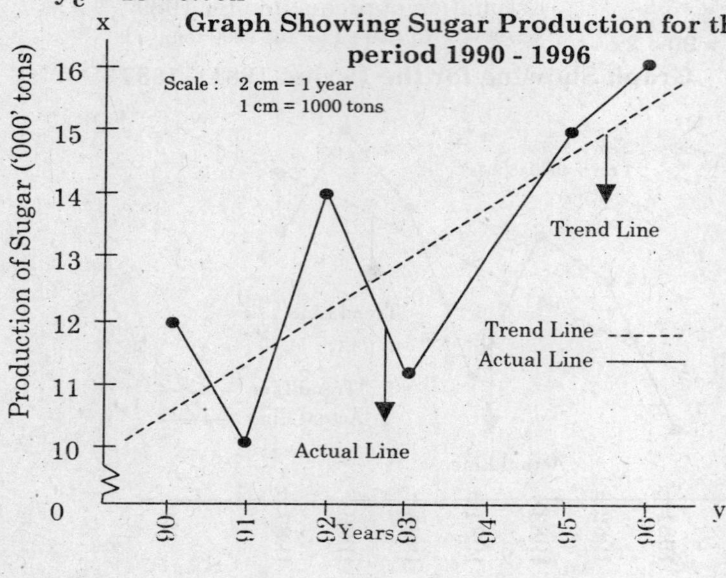

Example 15.19. *Apply the method of least squares and determine the sales for the year 1976 from the following data:*

Year	:	*1968*	*1969*	*1970*	*1971*	*1972*	*1973*	*1974*
Sales of Refrigerators	:	*100*	*110*	*130*	*125*	*170*	*168*	*191*

Plot the actual values and trend values on the graph (BU-A87)

Solution: Computation of Trend Values

Year	Sales (y)	x	x^2	xy	Trend Values Table
1968	100	-3	9	-300	$y_c = 142 + 15.3214(-3) = 96.0358$
1969	110	-2	4	-220	$y_c = 142 + 15.3214(-2) = 111.3572$
1970	130	-1	1	-130	$y_c = 142 + 15.3214(-1) = 126.6786$
1971	125	0	0	0	$y_c = 142 + 15.3214(0) = 142.0000$
1972	170	+1	1	+170	$y_c = 142 + 15.3214(+1) = 157.3214$
1973	168	+2	4	+336	$y_c = 142 + 15.3214(+2) = 172.6428$
1974	191	+3	9	+573	$y_c = 142 + 15.3214(+3) = 187.9642$
	994 $\Sigma y =$	0 $\Sigma x =$	28 $\Sigma x^2 =$	+429 $\Sigma xy =$	$\Sigma y_c = 994.0000$

$$'a' = \frac{\Sigma y}{n} = \frac{994}{7} = \mathbf{142} \qquad 'b' = \frac{\Sigma xy}{\Sigma x^2} = \frac{429}{28} = \mathbf{15.3214}$$

Sales for 1976 : $y = 142 + 15.3214(+5) = 142 + 76.607 = \mathbf{218.607}$ units

Graph Showing Sales for the Period 1981 – 1887

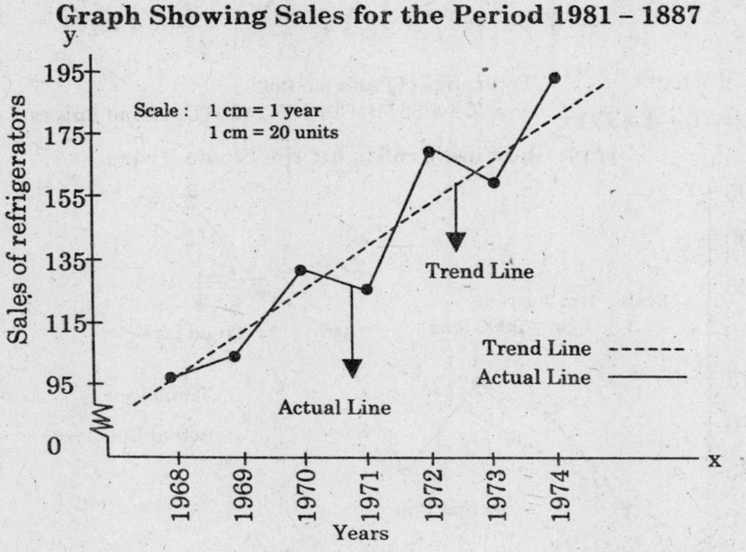

Example 15.20. *The following are the annual profits in thousands of rupees in a certain business:* (BU-N90)

Year	: 1981	1982	1983	1984	1985	1986	1987
Profits (Rs. `000'):	60	72	75	65	80	85	95

(a) Fit a straight line trend to these figures by the method of least squares.

(b) Plot the actual and trend values on a graph.

(c) Estimate the profits for the year 1990.

Solution: **Compuation of Trend Values**

Year	Profits (Rs.'000' (y)	x	x^2	xy	Trend Values (y_c)
1981	60	-3	9	-180	$y_c = 76+4.8571(-3) = 61.4287$
1982	72	-2	4	-144	$y_c = 76+4.8571(-2) = 6.4858$
1983	75	-1	1	-75	$y_c = 76+4.8571(-1) = 71.1429$
1984	65	0	0	0	$y_c = 76+4.8571(0) = 76.0000$
1985	80	+1	1	+80	$y_c = 76+4.8571(+1) = 80.8571$
1986	85	+2	4	+170	$y_c = 76+4.8571(+2) = 85.7142$
1987	95	+3	9	+285	$y_c = 76+4.8571(+3) = 90.5713$
	532 $\Sigma y =$	0 $\Sigma x =$	28 $\Sigma x^2 =$	+136 $\Sigma xy =$	$\Sigma y_c = 532.0000$

$$'a' = \frac{\Sigma y}{n} = \frac{532}{7} = \mathbf{76} \qquad 'b' = \frac{\Sigma xy}{\Sigma x^2} = \frac{136}{28} = \mathbf{4.8571}$$

$y = a + bx$

$\mathbf{y_c = 76 + 4.8571x}$

Estimation of Profit for 1990

$y = 76 + 4.8571(+6) = \mathbf{105.1426}$ (Thousand Rupees)

Graph Showing Profits for the Seven Years

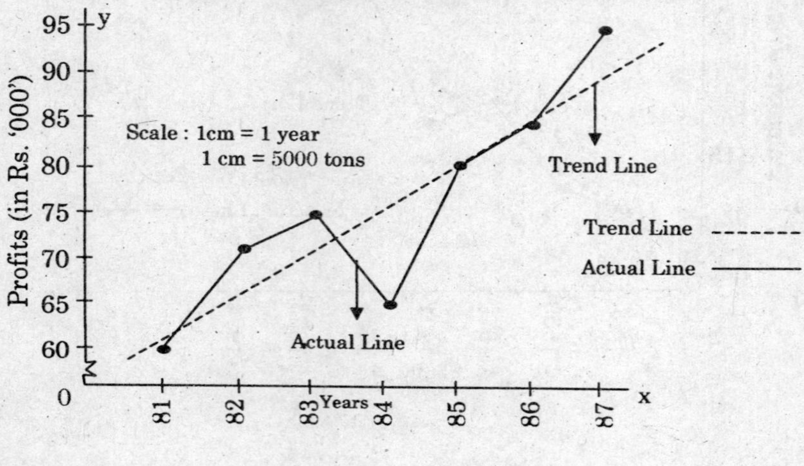

Example 15.21. *For the following table,*

(i) Fit a straight line trend by the method of least squares.

(ii) Show the trend line on a graph. (BU-A91)

Year	:	*1980*	*1981*	*1982*	*1983*	*1984*	*1985*	*1986*
Income(Rs `000')	:	*300*	*700*	*600*	*800*	*900*	*700*	*1000*

Solution: **Computation of Trend Values**

Year	Profits (Rs.'000' (y))	x	x^2	xy	Trend Values (y_c)
1980	300	-3	9	-900	$y_c = 714.2857 + 85.7142(-3) = 457.1431$
1981	700	-2	4	-1400	$y_c = 714.2857 + 85.7142(-2) = 542.8573$
1982	600	-1	1	-600	$y_c = 714.2857 + 85.7142(-1) = 628.5715$
1983	800	0	0	0	$y_c = 714.2857 + 85.7142(0) = 714.2857$
1984	900	+1	1	+900	$y_c = 714.2857 + 85.7142(+1) = 799.9999$
1985	700	+2	4	+1400	$y_c = 714.2857 + 85.7142(+2) = 885.7141$
1986	1000	+3	9	+3000	$y_c = 714.2857 + 85.7142(+3) = 971.4283$
	5000 $\Sigma y =$	0 $\Sigma x =$	28 $\Sigma x^2 =$	+2400 $\Sigma xy =$	$\Sigma y_c' = 4999.9999$

$$'a' = \frac{\Sigma y}{n} = \frac{5000}{7} = 714.2857 \qquad 'b' = \frac{\Sigma xy}{\Sigma x^2} = \frac{2400}{28} = 85.7142$$

$$y = a + bx$$

$$y_c = 5000 + 85.7142x$$

Graph Showing Income for the Period 1980 - 1986

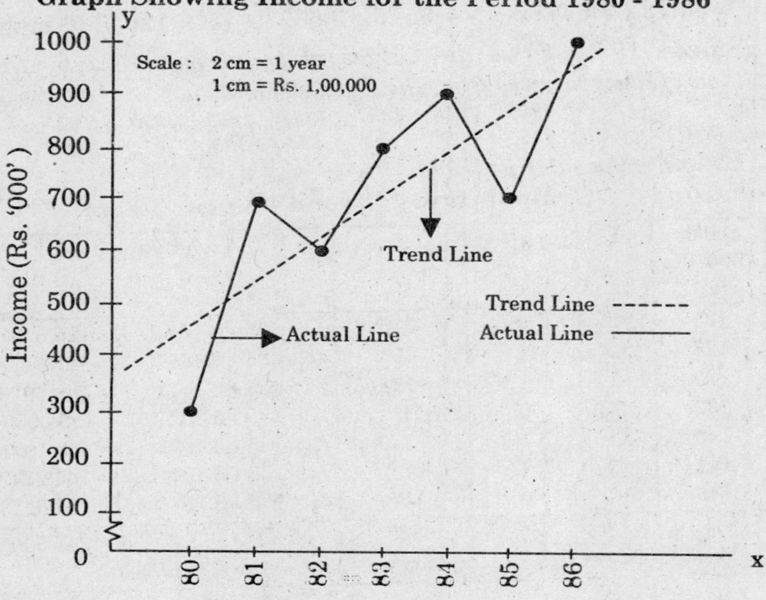

Example 15.22. *Fit a straight line trend by the least squares method to the following data. Assuming that same rate of change continues, state what would be the predicted earning for the year, 1992.* (BU-N92)

Year	: *1981*	*1982*	*1983.*	*1984*	*1985*	*1986*	*1987*	*1988*
Earnings (lakhs Rs)	: *38*	*40*	*65*	*72*	*69*	*60*	*87*	*95*

Solution: **Computation of Trend Values**

Year	Earnings (Rs.lakhs)	x	x^2	xy	Trend Values (y_c)
1981	38	-7	49	-266	$y_c = 65.75 + 3.6667(-7) = 40.0831$
1982	40	-5	25	-200	$y_c = 65.75 + 3.6667(-5) = 47.4165$
1983	65	-3	9	-195	$y_c = 65.75 + 3.6667(-3) = 54.7499$
1984	72	-1	1	-72	$y_c = 65.75 + 3.6667(-1) = 62.0833$
1985	69	+1	1	+69	$y_c = 65.75 + 3.6667(+1) = 69.4167$
1986	60	+2	9	+180	$y_c = 65.75 + 3.6667(+3) = 76.7501$
1987	87	+5	25	+435	$y_c = 65.75 + 3.6667(+5) = 84.0835$
1988	95	+7	49	+665	$y_c = 65.75 + 3.6667(+7) = 91.4169$
	526 $\Sigma y =$	0 $\Sigma x =$	168 $\Sigma x^2 =$	+616 $\Sigma xy =$	$\Sigma y_c = 526.0000$

$$'a' = \frac{\Sigma y}{n} = \frac{526}{8} = \mathbf{65.75} \qquad 'b' = \frac{\Sigma xy}{\Sigma x^2} = \frac{616}{168} = \mathbf{3.6667}$$

$y = a + bx$

Predicted earnings

$$\mathbf{y_c = 65.75 + 3.6667x} \qquad y = \mathbf{6575} + 3.6667(+15) = \mathbf{120.7505} \text{ lakhs}$$

Example 15.23. *Find the values of trend ordinates by the method of least squares from the data given below:* (BU-N94)

Year	:	*1985*	*1986*	*1987*	*1988*	*1989*	*1990*	*1991*
Sales (000 Rs)	:	*125*	*128*	*133*	*135*	*140*	*141*	*143*

Estimate the sales for 1993.

Solution : **Computation of Trend Values**

Year	Sales ('000' Rs (y))	x	x^2	xy	Trend Values (y_c)
1985	125	-3	9	-375	$y_c = 135 + 3.1071(-3) = 125.6787$
1986	128	-2	4	-256	$y_c = 135 + 3.1071(-2) = 128.7858$
1987	133	-1	1	-133	$y_c = 135 + 3.1071(-1) = 131.8929$
1988	135	0	0	0	$y_c = 135 + 3.1071(0) = 135.0000$
1989	140	+1	1	+140	$y_c = 135 + 3.1071(+1) = 138.1071$
1990	141	+2	4	+282	$y_c = 135 + 3.1071(+2) = 141.2142$
1991	143	+3	9	+429	$y_c = 135 + 3.1071(+3) = 144.3213$
	945 $\Sigma y =$	0 $\Sigma x =$	28 $\Sigma x^2 =$	+ 87 $\Sigma xy =$	$\Sigma y_c = 945.0000$

$'a' = \frac{\Sigma y}{n} = \frac{945}{7} = \mathbf{135}$ $\quad\quad$ $'b' = \frac{\Sigma xy}{\Sigma x^2} = \frac{87}{28} = \mathbf{3.1071}$

$y = a + bx \quad\quad y_c = \mathbf{135 + 3.1071x}$

Estimation of sales for 1993

$y = 135 + 3.1071(+5) = \mathbf{150.5355}$ '000' Rs.

Questions :

1. What are the elements of time series? (BU-A85)
2. What are the uses of Analysis of Time Series? (BU-N85,A90,N93,A94)
3. Name the components of Time Series. (BU-N86, N87)
4. Indicate with reasons with which component of a time series would you mainly associate the following :

   (i) Delay in production in a factory owing to a strike by workers for a period of one month.

   (ii) A sudden spurt in sales of ready made uniforms of school children at the time of re-opening of schools. (BU-A87)
5. What is a 'Secular Trend'? (BU-A89)
6. What are the cyclical fluctuations? (BU-N89)
7. Define a Time Series? What are its components? (BU-A92, A93, N95)
8. What do you mean by a 'trend'? (BU-A95)
9. What is a `Seasonal Variation'? What are its causes? (BU-N97)
10. State any two merits of the method of least squares? (BU-A84)
11. Define a 'trend'? (BU-N84)
12. What does it signify in the equation of straight line trend – $y = a + bx$? (BU-A89)
13. $y_c = a + bx$, where it is used? (BU-A86)
14. Fit a straight line trend and show the data graphically with trend values from the following data:

Year	:	1992	1993	1994	1995	1996	1997
Assets	:	83	92	71	90	169	191

Estimate the assets for 2000 years.

($y = 116 + 22.6x$. Estimation for 2000 years = 240.3)

15. Following are the profits of a concern from 1991 to 1997. Compute trend ordinates from the data:

Years	:	1991	1992	1993	1994	1995	1996	1997
Profits (in '000')	:	75	70	72	65	50	54	41

(y = 61 - 5.57x)

16. Calculate trend values from the data given below by applying the method of Least Squares.

Years	:	1992	1993	1994	1995	1996	1997	1998
Income (`000" Rs)	:	20	23	22	25	26	29	30

Estimate the likely income for the year 1999.
(y = 25 + 1.64x, Income for 1999 = 31.56)

17. Fit the straight line trends to the following figures by the method of least squares:

Years :	1993	1994	1995	1996	1997	1998
Sales ('000' Tonnes) :	50	60	65	63	68	70

[y = 64 + 3.18x]

18. Calculate trend values by the method of least squares from the data given below and estimate the sales for 2000.

Year	:	1993	1994	1995	1996	1997
Sales (Rs.lakhs)	:	70	74	80	86	90

(y = 80 + 5.2x, year 2000 = Rs. 160 lakhs)

19. The following table shows the number of salesmen working in a certain concern:

Year	:	1994	1995	1996	1997	1998
No. of Salesmen	:	28	38	46	40	56

(y = 41.6 + 5.8x)

20. Calculate trend values by the method of least squares from the data given below and estimate the sales for 2001:

Year	:	1994	1995	1996	1997	1998
Sales (in lakhs Rs):		4	6	7	8	10

(y = 7 + 1.4x, 2001 Sales = Rs. 14 lakhs)

21. The following figures are given relating to the output in a factory. Draw a trend line with the help of semi-average method.

Years	:	1992	1993	1994	1995	1996	1997	1998
Output Units	:	600	80	1000	800	1200	1000	1400

(Semi-averages – 800 and 1200)

22. Apply the method of semi-averages for measuring trend from the following data:

Year	:	1993	1994	1995	1996	1997	1998
Sales ('000' Rs.)	:	20	24	22	30	28	30

(Semi averages – 22 and 30)

23. Take five yearly period of moving averages and determine the trend line.

Year	1	2	3	4	5	6	7	8	9	10	11	12
Production (in 000 units):	14	17	22	28	26	18	29	24	25	29	30	23

(21.4, 22.2, 22.8, 23.2, 22.6, 23.2, 25.6, 26.2)

24. Find the centered four yearly moving averages for the following data:

Year	1991	1992	1993	1994	1995	1996	1997	1998
Values :	30.1	45.4	39.3	41.4	42.2	46.4	46.6	49.2

(40.6, 42.2, 43.2, 45.1)

25. Fit a straight line trend by the method of least squares to the following data:

Years	1	2	3	4	5	6	7	8	9	10	11
Output ('000' nos.):	17	20	19	26	24	40	35	55	50	74	69

(y = 39 + 5.8 x, output = 97,000 nos.)

Estimate output for the 16th year.

26. Compute the trend value by the method of least squares from the data given below:

Years	: 1992	1993	1994	1995	1996	1997	1998	
Profits (Rs.lakhs):	56	55	51	47	42	38	35	32

(y = 44.5 – 1.86x)

27. Fit a straight line by the method of least squares from the data given below. Find the trend values and predict the sales for 2000.

Years	:	1992	1993	1994	1995	1996	1997	1998
Sales ('000' units)	:	35	42	44	48	46	49	51

(y = 45 + 2.286x, 2000 sales = 56.43)

28. Compute the straight line trend equation for the data given below by the method of least squares; determine the annual trend estimates for each year.

Years	:	1994	1995	1996	1997	1998
Sales (Rs. '000')	:	25	30	40	50	45

(y = 38 + 6x, Annual Trend – 26, 32, 38, 44, 50)

29. Fit a straight line trend to the following data using the method of least squares:

Years	:	1992	1993	1994	1995	1996	1997	1998
Sales ('000' units)	:	83	60	54	21	22	13	23

(y = 39.429 – 10.929x)

30. Fit a straight line trend by the method of least squares to the following data and estimate the value for 2000.

Years	:	1994	1995	1996	1997	1998
Values	:	4	6	7	8	10

(y = 7 + 1.4x, 2000 year = 12.6)

16

Interpolation and Extrapolation

Interpolation and Extrapolation are the statistical techniques of obtaining the most likely estimate of a certain quantity from the relevant facts under certain assumptions. Mode and median are interpolated in the modal and the median classes respectively; but it was also done by starting with certain assumptions. In locating the mode in a continuous series, it is assumed that mode is influenced by the neighbouring class intervals. In locating the median it is assumed that the class interval is uniformly distributed over its frequencies. The same device of assumption is also useful for estimating some figures that are either missing or not available.

I. Interpolation

'Interpolation' stands for the "insertion of the most likely estimate under certain assumptions". In the absence of complete data at our disposal there would be no way out except that of resorting to interpolation. In some of the records, there may be either figures missing or insufficient or have been destroyed. In some other cases, the figures may be wanted for any intervening period or time or year concerned. So an estimate has to be made of the most likely figures from the available data.

Thus, interpolation is the estimation of missing or unrecorded information within the range of a given set of observed data. It is a process of inserting the most likely estimate of the figure for an intermediate period or point in between the two periods. It refers to the reading of the value which lies between the two points of data and which simplifies the missing link within the given range.

II. Extrapolation

' Extrapolation' stands for the `estimation' of the past or future figures that lie outside the two extreme points". It consists in reading the value that lies outside the given range of data. It is simply projects the past or future figures on the basis of given data. So it refers to the computation of values which lie beyond the first item or last item of the available data.

Distinction Between Interpolation and Extrapolation

Interpolation	Extrapolation
1. Estimation of figure within the given range of data.	1. Estimation of figure outside the given range of figure.
2. The technique is also extended to know the past and future figures (i.e outside the given range of data).	2. The technique cannot be extended to know the figures within the given range of data.

However, both the techniques aim at estimation or forecasting or predicting the unknown values.

III. Importance

The tools of interpolation and extrapolation are of great practical use. Following are the uses of these techniques:

(i) The techniques are helpful in filling the gaps that exist in statistical data. The gaps arise due to missing figures.

(ii) They are helpful in obtaining the median and mode in continuous series.

(iii) They are useful for forecasting the future events--sales, production, demand and other economic phenomena.

(iv) They are required when the data are insufficient due to difficulties in collecting the them.

(v) They are useful in obtaining the likely figures for any intervening period.

IV. Assumptions

The application of the techniques of interpolation and extrapolation is based on the following assumptions:

(i) There are no sudden jumps, from one period to another period, in the values of variable. It means there are no violent disturbances in the values of variable.

(ii) There is a sort of uniformity in the rise or fall of the values of variable. It means there is uniformity in the rate of change in the values of variable.

(iii) There is a definite and stable relationship between the two variables.

On the basis of these above assumptions, the figures can be interpolated or extrapolated within a reasonable degree of accuracy. The estimated figures, however, are not substitutes for original figures. They are just used for convenience in the process of further statistical analysis.

V. Methods of Interpolation (and Extrapolation)

Broadly speaking there are two methods of interpolation and extrapolation. They are,

(i) Graphic Method and (ii) Algebraic methods.

(i) Graphic method : The figures can be interpolated by the graphic method when the values of variable are influenced by the cyclical fluctuations. The given data is plotted on the graph. A continuous smooth curve or a straight line is drawn joining the plotted points. The year for which the value to be interpolated will be selected on the OX-axis. A perpendicular line, if drawn on OX-axis, will cut the curve or line. That intersecting point of value on OY-axis will be the estimate.

(ii) Algebraic methods : Algebraic methods of interpolation or extrapolation are more accurate than the graphic method. Following are the two important algebraic methods :

(a) Binomial Expansion Method.

(b) Newton`s Method of Advancing Differences.

VI. Binomial Expansion Method

This method is used for both the techniques- interpolation and extrapolation. It is easy to understand and simple to calculate. It is applicable when,

(i) The independent variable (x) advances by equal intervals like 2, 4, 6, 8 or 10, 15, 20, 25 or 6, 12, 18, 24 and so on.

(ii) The value of (x), for which the value of (y) is to be interpolated, is one of the class limits of x series.

Following is the distribution

X	:	8	12	16	20	24	28
Y	:	30	36	44	?	56	64

In the above distribution, `x' values are advancing by equal interval of 4. The value `y' for the value of `x' (i.e., 20) is missing. It means we have to interpolate `y' for `x' (i.e., 20). The value 20 is one of the class limits of the `x' series. In a similar way, we can also extrapolate the value of `y' for 'x' i.e., 4 or 32 but not 3, 5, or 30.

The Binomial Expansion Method is based on the Binomial Theorem which itself is based on the concept of "finite differences", let us study the following table,

x	y		Leading Difference					
			Δ^1		Δ^2		Δ^3	
1	4	y_0	$(y_1 - y_0) = +4$	$\Delta^1{}_0$	$(\Delta^1{}_1 - \Delta^1{}_0) = 2$	$\Delta^2{}_0$	$(\Delta^2{}_1 - \Delta^2{}_0) = 0$	$\Delta^3{}_0$
2	8	y_1	$(y_2 - y_1) = +6$	$\Delta^1{}_1$	$(\Delta^1{}_2 - \Delta^1{}_1) = 2$	$\Delta^2{}_1$		
3	14	y_2	$(y_3 - y_2) = +8$	$\Delta^1{}_2$				
4	22	y_3						

Analysis of the Difference

$$\Delta^3 = 0$$
$$\Delta^2{}_1 - \Delta^2_0 = 0$$
$$(\Delta^1{}_2 - \Delta^1{}_1) - (\Delta^1{}_1 - \Delta^1{}_0) = 0$$
$$[(y_3 - y_2) - (y_2 - y_1)] - [(y_2 - y_1) - (y_1 - y_0)] = 0$$
$$(y_3 - y_2 - y_2 - y_1) - (y_2 - y_1 - y_1 + y_0) = 0$$
$$y_3 - y_2 - y_2 - y_1 - y_2 + y_1 + y_1 - y_0 = 0$$
$$y_3 - 3y_2 + 3y_1 - y_0 = 0$$

In the above table, there are four `y' values. If any one is missing we can find it by using the above equation.

For instance,

X	Y		
1	4	y_0	"known values are 3." "y_2 is to be interpolated"
2	8	y_1	
3	--	y_2	
4	22	y_3	

$$y_3 - 3y_2 + 3y_1 - y_o = 0$$
$$22 - 3y_2 + 3(8) - 4 = 0$$
$$22 - 3y_2 + 24 - 4 = 0$$
$$42 - 3y_2 = 0$$
$$3y_2 = 42$$
$$y_2 = \mathbf{14}$$

In the above analysis, it is assumed that the last leading difference would be zero. The values are y_0, y_1, y_2 and y_3. The formula used is $y_3 - 3y_2 + 3y_1 - y_0 = 0$

In the similar way we can have the following formulas,

Known values	Δ	Expansion of the formulas	Symbol
2	$\Delta^2{}_0$	$y_2 - 2y_1 + y_0 = 0$	$(y-1)^2 = 0$
3	$\Delta^3{}_0$	$y_3 - 3y_2 + 3y_1 - y_0 = 0$	$(y-1)^3 = 0$
4	$\Delta^4{}_0$	$y_4 - 4y_3 + 6y_2 - 4y_1 + y_0 = 0$	$(y-1)^4 = 0$
5	$\Delta^5{}_0$	$y_5 - 5y_4 + 10y_3 - 10y_2 + 5y_1 - y_0 = 0$	$(y-1)^5 = 0$
6	$\Delta^6{}_0$	$y_6 - 6y_5 + 15y_4 - 20y_3 + 15y_2 - 6y_1 + y_0 = 0$	$(y-1)^6 = 0$
7	$\Delta^7{}_0$	$y_7 - 7y_6 + 21y_5 - 35y_4 + 35y_3 - 21y_2 + 7y_1 - y_0 = 0$	$(y-1)^7 = 0$
8	$\Delta^8{}_0$	$y_8 - 8y_7 + 28y_6 - 56y_5 + 70y_4 - 56y_3 + 28y_2 - 8y_1 + y_0 = 0$	$(y-1)^8 = 0$

The formulas can be remembered with reference to the coefficients and subscripts existing in them. Let us start with,

(i) $\Delta^2{}_0 = y_2 - 2y_1 + y_0 = 0 = (y-1)^2$

Coefficients are	1	2	1
Subscripts are	2	1	0

(ii) $\Delta^3{}_0 = y_3 - 3y_2 + 3y_1 - y_0 = (y-1)^3$

Coefficients are	1	3	3	1
Subscripts are	3	2	1	0

Similarly the coefficients can be obtained with the help of the **"Pascal's Triangle"** as under,

1

1 1

1 2 1

1 3 3 1

1 4 6 4 1

1 5 10 10 5 1

1 6 15 20 15 6 1

1 7 21 35 35 21 7 1

Expansion Procedure

1

1 1

1 2 1

1 3 3 1

1 4 6 4 1

1 5 10 10 5 1

1 6 15 20 15 6 1

We can also expand the formula by following the simple procedure as under,

(i) Record the `y' alphabets with the subscripts (equivalent to known values) up to `y_0'.

$$y_6 \quad y_5 \quad y_4 \quad y_3 \quad y_2 \quad y_1 \quad y_0 = 0$$

(ii) Place the signs alternatively starting from the first (which will be plus).

$$+y_6 \quad -y_5 \quad +y_4 \quad -y_3 \quad +y_2 \quad -y_1 \quad +y_0 = 0$$

(iii) Determine the coefficients being 1 the coefficients of the first item. The ranks are given to each item starting from the first item;

y_6	$-y_5$	$+y_4$	$-y_3$	$+y_2$	$-y_1$	$+y_0 = 0$
(1)	(2)	(3)	(4)	(5)	(6)	(7)

Apply the formula as under

$$\frac{\text{Previous Coefficient} \times \text{Previous Subscript}}{\text{Previous Rank}}$$

First Item is given	$\frac{1\times6}{1}=6$	$\frac{6\times5}{2}=15$	$\frac{15\times4}{3}=20$	$\frac{20\times3}{4}=15$	$\frac{15\times2}{5}=6$	$\frac{6\times1}{6}=1$
↓ y_6	$-6y_5$	$+15y_4$	$-20y_3$	$+15y_2$	$-6y_1$	$-y_o = 0$

Example16:1. *Find the figures of sales in Karnataka for the Year 1984 from the data given below:*

Year :	1978	1979	1980	1981	1982	1983
Sales : (`000'units)	240	300	320	360	400	450

(BU-A84, A96)

Solution : Since the known values are 6, the equation is $(y-1)^6 = 0$

Year	Sales in ('000' units)		Extrapolating the figure for 1984
1978	240	y_0	$y_6 - 6y_5 + 15y_4 - 20y_3 + 15y_2 - 6y_1 + y_0 = 0$
1979	300	y_1	$y_6 - 6(450) + 15(400) - 20(360) + 15(320) - 6(300) + 240 = 0$
1980	320	y_2	$y_6 - 2700 + 6000 - 7200 + 4800 - 1800 + 240 = 0$
1981	360	y_3	$y_6 - 11{,}700 + 11{,}040 = 0$
1982	400	y_4	$y_6 - 660 = 0$......... $\therefore$ $y_6 =$ **660 000** units of sales for the year 1984
1983	450	y_5	
1984	--	y_6	

Example 16.2. *Extrapolate the business done in 1982 from the following data:*

Years :	1979	1980	1981	1982	1983	1984	
Business done in (Rs lakhs) :	150	235	365	--	525	780	(BU-A85)

Solution : Since the known values are 5, the equation is $(y-1)^5 = 0$.

Year	Business Done (Rs.lakhs)		Interpolating the figure for 1982
1979	150	y_0	$y_5 - 5y_4 + 10y_3 - 10y_2 + 5y_1 - y_0 = 0$
1980	235	y_1	$780 - 5(525) + 10y_3 - 10(365) + 5(235) - 150 = 0$
1981	365	y_2	$780 - 2625 + 10y_3 - 3650 + 1175 - 150 = 0$
1982	---	y_3	$1955 - 6425 + 10y_3 = 0$
1983	525	y_4	$10y_3 - 4470 = 0$
1984	780	y_5	$10y_3 = 4470$.....$y_3 =$ **Rs. 447** lakhs for 1982

Example 16.3. *The following data shown is the monthly average number of deaths under one year in Bangalore City. Interpolate the monthly average number of deaths for the year 1981.*

Year :	1980	1981	1982	1983	1984	
M.A.No. of Death :	940	--	907	843	798	(BU- N85)

Solution : Since the known values are 4, the equation is $(y-1)^4 = 0$.

Interpolating the figure for 1981

Year	M.A. No. of. Deaths		
1980	940	y_0	$y_4 - 4y_3 + 6y_2 - 4y_1 + y_0 = 0$
1981	---	y_1	$798 - 4(843) + 6(907) - 4y_1 + 940 = 0$
1982	907	y_2	$798 - 3372 + 5442 - 4y_1 + 940 = 0$
1983	843	y_3	$7180 - 3372 - 4y_1 = 0$
1984	798	y_4	$3808 - 4y_1 = 0$

$4y_1 = 3808$

$y_1 = 952$....... **For 1981 MADR = 952.**

Example 16.4. *Interpolate the missing Index Number for the Year 1986:*

Year :	1984	1985	1986	1987	1988
Index No. :	3248.56	3134.59	--	2812.46	2789.96

(BU-A89)

Solution : Since the known values are 4, the equation is $(y-1)^4 = 0$.

Interpolating the figure for 1986

Year	Index No.		
1984	3248.60	y_0	$y_4 - 4y_3 + 6y_2 - 4y_1 + y_0 = 0$
1985	3134.59	y_1	$2789.97 - 4(2812.46) + 6y_2 - 4(3134.59) + 3248.56 = 0$
1986	---	y_2	$2{,}789.96 - 11{,}249.84 + 6y_2 - 12538.36 + 3248.56 = 0$
1987	2812.46	y_3	$6038.52 - 23788.20 + 6y_2 = 0$
1988	2789.96	y_4	$6y_2 = 17749.68$

$y_2 = 2958.28$ I.No. for 1986 is **2958.28**

Example 16.5. *Estimate the production for the year 1985 with the help of the following table:*

Year :	1960	1965	1970	1975	1980	1985	1990
Production in tonnes):	20	22	26	30	35	--	43

(BU- A98)

Solution : Since the known values are 6, the equation is $(y-1)^6 = 0$.

Year	Production (in tonnes)	
1960	20	y_0
1965	22	y_1
1970	26	y_2
1975	30	y_3
1980	35	y_4
1985	--	y_5
1990	43	y_6

Interpolation of the figure for 1985

$$y_6 - 6y_5 + 15y_4 - 20y_3 + 15y_2 - 6y_1 + y_0 = 0$$

$$43 - 6y_5 + 15(35) - 20(30) + 15(26) - 6(22) + 20 = 0$$

$$43 - 6y_5 + 525 - 600 + 390 - 132 + 20 = 0$$

$$-6y_5 + 978 - 732 = 0$$

$$-6y_5 + 246 = 0$$

$$6y_5 = 246 .... y_5 = \frac{246}{6} = 41$$

$\therefore$ 1985 figure is **41** tonnes.

Example 16.6. *Estimate the population of India for the Year 1991 from the following data:*

Census Year :	1941	1951	1961	1971	1981
Population in crores) :	31.9	36.1	43.9	54.8	68.4

(BU - N90)

Solution : Since the known values are 5, the equation is $(y-1)^5 = 0$

Census Year	Population (in crores)	
1941	31.9	y_0
1951	36.1	y_1
1961	43.9	y_2
1971	54.8	y_3
1981	68.4	y_4
1991	--	y_5

Extrapolating the figure for 1991

$$y_5 - 5y_4 + 10y_3 - 10y_2 + 5y_1 - y_0 = 0$$

$$y_5 - 5(68.4) + 10(54.8) - 10(43.9) + 5(36.1) - 31.9 = 0$$

$$y_5 - 342 + 548 - 439 + 180.5 - 31.9 = 0$$

$$y_5 - 812.9 + 728.5 = 0$$

$$y_5 - 84.4 = 0 .... \quad y_5 = 84.4$$

$\therefore$ 1991 population will be **84.4** crores.

Example 16.7. *Estimate the production for the years 1975 and 1985 with the help of the following table:*

Year :	1960	1965	1970	1975	1980	1985	1990
Production (ooo tonnes) :	20	22	26	--	35	--	43

(BU-N83,N89, N93)

Solution : There are two values missing. The known values are 5. The equation is $(y-1)^5 = 0$ which is used twice.

Year	Production (in '000' tonnes)	
1960	20	y_0 (i)
1965	22	y_1
1970	26	y_2 (ii)
1975	--	y_3
1980	35	y_4
1985	--	y_5
1990	43	y_6

Interpolating figures for 1975 & 1985

$y_5 - 5y_4 + 10y_3 - 10y_2 + 5y_1 - y_0 = 0$

(Now change the subscripts only)

$y_6 - 5y_5 + 10y_4 - 10y_3 + 5y_2 - y_1 = 0$

Using both the questions

$y_6 - 5y_5 + 10y_4 - 10y_3 + 5y_2 - y_1 = 0$

Add .... $y_5 - 5y_4 + 10y_3 - 10y_2 + 5y_1 - y_0 = 0$

After Addition = $\mathbf{y_6 - 4y_5 + 5y_4 - 5y_2 + 4y_1 - y_0 = 0}$

$43 - 4y_5 + 5(35) - 5(26) + 4(22) - 20 = 0$

$43 - 4y_5 + 175 - 130 + 88 - 20 = 0$

$306 - 105 - 4y_5 = 0 .... 4y_5 = 156$

$y_5 = \frac{156}{4} = \mathbf{39}$

Substitute the value of y_5

In (i) equation.

$39 - 5y_4 + 10y_3 - 10y_2 + 5y_1 - y_0 = 0$

$39 - 5(35) + 10y_3 - 10(26) + 5(22) - 20 = 0$

$39 - 175 + 10y_3 - 260 + 110 - 20 = 0$

$149 - 455 + 10y_3 = 0$

$10y_3 - 306 = 0 .... 10y_3 = 306$

$y_3 = \frac{306}{10} = \mathbf{30.6}$

$\therefore$ Production figures for 1975 = **30,600** tonnes and 1985 = **39,000** tonnes.

Example 16.8. *Estimate the production for the year 1965 and 1975 from the following data:*

Year :	1950	1955	1960	1965	1970	1975	1980
Production (ooo tonnes):	100	120	150	--	210	--	320

Solution : There are two values missing. The known values are 5. The equation is $(y-5)^5 = 0$ which is used twice.

Year	Production (in '000' tonnes)	
1950	100	y_0
1955	120	y_1
1960	150	y_2
1965	--	y_3
1970	210	y_4
1975	--	y_5
1980	320	y_6

Interpolating figures for 1965 & 1975

(i) $y_5 - 5y_4 + 10y_3 - 10y_2 + 5y_1 - y_0 = 0$

(Now change the subscripts)

(ii) $y_6 - 5y_5 + 10y_4 - 10y_3 + 5y_2 - y_1 = 0$

Substituting the values :

(i) $y_5 - 5(210) + 10y_3 - 10(150) + 5(120) - 100 = 0$

$y_5 - 1050 + 10y_3 - 1500 + 600 - 100 = 0$

$y_5 + 10y_3 = 1050 + 1500 + 100 - 600$

$\mathbf{y_5 + 10y_3 = 2050}$

(ii) $y_6 - 5y_5 + 10y_4 - 10y_3 + 5y_2 - y_1 = 0$

$320 - 5y_5 + 10(210) - 10y_3 + 5(150) - 120 = 0$

$320 - 5y_5 + 2100 - 10y_3 + 750 - 120 = 0$

$-5y_5 - 10y_3 = -2100 - 320 - 750 + 120$

$\mathbf{5y_5 + 10y_3 = 3050}$

Using Simultaneous Equations

(ii) $5y_5 + 10y_3 = 3050$

$5 \times$ (i) $\underline{{}_{-}5y_5 \pm 50y_3 =_{-} 10250}$

$-40y_3 = -7200$

$y_3 = 180$

Substituting y_3 value in (i)

$y_5 + 10y_3 = 2050$

$y_5 + 10(180) = 2050$

$y_5 + 1800 = 2050$

$y_5 = 2050 - 1800$

$y_5 = \mathbf{250}$

The production figures
for 1965 = **1,80,000** tonnes & for 1980 = **2,50,000** tonnes

Alternatively, using both the formulas independently.

(i) $(y-1)^6 = 0$ ..... as already obtained $\mathbf{y_5 + 10y_3 = 2050}$ (ii) $(y-1)^6 = 0$

$y_6 - 6y_5 + 15y_4 - 20y_3 + 15y_2 - 6y_1 + y_0 = 0$

$320 - 6y_5 + 15(210) - 20y_3 + 15(150) - 6(120) + 100 = 0$

$320 - 6y_5 + 3150 - 20y_3 + 2250 - 720 + 100 = 0$

$-6y_5 - 20y_3 + 5820 - 720 = 0$

$-6y_5 - 20y_3 + 5100 = 0$

$6y_5 + 20y_3 = \mathbf{5100}$

Using simultaneous equations ;

(ii) $6y_5 + 20y_3 = 5100$

$-2\times$(i) $\underline{2y_5 + 20y_3 = 4100}$

$4y_5 = 1000$

$y_5 = 250$ ('000' tonnes)

Example 16.9. *Interpolate the production for the years 1989 and 1991 with the help of the following table:*

Year	:	1986	1987	1988	1989	1990	1991	1992
Production (ooo tonnes)	:	120	122	126	--	135	--	143

(BU - N94)

Solution : Since the known values are 5 the equation is $(y-1)^5 = 0$. As there are two figures missing, simultaneous equations are used.

Year	Production (in '000' tonnes)	
1986	120	y_0
1987	122	y_1
1988	126	y_2
1989	--	y_3
1990	135	y_4
1991	--	y_5
1992	143	y_6

Interpolating figures for 1989 & 1991

(i) $y_5 - 5y_4 + 10y_3 - 10y_2 + 5y_1 - y_0 = 0$

(Now change the subscripts)

(ii) $y_6 - 5y_5 + 10y_4 - 10y_3 + 5y_2 - y_1 = 0$

(After addition of (i) to (ii))

$\therefore\ y_6 - 4y_5 + 5y_4 - 5y_2 + 4y_1 - y_0 = 0$

$143 - 4y_5 + 5(135) - 5(126) + 4(122) - 120 = 0$

$143 - 4y_5 + 775 - 630 + 488 - 120 = 0$

$-4y_5 + 1406 - 750 = 0$

$-4y_5 + 656 = 0$

$4y_5 = 656$

$y_5 = \mathbf{164}$

Substituting the value of y_5 in (i)

$164 - 5(135) + 10y_3 - 10(126) + 5(122) - 120 = 0$

$164 - 675 + 10y_3 - 1260 + 610 - 120 = 0$

$10y_3 + 774 - 2055 = 0 \ldots\ldots\ldots\ldots 10y_3 - 1281 = 0$

$10y_3 = 1281 \ldots\ldots\ldots\ldots y_3 = \mathbf{128.10}$

So Production for 1989 is **1,64,000** tonnes and for 1991 is **1,28,000** tonnes.

VII. Newtons`s Method of Advancing Differences

This method is used only in interpolation. It is also applicable when the independent variable (x) advances by equal intervals as in case of the Binomial Expansion method. However the (x) value for which the (y) value to be interpolated need not be one of the class limits of `x' series. It is more concerned with the interpolation of figures of (y) between the two values of `x' variable. It is based on the finite or advancing differences. We have to proceed with the obtaining of differences between the `y' values extending the process till only one difference remains in the end i.e., "The Last Leading Difference".

"If the `x` series are in descending order of values, reverse the series so as to bring them in an ascending order, and then apply Newton`s formula".

The Newtons Method of Advancing Differences is based on "finite differences".To know exactly the concept of the leading differences let us study the Newtons formula.

x	y	Δ^1		Δ^2		Δ^3		Δ^4	
x_0	y_0	$(y_1 - y_0)$	Δ^1_0						
x_1	y_1	$(y_2 - y_1)$	Δ^1_1	$\Delta^1_1 - \Delta^1_0$	Δ^2_0	$\Delta^2_1 - \Delta^2_0$			
x_2	y_2	$(y_3 - y_2)$	Δ^1_2	$\Delta^1_2 - \Delta^1_1$	Δ^2_1	$\Delta^2_2 - \Delta^2_1$	Δ^3_0	$\Delta^3_1 - \Delta^3_1$	Δ^4_0
x_3	y_3	$(y_4 - y_3)$	Δ^1_3	$\Delta^1_3 - \Delta^1_2$	Δ^2_2	$\Delta^2_3 - \Delta^2_2$	Δ^3_1		
x_4	y_4	$(y_5 - y_4)$	Δ^1_4	$\Delta^1_4 - \Delta^1_3$	Δ^2_3				
x_4	y_5								

(a) Value of 'x' to be obtaind... $x = \dfrac{\text{Item of Interpolation - Item of Origin}}{\text{Difference Between Adjoining Items}}$

(b) Leading Differences are $\Delta^1_0,\ \Delta^2_0,\ \Delta^3_0,\ \Delta^4_0$....... so on

(c) Newton's formula : $y = y_o + x\Delta^1_0 + \dfrac{x(x-1)}{1\times 2}\Delta^2_0 + \dfrac{x(x-1)(x-2)}{1\times 2\times 3}\Delta^3_0$

$$+\frac{x(x-1)(x-2)(x-3)}{1\times 2\times 3\times 4}\Delta^4_0 \text{.............soon}$$

Illustration Table :

x	y		Δ^1		Δ^2		Δ^3		Δ^4		Δ^5	
10	9	y_0	+6	Δ^1_0								
20	15	y_1	+8	Δ^1_1	+ 2	Δ^2_0	−15	Δ^3_0				
30	23	y_2	−5	Δ^1_2	−13	Δ^2_1	+20	Δ^3_1	+35	Δ^4_0	-69	Δ^5_0
40	18	y_3	+2	Δ^1_3	+ 7	Δ^2_2	−14	Δ^3_2	−34	Δ^4_1		
50	20	y_4	−5	Δ^1_4	− 7	Δ^2_3						
60	25	y_5										

Let us interpolate y for x_{60} (in the table it is 25)

$$x_{60} = \frac{\text{Item of Interpolation - Item of Origin}}{\text{Difference Between Adjoinging values}} = \frac{60-10}{10} = \frac{50}{10} = 5$$

$$y_{60} = y_0 + x\Delta^1_0 + \frac{x(x-1)}{1\times 2}\Delta^2_0 + \frac{x(x-1)(x-2)}{1\times 2\times 3}\Delta^3_0$$

$$+\frac{x(x-1)(x-2)(x-3)}{1\times 2\times 3\times 4}\Delta^4_0 + \frac{x(x-1)(x-2)(x-3)(x-4)}{1\times 2\times 3\times 4\times 5}\Delta^5_0$$

$$= 9 + 5(+6) + \frac{5(5-1)}{1\times 2}(+2) + \frac{5(5-1)(5-2)}{1\times 2\times 3}(-15)$$

$$+\frac{5(5-1)(5-2)(5-3)}{1\times 2\times 3\times 4}(+35) + \frac{5(5-1)(5-2)(5-3)(5-4)}{1\times 2\times 3\times 4\times 5}(-69)$$

$=9+30+20-150+175-69=234-219=15$

Note : Leading differences are +6, +2, -15, +35, -69. The last leading difference is –69.

Example 16.10. *Below are given the wages earned by workers per month in a certain factory. Interpolate the number of workers earning in between Rs 25 and Rs 35.*

Earnings per day up to Rs :	10	20	30	40	50	60
No. of Workers :	50	150	300	500	700	800

(BU-A83 ,A93)

Solution :

x	y		Δ^1		Δ^2		Δ^3		Δ^4		Δ^5	
10	50	y_0	+100	Δ^1_0								
20	150	y_1	+150	Δ^1_1	+50	Δ^2_0						
30	300	y_2	+200	Δ^1_2	+50	Δ^2_1	0	Δ^3_0				
40	500	y_3	+200	Δ^1_3	0	Δ^2_2	– 50	Δ^3_1	–50	Δ^4_0	0	Δ^5_0
50	700	y_4	+100	Δ^1_4	–100	Δ^2_3	–100	Δ^3_2	–50	Δ^4_1		
60	800	y_5										

a) No. of workers earning more than Rs. 35

$$x = \frac{35-10}{10} = \frac{25}{10} = 2.5$$

$$Y_x = y_0 + x\Delta^1_0 + \frac{x(x-1)}{1\times 2}\Delta^2_0 + \frac{x(x-1)(x-2)}{1\times 2\times 3}\Delta^3_0 + \frac{x(x-1)(x-2)(x-3)}{1\times 2\times 3\times 4}\Delta^4_0 + \frac{x(x-1)(x-2)(x-3)(x-4)}{1\times 2\times 3\times 4\times 5}\Delta^5_0$$

Leading Difference $\Delta^3_0 = 0$ and $\Delta^5_0 = 0$

∴ The calculations for the same parts remain zero.

$$y_x = 50 + 2.5(+100) + \frac{2.5(2.5-1)}{1\times 2}(+50) + 0 + 2.5\frac{(2.5-1)(2.5-2)(2.5-3)}{1\times 2\times 3\times 4}(-50) + 0$$

$$= 50 + 250 + 93.75 + 0 + 1.9531 + 0$$

$$= 395.7031 \text{ or } \mathbf{396} \text{ workers}$$

b) No. of workers earning more than Rs.25

$$x = \frac{25-10}{10} = \frac{15}{10} = 1.5$$

$$y_x = 50 + 1.5(+100) + \frac{1.5(1.5-1)}{2}(+50) + 0 + \frac{1.5(1.5-1)(1.5-2)(1.5-3)}{1\times 2\times 3\times 4}(-50) + 0$$

$$= 50 + 150 + 18.75 + 0 - 1.1719 + 0 = 217.5781 \text{ or } \mathbf{218} \text{ workers}$$

Thus No. of workers earning in between Rs.25 and Rs.35 are,

	No. of workers earning more than	Rs. 25 → 396
Less :	No. of workers earning more than	Rs. 35 → 218
		= **178**

Example 16.11. *From the data given below estimate the number of persons living between the age of 35 and 42:*

Age in Years :	20	30	40	50	
No. of persons:	513	439	346	243	(BU-A86)

Solution :

Age in years	No. of persons		Δ^1		Δ^2		Δ^3_0	
20	513	y_0	– 74	Δ^1_0				
30	439	y_1	– 93	Δ^1_1	–19	Δ^2_0	+9	Δ^3_0
40	346	y_2	–103	Δ^1_2	–10	Δ^2_1		
50	243	y_3						

(a) No of persons living at 35 years :

$$x = \frac{35-20}{10} = \frac{15}{10} = \mathbf{1.5}$$

$$y_x = y_0 + x\Delta^1_0 + \frac{x(x-1)}{1\times 2}\Delta^2_0 + \frac{x(x-1)(x-2)}{1\times 2\times 3}\Delta^3_0$$

$$= 513 + 1.5(-74) + \frac{1.5(1.5-1)}{1\times 2}(-19) + \frac{1.5(1.5-1)(1.5-2)}{1\times 2\times 3}(+9)$$

$$= 513 - 111 - 7.125 - 0.5625 = 513 - \mathbf{118.6875}$$

$$= 394.3125 \text{ or } \mathbf{394}$$

(b) No. of persons living at 42 years :

$$x = \frac{42-20}{10} = \frac{22}{10} = \mathbf{2.2}$$

$$y_x = 513 + 2.2(-74) + \frac{2.2(2.2-1)}{1\times 2}(-19) + \frac{2.2(2.2-1)(2.2-2)}{1\times 2\times 3}(+9)$$

$$= 513 - 162.8 - 25.08 + 0.792 = 513.792 - \mathbf{187.88}$$

$$= 325.912 \text{ or } \mathbf{326}$$

Thus No. of persons living between the age of 35 and 42 are,

	No. of persons living at	35 → 394
Less	No. of persons living at	42 → -326
		= 68

Example 16.12. *From the following table find the number of students who have obtained less than 45 marks:*

Marks :	30-40	40- 50	50-60	60-70	70-80
No. of students :	31	42	51	35	31

(BU-N86)

Solution: The distribution is converted into cumulative frequencies.

Marks	No. of Students		Δ^1		Δ^2		Δ^3		Δ^4	
Less than 40	31	y_0	+ 42	Δ^1_0	+ 9	Δ^2_0				
Less than 50	73	y_1	+ 51	Δ^1_1	− 16	Δ^2_1	− 25	Δ^3_0	+ 37	Δ^4_0
Less than 60	124	y_2	+ 35	Δ^1_2	− 4	Δ^2_2	+ 12	Δ^3_1		
Less than 70	159	y_3	+ 31	Δ^1_3						
Less than 80	190	y_4								

$$x = \frac{45-40}{10} = \frac{5}{10} = \mathbf{0.5}$$

$$y_x = y_0 + x\Delta^1_0 = \frac{x(x-1)}{1\times2}\Delta^2_0 + \frac{x(x-1)(x-2)}{1\times2\times3}\Delta^3_0 + \frac{x(x-1)(x-2)(x-3)}{1\times2\times3\times4}\Delta^3_0$$

$$= 31 + 0.5(+42) + \frac{0.5(0.5-1)}{1\times2}(+9) + \frac{0.5(0.5-1)(0.5-2)}{1\times2\times3}(-25) + \frac{0.5(0.5-1)(0.5-2)(0.5-3)}{1\times2\times3\times4}(+37)$$

$$= 31 + 21 - 1.125 - 1.5625 - 1.4453$$

$$= 52 - 4.1328 = 47.8672 \text{ or } \mathbf{48}$$

Hence the number of students who have obtained less than 45 marks is 48.

Example 16.13. *From the following data estimate the number of persons in the income group of Rs. 20 to Rs. 25.*

Income (in Rs)	:	0-10	10-20	20-30	30-40	40-50	
No. of Persons	:	20	25	70	95	115	(BU-A-87)

Solution : The distribution is converted into cumulative frequencies.

Income Rs.	No. of persons		Δ^1		Δ^2		Δ^3		Δ^4	
Less than 10	20	y_0	+ 25	Δ^1_0	+ 45	Δ^2_0				
Less than 20	45	y_1	+ 70	Δ^1_1	+ 25	Δ^2_1	− 20	Δ^3_0	+ 15	Δ^4_0
Less than 30	115	y_2	+ 95	Δ^1_2	+ 20	Δ^2_2	− 5	Δ^3_1		
Less than 40	210	y_3	+ 115	Δ^1_3						
Less than 50	325	y_4								

$$x = \frac{25-10}{10} = \frac{15}{10} = \mathbf{1.5}$$

$$y_x = y_0 + x\Delta^1_0 + \frac{x(x-1)}{1\times2}\Delta^2_0 + \frac{x(x-1)(x-2)}{1\times2\times3}\Delta^3_0 + \frac{x(x-1)(x-2)(x-3)}{1\times2\times3\times4}\Delta^4_0$$

$$y_x = 20 + 1.5(+25) + \frac{1.5(1.5-1)}{1\times2}(+45)$$

$$+\frac{1.5(1.5-1)(1.5-2)}{1\times2\times3}(-20) + \frac{1.5(1.5-1)(1.5-2)(1.5-3)}{1\times2\times3\times4}(+15)$$

$$= 20 + 37.5 + 16.875 + 1.25 + 0.3516$$

$$= 75.9766 \text{ or } \mathbf{76 \text{ persons}}$$

<u>No. of persons getting income in between Rs.20 & Rs.25 the</u>

	No. of persons getting less than	Rs.25 → 76
Less :	No. of persons getting less than	Rs 20 → 45 (given)
		= 31

Example 16.14. *The following table shows the expectation of life at different ages. Find the expectation of life at the age 26.*

Age (in years)	:	15	20	25	30	35	
Expectation of life (in years)	:	30	29	27	22	20	(BU-A90,N97)

Solution:

Age (in years)	Expectation of life		Δ^1		Δ^2		Δ^3		Δ^4	
15	30	y_0								
			−1	Δ^1_0						
20	29	y_1			−1	Δ^2_0				
			−2	Δ^1_1			−2	Δ^3_0		
25	27	y_2			−3	Δ^2_1			+8	Δ^3_0
			−5	Δ^1_2			+6	Δ^3_1		
30	22	y_3			+3	Δ^2_2				
			−2	Δ^1_3						
35	20	y_4								

$$x = \frac{26-15}{5} = \frac{11}{5} = \mathbf{2.2}$$

$$y_x = y_0 + x\Delta^1_0 + \frac{x(x-1)}{1\times2}\Delta^2_0 + \frac{x(x-1)(x-2)}{1\times2\times3}\Delta^3_0$$

$$+\frac{x(x-1)(x-2)(x-3)}{1\times2\times3\times4}\Delta^4_0$$

$$= 30 + 2.2(-1) + \frac{2.2(2.2-1)}{1\times2}(-1) + \frac{2.2(2.2-1)(2.2-2)}{1\times2\times3}(-2)$$

$$+\frac{2.2(2.2-1)(2.2-2)(2.2-3)}{1\times2\times3\times4}(+8)$$

$$= 30 - 2.2 - 1.32 - 0.176 - 0.1408$$

$$= 30 - 3.8368 = 25.1632 \text{ or } \mathbf{26 \text{ years}}$$

Thus, the expectation of life at 26 years is **26** years.

Example 16.15. *Estimate the number of students who have scored more than 48 marks but not more than 50 marks from the following data:*

Marks upto	:	45	50	55	60	65	
No. of Student	:	447	484	505	511	514	(BU- A91)

Solution :

Marks Upto	No. of Students	Δ^1	Δ^2	Δ^3	Δ^4
45	447 y_0				
		+37 Δ^1_0			
50	484 y_1		−16 Δ^2_0		
		+21 Δ^1_1		+1 Δ^3_0	
55	505 y_2		−15 Δ^2_1		+11 Δ^4_0
		+6 Δ^1_2		+12 Δ^3_1	
60	511 y_3		−3 Δ^2_2		
		+3 Δ^1_3			
65	514 y_4				

$$x = \frac{48-45}{5} + \frac{3}{5} = 0.6$$

$$y_x = y_0 + x\Delta^1_0 + \frac{x(x-1)}{1\times 2}\Delta^2_0 + \frac{x(x-1)(x-2)}{1\times 2\times 3}\Delta^3_0 + \frac{x(x-1)(x-2)(x-3)}{1\times 2\times 3\times 4\times}\Delta^4_0$$

$$= 447 + 0.6(+37) + \frac{0.6(0.6-1)}{1\times 2}(-16) + \frac{0.6(0.6-1)(0.6-2)}{1\times 2\times 3}(+1)$$

$$+ \frac{0.6(0.6-1)(0.6-2)(0.6-3)}{1\times 2\times 3\times 4}(+11)$$

$$= 447 + 22.2 + 1.92 + 0.056 - 0.3696 = 471.176 - 0.3696 = 470.80 \text{ or } 471$$

No. of students scoring between 48 and 50 marks	
No. of students upto	50 marks → 484
Less No. of students upto	48 marks → 471
	= **13**

Example 16.16. *Below are given the wages earned by workers per week in a certain factory:*

Weekly Income up to (Rs)	:	10	15	20	25	30
No. of workers	:	40	160	220	340	440

Calculate the number of workers earning between Rs.18 and Rs.23 (BU-N91, A95)

Solution :

Weekly Income (Rs.) Upto	No. of workers		Δ^1		Δ^2		Δ^3		Δ^4	
10	40	y_0								
			+120	Δ^1_0						
15	160	y_1			−60	Δ^2_0				
			+ 60	Δ^1_1			+120	Δ^3_0		
20	220	y_2			+60	Δ^2_1			−200	Δ^4_0
			+120	Δ^1_2			− 80	Δ^3_1		
25	340	y_3			−20	Δ^2_2				
			+100	Δ^1_3						
30	440	y_4								

(a) No. of workers earning up to Rs.18 :

$$x = \frac{18-10}{5} = \frac{8}{5} = 1.6$$

$$y_x = y_0 + x\Delta^1{}_0 + \frac{x(x-1)}{1\times 2}\Delta^2{}_0 + \frac{x(x-1)(x-2)}{1\times 2\times 3}\Delta^3{}_0 \frac{x(x-1)(x-2)(x-3)}{1\times 2\times 3\times 4}\Delta^4{}_0$$

$$= 40 + 1.6(+120) + \frac{1.6(1.6-1)}{1\times 2}(-60) + \frac{1.6(1.6-1)(1.6-2)}{1\times 2\times 3}(+120)$$

$$+ \frac{1.6(1.6-1)(1.6-2)(1.6-3)}{1\times 2\times 3\times 4}(-200)$$

$$= 40 + 192 - 28.8 - 7.68 - 4.48 = 232 - 40.96 = 191.04 \text{ or } 191$$

(b) No. of workers earning up to Rs.23

$$x = \frac{23-10}{5} = \frac{13}{5} = 2.6$$

$$y_x = 40 + 2.6(+120) + \frac{2.6(2.6-1)}{1\times 2}(-60) + \frac{2.6(2.6-1)(2.6-2)}{1\times 2\times 3}(+120)$$

$$+ \frac{2.6(2.6-1)(2.6-2)(2.6-3)}{1\times 2\times 3\times 4}(-200)$$

$$= 40 + 312 - 124.8 + 49.92 + 8.32 = 410.24 - 124.8 = 2855.44 \text{ or } 285$$

No. of workers earning between Rs.18 & 23

No. of workers earning up to	Rs.23 → 285
Less : No. of workers earning up to	Rs.18 → 191
	= 94

Example 16.17. *The following are the amounts of income tax paid by 600 college teachers in the year 1990. Find out the number of teachers who have paid more than Rs.1200 but not more than Rs.2400 as income tax.*

Income Tax(Rs)							
More than :	500	1000	1500	2000	2500	3000	
No. of Teachers :	600	550	425	275	100	25	(BU-A92)

Solution:

Income tax (Rs.) more than	No. of Teachers	Δ^1	Δ^2	Δ^3	Δ^4	Δ^5
500	600 y_0					
		-50 $\Delta^1{}_0$				
1000	550 y_1		-75 $\Delta^2{}_0$			
		-125 $\Delta^1{}_1$		$+50$ $\Delta^3{}_0$		
1500	425 y_2		-25 $\Delta^2{}_1$		-50 $\Delta^4{}_0$	
		-150 $\Delta^1{}_2$		0 $\Delta^3{}_1$		$+175$ $\Delta^5{}_0$
2000	275 y_3		-25 $\Delta^2{}_2$		$+125$ $\Delta^4{}_1$	
		-175 $\Delta^1{}_3$		$+125$ $\Delta^3{}_2$		
2500	100 y_4		$+100$ $\Delta^2{}_3$			
		-75 $\Delta^1{}_4$				
3000	25 y_5					

(a) No. of teachers paying tax more than Rs.1200

$$x = \frac{1200-500}{500} = \frac{700}{500} = 1.4$$

$$y_x = y_0 + x\Delta^1{}_0 + \frac{x(x-1)}{1\times 2}\Delta^2{}_0 + \frac{x(x-1)(x-2)}{1\times 2\times 3}\Delta^3{}_0 + \frac{x(x-1)(x-2)(x-3)}{1\times 2\times 3\times 4}\Delta^4{}_0 + \frac{x(x-1)(x-2)(x-3)(x-4)}{1\times 2\times 3\times 4\times 5}\Delta^5{}_0$$

$$= 600 + 1.4(-50) + \frac{1.4(1.4-1)}{1\times 2}(-75) + \frac{1.4(1.4-1)(1.4-2)}{1\times 2\times 3}(+50) + \frac{1.4(1.4-1)(1.4-2)(1.4-3)(1.4-3)}{1\times 2\times 3\times 4}(-50) + \frac{1.4(1.4-1)(1.4-2)(1.4-3)(1.4-3)(1.4-4)}{1\times 2\times 3\times 4\times 5}(+175)$$

$$= 600 - 70 - 21 - 2.8 - 1.12 - 2.0384 = 600 - 96.9584 = \mathbf{503}$$

(b) No. of teachers paying tax more than Rs.2400

$$x = \frac{2400-500}{500} = \frac{1900}{500} = 3.8$$

$$y_x = 600 + 3.8(-50) + \frac{3.8(3.8-1)}{1\times 2}(-75) + \frac{3.8(3.8-1)(3.8-2)}{1\times 2\times 3}(+50) + \frac{3.8(3.8-1)(3.8-2)(3.8-3)}{1\times 2\times 3\times 4}(-50) + \frac{3.8(3.8-1)(3.8-2)(3.8-3)(3.8-4)}{1\times 2\times 3\times 4\times 5}(+175)$$

$$= 600 - 190 - 399 + 159.6 - 31.92 - 4.4688 = 759.6 - 625.3888 = 134.2112 \text{ or } \mathbf{134}$$

No. of Teachers paying tax in between Rs.1200 and Rs.2,400	
No of Teachers paying tax more than	Rs.1200 → 503
Less : No of Teachers paying tax more than	Rs.2400 → 134
	= 369

Example 16.18. *The following are the marks obtained by 492 candidates in an examination.*

Marks not more than	:	40	45	50	55	60	65
No. of candidates	:	210	253	307	381	413	492

Find out the number of candidates who have secured more than 48 but not more than 50 marks. (BU- N92 N96)

Solution :

Marks not more than	No. of candidates		Δ^1		Δ^2		Δ^3		Δ^4		Δ^5	
40	210	y_0	+43	$\Delta^1{}_0$								
45	253	y_1	+54	$\Delta^1{}_1$	+11	$\Delta^2{}_0$	+ 9	$\Delta^3{}_0$				
50	307	y_2	+74	$\Delta^1{}_2$	+20	$\Delta^2{}_1$	−62	$\Delta^3{}_1$	−71	$\Delta^4{}_0$	+222	$\Delta^5{}_0$
55	381	y_3	+32	$\Delta^1{}_3$	−42	$\Delta^2{}_2$	+89	$\Delta^3{}_2$	+151	$\Delta^4{}_1$		
60	413	y_4	+79	$\Delta^1{}_4$	+47	$\Delta^2{}_3$						
65	492	y_5										

$$x = \frac{48-40}{5} = \frac{8}{5} = \mathbf{1.6}$$

$$y_x = y_0 + x\Delta^1_0 + \frac{x(x-1)}{1\times 2}\Delta^2_0 + \frac{x(x-1)(x-2)}{1\times 2\times 3}\Delta^3_0$$

$$+\frac{x(x-1)(x-2)(x-3)}{1\times 2\times 3\times 4}\Delta^4_0 + \frac{x(x-1)(x-2)(x-3)(x-4)}{1\times 2\times 3\times 4\times 5}\Delta^5_0$$

$$= 210 + 1.6(+43) + \frac{1.6(1.6-1)}{1\times 2}(+11) + \frac{1.6(1.6-1)(1.6-2)}{1\times 2\times 3}(+9)$$

$$+\frac{1.6(1.6-1)(1.6-2)(1.6-3)}{1\times 2\times 3\times 4}(-71)$$

$$+\frac{1.6(1.6-1)(1.6-2)(1.6-3)(1.6-4)}{1\times 2\times 3\times 4\times 5}(+222)$$

$$= 210 + 68.8 + 5.28 - 0.576 - 1.5904 - 2.3869$$

$$= 284.08 - 3.9773 = 280.1027 \text{ or } \mathbf{280}$$

No. of candidates scoring Marks in between 45 & 50

No. of candidates scoring marks not more than 50 →	307
Less : No. of candidates scoring marks not more than 48 →	280
	= **27**

Example 16.19. *The weekly wages paid to 460 employees of a factory are as under,*

wages (Rs)

Not more than	: 40	45	50	55	60	65	70	75
No. of Employees	: 212	296	368	429	460	481	490	492

Estimate the number of employees who got more than Rs.57 but not more than Rs.60. (BU-A94)

Solution :

Weekly wages Rs not more than	No. of workers		Δ^1		Δ^2		Δ^3		Δ^4		Δ^5		Δ^6		Δ^7	
40	212	y_0	+84	Δ^1_0	−12	Δ^2_0	+ 1	Δ^3_0	−20	Δ^4_0	+59	Δ^5_0	−120	Δ^6_0	+210	Δ^7_0
45	296	y_1	+ 72	Δ^1_1	− 11	Δ^2_1	− 19	Δ^3_1	+ 39	Δ^4_1	− 61	Δ^5_1	+ 90	Δ^6_1		
50	368	y_2	+ 61	Δ^1_2	− 30	Δ^2_2	+ 20	Δ^3_2	− 22	Δ^4_2	+ 29	Δ^5_2				
55	429	y_3	+ 31	Δ^1_3	− 10	Δ^2_3	− 2	Δ^3_3	+ 7	Δ^4_3						
60	460	y_4	+ 21	Δ^1_4	− 12	Δ^2_4	+ 5	Δ^3_4								
65	481	y_5	+ 9	Δ^1_5	− 7	Δ^2_5										
70	490	y_6	+ 2	Δ^1_6												
75	492	y_7														

$$x = \frac{57-40}{5} = \frac{17}{5} = \mathbf{3.4}$$

$$y_x = y_0 + x\Delta^1_0 + \frac{x(x-1)}{1\times 2}\Delta^2_0 + \frac{x(x-1)(x-2)}{1\times 2\times 3}\Delta^3_0 + \frac{x(x-1)(x-2)(x-3)}{1\times 2\times 3\times 4}\Delta^4_0$$
$$+ \frac{x(x-1)(x-2)(x-3)(x-4)}{1\times 2\times 3\times 4\times 5}\Delta^5_0 + \frac{x(x-1)(x-2)(x-3)(x-4)(x-5)}{1\times 2\times 3\times 4\times 5\times 6}\Delta^6_0$$
$$+ \frac{x(x-1)(x-2)(x-3)(x-4)(x-5)(x-6)}{1\times 2\times 3\times 4\times 5\times 6\times 7}\Delta^7_0$$
$$= 212 + 3.4(+84)\frac{3.4(3.4-1)}{1\times 2}(-12) + \frac{3.4(3.4-1)(3.4-2)}{1\times 2\times 3}(+1)$$
$$+ \frac{3.4(3.4-1)(3.4-2)(3.4-3)}{1\times 2\times 3\times 4}(-20)$$
$$+ \frac{3.4(3.4-1)(3.4-2)(3.4-3)(3.4-4)}{1\times 2\times 3\times 4\times 5}(+59)$$
$$+ \frac{3.4(3.4-1)(3.4-2)(3.4-3)(3.4-4)(3.4-5)}{1\times 2\times 3\times 4\times 5\times 6}(-120)$$
$$+ \frac{3.4(3.4-1)(3.4-2)(3.4-3)(3.4-4)(3.4-5)(3.4-6)}{1\times 2\times 3\times 4\times 5\times 6\times 7}(+210)$$
$$= 212 + 285.60 - 48.96 + 1.904 - 3.808 - 1.3480323 - 0.731136 - 0.4752383$$
$$= 499.50 - 55.31 = 444.19 \text{ or } \mathbf{444}$$

No. of workers getting wages in between Rs.57 and Rs.60

No. of workers getting wages not more than	Rs 60 → 460
Less : No of workers getting wages not more than	Rs 57 → 444
	= **16**

Example 16.20. *From the following data estimate the number of persons earning wages between Rs.70 and Rs.90 per day:*

Wages(Rs) per Day :	Below 40	40-60	60-80	80-100	100-120
No of persons :	500	240	200	140	100

(BU-N95)

Solution: The distribution is converted from class interval cumulative frequencies:

Wages per Day (Rs.) Below	No. of persons		Δ^1		Δ^2		Δ^3		Δ^4	
40	500	y_0								
			+240	Δ^1_0						
60	740	y_1			−40	Δ^2_0				
			+200	Δ^1_1			−20	Δ^3_0		
80	940	y_2			−60	Δ^2_1			+40	Δ^4_0
			+140	Δ^1_2			+20	Δ^3_1		
100	1080	y_3			−40	Δ^2_2				
			+100	Δ^1_3						
120	1180	y_4								

(a) No. of persons earning wages below Rs.70

$$x = \frac{70-40}{20} = \frac{30}{20} = \mathbf{1.5}$$

$$y_x = y_0 + x\Delta^1_0 + \frac{x(x-1)}{1\times 2}\Delta^2_0 + \frac{x(x-1)(x-2)}{1\times 2\times 3}\Delta^3_0 + \frac{x(x-1)(x-2)(x-3)}{1\times 2\times 3\times 4}\Delta^4_0$$

$$= 500 + 1.5(+240) + \frac{1.5(1.5-1)}{1\times 2}(-40) + \frac{1.5(1.5-1)(1.5-2)}{1\times 2\times 3}(-20) + \frac{1.5(1.5-1)(1.5-2)(1.5-3)}{1\times 2\times 3\times 4}(+40)$$

$$= 500 + 360 - 15 + 1.25 + 0.9375 = 862.1875 - 15 = 847.19$$

(b) No. of persons earning wages below Rs.90

$$x = \frac{90-40}{20} = \frac{50}{20} = \mathbf{2.5}$$

$$y_x = 500 + 2.5(+240) + \frac{2.5(2.5-1)}{1\times 2}(-40) + \frac{2.5(2.5-1)(2.5-2)}{1\times 2\times 3}(-20) + \frac{2.5(2.5-1)(2.5-2)(2.5-3)}{1\times 2\times 3\times 4}(+40)$$

$$= 500 + 600 - 75 - 6.25 - 1.5625 = 1100 - 7.8125 = \mathbf{1092.18}$$

No. of workers earning wages in between Rs.90 & Rs.70

No. of workers earning wages Below	Rs.90 →	1092
Less : No. of workers earning wages Below	Rs 70 →	847
		= **245**

Example 16.21. *Interpolate the value of premium to be paid for a policy (of Rs 1000) at the age of 17 years from the following data:*

Age in years :	15	25	35	45	55	
Premium (Rs.) (for Rs 1000 policy) :	11.1	12.6	14.3	16.1	18.3	(BU-A97)

Solution:

Age (in years)	Premium (Rs.)		Δ^1		Δ^2		Δ^3		Δ^4	
15	11.1	y_0	+1.5	Δ^1_0	+0.2	Δ^2_0	−0.1	Δ^3_0	+0.4	Δ^4_0
25	12.6	y_1	+1.7	Δ^1_1	+ 0.1	Δ^2_1	+0.3	Δ^3_1		
35	14.3	y_2	+1.8	Δ^1_2	+ 0.4	Δ^2_2				
45	16.1	y_3	+ 2.2	Δ^1_3						
55	18.3	y_4								

$$x = \frac{17-15}{10} = \frac{2}{10} = 0.2$$

$$y_x = y_0 + x\Delta^1_0 + \frac{x(x-1)}{1\times 2}\Delta^2_0 + \frac{x(x-1)(x-2)}{1\times 2\times 3}\Delta^3_0 + \frac{x(x-1)(x-2)(x-3)}{1\times 2\times 3\times 4}\Delta^4_0$$

$$= 11.1 + 0.2(+1.5) + \frac{0.2(0.2-1)}{1\times 2}(+0.2) + \frac{0.2(0.2-1)(0.2-2)}{1\times 2\times 3}(-0.1)$$

$$+ \frac{0.2(0.2-1)(0.2-2)(0.2-3)}{1\times 2\times 3\times 4}(+0.4)$$

$$= 11.1 + 0.3 - 0.016 - 0.0048 - 0.01344 = 11.4 - 0.03424$$

= Rs.11.36576 or **Rs.11.36 premium**

Questions

1. What is interpolation ? (BU-A84, 86)
2. What are the assumptions on which methods of interpolation are based ? (BU-A87, A90, N95, A 96, N97)
3. What you mean by interpolation ? When do you apply Binomial Expansion Method of Interpolation. (BU-A88)
4. Distinguish between Interpolation and Extrapolation. (BU-N89,A91, N92, A94, A97)
5. Expand $(Y-1)^5$. (BU-N91)
6. Expand $(Y-1)^6$. (BU-A94)
7. Under what conditions the Binomial Expansion Method of Interpolation is applied ? (BU-N96)

8. The following data gives the amount of cement in thousands of tonnes manufactured in India. Find the missing figure?

Year	1993	1994	1995	1996	1997	1998
Production (in ooo" tonnes)	39	85	--	151	264	388

(Ans : 96.4)

9. Using any algebraic method of interpolation find the population of educated for 1971.

Year	1951	1961	1971	1981	1991
Population (in lakhs)	2522	2514	--	3168	3613

(Ans:2765.5)

10. The working class cost of living index numbers are given below for certain years.

Year	1993	1994	1995	1996	1997	1998
I. Nos.	320	300	--	280	278	250

(Ans:284)

11. Find the number of workers earning between Rs.650 and Rs.680 from the following data by applying a suitable formula for interpolation:

Earning	:	Less than Rs.600	650	700	750	800
No. of Workers	:	38	120	174	190	250

(Ans:38)

12. The expectation of life at different ages for males in India is shown below:

Age (in years)	:	20	25	30	35	40
Expectation of life (years)	:	33.0	29.8	26.6	23.5	20.5

(Ans : 25.34)

Use Newton's formula to estimate the expection of life at age 32.

13. The following table gives index numbers of industrial production for a few years:

Year	:	1993	1994	1995	1996	1997	1998
I. Nos.	:	120.2	141.0	157.3	177.8	--	212.6

(Ans : 200.48)

Using all the given figures interpolate the figure of index number of industrial production for the year 1997.

14. Interpolate the missing figure in the following table of wheat cultivation:

Year	:	1992	1993	1994	1995	1996	1997	1998
Area (in hectares)	:	60	68	--	70	75	--	82

(Ans.:68.65 & 81.5)

15. Extrapolate the population of the city A for 2001 from the following data

Year	:	1951	1961	1971	1981	1991
Population (in 000')	:	425	453	470	484	504

(Ans:540)

16. Estimate the number of persons whose incomes are between Rs.400 and Rs.500 from the following figures:

Income Rs.	: below 200	200-400	400-600	600-800	800-1000
(No.of persons)	120	145	200	250	150

(Ans:89)

17. From the following data interpolate the missing figure of production for 1995 and 1997.

Year	:	1992	1993	1994	1995	1996	1997	1998
Production (in tonnes)	:	100	110	130	--	175	--	215

(Ans : 153 and 195)

18. From the following table of yearly premium for polices maturing at different years estimate the premium for the policies maturing at the age of 47 years.

Age (in years)	:	45	50	55	60	65
Premium (in Rs.)	:	287	240	208	186	171

(Ans:266)

19. Given below are the marks obtained by 200 students of a university in the Business Statistics paper.

Marks	:	40-50	50-60	60-70	70-80	80-90
No.of students	:	32	42	55	40	31

Interpolate the number of students who have obtained less than 65 marks.

[Hint: Prepare less than frequencies.] (Ans:102.43)

20. Estimate the probable number of persons earning between Rs.450 and Rs.480 from the following table:

Income Rs.	less than400	400-450	450-500	500-550	550-600
No.of persons:	38	82	54	16	60

[Hint: Prepare less than frequencies] (Ans:38)

21. Calculate the likely minimum temperature for a maximum of 35° degree `c' by Newton's Finite Difference Method.

Maximum Temperature	:	36°	34°	32°	30°	28°
Minimum Temperature	:	21°	19°	16°	12°	11°

[Hint:Reverse the series to bring the `x' series in ascending order.]

(Ans:20degree 'c')

17

Index Numbers

'Index Numbers' or **'Indices'** are the statistical devices designed to measure the relative changes in the level of a certain phenomenon. They are the specialized averages or rates or ratios or percentages which indicate the general level of magnitude of a statistical group of variables. They reflect the changes in certain economic factors in the form of a single ratio or percentage. They are nothing but percentage relatives which study relative changes in the economic activities over a period time. They give quick and overall picture of economic changes from time to time and place to place in a single figure.

Thus, Index Numbers are "*specialised averages*" which study the changes in prices of different commodities and represent the same in a single figure. They are "*expressed in percentages*" or reduced to a common denominator, with reference to some base year, ignoring % sign. They "*measure changes*" in the economic activities, and cost of living. They give a "*comparative picture*" of two periods relating to changes. They make the complicated data converted into a "*simplified data*". They exhibit the relative rather than absolute aspect of any phenomenon which is stretched over a period of time.

I. Meaning

"*An Index Number is a number which indicates the level of a certain phenomenon at any given date in comparison with the level of the same phenomenon at some standard date.*"

"*An Index Number is a single ratio (usually in percentages) which measures the combined (i.e. averaged) change of several variables between the two different times, places or situations.*"

"*An Index Number is a quantity which, by reference to a base period, shows its variations or changes in the magnitude over a period of time.*"

An Index number offers a device for estimating the relative changes of a variable in cases where measurement of its actual changes is impossible or inconvenient. It throws some light on the incommensurable and hidden factor about which we desire information. It is an average linked with percentages measuring the general changes in the economic activities.

II Purpose

It will be better to know the prime motive of constructing the index numbers. We must know what we really want to measure and how we intend to put to use the compiled index numbers. An index number, if not properly designed and constructed, becomes a dangerous tool to apply. Following are the different purposes for which the index numbers are computed:

(i) To measure and compare changes in a variable or a set of variables with some base year.

(ii) To measure the purchasing power of money which is of great help in finding out the real wages or incomes of the people.

(iii) To provide guidelines to policy making in business field.

III. Importance

Index numbers are called **"Economic Barometers"** as they indicate the pulses of economy and tendencies in price fluctuations. They measure the pressure of economic activities of the country. In studying the trends or tendencies in the level of any phenomenon they are helpful. They are useful in formulating the business policies and forecasting the future events. They provide a good basis for comparison as they are expressed in abstract units (short figures) of measurement.

Index numbers are not only useful in the field of business but also they are useful in the field of agriculture, employment and governance. They reduce the complex form of measurement to the simple numbers. They provide a useful method of combining units of dissimilar nature into one meaningful value. They measure the purchasing power of money and help in finding out the real wages or incomes of the people. Importance of index numbers is increasing day by day as they are used constantly by the government departments, business men, economists, professional men, contractors, engineers and industrialists. Today, they are one of the most widely used important statistical devices.

IV. Limitations

In spite of the importance of Index Numbers, they suffer from the number of limitations as under:

(i) Biased Sampling: In the process of biased sampling an error is systematically incorporated. This makes the index numbers reflect the economic activities in a wrong way.

(ii) Passage of Time: The period between the base year and the current year is not having the constant standard of living. Changes do take place in fashion, efficiency, attitude, behaviour and technology. These changes are not taken into consideration as they are influencing the changes in economic activities.

(iii) Common Index Number: We cannot compute a single or standard index number common to all the economic activities. For each phenomenon under study, we have to constuct a special index number.

(iv) Common Method: There is no common method for computing the index numbers for different activities. The methods of computation varies according the nature of data available.

(v) Change in the Items: The items selected in the base year may not be in continuous use and there may appear substitutes. Even then if the commodities remain the same in current year, their qualities might have been changed drastically.

(vi) Base Year: It is a problem to select the correct base year. There is no suitable or normal or ideal year to be considered as the base year. There will be different index numbers for different base years for the same current year.

V. Types of Index Numbers

Index numbers are broadly classified into various categories depending upon the type of the phenomenon or variable in which the relative changes are to be studied.

Index Numbers

- Price
  - Wholesale (General)
  - Retail (Cost of living)
- Quantity
  - Agricultural Production
  - Industrial production
- Value
  - Price x Quality
- Others
  - Others

(A) Wholesale Price Index Numbers : The Wholesale Price Index Numbers reflect the changes in the general price level of a country. They cover a number of commodities and markets, and intended to measure wholesale prices of specific commodities. They are designed to show price changes for the commodities sold at a particular place in a particular year with reference to a base year. They are often used in the periodic adjustment of long-term purchases or rental agreements as they serve as an indicator of general economic change.

(B) Retail Price Index Numbers : The Retail Price Index Numbers reflect the changes in the retail prices of various commodities, such as consumption goods, stocks, shares, deposits, bonds and other goods of daily use by a common man. They are popularly known as the *"Cost of Living Index Numbers"* or *"Consumer Price Index Numbers"*. They enable us to study the effect of changes in the retail prices over a period of time. The prices relate to a basket of goods or commodities on the purchasing power or cost of living of a class of people.

The consumer price index numbers are widely used as escalators for adjustment of wages of workers and employees. They give an exact idea of the effect of the change in retail prices on the cost of living of various classes of people.

(C) Quantity Index Numbers : The Quantity Index Numbers study the changes in the volume of goods produced, distributed and consumed. They cover both the industrial and agricultural goods and take into account the imports and exports also. They measure the level of physical output of a country for a period of time.

(D) Value Index Number : The Value Index Numbers study the changes in the total value (price x quantity) of the commodities concerned for a period of time. However, these indices are not in common use like other indices.

(E) Specific Purpose Index Numbers : There are various index numbers to measure the changes in different phenomena such as profits, sales, production, expenditure and other business activities to serve the specific purpose. They are of great help for the business community in forecasting the future events. The purpose of constructing these index numbers is specific and they are not regularly used. They are used for forming business policies by private organisations.

VI. Steps in Constructing Index Numbers

The technique of constructing index numbers involves a number steps which are to be observed. These steps are,

(i) Objectives : The first and the foremost step is to define clearly the objectives for which the index numbers are required. The purpose of constructing the index numbers must be specifically mentioned well in advance.

(ii) Base Year : The choice of the base year or reference year is very important in constructing the index numbers. The "Base year" is a year with which index numbers are to be compared or to which they are to be referred. It should be a period which is having normal or stable economic activities. It should not be characterised by abnormal economic activities. The year selected as the base year shall not be too far from the current year under study.

The data is used as the base for the base year in calculating the index number. The length of the period between the base year and the current year will be governed by the nature of the index number. There are two methods of base year -- Fixed Base Method and Chain Base Method.

"*Fixed Base Method*" refers to the base year, which is common to all the prices that are changing. The fixed base year serves as a common standard of comparision. It remains unchanged for the calculations during the period of index number. For price indices and cost of living indices, the fixed base year will be appropriate for calculations.

"*Chain Base Method*" refers to the base year which goes on shifting from one period to another. The base year is not fixed. Generally, the previous year will be the base year for the calculation of index number for the current year. So base year changes from year to year. It is used in case of time series where index numbers are considered.

Thus the base year is some specific year or period of time with reference to which the current year changes are based. The base year represents the value 100 and the current year changes are based on it.

(iii) Selection of Items : The items or commodities selected should be relevant to the purpose of the index number. In computing cost of living index numbers, we should select only those items which are consumed by the consumers. In calculating wholesale price index numbers, we should consider only those items which enter into the wholesale market. However, the number of items selected should neither be too small or too large. Only standardised and related items should be selected.

(iv) Price Quotation : The prices referred to for constructing the index numbers should be relevant to the purpose and period under study. The retail prices are appropriate for calculating the cost of living index numbers. The prices quoted may be relating to any time – opening, closing, average of day, average of week and other periods. While obtaining the price quotations, the reliability of sources are viewed properly.

(v) Choice of Average : The index numbers are calculated by using the number of averages. The arithmetic average is the most appropriate average for calculating the index numbers. However, the geometric mean possesses some of the important characteristics superior to that of the arithmetic mean.

(vi) System of Weights : The items collected for computing the index numbers are always not of equal importance. To bring all the items in equal importance, weights are properly assigned to each item. The system of weighting the items is of utmost importance in constructing the index numbers. So weights are suitably assigned to each commodity on the basis of quantity consumed, quantity sold, quantity purchased, quantity produced or quantity spent. The weights differ from one item to another according to their use or significance or importance. Generally quantity weights are assigned when the items are varying in quantity while consuming, purchasing or selling. The value weights are assigned when expenditure incurred on different items varies. The assignments of weights bring in the uniformity in the calculation of index numbers.

(vii) Choice of Method : There are various methods used in computing the different types of index numbers. The suitability of each method depends upon the factors such as availability of data, purpose for which index numbers are required and resources at disposal for constructing index numbers. Following are some of the important methods of computing the index numbers:

(a) Simple Aggregative Method.

(b) Weighted Aggregative Method.

(c) Simple Average of Price Relatives Method.

(d) Weighted Average of Price Relatives Method.

Methods of Computation of Index Numbers

- Aggregative
  - Simple
  - Weighted
- Average of Price Relatives
  - Simple
  - Weighted

VII. Methods of Calculating Index Numbers

Let us discuss about the terminologies and notations used in the index number formulas. **'0'** denotes base year. **'1'** denotes current year.

P_{01} = Price Index number for the current year with reference to the base year.

P_{10} = Price Index number for the base year with reference to the current year.

Q_{01} = Quantity Index number for the current year with reference to the base year.

Q10 = Quantity Index number for the base year with reference to the current year.

V_{01} = Value Index number for the current year with reference to the base year.

P_0 = Price of an item in the base year.

P_1 = Price of an item in the current year.

q_0 = Quantity of an item (consumed or purchased) in the base year.

q_1 = Quantity of an item (consumed or purchased) in the current year.

W = Weight assigned to an item with reference to its significance or importance.

(The base year, with which the comparisons of the current year are made, indicates 100)

I = Simple (single item) Index Number or Price Relatives. It is obtained as under,

$$I = \text{Price Relative } \frac{p_1}{p_0} \times 100$$

(a) Simple Aggregative Method : Under this method, the aggregate of prices of various commodities, in a given year, is expressed as a percentage of the same with reference to the base year. Several values of variables are combined together and the index number is obtained by means of an average. The prices of each commodity in a given current year are simply added together to and divided by the total of prices in given base year. The resultant figure is expressed as a percentage.

The formula is, $P_{01} = \frac{\Sigma p_1}{\Sigma p_0} \times 100$

P_{01} = Index Number.

Σp_1 = Aggregate of prices of the current year.

Σp_0 = Aggregate of prices of the base year.

Example 17.1. *Calculate the price index for the years 1991, 1994 and 1997 by using the simple aggregative method on the basis of 1980 from the following data:* (Prices per unit)

Commodities	Units	1980	1991	1994	1997
Rice	Kg	Rs. 10.50	Rs. 12.10	Rs. 14.30	Rs. 18.60
Wheat	Kg	Rs. 9.25	Rs. 11.40	Rs. 12.70	Rs. 13.40
Milk	Liters	Rs. 4.75	Rs. 7.00	Rs. 9.00	Rs. 10.50
Sugar	Kg	Rs. 8.60	Rs. 14.00	Rs. 16.00	Rs. 17.00
Oil	Kg	Rs. 27.50	Rs. 32.00	Rs. 35.00	Rs. 36.50
Pulses	Kg	Rs. 11.20	Rs. 12.80	Rs. 13.10	Rs. 14.00

Solution :

Computation of Index Numbers for the years 1991, 1994 and 1997.

Commodities	Units	1980 p_0	1991 p_1	1994 p_1	1997 p_1
Rice	Kg	Rs. 10.50	Rs. 12.10	Rs. 14.30	Rs. 18.60
Wheat	Kg	Rs. 9.25	Rs. 11.40	Rs. 12.70	Rs. 13.40
Milk	Liters	Rs. 4.75	Rs. 7.00	Rs. 9.00	Rs. 10.50
Sugar	Kg	Rs. 8.60	Rs. 14.00	Rs. 16.00	Rs. 17.00
Oil	Kg	Rs. 27.50	Rs. 32.00	Rs. 35.00	Rs. 36.50
Pulses	Kg	Rs. 11.20	Rs. 12.80	Rs. 13.10	Rs. 14.00
		$\Sigma p_0 = 71.80$	$\Sigma p_1 = 89.30$	$\Sigma p_1 = 100.10$	$\Sigma p_1 = 110.00$

(i) $P_{01} = \frac{\Sigma p_1}{\Sigma p_0} \times 100 = \frac{89.30}{71.80} \times 100 = \mathbf{124.37}$ for 1991.

(ii) $P_{01} = \frac{\Sigma p_1}{\Sigma p_0} \times 100 = \frac{100.10}{71.80} \times 100 = \mathbf{139.42}$ for 1994.

(iii) $P_{01} = \frac{\Sigma p_1}{\Sigma p_0} \times 100 = \frac{110.00}{71.80} \times 100 = \mathbf{153.20}$ for 1997.

(b) Weighted Aggregative Method : Under this method, the appropriate weights are assigned to various commodities to reflect their importance individually in the group. The *'weight'* may refer to the consumption, purchase or production. Generally, quantities are used as weights in computing the price index numbers. The current year prices are multiplied by the base year quantities or weights (p_1q_0). The base year prices are multiplied by the base year quantities (p_0q_0).

The sum of the **'p_1q_0'** is divided by the sum of the **'p_0q_0'** and the resultant is expressed in percentage. The formula is,

$$P_{01} = \frac{\Sigma p_1 q_0}{\Sigma p_0 q_0} \times 100$$

Σp_1q_0= The sum of the products of p_1q_0

Σp_0q_0= The sum of the products of p_0q_0

Example 17.2. *Calculate the weighted aggregative index number for a group of commodities for the year 1991 and 1998 taking the year 1981 as the base year.*

Commodities in the group	Quantity consumed in 1981 (q_0)	(Price per unit Rs.) 1981 (p_0)	1991 (p_1)	1998 (p_1)
Rice	10 kg	11.00	16.50	18.00
Wheat	5 kg	10.20	12.25	14.00
Gram	3 kg	5.00	7.00	9.00
Milk	30 liters	6.70	9.00	10.50
Ghee	4 kg	29.00	32.00	38.00
Sugar	12 kg	8.80	11.30	16.30

Solution :

Computation of Index Numbers for the years 1991 and 1998.

Commodities	Weights q_0	1981 p_0	1991 p_1	1998 p_1	1981 p_0q_0	1991 p_1q_0	1998 p_1q_0
Rice	10	11.00	16.50	18.00	110.00	165.00	180.00
Wheat	5	10.20	12.25	14.00	51.00	61.25	70.00
Gram	3	5.00	7.00	9.00	15.00	21.00	27.00
Milk	30	6.70	9.00	10.50	201.00	270.00	315.00
Ghee	4	29.00	32.00	38.00	116.00	128.00	152.00
Sugar	12	8.80	11.30	16.30	105.60	135.60	195.60
					598.60 $=\Sigma p_0q_0$	780.85 $=\Sigma p_1q_0$	939.60 $=\Sigma p_1q_0$

(i) $P_{01} = \dfrac{\Sigma p_0q_0}{\Sigma p_0q_0} \times 100 = \dfrac{780.85}{598.60} \times 100 = \mathbf{130.45}$ for 1991

(ii) $P_{01} = \dfrac{\Sigma p_1q_0}{\Sigma p_0q_0} \times 100 = \dfrac{939.60}{598.60} \times 100 = \mathbf{156.97}$ for 1998

(c) Simple Average of Price Relatives Method : Under this method, "Price Relatives" (**I**) are obtained for each commodity. All the price relatives added together (**ΣI**). To obtain the index number, the sum of price relatives (**ΣI**) is divided by the number of items (**n**).

A ***price relative*** is an index number of the individual item or commodity in a group. It is the price of the current year expressed as a percentage of the base year (if fixed base year) or the previous year (if chain base year).

The formula is,

i) Fixed Base Year ... $P_{01} = \frac{\Sigma I}{n}$ ... $I = \frac{\textbf{Current Year Price}}{\textbf{Base Year Price}} \times 100 = \frac{p_1}{p_0} \times 100$

ii) Chain Base Year ... $P_{01} = \frac{\Sigma I}{n}$ ... $I = \frac{\text{Current Year Price}}{\text{Pevious Year Price}} \times 100 = \frac{p_1}{p_0} \times 100$

'n' being the number of items

$$\text{Index Number} = P_{01} = \frac{\Sigma I}{n} = \frac{\Sigma\left(\frac{p_1}{p_0} \times 100\right)}{n}$$

Example 17.3. *Compute the price index number for the following data by using a simple average of price relative method by (a) Arithmetic mean and (b) Geometric mean.*

Items :	Bricks	Timber	Board	Sand	Cement
Prices					
1991 :	10	20	5	2	7
1997 :	16	21	6	3	14
1998 :	18	22	7	5	21

Solution: **Computation of Index Number**

Items	1991 p_0	1997 p_1	Price Relatives I (1997)	1998 p_1	Price Relatives I (1998)
Bricks	10	16	$\frac{16}{10} \times 100 = 160$	18	$\frac{18}{10} \times 100 = 180$
Timber	20	21	$\frac{21}{20} \times 100 = 105$	22	$\frac{212}{20} \times 100 = 110$
Board	5	6	$\frac{6}{5} \times 100 = 120$	7	$\frac{7}{5} \times 100 = 140$
Sand	2	3	$\frac{3}{2} \times 100 = 150$	5	$\frac{5}{2} \times 100 = 250$
Cement	7	14	$\frac{14}{7} \times 100 = 200$	21	$\frac{21}{7} \times 100 = 300$
			$\Sigma I = 735$		$\Sigma I = 980$

(a) Using the Arithmetic Mean,

Index No. for 1997

$$P_{01} = \frac{\Sigma I}{n} = \frac{735}{5} = \mathbf{147}$$

Index No. for 1998

$$P_{01} = \frac{\Sigma I}{n} = \frac{980}{5} = \mathbf{196}$$

(b) Using the Geometric Mean,

1997 (I)	Log (I)
160	2.2041
105	2.0212
120	2.0792
150	2.1761
200	2.3010
	$\Sigma \log I = 10.7816$

$$\text{G.M.} = \text{Antilog of } \frac{10.7816}{5}$$

$$= \text{Antilog of } 2.15632$$

$$= \mathbf{143.30}$$

1998 (I)	Log (I)
180	2.2553
110	2.0414
140	2.1461
250	2.3979
300	2.4771
	$\Sigma \log I = 11.3178$

$$\text{G.M.} = \text{Antilog of } \frac{11.3178}{5}$$

$$= \text{Antilog of } 2.2635$$

$$= \mathbf{184.40}$$

(d) Weighted Average of Price Relative Method : Under this method, appropriate weights are assigned to the price relatives according to the importance of each commodity. Multiply the weights (W) by the price relatives (I). We get `IW'product for each commodity. Then obtain the sum of the prodicts (ΣIW) which is divided by the sum of the weights (ΣW). The formula is,

$$P_{01} = \frac{\Sigma IW}{\Sigma W} = \frac{\Sigma\left(\frac{p_1}{p_0} \times 100 \times W\right)}{\Sigma W}$$

Example 17.4. *An enquiry into the budgets of middle class families in Bangalore provides the following information:*

Items	Food	Rent	Clothing	Fuel	Others
Expenses (%)	35	15	20	10	20
Prices 1991.	30	10	20	4	12
Prices 1998.	34.8	12	25	5	18

What changes in the cost of living index number of 1998 have taken place as compared to the year 1991.?

Solution: Computation of Cost of Living Index Number

Items	1991 p_0	1998 p_1	Price Relatives (I)	Weights (W)	IW
Food	30	34.8	$\frac{34.8}{30} \times 100 = 116$	35	4,060
Rent	10	12	$\frac{12}{10} \times 100 = 120$	15	1,800
Clothing	20	25	$\frac{25}{20} \times 100 = 125$	20	2,500
Fuel	4	5	$\frac{5}{4} \times 100 = 125$	10	1,250
Others	12	18	$\frac{18}{12} \times 100 = 150$	20	3,000
				$\Sigma W = 100$	$\Sigma IW = 12{,}610$

$$P_{01} = \frac{\Sigma IW}{\Sigma W} = \frac{12160}{100} = \mathbf{126.10}$$

VIII. (A) Consumer Price Index Number

Consumer price index number (Cost of living index number) is designed to study the effect of changes in prices on the working class families or consumers. It is the ratio of monetary expenditures of an individual which secure for him the same standard of living in two situations differing only in respect of prices. This index number shall be compiled carefully considering the following factors:

(i) Class of People: We have to decide the class of people for which the index number should be prepared. The working class has got different pattern of living as compared to the middle class and the rich class. Even the working class in Mysore has got different pattern of living as compared to the working class in Bangalore or Madras.

(ii) *Base Year :* Generally, the year that is having normal economic activities will be selected as the base year. There should not be any fluctuation in the prices of retail commodities.

(iii) *Family Budget Enquiry:* The consumption pattern of a particular class of people can be ascertained by conducting a family budget enquiry. The enquiry should have been conducted in the base year.

(iv) *Commodities:* The selection of the commodities that are included in the computation of index number is the most important consideration. The family budget enquiry provides for the number of commodities used in the index number. The detailed information about the expenditure of the family on different items will be provided by the enquiry. Generally, the commodities are *Food, Fuel and Lighting, Clothing and Footwear, Housing and Miscellaneous.* The Percentage expenditure on different items constitutes the weightage to be assigned to each item.

(v) *Methods of Computation :* There are two methods of computing the consumer price index number -- Aggregate Expenditure Method and Family Budget Method. Formulas are,

(a) Aggregate Expenditure Method... $\mathbf{P_{01}} = \dfrac{\Sigma \mathbf{p_1 q_0}}{\Sigma \mathbf{p_0 q_0}} \times \mathbf{100}$

(b) Family Budget Method... $\mathbf{P_{01}} = \dfrac{\Sigma \mathbf{IW}}{\Sigma \mathbf{W}}$

These two formulas are discussed already in this chapter. Further, it is noted that the consumer price indices are also used to determine the purchasing power of money and real wages. They are helpful in announcing Dearness Allowance to the employees, in formulating price policies, wage policies and other business policies.

The Aggregate Expenditure Method and Family Budget Method will give us the same result. So we may put the formulas as under, $P_{01} = \dfrac{\Sigma p_1 q_0}{\Sigma p_1 q_0} \times 100 = \dfrac{\Sigma IW}{\Sigma W}$

Let us consider the three items for calculating the consumer price index number as under,

Items	q_0	p_0	p_1	p_0q_0	p_1q_0
A	5	8	15	40	75
B	2	9	12	18	24
C	3	16	20	48	60
				$\Sigma P_0q_0 = 106$	$\Sigma p_1q_0 = 159$

Aggregate Expenditure Method ...

$$P_{01} = \frac{\Sigma p_1q_0}{\Sigma p_0q_0} \times 100 = \frac{159}{106} \times 100 = \mathbf{150}$$

Items	q_0	p_0	p_1	$(p_0 \times q_0)W$	Price Relatives (I)	IW
A	5	8	15	40	$\frac{15}{8} \times 100 = 187.500$	7,500.00
B	2	9	12	18	$\frac{12}{9} \times 100 = 133.333$	2,399.99
C	3	16	20	48	$\frac{20}{16} \times 100 = 125.000$	6,000.00
				$\Sigma W = 106$		$\Sigma IW = 15{,}899.99$

Family Budget Method ...

$$P_{01} = \frac{\Sigma IW}{\Sigma W} = \frac{15{,}899.99}{106} = \mathbf{149.99}$$

(Note : Weight = Expenditure = p_0q_0)

Uses of Consumer Price Index Number.

The consumer price indices are used in solving the various problems by different people in different fields. Following are the uses of consumer price indices,

(i) They are useful in wage negotiatations and settlements. The wages are adjusted and dearness allowances are announced on the bases of these indices.

(ii) They are helpful to the government in forming the wage policy, income policy, price policy, rent control, taxation and general economic policies.

(iii) They are used in measuring the purchasing power of money and real wages or income.

(iv) They are of much use in analysing the markets for particular type of goods and services.

Example 17.5: *An enquiry into the budgets of the Middle class families of a certain city revealed that on an average the percentage of expenses on the different groups were : Food 45, Rent 15, Clothing 12, Fuel and Lighting 8 and Miscellaneous 20 during the year 1981. The group index for the current year 1982, as compared with the base year 1981, were respectively 410, 150, 343, 248 and 285.*

Calculate the consumer price index number for the current year 1982. Mr. X was getting Rs.240 wages in the base year. State how much he should get to maintain his former standard of living during the current year. (BU-A83)

Solution:

Computation of Consumer Price Index Number for 1982

Commodities	Percentage Expenses (W)	Group Index (I)	IW
Food	45	410	18,450
Rent	15	150	2,250
Clothing	12	343	4,116
Fuel and Lighting	8	248	1,984
Miscellaneous	20	285	5,700
	$\Sigma W = 100$		$\Sigma IW = 32{,}500$

$$P_{01} = \text{CPI} = \frac{\Sigma IW}{\Sigma W} = \frac{32{,}500}{100} = \mathbf{325}$$

Mr.X should get the wages in 1982 ... $\frac{325 \times 240}{100}$ = Rs.**780**

[During the base year (100) he is getting Rs.240 and during the current year (325) he should get Rs.780].

Example 17.6. *An enquiry into the budgets of middle class families in Bombay gave the following information :*

Expenses on (1975) :	Food	Rent	Clothing	Fuel	Miscellaneous
	35%	15%	20%	10%	20%
Price Relatives 1976 :	116	120	125	125	150

What changes in the cost of living index of 1976 have taken place as compared to 1975.? How much dearness allowance should be given to a worker who was drawing Rs.200 wages in the base year 1975.? (BU-N83, A95)

Solution :

Computation of consumer Price Index Number for 1976

Items of Expenditure	W	I	IW
Food	35	116	4,060
Rent	15	120	1,800
Clothing	20	125	2,500
Fuel	10	125	1,250
Miscellaneous	20	150	3,000
	$\Sigma W = 100$		$\Sigma IW = 12{,}610$

$$C.L.I = \frac{\Sigma IW}{\Sigma W} = \frac{12{,}610}{100}$$

$= \mathbf{126.10}$.....1976

A worker who was drawing Rs.200 wages in 1975 (100), should get wages in 1976 (126.10) as under:

$$1976\ldots \text{ wages } \frac{126.10 \times 200}{100} = \text{Rs.}252.20$$

Now he is getting in 1976... Rs. 200.00

∴ He should get D.A. Rs. 52.20

Rs. 252.20 D.A. = **Rs. 52.20**

Example 17.7. *An enquiry into the budget of middle class families in Bangalore gave the following information:*

Expenses on (1982) :	Food	Rent	Clothing	Fuel	Miscellaneous
	40%	10%	15%	10%	25%
Price 1982 :	Rs. 300	100	100	40	120
Price 1983 :	Rs. 500	200	300	80	220

What changes in the cost of living index of 1983 have taken place as compared to 1982? (BU-A84)

Solution :

Computation of Consumer Price Index Number for 1983.

Items	W	1982 p_0	1983 p_1	Price Relatives (I)	IW
Food	40	300	500	$\frac{500}{300}\times 100 = 166.67$	6,666.80
Rent	10	100	200	$\frac{200}{100}\times 100 = 200.00$	2,000.00
Clothing	15	100	300	$\frac{300}{100}\times 100 = 300.00$	4,500.00
Fuel	10	40	80	$\frac{80}{40}\times 100 = 200.00$	2,000.00
Miscellaneous	25	120	220	$\frac{220}{120}\times 100 = 183.33$	4,583.25
	$\Sigma W = 100$				$\Sigma IW = 19,750.05$

$$C.P.I = \frac{\Sigma IW}{\Sigma W} = \frac{19.750.05}{100} = \mathbf{197.51}$$

Example 17.8. *Following information relating to workers in industrial town is given:*

Items of Consumption :	Food & Drinks	Clothing	Fuel & Lighting	Housing	Miscellaneous
Group Index in 1985 (Base 1980) :	225	185	150	200	180
Proportion of Expenditure :	50%	10%	10%	15%	15%

Average wage per month in 1980 is Rs.750. What should be the average wage per worker in 1985 in that town so that the standard of living of the workers does not fall below the year 1980 level? (BU-A87,A94)

Solution :

Computation of Consumer Price Index Number for 1985.

Items of Consumption	(1980) proportion of Exp. (W)	Group Index in 1985 (I)	IW
Food & Drinks	50	225	11,250.00
Clothing	10	185	1,850.00
Fuel & Lighting	10	150	1,500.00
Housing	15	200	3.000.00
Miscellaneous	15	180	2,700.00
	ΣW = 100		ΣIW = 20,300.00

$$\text{C.P.I} = \frac{\Sigma IW}{\Sigma W} = \frac{20{,}300}{100} = \mathbf{203} \text{ in } 1985$$

If average wage per month in 1980 (100) is Rs750, the average wage per month in 1985 (203) should be,

$$\text{Average wages in 1985} = \frac{750 \times 203}{100} = \text{Rs.}\mathbf{1,522.50}$$

Example 17.0 *Construct the Price Index Number for 1982 on the basis of 1981 from the following data using:* *(BU-N86)*

(i) Aggregate Expenditure Method and

(ii) Family Budget Method.

Commodity	1981 Quantity Consumed	Unit	Price In 1981	Price In 1982
A	6 quintals	Qunital	5.75	6.00
B	6 quintals	Quintal	5.00	8.00
C	1 qunitals	Quintal	6.00	9.00
D	6 quintals	Quintal	8.00	10.00
E	4 kg	Kg	2.00	1.50
F	1 qunital	Quintal	20.00	15.00

Solution :

(i) Aggregate Expenditure Method

Commodity	q_0	p_0	p_1	p_0q_0	p_1q_0
A	6	5.75	6.00	34.50	36.00
B	6	5.00	8.00	30.00	48.00
C	1	6.00	9.00	6.00	9.00
D	6	8.00	10.00	48.00	60.00
E	4	2.00	1.50	8.00	6.00
F	1	20.00	15.00	20.00	15.00
				Σp_0q_0 = 146.50	Σp_1q_0 = 174.00

$$\text{C.P.I. for 1982} = \frac{\Sigma p_1q_0}{\Sigma p_0q_0}\times 100 = \frac{174}{146.5}\times 100 = \mathbf{118.77}$$

(ii) Family Budget Method

Items	q_0	p_0	W $(p_0 \times q_0)$	p_1	Price Relatives (I)		IW
A	6	5.75	34.50	6.00	$\frac{6}{5.75}\times 100$	104.3478	3,599.99
B	6	5.00	30.00	8.00	$\frac{8}{5}\times 100$	160.0000	4,800.00
C	1	6.00	6.00	9.00	$\frac{9}{6}\times 100$	150.0000	900.00
D	6	8.00	48.00	10.00	$\frac{10}{8}\times 100$	125.0000	6,000.00
E	4	2.00	8.00	1.50	$\frac{1.5}{2}\times 100$	75.0000	600.00
F	1	20.00	20.00	15.00	$\frac{15}{20}\times 100$	75.0000	1,500.00
			ΣW = 146.50				ΣIW = 17399.99

$$\text{C.P.I.} = \frac{\Sigma IW}{\Sigma W} = \frac{17{,}399.99}{146.50} = \mathbf{118.77}$$

Example 17.10. *From the following data, calculate the Index Number:* (BU-N87)

Commodities	1985 Price Per unit	1985 Total Expenditure	1986 Price Per Unit
A	Rs.2	Rs.40	Rs.5
B	Rs.4	Rs.16	Rs.8
C	Rs.1	Rs.10	Rs.2
D	Rs.5	Rs.25	Rs.10

Solution : Base Year expenditure is given (i.e.p_0q_0)

Computation of Consumer Price Index Number for 1986 Commodities

Commodities	* p_0	* q_0	p_1	p_0q_0	p_1q_0
A	2	20	5	40	100
B	4	4	8	16	32
C	1	10	2	10	20
D	5	5	10	25	50
				$\Sigma p_0q_0 = 91$	$\Sigma p_1q_0 = 202$

$$*q_0 \text{ is obtained by, } q_0 = \frac{\text{Expenditure}}{\text{Price}} = \frac{p_0q_0}{p_0}$$

$$\text{C.P.I} = \frac{\Sigma p_1q_0}{\Sigma p_0q_0}\times 100 = \frac{202}{91}\times 100 = \mathbf{221.98}$$

Example 17.11. *The cost of living index number on a certain data was 200. From the base period, the percentage increase in prices were -- Rent Rs.60, clothing Rs.250, Fuel and Light Rs.150 and Miscellaneous Rs.120. The weights for different groups were food 60, Rent 16, clothing 12, Fuel and Light 8 and Miscellaneous 4.*

What was the percentage increase in the food group?

(BU-A88, A97)

Solution :

Computation of cost of living Index Number and Food Item

Items	Base Year (W)	Group Index Numbers (I)	IW
Food	60	(f)	60f
Rent	16	60	960
Clothing	12	250	3,000
Fuel & Light	8	150	1,200
Miscellaneous	4	120	480
	$\Sigma W = 100$		$\Sigma IW = 5{,}640 + 60f$

f = Assumed figure for Food Index Number

$$\text{Cost of Living Index} = \frac{\Sigma IW}{\Sigma W}$$

$$200 = \frac{5640 + 60f}{100}$$

$$5640 + 60f = 20{,}000$$

$$6f = 20{,}000 - 5640 = 14{,}360$$

$$f = \mathbf{239.33}$$

Example 17.12. *Construct a cost of living Index Number for the current year on the basis of the family budget method from the following:*

Articles	Quantity	Unit	Base year Price	Current year Price
Rice	200 kg	Per quintal	200.00	250.00
Wheat	300 kg	Per quintal	250.00	300.00
Jower	100 kg	Per quintal	100.00	150.00
Pulses	20 kg	Per kg	12.00	14.00
Sugar	10 kg	Per kg	3.50	4.00
Oil	4 kg	Per kg	0.50	0.75
Cloth	50 Mtr	Per meter	8.00	12.00
Fuel	15 kg	Per kg	5.00	8.00
Kerosine	1 tin	Per tin	60.00	62.00
Rent	1 House	Per house	400.00	500.00

(Note : 1 quintal = 100 kilograms) (BU –A89)

Solution: Prince of first three items are to be converted into Kq.

Articles	Quantity (q_0)	(p_0)	(p_1)	$\left(\frac{p_1}{p_0} \times 100 = I\right)$	$\left(p_0 q_0 = W\right)$	IW
Rice	200	2.00	2.50	125.00	400	50,000.00
Wheat	300	2.50	3.00	120.00	750	90,000.00
Jowar	100	1.00	1.50	150.00	100	15,000.00
Pulses	20	12.00	14.00	116.67	240	28,000.00
Sugar	10	3.50	4.00	114.29	35	4,000.15
Oil	4	0.50	0.75	150.00	2	300.00
Cloth	50	8.00	12.00	150.00	400	60,000.00
Fuel	15	5.00	8.00	160.00	75	12,000.00
Kerosene	1	60.00	62.00	103.33	60	6,199.80
Rent	1	400.00	500.00	125.00	400	50,000.00
					$\Sigma W =$ 2462	$\Sigma IW =$ 3,51,500.75

$$\text{C.P.I.} = \frac{\Sigma IW}{\Sigma W} = \frac{3{,}15{,}500.75}{2{,}462} = \mathbf{128.15}$$

Example 17.13. *Construct the cost of living index number by using family Budget method for the year 1975 with 1970 as the base year from the following:* *(BU – A90)*

Commodity	A	B	C	D	E
Quantity (units) 1970 :	50	100	60	30	40
Price (per unit) 1970 :	6	2	4	10	8
Price (per unit) 1975 :	10	2	6	12	12

Solution : Computation of Cost of Living Index Number for 1970.

Commodity	q_0	p_0	$p_0 q_0$ (W)	p_1	Price Relatives $\left(\frac{p_1}{p_0} \times 100 = I\right)$	IW
A	50	6	300	10	166.67	50,001
B	100	2	200	2	100.00	20,000
C	60	4	240	6	150.00	36,000
D	30	10	300	12	120.00	36,000
E	40	8	320	12	150.00	48,000
			$\Sigma W =$ 1360			$\Sigma IW =$ 1,90,001

$$\text{C.P.I or C.L.I} = \frac{\Sigma IW}{\Sigma W} = \frac{1{,}90{,}001}{1{,}360} = \mathbf{139.71}$$

Example 17.14. *From the following data calcutale the index number:* (BU – A91)

Commodities :	Food	Rent	Clothing	Fuel
Price Per unit 1989 (Rs.) :	200	300	20	50
Expenditure 1989 (Rs.) :	8,000	4,800	2,000	1,500
Price per unit 1990 (Rs) :	280	345	50	75

Solution : Base year expenditure (i.e.p_0q_0) is given.

Computation of Cconsumer Price Index Number

Commodities	p_0	1989 $*q_0$	1990 p_1	p_0q_0	p_1q_0
Food	200	40	280	8,000	11,200
Rent	300	16	345	4,800	5,520
Clothing	20	100	50	2,000	5,000
Fuel	50	30	75	1,500	2,250
				Σp_0p_0 = 16,300	Σp_1p_0 = 23,970

$*q_0$ is obtained by $q_0 = \frac{\text{Expenditure}}{\text{Price}} = \frac{p_0q_0}{p_0}$

$$\text{C.P.I} = \frac{\Sigma p_1q_0}{\Sigma p_0q_0} \times 100 = \frac{23{,}970}{16{,}300} \times 100 = \mathbf{147.06}$$

Example 17.15. *The data below show the percentage increases in prices of a few selected food items and the weights attached to each of them. Calculate the index number for the food group.*

Food Items :	*Rice*	*Wheat*	*Dal*	*Ghee*	*Oil*
Weights :	*33*	*11*	*8*	*5*	*5*
Increase in Price % :	*180*	*202*	*115*	*212*	*175*
Food Items :	*Spices*	*Milk*	*Fish*	*Veg.*	*Refr.*
Weights :	*3*	*7*	*9*	*9*	*10*
Increase in Price% :	*517*	*260*	*426*	*332*	*279*

Using the above food index and information given below calculate the cost of living index number. *(BU-A96)*

Group :	*Food*	*Clothing*	*Lighting*	*Rent*	*Miscellaneous*
I.No. :	--	*310*	*220*	*150*	*300*
Weight :	*60*	--	*8*	*9*	*18*

Solution :

First, We have to calculate the food index number. The same is substituted in the Group. Weights are assigned and the total is assumed to be 100. So the difference is 5 for clothing.

Calculation of Food Index Number

Food Items	Weights (W)	% Increase	*Current Index (I)	IW
Rice	33	180	280	9,240
Wheat	11	202	302	3,322
Dal	8	115	215	1,720
Ghee	5	212	312	1,560
Oil	5	175	275	1,375
Spices	3	517	617	1,851
Milk	7	260	360	2,520
Fish	9	426	526	4,734
Vegetables	9	332	432	3,888
Refreshments	10	279	379	3,790
	$\Sigma W = 100$			$\Sigma IW = 34,000$

* Current Index is obtained by adding 100 to the percentage increase in the prices of each item.

$$\text{Food Index Number} = \frac{\Sigma IW}{\Sigma W} = \frac{34,000}{100} = \mathbf{340}^{\star}$$

Calculation of Cost of Living Index (Substitute Food Index Number 340)

Group	Index (I)	Weights (W)	IW
Food	340✩	60	20,400
Clothing	310	5♦	1,550
Lighting	220	8	1,760
Rent	150	9	1,350
Miscellaneous	300	18	5,400
		$\Sigma W = 100$	$\Sigma IW = 30,460$

[(*100 – 95)] $$\text{C.L.I} = \frac{\Sigma IW}{\Sigma W} = \frac{30{,}460}{100} = \mathbf{304.60}$$

Example 17.16. *The relative importance of the following 8 groups of family expenditure was found to be.*

Food	Rent	Clothing	Fuel & Light	House hold	Miscella neous	Services	Drink & Tobacco
348	88	97	65	71	35	79	217

The corresponding increase in price for February, 1992. based on January, 92, gave the following 8 percentage values respectively,

25, 01, 22, 18, 14, 13, 11 and 04

Calculate the average percentage increase for the whole group. (BU-A93)

Solution :

Family expenditure gives the weights, Index numbers for each item will be obtained by adding 100 to the percentage increase in price.

Computation of Consumer Price Index Number Commodities

Commodities	Weights (W)	Index No. (I)	IW
Food	348	125	43,500
Rent	88	101	8,888
Clothing	97	122	11,834
Fuel and Light	65	118	7,670
Household Goods	71	114	8,094
Miscellaneous	35	113	3,955
Service	79	111	8,769
Drinks & Tobacco	217	104	22,568
	ΣW = 1000		ΣIW = 1,15,278

Cost of living Index No. for February 1992

$$= \frac{\Sigma IW}{\Sigma W} = \frac{1{,}15{,}278}{1{,}000} = \mathbf{115.28}$$

Example 17.17. *A textile worker earns Rs.350 per month. The cost of living index for that particular month is known as 136.*

Using the following data find the amounts spent by him on house rent and clothing. (BU N-92, N96)

Group :	Food	Clothing	House Rent	Fuel	Miscellaneous
Expenditure (Rs.) :	140	?	?	56	63
Group Index :	180	150	100	110	80

Solution : Assume the amounts spent on Clothing and House Rent as `A' and `B' respectively. The total wages spent will also be assumed as his total earnings. Thus we can have the following equation.

$$140 + A + B + 56 + 63 = 350$$

$$A + B + 259 = 350$$

$$A + B = 350 - 259$$

$$\text{(i)}.... \mathbf{A + B = 91}$$

Computation of Cost of Living Index.

Group	Expenditure (W)	I	IW
Food	140	180	25,200
Clothing	A	150	(150 A)
H. Rent	B	100	(100 B)
Fuel	56	110	6,160
Misscelaneous	63	80	5,040
	ΣW = 350		ΣIW = 36,400 + 150A + 100B

$$C.L.I = \frac{\Sigma IW}{\Sigma W}$$

$$136 = \frac{36,400 + 150A + 100B}{350}$$

$$47,600 = 36,400 + 150A + 100B$$

$$150A + 100B = 47,600 - 36,400$$

$$\text{(ii)} .... \mathbf{150A + 100B = 11,200}$$

Using the simultaneous equations and multiplying equation (i) by 100, we get,

$$150A + 100B = 11{,}200$$
$$(-)\ 100A + 100B = 9{,}100$$
$$50A = 2{,}100$$
$$\mathbf{A = 42}$$

Substitute 'a' value in

$$A + B = 91$$
$$42 + B = 91$$
$$B = 91 - 42$$
$$\mathbf{B = 49}$$

Thus, the worker has spent **Rs.42** on Clothing and **Rs.49** on House Rent.

Example 17.18. *A worker earns Rs.750 p.m. The cost the living for January, 1989, is given as 160. Using the following data find out the amounts he has spent on (i) Food and (ii) Rent.* *(BU-A92)*

Group :	Food	Clothing	Rent	Fuel & Light	Miscellaneous
Expenditure (Rs.) :	?	125	?	100	75
Group Index (Rs.) :	190	181	140	118	101

Solution : Assume the amounts spent on Food and Rent as 'A' and 'B' respectively. The total earnings will be assumed as spent on all the items. Thus we can have the following equation:

$$A + 125 + B + 100 + 75 = 750$$
$$A + B + 300 = 750$$
$$A + B = 750 - 300$$
$$\textbf{(i) .... } \mathbf{A + B = 450}$$

Computation of Cost of Living Index

Group	Expenditure (W)	I	IW
Food	A	190	(190A)
Clothing	125	181	22,625
Rent	B	140	(140 B)
Fuel & Light	100	118	11,800
Misscelaneous	75	101	7,757
	$\Sigma W = 750$		$\Sigma IW = 42{,}000 + 190A + 140B$

$$C.L.I = \frac{\Sigma IW}{\Sigma W}$$

$$160 = \frac{42,000 + 190A + 140B}{750}$$

$$1,20,000 = 42,000 + 190A + 140B$$

$$190A + 140B = 1,20,000 - 42,000$$

$$\textbf{(ii) .... } \mathbf{190A + 140B = 78,000}$$

Using the simultaneous equations and multiplying equation (i) by 140, we get

$$\begin{array}{r} 190 \quad + 140B = 78,000 \\ (-)\ 140A + 140B = 63,000 \\ \hline 50A = 15,000 \\ A = \mathbf{300} \end{array}$$

Substitute 'A' value in

$$A + B = 450$$

$$300 + B = 450$$

$$B = 450 - 300$$

$$B = \mathbf{150}$$

Thus, the worker has spent Rs.300 on Food and Rs.150 on Rent .

Purchasing Power of Money

The value of money goes on changing from time to time with the changes in the price line. If the price line rises, the value of money comes down, and vice versa. The purchasing power of money index indicates the value of money rather than the number of rupees required to buy a specified quantity. For example, if the price index is Rs.185, it means we have to pay Rs.85 more to buy the quantity of goods that was brought in the base year.

$$\text{Purchasing Power of Money } \frac{100}{\text{Price Index}} = \frac{100}{185} = \mathbf{0.54} \text{ Paise}$$

Index Number also serves as an important tool in transforming the money income into the real income. The real income is expressed in terms of value of money. It is obtained by dividing the money income by the appropriate Price Index. This process is called **"statistical deflation"**.

$$\text{Real Income (wage)} = \frac{\text{Money Income (wage)}}{\text{Price Index}} \times 100$$

Example 17.19. *From the figures given below calculate the index number of real wages taking 1981 base :* *(BU-A84)*

Year	*Average Monthly wages (Rs.)*	*C. P. Index (Base 1981)*
1981	*240*	*100*
1982	*264*	*240*
1983	*286*	*260*

Solution :

Year	Wages	I. No.	Conversion	Real Wage	Conversion	Real Wage Index
1981	240	100	$\frac{240}{100}\times 100$	240	--	100
1982	264	240	$\frac{264}{240}\times 100$	110	$\frac{110}{240}\times 100$	45.83
1983	286	260	$\frac{286}{260}\times 100$	110	$\frac{110}{240}\times 100$	45.83

(B) Weighted Aggregative Methods

We have already studied the weighted aggregative method in this chapter. The formula used is,

$$P_{01} = \frac{\Sigma p_1 q_0}{\Sigma p_0 q_0} \times 100$$

In the above formula, we have considered the quantity in base year as the weight assigned in computation (i.e., q_0). There are other systems of assigning the weights considered by different experts. Let us study these formulas as under,

(1) Laspeyre's Method : Under this method, as already explained, the base year quantities are used as weights. The formula is,

$$P_{01} = \frac{\Sigma p_1 q_0}{\Sigma p_0 q_0} \times 100$$

Laspeyre, the French Economist, devised the above formula in 1871 for calculating the index number. He took the base year quantities as weights assigned to prices.

(2) Paasche's Method : Under this method, the current year quantities are used as weights. The formula is

$$P_{01} = \frac{\Sigma p_1 q_1}{\Sigma p_0 q_1} \times 100$$

Paasche, the German Statistician, introduced the above formula in 1874 for calculating the index number. He took the current year quantities as weights assigned to prices.

(3) Marshall – Edgeworth's Method : Under this method the quantities of base year and the current year are averaged and the average is taken as the weights. The formula is

$$P_{01} = \frac{\Sigma p_1 \left(\frac{q_0 + q_1}{2}\right)}{\Sigma p_0 \left(\frac{q_0 + q_1}{2}\right)} \times 100 = \frac{\Sigma p_1 q_0 + \Sigma p_1 q_1}{\Sigma p_0 q_0 + \Sigma p_0 q_1} \times 100$$

Marshall – Edgeworth, the two economists considered both the current year as well as the base year quantities as weights to avoid the controversy with respect to fixation of weights. This method considers the ratio of the sum of the numerators of Laspeyre's and Paasche's method to the sum of their denominators.

(4) Fisher's Method : **Prof. Irving Fisher,** considered both the Laspeyre's Method and the Paasche's Method, and applied the geometric mean (i.e., the root of the product of both the methods). He attempted to find an ideal index number as it confirms the tests of consistency and behaviour. That is why his formula is called "Fisher's Ideal Formula". It is also called a "cross – weight" formula shown as under,

$$P_{01} = \sqrt{\frac{\Sigma p_1 q_0}{\Sigma p_0 q_0} \times \frac{\Sigma p_1 q_1}{\Sigma p_0 q_1}} \times 100$$

Fisher's formula is considered to be an ideal formula of calculating the index number because,

(i) It is based on the appropriate average for index number i.e., the geometric mean.

(ii) It considers the quantities of both the base year and current year

(iii) It is free from bias, as it satisfies the two tests :

(a) Time Reversal Test.

(b) Factor Reversal Test.

The formula obeys the Time Reversal Test and the Factor Reversal Test (without the use of 100). These two tests are the real tools of confirming the formula as an ideal method of index number. Reversability means changing the base year to the current year and current year to the base year or changing the place of the prices in the place of quantities and the place of the quantities in the place of the prices. The system of 'reciprocal' is applied in tests.

An idea formula ought to permit interchanging the prices and quantities or the base year and current year without giving inconsistent result. Arithmetic average of relatives has no such reversability character or test. Geometric Mean of relatives has the reversability test. The Fisher's Index Number satisfies the reversability tests.

(a) Time Reversal Test : The formula should give the same ratio, if the index number reckoned either forward or backward. The formula should work both ways – Base year to Current year and Current year to Base year – resulting into the same ratio. It should give the same ratio between one point of comparison and the other, no matter which of the two is taken as base. When the formula is recknoed forward, it should be the reciprocal of that when reckoned backward (without 100). This can be presented in the form of equation as under,

$$P_{01} \times P_{10} = \sqrt{\frac{\Sigma p_1 q_0}{\Sigma p_0 q_0} \times \frac{\Sigma p_1 q_1}{\Sigma p_0 q_1}} \times \sqrt{\frac{\Sigma p_0 q_1}{\Sigma p_1 q_1} \times \frac{\Sigma p_0 q_0}{\Sigma p_1 q_0}}$$

$$= \sqrt{\frac{\Sigma p_1 q_0}{\Sigma p_0 q_0} \times \frac{\Sigma p_1 q_1}{\Sigma p_0 q_1} \times \frac{\Sigma p_0 q_1}{\Sigma p_1 q_1} \times \frac{\Sigma p_0 q_0}{\Sigma p_1 q_0}} = \sqrt{1} = \mathbf{1}$$

(without 100)

P_{01} = Price index for current year on the base year.

P_{10} = Price index for base year (treating as current year) on the current year (treating as base year).

(b) Factor Reversal Test : The formula should give the true value ratio, if the price index number is multiplied by the quantity index number. The Factor Reversal Test (interchanging the price and quantity) holds that the product of the price index number and the corresponding quantity index number should accurately measure the relative total value (without 100). The formula ought to permit interchange of the prices and quantities (i.e., the two factors) without giving inconsistent results. This can be presented in the form of equation as under,

$$P_{01} \times Q_{01} = \sqrt{\frac{\Sigma p_1 q_0}{\Sigma p_0 q_0} \times \frac{\Sigma p_1 q_1}{\Sigma p_0 q_1}} \times \sqrt{\frac{\Sigma p_0 q_1}{\Sigma p_0 q_0} \times \frac{\Sigma p_1 q_1}{\Sigma p_1 q_0}}$$

$$= \sqrt{\frac{\Sigma p_1 q_0}{\Sigma p_0 q_0} \times \frac{\Sigma p_1 q_1}{\Sigma p_0 q_1} \times \frac{\Sigma p_0 q_1}{\Sigma p_0 q_o} \times \frac{\Sigma p_1 q_1}{\Sigma p_1 q_0}}$$

$$= \sqrt{\frac{\Sigma p_1 q_1}{\Sigma p_0 q_0} \times \frac{\Sigma p_1 q_1}{\Sigma p_0 q_0}} = \frac{\boldsymbol{\Sigma p_1 q_1}}{\boldsymbol{\Sigma p_0 q_0}} \quad \text{(.... without 100)}$$

P_{01} = Price index for current year on the base year

Q_{01} = Quantity index for current year on the base year

Let us consider the following illustration in which we can see the confirmity of reversability tests and the suitability of the geometric average.

Commodities	Base year		Current year		p_0q_0	p_1q_0	p_0q_1	p_1q_1
	q_0	p_0	q_1	p_1				
A	8	5	11	7	40	56	55	77
B	12	3	13	6	36	72	39	78
					76	128	34	155
					Σp_0q_0	Σp_1q_0	Σp_0q_1	Σp_1q_1

1. *Laspeyre's Method :*

$$P_{01} = \frac{\Sigma p_1q_0}{\Sigma p_0q_0} \times 100 = \frac{128}{76} \times 100 = \mathbf{168.4211}$$

2. *Paasche's Method :*

$$P_{01} = \frac{\Sigma p_1q_1}{\Sigma p_0q_0} \times 100 = \frac{155}{94} \times 100 = \mathbf{164.8936}$$

3. *Marshall-Edgeworth's Method :*

$$P_{01} = \frac{\Sigma p_1q_0 + \Sigma p_1q_1}{\Sigma p_0q_0 + \Sigma p_0q_1} \times 100 = \frac{128+155}{76+94} \times 100$$

$$= \frac{283}{170} \times 100 = \mathbf{166.4706}$$

4. *Fisher's Ideal Method :*

$$P_{01} = \sqrt{\frac{\Sigma p_1q_0}{\Sigma p_0q_0} \times \frac{\Sigma p_1q_1}{\Sigma p_0q_1}} \times 100 = \sqrt{\frac{128}{76} \times \frac{155}{94}} \times 100$$

$$= \sqrt{1.684211 \times 1.648936} \times 100 = \sqrt{2.7771561} \times 100$$

$$= \mathbf{166.6480}$$

(a) Time Reversal Test $(P_{01} \times P_{10} = 1)$.... Without '100'

1. **Laspeyre's Method : $P_{01} \times P_{10} =$**

$$= \frac{\Sigma p_1q_0}{\Sigma p_0q_0} \times \frac{\Sigma p_1q_1}{\Sigma p_0q_1} = \frac{128}{76} \times \frac{94}{155}$$

$$= 1.6842 \times 0.6065 = \mathbf{0.3601}\ (\neq \mathbf{1})$$

2. Paasche's Method :

$$P_{01} \times P_{10} = \frac{\Sigma p_1q_1}{\Sigma p_0q_1} \times \frac{\Sigma p_0q_0}{\Sigma p_1q_0} = \frac{155}{94} \times \frac{76}{128}$$

$$= 1.648936 \times 0.59375 = \mathbf{0.97906}\ (\neq \mathbf{1})$$

3. Marshal-Edgeworth's Method :

$$P_{01} \times P_{10} = \frac{\Sigma p_1q_0 + \Sigma p_1q_1}{\Sigma p_0q_0 + \Sigma p_0q_1} \times \frac{\Sigma p_0q_1 + \Sigma p_0q_0}{\Sigma p_1q_1 + \Sigma p_1q_0}$$

$$= \frac{128 + 155}{76 + 94} \times \frac{94 + 76}{155 + 128} = \frac{283}{170} \times \frac{170}{283} = \mathbf{1}$$

4. Fisher's Ideal Method :

$$P_{01} \times P_{10} = \sqrt{\frac{\Sigma p_1q_0}{\Sigma p_0q_0} \times \frac{\Sigma p_1q_1}{\Sigma p_0q_1} \times \frac{\Sigma p_0q_1}{\Sigma p_1q_1} \times \frac{\Sigma p_0q_0}{\Sigma p_1q_0}} = \sqrt{1} = \mathbf{1}$$

(Note : The numerators and denominators are settled by multiplication)

Thus, the two methods – Marshall – Edgeworth's and Fisher's – satisfy the Time Reversal Test. So (P_{01}) should be the reciprocal of (P_{10}).

(b) Factor Reversal Test :

$$\left(P_{01} \times Q_{01} = \frac{\Sigma p_1q_1}{\Sigma p_0q_0} = \frac{155}{76} = \mathbf{2.03947}\right) \text{...... without 100}$$

1. Laspeyer's Method :

$$P_{01} \times Q_{01} = \frac{\Sigma p_1q_0}{\Sigma p_0q_0} \times \frac{\Sigma p_0q_1}{\Sigma p_0q_0} = \frac{128}{76} \times \frac{94}{76}$$

$$= 1.684211.236842 = \mathbf{2.083103}\ (\text{not in true ratio})$$

2. **Paasche's Method :**

$$P_{01} \times Q_{01} = \frac{\Sigma p_1 q_1}{\Sigma p_0 q_1} \times \frac{\Sigma p_1 q_1}{\Sigma p_1 q_0} = \frac{155}{94} \times \frac{155}{128}$$

$$= 1.648936 \times 1.2109375 = \mathbf{1.996758} \text{ (not in true ratio)}$$

3. **Marshall- Edgewordth's Method :**

$$P_{01} \times Q_{01} = \frac{\Sigma p_1 q_0 + \Sigma p_1 q_1}{\Sigma p_0 q_0 + \Sigma p_0 q_1} \times \frac{\Sigma p_0 q_1 + \Sigma p_1 q_1}{\Sigma p_0 q_0 + \Sigma p_1 q_0}$$

$$= \frac{128 + 155}{76 + 94} \times \frac{94 + 155}{76 + 128} = \frac{283}{170} \times \frac{249}{204}$$

$$= 1.664706 \times 1.220588 = \mathbf{2.03192} \text{ (not in true ratio)}$$

4. **Fisher's Method :**

$$P_{01} \times Q_{01} = \sqrt{\frac{\Sigma p_1 q_0}{\Sigma p_0 q_0} \times \frac{\Sigma p_1 q_1}{\Sigma p_0 q_1} \times \frac{\Sigma p_0 q_1}{\Sigma p_0 q_0} \times \frac{\Sigma p_1 q_1}{\Sigma p_1 q_0}}$$

$$= \sqrt{\frac{\Sigma p_1 q_1}{\Sigma p_0 q_0} \times \frac{\Sigma p_1 q_1}{\Sigma p_0 q_0}} = \frac{\Sigma p_1 q_1}{\Sigma p_0 q_0} \text{ (It is in true ratio)}$$

Thus, only the Fisher's Method satisfies the Factor Reversal Test. So, the Fisher's method satisfies both the tests – Time as well as Factor Reversal Test.

(c) Suitability of Geometric Mean

Index Number (using G.M.)

Two I. No.	log P_{01}	
$P_{01} = \frac{\Sigma p_1 q_0}{\Sigma p_0 q_0} \times 100 = \mathbf{168.4211}$	2.2263	$G.M = \text{Anti log} \frac{4.4432}{2}$
$P_{01} = \frac{\Sigma p_0 q_1}{\Sigma p_0 q_1} \times 100 = \mathbf{164.8936}$	2.2169	$= \text{Anti log } 2.2216 = \mathbf{166.5}$
	$\Sigma \log P_{01} = 4.4432$	

Summary of fisher's Index Number (T.R.T)

$$P_{01} = \sqrt{\frac{128}{76} \times \frac{155}{94}} \times 100 = \mathbf{166.6480}$$

$$P_{10} = \sqrt{\frac{94}{155} \times \frac{76}{128}} \times 100 = \mathbf{60.0067}$$

Index No.	Base year	Current year	Increase / Decrease (%)	For base year	Computation	Result
P_{01}	100	166.6480	+66.6480%	100	$\frac{100 \times 66.6480}{100}$	+66.6480
P_{10}	100	60.00671	-39.9933%	166.6480	$\frac{166.648 \times 39.9933}{100}$	-66.6480

Reciprocal of 1.666480 = 0.600671. ... (without 100)
Reciprocal of 0.600671 = 1.66480 ... (without 100)
(without 100 index number)

Example 17.19. *The following information relates to the weekly pay of the wage earners of a company.*

Age in years	*April, 1980 Number*	*Total pay (Rs)*	*April, 1981 Number*	*Total pay (Rs.)*
Men above 21	*350*	*2,500*	*300*	*4,200*
Women above 18	*400*	*1,600*	*1,200*	*8,000*
Youths (Boys)	*150*	*450*	*100*	*560*
Youths (Girls)	*100*	*250*	*400*	*1,540*

You are required to construct an index of weekly earnings by using : (BU – N93)

(i) *Base Year Weighting, and*

(ii) *Current Year Weighting*

Solution : Computation of Index of Weekly Earnings

April 1980 No. (q_0)	April 1980 Pay (p_0)	April 1981 No. (q_1)	April 1981 Pay (p_1)
350	2,500	300	4,200
400	1,600	1,200	8,000
150	450	100	560
100	250	400	1,540

p_0q_0	p_1q_0	p_0q_1	p_1q_1
8,75,000	14,70,000	7,50,000	12,60,000
6,40,000	32,00,000	19,20,000	96,00,000
67,500	84,000	45,000	56,000
25,000	1,54,000	1,00,000	6,16,000
16,07,500	49,08,000	28,15,000	1,15,32,000
$\Sigma p_0q_0 =$	$\Sigma p_1q_0 =$	$\Sigma p_0q_1 =$	$\Sigma p_1q_1 =$

(i) Base year weighted Index Number

(Laspeyre's Method)

$$P_{01} = \frac{\Sigma p_1 q_0}{\Sigma p_0 q_0} \times 100 = \frac{49,08,000}{16,07,500} \times 100 = \mathbf{305.3188}$$

(ii) Current year weighted Index Number

(Paasche's Method)

$$P_{01} = \frac{\Sigma p_1 q_1}{\Sigma p_0 q1} \times 100 = \frac{1,15,32,000}{28,15,000} \times 100 = \mathbf{409.6625}$$

Example 17.20. *Calculate from the following data the Fisher's Index Number :* (BU – N84)

Items	*Price*		*Quantity*	
	1975 (p_0)	*1983* (p_1)	*1975* (q_0)	*1983* (q_1)
A	*16*	*40*	*100*	*120*
B	*4*	*12*	*30*	*20*
C	*2*	*4*	*40*	*50*
D	*4*	*10*	*20*	*16*
E	*2*	*10*	*80*	*60*

Solution : Computation of Fisher's Ideal Index Number

Items	*Price*		*Quantity*	
	(p_0)	(p_1)	(q_0)	(q_1)
A	*16*	*40*	*100*	*120*
B	*4*	*12*	*30*	*20*
C	*2*	*4*	*40*	*50*
D	*4*	*10*	*20*	*16*
E	*2*	*10*	*80*	*60*

p_1q_0	p_0q_0	p_1q_1	p_0q_1
4,000	1600	4800	1920
360	120	240	80
160	80	200	100
200	80	160	64
800	160	600	120
= 5520	= 2,040	= 6,000	= 2,484
$\Sigma p_1 q_0$	$\Sigma p_0 q_0$	$\Sigma p_1 q_1$	$\Sigma p_0 q_1$

Fisher's Index Number :

$$P_{01} = \sqrt{\frac{\Sigma p_1 q_0}{\Sigma p_0 q_0} \times \frac{\Sigma p_1 q_1}{\Sigma p_0 q_1}} \times 100 = \sqrt{\frac{5520}{2040} \times \frac{6000}{2,284}} \times 100$$

$$= \sqrt{2.70588 \times 2.627} \times 100 = \sqrt{7.10835} \times 100$$

$$= 2.66615 \times 100 = \mathbf{266.615}$$

Example 17.21. *Calculate Fisher's Index Number from the data given below and show that it satisfies the Time Reversal Test and Factor Reversal Test.* *(BU-A85)*

Commodities:	*A*	*B*	*C*	*D*	*E*
1982 Price :	*10*	*12*	*18*	*20*	*22*
Quantity :	*49*	*25*	*10*	*5*	*8*
1983 Price :	*12*	*15*	*20*	*40*	*45*
Quantity :	*50*	*20*	*12*	*2*	*5*

Solution : Computation of Fisher's Ideal Index Number

Items	*1982*		*1983*	
	q_0	p_0	q_1	p_1
A	*49*	*10*	*50*	*12*
B	*25*	*12*	*20*	*15*
C	*10*	*18*	*12*	*20*
D	*5*	*20*	*2*	*40*
E	*8*	*22*	*5*	*45*

p_1q_0	p_0q_0	p_1q_1	p_0q_1
588	490	600	500
375	300	300	240
200	180	240	216
200	100	80	40
360	176	225	110
= 1723	= 1,246	= 1,445	= 1,106
Σp_1q_0	Σp_0q_0	Σp_1q_1	Σp_0q_1

Fisher's Ideal Index Number :

$$P_{01} = \sqrt{\frac{\Sigma p_1q_0}{\Sigma p_0q_0} \times \frac{\Sigma p_1q_1}{\Sigma p_0q_1}} \times 100 = \sqrt{\frac{1723}{1246} \times \frac{1445}{1106}} \times 100$$

$$= \sqrt{1.382825 \times 1.30651} \times 100 = \sqrt{1.8066746} \times 100$$

$$= 1.344126 \times 100 = \mathbf{134.4126}$$

(1) Time Reversal Test : This test is satisfied when, $P_{01} \times P_{10} = 1$

$$P_{01} \times P_{10} = \sqrt{\frac{\Sigma p_1q_0}{\Sigma p_0q_o} \times \frac{\Sigma p_1q_1}{\Sigma p_0q_1}} \times \sqrt{\frac{\Sigma p_0q_1}{\Sigma p_1q_1} \times \frac{\Sigma p_0q_0}{\Sigma p_1q_0}}$$

$$= \sqrt{\frac{1723}{1246} + \frac{1445}{1106} \times \frac{1106}{1445} \times \frac{1246}{1723}} = \sqrt{1} = \mathbf{1}$$

(2) Factor Reversal Test : This test is satisfied when

$$P_{01} \times Q_{01} = \frac{\Sigma p_1q_1}{\Sigma p_0q_0}$$

$$P_{01} \times Q_{01} = \sqrt{\frac{\Sigma p_1q_0}{\Sigma p_0q_0} \times \frac{\Sigma p_1q_1}{\Sigma p_0q_1}} \times \sqrt{\frac{\Sigma p_0q_1}{\Sigma p_0q_0} \times \frac{\Sigma p_1q_1}{\Sigma p_1q_0}}$$

$$= \sqrt{\frac{1723}{1246} \times \frac{1445}{1106} \times \frac{1106}{1246} \times \frac{1445}{1723}}$$

$$= \sqrt{\frac{1445}{1246} \times \frac{1445}{1246}} = \frac{1445}{1246} = \frac{\mathbf{\Sigma p_1q_1}}{\mathbf{\Sigma p_0q_0}}$$

Example 17.22. *Construct the Index Number using the Fisher's Ideal Formula and show how it satisfies Factor Reversal Test.*

(BU-N85)

Commodities		*A*	*B*	*C*	*D*	*E*
(Values in Rs.)	:					
Base year	:	*300*	*200*	*240*	*300*	*320*
Current year	:	*560*	*240*	*360*	*288*	*432*
Quantity (Base year)	:	*53*	*100*	*60*	*30*	*40*
Price (Current year)	:	*10*	*6*	*2*	*12*	*12*

Solution : In the above problem Base Year and Current Year values are given. We have to obtain the Base Year Prices and Current Year Quantities.

Computation Fisher's Ideal Index Number

Commodities	Values		q_0
	p_0q_0	p_1q_1	
A	300	560	53
B	200	240	100
C	240	360	60
D	300	288	30
E	320	432	40
	1360	1,880	
	$\Sigma p_0q_0 =$	$\Sigma p_1q_1 =$	

$\left(\frac{p_0q_0}{q_0}\right)$ p_0	p_1	$\left(\frac{p_1q_1}{p_1}\right)$ q_1	p_1q_0	p_0q_1
5.6604	10	56	530	317
2.0000	6	40	600	80
4.0000	2	180	120	720
10.0000	12	24	360	240
8.0000	12	36	480	288
			= 2090	= 1645
			Σp_1q_0	Σp_0q_1

Fisher's Index Number :

$$P_{01} = \sqrt{\frac{\Sigma p_1q_0}{\Sigma p_0q_0} \times \frac{\Sigma p_1q_1}{\Sigma p_0q_1}} \times 100 = \sqrt{\frac{2090}{1360} \times \frac{1880}{1645}} \times 100$$

$$= \sqrt{1.536765 \times 1.14286} \times 100 = \sqrt{1.75631} \times 100$$

$$= 1.325258 \times 100 = \mathbf{132.5258}$$

Factor Reversal Test : This test is satisfied when

$$P_{01} \times Q_{01} = \frac{\Sigma p_1q_1}{\Sigma p_0q_0}$$

$$P_{01} \times Q_{01} = \sqrt{\frac{\Sigma p_1 q_0}{\Sigma p_0 q_0} \times \frac{\Sigma p_1 q_1}{\Sigma p_0 q_1}} \times \sqrt{\frac{\Sigma p_0 q_1}{\Sigma p_0 q_0} \times \frac{\Sigma p_1 q_1}{\Sigma p_1 q_0}}$$

$$= \sqrt{\frac{2090}{1360} \times \frac{1880}{1645} \times \frac{1645}{1360} \times \frac{1880}{2090}}$$

$$= \sqrt{\frac{1880}{1360} \times \frac{1880}{1360}} = \frac{1880}{1360} = \frac{\Sigma p_1 q_1}{\Sigma p_0 q_0}$$

Example 17.23. *Calculate Fisher's Index Number from the data given below and show that it satisfies the Time Reversal Test and the Factor Reversal Test :* *(BU-A86, A98)*

Commodities	:	*A*	*B*	*C*	*D*	*E*
Base Year (Price)	:	*6*	*2*	*4*	*10*	*8*
Base Year Quantity	:	*50*	*100*	*60*	*30*	*40*
Current Year (Price)	:	*10*	*2*	*6*	*12*	*12*
Current Year Quantity	:	*56*	*120*	*60*	*24*	*36*

Solution : Computation of Fisher's Ideal Index Number

Commodity	Base Year		Current Year	
	q_0	p_0	q_1	p_1
A	50	6	56	10
B	100	2	120	2
C	60	4	60	6
D	30	10	24	12
E	40	8	36	12

p_1q_0	p_0q_0	p_1q_1	p_0q_1
500	300	560	336
200	200	240	240
360	240	360	240
360	300	288	240
480	320	432	288
= 1,900	= 1,360	= 1,880	= 1,344
Σp_1q_0	Σp_0q_0	Σp_1q_1	Σp_0q_1

Fisher's Index Number :

$$P_{01} = \sqrt{\frac{\Sigma p_1 q_0}{\Sigma p_0 q_0} \times \frac{\Sigma p_1 q_1}{\Sigma p_0 q_1}} \times 100 = \sqrt{\frac{1900}{1360} \times \frac{1880}{1344}} \times 100$$

$$= \sqrt{1.397059 \times 1.3988095} \times 100 = \sqrt{1.9542194} \times 100$$

$$= 1.3979339 \times 100 = \mathbf{139.7934}$$

(1) Time Reversal Test : This test is satisfied when,

$$P_{01} \times P_{10} = 1$$

$$P_{01} \times P_{10} = \sqrt{\frac{\Sigma p_1 q_0}{\Sigma p_0 q_0} \times \frac{\Sigma p_1 q_1}{\Sigma p_0 q_1}} \times \sqrt{\frac{\Sigma p_0 q_1}{\Sigma p_1 q_1} \times \frac{\Sigma p_0 q_0}{\Sigma p_1 q_0}}$$

$$= \sqrt{\frac{1900}{1360} \times \frac{1880}{1344} \times \frac{1344}{1880} \times \frac{1360}{1990}} = \sqrt{1} = \mathbf{1}$$

(2) Factor Reversal Test : This test is satisfied when,

$$P_{01} \times Q_{01} = \frac{\Sigma p_1 q_1}{\Sigma p_0 q_0}$$

$$P_{01} \times Q_{01} = \sqrt{\frac{\Sigma p_1 q_0}{\Sigma p_0 q_0} \times \frac{\Sigma p_1 q_1}{\Sigma p_0 q_1}} \times \sqrt{\frac{\Sigma p_0 q_1}{\Sigma p_0 q_0} \times \frac{\Sigma p_1 q_1}{\Sigma p_1 q_0}}$$

$$= \sqrt{\frac{1900}{1360} \times \frac{1880}{1344} \times \frac{1344}{1360} \times \frac{1880}{1900}}$$

$$= \sqrt{\frac{1880}{1360} \times \frac{1880}{1360}} = \frac{1880}{1360} = \frac{\mathbf{\Sigma p_1 q_1}}{\mathbf{\Sigma p_0 q_0}}$$

Example 17.24. *From the following data construct an appropriate index number :* *(BU-N89)*

Commodities	:	*Wheat*	*Gram*	*Jowar*
Prices (1985)	:	*4*	*3*	*2*
Prices (1988)	:	*10*	*8*	*4*
Quantity (1985)	:	*50*	*10*	*5*
Quantity (1988)	:	*40*	*8*	*4*

***Solution* : Computation of Fisher's Ideal Index Number**

Commodities	1985		1988	
	q_0	p_0	q_1	p_1
Wheat	50	4	40	10
Gram	10	3	8	8
Jowar	5	2	4	4

p_1q_0	p_0q_0	p_1q_1	p_0q_1
500	200	400	160
80	30	64	24
20	10	16	8
= 600	= 240	= 480	= 192
Σp_1q_0	Σp_0q_0	Σp_1q_1	Σp_0q_1

Fisher's Index Number :

$$P_{01} = \sqrt{\frac{\Sigma p_1q_0}{\Sigma p_0q_0} \times \frac{\Sigma p_1q_1}{\Sigma p_0q_1}} \times 100 = \sqrt{\frac{600}{240} \times \frac{480}{192}} \times 100$$

$$= \sqrt{2.5 \times 2.5} \times 100 = 2.5 \times 100 = \mathbf{250}$$

Example 17.25. *Compute Fisher's Ideal Index from the following data and show how it satisfies Time Reversal Test and Factor Reversal Test :* *(BU-N90)*

Commodities		*A*	*B*	*C*	*D*
Base Year Price	:	*12*	*4*	*8*	*20*
Base Year Quantity	:	*10*	*20*	*12*	*6*
Current Year Price	:	*20*	*4*	*12*	*24*
Current Year Quantity	:	*12*	*24*	*15*	*2*

Solution : Computation of Fisher's Ideal Index Number

Commodities	Base year		Current year	
	q_0	p_0	q_1	p_1
A	10	12	12	20
B	20	4	24	4
C	12	8	15	12
D	6	20	2	24

p_1q_0	p_0q_0	p_1q_1	p_0q_1
200	120	240	144
80	80	96	96
144	96	180	120
144	120	48	40
= 568	= 46	= 564	= 400
Σp_1q_0	Σp_0q_0	Σp_1q_1	Σp_0q_1

Fisher's Index Number :

$$P_{01} = \sqrt{\frac{\Sigma p_1q_0}{\Sigma p_0q_0} \times \frac{\Sigma p_1q_1}{\Sigma p_0q_1}} \times 100 = \sqrt{\frac{568}{416} \times \frac{564}{400}} \times 100$$

$$= \sqrt{1.365385 \times 1.41} \times 100 = \sqrt{1.925193} \times 100$$

$$= 1.387513 \times 100 = \mathbf{138.7513}$$

(1) Time Reversal Test : This test is satisfied when,

$$P_{01} \times P_{10} = 1$$

$$P_{01} \times P_{10} = \sqrt{\frac{\Sigma p_1q_0}{\Sigma p_0q_0} \times \frac{\Sigma p_1q_1}{\Sigma p_0q_1}} \times \sqrt{\frac{\Sigma p_0q_1}{\Sigma p_1q_1} \times \frac{\Sigma p_0q_0}{\Sigma p_1q_0}}$$

$$= \sqrt{\frac{568}{416} \times \frac{564}{400} \times \frac{400}{564} \times \frac{416}{568}} = \sqrt{1} = \mathbf{1}$$

(2) Factor Reversal Test : This test is satisfied when,

$$P_{01} \times Q_{01} = \frac{\Sigma p_1q_1}{\Sigma p_0q_0}$$

$$P_{01} \times Q_{01} = \sqrt{\frac{\Sigma p_1q_0}{\Sigma p_0q_0} \times \frac{\Sigma p_1q_1}{\Sigma p_0q_1}} \times \sqrt{\frac{\Sigma p_0q_1}{\Sigma p_0q_0} \times \frac{\Sigma p_1q_1}{\Sigma p_1q_0}}$$

$$= \sqrt{\frac{568}{416} \times \frac{564}{400} \times \frac{400}{416} \times \frac{564}{568}} = \sqrt{\frac{564}{416} \times \frac{564}{416}}$$

$$= \frac{564}{416} = \frac{\mathbf{\Sigma p_1q_1}}{\mathbf{\Sigma p_0q_0}}$$

Example 17.26. *Construct a suitable Index Number with the help of the following data and state how it satisfies the factor Reversal Test :* *(BU-N91)*

Commodities	*Rice*	*Sugar*	*Ghee*
1980 (Value)	*210*	*100*	*40*
1980 (Price)	*14*	*20*	*4*
1985 (Value)	*300*	*108*	*56*
1985(Price)	*25*	*27*	*7*

Solution : In the above problem Base Year and Current Year quantities are not given. We have to obtain them from the values and prices.

Computation of Fisher's Ideal Index Number

Commodities	1980 p_0	p_0	$\left(\frac{p_0q_0}{p_0}\right)$ q_0	1985 p_1q_1
Rice	210	14	15	300
Sugar	100	20	5	108
Ghee	40	4	10	56
	= 350 Σp_0q_0			= 464 Σp_1q_1

p_1	$\left(\frac{p_1q_1}{p_1}\right)$ q_1	p_1q_0	p_0q_1
25	12	375	168
27	4	135	80
7	8	70	32
		= 580 Σp_1q_0	280 = Σp_0q_1

Fisher's Index Number :

$$P_{01} = \sqrt{\frac{\Sigma p_1q_0}{\Sigma p_0q_0} \times \frac{\Sigma p_1q_1}{\Sigma p_0q_1}} \times 100 = \sqrt{\frac{580}{350} \times \frac{464}{280}} \times 100$$

$$= \sqrt{1.657143 \times 1.6571428} \times 100 = \sqrt{2.746123} \times 100$$

$$= 1.657143 \times 100 = \mathbf{165.7143}$$

Factor Reversal Test : This test is satisfied when,

$$P_{01} \times Q_{01} = \frac{\Sigma p_1 q_1}{\Sigma p_0 q_0}$$

$$P_{01} \times Q_{10} = \sqrt{\frac{\Sigma p_1 q_0}{\Sigma p_0 q_0} \times \frac{\Sigma p_1 q_1}{\Sigma p_0 q_1}} \times \sqrt{\frac{\Sigma p_0 q_1}{\Sigma p_0 q_0} \times \frac{\Sigma p_1 q_1}{\Sigma p_1 q_0}}$$

$$= \sqrt{\frac{580}{350} \times \frac{464}{280} \times \frac{280}{350} \times \frac{464}{580}} = \sqrt{\frac{464}{350} \times \frac{464}{350}}$$

$$= \frac{464}{350} = \frac{\Sigma \mathbf{p_1 q_1}}{\Sigma \mathbf{p_0 q_0}}$$

Example 17.27. *Construct Fisher's Index for the following and verify whether it satisfies Time Reversal Test and Factor Reversal Test :* *(BU-A-92)*

Commodities		*A*	*B*	*C*	*D*	*E*
Base year (price)	:	*12*	*4*	*8*	*20*	*16*
Base Year (Quantity)	:	*100*	*200*	*120*	*60*	*80*
Current Year (Price)	:	*20*	*4*	*12*	*24*	*24*
Current Year (Quantity)	:	*112*	*240*	*120*	*48*	*52*

Solution : Computation of Fisher's Ideal Index Number

Commodities	Base Value		Current Year	
	q_0	p_0	q_1	p_1
A	100	12	112	20
B	200	4	240	4
C	120	8	120	12
D	60	20	48	24
E	80	16	52	24

p_1q_0	p_0q_0	p_1q_1	p_0q_1
2,000	1,200	2,240	1,344
800	800	960	960
1,440	960	1,440	960
1,440	1,200	1,152	960
1,920	1,280	1,248	832
= 7,600	= 5440	= 7,040	= 5,056
Σp_1q_0	Σp_0q_0	Σp_1q_1	Σp_0q_1

Fisher's Index Number :

$$P_{01} = \sqrt{\frac{\Sigma p_1 q_0}{\Sigma p_0 q_0} \times \frac{\Sigma p_1 q_1}{\Sigma p_0 q_1}} \times 100 = \sqrt{\frac{7600}{5440} \times \frac{7040}{5056}} \times 100$$

$$= \sqrt{1.397059 \times 1.392405} \times 100 = \sqrt{1.9452719} \times 100$$

$$= 1.39473 \times 100 = \mathbf{139.473}$$

(1) Time Reversal Test : This test is satisfied when

$$P_{01} \times P_{10} = 1$$

$$P_{01} \times P_{10} = \sqrt{\frac{\Sigma p_1 q_0}{\Sigma p_0 q_0} \times \frac{\Sigma p_1 q_1}{\Sigma p_0 q_1}} \times \sqrt{\frac{\Sigma p_0 q_1}{\Sigma p_1 q_1} \times \frac{\Sigma p_0 q_0}{\Sigma p_1 q_0}}$$

$$= \sqrt{\frac{7600}{5440} \times \frac{7040}{5056} \times \frac{5056}{7040} \times \frac{5440}{7600}} = \sqrt{1} = \mathbf{1}$$

(2) Factor Reversal Test : This test is satisfied when,

$$P_{01} \times Q_{01} = \frac{\Sigma p_1 q_1}{\Sigma p_0 q_0}$$

$$P_{01} \times Q_{01} = \sqrt{\frac{\Sigma p_1 q_0}{\Sigma p_0 q_0} \times \frac{\Sigma p_1 q_1}{\Sigma p_0 q_0}} \times \sqrt{\frac{\Sigma p_0 q_1}{\Sigma p_1 q_1} \times \frac{\Sigma p_1 q_1}{\Sigma p_0 q_0}}$$

$$= \sqrt{\frac{7600}{5440} \times \frac{7040}{5056} \times \frac{5056}{5440} \times \frac{7040}{7600}} = \sqrt{\frac{7040}{5440} \times \frac{7040}{5440}}$$

$$= \frac{7040}{5440} = \mathbf{\frac{\Sigma p_1 q_1}{\Sigma p_0 q_0}}$$

Example 17.28. *Construct Fisher's Index for the following and show that it satisfies the Factor Reversal Test :* *(BU-N92)*

Commodities		*A*	*B*	*C*	*D*	*E*
Base Year (Price)	:	*8*	*2*	*1*	*2*	*1*
Base Year (Quantity)	:	*50*	*15*	*20*	*10*	*40*
Current Year (Price)	:	*20*	*6*	*2*	*5*	*3*
Current Year (Quantity)	:	*26*	*10*	*25*	*8*	*30*

Solution : Computation of Fisher's Ideal Index Number

Commodities	Base Year		Current Year	
	q_0	p_0	q_1	p_1
A	50	8	26	20
B	15	2	10	6
C	20	1	25	2
D	10	2	8	5
E	40	1	30	3

p_0q_0	p_1q_0	p_1q_1	p_0q_1
400	1,000	520	208
30	90	60	20
20	40	50	25
20	50	40	16
40	120	90	30
= 510	= 1300	= 760	= 299
Σp_0q_0	Σp_1q_0	Σp_1q_1	Σp_0q_1

Fisher's Index Number :

$$P_{01} = \sqrt{\frac{\Sigma p_1q_0}{\Sigma p_0q_0} \times \frac{\Sigma p_1q_1}{\Sigma p_0q_1}} \times 100 = \sqrt{\frac{1300}{510} \times \frac{760}{299}} \times 100$$

$$= \sqrt{2.59402 \times 2.54181} \times 100 = \sqrt{6.479125} \times 100$$

$$= 2.5454125 \times 100 = \mathbf{254.541}$$

Factor Reversal Test : This test is satisfied when,

$$P_{01} \times Q_{01} = \frac{\Sigma p_1q_1}{\Sigma p_0q_0}$$

$$P_{01} \times Q_{01} = \sqrt{\frac{\Sigma p_1q_0}{\Sigma p_0q_0} \times \frac{\Sigma p_1q_1}{\Sigma p_0q_1}} \times \sqrt{\frac{\Sigma p_0q_1}{\Sigma p_0q_0} \times \frac{\Sigma p_1q_1}{\Sigma p_1q_0}}$$

$$= \sqrt{\frac{1300}{510} \times \frac{760}{299} \times \frac{299}{510} \times \frac{760}{1300}} = \sqrt{\frac{760}{510} \times \frac{760}{510}}$$

$$= \frac{760}{510} = \frac{\mathbf{\Sigma p_1q_1}}{\mathbf{\Sigma p_0q_0}}$$

Example 17.29. *Construct Fisher's Index for the following and prove that it satisfies the Factor Reversal Test :* *(BU-A93)*

Items	*Price per kg.(Rs.)*		*Consumption in Kg.*	
	1979	*1989*	*1979*	*1989*
A	*3.30*	*6.90*	*185.00*	*152.00*
B	*2.25*	*3.31*	*192.00*	*191.00*
C	*17.40*	*55.70*	*10.50*	*10.90*
D	*6.40*	*9.70*	*94.70*	*98.10*
E	*34.50*	*65.00*	*3.70*	*6.80*
F	*26.80*	*61.40*	*3.40*	*3.30*
G	*18.60*	*30.10*	*7.40*	*5.90*

Solution : **Computation of Fisher's Ideal Index Number**

Items	Base Year		Current Year	
	q_0	p_0	q_1	p_1
A	*185.00*	*3.30*	*152.00*	*6.90*
B	*192.00*	*2.25*	*191.00*	*3.31*
C	*10.50*	*17.40*	*10.90*	*55.70*
D	*94.70*	*6.40*	*98.10*	*9.70*
E	*3.70*	*34.50*	*6.80*	*65.00*
F	*3.40*	*26.80*	*3.30*	*61.40*
G	*7.40*	*18.60*	*5.90*	*30.10*

p_1q_0	p_0q_0	p_1q_1	p_0q_1
1276.50	610.50	1048.80	501.60
635.52	432.00	632.21	429.75
584.85	182.70	607.13	189.66
918.59	606.08	951.57	627.84
240.50	127.65	442.00	234.60
208.76	91.12	202.62	88.44
222.74	137.64	177.59	109.74
4,087.46	2,187.69	4061.92	2181.63
$\Sigma p_1q_0 =$	$\Sigma p_0q_0 =$	$\Sigma p_1q_1 =$	$\Sigma p_0q_1 =$

Fisher's Index Number :

$$P_{01} = \sqrt{\frac{\Sigma p_1 q_0}{\Sigma p_0 q_0} \times \frac{\Sigma p_1 q_1}{\Sigma p_0 q_1}} \times 100 = \sqrt{\frac{4087.46}{2187.69} \times \frac{4061.92}{2181.00}} \times 100$$

$$= \sqrt{1.868391 \times 1.861874} \times 100 = \sqrt{3.4787086} \times 100$$

$$= 1.8651296 \times 100 = \mathbf{186.513}$$

Factor Reversal Test : This test is satisfied when,

$$P_{01} \times Q_{01} = \frac{\Sigma p_1 q_1}{\Sigma p_0 q_0}$$

$$P_{01} \times Q_{01} = \sqrt{\frac{\Sigma p_1 q_0}{\Sigma p_0 q_0} \times \frac{\Sigma p_1 q_1}{\Sigma p_0 q_1}} \times \sqrt{\frac{\Sigma p_0 q_1}{\Sigma p_0 q_0} \times \frac{\Sigma p_1 q_1}{\Sigma p_1 q_0}}$$

$$= \sqrt{\frac{4087.46}{2187.69} \times \frac{4061.92}{2181.63} \times \frac{2181.63}{2187.69} \times \frac{4061.92}{4087.46}}$$

$$= \sqrt{\frac{4061.92}{2187.69} \times \frac{4061.92}{2187.69}} = \frac{4061.92}{2187.69} = \frac{\mathbf{\Sigma p_1 q_1}}{\mathbf{\Sigma p_0 q_0}}$$

Example 17.30. *Prices and quantities of base year and current year for 8 groups of commodities are given below :*

Groups	*Price*		*Quantity*	
	Base Year	*Current year*	*Base year*	*Current year*
A	12	20	55	120
B	10	12	100	80
C	14	15	60	80
D	16	18	30	70
E	18	20	40	40
F	20	15	70	60
G	20	16	90	100
H	15	18	80	80

Calculate the Fisher's Ideal Index Number and verify both the tests.

Solution : Computation of Fisher's Ideal Index Number

Groups	Price		Quantity	
	p_0	p_1	q_0	q_1
A	12	20	55	120
B	10	12	100	80
C	14	15	60	80
D	16	18	30	70
E	18	20	40	40
F	20	15	70	60
G	20	16	90	100
H	15	18	80	80

p_1q_0	p_0q_0	p_1q_1	p_0q_1
1,100	660	2,400	1,440
1,200	1000	960	800
900	840	1,200	1,120
540	480	1,260	1,120
800	720	800	720
1050	1,400	900	1,200
1440	1,800	1,600	2,000
1440	1,200	1,440	1,200
8,470	8,100	10,560	9,600
$\Sigma p_1q_0 =$	$\Sigma p_0q_0 =$	$\Sigma p_1q_1 =$	$\Sigma p_0q_1 =$

Fisher's Index Number :

$$P_{01} = \sqrt{\frac{\Sigma p_1q_0}{\Sigma p_0q_0} \times \frac{\Sigma p_1q_1}{\Sigma p_0q_1}} \times 100 = \sqrt{\frac{8470}{8100} \times \frac{10,560}{9,600}} \times 100$$

$$= \sqrt{1.045679 \times 1.1} \times 100 = \sqrt{1.1502469} \times 100$$

$$= 1.0724956 \times 100 = \mathbf{107.2496}$$

(1) Time Reversal Test : This test is satisfied when,

$$P_{01} \times Q_{01} = 1$$

$$P_{01} \times Q_{01} = \sqrt{\frac{\Sigma p_1q_0}{\Sigma p_0q_0} \times \frac{\Sigma p_1q_1}{\Sigma p_0q_1}} \times \sqrt{\frac{\Sigma p_0q_1}{\Sigma p_1q_1} \times \frac{\Sigma p_0q_0}{\Sigma p_1q_0}}$$

$$= \sqrt{\frac{8470}{8100} \times \frac{10,560}{9,600} \times \frac{9,600}{10,560} \times \frac{8,100}{8470}} = \sqrt{1} = 1$$

(2) Factor Reversal Test : This test is satisfied when

$$P_{01} \times Q_{01} = \frac{\Sigma p_1 q_1}{\Sigma p_0 q_0}$$

$$P_{01} \times Q_{01} = \sqrt{\frac{\Sigma p_1 q_0}{\Sigma p_0 q_0} \times \frac{\Sigma p_1 q_1}{\Sigma p_0 q_1}} \times \sqrt{\frac{\Sigma p_0 q_1}{\Sigma p_0 q_0} \times \frac{\Sigma p_1 q_1}{\Sigma p_1 q_0}}$$

$$= \sqrt{\frac{8470}{8100} \times \frac{10560}{9600} \times \frac{9600}{8100} \times \frac{10560}{8470}} = \sqrt{\frac{10560}{8100} \times \frac{10560}{8100}}$$

$$= \frac{10560}{8100} = \frac{\mathbf{\Sigma p_1 q_1}}{\mathbf{\Sigma p_0 q_0}}$$

Example 17.31. *Calculate Fisher's Index from the following data and show that it satisfies both the Reversal Tests.* *(BU-N94)*

Commodities	*A*	*B*	*C*	*D*	*E*
Base Year (Price)	*10*	*8*	*20*	*18*	*35*
Base Year (Value)	*200*	*108*	*160*	*144*	*280*
Current Year (Value)	*300*	*220*	*250*	*140*	*300*
Current Year (Quantity)	*25*	*22*	*10*	*7*	*10*

Solution : In the above problem, Base year quantity and Current year price are not given. They are obtained with the help of values.

Computation of Fishers Ideal Index Number

Commodities	Base year p_0	p_0	$\left(\frac{p_0 q_0}{p_0}\right)$ q_0	Current year $p_1 q_1$
P	10	200	20.0	300
Q	8	108	13.5	220
R	20	160	8.0	250
S	18	144	8.0	140
T	35	280	8.0	300
		= 892 $\Sigma p_0 q_0$		= 1210 $\Sigma p_1 q_1$

Current year $\left(\frac{p_1q_1}{p_1}\right)$			
q_1	p_1	p_1q_0	p_0q_1
25	12	240	250
22	10	135	176
10	25	200	200
7	20	160	126
10	30	240	350
		= 975	= 1,102
		Σp_1q_0	Σp_0q_1

Fisher's Index Number :

$$P_{01} = \sqrt{\frac{\Sigma p_1q_0}{\Sigma p_0q_0} \times \frac{\Sigma p_1q_1}{\Sigma p_0q_1}} \times 100 = \sqrt{\frac{975}{892} \times \frac{1210}{1102}} \times 100$$

$$= \sqrt{1.0.9305 \times 1.098} \times 100 = \sqrt{1.2001689} \times 100$$

$$= 1.09.5522 \times 100 = \mathbf{109.5522}$$

(1) ***Time Reversal Test :*** This test is satisfied when,

$$P_{01} \times P_{10} = 1$$

$$P_{01} \times P_{10} = \sqrt{\frac{\Sigma p_1q_0}{\Sigma p_0q_0} \times \frac{\Sigma p_1q_1}{\Sigma p_0q_1}} \times \sqrt{\frac{\Sigma p_0q_1}{\Sigma p_1q_1} \times \frac{\Sigma p_0q_0}{\Sigma p_1q_0}}$$

$$= \sqrt{\frac{975}{892} \times \frac{1210}{1102} \times \frac{1102}{1210} \times \frac{892}{975}} = \sqrt{1} = \mathbf{1}$$

(2) Factor Reversal Test : This test is satisfied when,

$$P_{01} \times Q_{01} = \sqrt{\frac{\Sigma p_1q_0}{\Sigma p_0q_0} \times \frac{\Sigma p_1q_1}{\Sigma p_0q_1}} \times \sqrt{\frac{\Sigma p_0q_1}{\Sigma p_0q_0} \times \frac{\Sigma p_1q_1}{\Sigma p_1q_0}}$$

$$= \sqrt{\frac{975}{892} \times \frac{1210}{1102} \times \frac{1102}{892} \times \frac{1210}{975}} = \sqrt{\frac{1210}{892} \times \frac{1210}{892}}$$

$$= \frac{1210}{892} = \frac{\mathbf{\Sigma p_1q_1}}{\mathbf{\Sigma p_0q_0}}$$

Example 17.32. *From the data given below, construct index number of the group of four commodities by using Fisher's formula and show that it satisfies both the reversal tests :*

(BU-N95)

Commodities	:	*A*	*B*	*C*	*D*
Base Year (Price)	:	*20*	*40*	*10*	*50*
Base year (Expenditure)	:	*400*	*160*	*100*	*250*
Current Year (Price)	:	*50*	*80*	*20*	*100*
Current Year (Expenditure)	:	*750*	*400*	*240*	*600*

Solution : In the above problem, quantities are not given. We have to obtain the quantities with the help of expenditure.

Computation of Fisher's Ideal Index Number

Commodities	Base year		$\left(\frac{p_0q_0}{p_0}\right)$
	p_0	p_0q_0	q_0
A	20	400	20
B	40	160	4
C	10	100	10
D	50	250	5
		= 910 Σp_0q_0	

Current year		$\left(\frac{p_1q_1}{p_1}\right)$		
p_1	p_1q_1	q_1	p_1q_0	p_0q_1
50	750	15	1000	300
80	400	5	320	200
20	240	12	200	120
100	600	6	500	300
	= 1990 Σp_1q_1		= 2,020 Σp_1q_0	= 920 Σp_1q_1

Fisher's Index Number :

$$P_{01} = \sqrt{\frac{\Sigma p_1 q_0}{\Sigma p_0 q_0} \times \frac{\Sigma p_1 q_1}{\Sigma p_0 q_1}} \times 100 = \sqrt{\frac{2020}{910} \times \frac{1990}{920}} \times 100$$

$$= \sqrt{2.21978 \times 2.16304} \times 100 = \sqrt{4.8014729} \times 100$$

$$= 2.191226 \times 100 = \mathbf{219.1226}$$

(1) ***Time Reversal Test*** **:** This test is satisfied when, $P_{01} \times P_{10} = 1$

$$P_{01} \times P_{10} = \sqrt{\frac{\Sigma p_1 q_0}{\Sigma p_0 q_0} \times \frac{\Sigma p_1 q_1}{\Sigma p_0 q_1}} \times \sqrt{\frac{\Sigma p_0 q_1}{\Sigma p_1 q_1} \times \frac{\Sigma p_0 q_0}{\Sigma p_1 q_0}}$$

$$= \sqrt{\frac{2020}{910} \times \frac{1990}{920} \times \frac{920}{1990} \times \frac{910}{2020}} = \sqrt{1} = \mathbf{1}$$

(2) ***Factor Reversal Test*** **:** This test is satisfied when,

$$P_{01} \times Q_{01} = \frac{\Sigma p_1 q_1}{\Sigma p_0 q_0}$$

$$P_{01} \times Q_{01} = \sqrt{\frac{\Sigma p_1 q_0}{\Sigma p_0 q_0} \times \frac{\Sigma p_1 q_1}{\Sigma p_0 q_1}} \times \sqrt{\frac{\Sigma p_0 q_1}{\Sigma p_0 q_0} \times \frac{\Sigma p_1 q_1}{\Sigma p_1 q_0}}$$

$$= \sqrt{\frac{2020}{910} \times \frac{1990}{920} \times \frac{920}{910} \times \frac{1990}{2020}} = \sqrt{\frac{1990}{910} \times \frac{1990}{910}}$$

$$= \frac{1990}{910} = \frac{\mathbf{\Sigma p_1 q_1}}{\mathbf{\Sigma p_0 q_0}}$$

Example 17.33. *From the data given below construct Index Number of the group by using the Fisher's method and show that it satisfies both the Time Reversal Test and Factor Reversal Test:*

Commodities	*A*	*B*	*C*	*D*
Price per unit (Rs.) 1981:	*2*	*4*	*1*	*5*
Price per unit (Rs.) 1991:	*5*	*8*	*2*	*10*
Expenditure (Rs.) 1981 :	*40*	*16*	*10*	*25*
Expenditure (Rs.) 1991 :	*75*	*40*	*24*	*60*

(BU-N97)

Solution : In the above problem, quantities are to be obtained with the help of expenditure.

Computation of Fisher's Ideal Index Number

Commodities	(1981) Base year p_0	p_0q_0	$\left(\frac{P_0q_0}{P_0}\right)$ q_0
A	2	40	20
B	4	16	4
C	1	10	10
D	5	25	5
		= 91 Σp_0q_0	

(1991) Current Year p_1	p_1q_1	$\left(\frac{p_1q_1}{p_1}\right)$ q_1	p_1q_0	p_0q_1
5	75	15	100	30
8	40	5	32	20
2	24	12	20	12
10	60	6	50	30
	= 199 Σp_1q_1		= 202 Σp_1q_0	= 92 Σp_0q_1

Fisher's Index number :

$$P_{01} = \sqrt{\frac{\Sigma p_1q_0}{\Sigma p_0q_0} \times \frac{\Sigma p_1q_1}{\Sigma p_0q_1}} \times 100 = \sqrt{\frac{202}{91} \times \frac{199}{92}} \times 100$$

$$= \sqrt{2.219781 \times 2.163043} \times 100 = \sqrt{4.8014817} \times 100$$

$$= 2.191228 \times 100 = \mathbf{219.1228}$$

(1) Time Reversal Test : This test is satisfied when, $P_{01} \times P_{10} = 1$

$$P_{01} \times P_{10} = \sqrt{\frac{\Sigma p_1q_0}{\Sigma p_0q_o} \times \frac{\Sigma p_1q_1}{\Sigma p_0q_1}} \times \sqrt{\frac{\Sigma p_0q_1}{\Sigma p_1q_1} \times \frac{\Sigma p_0q_0}{\Sigma p_1q_0}}$$

$$= \sqrt{\frac{202}{91} \times \frac{199}{92} \times \frac{92}{199} \times \frac{91}{202}} = \sqrt{1} = \mathbf{1}$$

(2) Factor Reversal Test : This test is satisfied when

$$P_{01} \times Q_{01} = \frac{\Sigma p_1 q_1}{\Sigma p_0 q_0}$$

$$P_{01} \times Q_{01} = \sqrt{\frac{\Sigma p_1 q_0}{\Sigma p_0 q_0} \times \frac{\Sigma p_1 q_1}{\Sigma p_0 q_1}} \times \sqrt{\frac{\Sigma p_0 q_1}{\Sigma p_0 q_0} \times \frac{\Sigma p_1 q_1}{\Sigma p_1 q_0}}$$

$$= \sqrt{\frac{202}{91} \times \frac{199}{92} \times \frac{92}{91} \times \frac{199}{202}} = \sqrt{\frac{199}{91} \times \frac{199}{91}}$$

$$= \frac{199}{91} = \frac{\Sigma p_1 q_1}{\Sigma p_0 q_0}$$

Question

1. What is an Index Number? (BU-N84, A95)
2. Mention any four problems that need a careful thought before constructing index numbers. (BU – A85)
3. State the uses of Index Numbers. (BU – N85, N91)
4. Why are index numbers called "Economic Barometers"? (BU-A87, A89, N90)
5. Why are weights used in index numbers? (BU – N89)
6. What do you understand by consumer price index number? (BU – A90)
7. Why the Fisher's formula is called "ideal"? (BU-A92, A97)
8. Define "index number". What are its uses? (BU – N92)
9. What do you mean by Time Reversal Test? Show how Fisher's Formula satisfies this test. (BU – A93)
10. What is base year? What points are considred in the selection of the base year? (BU – N93, N97)
11. What are the uses of consumer price index number? (BU-N94)
12. What do you mean by the Factor Reversal Test? (BU- A96)
13. What is the Time Reversal Test? (BU - N96)
14. Construct the Index Number for 1998 taking 1997 as the base year from the following data :

Commodities	A	B	C	D
Prices in 1997	90	40	90	30
Prices in 1998	95	50	110	35

$(P_{01} = 116)$

15. Compute the price index numbers for the following data by using the average of price relatives method.

Commodities	:	A	B	C	D	E	F
Prices in 1997	:	4	6	2	5	8	10
Prices in 1998	:	5	6	3	7	9	11

$(P_{01} = 122.92)$

16. Calculate the weighted aggregative price index number from the following data : $(P_{01} = 148)$

Commodities	P	Q	R	S
Weights	50	200	5	2000
Prices in 1991	0.5	0.95	3.4	1.2
Prices in 1998	0.8	1.42	4.2	2.4

17. From the following data, prepare the "quantity index numbers for the year 1998 taking 1988 as the base year :

Year	Commodity I		Commodity II		Commodity II	
	Price	Quantity	Price	Quantity	Price	Quantity
1988	5	10	8	6	6	3
1998	4	12	7	7	5	4

(Laspeyre's = 120.68, Paasche's 120.62, Fisher's – 120.65)

18. Calculate index number from the following data :

Items	:	A	B	C
Base Year Quantity	:	5.0	2.0	1.0
Base Year Price	:	1.5	7.5	12.5
Current Year Quantity	:	4.0	7.5	1.5
Current Year Price	:	1.625	10.0	11.5

(Laspeyre's = 125.9, Paasche's = 121.9, Fisher's 123.88)

19. Given the data below construct the Index Number.

Commodities	p_0	q_0	p_1	q_1
A	10	100	20	50
B	10	50	40	20

(Laspeyre's = 266.667, Paasche's = 257.143, Fisher's 261.8615)

20. From the data given below construct the Fisher's Index Number :

Commodities		A	B	C	D
Base Year (Price)	:	8	12	6	4
Base Year (Quantity)	:	20	10	16	8
Current Year (Price)	:	10	15	8	6
Current Year (Quantity)	:	30	10	20	10

$(P_{01} = 128.85)$

21. Construct the Fisher's Index Number from the following data and state how it satisfies the Time Reversal and Factor Tests :

Commodities		A	B	C	D
Base Year (Price)	:	15	12	60	20
Base Year (Quantity)	:	2.5	1	0.2	0.1
Current Year (Price)	:	30	20	100	30
Current Year (Quantity)	:	3	1.2	0.3	0.2

$(P_{01} = 185)$

22. Construct the appropriate index number and show if it satisfies the reversability tests.

Commodity	1997		1998	
	Price	Quantity	Price	Quantity
Rice	6	10	6.4	10
Sugar	5	8	6	7
Wheat	3.6	10	3.2	11

$(P_{01} = 111.0742)$

23. From the following group index numbers calculate the Cost of Living Index Number :

Group	Food	Fuel	Clothing	Rent	Miscellaneous
I.No.	350	200	240	160	250
Weights	5	1	1	1	2

$(P_{01} = 285)$

24. Compute the price index number for the following data by using weighted average of price relative :

Items	Price in 1991	Price in 1998	Quantity in 1991
Wheat	2.00	2.50	40 kg.
Rice	3.00	3.25	20 kg.
Dal	1.50	1.75	10 liters

$(P_{01} = 111.074)$

25. Compute the consumer price index number from the following information :

Items :	Food	Clothing	Rent	Miscellaneous
Weights :	55%	25%	8%	12%
Price Relatives:	150	120	175	168

$(P_{01} = 146.66)$

26. Calculate the index number for 1998 with 1991 as the base, by using (i) simple average of price relatives, and (ii) weighted average of price relatives.

Commodity	Weight	Prices (1991)	Prices (1998)
A	5	Rs.4.50	Rs.2.00
B	7	Rs.3.20	Rs.2.50
C	6	Rs.4.50	Rs.3.00
D	2	Rs.1.80	Rs.1.00

[(i) = 170.75 (ii) = 164.05]

TABLE I
LOGARITHMS

	0	1	2	3	4	5	6	7	8	9	Mean Differences 1	2	3	4	5	6	7	8	9
10	0000	0043	0086	0128	0170	0212	0253	0294	0334	0374	4	8	12	17	21	25	29	33	37
11	0414	0453	0492	0531	0569	0607	0645	0682	0719	0755	4	8	11	15	19	23	26	30	34
12	0792	0828	0864	0899	0934	0969	1004	1038	1072	1106	3	7	10	14	17	21	24	28	31
13	1139	1173	1206	1239	1271	1303	1335	1367	1399	1430	3	6	10	13	16	19	23	26	29
14	1461	1492	1523	1553	1584	1614	1644	1673	1703	1732	3	6	9	12	15	18	21	24	27
15	1761	1790	1818	1847	1875	1903	1931	1959	1987	2014	3	6	8	11	14	17	20	22	25
16	2041	2068	2095	2122	2148	2175	2201	2227	2253	2279	3	5	8	11	13	16	18	21	24
17	2304	2330	2355	2380	2405	2430	2455	2480	2504	2529	2	5	7	10	12	15	17	20	22
18	2553	2577	2601	2625	2648	2672	2605	2718	2742	2765	2	5	7	9	12	14	16	19	21
19	2788	2810	2833	2856	2878	2900	2923	2945	2967	2989	2	4	7	9	11	13	16	18	20
20	3010	3032	3054	3075	3096	3118	3139	3160	3181	3201	2	4	6	8	11	13	15	17	19
21	3222	3243	3263	3284	3304	3324	3345	3365	3385	3404	2	4	6	8	10	12	14	16	18
22	3424	3444	3464	3483	3502	3522	3541	3560	3579	3598	2	4	6	8	10	12	14	15	17
23	3617	3636	3655	3674	3692	3711	3729	3747	3766	3784	2	4	6	7	9	11	13	15	17
24	3802	3820	3838	3856	3874	3892	3909	3927	3945	3962	2	4	5	7	9	11	12	14	16
25	3979	3997	4014	4031	4048	4065	4082	4099	4116	4133	2	3	5	7	9	10	12	14	15
26	4150	4166	4183	4200	4216	4232	4249	4265	4281	4298	2	3	5	7	8	10	11	13	15
27	4314	4330	4346	4362	4378	4393	4409	4425	4440	4456	2	3	5	6	8	9	11	13	14
28	4472	4487	4502	4518	4533	4548	4564	4579	4594	4609	2	3	5	6	8	9	11	12	14
29	4624	4639	4654	4669	4683	4698	4713	4728	4742	4757	1	3	4	6	7	9	10	12	13
30	4771	4786	4800	4814	4829	4843	4857	4871	4886	4900	1	3	4	6	7	9	10	11	13
31	4914	4928	4942	4955	4969	4983	4997	5011	5024	5038	1	3	4	6	7	8	10	11	12
32	5051	5065	5079	5092	5105	5119	5132	5145	5159	5172	1	3	4	5	7	8	9	11	12
33	5185	5198	5211	5224	5237	5250	5263	5276	5289	5302	1	3	4	5	6	8	9	10	12
34	5315	5328	5340	5353	5366	5378	5391	5403	5416	5428	1	3	4	5	6	8	9	10	11
35	5441	5453	5465	5478	5490	5502	5514	5527	5539	5551	1	2	4	5	6	7	9	10	11
36	5563	5575	5587	5599	5611	5623	5635	5647	5658	5670	1	2	4	5	6	7	8	10	11
37	5682	5694	5705	5717	5729	5740	5752	5763	5775	5786	1	2	3	5	6	7	8	9	10
38	5798	5809	5821	5832	5843	5855	5866	5877	5888	5899	1	2	3	5	6	7	8	9	10
39	5911	5922	5933	5944	5955	5966	5977	5988	5299	6010	1	2	3	4	5	7	8	9	10
40	6021	6031	6042	6053	6064	6075	6085	6096	6107	6117	1	2	3	4	5	6	8	9	10
41	6128	6138	6149	6160	6170	6180	6191	6201	6212	6222	1	2	3	4	5	6	7	8	9
42	6232	6243	6253	6263	6274	6284	6294	6304	6314	6325	1	2	3	4	5	6	7	8	9
43	6335	6345	6355	6365	6375	6385	6395	6405	6415	6425	1	2	3	4	5	6	7	8	9
44	6435	6444	6454	6464	6474	6484	6493	6503	6513	6522	1	2	3	4	5	6	7	8	9
45	6532	6542	6551	6561	6571	6580	6590	6599	6609	6618	1	2	3	4	5	6	7	8	9
46	6628	6637	6646	6656	6665	6675	6684	6693	6702	6712	1	2	3	4	5	6	7	7	8
47	6721	6730	6739	6749	6758	6767	6776	6785	6794	6803	1	2	3	4	5	5	6	7	8
48	6812	6821	6830	6839	6848	6857	6866	6875	6884	6893	1	2	3	4	4	5	6	7	8
49	6902	6911	6920	6928	6937	6946	6955	6964	6972	6981	1	2	3	4	4	5	6	7	8
50	6990	6998	7007	7016	7024	7033	7042	7050	7059	7067	1	2	3	3	4	5	6	7	8
51	7076	7084	7093	7101	7110	7118	7126	7135	7143	7152	1	2	3	3	4	5	6	7	8
52	7160	7168	7177	7185	7193	7202	7210	7218	7226	7235	1	2	2	3	4	5	6	7	7
53	7243	7251	7259	7267	7275	7284	7292	7300	7308	7316	1	2	2	3	4	5	6	6	7
54	7324	7332	7340	7348	7356	7364	7372	7380	7388	7396	1	2	2	3	4	5	6	6	7

TABLE I
LOGARITHMS

	0	1	2	3	4	5	6	7	8	9	Mean Differences								
											1	2	3	4	5	6	7	8	9
55	7404	7412	7419	7427	7435	7443	7451	7459	7466	7474	1	2	2	3	4	5	5	6	7
56	7482	7490	7497	7505	7513	7520	7528	7536	7543	7551	1	2	2	3	4	5	5	6	7
57	7559	7566	7574	7582	7589	7597	7604	7612	7619	7627	1	2	2	3	4	5	5	6	7
58	7634	7642	7649	7657	7664	7672	7679	7686	7694	7701	1	1	2	3	4	4	5	6	7
59	7709	7716	7723	7731	7738	7745	7752	7760	7767	7774	1	1	2	3	4	4	5	6	7
60	7782	7789	7796	7803	7810	7818	7825	7832	7839	7846	1	1	2	3	4	4	5	6	6
61	7853	7860	7868	7875	7882	7889	7896	7903	7910	7917	1	1	2	3	4	4	5	6	6
62	7924	7931	7938	7945	7952	7959	7966	7973	7980	7987	1	1	2	3	3	4	5	6	6
63	7993	8000	8007	8014	8021	8028	8035	8041	8048	8055	1	1	2	3	3	4	5	5	6
64	8062	8069	8075	8082	8089	8096	8102	8109	8116	8122	1	1	2	3	3	4	5	5	6
65	8129	8136	8142	8149	8156	8162	8169	8176	8182	8189	1	1	2	3	3	4	5	5	6
66	8195	8202	8209	8215	8222	8228	8235	8241	8248	8254	1	1	2	3	3	4	5	5	6
67	8261	8267	8274	8280	8287	8293	8299	8306	8312	8319	1	1	2	3	3	4	5	5	6
68	8325	8331	8338	8344	8351	8357	8363	8370	8376	8382	1	1	2	3	3	4	4	5	6
69	8388	8395	8401	8407	8414	8420	8426	8432	8439	8445	1	1	2	2	3	4	4	5	6
70	8451	8457	8463	8470	8476	8482	8488	8494	8500	8506	1	1	2	2	3	4	4	5	6
71	8513	8519	8525	8531	8537	8543	8549	8555	8561	8567	1	1	2	2	3	4	4	5	5
72	8573	8579	8585	8591	8597	8603	8609	8615	8621	8627	1	1	2	2	3	4	4	5	5
73	8633	8639	8645	8651	8657	8663	8669	8675	8681	8686	1	1	2	2	3	4	4	5	5
74	8692	8698	8704	8710	8716	8722	8727	8733	8739	8745	1	1	2	2	3	4	4	5	5
75	8751	8756	8762	8768	8774	8779	8785	8791	8797	8802	1	1	2	2	3	3	4	5	5
76	8808	8814	8820	8825	8831	8837	8842	8848	8854	8859	1	1	2	2	3	3	4	5	5
77	8865	8871	8876	8882	8887	8893	8899	8904	8910	8915	1	1	2	2	3	3	4	4	5
78	8921	8927	8932	8938	8943	8949	8954	8960	8965	8971	1	1	2	2	3	3	4	4	5
79	8976	8982	8987	8993	8998	9004	9009	9015	9020	9025	1	1	2	2	3	3	4	4	5
80	9031	9036	9042	9047	9053	9058	9063	9069	9074	9079	1	1	2	2	3	3	4	4	5
81	9085	9090	9096	9101	9106	9112	9117	9122	9128	9133	1	1	2	2	3	3	4	4	5
82	9138	9143	9149	9154	9159	9165	9170	9175	9180	9186	1	1	2	2	3	3	4	4	5
83	9191	9196	9201	9206	9212	9217	9222	9227	9232	9238	1	1	2	2	3	3	4	4	5
84	9243	9248	9253	9258	9263	9269	9274	9279	9284	9289	1	1	2	2	3	3	4	4	5
85	9294	9299	9304	9309	9315	9320	9325	9330	9335	9340	1	1	2	2	3	3	4	4	5
86	9345	9350	9355	9360	9365	9370	9375	9380	9385	9390	1	1	2	2	3	3	4	4	5
87	9395	9400	9405	9410	9415	9420	9425	9430	9435	9440	0	1	1	2	2	3	3	4	4
88	9445	9450	9455	9460	9465	9469	9474	9479	9484	9489	0	1	1	2	2	3	3	4	4
89	9494	9499	9504	9509	9513	9518	9523	9528	9533	9538	0	1	1	2	2	3	3	4	4
90	9542	9547	9552	9557	9562	9566	9571	9576	9581	9586	0	1	1	2	2	3	3	4	4
91	9590	9595	9600	9605	9609	9614	9619	9624	9628	9633	0	1	1	2	2	3	3	4	4
92	9638	9643	9647	9652	9657	9661	9666	9671	9675	9680	0	1	1	2	2	3	3	4	4
93	9685	9689	9694	9699	9703	9708	9713	9717	9722	9727	0	1	1	2	2	3	3	4	4
94	9731	9736	9741	9745	9750	9754	9759	9763	9768	9773	0	1	1	2	2	3	3	4	4
95	9777	9782	9786	9791	9795	9800	9805	9809	9814	9818	0	1	1	2	2	3	3	4	4
96	9823	9827	9832	9836	9841	9845	9850	9854	9859	9863	0	1	1	2	2	3	3	4	4
97	9868	9872	9877	9881	9886	9890	9894	9899	9903	9908	0	1	1	2	2	3	3	4	4
98	9912	9917	9921	9926	9930	9934	9939	9943	9948	9952	0	1	1	2	2	3	3	4	4
99	9956	9961	9965	9969	9974	9978	9983	9987	9991	9996	0	1	1	2	2	3	3	3	4

TABLE II
ANTI-LOGARITHMS

	0	1	2	3	4	5	6	7	8	9	Mean Differences								
											1	2	3	4	5	6	7	8	9
00	1000	1002	1005	1007	1009	1012	1014	1016	1019	1021	0	0	1	1	1	1	2	2	2
01	1023	1026	1028	1030	1033	1035	1038	1040	1042	1045	0	0	1	1	1	1	2	2	2
02	1047	1050	1052	1054	1057	1059	1062	1064	1067	1069	0	0	1	1	1	1	2	2	2
03	1072	1074	1076	1079	1081	1084	1086	1089	1091	1094	0	0	1	1	1	1	2	2	2
04	1096	1099	1102	1104	1107	1109	1112	1114	1117	1119	0	1	1	1	1	2	2	2	2
05	1122	1125	1127	1130	1132	1135	1138	1140	1143	1146	0	1	1	1	1	2	2	2	2
06	1148	1151	1153	1156	1159	1161	1164	1167	1169	1172	0	1	1	1	1	2	2	2	2
07	1175	1178	1180	1183	1186	1189	1191	1194	1197	1199	0	1	1	1	1	2	2	2	2
08	1202	1205	1208	1211	1213	1216	1219	1222	1225	1227	0	1	1	1	1	2	2	2	2
09	1230	1233	1236	1239	1242	1245	1247	1250	1253	1256	0	1	1	1	1	2	2	2	3
10	1259	1262	1265	1268	1271	1274	1276	1279	1282	1285	0	1	1	1	1	2	2	2	3
11	1288	1291	1294	1297	1300	1303	1306	1309	1312	1315	0	1	1	1	2	2	2	2	3
12	1318	1321	1324	1327	1330	1334	1337	1340	1343	1346	0	1	1	1	2	2	2	2	3
13	1349	1352	1355	1358	1361	1365	1368	1371	1374	1377	0	1	1	1	2	2	2	3	3
14	1380	1384	1387	1390	1393	1396	1400	1403	1406	1409	0	1	1	1	2	2	2	3	3
15	1413	1416	1419	1422	1426	1429	1432	1435	1439	1442	0	1	1	1	2	2	2	3	3
16	1445	1449	1452	1455	1459	1462	1466	1469	1472	1476	0	1	1	1	2	2	2	3	3
17	1479	1483	1486	1489	1493	1496	1500	1503	1507	1510	0	1	1	1	2	2	2	3	3
18	1514	1517	1521	1524	1528	1531	1535	1538	1542	1545	0	1	1	1	2	2	2	3	3
19	1549	1552	1556	1560	1563	1567	1570	1574	1578	1581	0	1	1	1	2	2	3	3	3
20	1585	1589	1592	1596	1600	1603	1607	1611	1614	1618	0	1	1	1	2	2	3	3	3
21	1622	1626	1629	1633	1637	1641	1644	1648	1652	1656	0	1	1	2	2	2	3	3	3
22	1660	1663	1667	1671	1675	1679	1683	1687	1690	1694	0	1	1	2	2	2	3	3	3
23	1698	1702	1706	1710	1714	1718	1722	1726	1730	1734	0	1	1	2	2	2	3	3	4
24	1738	1742	1746	1750	1754	1758	1762	1766	1770	1774	0	1	1	2	2	2	3	3	4
25	1778	1782	1786	1791	1795	1799	1803	1807	1811	1816	0	1	1	2	2	2	3	3	4
26	1820	1824	1828	1832	1837	1841	1845	1849	1854	1858	0	1	1	2	2	3	3	3	4
27	1862	1866	1871	1875	1879	1884	1888	1892	1897	1901	0	1	1	2	2	3	3	3	4
28	1905	1910	1914	1919	1923	1928	1932	1936	1941	1945	0	1	1	2	2	3	3	4	4
29	1950	1954	1959	1963	1968	1972	1977	1982	1986	1991	0	1	1	2	2	3	3	4	4
30	1995	2000	2004	2009	2014	2018	2023	2028	2032	2037	0	1	1	2	2	3	3	4	4
31	2042	2046	2051	2056	2061	2065	2070	2075	2080	2084	0	1	1	2	2	3	3	4	4
32	2089	2094	2099	2104	2109	2113	2118	2123	2128	2133	0	1	1	2	2	3	3	4	4
33	2138	2143	2148	2153	2158	2163	2168	2173	2178	2183	0	1	1	2	2	3	3	4	4
34	2188	2193	2198	2203	2208	2213	2218	2223	2228	2234	1	1	2	2	3	3	4	4	5
35	2239	2244	2249	2254	2259	2265	2270	2275	2280	2286	1	1	2	2	3	3	4	4	5
36	2291	2206	2301	2807	2312	2317	2323	2328	2333	2339	1	1	2	2	3	3	4	4	5
37	2344	2350	2355	2360	2366	2371	2377	2382	2388	2393	1	1	2	2	3	3	4	4	5
38	2399	2404	2410	2415	2421	2427	2432	2438	2443	2449	1	1	2	2	3	3	4	4	5
39	2455	2460	2466	2472	2477	2483	2489	2495	2500	2506	1	1	2	2	3	3	4	5	5
40	2512	2518	2523	2529	2535	2541	2547	2553	2559	2564	1	1	2	2	3	4	4	5	5
41	2570	2576	2582	2588	2594	2600	2606	2612	2618	2624	1	1	2	2	3	4	4	5	5
42	2630	2636	2642	2649	2655	2661	2667	2673	2679	2685	1	1	2	2	3	4	4	5	6
43	2692	2698	2704	2710	2716	2723	2729	2735	2742	2748	1	1	2	3	3	4	4	5	6
44	2754	2761	2767	2773	2780	2786	2793	2799	2805	2812	1	1	2	3	3	4	4	5	6
45	2813	2825	2831	2838	2844	2851	2858	2864	2871	2877	1	1	2	3	3	4	5	5	6
46	2884	2891	2897	2904	2911	2917	2924	2931	2938	2944	1	1	2	3	3	4	5	5	6
47	2951	2958	2965	2972	2979	2985	2992	2999	3006	3013	1	1	2	3	3	4	5	5	6
48	3020	3027	3034	3041	3048	3055	3062	3069	3076	3083	1	1	2	3	4	4	5	6	6
49	3090	3097	3105	3112	3119	3126	3133	3141	3148	3155	1	1	2	3	4	4	5	6	6

TABLE II
ANTI-LOGARITHMS

	0	1	2	3	4	5	6	7	8	9	Mean Differences 1	2	3	4	5	6	7	8	9
50	3162	3170	3177	3184	3192	3199	3206	3214	3221	3228	1	1	2	3	4	4	5	6	7
51	3236	3243	3251	3258	3266	3273	3281	3289	3296	3304	1	2	2	3	4	5	5	6	7
52	3311	3319	3327	3334	3342	3350	3357	3365	3373	3381	1	2	2	3	4	5	5	6	7
53	3388	3396	3404	3412	3420	3428	3436	3443	3451	3459	1	2	2	3	4	5	6	6	7
54	3467	3475	3483	3491	3499	3508	3516	3524	3532	3540	1	2	2	3	4	5	6	6	7
55	3548	3556	3565	3573	3581	3589	3597	3606	3614	3622	1	2	2	3	4	5	6	7	7
56	3631	3639	3648	3656	3664	3673	3681	3690	3698	3707	1	2	3	3	4	5	6	7	8
57	3715	3724	3733	3741	3750	3758	3767	3776	3784	3793	1	2	3	3	4	5	6	7	8
58	3802	3811	3819	3828	3837	3846	3855	3864	3873	3882	1	2	3	4	4	5	6	7	8
59	3890	3899	3908	3917	3926	3936	3945	3954	3963	3972	1	2	3	4	5	5	6	7	8
60	3981	3990	3999	4009	4018	4027	4036	4046	4055	4064	1	2	3	4	5	6	6	7	8
61	4074	4083	4093	4102	4111	4121	4130	4140	4150	4159	1	2	3	4	5	6	7	8	9
62	4169	4178	4188	4198	4207	4217	4227	4236	4246	4256	1	2	3	4	5	6	7	8	9
63	4266	4276	4285	4295	4305	4315	4325	4335	4345	4355	1	2	3	4	5	6	7	8	9
64	4365	4375	4385	4395	4406	4416	4426	4436	4446	4457	1	2	3	4	5	6	7	8	9
65	4467	4477	4487	4498	4508	4519	4529	4539	4550	4560	1	2	3	4	5	6	7	8	9
66	4571	4581	4592	4603	4613	4624	4634	4645	4656	4667	1	2	3	4	5	6	7	9	10
67	4677	4688	4699	4710	4721	4732	4742	4753	4764	4775	1	2	3	4	5	7	8	9	10
68	4786	4797	4808	4819	4831	4842	4853	4864	4875	4887	1	2	3	4	6	7	8	9	10
69	4898	4909	4920	4932	4943	4955	4966	4977	4989	5000	1	2	3	5	6	7	8	9	10
70	5012	5023	5035	5047	5058	5070	5082	5093	5105	5117	1	2	4	5	6	7	8	9	11
71	5129	5140	5152	5164	5176	5188	5200	5212	5224	5236	1	2	4	5	6	7	8	10	11
72	5248	5260	5272	5284	5297	5309	5321	5333	5346	5358	1	2	4	5	6	7	9	10	11
73	5370	5383	5395	5408	5420	5433	5445	5458	5470	5483	1	3	4	5	6	8	9	10	11
74	5495	5508	5521	5534	5546	5559	5572	5585	5598	5610	1	3	4	5	6	8	9	10	12
75	5623	5636	5649	5662	5675	5689	5702	5715	5728	5741	1	3	4	5	7	8	9	10	12
76	5754	5768	5781	5794	5808	5821	5834	5848	5861	5875	1	3	4	5	7	8	9	11	12
77	5888	5902	5916	5929	5943	5957	5970	5984	5998	6012	1	3	4	5	7	8	10	11	12
78	6026	6039	6053	6067	6081	6095	6109	6124	6138	6152	1	3	4	6	7	8	10	11	13
79	6166	6180	6194	6209	6223	6237	6252	6266	6281	6295	1	3	4	6	7	9	10	11	13
80	6310	6324	6339	6353	6368	6383	6397	6412	6427	6442	1	3	4	6	7	9	10	12	13
81	6457	6471	6486	6501	6516	6531	6546	6561	6577	6592	2	3	5	6	8	9	11	12	14
82	6607	6622	6637	6653	6668	6683	6699	6714	6730	6745	2	3	5	6	8	9	11	12	14
83	6761	6776	6792	6808	6823	6839	6855	6871	6887	6902	2	3	5	6	8	9	11	13	14
84	6918	6934	6950	6966	6982	6998	7015	7031	7047	7063	2	3	5	6	8	10	11	13	15
85	7079	7096	7112	7129	7145	7161	7178	7194	7211	7228	2	3	5	7	8	10	12	13	15
86	7244	7261	7278	7295	7311	7328	7345	7362	7379	7396	2	3	5	7	8	10	12	13	15
87	7413	7430	7447	7464	7482	7499	7516	7534	7551	7568	2	3	5	7	9	10	12	14	16
88	7586	7603	7621	7638	7656	7674	7691	7709	7727	7745	2	4	5	7	9	11	12	14	16
89	7762	7780	7798	7816	7834	7852	7870	7889	7907	7925	2	4	5	7	9	11	13	14	16
90	7943	7962	7980	7998	8017	8035	8054	8072	8091	8110	2	4	6	7	9	11	13	15	17
91	8128	8147	8166	8185	8204	8222	8241	8260	8279	8299	2	4	6	8	9	11	13	15	17
92	8318	8337	8356	8375	8395	8414	8433	8453	8472	8492	2	4	6	8	10	12	14	15	17
93	8511	8531	8551	8570	8590	8610	8630	8650	8670	8690	2	4	6	8	10	12	14	16	18
94	8710	8730	8750	8770	8790	8810	8831	8851	8872	8892	2	4	6	8	10	12	14	16	18
95	8913	8933	8954	8974	8995	9016	9036	9057	9078	9099	2	4	6	8	10	12	15	17	19
96	9120	9141	9162	9183	9204	9226	9247	9268	9290	9311	2	4	6	8	11	13	15	17	19
97	9333	9354	9376	9397	9419	9441	9462	9484	9506	9528	2	4	7	9	11	13	15	17	20
98	9550	9572	9594	9616	9638	9661	9683	9705	9727	9750	2	4	7	9	11	13	16	18	20
99	9772	9795	9817	9840	9863	9886	9908	9931	9954	9977	2	5	7	9	11	14	16	18	20

TABLE III
POWERS, ROOTS AND RECIPROCALS

n	n^2	n^3	$\sqrt{n}$	$\sqrt[3]{n}$	$\frac{1}{n}$	$\sqrt{10n}$	$\frac{1}{\sqrt{n}}$	$\frac{1}{\sqrt{10n}}$
1	1	1	1·0000	1·0000	1·00000	3·1623	1·00000	0·31623
2	4	8	1·4142	1·2599	0·50000	4·4721	0·70711	0·22361
3	9	27	1·7321	1·4422	0·33333	5·4772	0·57735	0·18257
4	16	64	2·0000	1·5874	0·25000	6·3245	0·50000	0·15811
5	25	125	2·2361	1·7100	0·20000	7·0711	0·44721	0·14142
6	36	216	2·4495	1·8171	0·16667	7·7460	0·40825	0·12910
7	49	343	2·6458	1·9129	0·14286	8·3666	0·37796	0·11952
8	64	512	2·8284	2·0000	0·12500	8·9443	0·35355	0·11180
9	81	729	3·0000	2·0801	0·11111	9 4868	0·33333	0·10541
10	100	1000	3·1623	2·1544	0·10000	10·0000	0·31623	0·10000
11	121	1331	3·3166	2·2240	0·09091	10·4881	0·30151	0·09535
12	144	1728	3·4641	2·2894	0·08333	10·9545	0·28868	0·09129
13	169	2197	3·6056	2·3513	0·07692	11·4018	0·27735	0·08771
14	196	2744	3·7417	2·4101	0·07143	11·8322	0·26726	0·08452
15	225	3375	3·8730	2·4662	0·06667	12·2474	0·25820	0·08165
16	256	4096	4·0000	2·5198	0·06250	12·6491	0·25000	0·07906
17	289	4913	4·1231	2·5713	0·05882	13·0384	0·24253	0·07670
18	324	5832	4·2426	2·6207	0·05556	13·4164	0·23570	0·07454
19	361	6859	4·8589	2·6684	0·05263	13·7840	0·22942	0·07255
20	400	8000	4·4721	2·7144	0·05000	14·1421	0·22361	0·07071
21	441	9261	4·5826	2·7589	0·04762	14·4914	0·21822	0·06901
22	484	10648	4·6904	2·8020	0·04545	14·8324	0·21320	0·06742
23	529	12167	4·7958	2·8439	0·04348	15·1658	0·20851	0·06594
24	576	13824	4·8990	2·8845	0·04167	15·4919	0·20412	0·06455
25	625	15625	5·0000	2·9240	0·04000	15·8114	0·20000	0·06325
26	676	17576	5·0990	2·9625	0·03846	16·1245	0·19612	0·06202
27	729	19683	5·1962	3·0000	0·03704	16·4317	0·19245	0·06086
28	784	21952	5·2915	3·0366	0·03571	16·7332	0·18898	0·05976
29	841	24389	5·3852	3·0723	0·03448	17·0294	0·18570	0·05872
30	900	27000	5·4772	3·1072	0·03333	17·3205	0·18257	0·05774
31	961	29791	5·5678	3·1414	0·03226	17·6068	0·17961	0·05680
32	1024	32768	5·6569	3·1748	0·03125	17·8885	0·17678	0·05590
33	1089	35937	5·7446	3·2075	0·03030	18·1659	0·17408	0·05505
34	1156	39304	5·8310	3·2396	0·02941	18·4391	0·17150	0·05423
35	1225	42875	5·9161	3·2711	0·02857	18·7083	0·16903	0·05345
36	1296	46656	6·0000	3·3019	0·02778	18·9737	0·16667	0·05270
37	1369	50653	6·0828	3·3322	0·02703	19·2354	0·16440	0·05199
38	1444	54872	6·1644	3·3620	0·02632	19·4936	0·16222	0·05130
39	1521	59319	6·2450	3·3912	0·02564	19·7484	0·16013	0·05064
40	1600	64000	6·3245	3·4200	0·02500	20·0000	0·15811	0·05000
41	1681	68921	6·4031	3·4482	0·02439	20·2485	0·15617	0·04939
42	1764	74088	6·4807	3·4760	0·02381	20·4939	0·15430	0·04880
43	1849	79507	6·5574	3·5034	0·02326	20·7364	0·15250	0·04822
44	1936	85184	6·6332	3·5303	0·02273	20·9762	0·15076	0·04767
45	2025	91125	6·7082	3·5569	0·02222	21·2132	0·14907	0·04714
46	2116	97336	6·7823	3·5830	0·02174	21·4476	0·14744	0·04663
47	2209	103823	6·8557	3·6088	0·02128	21·6795	0·14587	0·04613
48	2304	110592	6·9282	3·6342	0·02083	21·9089	0·14434	0·04564
49	2401	117649	7·0000	3·6593	0·02041	22·1359	0·14286	0·04518
50	2500	125000	7·0711	3·6840	0·02000	22·3607	0·14142	0·04472

TABLE III
POWERS, ROOTS AND RECIPROCALS

n	n^2	n^3	$\sqrt{n}$	$\sqrt[3]{n}$	$\frac{1}{n}$	$\sqrt{10n}$	$\frac{1}{\sqrt{n}}$	$\frac{1}{\sqrt{10n}}$
51	2601	132651	7·1414	3·7084	0·01961	22·5832	0·14003	0·04428
52	2704	140608	7·2111	3·7325	0·01923	22·8035	0·13868	0·04385
53	2809	148877	7·2801	3·7563	0·01887	23·0217	0·13736	0·04344
54	2916	157464	7·3485	3·7798	0·01852	23·2379	0·13608	0·04303
55	3025	166375	7·4162	3·8030	0·01818	23·4521	0·13484	0·04264
56	3136	175616	7·4833	3·8259	0·01786	23·6643	0·13363	0·04226
57	3249	185193	7·5498	3·8485	0·01754	23·8747	0·13245	0·04189
58	3364	195112	7·6158	3·8709	0·01724	24·0832	0·13131	0·04152
59	3481	205379	7·6811	3·8930	0·01695	24·2899	0·13019	0·04117
60	3600	216000	7·7460	3·9149	0·01667	24·4949	0·12910	0·04082
61	3721	226981	7·8102	3·9365	0·01639	24·6982	0·12804	0·04049
62	3844	238328	7·8740	3·9579	0·01613	24·8998	0·12700	0·04016
63	3969	250047	7·9373	3·9791	0·01587	25·0998	0·12599	0·03984
64	4096	262144	8·0000	4·0000	0·01563	25·2982	0·12500	0·03953
65	4225	274625	8·0623	4·0207	0·01538	25·4951	0·12403	0·03922
66	4356	287496	8·1240	4·0412	0·01515	25·6905	0·12309	0·03892
67	4489	300763	8·1854	4·0615	0·01493	25·8844	0·12217	0·03863
68	4624	314432	8·2462	4·0817	0·01471	26·0768	0·12127	0·03835
69	4761	328509	8·3066	4·1016	0·01449	26·2679	0·12039	0·03807
70	4900	343000	8·3666	4·1213	0·01429	26·4575	0·11952	0·03780
71	5041	357911	8·4261	4·1408	0·01408	26·6458	0·11868	0·03753
72	5184	373248	8·4853	4·1602	0·01389	26·8328	0·11785	0·03727
73	5329	389017	8·5440	4·1793	0·01370	27·0185	0·11704	0·03701
74	5476	405224	8·6023	4·1983	0·01351	27·2029	0·11625	0·03676
75	5625	421875	8·6603	4·2172	0·01333	27·3861	0·11547	0·03651
76	5776	438976	8·7178	4·2358	0·01316	27·5681	0·11471	0·03627
77	5929	456533	8·7750	4·2543	0·01299	27·7489	0·11396	0·03604
78	6084	474552	8·8318	4·2727	0·01282	27·9285	0·11323	0·03581
79	6241	493039	8·8882	4·2908	0·01266	28·1069	0·11251	0·03558
80	6400	512000	8·9443	4·3089	0·01250	28·2843	0·11180	0·03536
81	6561	531441	9·0000	4·3267	0·01235	28·4604	0·11111	0·03514
82	6724	551368	9·0554	4·3445	0·01220	28·6356	0·11043	0·03492
83	6889	571787	9·1104	4·3621	0·01205	28·8097	0·10976	0·03471
84	7056	592704	9·1652	4·3795	0·01190	28·9828	0·10911	0·03450
85	7225	614125	9·2195	4·3968	0·01176	29·1548	0·10847	0·03430
86	7396	636056	9·2736	4·4140	0·01163	29·3258	0·10783	0·03410
87	7569	658503	9·3274	4·4310	0·01149	29·4958	0·10721	0·03390
88	7744	681472	9·3808	4·4480	0·01136	29·6648	0·10660	0·03371
89	7921	704969	9·4340	4·4647	0·01124	29·8329	0·10600	0·03352
90	8100	729000	9·4868	4·4814	0·01111	30·0000	0·10541	0·03333
91	8281	753571	9·5394	4·4979	0·01099	30·1662	0·10483	0·03315
92	8464	778688	9·5917	4·5144	0·01087	30·3315	0·10426	0·03297
93	8649	804357	9·6437	4·5307	0·01075	30·4959	0·10370	0·03279
94	8836	830584	9·6954	4·5468	0·01064	30·6594	0·10314	0·03262
95	9025	857375	9·7468	4·5629	0·01053	30·8221	0·10260	0·03244
96	9216	884736	9·7980	4·5789	0·01042	30·9839	0·10206	0·03227
97	9409	912673	9·8489	4·5947	0·01031	31·1448	0·10153	0·03211
98	9604	941192	9·8995	4·6104	0·01020	31·3050	0·10102	0·03194
99	9801	970299	9·9499	4·6261	0·01010	31·4643	0·10050	0·03178
100	10000	1000000	10·0000	4·6416	0·01000	31·6228	0·10000	0·03162

Formulae

1. Central Tendencies

(A) Arthmetic Mean:($\bar{x}$)

(a) Individual series $\bar{x} = \frac{\Sigma x}{n}$

(short-cut) $\bar{x} = A + \frac{\Sigma d}{n}$

(b) Discret and Continuous series $\bar{x} = \frac{\Sigma fx}{n}$

(short-cut) $\bar{x} = A + \frac{\Sigma fd}{n}$

[Weighted A.M. $\bar{x}w = \frac{\Sigma wx}{\Sigma w}$]

(B) Geometric Mean (G.M)

$$G.M. = \sqrt[n]{x_1 \times x_2 \times x_2 \ldots\ldots \times x_n}$$

or

$$G.M. = \text{Anti-log}\left[\frac{\log x_1 + \log x_2 + \ldots\ldots + \log x_n}{n}\right]$$

$$= \text{Anti log of } \frac{\Sigma \log x}{n}$$

(C) Harmonic Mean (H.M)

$$H.M = \frac{n}{\frac{1}{x_1} + \frac{1}{x_2} + \frac{1}{x_3} + \ldots + \frac{1}{x_n}}$$

$$= \text{Reciprocal of} \ldots \frac{\frac{1}{x_1} + \frac{1}{x_2} + \frac{1}{x_3} + \ldots + \frac{1}{x_n}}{n}$$

$$= \frac{n}{\Sigma Rx} \text{ or R. of } \frac{\Sigma Rx}{n}$$

(D) Median (Me)

(a) Individual Series

(i) Odd Numbers $\left(\frac{n+1}{2}\right)$ th item.

(ii) Even Number mean of the middle two values.

(b) Discret Series

(Definite values No fraction) (Frequencies are converted into cumulative.) $\left(\frac{n+1}{2}\right)$ th item and its Value.

(c) Continuous Series

(Frequencies are converted into cumulative.) $\left(\frac{n}{2}\right)$ th item and its class interval

$$Me = l + \frac{\frac{n}{2} - m}{f} \times c$$

Similarly Quartiles and other partitioned values.

$$Q_1 = l + \frac{n/4 - m}{f} \times c \qquad Q_3 = l + \frac{3n/4 - m}{f} \times c$$

(E) Mode (Z)

(a) Individual series → The value which occurs frequently

(b) Discrete series → The value against which there is a highest frequency.

(For irregularities in frequency apply grouping system)

(c) Continuous series → The value lies in the class interval against which there is a highest frequency.

(No Negative Result)

General Formula

$$Z = l + \frac{f_1 - f_0}{2f_1 - f_0 - f_2} \quad \text{or} \quad Z = l + \frac{f_1 - f_0}{(f_1 - f_0) - (f_1 - f_2)} \times c \text{ (diff. only)}$$

f_0= frequency of the class preceeding the modal class.

f_2= frequency of the class succeeding the modal class.

f_1= frequency of the MODAL CLASS.

(i) If differency between the neighbouring frequencies (f_2 and f_0) and the modal frequency is not relatively very large, the following formula is preferably used

$$Z = l + \frac{f_2}{f_2 + f_0} \times c$$

(ii) When f_1 is less than f_0 or f_2 and $2f_1$ is less than $(f_0 + f_2)$ use the formula for mode.

$$Z = l + \frac{\Delta_1}{\Delta_1 + \Delta_2} \times c \qquad \Delta_1 = (f_1 - f_0) \text{ diff} \qquad \Delta_2 = (f_1 - f_2) \text{ diff}$$

It is similar to that of the General Formula

(Ignore Negative Sign & Diff.)

(iii) When $f_0 = f_2$, than take the mid-point (as mode) of the class interval of the modal class.

(iv) When $2f_1 = f_0 + f_2$ $2f_1 - f_0 - f_2 = 0$, [Use (ii) formula]

When mode is (Bio-modal or Multi-Modal) ill-defined, use Karl Pearson's Empirical formuld.

Mode = 3 Median - 2 Mean By-formulae

$\bar{x} = \frac{1}{2}(3\ Me - z)$.	$Me = \frac{1}{3}(2\bar{x} + z)$
$\bar{x} - z = 3(\bar{x} - Me)$.	$Me = \frac{2}{3}(\bar{x} - z) + z$
$\bar{x} - Me = \frac{1}{3}(Me - z)$.	$\bar{x} - Me = \frac{1}{3}(\bar{x} - z)$

---

2. Measures of Dispersion

(i) *Range:*- Range = Largest value - Smallest value

R=L-S....Absolute measure

(ii) Coefficient of Range (Relative Measures $= \frac{\text{Largest value - Smallest value}}{\text{Largest value - Smallest value}}$

C. of R $= \frac{L - S}{L+S}$ ... Relative measure

(B) Quartile Deviation :- (Semi-inter-quartile- range)

Q.D. $= \frac{Q_3 - Q_1}{2}$ (Absolute Measure)

Coefficient of Q.D. (Relative Measure) $= \frac{Q_3\text{-}Q_1}{Q_3\text{-}Q_1}$ x100

(Formula is applicable for all the series)

(C) Mean Deviation :- (δ)

(Negative signs are ignored in finding the Σd). Deviations are are taken either from $\overline{x}$, Me or *z*.

(a) Individual Series :- $\delta = \frac{\Sigma d}{n}$ (Absulute Measure)

Coefficient of δ $= \frac{\delta}{\overline{x}}$ or $\frac{\delta}{Me}$ or $\frac{\alpha}{Z}$ (Relative Measure)

(b) Discret Series & Continuous Series:- $\delta = \frac{\Sigma fd}{n}$ (Absulute Measure)

Coefficient of δ $= \frac{\delta}{\overline{x}}$ or $\frac{\delta}{Me}$ or $\frac{\delta}{Z}$ (Relative Measure)

Note: Deviations are taken preferably from median

When the averages are fractional, we can use the short-cut methods,

(i) Deviations are taken from assumed. $\overline{x}$, or Me or *Z*.

$$\delta = \frac{\Sigma fxA - \Sigma fxB - (\Sigma fA - \Sigma fB)\,\overline{x}}{n}$$

(ii) Without deviation, *x* values are directly taken.

$$\delta = \frac{\Sigma fd^1 - (\overline{x}\text{-}A) - (\Sigma fB - \Sigma fA)}{n}$$

$$\delta = \frac{\Sigma fd'(c) - (*\overline{x}\text{-}A) - (\Sigma fB - \Sigma fA)}{n}$$ ..... * Any average

Note: Divide the entire frequencies into two parts - A & B.

A= Total frequencies (inclusive of average part)

B= Total frequencies (exclusive of average part)

(D) Standard Deviation :- (σ)

Deviations are always taken from the $\overline{x}$. Then each 'd' is squared and 'd_2' are totalled.

Indi. Series $\sigma = \sqrt{\frac{\Sigma(x-\overline{x})^2}{n}}$ $\sigma = \sqrt{\frac{\Sigma d^2}{n}}$ (Absolute Measure)

Disc & Cont cont. Series $\sigma=\sqrt{\frac{\Sigma f(x-\bar{x})^2}{n}}$ $\sigma=\sqrt{\frac{\Sigma fd^2}{n}}$ (Absolute Measure)

Coefficient of variation σ CV $=\frac{\sigma}{\bar{x}} \times 100$ (Relative Measure)

---

3. Skewness (SK)

Tests:- (i) $\bar{x}$ & Z pulled apart and Me. lies in between the two.
(ii) Curve is not bell - shaped.
(iii) Q3 - Me ≠ Me - Q1
(iv) Σd(+) ≠ Σd(-)
(v) Frequencies on either side of z are not equal.

(A) Absolute Measures :- These are not of much use in practice. mean-mode, median-mode, Mean-median. (Not importantant)

(B) Relative Measures :- These are useful practically.

(i) Karl pearson's co-efficient of SK

(Based on $\bar{x}, z, \sigma$) $Skp = \frac{\bar{x}-z}{\sigma}$

If Z is ill-defined. $Skp = \frac{3(x-Me)}{\sigma}$

(ii) Bowley's Coefficient of SK

(Based on Q_1, Q_3, Me) $Sk = \frac{Q_3+Q_1-2Me}{Q_3-Q_1}$

---

4. Correlation (γ)

(A) Karl Pearson's Coefficient of correlation.

$$r = \frac{\Sigma dxdy}{n\ \sigma x \times \sigma y} \quad or\ r = \frac{\Sigma dxdy}{\sqrt{\Sigma dx^2 \times \Sigma dy^2}} \quad r = \frac{\Sigma dxdy}{\sqrt{\Sigma dx^2} \times \sqrt{\Sigma dy^2}}$$

dx = diviations of x from $\bar{x}$
dy = deviations of y from y
$dxdy = dx \times dy$ [⊕ &⊝ settled]

Based on Assumed Mean

$$r = \frac{\Sigma dxdy - \frac{(\Sigma dx)(\Sigma dy)}{n}}{\sqrt{\Sigma dx^2 - \frac{(\Sigma dx)^2}{n}}\sqrt{\Sigma dy^2 - \frac{(\Sigma dy)^2}{n}}}$$

Probable Error $= 0.6745\ \frac{1-r^2}{\sqrt{n}}$

(B) Spearman's Rank Correlation.

$$r = 1 - \frac{6(\Sigma d^2)}{n(n^2-1)} \quad \frac{(6 = \Sigma D^2)}{n^3-n}$$ ... (6 = Number Six)

For similar ranking (common ranks) corrections are made by adding the following values to Σd^2.
For 2 similar ranks $[\frac{1}{12}(m^3-m)]$ ... i.e. m=2

For 3 similar ranks $[^1/_{12}(m^3\text{-}m)]$ ... i.e. m=2

So $\Sigma d^2 + [^1/_{12}(m^3\text{-}m)] + \ldots$ so on.

5. Regression (Equations)

(A) y on x — *(B)* x on y

y = a+bx — x = a+by

To obtain the values of 'a' & 'b'

$\Sigma y = na + b\Sigma x$ — $\Sigma x = na + b\Sigma y$

$\Sigma xy = a\Sigma x + b\Sigma x^2$ — $\Sigma xy = a\Sigma y + b\Sigma y^2$

If deviation is from assumed x

$y = bX$ — $X = bY$

$b = \dfrac{\Sigma XY}{X^2}$ — $b = \dfrac{\Sigma XY}{Y^2}$

[Y=(y-y) — X=(x-x)]

Relationship between

6x	γ	byx	'b' is called Regression Coefficient.
6y		bxy	

(i) $byx = \dfrac{\Sigma XY}{\Sigma x^2}$ (ii) $bxy = \dfrac{\Sigma XY}{\Sigma Y^2}$

(iii) $byx = \gamma \dfrac{\sigma y}{\sigma x}$ (iv) $bxy = \gamma \dfrac{\sigma x}{\sigma y}$

(v) $\gamma = \sqrt{byx \text{ x } bxy}$ (vi) $byx = \dfrac{n\Sigma xy - (\Sigma x)(xy)}{n\Sigma x^2 - (\Sigma x)^2}$

(vi) $byx = \dfrac{n\Sigma xy - (\Sigma x)(xy)}{n\Sigma y^2 - (\Sigma y)^2}$

---

6. Time Series

Apply *y* on *x* formula (above for finding the trend values for *y* depending on *x* or follwing.

$y = a + bx \qquad a = \dfrac{\Sigma Y}{n} \qquad b = \dfrac{\Sigma xy}{\Sigma X^2}$

Note: (i) In *x* series the peirod is changing constantly. If we take exactly middle period as zero '0' the step deviation is $\Sigma x = 0$.

$\therefore \Sigma y = na + b\Sigma x$
$\Sigma y = na + b(0)$
$\Sigma y = na$ $\Big\}$ $S_o\, a = \dfrac{\Sigma y}{n}$

$\therefore \Sigma xy = a\Sigma x + b\Sigma x^2$
$\Sigma xy = a(0) + b\Sigma x^2$
$\Sigma xy = b\Sigma x^2$ $\Big\}$ $S_o\, b = \dfrac{\Sigma xy}{\Sigma x^2}$

---

7. Interpolation & Extrapolation

Interpolation:-(i) Estimation of missing or odd value of '*y*' (dependent) for the given value of '*x*' (independent).

If known values are	To find out unknown value of *y* use respective formula

2. ⟶ $y_2-2y_1+y_0=0$

3. ⟶ $y_3-3y_2+3y_1-y_0=0$

4. ⟶ $y_4-4y_3+6y_2-4y_1-y_0=0$

5. ⟶ $y_5-5y_4+10y_3-10y_2+5y_1-y_0=0$

6. ⟶ $y_6-6y_5+15y_5-20y_3-15y_2-6y_1+y_0=0$

7. ⟶ $y_7-7y_6+21y_5-35y_4+35y_3-21y_2+7y_1-y_0=0$

Bionomial Expansion Method

(ii) Estimation of probable value of 'y' (dependent) for the intermediate period of 'x' (independent) value NEWTON's Advancing differences formula is used.

$$x = \frac{\text{Year of item to be interpolated - Year of item of origin}}{\text{Difference between adjoining } x \text{ values.}}$$

Then apply the following formula,

$$y_x=y+x\Delta_1 + \frac{x(x-1)}{1x2}\Delta_2 + \frac{x(x-1)(x-2)}{1x2x3}\Delta_3 + \frac{x(x-1)(x-2)(x-3)}{1x2x3x4}\Delta_4 \text{ so on ......}$$

Δ_1, Δ_2, Δ_3 } *These are Leading Differences*

Thus, interpolation is the estimation of y value within the range.

Extraporation:- It is the estimation of y value for the x value which future values).

For the Binomial expansion method is used.

---

8. Index Numbers.

(i) Simple Aggregative Method ..... $Po_1 = \frac{\Sigma P_1}{\Sigma P_0} \text{ x } 100$

(ii) Weighted Aggregative Method ..... $Po_1 = \frac{\Sigma P_1 q_0}{\Sigma P_0 q_0} \text{ x } 100$

(iii) Simple Price Relative method .... $Po_1 = \frac{\Sigma PR}{n}$

PR=($^{P_1}/_{P_0}$ x100)

(iv) Weighted Price Relative method .... $Po_1 = \frac{\Sigma WPR}{\Sigma W}$

WPR=($^{P_1}/_{P_0}$ x100xW)

Fisher's Idea Formula

$$Po_1 = \sqrt{\frac{\Sigma P_1 q_0}{\Sigma P_0 q_0} \text{ x } \frac{\Sigma P_1 q_1}{\Sigma P_0 q_1}} \text{ x100}$$

1. *Time Reversal Test*:- Interchange the current year and Base year. So I.No. for C.Y. should be the reciprocal of the I.No. for B.Y.(*without 100*)

$\therefore P_{01} \text{ x } P_{10} = 1$

i.e. $= \sqrt{\frac{\Sigma P_1 q_0}{\Sigma P_0 q_0} \text{ x } \frac{\Sigma P_1 q_1}{\Sigma P_0 q_1}} \text{ x } \sqrt{\frac{\Sigma P_0 q_1}{\Sigma P_1 q_1} \text{ x } \frac{\Sigma P_0 q_0}{\Sigma P_1 q_0}} = 1$

Fisher's formula satisfies this test.

2. *Factor Reversal Test*:- Inter change the price and quantity. The product of the price index and quantity index is equal to the ratio of the aggregate value in the current year to the aggregate value in the base year (without 100)

$$\therefore P_{01} \times P_{10} = \frac{\Sigma P_1 q_1}{\Sigma P_0 q_0}$$

$$\text{i.e.} = \sqrt{\frac{\Sigma P_1 q_0}{\Sigma P_0 q_0} \times \frac{\Sigma P_1 q_1}{\Sigma P_0 q_1}} \times \sqrt{\frac{\Sigma P_0 q_1}{\Sigma P_1 q_1} \times \frac{\Sigma P_0 q_0}{\Sigma P_1 q_0}} = \frac{\Sigma P_1 q_1}{\Sigma P_0 q_0}$$

9. Miscellaneous

(A) *Relation between*: x, G.M., and H.M.

x is the sum total of all observations divided by the number of observations divided by the number of observations. G.M. is the 'n[th]' root of the product of 'n' values of items. H.M. is the reciprocal of the arithmetic average of the reciprocals of the items.

$$\text{A.M.} = \frac{a+b}{2} \qquad \text{G.M.} = \sqrt{ab} \qquad \text{H.M.} = \frac{2ab}{a+b}$$

If there are 'a' and 'b' two items, x = 25 and G.M = 15 find H,M.

$$\text{A.M.} = \frac{a+b}{2} \qquad \text{G.M.} = \sqrt{ab} \qquad \text{H.M.} = \frac{2(225)}{50}$$

$$25 = \frac{a+b}{2} \qquad 15 = \sqrt{ab} \qquad = 9$$

$$a+b = 50 \qquad ab = 15^2 = 225$$

(B) *Sturge's Rule*: From the available data continuous series table is to be prepared. So to find out the number of class intervals sturge's Rue is applied.

$$\text{Number of class Intervals} = \frac{\text{Range}}{1+3.322 \log N}$$

$$\text{Number of class Intervals} = \frac{\text{Range}}{\text{Width of C.I.}}$$

$$\text{Width of C.I} = \frac{\text{Range}}{\text{No. of C.I.}}$$

(C) *Regression Equations*

y on x

$$(y-\bar{y}) = \gamma \frac{\sigma y}{\sigma x} (x-\bar{x})$$

$$(y-\bar{y}) = byx\,(x-\bar{x})$$

x on y

$$(x-\bar{x}) = \gamma \frac{\sigma x}{\sigma y} (y-\bar{y})$$

$$(x-\bar{x}) = bxy\,(y-\bar{y})$$

(Coefficient of Correlation)

$$\gamma = \frac{\text{C.V.}}{\sigma x\, \sigma y} \qquad \frac{\text{Covariatance}}{\sigma x\, \sigma y}$$

(D) *Properties of Correlation*

The coefficient of correlation lies between (+1) and (-1)

when $\gamma = +1$ (perfect (+) correlation)

when $\gamma = -1$ (perfect (-) correlation)

when $\gamma = 0$ No correlation.

(E) *Binomial Expansion Method*

$(y-1)^2=0 \rightarrow y_2 - 2y_1 + y_0 = 0$

$(y-1)^3=0 \rightarrow y_3 - 3y_2 + 3y_1 - y_0 = 0$

$(y-1)^4=0 \rightarrow$ Formula of 4 known values

$(y-1)^5=0 \rightarrow$ Formula of 5 known values

$(y-1)^6=0 \rightarrow$ Formula of 6 known values

II B.Com Examination, April/May 1999
(1997-1998 Scheme)
COMMERCE
Business Statistics

Time: 3 Hours | Max. Marks: 100

SECTION - A (8 x 2 = 16)

1. a. "The proper functions of statistics is to enlarge individual experience" - Explain.

Ans. It arranges the data in a proper form, makes its clear to understand, describes it to conclude and enlarges human knowledge.

b. What is Random Sampling?

Ans. A chance of selection of items from the mass on random basis which should be free from personal bias.

c. Secondary data should not be accepted at their face value. Explain.

Ans. Secondary data should be used with caution. Edit them to find out errors, omissions and inconsistencies.

d. Mention the types of classification.

Ans.

- Qualitative(Descriptive)
  - Simple (2-fold)
  - Composite (manifold)
  - Arbitrary (Notinal)
- Qualitative(Numerical)
  - Discrete (Integers)
  - Continuous (Fractional)

e. What is false base line?

Ans. A line which indicates a portion of the scale in a graph which is unwanted and thus omitted to reduce the space.

f. Define Harmonic Mean.

Ans. A specialised average in which the number of items is divided by the sum of the reciprocals of the values of the variables.

g. Mean = 12, Mode = 13; find Median.

Ans. $Me = \frac{2}{3}(\overline{X} - z) + Z$. ...... **12.3333** $= -0.6666 + 13$

or $Z = 3Me - 2\overline{X}$ .... **12.333** $= \frac{13+24}{3}$

h. Mention the uses of Rank Correlation.

Ans. In all the contests-beauty, cooking, flower show and interview we can use the rank correlation coefficient.

i. What is moving average?

Ans. Trend values are obtained by using arithmetic mean of the series except at the two ends of the series.

j. Define Index Numbers.

Ans. The specialised averages which study the relative changes in the economic activities over a period of the

k. Given the two numbers 20 and 5. Find their G.M.

Ans. G.M $=$ Anti log of $\dfrac{\Sigma \log X}{n}$ $=$ Anti. log. of $\dfrac{2}{2} = 1$

(1.3010 + 0.6990 = 2) $= 10 \quad = 10$

l. What is probable error?

Ans. A measure which when "added to" and "substracted from", gives us the two limits, within which it is probable that all the results of the sample will fall.

SECTION - B (3 x 8 = 24)

2. Prepare a histogram and a frequency polygon from the following data:

x	0-10	10-20	20-30	30-40	40-50
f	13	17	15	13	10

Ans.

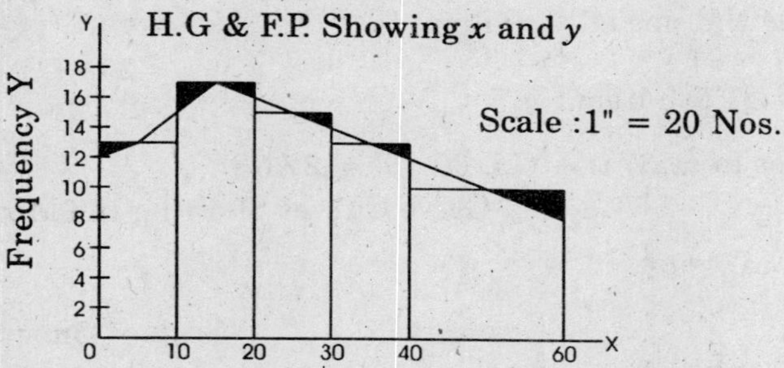

3. (a) Mean of the 20 values is 45. If one of these values is to be taken 64 instead of 46. Find the corrected mean.

(b) The Mean age of a Group of 100 children was 9.35 years. The Mean age of 25 of them was 8.75 and that of 65 was 10.51 years. What was the mean age for the remainder?

Ans. (a) $\bar{X} = \dfrac{\Sigma x}{n} \ldots 45 = \dfrac{\Sigma x}{20} \ldots \Sigma x = 900$

Corr. Σx = Incorr. $\Sigma x - 46 + 64 = 900 - 46 + 64$

$= 918. \therefore \bar{X} = \dfrac{918}{20} = 45.9$

(b) $\bar{X}_{100} = \dfrac{\Sigma x}{n} \qquad \bar{X}_{25} = \dfrac{\Sigma x}{n} \qquad \bar{X}_{65} = \dfrac{\Sigma x}{n}$

$9.35 = \dfrac{\Sigma x}{100} \quad 8.75 = \dfrac{\Sigma x}{25} \quad 10.51 = \dfrac{\Sigma x}{65}$

$\Sigma x_{100} = 935 \quad \Sigma x_{25} = 218.75 \quad \Sigma x_{65} = 683.15$

$\Sigma x_{10} = \Sigma x_{100} - \Sigma x_{25} - \Sigma x_{65}$

$= 935 - 218.75 - 683.15 = 33.10$

$\therefore \bar{X}_{10} = \dfrac{\Sigma x}{n} = \dfrac{33.10}{10} =$ **3.31 years**

4. Draw a Ogive curves from the following data and measure the median value. Verify it by actual calculations.

Central Size	5	15	25	35	45
Frequency	5	11	21	16	10

Ans. Conversion Table

Central Size	Class Interval	f	(LT) *c.f.*	(MT) *c.f.*
5	0-10	5	5	63
15	10-20	11	16m	58
25	l20-30	21f	37	47
35	30-40	16	53	26
45	40-50	10	63	10
		T=63		

$$Me = l + \frac{\frac{n}{2} - m}{f} \times c$$

$$= 20 + \frac{31.5 - 16}{21} \times 10$$

$$= 20 + \frac{15.5}{21} \times 10$$

$$= 20 + \frac{155}{21}$$

$$= 20 + 7.38095$$

$$= 20 + 7.381$$

$$= \mathbf{27.38}$$

Me is the size of $\frac{n}{2}$ th item

$\frac{63}{2}$ = 31.5th item

It lies in *c.f.37 (i.e. C.I. 20-30)* = ***27.38***

Ogive Curves Showing the Median

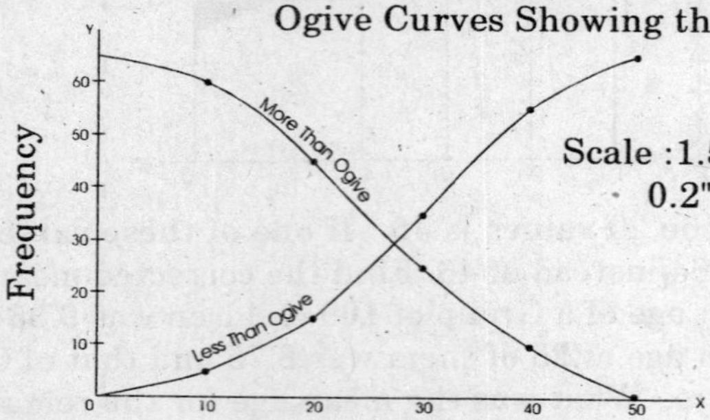

Scale :1.5m=10 Value
0.2"=5 Nos.

(Values) Me= 27.38

5. The following table shows the number of Salesmen working for a certain concern.

Year :	1990	1991	1992	1993	1994
Number :	28	38	46	40	56

Use the method of least squares to fit a straight line.

Ans. Computation of Trend values

Year	No.of. SM	Devi(92)(x=x-A)	x^2	xy	T.V.
1990	28	-2	4	-56	30.0
1991	38	-1	1	-38	35.8
1992	46	0	0	0	41.6
1993	40	+1	1	-40	47.4
1994	56	+2	4	-112	53.2
n=0	***Σy=208***	***Σx=0***	***Σx²=10***	***Σxy=58***	***208.0***

T.V. Yc = a+ bx

Yc = 41.6+5.8x

Y_{1990} = 41.6+5.8(-2)

= 41.6-11.6 = 30 . . . so on

$$a = \frac{\Sigma y}{n} = \frac{208}{5} = 41.6$$

$$b = \frac{\Sigma xy}{\Sigma x^2} = \frac{58}{10} = 5.8$$

6. Estimate the profits for the year 1993 from the following:

Year	1991	1992	1994
Profit(lakh or Rs.	8.5	12	10

Ans. Since the known values are 3, use the, equation of,

Year	Profit(Rs.lak)	
1991	8.5	y_0
1992	12.0	y_1
1993	-	y_2
1994	10.0	y_3

$y_3 - 3y_2 + 3y_1 - y_0 = 0$

$10 - 3y_2 + 3(12) - 8.5 = 0$

$3y_2 = 10 + 36 - 8.5$

$3y_2 = 46 - 8.5 = 37.5$

$$\therefore y_2 = \frac{37.5}{3} = \text{Rs.}12.5 \text{ lakhs}$$

SECTION - C (4 x 15 = 60)

7. Calculate co-efficient of correlation under Rank difference method for the following data:

X	53	98	95	81	70	81	65	81
Y	25	47	82	76	53	61	75	70

Ans. Conversion Table

x	y	R_x	R_y	$(R_x - R_y)$ d	d^2
53	25	8	8	0	0
98	47	1	7	-6	36
95	82	2	1	+1	1
81	76	4	2	+2	4
70	53	6	6	0	0
81	61	4	5	-1	1
65	75	7	3	+4	16
81	70	4	4	0	0
				Σd=0	Σd²=58

Tied ranks in *x* series 3rd, 4th & 5th common rank 4,4 &4 is given ***m*=3** ***n*=8**

$$r_5 = 1 - \frac{6\,[\Sigma d^2 + {}^1/_{12}\,(m^3 - m)]}{(n^3 - n)}$$

$$= 1 - \frac{6\,[58 + {}^1/_{12}\,(3^3 - 3)]}{(8^3 - 8)}$$

$$= 1 - \frac{6\,[58 + {}^1/_{12}\,(24)]}{(512-8)} = 1 - \frac{6(58+2)}{504}$$

$$= 1 - \frac{6(60)}{504} = 1 - \frac{360}{504} = 1 - 0.7143$$

= **0.2857**positively showed

8. Calcualte one measure of central tendency dispersion and skewness for the following data:

Year	No. of Workers
less than 5	449
less than 10	1154
less than 15	1661
15-20	281
20-25	109
25 and above	64
30 and above	11

Ans. Conversion Table

	No.of Workers	*c.f.*
Less Than 5	449	449
5-10	705	1154
10-15	507	1161
15-20	281	1942
20-25	109	2051
25-30	53	2104
30 & above	11	2115
	n=2115	

Since the distrubution is having open end calss intervals, Median is the accurate average.

Hence, Quartile Deviation is the suitable measure of dispersion, and Bowley's Coefficient of Skewness is the suitable measure of skewness.

Q_1 is the size of $^n/_4$ th item.

$\therefore$ $^{2115}/_4$ th item,

$\therefore$ 528.75 th item. It lies in (1154) *c.f.*

$\therefore$ The Q_1 lies in (5-10) class interval.

$$Q_1 = l + \frac{^n/_4 - m}{f} \times c. \ldots = 5 + \frac{528.75-499}{705} \times 5$$

$$= 5 + \frac{79.75}{705} \times 5. \ldots = 5 + \frac{79.75}{141} = 5+0.5656$$

= **5.5656** is Q_1

Q_2 Me is the size of $^n/_2$ th item.

$\therefore$ $^{2115}/_2$ th item,

$\therefore$ 1057.5 th item. It lies in (1154) *c.f.*

$\therefore$ The *Me* lies in (5-10) class interval.

$$Me = l + \frac{^n/_2 - m}{f} \times c. \ldots = 5 + \frac{1057.50-449}{705} \times 5$$

$$= 5 + \frac{608.5}{705} \times 5. \ldots = 5 + \frac{608.5}{141} = 5+4.3156$$

= **9.3156** is Me

Q_3 is the size of $^{3n}/_4$ th item.

$\therefore$ $^{3(2115)}/_4$ th item,

$\therefore$ 1586.25 th item. It lies in (1661) *c.f.*

$\therefore$ The Q_3 lies in (10-15) class interval.

$$Q_1 = l + \frac{^{3n}/_4 - m}{f} \times c \ldots = 10 + \frac{1586.25-1154}{507} \times 5$$

$$= 10 + \frac{432.25}{507} \times 5 \ldots = 10 + \frac{432.25}{101.4} = 10 + 4.2628$$

= **14.2628** is Q_3

$$Q.D. = \frac{Q_3 - Q_1}{2} = \frac{14.2628-5.5656}{2} = \frac{8.6972}{2} = \mathbf{4.3486}$$

$$\text{Coeff. } Q.D. = \frac{Q_3 - Q_1}{Q_3 + Q_1} = \frac{8.6972}{19.8284} = \mathbf{4.3486}$$

$$Skb = \frac{Q_3 + Q_1 - 2Me}{Q_3 - Q_1} = \frac{19.8284-2(9.3156)}{8.6972}$$

$$= \frac{19.824 - 18.6312}{8.6972} = \frac{1.1928}{8.6972} = \mathbf{0.13715}$$

9. The table below gives the distribution by size

No. of Workmen	No. of Companies
0 - 50	13
50 - 100	9
100 - 150	0
150 - 200	7
200 - 250	4
250 - 300	5
300 and above	2

Calculate:

(a) The total number of persons employed in these companies.

(b) The standard deviation.

(c) Co-efficient of variation.

Ans. Computation or $\overline{X}$, σ *and C.V*

No. of W	*No. of Co*	M	*d*	*fd*	*fd²*
0-50	*13*	*25*	*-2*	*-26*	*52*
50-100	*9*	*75*	*-1*	*-9*	*9*
100-500	*0*	*125*	*0*	*0*	*0*
150-200	*7*	*175*	*+1*	*+7*	*7*
200-250	*4*	*225*	*+2*	*+8*	*16*
250-300	*5*	*275*	*+3*	*+15*	*45*
300 & above	*2*	*325*	*+4*	*+8*	*32*
	n = 40			***Σfd=+3***	***Σfd²=161***

$\overline{X}$

$$= A + \frac{\Sigma fd}{n} \times c$$

$$= 125 + \frac{3}{40} \times 50$$

$$= 125 + \frac{150}{40}$$

= 125 + 3.75

= **128.75**

Total No of Co.

128.75x40=5150

$$\sigma = \sqrt{\frac{\Sigma fd^2}{n} - \left(\frac{\Sigma fd}{n}\right)^2} \text{ X } c \ldots \sqrt{\frac{161}{40} - \left(\frac{3}{40}\right)^2} \text{ X } 50$$

$$= \sqrt{4.025 - 0.005625} \text{ X } 50 \quad = \sqrt{4.019375} \text{ X } 50$$

$$= 2.0048378 \text{ X } 50 \quad = \mathbf{100.24189}$$

$$C.V. = \frac{\sigma}{x} = \frac{100.24189}{128.75} \text{ X } 100 = \mathbf{77.8578\%}$$

10. The following table depicts the number of persons earning certain grades of wages. Estimate the number of persons earning wages between Rs.60 and Rs.75 per Mensem.

Wages per Mensem in Rupees	**No. of persons earning(Rs.000)**
Below 40	250
40 - 60	120
60 - 80	100
80 - 100	70
100 - 120	50

Ans. Conversion of C.I into L.T. Cumulative

Wages Per Men(Rs.)	*No.of Persons (in 000')*	Δ^1	Δ^2	Δ^3	Δ^4
Below 40	250 Y_0				
		+120			
Below 60	370 Y_1		-20		
		+100		-10	
Below 80	470 Y_2		-30		+20
		+70		+10	
Below 100	540 Y_3		-20		
		+50			
Below 120	590 Y_4				

No. of persons earning below Rs.75/- per men.

$$x = \frac{75-40}{20} = 1.75 \quad y_x = y_0 + x\Delta^1_0 + \frac{x(x-1)}{1x2} \Delta^2_0$$

$$+ \frac{x(x-1)(x-2)}{1x2x3} \Delta^3_0 + \frac{x(x-1)(x-2)(x-3)}{1x2x3x4} \Delta^4_0$$

$$y_{75} = 250 + 1.75(120) + \frac{1.75(1.75-1)}{1x2} (-20)$$

$$+ \frac{1.75(1.75-1)(1.75-2)}{1x2x3} (-10) \frac{1.75(1.75-1)(1.75-2)(1.75-3)}{1x2x3x4} (+20)$$

$$y_{75} = 250 + 210 - 13.125 + 0.546875 + 0.347968$$

$$= 460.8887 - 13.125 = 447.7637$$

Appro. 448

Persons Earning Between Rs.60 and Rs.75

No. of persons below Rs.75	*448*
Less No. of persons below Rs.60.	*-370*
(78,000 persons)	***78***

11. In calculating a certain cost of living index number, the following weights were used. Food 15, Clothing 3, Rent 4, Fuel and Light 2, Misc. 1, calculate index for a data when the average percentage increases in prices of items in the various groups over the base period were 32, 54, 47, 78 and 50 respectively. Suppose a business executive was earning Rs.2,050 in the base period, what should be his salary in the current period if his standard of living is to remain the same?

Ans. Computation of Cost of Living Index

Group	*Average% Incre. in Pri.*	*Group Ind.(I)*	*Weight (W)*	*IW*
Food...	32	132	15	1980
Clothing...	54	154	3	462
Rent...	47	147	4	588
F&Light	78	178	2	356
Misc...	50	150	1	150
			ΣW=25	*ΣIW=3536*

Cost of Living index $= \frac{\Sigma IW}{\Sigma W} = \frac{3536}{25} = \mathbf{141.44}$

A Business executive should get $= \frac{2050 \times 141.44}{100} = \mathbf{2899.25}$

12. The following table shows the results of B.Com. students of a college for the last three years. Present the same by a suitable diagram.

Years	**1st Class**	**2nd Class**	**Pass Class**	**Failed**
1996	20	30	40	10
1997	30	50	20	20
1998	25	60	40	25

Ans. The data is converted into cumulative figures for showing the different components and their break up.

Year	*I Class*	*I& II Class*	*I,II,III Class*	*I,II,III,f. Total*
1996	20	50	90	100
1997	30	80	100	120
1998	25	85	125	150

Diagram showing results of B.Com students of a college for the years 1996, 1997 & 1998

Scale : 1mm = 20 persons

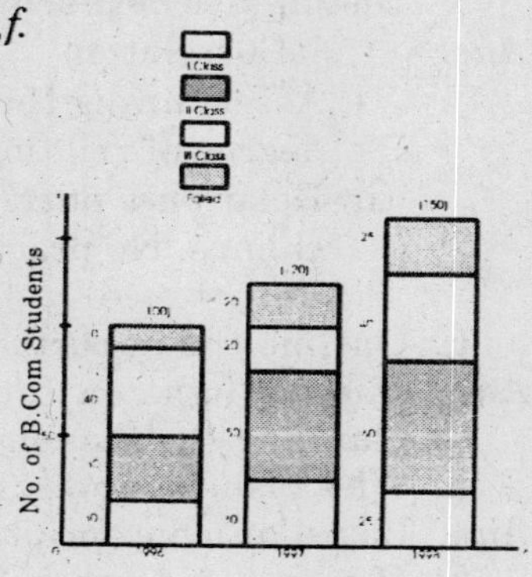

II B.Com. Examination, Oct/Nov. 1998
(1989-90 Onwards Scheme)(New)
BUSINESS STATISTICS

Time: 3 Hours | Max. Marks:100

SECTION - A (8 x 2 = 16)

1. a. State any four functions of statistics.

Ans. *Simplifies*: unwieldy and complex mass data.
Enlarges: individual experience for making decisions
Indicates: tendencies or trends or positions or directions
Presents: data systematically in a suitable manner.

b. Name the types of classification.

Ans. *Qualitative:* Simple, Composite, Arbitrary
Quantitative: Discrete and continuous

c. What is meant by Ogive? What are its uses?

Ans. A graphic presentation of cumulative frequency distribution of continuous series.
Used for the purpose of comparing groups statistics.
Determine the positional averages.

d. Find the co-efficient of variation if variance is 16, number of items is 20 and sum of the items is 160.

Ans. $\bar{X} = \frac{\Sigma x}{n} = \frac{160}{20} = 80$ $\sigma = \sqrt{\text{variance}} = \sqrt{16} = 4$

$$C.V. = \frac{\sigma}{\bar{x}} \times 100$$

$$= \frac{4}{8} \times 100 = 50$$

e. Define skewness. What are the types of skewness?

Ans. A tendency of 'Twist' or 'Turn' or 'Not Being Straight'.
A refined measure of dispersion.
Positive and Negative skewness.

f. Distinguish between Correlation and Regression Analysis.

Ans.

Correlation	Regression
(i) Assertaining the degree of relation	(i) Also studies cause and effect of relation
(ii) Relation-a purely chance. No practical importance	(ii) Relation is perfect. Practically it has importance

g. Outline the importance of Time Series Analysis.

Ans. Throws light on future economic behaviour useful for planning the economic activities.

h. Why Fisher's Index is ideal?

Ans. Based on appropriate average-G.M. considers quantities of both 0 & 1 years. Satisfies TRT and FRT.

i. Mention the differences between Diagrams and Graphs.

Ans.

Diagram	Graph
(i) Drawn on plane paper & graph paper	(i) Drawn on only a graph paper
(ii) Depict categorical & geographical data	(ii) Depict time series & Frequency Distribution
(iii) Difficult to draw	(iii) Easy to draw

j. What are the assumptions on which methods of interpolation are based?

Ans. No sudden jumps from one to another time. Existence of a sort of uniformity in series. Existence of definite and stable relation-x & y.

k. What is Rank Correlation?

Ans. Ranking the values of variables and establishing the correlation that can be measured.

l. State the Limitations of Geometric Mean.

Ans. Not used when one of the values is '0'. It entails much work of calculation. Not easily understood.

SECTION - B (3 x 8 = 24)

2. The following table gives the marks obtained by 65 students in statistics in a certain examination. Find Mean and Median from the data:

Examination Marks	**No.of students**
More than 70%	7
More than 60%	18
More than 50%	40
More than 40%	40
More than 30%	63
More than 20%	65

Ans.

Marks	***f***	**M**	***d'*(x-A)**	***fd'***	***cf***
20-30	2	25	-2	-4	2
30-40	23	35	-1	-23	25
40-50	0	45	0	0	25
50-60	22	55	+1	+22	47
60-70	11	65	+2	+22	58
70 & above	7	75	+3	+21	65

$\frac{n}{2} = \frac{65}{2}$ =32.514

Lics in 47%-c.f. So, 50-60 is Me.C.I.

$n=65$ $\Sigma fd'=38$

$X = A + \frac{\Sigma fd'}{n} \times C$

$= 45 + \frac{38}{65} \times 10$

$= 45 + 5.8462$

$= 50.8462$

$Me = l + \frac{\frac{n}{2} - m}{f} \times C$

$= 50 + \frac{32.5 - 25}{22} \times 10$

$= 50 + \frac{7.5}{22} \times 10$

$= 53.4091$ (or 53.9091)

3. The number of students in a college in 1972 was 510. Of these 480 were boys. In 1982, the number of boys increased by 100% and that of girls increased by 300% of that of 1972. In 1992 the total number of students in the college was 1200, the number of boys being double the number of girls. Present the above data in a tabular form.

Ans. No.of students in a college for 3 decades

Sex\Year	1972	1982	1992
Boys	480	960	800
Girls	30	120	400
Total	510	1080	1200

4. Calculate Geometric Mean and Harmonic Mean for the following:
2574, 475, 5, 0.8, 0.08, 0.005, 0.0009

Ans. a. *G.M.*

X(values)	*log X*
2574.0000	3.4104
415.0000	2.6767
5.0000	0.6990
0.8000	$\bar{1}.9031$
0.0800	$\bar{2}.9031$
0.0050	$\bar{3}.6970$
0.0009	$\bar{4}.9592$
$\Sigma \log x$	0.2457

G.M. Anti log of $\frac{\Sigma \log X}{n}$

G.M. Anti log $= \frac{0.2457}{7}$

G.M. Anti log $= 0.0351$
1.084

b. *H.M*

X(values)	*Rx*
2574.0000	0.0003885
475.0000	0.0021052
5.0000	0.2000000
0.8000	1.2500000
0.0800	12.500000
0.0050	200.0000000
0.0009	1111.1111111
ΣRx	1325.0524847

$$\text{H.M.} = \frac{n}{\Sigma Rx} = \frac{7}{1325.0524} = \mathbf{0.0052809}$$

5. a. The average marks of the Pre-University students is 68.4 and that of the Degree students is 71.2. If the combined average of all these students be 70, find the percentage of the number of students in Pre-university and Degree.

a. $\bar{x}_{12} = \frac{N_1 x_1 + N_2 x_2}{N_1 + N_2}$ $\qquad \frac{N_1}{N_2} = \frac{1.2}{1.6}$

$70 = \frac{N_1\, 68.4 + N_2\, 71.2}{N_1 + N_2}$

$70N_1+70N_2=68.4N_1+71.2N_2$ 3:4

$70N_1-68.4N_1=71.2N_2-70N_2$ 42.8571 (PU)

$1.6N_1=1.2N_2$ 57.1429 (Deg.)

b. **In a class of 60 students 10 have failed with an average mark of 15. If the total marks of all students was 1800, find the average marks of those who have passed.**

Ans. Total Marks = Failed Marks + Passed Marks.

1800 = 150 + 1650

$$\bar{x}_{50} = \frac{\Sigma x}{n} = \frac{1650}{50} = 33$$

6. **From the following data compute the consumer's price index numbers using (i) Aggregate expenditure method (ii) Family Budget method.**

Items	Units Consumed in Base Year	Price in Base Year	Price in Current Year
1. Rice	20	1.00	1.20
2. Wheat	50	3.00	3.50
3. Pulses	50	4.00	5.00
4. Ghee	20	20.00	30.00
5. Sugar	40	2.50	5.00
6. Oil	50	10.00	15.00
7. Fuel	60	2.00	2.50
8. Vegetable	40	15.00	18.00

Ans.

Items	q_o	p_o	p_1	p_oq_o	p_1q_o	I	IW
Rice	20	1.00	1.20	20	24	120	2400
Wheat	50	3.00	3.50	150	115	116	17500
Pulses	50	4.00	5.00	200	250	125	25000
Ghee	20	20.00	30.00	400	600	150	60000
Sugar	40	2.50	5.00	100	200	200	20000
Oil	50	10.00	15.00	500	750	150	75000
Fuel	60	2.00	2.50	120	150	125	15000
Veg.	40	15.00	18.00	600	720	120	72000
				2090	2869		2,86,900

a. Aggregate Expenditure Method

$$po1 = \frac{\Sigma p_1q_0}{\Sigma p_0q_0} \times 100 = \frac{2869}{2090} \times 100 = 137.273$$

b. Family Budget Method

$$p_{01} = \frac{\Sigma IW}{W} = \frac{2,86,900}{2090} = 137.273$$

SECTION - C (4 x 15 = 60)

7. Assuming the variable to be of continuous order find Bowley's co-efficient of skewness from the following data:

		No.of items
Equal to & more than	100	1000
Equal to & more than	200	950
Equal to & more than	300	700
Equal to & more than	400	600
Equal to & more than	500	500
Equal to & more than	600	200
Equal to & more than	700	150
Equal to & more than	800	100
Equal to & more than	900	50
Equal to & more than	1000	0

Ans.

C.I	f	Cf
100-200	50	50
200-300	250	300
300-400	100	400
400-500	100	500
500-600	300	800
600-700	50	850
700-800	50	900
800-900	50	950
900-1000	50	1000
	$n = 1000$	

$$Q_1 = 200 + \frac{250\text{-}50}{250} \times 100$$

$$= 200 + 80 = \mathbf{280}$$

$$Q_3 = 500 + \frac{750\text{-}500}{300} \times 100$$

$$= 500 + 83.333 = \mathbf{583.333}$$

$$Me = 400 + \frac{500\text{-}400}{100} \times 100$$

$$= 400 + 100 = \mathbf{500}$$

$$Skb = \frac{Q_3 + Q_1 - 2Me}{Q_3 - Q_1} = \frac{863.333 - 1000}{303.333}$$

$$= \frac{-136.667}{303.333} = \mathbf{-0.4506}$$

8. From the following data obtain the two regression equations:

Sales	Purchases
91	71
97	75
108	69
121	97
67	70
124	91
51	39
73	61
111	80
57	47

Also find the correlation co-efficient between the Sales and Purchases.

Ans. *Sales*	*x*	*y*	*x-x̄*	*x²*	*y-ȳ*	*y²*	*xy*	
	91	71	1	1	1	1	1	$\bar{x} = 90$
	97	75	7	49	5	25	35	
	108	69	18	324	-1	1	-18	
	121	97	31	961	27	729	837	$\bar{y} = 70$
	67	70	-23	529	0	0	0	
	124	91	34	1156	21	441	714	
	51	39	-39	1521	-31	961	1209	
	73	61	-17	289	-9	81	153	
	111	80	21	441	10	100	210	
	57	47	-33	1089	-23	529	759	
			0	**6360**	**0**	**2868**	**3900**	

y on *x* $(y-\bar{y})=\frac{\Sigma xy}{x^2}(x-\bar{x})$

$(y-70)=\frac{3760}{6360}(x-90)$ $\qquad = y-70 = 0.6026\text{ x } -54.2308$

$y=0.6026\text{ x}+15.7692$

x on*y* $(x-\bar{x})=\frac{\Sigma xy}{\Sigma y^2}(y-\bar{y})$

$(x-90)=\frac{3760}{2868}(y-70)$ x -90 = 1.311*y* - 91.7713

$x=1.311\,y-1.7713$

$r=\sqrt{byx \text{ x } bxy}=\sqrt{0.6132 \text{ x } 1.311}$

$=\sqrt{0.790001} \qquad = 0.8888$

9. **Fit a straight line trend to the following data by the method of least square:**

Year	Sales
1990	80
1991	90
1992	92
1993	83
1994	94
1995	99
1996	92

i. Plot the given data and the trend values on the graph paper:

ii. Estimate the sales for 1999.

Ans. **Year**	**Sales**	***x***	***x²***	***xy***	**Trend Values**
1990	80	-3	9	-240	$Y_c=90+2(-3) = 84$
1991	90	-2	4	-180	$Y_c=90+2(-2) = 86$
1992	92	-1	1	-92	$Y_c=90+2(-1) = 88$
1993	83	0	0	0	$Y_c=90+2(0) = 90$
1994	94	+1	1	+94	$Y_c=90+2(1) = 92$
1995	99	+2	4	+198	$Y_c=90+2(2) = 94$
1996	92	+3	9	+276	$Y_c=90+2(3) = 96$
	Σy = 630		28	+56	$\Sigma y_c=630$

$a=\frac{\Sigma y}{n}$

$=\frac{630}{7}$

=90

$b=\frac{\Sigma xy}{\Sigma x^2}$

$=\frac{56}{28}$

2

Graph Showing
Sales for 7 Years

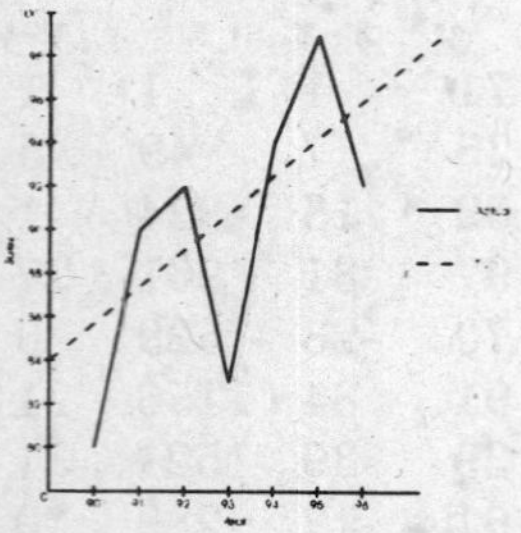

Estimation - 99
$Y_{99} = 90 + 2(6) = 102$
102

10. Draw a percentage sub-divided Rectangular Diagram to represent the following data:

Item of Expenditure Rs.	Expenditure in Rs. Family A Rs.	Family B
1. Food	2000	3000
2. Clothing	480	750
3. Education	320	400
4. House Rent	400	750
5. Travelling	600	900
6. Miscellaneous	200	200
Total Expenditure	4000	6000
Total Income	5000	8000
Total Savings	1000	2000

Ans. Diagram Showing Exp.of A&B Families

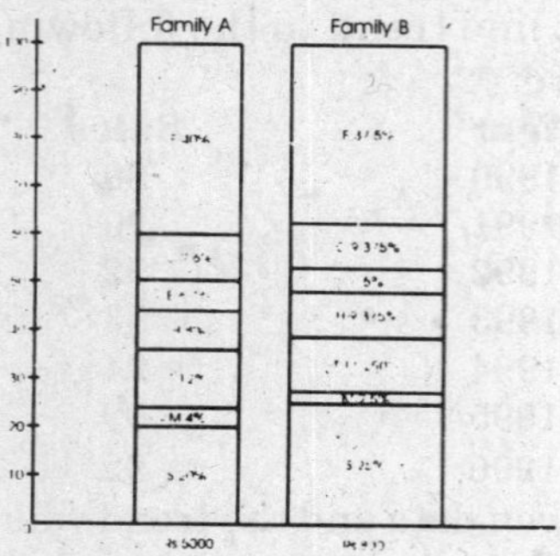

Items	A	%	Cum.	B	%	Cum.
F	2000	40	100.0	3000	37.500	100.000
C	480	9.6	60.0	750	9.375	62.500
E	320	6.4	50.4	400	5.000	53.125
H	400	8	44.0	750	9.375	48.125
T	600	12	36.0	900	11.250	38.750
M	200	4	24.0	200	2.500	27.500
S	1000	20	20.0	2000	25.000	25.000
	5000			8000		

11. Below are given the wages earned by workers per month in a certain factory. Calculate the number of workers earning more than Rs.75 per month. Apply Newton's method.

Monthly Income	No. of Workers
Upto Rs.50	50
Upto Rs.60	150
Upto Rs.70	300
Upto Rs.80	500
Upto Rs.90	700
Upto Rs.100	800

Ans.

x	y	Δ^1	Δ^2	Δ^3	Δ^4	Δ^5
50	50	+100	+50	0	-50	0
60	150	+150	+50	-50	-50	
70	300	+200	0	-100		
80	500	+200	-100			
90	700	+100				
100	800					

$$x = \frac{7550}{10} = \frac{25}{10} = 2.5$$

$$y_x = y_0 + x\Delta_0^1 + \frac{x(x-1)}{1x2}\Delta_0^2 + \frac{x(x-1)(x-2)}{1x2x3}\Delta_0^3$$

$$+ \frac{x(x-1)(x-2)(x-3)}{1x2x3x4}\Delta_0^4 + 0$$

$$= 50 + 2.5(+100) + \frac{2.5(2.5-1)}{1x2}(+50) + 0$$

$$+ 2.5\frac{(2.5-1)(2.5-2)(2.5-3)}{1x2x3x4}(-50) + 0$$

= 50+250+93.75+0+1.9531+0 =395.7031 or **396** workers

No. of workers earning more than 75m.

No. of workers earning up to Rs.100	=	800
Less workers earning up to Rs.75	=	396
Total	=	**404**

12. Find which of the following Batsmen is more consistent in scoring. Would you also accept him as a better run getter? Why?

Batsman A	Batsman B
5	0
7	4
16	16
27	21
39	41
53	43
56	57
61	78
80	83
101	90
105	95

	Batsman A			**Batsman B**	
	(d)			(d)	
x	$x-\bar{x}$	d^2	y	$y-\bar{y}$	d^2
5	-45	2025	0	-48	2304
7	-43	1849	4	-44	1736
16	-34	1156	16	-32	1024
27	-23	529	21	-27	729
39	-11	121	41	-7	49
53	+3	9	43	-5	25
56	+6	36	57	+9	81
61	+11	121	78	+30	900
80	+30	900	83	+35	1225
101	+51	2601	90	+42	1764
105	+55	3025	95	+47	2209
550		12372	528		12,246
$x=50$		Σd^2	$\bar{y}=48$		Σd^2

$$\sigma_a = \sqrt{\frac{\Sigma d^2}{n}} \qquad \sigma_b = \sqrt{\frac{\Sigma d^2}{n}}$$

$$= \sqrt{1,124.7272} \qquad = \sqrt{1,113.2727}$$

$$= \mathbf{33.536752} \qquad = \mathbf{33.365741}$$

$$\text{C.V.} = \frac{\sigma}{x_n} \times 100 \qquad \text{C.V.} = \frac{\sigma}{x_B} \times 100$$

$$= \frac{33.537}{50} \times 100 \qquad = \frac{33.366}{48} \times 100$$

$$= \mathbf{67.074\%} \qquad = \mathbf{69.5125}$$

(i) Batsman 'A' more consistent.

(ii) Of course not, because consistency is determined by C.V. not by average.

However, in this case, 'A' is a better run getter also as his average is more.